T0210667

Lecture Notes in Computer Science 9637

Commenced Publication in 1973
Founding and Former Series Editors:
Gerhard Goos, Juris Hartmanis, and Jan van Leeuwen

More information about this series at http://www.springer.com/series/7407

Frank Hannig · João M.P. Cardoso
Thilo Pionteck · Dietmar Fey
Wolfgang Schröder-Preikschat · Jürgen Teich (Eds.)

Architecture of Computing Systems – ARCS 2016

29th International Conference
Nuremberg, Germany, April 4–7, 2016
Proceedings

 Springer

Editors

Frank Hannig
Friedrich-Alexander University
  Erlangen-Nürnberg
Erlangen
Germany

João M.P. Cardoso
Faculty of Engineering (FEUP)
University of Porto
Porto
Portugal

Thilo Pionteck
Universität zu Lübeck
Lübeck
Germany

Dietmar Fey
Friedrich-Alexander University
  Erlangen-Nürnberg
Erlangen
Germany

Wolfgang Schröder-Preikschat
Friedrich-Alexander University
  Erlangen-Nürnberg
Erlangen
Germany

Jürgen Teich
Friedrich-Alexander University
  Erlangen-Nürnberg
Erlangen
Germany

ISSN 0302-9743   ISSN 1611-3349   (electronic)
Lecture Notes in Computer Science
ISBN 978-3-319-30694-0   ISBN 978-3-319-30695-7   (eBook)
DOI 10.1007/978-3-319-30695-7

Library of Congress Control Number: 2016932341

LNCS Sublibrary: SL1 – Theoretical Computer Science and General Issues

Printed on acid-free paper

This Springer imprint is published by SpringerNature
The registered company is Springer International Publishing AG Switzerland

Preface

The 29th International Conference on Architecture of Computing Systems (ARCS 2016) was hosted by the Department of Computer Science at Friedrich-Alexander University Erlangen-Nürnberg (FAU), Germany, during April 4–7, 2016. ARCS took place in Nuremberg, a beautiful city where medieval vistas meet modernism and technology. The conference continued the long-standing ARCS tradition of reporting top-notch results in computer architecture and other related areas. ARCS was founded in 1970 by the German computer pioneer Prof. Wolfgang Händler, who also founded the Computer Science Department at FAU in 1966. It was a privilege to have brought ARCS back to its roots in honor of the CS Department's 50th anniversary. The conference was organized by the Special Interest Group on Architecture of Computing Systems of the GI (Gesellschaft für Informatik e. V.) and ITG (Informationstechnische Gesellschaft im VDE), which held the financial responsibility for this ARCS edition. The conference was also supported by IFIP (International Federation of Information Processing).

"Heterogeneity in Architectures and Systems – From Embedded to HPC" was the specific focus of ARCS 2016. This leitmotif reflected the ongoing progress in semiconductor technology that allows for building fascinating, complex computing systems, including multiple (heterogeneous) microprocessors, large on-chip memory hierarchies, advanced interconnection networks, and peripherals. The downside to this technological progress is that computing has already hit a power and complexity wall. Thus, energy efficiency has become the key driver behind performance scaling across all areas, from portable devices, such as smartphones and tablet PCs, to high-performance computing (HPC) systems. This is why computing systems have begun to include more and more heterogeneous hardware with various, specialized resources, such as accelerators (e.g., GPUs or FPGAs) dedicated to one application domain. However, designing and testing as well as the parallel programming of such heterogeneous computing systems are challenging tasks. Aside from energy efficiency, predictability, fault tolerance, accuracy, and security are often at least equally important aspects when designing hardware and software. Thus, novel concepts as well as long-reaching research in the areas of computer architecture design, computation models, parallelization methods, software stacks, and programming and debugging tools are required.

The ARCS 2016 program included an exciting collection of contributions resulting from a successful call for papers. In response to the call for papers, 87 submissions were received with affiliations to 31 countries. Each submission was subjected to rigorous review from four Program Committee members. After having intensely scrutinized the reviews, we were pleased to present a high-quality technical program that included a total of 29 papers at the conference. The selected papers were divided into thematic areas (nine sessions), which highlighted the, at the time, current focus of research endeavors within computing systems. The sessions covered topics on architecture design (accelerators, NoCs, caches, security components), approximate and energy-efficient computing, organic computing systems, parallelization and mapping approaches, including various aspects on timing, performance modeling, and reliability. The strong technical program was complemented by three keynote talks on: "Knights Landing Intel Xeon Phi CPU: Path to Parallelism with General Purpose Programming" by Avinash Sodani, Intel, USA; "Massive Parallelism – C++ and OpenMP Parallel Programming Models of Today and Tomorrow" by Michael Wong, IBM, Canada; and "Heterogeneous Systems Era" by John Glossner, Optimum Semiconductor Technologies, USA. The five workshops focusing on specific sub-topics within ARCS were organized in conjunction with the main conference, one on parallel systems and algorithms, one on dependability and fault tolerance, one on self-optimization in autonomic and organic computing systems, one on multi-objective many-core design, and one on improvements to safe, multi-core, and software-intensive systems.

We would like to thank the many individuals who contributed to the success of the conference, in particular the authors who responded to our call for papers, the members of the Program Committee and the additional external reviewers who, with their opinion and expertise, ensured a program of the highest quality. The workshops and tutorials were coordinated by Ana Lucia Varbanescu, while Thilo Pionteck assisted in organizing the proceedings. Many thanks to the team at FAU, which substantially helped in the local arrangements. In particular, Ina Derr's and Ina Hümmer's organizational talent was greatly appreciated and Dominik Schönwetter ensured that the Web interactivity remained engaging and responsive. Thank you all.

April 2016

Frank Hannig
João M.P. Cardoso
Dietmar Fey
Wolfgang Schröder-Preikschat
Jürgen Teich

Organization

General Co-chairs

Dietmar Fey	Friedrich-Alexander University Erlangen-Nürnberg, Germany
Wolfgang Schröder-Preikschat	Friedrich-Alexander University Erlangen-Nürnberg, Germany
Jürgen Teich	Friedrich-Alexander University Erlangen-Nürnberg, Germany

Program Co-chairs

Frank Hannig	Friedrich-Alexander University Erlangen-Nürnberg, Germany
João M.P. Cardoso	University of Porto, Portugal

Workshop and Tutorial Chair

Ana Lucia Varbanescu	University of Amsterdam, The Netherlands

Publication Chair

Thilo Pionteck	Universität zu Lübeck, Germany

Program Committee

Michael Beigl	Karlsruhe Institute of Technology, Germany
Mladen Berekovic	Technische Universität Braunschweig, Germany
Simon Bliudze	École Polytechnique Fédérale de Lausanne, Switzerland
Florian Brandner	École Nationale Supérieure de Techniques Avancées, France
Jürgen Brehm	Leibniz Universität Hannover, Germany
Uwe Brinkschulte	Universität Frankfurt, Germany
João M.P. Cardoso	University of Porto, Portugal
Luigi Carro	Universidade Federal do Rio Grande do Sul, Brasil
Albert Cohen	Inria, France
Nikitas Dimopoulos	University of Victoria, Canada
Ahmed El-Mahdy	Egypt-Japan University for Science and Technology, Egypt
Fabrizio Ferrandi	Politecnico di Milano, Italy

Pedro Trancoso	University of Cyprus, Cyprus
Carsten Trinitis	Technische Universität München, Germany
Sascha Uhrig	Airbus, Germany
Theo Ungerer	Universität Augsburg, Germany
Hans Vandierendonck	Queen's University Belfast, UK
Stephane Vialle	CentraleSupelec and UMI GT-CNRS 2958, France
Lucian Vintan	Lucian Blaga University of Sibiu, Romania
Klaus Waldschmidt	Universität Frankfurt am Main, Germany

Additional Reviewers

Akesson, Benny	Hamza, Hamza
Al Nahas, Beshr	Hassan, Ahmad
Becker, Thomas	Hedrich, Lars
Behere, Sagar	Heid, Kris
Benjamin, Betting	Horsinka, Sven
Berezovskyi, Kostiantyn	Hönig, Timo
Betting, Benjamin	Iacovelli, Saverio
Bletsas, Konstantinos	Izosimov, Viacheslav
Blochwitz, Christopher	Jean, Xavier
Bromberger, Michael	Jooya, Ali
Buschhoff, Markus	Joseph, Moritz
Cebrián Márquez, Gabriel	Kantert, Jan
Chalios, Charalampos	Karavadara, Nilesh
Chen, Dejiu	Karray, Hassen
Chi, Chi Ching	Keshavarz, Babak
Cosenza, Biagio	Khoshbakht, Saman
Damschen, Marvin	Kicherer, Mario
de Souza, Diego F.	Klaus, Tobias
Eckert, Marcel	Kuznetsov, Max
Eibel, Christopher	Lal, Sohan
Falk, Joachim	Le Rhun, Jimmy
Feng, Lei	Lucas, Jan
Franzmann, Florian	Lund, Andreas
Freitag, Johannes	Martins, Paulo
Frieb, Martin	Maurer, Simon
Gabriel, Dirk	Meumeu Yomsi, Patrick
Gante, João	Meyer, Dominik
Georgakoudis, Giorgis	Mische, Jörg
Girbal, Sylvain	Mohanty, Jaganath
Goebel, Matthias	Mukhanov, Lev
Guerreiro, João F.D.	Naghmouchi, Jamin
Gurdur, Didem	Naji, Amine
Gómez Luna, Juan	Nelis, Vincent
Haas, Florian	Nelissen, Geoffrey

Neves, Nuno
Niazmand, Behrad
Niemann, Sebastian
Nikolic, Borislav
Pathania, Anuj
Payandeh Azad, Siavoosh
Penschuck, Manuel
Preußer, Thomas
Rao, Srinivas
Rashid, Syed Aftab
Reiche, Oliver
Rochange, Christine
Ruschke, Tajas
Sabel, David
Samie, Farzad
Schirmeier, Horst

Shuka, Romeo
Siegl, Patrick
Sreekar Shenoy, Govind
Stegmeier, Alexander
Ulbrich, Peter
Versick, Daniel
Wagner, Jan
Weidendorfer, Josef
Weis, Sebastian
Wenzel, Volker
Westman, Jonas
Wildermann, Stefan
Wolf, Dennis
Zabel, Martin
Zaichenkov, Pavel
Zhang, Hongyan

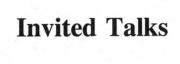

Invited Talks

Avinash Sodani, Chief Architect 'Knights Landing' Xeon-Phi Processor at Intel Corporation

Knights Landing Intel Xeon Phi CPU: Path to Parallelism with General Purpose Programming

Abstract of Talk: The demand for high performance will continue to skyrocket in the future fueled by the drive to solve the challenging problems in science and to provide the horsepower needed to support the compute-hungry use cases that are emerging in consumer and commercial space. Exploiting parallelism will be crucial in achieving the massive amounts of performance required to solve these problems. This talk will present the new Xeon Phi Processor, called Knights landing, which is architected to provide huge amounts of parallelism in a manner that is accessible with general purpose programming. The talk will provide insight into the important architecture features of the processor and explain their implications on software. It will provide the inside story on the various architecture decisions made on Knights Landing - why we architected the processor the way we did. It will show measured performance numbers from the Knights Landing silicon on range of workloads. The talk will conclude with showing the historical trends in architecture and what they mean for software as we extend the trends into the future.

Avinash Sodani is a Senior Principal Engineer at Intel Corporation and the chief architect of the Xeon-Phi Processor called Knights Landing. He specializes in the field of High Performance Computing (HPC). Previously, he was one of the architects of the 1st generation Core processor, called Nehalem, which has served as a foundation for today's line of Intel Core processors. Avinash is a recognized expert in computer architecture and has been invited to deliver several keynotes and public talks on topics related to HPC and future of computing. Avinash holds over 20 US Patents and is known for seminal work on the concept of "Dynamic Instruction Reuse". He has a PhD and MS in Computer Science from University of Wisconsin-Madison and a B.Tech (Hon's) in Computer Science from Indian Institute of Technology, Kharagpur in India.

Michael Wong, IBM Corporation, XL C++ Compiler Kernel Development

Massive Parallelism - C++ and OpenMP Parallel Programming Models of Today and Tomorrow

Abstract of Talk: Why is the world rushing to add Parallelism to base languages when consortiums and companies have been trying to fill that space for years? How is the landscape of Parallelism changing in the various standards, and specifications? I will give an overview as well as a deep dive into what C/C++ is doing to add parallelism such as the proposaed Vector/SIMD model that employs implicit Wavefront, but also how consortiums like OpenMP is pushing forward into the world's first High-level Language support for GPGPU/Accelerators and SIMD programming. Both are necessary to express the Massive Parallelism of tomorrow. GPU/Accelerator computing looks to be here to stay. Whether it is a flash in the pan or not, data parallelism is never going to be stale, especially for high-performance computing. The good news is that Clang 3.7 has OpenMP 3.1 support through a collaborative effort between many institutions, and Clang 3.8 or later will have some form of support for OpenMP 4 accelerators that targets many different devices, including Intel Xeon Phi and NVIDIA GPUs. Other compilers with high-level accelerator support will be GCC 6. The OpenMP model was designed to fit all possible forms of accelerators. However, in a changing world where discrete GPUs are transitioning into accelerated processing units (APUs), and being combined with various forms of high-bandwidth memory (HBM), is the OpenMP model, or even the OpenACC model, the best model? Should we begin programming future devices with a new programming model that ignores the "legacy" discrete systems and aims for the future? I'll contrast the OpenMP design with the emerging C++ Standard design and how we can merge the design experience from both HPC and consumer devices. As Chair of C++ Standard's SG14: Games Dev and Low Latency, I will show where we might be going in five years with an accelerator model that is appropriate for the future with description of Agency, SYCL, HCC, and HPX based on an outline of future goals.

Michael Wong is the CEO of OpenMP. He is the IBM and Canadian representative to the C++ Standard and OpenMP Committee. He is also a Director of ISOCPP.org and a VP, Vice-Chair of Programming

Languages for Canada's Standard Council. He has so many titles, it's a wonder he can get anything done. He chairs the WG21 SG5 Transactional Memory and SG14 Games Development/Low Latency, and is the co-author of a number C++11/ OpenMP/ Transactional Memory features including generalized attributes, user-defined literals, inheriting constructors, weakly ordered memory models, and explicit conversion operators. Having been the past C++ team lead to IBM's XL C++ compiler means he has been messing around with designing C++ compilers for twenty years. His current research interest, i.e. what he would like to do if he had time is in the area of parallel programming, transactional memory, C++ benchmark performance, object model, generic programming and template metaprogramming. He holds a B.Sc from University of Toronto, and a Masters in Mathematics from University of Waterloo. He has been asked to speak at ACCU, C++Now, Meeting C++, ADC++, CASCON, Bloomberg, CERN, and many Universities, research centers and companies.

John Glossner, President of HSAF and CEO of Optimum Semiconductor Technologies

Heterogeneous Systems Era

Abstract of Talk: Heterogeneous processing represents the future of computing, promising to unlock the performance and power efficiency of parallel computing engines found in most modern electronic devices. This talk will detail the HSA Foundation (HSAF) computing platform infrastructure including features/advantages across computing platforms from mobile and tablets to desktops to HPC and servers. The talk will focus on technical issues solved by HSAF technologies. The presentation will also discuss important new developments that are bringing the industry closer to broad adoption of heterogeneous computing.

Dr. John Glossner is President of the Heterogeneous System Architecture Foundation (HSAF) and CEO of Optimum Semiconductor Technologies. OST and its processor division General Processor Technologies (GPT-US). He is also a professor of Computer Science at Daniel Webster College. Previously he served as Chair of the Board of the Wireless Innovation Forum. In 2010 he joined Wuxi DSP (a licensee of Sandbridge technology and parent company of OST) and was named a China 1000 Talents. He previously co-founded Sandbridge Technologies and received a World Economic Forum award. Prior to Sandbridge, John managed both technical and business activities in IBM and Lucent/Starcore. John received a Ph.D. in Electrical Engineering from TU Delft in the Netherlands, M.S degrees in E.E. and Eng. Mgt from NTU, and a B.S.E.E. degree from Penn State. He has more than 40 patents and 120 publications.

Contents

Mapping of Applications on Heterogeneous Architectures and Real-Time Tasks on Multiprocessors

All About Time: Timing, Tracing, and Performance Modeling

Approximate and Energy-Efficient Computing

Configurable and In-Memory Accelerators

Towards Multicore Performance
with Configurable Computing Units

Anita Tino[✉] and Kaamran Raahemifar

Department of Electrical and Computer Engineering,
Ryerson University, 350 Victoria St, Toronto, ON, Canada
a2tino@ee.ryerson.ca

Abstract. Energy efficiency and the need for high performance has steered computing platforms toward customization. General purpose computing however remains a challenge as on-chip resources continue to increase with a limited performance improvement. In order to truly improve processor performance, a major reconsideration at the microarchitectural level must be sought with regards to the compiler, ISA, and general architecture without an explicit dependence on transistor scaling and increased cache levels. In attempts to assign the processor transistor budget towards engineering ingenuity, this paper presents the concept of Configurable Computing Units (CCUs). CCUs are designed to make reconfigurability in general purpose computing a reality by introducing the concept of logical and physical compilation. This concept allows for both the application and underlying architecture to be considered during the compilation process. Experimental results demonstrate that a single CCU core (consisting of double engines) achieves dual core performance, with half the area and power consumption required of a conventional monolithic CPU.

1 Introduction

Traditional microprocessors have long benefited from the transistor density gains of Moore's law. Diminishing transistor speeds and practical energy limits however have created new challenges in technology, where the exponential performance improvements we have been accustomed to from previous computing generations continue to slowly cease. A common response to addressing various issues in computing has revolved around increasing core counts in multiprocessors and employing heterogeneity (i.e. including accelerated units such as GPUs, FPGAs etc.) for offloading and executing dataflow-like phases of an application. This type of computing has been made possible with parallel programming models and languages such as OpenCL, OpenMP, CUDA, and OmpSs [2, 7]. Much research in Chip Multiprocessors (CMP) has also revolved around energy efficiency and specialization, noting that processor performance improvement is attributed to increased cache levels and transistor scaling [1, 3]. Although these concepts have increased performance to an extent, there is still the fundamental problem of how a single core's organization and design may be improved and applied to the multiprocessor domain [4, 5, 8–10].

Conventional CPU architectures possess a boundary between the compiler and underlying hardware due to a processor's Instruction Set Architecture (ISA). Current

© Springer International Publishing Switzerland 2016
F. Hannig et al. (Eds.): ARCS 2016, LNCS 9637, pp. 3–18, 2016.
DOI: 10.1007/978-3-319-30695-7_1

ISAs are limited by program counters, control-flow, and fine-grained instruction execution, lacking the richness needed to express a programmer's intent. Specifically, the programmer and software may provide a considerable amount of information about an application prior to compilation, however ISAs are unable to express this information during code generation and consequently the compiler is not able to exploit this knowledge to the underlying CPU [10]. Majority of the processor's hardware units must then try to rediscover the program's characteristics at the cost of power and area overhead. Hence, there is much ingenuity to be discovered based on these limitations if transistor budgets are put towards improving and sophisticating processing element performance, versus adopting the mantra of integrating more simple cores and memory on a single die [5].

Given these factors, this work presents a nuanced approach to general purpose computing using the concepts of Configurable Computing Units (CCUs), and *logical* and *physical* compilation. CCUs are configurable processors that execute tasks which are formed using the OmpSs programming model (Sect. 3.1). Each CCU processor consists of multiple variable sized engines, where each engine comprises of unique functional units (FUs) that are connected through a registerSwitch (rS) interconnect as shown in Fig. 1. The rS interconnect provides *distributed storage* and single-cycle multi-hop data communication amongst its FUs. Thus the rS interconnect avoids the need to constantly access centralized register files, bypass networks, and tile-based hotspots by revising the datapath layout. The engines are able to configure to a general purpose application's communication patterns using the programmable rS interconnect and information of the underlying architecture, transferring data amongst the functional units only when necessary. Therefore the configuration data (generated by the physical compiler) allows the engine to temporally configure itself on every clock cycle to support various data transfers and storages as required. To maintain memory ordering imposed by the logical compiler, a small external register file and load/store unit(s) are also included in the CCU back-end. A banked memory setup for storing configuration data is also used to reduce configuration times and allow for reconfigurability in general purpose processors.

The focus of this work pertains to the CCU back-end which will be prototyped in hardware, with the full CCU simulated in software and compared to a conventional monolithic CPU and multiprocessor.

2 Overview

2.1 Design Flow and CCU Microarchitecture

Figure 2 provides the CCU design flow implemented in this work. In the first stage of the design flow, a benchmark is input to the *logical* compiler which generates a binary and sends it to the physical compiler (and software simulator for testing). General profiling information of the tasks is then obtained in the physical compiler using the provided binary and embedded OmpSs pragmas. Exploiting the underlying processor information, the physical compiler then **(1)** generates tasks, **(2)** analyzes the instructions within the tasks to obtain statistical data and eliminate Write-After-Write

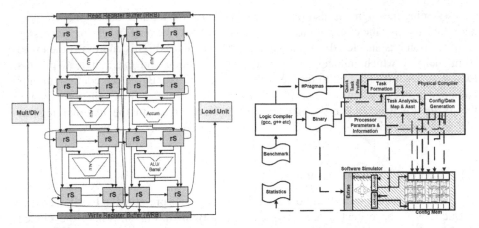

Fig. 1. Six FU (Single) engine CCU architecture

Fig. 2. Proposed CCU processor design flow

(WAW) hazards, which is then used to **(3)** extract producer-consumer dependencies, **(4)** assign tasks to the most suitable engines, and finally **(5)** generate configuration and task data to be used by the CCU engines for configuration and execution of task instructions. Thus once successfully compiled, the generated configuration data is stored to its respective engine's (banked) configuration memory. Similarly, the addresses used to store the configuration data are saved to a lookup table based on the task's ID (Fig. 2).

As execution in a CCU is task based and the "instructions" to be executed are essentially the configuration bits generated by the physical compiler, the scheduler must then simply keep track of task related dependencies for dispatch/execution. As seen in the microarchitectural pipeline provided in Fig. 3, when a task is ready, the scheduler outputs the corresponding task's ID to the engine designated by the physical compiler. Note that the scheduler may keep track of two engines concurrently. For this work, the Extra instrumentation tool [6] is used by the software simulator's scheduler to obtain traces and determine ready tasks and dependencies to reduce design complexity.

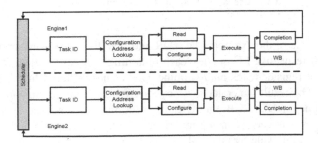

Fig. 3. CCU microarchitectural pipeline

Assuming the engine is also ready, the task ID is then input to the engine's lookup table to determine the configuration memory addresses to be read (where the necessary configuration bits are stored contiguously from that address). This address is then read from memory which initiates the engine's configuration and external read process (where external data is sent to the Read Register Buffer (RRB)). Once configuration is complete, task execution commences. Subsequent to execution, final values pending in the Write Register Buffer (WRB) are written/stored back to the external register file/cache, respectively.

2.2 Backend Execution Example

An example datapath execution flow for a six FU engine is presented in Fig. 4. The task instructions to be executed are provided to the right of Fig. 4, where the circled numbers signify an instruction's execution time. Instructions are displayed as: <operation, result, operand1, operand2>. The engine's "path" of execution for the listed instructions is provided on the engine's datapath. Note that this path is temporally and spatially configured with the configuration data provided by the physical compiler. The various dashed lines used in the figure represent execution in different cycles.

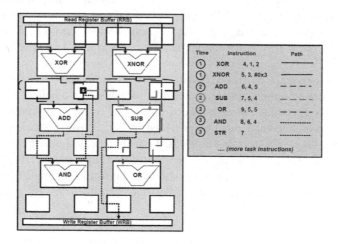

Fig. 4. CCU execution example (torus connection not shown)

In the first cycle of the example, the XOR and XNOR instructions are executed (as buffered in their respective FU queue), each obtaining their source data from the RRB (i.e. the external register reads and/or immediate values buffered to the RRB during configuration). The result generated by the XNOR instruction is thereafter needed by the three consumers ADD, SUB, and OR, all executing in the second cycle. The XOR instruction however is needed in the next clock cycle by the ADD and SUB instructions, and in the third cycle by the AND instruction. The operand result ('4') therefore requires both propagation and temporary storage for its consumers in the 2nd and 3rd clock cycle respectively. Therefore during the 3rd clock cycle when AND executes, the operand is selected from the rS unit storage (marked 'S' in the 2nd row, 2nd column), and propagated to its consumer as programmed during configuration.

This process continues for all instructions until completion, where each FU contains a queue to buffer multiple task instructions. In terms of distributed storage, the rS units may temporally store up to 3 values each (i.e. 3 input ports) where the torus connection is used to transfer results from opposite edges of the rS interconnect (right to left, and bottom to top) for a continuing stream of dataflow execution using the xy protocol. Note that stores are also sent to the WRB during execution, which are then forwarded to the store unit to handle writebacks. Once all instructions have finished executing, the final register values present in the WRB are written to the external register file as required.

3   Compilers

3.1   OmpSs Programming Model

OmpSs is a task-based programming model which exploits task-level parallelism on a shared-memory architecture. OmpSs enables programmers to annotate standard sequential-based applications with pragmas to help the compiler and runtime identify dependent and independent tasks for parallel execution while maintaining programming familiarity. Therefore the programmer does not need to synchronize or manage task execution, but rather expose task side-effects by simply annotating each kernel's operands with *input*, *output*, or *inout* (bidirectional) [7]. Using the clauses specified by the programmer, communication patterns amongst the tasks are obtained and analyzed by the physical compiler to determine inter-dependencies.

3.2   Logical Compiler

A logical compiler is a standard compiler that may be used by any modern computing system. Although any compiler may be chosen for a CCU, the logical (and physical) compiler will likely benefit from a more RISC-like target architecture as more Instruction Level Parallelism (ILP) may be extracted based on the structure of the ISA's layout, i.e. it is generally easier to eliminate false data dependencies, analyze register usage etc. in RISC. Conversely, x86 (a more CISC-like ISA) relies on an accumulator-based register architecture making it slightly more difficult for the physical compiler to extract parallelism from a fairly sequential instruction stream.

For this work, the ARMv7 ISA was selected for both the physical and logical compiler target architecture, with other ISA plugins remaining future work. To maintain compatibility with the OmpSs model, the Mecurium compiler (gcc-based) was also embedded into the logical compiler. Therefore the logical compiler may compile any C, C++, and Fortran language with either a sequential, OpenMP, OmpSs and/or MPI based programming model.

3.3   Physical Compiler

A physical compiler is the joint effort between compiler designers and computer architects, used for a smarter compilation process. The overall goal of the CCU's physical compiler is to form and map tasks according to specifications of the underlying architecture for higher performance and energy efficiency. Therefore the physical compiler is responsible for forming tasks by decoding instructions, eliminating false dependencies, and considering task dependencies and their effect on the underlying architecture.

As standard with majority of task-based compilers, the first stage of physical compilation requires tasks to be formed (and respective instructions gathered) based on the binary and task information gathered with the OmpSs model. The physical compiler then packs task instructions until a *conditional* branch is reached, eliminating all unconditional branches while maintaining program correctness (i.e. following the unconditional flow of control). Architecturally, this allows each engine's branch unit to possess low hardware complexity, and for a substantial amount of instructions to be present per task. The physical compiler then assesses dependencies within the intra-task instructions, eliminating false dependencies, extracting ILP, and creating a producer-consumer dependency matrix for every task.

To appropriately assign tasks to engines, the task's respective instructions and inter-dependencies are analyzed and compared to the available (and ideal) CCU engines for execution. The physical compiler invokes a demand-type algorithm to map tasks to an engine - i.e. if a task contains a high instruction count and ILP, the algorithm will give preference to assigning the task to a larger engine in the CCU that can exploit the ILP and not overload the rS and FU buffers. Similarly, if an instruction requires a specialized FU, the task will be mapped to the engine which possesses the FU. Thus tasks are mapped in this way while following inter-dependencies. Note that large tasks which do not fit into the FU buffers are divided into smaller tasks and assigned accordingly.

Once the tasks have been mapped to an appropriate engine, the internal instructions are assessed and mapped to FUs according to the instruction dependency matrix generated and/or any functional unit dependencies. The technique employed by the physical compiler is to place independent instructions side-by-side in the x direction (spatially adjacent FUs), and dependent instructions in the y direction (FUs in the following engine row(s)) so that the results may traverse with minimal hops. If an adjacent FU is unavailable, the compiler will then search for the closest available FU to its dependency.

Once the instructions have been successfully mapped, the physical compiler then evaluates the mappings to determine how each rS unit should be temporally and spatially configured for data propagation and/or storage of dependent instructions. Once the rS have been successfully mapped, the configuration data needed by the CCU engine is generated for each rS, FU (instruction opcodes), RRB, and WRB. Each task's configuration data is then stored in its respective memory bank located in the processor back-end, with each task's configuration address stored to the engine's lookup table.

It is important to note that load (and store) instructions within tasks are extracted prior to the rS mapping stage as these instructions must execute on an externally dedicated unit (See Fig. 1). Loads may be divided into two categories: External (a load which is needed to start task execution) or internal (load requested by an inter-task instruction). *External* loads possess a separate configuration memory bank which is used to read data values during configuration, occurring concurrently while the other units are configured. These loaded values are then written to the *RRB* so that they may propagate to their consumers as required during the execution stage. Similarly, internal loads are configured in the WRB which must wait for their producer data to generate in the engine. Once ready, the address is then sent to the load unit, where the data is brought back to the RRB when successfully read. Store instructions are also buffered by the WRB during task execution and sent to the store unit when ready. Likewise, external "register" values to be read prior and/or written after task execution are configured in the RRB and WRB memory respectively (in the same manner as loads and stores). Note that the multiplier/divider unit does not need to be configured as the RRB and WRB units are configured in the same manner as loads.

4 Hardware Design

4.1 rS and Interconnect

The two types of units present in an engine's interconnect are referred to as *external* and *internal* rS. As seen in Fig. 1, *external* rS are found at the very top of the interconnect and consist of four ports - two input and two output. These rS act as an interface between the RRB and functional unit inputs, and connect the bottom rS units to the top of the torus topology. Therefore external switches do not require storage properties since they are directly connected to the RRB (which buffer data) and do not receive any FU output. Horizontal propagation is also not supported by the external switches due to the xy routing protocol. All these factors allow external switches to possess low hardware area and a reduced number of I/O ports.

Internal switches are present in the main communication network and consist of six ports- three inputs and three outputs. An example of an internal rS architecture is presented in Fig. 5. All internal rS input ports consist of a 2:1 multiplexer that may (1) propagate input data, (2) output a stored value, or (3) simultaneously store and propagate a value. Control bits for all multiplexers and registers are dictated by the configuration data generated by the physical compiler. As shown in Fig. 5, an output port multiplexes all input ports, and therefore all rS output ports may propagate data simultaneously to neighbouring rS. Conflicts involved in data traversal of results are minimal. However if conflicts do exist, they are resolved by the physical compiler which either reroutes the result, uses alternative storage locations, or in the worst case, delays execution by one clock cycle.

The rS interconnect was designed to support single cycle multi-hop traversal, signifying that any result may be sent to any functional unit source input (including its own) within one clock cycle. To support this feature, the frequency of operation is limited by an engine's critical path. As each engine within a CCU varies in topological size, its respective maximum frequency will also vary. As will be seen during experimental testing however, engine size accounts for slight variation in the CCU's

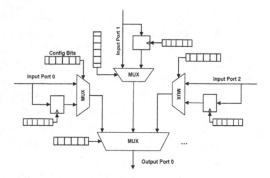

Fig. 5. Internal registerswitch (rs) architecture

maximum achievable frequency due to the simplistic design of the rS (Sect. 5.2.5, *Frequency of Operation*).

4.2 Functional Units

FUs present within an engine may be of any type including (but not limited to) ALUs, Multiplier/dividers, Multiplier-Accumulator Units (MAC), ALU/barrel shifter combinations etc. Each functional unit in an engine contains a buffer to hold its assigned task instruction opcodes. A low complexity *conditional* branch unit is also included in every engine. To support conditional branch execution, an engine contains a flag status register which is updated as instructions execute. External to each engine is a dedicated load unit(s) (see Fig. 1). A load takes approximately four clock cycles to execute, as standard in majority of conventional processors. Since multiply/divide instructions occur infrequently, one multiplier/divide unit is typically shared by the engines. Similar to the load unit, the operand data for mult/div is sent by the WRB, and the product/quotient is received by the RRB.

4.3 Read Register Buffer (RRB)

The RRB is responsible for managing (inputted) external data and communicating the data to the engine's components as needed during execution. Specifically, RRBs manage:

- External register file reads and loads during configuration and communicate these values to the required rS during execution.
- Internal loads (requested by the WRB) and communicate these loaded values to the required rS.
- The communication of immediate values to the required rS.
- Incoming external (i.e. multiply/divide) results and communicate the values to the correct rS.

The RRB is provided with configuration data so that its internal multiplexers, directly connected from the RRB to the rS interconnect, may communicate data to each of the four external rS inputs as required.

4.4 Write Register Buffer (WRB)

The WRB's main objectives are to manage store instructions issued by the engines and communicate the multiply/divide data and load requests to their respective external units. Although the WRB is not as complicated as the RRB design, it must properly interface these two external unit types and manage up to four concurrent requests made by the engine (i.e. the rS units directly connected). For this reason a queue is included in the WRB to manage pending requests, but is infrequently required due to the scheduling techniques provided by the physical compiler. The WRB must also handle the request and grant signals to the multiplier/divider when the unit is shared between multiple engines. Finally, the WRB is responsible for sending a signal to the RRB to specify that a load and/or mult/div has been sent. Based on this signal, if the RRB has not received the result after a specific time (i.e. four clock cycles for a load etc.), the engine stalls until the pending data is received. The WRB also handle final value writebacks to the external register file.

4.5 Configuration and Setup

Configuration of an engine is initiated when the configuration memory is signaled by the scheduler after address lookup. Each engine contains its own configuration memory which is banked into several partitions to quickly configure the engine. Specifically, each component and/or row within the engine is given a separate configuration memory so that the components may be configured concurrently. Separate memories are provided for the RRB, WRB, per row of ALUs, and two dedicated banks for every row of rS to reduce configuration time to a maximum of 10 clock cycles per engine (assuming a 64bit datawidth). The external register reads and loads possess their own memory bank as well so they may obtain their values concurrently during engine configuration. During experimental testing, the average register reads required per task was approximately three (2.88) with an average of one to two maximum external loads, easily meeting the 10 clock cycle requirement for configuration.

5 Experimental Testing

5.1 Methodology

To determine the benefits and characteristics of CCU processors, seven different combinations of engines were designed and tested as presented in Table 1. The engine configurations in this table are written as <engine$_i$ x engine$_{i+1}$> where the value of *engine$_i$* signifies the number of functional units present in the engine at that location. Including over 6 FUs did not show an advantage towards increasing performance as extracting ILP/DLP for greater than 6 instructions simultaneously was rare.

Table 1. CPU/CCU engine combinations tested

CCUs						
<6x2>	<4x6>	<6x6>	<4x4>	<4x2>	<6>	<4>
Each engine in a CCU contains: - 2 ld/str, 1 cond branch unit(s)/engine - 387KB of config cache / 12 banks - 2*(nFUs) + x*2 rS units/engine				Each CCU shares: - 1 Mul/Div Unit - 128KB 4-way D-cache (4 c.c) - 16-entry external Register File		
CPUs						
Dual Core (2 single OoO cores)				Single Core OoO Processor		
-Each processor contains: 2 ALUs (INT), 1 Branch Unit, 2 LD/STR units, 1 MUL/DIV, 36-entry issue queue, 48KB I$, 32KB D$ /core (4 c.c access time) - Based on 64-bit ARM Cortex-A57, 32-entry register file (ARF/PRF)						

An OoO single and dual core processor were also designed for baseline comparison invoking a sequentially consistent memory model. Specifically, the CCU, single, and dual core processors were all modeled using custom in-house software simulators coded in C++, where the back-end of each processor type was also implemented as a hardware prototype. This strategy was used to accurately determine the feasibility of a CCU processor in terms of area, timing, and power with RTL modeling, while being able to mitigate several front-end issues (i.e. branch prediction, cache misses etc.) to easily assess various performance characteristics, simulate several CCU engine combinations, and execute millions of instructions at a cycle accurate level.

5.1.1 Benchmarks

The benchmarks used for experimental testing were retrieved from the *Barcelona Application Repository* [10]. The applications selected use the OmpSs programming and shared memory model. As CCUs currently only support integer execution, the benchmarks tested were also integer based while those that used floating point were converted to its integer equivalent. The benchmarks and their field of application are provided in Table 2.

Table 2. Benchmark description

Benchmark	Field of application	Benchmark	Field of application
Barnes-Hut	N-Body particle simulations	Knights tour	Math/computer science
N-Binary	Binary search algorithm	Array	Reduction application
N Queens	Chess simulations/opt	Cholesky	Decomposition algorithm
SparseLU	LU decomposition	Arnoldi	Mathematics/orthogonality

5.1.2 Compilation

The benchmarks were logically compiled (-O2) using the Mecurium compiler (gcc-based) to support the OmpSs model, with the ARMv7-A ISA as the target architecture. The CCUs with two engines running simultaneously (and the baseline multicore) were profiled with Extra in the logical compiler using the NX_ARGS two processor, one thread option, with the single cores employing a single processor option. The physical compiler was also coded in C++, capable of decoding ARMv7 instructions. The average physical and logical compilation time was estimated to be approximately 0.253 s and 0.377 s respectively. Therefore results demonstrate that physical compilation on average requires less time than standard logical compilation.

5.1.3 Benchmark Analysis for Prototyping

The benchmark characteristics were analyzed to determine ideal CCU functional units that should be included in engines for executing general purpose applications. The average number of instructions per task was approximately 38. On average, arithmetic type instructions accounted for majority of the instructions. Bitwise operations accounted for a very small fraction of the total instruction count (1.15 %), and consequently were added to the arithmetic count. Loads and stores accounted for approximately 37.21 % of the instructions and are provided with their own external execution units accordingly. Mult/div on average only accounted for 0.27 % of the instruction count. Therefore, for reasons of power and area, only one mult/div unit was included per CCU processor, shared between the engines. Based on these trends, ALUs were included as all FUs within the engine, with one of the ALUs per engine possessing barrel shifting capabilities.

5.1.4 Software Simulators

Both the CPU and CCU simulators were run on a Ubuntu Linux operating system with an Intel Core i7-5820 K (3.3 GHz) and 16 GB RAM. An analyzer was built in to all simulators to gather statistics of performance, utilization, and various task and engine execution characteristics.

The CPU and multicore simulator were modeled after the ARM Cortex-A57 OoO processor, with specifications given in Table 1. Specifically, this processor consists of a 12 stage front-end with a two stage issue to dispatch. The back-end consists of two ALUs, a 4-stage multiplier/divider unit, two load/store units, and a branching unit. The NEON units were omitted as vector/SIMD processing was not implemented. The dual core processor was modeled as two Cortex-A57 CPUs running in parallel.

Perfect branch prediction is assumed for all processors during initial testing. Thereafter CCUs with no branch prediction are compared to a CPU with branch prediction (GShare - assuming a 92 % prediction accuracy). Regarding cache misses, CCU engines currently stall until the data is retrieved from the cache since a tag-less method is invoked. Future work involves (1) cache bit integration in the configuration data so that instructions which do not rely on the load may still execute, and (2) reducing register spilling in the logic binary for minimal cache access. With regards to page faults, interrupts, and exception handling, CCUs currently flush the engine to accommodate the context switch/exception with a 10 clock cycle reconfiguration cost (which overlaps the previous task's execution phase).

5.1.5 Hardware Prototypes

All CPU/CCU back-end hardware was implemented in VHDL and verified for correctness using ModelSim. The Synopsys Design Vision CAD flow was used to elaborate the RTL and obtain preliminary statistics on area, timing, and power consumption. This modeling was performed at the 45 nm technology node using the open source OpenPDK library (NCSU/OSU). The CPU and CCU back-ends were prototyped according to the specifications provided in Table 1. The CPUs include a register file (32 physical registers), a 36-entry issue queue (6 entries for 6 functional units) and bypass network. Configuration memory was not modeled and included during synthesis since this memory is synonymous to the instruction cache in a conventional processor (also not modeled). Hence the configuration memories and instructions/data dispatched to the CPU queues were stored into several Memory Initialization Files (.MIF) statically to replicate the execution of certain application phases and to verify the design in ModelSim. An example of a <4x6> CCU back-end prototyped for testing is given in Fig. 6.

5.2 Results

5.2.1 Area

Figure 7 presents the area, frequency and power consumption for the multicore and CCU processors normalized to the single core processor. As seen in the figure, the various CCU configurations were able to decrease area requirements of a single processor back-end by an average of 51 %, with single engine CCU configurations averaging around 37 % of the area required. This decrease in area overhead is mainly attributed to the elimination of the issue and dispatch queues (and their respective search and lookup logic), a smaller register file, and simple network for operand forwarding and bypassing.

5.2.2 Configuration Memory

The average configuration banked memory storage requirements are as follows:

ALUs: Configured in twos - 16 Kb (i.e. 8 Kb per ALU)
rS: Configured in twos - 16 Kb
RRB: 8 Kb
WRB: 1 Kb

The total memory requirements per engine component are outlined in Table 3, based on the average number of tasks per application. Overall, the statistics demonstrate that the scalability and reconfigurability of the engines and interconnect come at

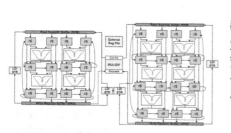

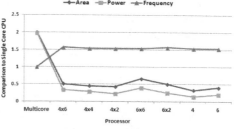

Fig. 6. <4x6> Engine CCU processor   **Fig. 7.** Normalized power, area and frequency

Table 3. Configuration specifications

Conf memory	Timing specification	Total storage required (**KB**)
Functional units	4 c.c per row (2 c.c/FU)	120
rS	10 c.c. per two (5 c.c/rS)	240
RRB	4 c.c	20
WRB	4 c.c	4
PreLoad	2-3 c.c per load	2
External reg file	2c.c per two reads (multi-port reads)	1

the cost of approximately 5 KB per additional row added to an engine, i.e. two FUs and four rS.

5.2.3 Performance

Figure 8 presents the normalized IPC improvement for a <4> and <6> single-engine CCU over a single CPU core. As displayed in Fig. 8, by using the physical compiler and revised engine datapath to extract additional ILP and DLP, the <4> and <6> CCUs were able to exceed an OoO single core processor on average by 1.321x and 1.350x respectively. Thus there is a clear benefit for increased performance with the simple design and methodology of CCUs in comparison to monolithic cores.

Next, the multi-engine performance of a CCU processor is assessed. Figure 9 presents the single CCU core (dual-engine) IPC speedup over the baseline single core, for the inclusion and exclusion of unconditional branch instructions. This factor was analyzed since unconditional branches accounted for approximately 14 % of the instruction count, adding to the single core's achievable IPC. The <ideal> configuration is also included, representative of the maximum possible performance achievable in a CCU for a given application (with each ideal configuration varying per benchmark).

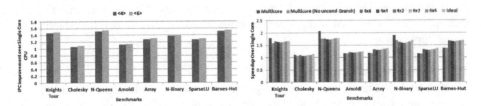

Fig. 8. Normalized IPC - single-thread CCUs **Fig. 9.** Normalized IPC - dual-engine CCUs

With the inclusion of all instructions, CCU (double engine) processors were able to achieve a 1.45x average speedup over an OoO single core, with the dual core architecture achieving approximately the same performance improvement (1.467x). When unconditional branches were eliminated from the instruction count, the CCU processors were able to achieve a 1.555x average performance improvement over the single core CPU, with a slight performance advantage over the dual core since its unconditional branches were also eliminated. In comparison to the ideal configurations, the <4x6> and <6x6> CCUs were able to meet performance within 6 %.

As CCU branch prediction techniques remain future work, we compare the per-formance of CCUs with no branch prediction to the OoO CPU performance with branch prediction. The normalized speedup per CCU configuration over the baseline CPU is provided in Fig. 10. As seen in Fig. 10, the CCUs on average were able to meet the performance ($\approx$1.01x) with less hardware units and power consumption than a conventional CPU. This comparable performance is mainly attributed to the cost of CPU misprediction (i.e. flush the pipeline and restore from a checkpoint), whereas the CCU simply suffers a constant 3 c.c penalty while extracting higher ILP/DLP in the back-end. Thus branch prediction techniques applied to the CCU will inevitably attain more performance advantages over conventional processors once implemented.

Figures 9 and 10 together display that the best performance attained for all benchmarks are the <4x6>, <6x2>, and <6x6> configured CCUs due to their FU sizes that can exploit higher ILP and DLP present in application instruction streams. In general however, the <4x6> configuration presents more flexibility and energy effi-ciency (over the <6x2> and <6x6> CCUs) due to its heterogeneous engine configuration.

5.2.4 Engine Utilization

The average utilization of various CCU engine configurations during benchmark execution is presented in Fig. 11. Single engine configurations were not shown in the Fig. 11 as they demonstrated 100 % utilization. As tasks (may) execute concurrently, Fig. 11 displays that CCUs with engines which possess 2-FUs (i.e.<4x2> and <6x2>) on average prefer to execute their tasks on larger engines (i.e.4- and 6-FUs) which is contrary to conventional processors which possess two ALUs. This fact is attributed to the physical compiler's ability to extract additional ILP and DLP. Thus when only one task is to be executed at a given time, preference to is given to the larger engine which can provide the processor with higher performance and more flexibility for executing the task. Overall, the most fair utilization found among the different engine configu-rations tested was the <4x6> CCU which delivered almost equal utilization of its engines. This signifies that using heterogeneous sized engines is key for adapting to various applications.

5.2.5 Frequency of Operation

Referring back to Fig. 7, operational frequency observed a slight change between the two, four, and six FU engine configurations. As stated previously, data may traverse any number of rS in an engine, where each rS consists of a set of multiplexers. There

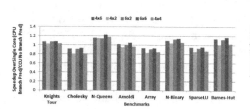

Fig. 10. Normalized IPC (branch prediction)

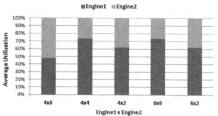

Fig. 11. Avg engine utilization

are 3 gates/mux*2mux/rS, and therefore a 6-FU engine's critical path will experience 42 gate delays (gd), a 4-FU engine 36 gd, and 2-FU engine 30gd. Assuming 4 ps per gd at the 45 nm node, there is an approximate 24 ps difference in critical path delay per engine type. This fact exemplifies that the CCU design is scalable in terms of frequency, area, and power.

As seen in Fig. 8, when compared to the single and dual core processors, the frequency was able to improve by approximately 1.51x. This increase is mainly due to the avoidance of a complex bypass network, issue queue and its search logic. This advantage however comes at the expense of implementing the physical compiler and the loss of a pure dynamic execution style typical of OoO processors.

5.2.6 Power
Power dissipation results are also presented in Fig. 7 with values normalized to the single core processor. As expected, the single FU engine CCUs consumed the least power, with the <6x6> engine consuming the most power. However even the largest <6x6> engine only consumed 66 % of the power required of the single core. The ideal engine <4x6> which achieved near multicore performance was also able to reduce single core and multicore power by 65 % and 82 % respectively.

6 Conclusion

This work presented the concept of a configurable processor architecture referred to as Configurable Computing Units (CCUs). CCUs employ logical compilation to maintain compatibility with current computing standards and apply physical compilation to support an underlying reconfigurable processor architecture. CCUs consist of a variety of execution engines and functional units, connected through a configurable single-cycle multi-hop registerSwitch (rS) interconnect for data propagation and distributed storage. Several CCU engine combinations were tested using the OmpSs programming model for applicability to parallel, shared memory applications. A software simulator was used to assess OoO single core and dual core processor performance and compare it to several engine combinations. The back-ends of the processors were prototyped as hardware RTL models to determine various factors of area, power, and performance. Results demonstrated that CCUs were able to improve performance in parallel applications on average by approximately 1.45–1.555x, in turn matching dual-core performance, while consuming 51 % of the area required of a conventional processor back-end and reducing power consumption by 65 %. Future work in CCUs involves branch prediction and a front-end hardware implementation.

Acknowledgement. The authors of this work would like to acknowledge the support and funding provided by the Ontario Graduate Scholarship (OGS) program and Ryerson University FEAS.

References

1. Esmaeilzadeh, H., Sampson, A., Ceze, L., Burger, D.: Neural acceleration for general-purpose approximate programs. In: IEEE/ACM International Symposium on Microarchi tecture (MICRO 45), pp. 449–460 (2012)
2. Dallou, T., Juurlink, B.: Hardware-based task dependency resolution for the starSs programming model. In: International Conference on Parallel Processing Works, pp. 367–374 (2012)
3. Borkar, S., Chien, A.: The future of microprocessors. Commun. ACM **54**(5), 67–77 (2011)
4. Flynn, M.J., Mencer, O., Milutinovic, V., Rakocevic, G., Stenstrom, P., Trobec, R., Valero, M.: Moving from petaflops to petadata. Commun. ACM **56**(5), 39–42 (2013)
5. Patt, Y.: Future microprocessors: what must we do differently if we are to effectively utilize multi-core and many-core chips. IPSI BGD Trans. Internet Res. **5**(1), 2–10 (2009)
6. Extra instrumentation package: www.bsc.es/computer-sciences/paraver
7. Duran, A., Ayguade, E., Badia, R., Labarta, J., et al.: OmpSs: a proposal for programming heterogeneous multicore architectures. Parallel Process. Lett. **21**, 173–193 (2011)
8. Tseng, F., Patt, Y.: Achieving out-of-order performance with almost in-order complexity. In: Proceedings of International Symposium of Computer Architecture (ISCA), pp. 3–12 (2008)
9. Barcelona Application Repository: pm.bsc.es/projects/bar
10. Torrellas, J., Oskin, M., Adve, S., et al.: workshop on advancing computer architecture research: laying a new foundation IT: computer architecture for 2025 and beyond. In: ACAR-II (2010)

Design and Evaluation of a Processing-in-Memory Architecture for the Smart Memory Cube

Erfan Azarkhish[1]([⊠]), Davide Rossi[1], Igor Loi[1], and Luca Benini[1,2]

[1] University of Bologna, Bologna, Italy
{erfan.azarkhish,davide.rossi,igor.loi}@unibo.it
[2] Swiss Federal Institute of Technology in Zurich, Zurich, Switzerland
luca.benini@iis.ee.ethz.ch

Abstract. 3D integration of solid-state memories and logic, as demonstrated by the Hybrid Memory Cube (HMC), offers major opportunities for revisiting near-memory computation and gives new hope to mitigate the power and performance losses caused by the "memory wall". Several publications in the past few years demonstrate this renewed interest. In this paper we present the first exploration steps towards design of the Smart Memory Cube (SMC), a new Processor-in-Memory (PIM) architecture that enhances the capabilities of the logic-base (LoB) die in HMC. An accurate simulation environment called SMCSim has been developed, along with a full featured software stack. The key contribution of this work is full system analysis of near memory computation including high-level software to low-level firmware and hardware layers, considering offloading and dynamic overheads caused by the operating system (OS), cache coherence, and memory management. A zero-copy pointer passing mechanism has been devised to allow low overhead data sharing between the host and the PIM. Benchmarking results demonstrate up to 2X performance improvement in comparison with the host System-on-Chip (SoC), and around 1.5X against a similar host-side accelerator. Moreover, by scaling down the voltage and frequency of PIM's processor it is possible to reduce energy by around 70 % and 55 % in comparison with the host and the accelerator, respectively.

Keywords: Processor-in-memory · Hybrid memory cube · Full system analysis · Software stack · Device driver

1 Introduction

The recent technological breakthrough represented by HMC is on its way to improve bandwidth, power consumption, and density [13]. This is while heterogeneous 3D integration also provides another opportunity for revisiting near memory computation to fill the gap between the processors and memories even further. Several research efforts in the past years demonstrate the renewed interest in moving part of the computation to where the data resides [4,5,11,22],

© Springer International Publishing Switzerland 2016
F. Hannig et al. (Eds.): ARCS 2016, LNCS 9637, pp. 19–31, 2016.
DOI: 10.1007/978-3-319-30695-7_2

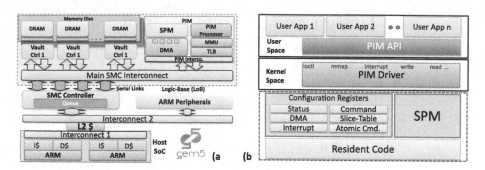

Fig. 1. An overview of the SMCSim environment for design space exploration of the smart memory cube (a), PIM's software stack (b).

specifically, in a 3D stacked memory context. Near memory computation can provide two main opportunities: (1) reduction in data movement by vicinity to the main storage resulting in reduced memory access latency and energy, (2) higher bandwidth provided by Through Silicon Vias (TSVs) in comparison with the interface to the host limited by the pins. Most recent works exploit the second opportunity by trying to accelerate data-intensive applications with large bandwidth demands [5]. In [22] and [4] also, networks of 3D stacked memories are formed and host processors are attached to their peripheries, providing even more hospitable platforms for processing-in-memory due to huge bandwidth internal to the memory-centric networks. These platforms, however, are highly costly and suitable for high-end products with extremely high performance goals [4]. Also, a look at the latest HMC Specifications [2] reveals that its ultra-fast serial interface is able to deliver as much bandwidth as is available in the 3D stack (Four serial links, 32 lanes each operating from 12.5 Gb/s to 30 Gb/s). For this reason, the same bandwidth available to a PIM on LoB is also theoretically available to the external host, and high-performance processing clusters or GPU architectures executing highly parallel and optimized applications can demand and exploit this huge bandwidth [25]. This puts PIM in a difficult but realistic position with its main obvious advantage over the external world being vicinity to the memory (lower access latency and energy) and not an increased memory bandwidth.

In this paper, we focus on this dark corner of the PIM research, and try to demonstrate that even if delivered bandwidth to the host can be as high as the internal bandwidth of the memory, PIM's vicinity to memory itself can provide interesting opportunities for energy and performance optimization. We focus on a scenario with a single PIM processor competing with a single thread on the host. In this scenario the caches of the host are not thrashed, the memory interface is not saturated, and the host can demand as much bandwidth as it requires. This is a worst-case scenario from PIM's point of view. Our PIM proposal (called the Smart Memory Cube) is built on top of the existing HMC standard with full compatibility with its IO interface specification. We have developed a full-system simulation environment called SMCSim and verified its accuracy against a Cycle-Accurate (CA) model [8]. We devised an optimized memory virtualization scheme for zero-copy data sharing between host and PIM; enhanced PIM's operations by the aid from atomic processing in-memory operations; and enhanced PIM's memory access by means of a flexible Direct Memory Access (DMA) engine. Up to 2X performance improvement in comparison with the host SoC, and around 1.5X against a similar host-side accelerator are achieved. Power consumption was reduced by about 70 % and 55 % in comparison with the host and the accelerator, respectively, when PIM's voltage and frequency were scaled down. Lastly, the overheads associated with offloading code and data from host to PIM were found to be negligible. Related works are presented in Sect. 2. SMCSim is introduced in Sect. 3. Design of PIM and its software stack is described in Subsect. 3.1. Experimental results and conclusions are presented in Sects. 4 and 5.

2 Related Works

The design space for near memory computation is enormous, and several different concerns need to be addressed such as the micro-architecture of the PIM processor, memory management scheme, and communication mechanisms with the host [17]. In [11] a Coarse-grain Reconfiurable Accelerator (CGRA) is located on a separate die and connected to the DRAM dies through TSVs. Segmented memory without caching is used and 46 % energy saving along with 1.6X performance gain for Big Data applications are reported. The main difference between our work and this work is flexible support for virtual memory as well as considering the offloading overheads in our analysis. Active Memory Cube (AMC) [22] extends the logic layer of the HMC with clusters of vector processors without caches. Hardware coherence is maintained with the host and virtual memory support has been provided. 2X performance improvement is reported for dense matrix operations, increasing to 5X when vicinity aware memory allocation is utilized. Tesseract [4] features a network of memory cubes each accommodating 32 in-order cores with L1 caches and two prefetchers, optimized for parallelizing the PageRank algorithm. Uncacheable regions are shared with PIM and segmented memory without paging is supported. Up to 10X performance improvement and 87 % energy reduction has been provided in comparison with high-performance server hosts. Unlike these works, we focus on a context which external memory interface is not bandwidth saturated and PIM's benefits are determined only by latency. In addition, we utilize atomic commands and consider the offloading overheads in our studies, as well. In [5], the memory stack has been augmented with low level atomic in-memory operations. Host instructions are augmented, and full virtual memory support and hardware cache coherence is provided. for Big Data workloads up to 20 % performance and 1.6X energy gain is obtained. The main difference between our proposal and this work is that our PIM supports flexible execution of different computation kernels and its acceleration is not limited to the atomic operations only. Moreover, our solution is not dependent on the ISA of the host and with a proper software any host platform can communicate with it through its memory-mapped interface.

In this paper the goal is to provide flexible near-memory computation with full virtual memory support through a full-featured software stack compatible with the Parallel Programming Application Programming Interfaces (API). This is the first PIM effort to accurately model all layers from high level user applications, to low level drivers, OS, and hardware. Besides, a comprehensive accuracy verification versus a CA model has been performed which improves the quality of the obtained results.

3   The SMC Simulation Environment

SMCSim is a high-level simulation environment developed based on gem5 [12], capable of modeling an SMC device attached to a complete host SoC. Figure 1a illustrates an example of one such platform modeled in this environment. SMCSim has been designed based on gem5's General Memory System model [12] exploiting its flexibility, modularity, and high simulation speed, as well as, features such as check-pointing and dynamic CPU switching. An extensive comparison with a CA model [8] has been performed, as well, which confirms its reasonable accuracy. Figure 1a highlights the most important components in this environment. The host is a Cortex-A15 SoC capable of booting a full-featured OS. Inside the SMC, the vault controllers and the main interconnect are modeled using pre-existing components and tuned based on the CA models in [8]. A PIM is located on the LoB layer with flexible and generic computational capabilities. This configuration is completely consistent with the current release of the HMC Specification [13]. Also, SMC is not dependent or limited to any ISA and it is exposed to the host via memory mapped regions. Therefore, any host platform should be able to communicate with it by the aid from a proper software stack. For the serial links: bandwidth, serialization latency, and packetization overheads are obtained from [2]. They accept the same address ranges and each packet can travel over any of them [2,3]. SMC/HMC controller is responsible for translating the host protocol (AXI for example) to the serial links protocol. Plus, it should have large internal buffers to hide the access latency of the cube. Different sources of latency are modeled in this environment and calibrated in Sect. 4.

3.1   Design of PIM and Its Software Stack

We have chosen an ARM Cortex-A15 core without caches or prefetchers for PIM, and augmented it with low cost components to enhance its capabilities. Our choice of ARM is because it offers a mature software stack, its system bridges (AXI) are well understood, and it is an energy-efficient architecture. Nevertheless, the architecture is not limited to it. As shown in Fig. 1a, PIM is attached to the main LoB interconnect through its own local interconnect, and features a Scratchpad Memory (SPM), a DMA engine, a Translation Look-aside Buffer (TLB) along with a Memory Management Unit (MMU).

PIM has been designed to directly access user-space virtual memory. Its TLB serves for this purpose. Apart from memory protection benefits, it replaces memory-copy from user's memory to PIM with a simple virtual pointer passing. Scalability and programmability are improved, and offloading overheads are reduced to a great extent. Since user's memory is paged in conventional architectures, PIM should support it, as well. To add more flexibility we introduce the concept of *slices* as a generalization to memory pages: a region of memory composed by 1 or more memory-pages which is contiguous in both virtual and physical memory spaces. With this definition, contiguous memory pages which map to contiguous page-frames can be merged to build larger slices, with arbitrary sizes. Note that, any change in page-size requires rebuilding the OS and all device drivers, while slices are transparent to the OS and other devices. PIM's memory management is done at the granularity of the slices. The first slice is devoted to PIM's SPM, and the rest of the memory space is mapped immediately after this region. Upon a TLB miss, a data structure in DRAM called the *slice-table* is consulted and the translation rules are updated on a Least Recently Used (LRU) basis. *Slice-table* is similar to page-tables and contains all translation rules for the computation kernel currently executing on PIM. It is built during the task offloading procedure by PIM's device-driver. Most host-side accelerators with virtual memory support rely on the host processor to refill the rules in their TLB. The OS consults its page-table to reprogram the IO-MMU of the device, and then wakes up the accelerator to continue its operation. Since PIM is far from the host processors, asking them for a refill upon every miss can result in a large delay. As an alternative, PIM's TLB contains a simple controller responsible for fetching the required rule from the slice-table. Apart from the performance benefits, this allows for fully independent execution of PIM.

A simple zero-load latency analysis (Sect. 4) reveals that the latency of directly accessing DRAM by PIM is harmful to its performance, therefore latency-hiding mechanisms are required. Caches and prefetchers provide a higher-level of abstraction without much control. This is desired for SoCs far from the memory and flexible enough to support different main memory configurations [6]. DMA engines plus SPMs, on the other hand, provide more control and can reduce energy consumption without much increase in the programming effort [18]. For this reason they make more sense in a near-memory processor. We have augmented PIM with a DMA engine capable of bulk data transfers between the DRAM vaults and its SPM (See Fig. 1a). It allows multiple outstanding transactions by having several DMA resources, and accepts virtual address ranges without any alignment or size restrictions. A complementary way to address this problem is to move some very specific arithmetic operations directly to the DRAM dies and ask the vault controller to do them "atomically". In-memory operations can reduce data movement when computation is local to one DRAM row [5], and they are easily implementable in the abstracted memory interface of HMC. We have augmented our vault controllers with three types of atomic commands suitable for the benchmarks under our study: *atomic-min*, *atomic-increment*, and *atomic-add-immediate*. These commands are implemented in the vault-controllers and their latency is hidden behind the DRAM timings. On the other side, instead of modifying PIM's ISA to support these commands, we added specific memory mapped registers to the PIM processor.

By configuring these registers PIM is able to send atomic operations towards the SMC vaults. For computations that need to gather information not fully localized to a single memory vault, DMA can be more beneficial. While, highly localized computations with low computational intensity are better performed as close as possible to the memory dies, by means of the atomic commands.

A software-stack has been developed for the user level applications to view PIM as a standard accelerator (See Fig. 1b). At the lowest level, a resident program runs on PIM performing the required tasks. A dynamic binary offloading mechanism has been designed to modify this code during runtime. PIM also features a set of configuration registers mapped in the physical address space and accessible by the host. PIM's device driver has been adopted from Mali GPU's driver [1] and is compatible with standard accelerators as well as parallel programming APIs such as OpenCL. This light-weight driver provides a low-overhead and high-performance communication mechanism between the API and PIM. An object-oriented user-level API has been designed, as well, to abstract away the details of the device driver and to facilitate user's interface. Offloading and coordinating the computations on PIM are initiated by this API.

PIM targets execution of medium sized computation kernels having less than a few kilobytes of instructions. The host processor parses the binary Executable and Linkable Format (ELF) file related to a precompiled computation kernel, and dynamically offloads .text and .rodata sections to PIM's memory map by the aid from the API. This procedure is called the *kernel-offloading*. On the other hand, the virtual pointer to preallocated user level data structures need to be sent to PIM for the actual execution to take place (*task-offloading*). PIM's API sends the page numbers associated with user data structures to the driver, and the driver builds the slice-table in the kernel memory space using the physical addresses. Next, caches are flushed and the virtual pointers are written to PIM's memory mapped registers. An interrupt is then sent to PIM to wake it up for execution. This mechanism prevents PIM from accessing unwanted physical memory locations, and allows it to traverse user-level data structures without any effort. A polling thread in PIM's API waits for completion of the offloaded task.

4   Experimental Results

Our baseline host system is composed of two Cortex-A15 CPU cores @2 GHz with 32 KB of instruction cache, 64 KB of data cache, and a shared 2 MB L2 cache with associativity of 8 as the last-level cache (LLC). The block size of all caches is increased to 256 B to match the row buffer size of the HMC model (effect of cache block size is studied later in this section). The memory cube model provides 512 MB of memory with 16 vaults, 4 stacked memory dies, and 2 banks per partition [8]. PIM has a single core processor similar to the host processors running at the same frequency, with the possibility of voltage and frequency scaling by means of dedicated clock and voltage domains on the LoB. Maximum burst size of PIM's DMA is set to 256 B by default. We performed a detailed accuracy comparison of the high-level SMC against a CA model [8].

We applied identical traffic patterns with various bandwidth demands to both CA and gem5-based models, and compared their delivered bandwidth and total execution time over a large design space defined by the architectural parameter. Several experiments demonstrated that total execution time and delivered bandwidth of the gem5-based model correlate well with the CA model: with low or medium traffic pressure, the difference was less than 1 %, and for high pressure saturating traffic the difference was bounded by 5 %, in all cases. Next, we calibrated the latency of the individual components based on the available data from the literature and the state of the art. The results are shown in Table 1.

Table 1. Zero-load latency breakdown of memory accesses from the host and PIM.

HOST: L2 cache refill latency - (Size: 256 B) [Total: 102.3 ns]			PIM: 4B read access latency (no caches) [Total: 39.1 ns]		
Membus	1 Cycle@2 GHz	Flit:64 b	PimBus	1 Cycle@1 GHz	Flit:32 b
SMCController	8 Cycles@2 GHz	Pipeline Latency [21]	SMCXbar	1 Cycle@1GHz	Flit:256 b [8]
SERDES	1.6 ns	SER = 1.6 DES = 1.6 [14]	Vault Ctrl. Front-end	4 Cycles@1.2 GHz	[8]
Packet Transfer	13.6 ns	16 Lanes@10 Gb/s, 128 b hdr [2]	tRCD	13.75 ns	Activate [14]
PCB Trace Latency	3.2 ns + 3.2 ns	Round Trip	tCL	13.75 ns	Issue Read Command [14]
SMCXBar	1 Cycle@1 GHz	Flit:256 b [8]	tBURST	3.2 ns	1 Beat [19]
VaultCtrl.frontend	4 Cycles@1.2 GHz	[8]	Vault Ctrl. Back-end	4 Cycles@1.2 GHz	[8]
tRCD	13.75 ns	Activate [14]	PimBus	1 Cycle@1 GHz	Flit:32 b
tCL	13.75 ns	Issue Read Command [8]			
tBURST	25.6 ns	256 B Burst [19]			
VaultCtrl.backend	4 Cycles@1.2 GHz	[8]			
SERDES	1.6 ns	SER = 1.6 DES = 1.6 [14]			
Packet Transfer	13.6 ns	16 Lanes@10 Gb/s, 128 b hdr [2]			
SMCController	1 Cycles@2 GHz	Pipeline Latency [21]			
Membus	1 Cycle@2 GHz	Flit:64 b			

Data intensive applications often categorized as "Big Data" workloads are widely chosen in the literature as the target for near memory acceleration [4,5,11]. The common trait shared by most of these applications is sensitivity to memory latency and high bandwidth demand. Graph traversal applications are an interesting example in this group due to their unpredictable memory access patterns and high ratio of memory access to computation [5]. A common use for these benchmarks is social network analysis. We have chosen four large-scale graph processing applications, and try to accelerate their main computing loop (i.e. the computation kernel) by offloading it to PIM for execution. Our results are also compared with simple matrix addition (MAT), as a reference with lowest possible memory access latency sensitivity. Here is the list of the graph bench-marks studied in this paper: *Average Teenage Follower (ATF)* [5] counts for each vertex the number of its teenage followers by iterating over all teenager. We have implemented an *atomic-increment* command inside the memory cube for this purpose. *Breadth-First Search (BFS)* [5] visits the vertices closer to a given source vertex first by means of a FIFO queue. No atomic operations were utilized to accelerate this kernel, however, the queue for visiting the nodes has been implemented in PIM's SPM, given that in sparse graphs the required queue size of BFS is determined by the maximum outage degree of the nodes and not the number of nodes. *PageRank (PR)* [4] is a well-known algorithm that calculates the importance of vertices in a graph. We have implemented a single-precision floating point version of this kernel, plus an atomic floating-point *add-immediate* on the vault side. *Bellman-Ford Shortest Path (BF)* [5] finds the shortest path from a given source vertex to other vertices in a graph. Vault con-trollers have been augmented with *atomic-min* to facilitate its execution. We have used randomly generated sparse graphs ranging from 4 K node to 512 K nodes with characteristics obtained from real world data sets [15], and imple-mented them using the List of Lists (LIL) representation format [20], as its easily parallelizable and scalable to many nodes, and does not have the scalability lim-itations of the adjacency matrices. We use two DMA resources to efficiently hide the latency of traversing the LIL.

First we study offloading overheads. ATF has been executed on the host side and then offloaded to PIM. In Fig. 2a, *kernel-offload* represents the overhead associated with reading the ELF file from the secondary storage of the host, parsing it, and offloading the binary code (as explained in Subsect. 3.1); *task-offload* is all overheads associated with virtual pointer passing to PIM for the graph to be analyzed; and *host-execution* is the absolute execution time of the kernel on host. It can be seen that the task-offload overhead decreases with the size of the graph and is always below 5 % of the total execution time of the ATF. Most of this overhead is due to cache flushing and less than 15 % of it belongs to building the slice-table and pointer passing. Also, kernel-offload is usually performed once per several executions, therefore, its cost is amortized among them. Plus, for kernels like PR with several iterations relative overheads becomes even lower. Next, we analyze the speed-up achieved by PIM in terms of host's execution time divided by PIM's. The number of graph nodes has been changed and Fig. 2b (left vertical axis) illustrates the results. Lightly shaded columns represent PIM's execution without any aid from the atomic HMC commands, while the highly shaded ones use them. PIM's frequency is equal to the host (2 GHz). An average speed-up of 2X is observable across different graph sizes, and as the size increases, speed-up increases as well. This can be associated with increase in cache misses in the LLC of the host (plotted on the right vertical axis). Furthermore, the average benefit of using *atomic-increment*, *atomic-min*, *atomic-float-add* is obtained as 10 %, 18 %, and 35 %, respectively. A cache line size of 256 Bytes was mentioned before for both cache levels in the host. We can see in Fig. 2c that this choice has been in favour of the host in terms of performance,

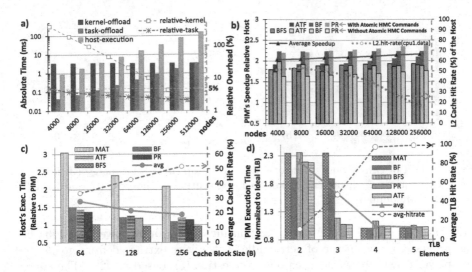

Fig. 2. Offloading overheads in execution of the ATF kernel (a), PIM's speed-up with/without SMC Atomic Commands [left axis] and LLC hit-rate associated with the data port of the executing CPU [right axis] (b), Host's execution time versus cache block size (c), and effect of PIM's TLB size on hit-rate and execution time (d) (Colour figure online).

leading to an increase in the LLC hit-rate. This is mainly due to sequential traversing of the graph nodes which results in a relatively high spatial locality (MAT in this plot represents simple 1000×1000 matrix addition as a reference for comparison). Two additional experiment on PIM identify its optimal TLB size (Fig. 2d) and the required DMA transfer size (Fig. 3a). Four TLB elements were found enough for the studied computation kernels and a nearly perfect TLB hit-rate was achieved. Also, transfer size was changed from 32 B to 512 B and the optimal point was found around 256 B transfers. This is because small transfers cannot hide memory access latency very well, and too large transfers incur larger queuing latency in the vault controllers, as the size of the row buffers is fixed at 256 B.

For estimation of the power consumption, we assumed 28 nm Low Power technology as the logic process. For the interconnects, energy/transaction was extracted from logic synthesis of the AXI-4.0 RTL model [8]. Cache power consumption was extracted from the latest release of CACTI [24]. Power consumed in the DRAM devices was extracted from DRAMPower [10]. The energy consumed in the vault controllers was estimated to be 0.75 pJ/bit [9]. SMC Controller was estimated to consume 10 pj/bit by scaling values obtained in [21]. For serial links, energy per transaction was considered 13.7 pj/bit [16], and an idle power consumption of 1.9 Watts (for transmission of the null flits) was estimated based on the maximum power reported in [13] and link efficiency in [19]. Also, since power state transition for the serial links introduces long sleep latency in the order of a few hundred nanoseconds, and a wakeup latency of a few microseconds [3], we assumed that during host's computations, links are

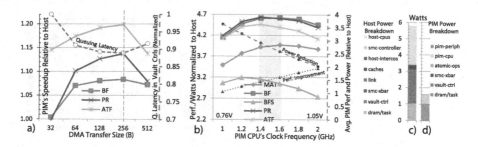

Fig. 3. Effect of DMA transfer size on PIM's speed-up (a), PIM's energy efficiency vs. its clock frequency (b), power breakdown for execution of the host (c) and PIM (d) (Colour figure online).

fully active, while when PIM starts computing, links can be power gated [3]. For the processors, percentage of active/idle cycles were extracted from gem5, and the power consumption for each one were estimated based on [23]. The energy consumed by the Floating Point operations was estimated based on [7], and the energy associated with atomic commands, PIM's TLB, and its DMA engine were estimated based on logic synthesis and plotted in Fig. 3d as "atomic-ops" and "pim-periphs".

To perform a fair analysis of the energy efficiency achieved by PIM, we omitted the system-background power and only considered the energy consumption related to the execution of tasks. Background power consists of all components which consume energy whether host is active or PIM, and can range from system's clocking circuits to peripheral devices, the secondary storage, the cooling mechanism, as well as, unused DRAM cells. One important observation was that for typical social graphs with less than 1 million nodes the total allocated DRAM size was always less than 100 MB (Using LIL representation). While, a significant amount of power is consumed in the unused DRAM cells. In fact, increasing stacked DRAM's size is one of the background sources which can completely neutralize the energy efficiency achieved by PIM. For this reason, we only consider the energy consumed in the "used" DRAM pages, all components in LoB of the memory cube, the serial links, the host processors, and their memory interface including the interconnects and the caches. Power consumption breakdown for execution of the task on PIM and the host are illustrated in Fig. 3c and d. The main contributors were found to be DRAM, the processors, and the serial links. The voltage and frequency of PIM's processor (on LoB) have been scaled down from 2 GHz@1.05 V to 1 GHz@0.76 V [23]. Under these circumstances, PIM can reduce power consumption by over 70 %. To find the optimal point in terms of energy efficiency we scaled the voltage and frequency of PIM's processor and plotted PIM's performance per watts (calculated as total execution time divided by consumed power) normalized to the host in Fig. 3b It can be seen that clocking PIM at around 1.5 GHz leads to highest energy efficiency in all cases.

As the final experiment, PIM was compared with a host-side accelerator with similar capabilities, to study the effect of vicinity to the main memory.

For this purpose, we detached the complete PIM subsystem from the cube and connected it to "Interconnect 2" (Fig. 1a) without any change in its capabilities. For matrix addition, no performance difference was observed, because the DMA engine effectively hides memory access latency. However, in all four graph traversal benchmarks PIM beats the host-side accelerator by a factor of 1.4X to 1.6X. This can be explained by the latency sensitivity of the graph traversal benchmarks (Average memory access latency from PIM to the main memory was measured as 46 ns, while for the host side accelerator this value had increased to 74 ns). Also, since the host side accelerator needs the serial links and the SMC Controller to be active, under the same conditions as the previous experiment (Considering power for the active banks of the DRAM and scaling down the voltage and frequency of PIM's processor), our PIM achieves an energy reduction of 55 % compared to a similar accelerator located on the host. Lastly, according to Little's law, the host side accelerator requires more buffering to maintain the same bandwidth, due to higher memory access latency. This results in increased manufacturing cost and energy.

5 Conclusions

In this paper we presented the first exploration steps towards design of SMC, a new PIM architecture that enhances the capabilities of the LoB die in HMC. An accurate simulation environment called SMCSim has been developed, along with a full featured software stack. A full system analysis considering offloading and all dynamic overheads demonstrated that even in a case where the only benefit of using PIM is latency reduction, up to 2X performance improvement in comparison with the host SoC, and around 1.5X against a similar host-side accelerator is achievable. Moreover, by scaling down the voltage and frequency of the proposed PIM it is possible to reduce energy by about 70 % and 55 % in comparison with the host and the accelerator, respectively.

Acknowledgment. This work was supported, in parts, by EU FP7 ERC Project MULTITHERMAN (GA no. 291125). We would also like to thank Samsung Electronics for their support and funding.

References

1. Mali-400/450 GPU device drivers. http://malideveloper.arm.com/resources/drivers
2. Hybrid memory cube specification 2.1 (2014). http://www.hybridmemorycube.org/
3. Ahn, J., Yoo, S., Choi, K.: Low-power hybrid memory cubes with link power management and two-level prefetching. IEEE Trans. Very Large Scale Integr. VLSI Syst. **99**, 1–1 (2015)
4. Ahn, J., Hong, S., Yoo, S., Mutlu, O., Choi, K.: A scalable processing-in-memory accelerator for parallel graph processing. In: Proceedings of the 42nd Annual International Symposium on Computer Architecture, ISCA 2015, pp. 105–117. ACM, New York, NY, USA (2015)

5. Ahn, J., Yoo, S., Mutlu, O., Choi, K.: PIM-enabled instructions: a low-overhead, locality-aware processing-in-memory architecture. In: Proceedings of the 42nd Annual International Symposium on Computer Architecture, ISCA 2015, pp. 336–348. ACM, New York, NY, USA (2015)
6. Alves, M.A.Z., Freitas, H.C., Navaux, P.O.A.: Investigation of shared L2 cache on many-core processors. In: 2009 22nd International Conference on Architecture of Computing Systems (ARCS), pp. 1–10, March 2009
7. Aminot, A., Lhuiller, Y., Castagnetti, A., et al.: Floating point units efficiency in multi-core processors. In: Proceedings, ARCS 2015 - The 28th International Conference on Architecture of Computing Systems, pp. 1–8, March 2015
8. Azarkhish, E., Rossi, D., Loi, I., Benini, L.: High performance AXI-4.0 based interconnect for extensible smart memory cubes. In: Proceedings of the 2015 Design, Automation and Test in Europe Conference and Exhibition, DATE 2015, pp. 1317–1322. EDA Consortium, San Jose, CA, USA (2015)
9. Boroujerdian, B., Keller, B., Lee, Y.: LPDDR2 memory controllerdesign in a 28 nm process. http://www.eecs.berkeley.edu/bkeller/~rekall.pdf
10. Chandrasekar, K., Akesson, B., Goossens, K.: Improved power modeling of DDR SDRAMs. In: 2011 14th Euromicro Conference on Digital System Design (DSD), pp. 99–108, August 2011
11. Farmahini-Farahani, A., Ahn, J.H., Morrow, K., Kim, N.S.: NDA: near-DRAM acceleration architecture leveraging commodity DRAM devices and standard memory modules. In: 2015 IEEE 21st International Symposium on High Performance Computer Architecture (HPCA), pp. 283–295, February 2015
12. Hansson, A., Agarwal, N., Kolli, A., et al.: Simulating DRAM controllers for future system architecture exploration. In: 2014 IEEE International Symposium on Performance Analysis of Systems and Software (ISPASS), pp. 201–210, March 2014
13. Jeddeloh, J., Keeth, B.: Hybrid memory cube new DRAM architecture increases density and performance. In: 2012 Symposium on VLSI Technology (VLSIT), pp. 87–88, June 2012
14. Kim, G., Kim, J., Ahn, J.H., Kim, J.: Memory-centric system interconnect design with hybrid memory cubes. In: 22nd International Conference on Parallel Architectures and Compilation Techniques (PACT), pp. 145–155, September 2013
15. Leskovec, J., Krevl, A.: SNAP Datasets: Stanford large network dataset collection, June 2014. http://snap.stanford.edu/data
16. Lloyd, S., Gokhale, M.: In-memory data rearrangement for irregular, data-intensive computing. Computer 48(8), 18–25 (2015)
17. Nair, R.: Evolution of memory architecture. Proc. IEEE 103(8), 1331–1345 (2015)
18. Paul, J., Stechele, W., Kroehnert, M., Asfour, T.: Improving efficiency of embedded multi-core platforms with scratchpad memories. In: 2014 27th International Conference on Architecture of Computing Systems (ARCS), pp. 1–8, February 2014
19. Rosenfeld, P.: Performance Exploration of the Hybrid Memory Cube. Ph.D. thesis, University of Maryland (2014)
20. Salihoglu, S., Widom, J.: GPS: A graph processing system. In: Proceedings of the 25th International Conference on Scientific and Statistical Database Management, SSDBM, pp. 22:1–22:12. ACM, New York, NY, USA (2013)
21. Schaffner, M., Gürkaynak, F.K., Smolic, A., Benini, L.: DRAM or no-DRAM? exploring linear solver architectures for image domain warping in 28 nm CMOS. In: Proceedings of the 2015 Design, Automation and Test in Europe Conference and Exhibition. DATE 2015, EDA Consortium (2015)

22. Sura, Z., Jacob, A., Chen, T., et al.: Data access optimization in a processing-in-memory system. In: Proceedings of the 12th ACM International Conference on Computing Frontiers. CF 2015, pp. 6:1–6:8. ACM, New York, NY, USA (2015)
23. Tudor, B.M., Teo, Y.M.: On understanding the energy consumption of ARM-based multicore servers. SIGMETRICS Perform. Eval. Rev. **41**(1), 267–278 (2013)
24. Wilton, S., Jouppi, N.: CACTI: an enhanced cache access and cycle time model. IEEE J. Solid-State Circuits **31**(5), 677–688 (1996)
25. Zhong, J., He, B.: Towards GPU-accelerated large-scale graph processing in the cloud. In: 2013 IEEE 5th International Conference on Cloud Computing Technology and Science (CloudCom), vol. 1, pp. 9–16, December 2013

Network-on-Chip and Secure Computing Architectures

CASCADE: Congestion Aware Switchable Cycle Adaptive Deflection Router

Gnaneswara Rao Jonna$^{(\boxtimes)}$, Vamana Murthi Thuniki, and Madhu Mutyam

PACE Laboratory, Department of Computer Science and Engineering,
Indian Institute of Technology Madras, Chennai 600036, India
{jonna,vaman,madhu}@cse.iitm.ac.in

Abstract. Shrinking process technology poses a challenge to network-on-chip design for high performance and energy efficient router architecture to interconnect multiple cores on a chip. Because of its importance, several router micro-architectures are proposed in the literature. In this paper, we propose a novel router architecture, *congestion aware switchable cycle adaptive deflection* (CASCADE) router, which dynamically reconfigures itself from single-cycle buffer-less router to two-cycle minimally-buffered router, and vice-versa, based on the router congestion level. The CASCADE router employs congestion aware cycle switching and power-gating to achieve both power and performance efficiency under varying network loads. Experimental results show that, when compared to SLIDER, the state of the art minimally buffered deflection router, the CASCADE router achieves on average 19 % power reduction and 26 % flit latency reduction with marginal area overhead.

1 Introduction and Related Work

With extensive integration of processing cores onto chips in the many-core era, there exists a great need for an efficient, reliable and scalable communication fabric. Packet switched Network-on-Chips (NoCs) are developed as a viable solution to address the on-chip communication issues [4]. Conventional input buffered Virtual Channel (VC) routers [5] offer low latency, high throughput and high load handling capacity, but at the cost of large area and power overheads due to the presence of the power hungry buffers. Approximately 30 % to 40 % of chip power is consumed by NoC alone, out of which router buffers constitute a significant amount [6,7].

Back-pressure-less routing techniques are employed in VC based routers to address the increased power consumption in them. These techniques eliminate the input buffers in the routers completely [11,12], thereby reducing NoC power consumption significantly. Furthermore it is observed that with the real workloads that have low injection rate, the VC routers are found to use less than 25 % of buffers for a majority of time (nearly 90 %) [1]. This indicates over-provisioning of the buffers in such routers. At low injection rates, buffer-less routers perform well because of low port contention [12]. Buffer-less routers handle port contention problem either by dropping or deflecting all the contending

© Springer International Publishing Switzerland 2016
F. Hannig et al. (Eds.): ARCS 2016, LNCS 9637, pp. 35–47, 2016.
DOI: 10.1007/978-3-319-30695-7_3

flits except one (winner). Deflection is preferred over dropping of flits because of the overhead associated with their acknowledgment and retransmission [8,9]. The concept of buffer-less deflection NoC routers is discussed in [20] and a detailed implementation is presented in BLESS [11].

Under high loads, performance of buffer-less routers degrades significantly as port contention increases. This leads to increased deflection rate and network activity, resulting in higher delay and early saturation. Minimally buffered routers came up as a design optimization to the buffer-less routers, by employing Side Buffer to buffer a fraction of deflected flits (MinBD [13]), leading to performance improvement. DeBAR [1] outperforms MinBD in terms of average flit latency by introducing a better priority mechanism. SLIDER [2] employs delayed injection and selective preemption to outperform DeBAR.

As an effort to reduce the flit traversal time in the NoC router, single-cycle routers are being proposed. Special permutation deflection network architecture is proposed in MinBSD [3], which performs all the router operations in a single cycle. Application aware topology reconfiguration using SMART links is proposed in SMART NoC [10]. Speculation based single-cycle buffered router architecture is proposed in [18], which employs virtual output queuing. Kumar et al. [19] propose a non-speculation based single-cycle buffered router. Hayenga et al. [9] propose SCARAB, a buffer-less adaptive single-cycle router architecture by using dropping protocol.

Centralized buffer router [21] incorporates a centralised buffer that can be bypassed and power gated at low loads. AFC [22] bypasses input buffers in a VC router to act as a buffer-less router depending on network load. Flexibuffer [23] uses power gating to dynamically vary the number of active buffers in a VC router. In all these techniques input buffers are physically present, leading to huge area overhead. Power gating mechanisms to optimize power efficiency are proposed in recent works [21,24]. Though there exist prior works on buffer-less [9,11,12,20], minimally buffered [1–3,13], single-cycle [3,9,18,19], multi-cycle [1,2,11,12], and adaptive [21–23] router microarchitectures, their design methodologies and objectives are different.

In this paper, we propose *congestion aware switchable cycle adaptive deflection* (CASCADE) router design, a novel minimally buffered deflection router architecture. It combines the benefits of buffer-less single cycle routers (at low loads) and minimally buffered two-cycle routers (at high loads). It employs congestion aware cycle switching and power gating to switch between single cycle buffer-less mode and two-cycle minimally buffered mode, adapting to the traffic dynamically at runtime. The CASCADE router consumes 19 % less power (on an average) compared to SLIDER, with a marginal area overhead of 5.7 %. Experimental results show that the CASCADE router outperforms SLIDER, MinBSD and DeBAR and extends saturation point on all synthetic traffic patterns. With real workloads, the CASCADE router reduces the average flit latency by 26 % and 10.7 % (on an average), compared to SLIDER and MinBSD, respectively.

2   Motivation

In this section, we present the motivation for an adaptive single/multi-cycle router by discussing the advantages and limitations of single-cycle, multi-cycle, buffer-less and minimally buffered routers.

Multi-Cycle Vs Single-Cycle Routers: Consider a flit that is n hops away from its destination in a mesh NoC. To reach the destination, the flit takes $kn+n$ cycles (kn cycles in routers, n cycles on links) when complex intelligent k-cycle router are used, whereas it takes only $n+n$ cycles (n cycles in router, n cycles on links) when a simple single-cycle router is considered, assuming the flit is neither buffered nor deflected in the path. At low loads, port contention is low or absent, hence flits are neither buffered nor deflected. So at low loads, a simple single-cycle router is preferred over a k-cycle router, because it can reduce the latency, area and power consumption. At high loads, as port contention can be high, a simple single-cycle router without any flit management provisions leads to heavy deflection rate, longer delay, and increased network activity, which in turn cause early saturation. Thus we need more intelligent, multi-cycle routers to employ effective flit management techniques under high loads. We target to overcome the shortcomings of single-cycle routers under high loads and multi-cycle routers under low loads.

Buffer-Less Vs Minimally-Buffered Routers: Minimally-buffered routers are equipped to buffer a fraction of deflected flits to minimize the deflection rate significantly as compared to buffer-less routers. At low loads, as port contention is low, buffer-less router design is an optimal design choice. Buffer segment in minimally-buffered routers is underutilized at low loads, as well as it incurs area and power overheads compared to buffer-less routers. But, at high loads, as port contention can be high, buffer-less router will encounter heavy deflection rate, longer delay, and increased network activity, which in turn cause early saturation. So we need minimally-buffered routers, to address these issues under high loads. We target to overcome the shortcomings of buffer-less routers under high loads and minimally-buffered routers under low loads.

Addressing these limitations, we propose a novel router design, CASCADE router, that intelligently chooses to operate in different modes at different congestion levels.

3   CASCADE Router Architecture

We propose CASCADE router design in which the router reconfigures itself from single-cycle buffer-less router to two-cycle minimally-buffered router at high loads and vice-versa. The reconfiguration can be done dynamically based on the level of congestion at runtime. The pipeline architecture of the CASCADE router is shown in Fig. 1. Figures 2 and 3 show the CASCADE router pipeline architecture in single-cycle and two-cycle mode. The detailed operation of various units in the CASCADE router are explained below.

Congestion Monitoring and Trigger Unit (CMTU): CMTU performs the following operations:

- *Congestion Monitoring*: CMTU takes the Occupancy bit of each channel from pipeline register **A** as an input and monitors congestion level in that particular router. Every channel has an Occupancy bit, which is set when the channel is occupied, otherwise it is reset.
- *Decide whether the router is congested or not*: We define two threshold values: Congestion Threshold (CT) and Congestion Free Threshold (CFT), based on the number of channels occupied. For certain number of cycles in a CW-cycle window (refer Sect. 4), if the number of channels occupied is greater than or equal to CT, the router is considered to be congested, and if the number of channels occupied is less than or equal to CFT, the router is considered to be congestion-free.
- *Trigger the cycle switching*: When a router is operated in the single-cycle mode and if it is congested, CMTU enables the trigger to convert it into the two-cycle mode. When a router is operated in the two-cycle mode and if it is congestion-free, the trigger is disabled to convert it into the single-cycle mode.

Pipeline Registers (A, B, C): These registers are used to buffer and forward flits in each router pipeline stage. Pipeline register **A** receives flits from neighboring routers. Pipeline register **C** sends flits to neighboring routers. Pipeline register **B** is an intermediate register that separates the two stages of the router. At the end of each clock cycle, flits are stored in the corresponding pipeline registers. Under single-cycle mode of operation, pipeline register **B** is bypassed and power-gated.

Routing Unit (RU): It performs the route computation for each incoming flit through **A**. RU extracts the destination address field from each flit, applies XY routing and computes its productive port. This information is local to each router and it is reset when the flit leaves the router.

Prioritization Unit (PU): It performs the priority computation for each incoming flit through **A**, based on hops-to-destination, which ensures fairness and progress in flit movement. It extracts the destination address field from each flit, determines hops-to-destination and assigns a priority value based on that. Flits closer to their destination are given higher priority which ensures that flits closer to destination are least deflected. Priority values computed are used for arbitration of flits in Permutation Deflection Network (PDN).

Ejection bit Set Unit (ESU): It sets an Eject flag, which is used by the Ejection Bypass Unit (EBU) of immediate neighbors of the current router. For each outgoing flit before **C**, if its productive port is same as the assigned port and the destination is one step away, Eject flag is set by the ESU.

Ejection Bypass Unit (EBU): It checks the Eject flag bit of all the incoming flits through **A**. If it finds a flit with Ejection flag bit set, it bypasses that flit

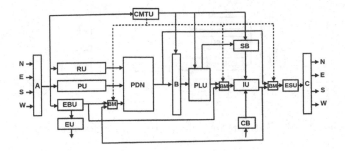

Fig. 1. CASCADE router pipeline architecture.

to EU and resets the Occupancy bit of that particular channel. If multiple flits have their Eject flag set, then one of them is selected in random.

Ejection Unit (EU): The flit that is bypassed by the EBU is directed to Ejection Unit (EU), which actually ejects the flit to the core. We consider one ejection port per router.

Permutation Deflection Network (PDN): It performs parallel allocation of the ports. We use a 4×4 PDN. After initial set of parallel operations (RU, PU, EBU & IU), flits reach the PDN. It has 4 arbiters, arranged in two stages as 2×2 arbiters with 4 inputs and 4 outputs. The PDN uses the priority and productive port information of flits computed by PU and RU to allocate the output port for each of the flits. At each arbiter, the highest priority flit is assigned to its productive port and the other flit is assigned to the left-out port. Hence the highest priority flit always gets the desired port. Other flits may get deflected or assigned productive ports based on port conflicts at each stage of the arbiter. The flit that receives its desired port is termed as a non-deflected flit, while the flit that is diverted from its original path is termed as the deflected flit.

Side Buffer (SB) and Core Buffer (CB): We have two kinds of buffer segments in the CASCADE router: SB and CB. SB is used to store the preempted flits and CB is used to store the flits injected by local node. We keep the buffer segment size same as that of MinBSD, SLIDER and DeBAR for fair evaluation purpose. Every flit in these buffers are given opportunity for injection, so the CB and SB are non-FIFO queues. We implement this by using a 2-bit flag for each flit in these buffers to represent the desired port of that flit. Under the single-cycle mode of operation, the SB is bypassed and power-gated.

Preemption Logic Unit (PLU): It performs both the redirection and buffer ejection operations of MinBD. One among the deflected flits, if any, is moved to side buffer per cycle. These flits in the side buffer are injected back into the router pipeline in subsequent cycles to acquire their desired ports. If there are no deflected flits and all channels are occupied, we cannot inject flits from either CB or SB. If this situation persists, the flits in CB and SB will be starved. To avoid this we maintain a threshold [2] on maximum number of cycles for which

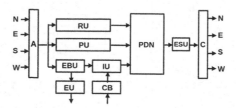

Fig. 2. CASCADE router architecture in single-cycle mode.

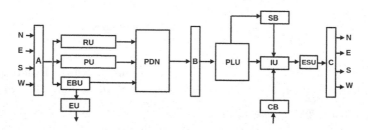

Fig. 3. CASCADE router architecture in two-cycle mode.

injection is blocked. Once the threshold is crossed, we forcefully preempt a flit from the router pipeline to allow starving flits. Under the single-cycle mode of operation, the PLU is bypassed and power-gated.

Injection Unit (IU): It injects flits from CB and SB into the router pipeline. If two or more channels are available, both CB and SB can inject. If only one channel is available, injection from CB is performed in even cycles, and injection from SB is performed in odd cycles. During the injection, we look for an ideal channel-flit mapping by comparing the 2-bit flag of each flit in buffers and the Occupancy bit of each channel. When the number of flits in CB is less than half of its capacity, we perform injection only if the flits in the buffers get their productive port. Otherwise, we perform injection even if the flits in the buffers do not get their productive port [2]. Under the single-cycle mode of operation, as we power-gate SB, in every cycle CB alone injects flits.

Bypass Multiplexer (BM): It chooses flits from one of its two inputs based on the select input from CMTU and forwards them in the router pipeline. BMs are used to bypass/include components (SB, B, PLU) in the CASCADE router pipeline to facilitate switching between different modes.

4   Congestion Monitoring and Cycle Switching

CASCADE router monitors the occupied channels in router pipeline continuously. Hence it is aware of the congestion level. Based on congestion level, it switches dynamically at runtime from single-cycle to two-cycle and vice-versa when required. Initially all the routers in the network are operated in

---

Algorithm 1. Single-cycle to two-cycle switching

1: **procedure** single_cycle_to_two_cycle_switching
2: **Input** CW, CC, CT, trigg=0 and k=1
3: **for** $k = 1$ **to** CW **do**
4:     **if** $number\_of\_channels\_occupied \geq CT$ **then**
5:        $trigg = trigg + 1$
6:     **end if**
7: **end for**
8: **if** $trigg \geq CC$ **and** $k == CW$ **then**
9:     Enable trigger input to convert single-cycle router into two-cycle router (Include PLU, SB, B)
10: **end if**
11: **if** $k == CW$ **then**
12:     reset k to 1, trigg to 0
13: **end if**
14: **end procedure**

---

single-cycle mode. We choose to operate the CASCADE router in two-cycle minimally-buffered mode under high loads to optimize power and performance. CMTU takes the occupancy bit for each channel as an input from pipeline register **A** in every cycle. It monitors the occupancy information of channels continuously for every CW-sized window of cycles. In a CW-cycle window if the router is congested for CC (congested cycles) cycles or more, CMTU enables the trigger to convert the CASCADE router from single-cycle to two-cycle mode and also enables PLU, SB, and pipeline register **B** in the router pipeline for effective flit management. Algorithm 1 gives the switching process of CASCADE router from single-cycle to two-cycle mode.

In a CW-cycle window if the router is congestion-free for CFC (congestion-free cycles) cycles or more, CMTU disables the trigger to convert the CASCADE router from two-cycle to single-cycle mode and bypass and power-gate PLU, SB, pipeline register **B**. Bypassing these components can be done immediately but power-gating is applied only after injecting the left out flits, if any, into the IU from these components. Algorithm 2 gives the switching process of the CASCADE router from two-cycle to single-cycle mode.

Design space exploration with various values of CW, CC, CFC, CT, and CFT provides us their optimal values for our design objective. Frequent switchings can be incurred for conservative values, while design can become insensitive to congestion for less strict values. We consider CW, CC, and CFC as 8, 5, and 5 cycles, respectively, and CT and CFT as 3 and 2 channels, respectively.

In the single-cycle mode there is no cyclic path, hence there is no cyclic movement of flits within the router. In the two-cycle mode, delayed injection towards the end of the router pipeline avoids cyclic movement of flits within the router. So the CASCADE router is both deadlock and live-lock free internally. Our routing and prioritization mechanisms ensure that there is no cyclic movement of flits among the routers. While moving across the routers, a flit gets

---

Algorithm 2. Two-cycle to single-cycle switching

1: **procedure** two_cycle_to_single_cycle_switching
2: **Input** CW, CFC, CFT, trigg=0 and k=1
3: **for** $k = 1$ **to** CW **do**
4:     **if** *number_of_channels_occupied* $\leq CFT$ **then**
5:         $trigg = trigg + 1$
6:     **end if**
7: **end for**
8: **if** $trigg \geq CFC$ **and** $k == CW$ **then**
9:     Disable trigger input to convert two-cycle router into single-cycle router (Bypass and power-gate PLU, SB, B)
10: **end if**
11: **if** $k == CW$ **then**
12:     reset k to 1, reset trigg to 0
13: **end if**
14: **end procedure**

---

either its productive port or deflected, avoiding cyclic dependency stalls among the routers. Hence, the CASCADE router is both deadlock and live-lock free.

Our design has the merits of both the worlds, buffer-less routers and minimally-buffered routers, as well as single-cycle routers and two/multi-cycle routers, overcoming their demerits at the same time. In addition, the other features of the CASCADE router are:

- Overlapped execution of independent operations (CMTU/RU/PU/EU&IU), reduces the pipeline latency.
- No communication overhead involved in switching and every router can switch independently.
- Delayed injection and selective preemption in two-cycle mode reduces the deflection rate, increases the effective utilization of idle channels [2].
- Power-gating and bypassing the components when required saves power and reduces latency.
- Dynamically reconfigurable at runtime and application awareness is not necessary for reconfiguration.

5   Experimental Setup

We modify the VC-based cycle accurate NoC simulator, Booksim [4], into two-cycle deflection router as mentioned in CHIPPER [12]. In deflection routing, each flit is routed independently, hence we consider every flit with necessary control information attached in the header. Out-of-order delivered flits are handled by necessary reassembly mechanism. The flit channel is 140-bit wide: 128-bit data field and 12-bit header field. We model DeBAR, SLIDER, MinBSD and CASCADE router by making necessary changes to this baseline router architecture.We implement the microarchitecture of DeBAR, MinBSD, SLIDER and

CASCADE router in Verilog and synthesize them using Synopsys Design Compiler with 65 nm CMOS library to obtain the area, latency and power information associated.

We evaluate the CASCADE router against SLIDER, MinBSD and DeBAR, using multiprogrammed (SPEC CPU2006 [15] benchmark mixes [1]) and multithreaded (SPLASH2 [16], PARSEC2.1 [17] benchmarks) workloads. We use Multi2Sim [14] to model 64-core CMP setup with CPU cores, cache hierarchy, coherence protocols in sufficient detail and accuracy. Each core has an out-of-order x86 processing unit with 64KB, 4-way set associative, 32 byte block, private L1 cache and a 512KB, 16-way set-associative, 64 byte block, shared distributed L2 cache. Each core is assigned with a SPEC CPU2006 benchmark application and misses per kilo instruction (MPKI) on L1 cache is calculated. We create 7 mixes (M1 to M7) with different proportions of MPKI. We consider similar setup with slight modifications to run multithreaded workloads (64-core CMP with 60 processing cores with private L1 cache and 4 shared distributed L2 cache cores at 4 corners of the network). We run 60 threads of each benchmark at a time, one thread on each processor core. After fast forwarding sufficiently, we capture the network events and provide this as traffic to simulate the NoC models developed.

We also analyze the performance of the CASCADE router against SLIDER, MinBSD and DeBAR, using synthetic traffic patterns on 8×8 mesh network. Average flit latency, deflection rate and overall throughput values are captured for each synthetic pattern by varying injection rate from zero load till saturation is reached.

6   Results and Analysis

As the CASCADE router is a minimally-buffered two-cycle router by architecture, we compare it with SLIDER (state of the art two-cycle minimally-buffered router) in general. Since the CASCADE router transforms itself into single-cycle router under low traffic, we compare its performance with MinBSD (state of the art single-cycle minimally-buffered router) as well. We also compare our router with DeBAR. Past analysis [1] indicate that DeBAR outperforms traditional input buffered VC Router, so we do not compare our technique with VC Router.

Figure 4 shows the average flit latency, deflection rate, and throughput vs injection rate of MinBSD, DeBAR, SLIDER and CASCADE router for different synthetic traffic patterns on 8×8 mesh network. For evaluation purposes routers under comparison are assumed to be operated at same frequency. From the latency graphs, we observe that at low and medium injection rates the CASCADE router outperforms SLIDER and DeBAR and performs almost similar to MinBSD. The CASCADE router has the advantage of single-cycle and bufferless architecture at low injection rates. As the injection rate increases, the CASCADE router starts working in two-cycle mode, which increases latency but handles traffic effectively, whereas in MinBSD, flits get buffered and deflected heavily because of forced buffering and fixed paths even at low latencies, leading to early saturation. The CASCADE router extends the saturation for all

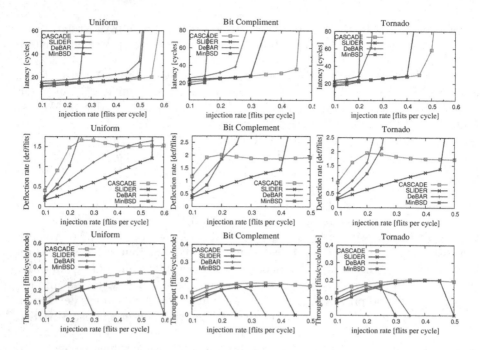

Fig. 4. Average latency, deflection rate and throughput comparison under various synthetic patterns on 8 × 8 mesh network.

synthetic patterns compared to all other routers. A mesh NoC with CASCADE routers reconfigures itself, router by router, based on congestion level in each router, unlike SLIDER and DEBAR, which are two-cycle routers throughout. Thus the CASCADE router manages flits more efficiently adapting to the traffic, accommodates more load and extends the saturation point.

From the deflection rate graphs, we observe that the deflection rate of the CASCADE router is high compared to other routers initially. As the injection rate increases further the deflection rate slowly reduces and becomes stable, unlike the other routers wherein the deflection rate increases gradually at initial periods and exponentially afterwards. Initially the CASCADE router operates in buffer-less mode, in which every contention leads to deflection. But as the traffic increases, routers convert from the single-cycle buffer-less mode to the two-cycle minimally-buffered mode, which slowly reduces and stabilizes the deflection rate.

The number of flits ejected per router per cycle amounts to throughput. From the throughput graphs, we observe that the CASCADE router maintains a better throughput compared to MinBSD, DeBAR and SLIDER because of its effective flit management and high load handling capacity.

Figure 5 shows the percentage reduction in latency of SLIDER, MinBSD and CASCADE routers with respect to DeBAR for different benchmarks from PARSEC2.1 and SPLASH2, and SPEC CPU2006. From the graphs, we observe that the CASCADE router outperforms all other routers for all the benchmarks.

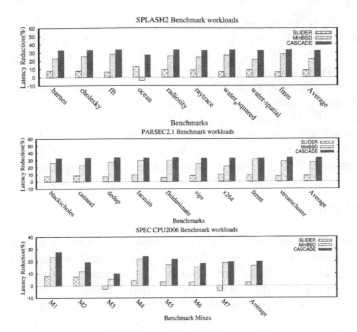

Fig. 5. Reduction in average latency comparison under multithreaded and multiprogrammed workloads with respect to DeBAR.

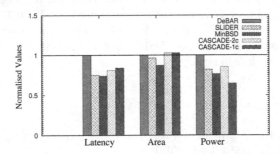

Fig. 6. Pipeline latency, area and power comparison of different routers normalized with respect to DeBAR.

Note that the injection rates are low in real workloads. The CASCADE router has the advantage of single-cycle and buffer-less router architecture at low loads. Though MinBSD is a single-cycle router, it has the disadvantage of forced buffering and fixed paths even at low latencies. The CASCADE router reduces the average flit latency by 26 % and 10.7 % compared to SLIDER and MinBSD, respectively.

Figure 6 compares the critical path latency, area and total power of SLIDER, MinBSD, CASCADE-2c and CASCADE-1c normalized with respect to DeBAR. We use additional logic for congestion monitoring and reconfiguring in the CASCADE router, which accounts to a marginal area overhead of 5.7 % over SLIDER.

The CASCADE router under both single-cycle mode (CASCADE-1c) and two-cycle mode (CASCADE-2c) will have the same area overhead. Critical path latency in the CASCADE router is slightly increased over SLIDER due to inclusion of reconfiguration logic. CASCADE-2c consumes 4.9 % more power than SLIDER due to additional logic, but when bypassing and power-gating is applied, CASCADE-1c consumes 21.5 %, 16 % and 35 % less power compared to SLIDER, MinBSD and DeBAR, respectively. Our experiments using the CASCADE router with benchmark workloads show that, on average, the CASCADE router operates in single-cycle mode for 94 % of the time because of low injection rates, which results in 19 % savings in power consumption as compared to SLIDER.

7   Conclusion

In this paper, we presented the CASCADE router, a novel low latency, robust, runtime reconfigurable, and power efficient minimally buffered deflection router architecture. The CASCADE router couples the benefits of single-cycle buffer-less and two-cycle minimally-buffered router architectures by switching between them adapting to the congestion level. The CASCADE router incorporates combination of congestion aware cycle switching and power-gating, which reduces power consumption by 19 % on average compared to SLIDER, the state of the art minimally-buffered router architecture. In terms of performance, the CASCADE router outperforms SLIDER and MinBSD on all workloads. It reduces the average flit latency by 26 % and 10.7 % compared to SLIDER and MinBSD, respectively. High performance, energy efficiency and extended saturation makes the CASCADE router robust and ideal choice for minimally-buffered routers under varying network utilization.

References

1. Jose, J., et al.: DeBAR: deflection based adaptive router with minimal buffering. In: DATE 2013, pp. 1583–1588 (2013)
2. Nayak, B., et al.: SLIDER: smart late injection DEflection router for mesh NoCs. In: ICCD 2013, pp. 377–383 (2013)
3. Jonna, G.R., et al.: MinBSD: minimally buffered single-cycle deflection router. In: DATE 2014, pp. 1–4 (2014)
4. Dally, W., Towles, B.: Principles and Practices of Interconnection Networks. Morgan Kaufmann Publishers Inc., San Francisco (2003)
5. Dally, W.: Virtual-channel flow control. IEEE Trans. Parallel Distrib. Syst. **3**, 194–205 (1992)
6. Hoskote, Y., et al.: A 5-GHz mesh interconnect for a teraflops processor. IEEE Micro **27**(5), 51–61 (2007)
7. Taylor, M.B., et al.: Evaluation of the raw microprocessor: an exposed-wire-delay architecture for ILP and streams. In: ISCA (2004)
8. Gomez, C., et al.: An efficient switching technique for NoCs with reduced buffer requirements. In: ICPADS, pp. 713–720 (2008)

9. Hayenga, M., et al.: SCARAB: a single cycle adaptive routing and bufferless network. In: MICRO, pp. 244–254 (2009)
10. Chen, C.-H.O., et al.: SMART: a single-cycle reconfigurable NoC for SoC applications. In: DATE 2013, pp. 338–343 (2013)
11. Moscibroda, T., Mutlu, O.: A case for bufferless routing in on-chip networks. In: ISCA, pp. 196–207 (2009)
12. Fallin, C., et al.: CHIPPER: a low complexity bufferless deflection router. In: HPCA, pp. 144–155 (2011)
13. Fallin, C., et al.: MinBD: minimally-buffered deflection routing for energy-efficient interconnect. In: NOCS, pp. 1–10 (2012)
14. Ubal, R., et al.: Multi2sim: a simulation framework to evaluate multicore-multithreaded processors. In: SBAC-PAD, pp. 62–68 (2007)
15. SPEC2006 CPU benchmark suite. http://www.spec.org
16. Woo, S.C., et al.: The splash-2 programs: characterization and methodological considerations. In: ISCA, pp. 24–36 (1995)
17. Bienia, C., et al.: The parsec benchmark suite: characterization and architectural implications. In: PACT, pp. 72–81 (2008)
18. Nguyen, S.T., et al.: A low cost single-cycle router based on virtual output queuing for on-chip networks. In: DSD, pp. 60–67 (2010)
19. Kumar, A., et al.: A 4.6 Tbits/s 3.6 GHz single-cycle NoC router with a novel switch allocator in 65 nm CMOS. In: ICCD, pp. 63–70 (2007)
20. Nilsson, E., et al.: Load distribution with the proximity congestion awareness in a network-on-chip. In: DATE, pp. 1126–1127 (2003)
21. Hassan, S.M., et al.: Centralized buffer router: a low latency, low power router for high radix NOCs. In: NOCS, pp. 1–6 (2013)
22. Jafri, S.A.R., et al.: Adaptive flow control for robust performance and energy. In: MICRO, pp. 433–444 (2010)
23. Kim, G., et al.: Flexibuffer: reducing leakage power in on-chip network routers. In: DAC, pp. 936–941 (2011)
24. Chen, L., et al.: Power punch: towards non-blocking power-gating of noc routers. In: HPCA, pp. 378–389 (2015)

An Alternating Transmission Scheme for Deflection Routing Based Network-on-Chips

Armin Runge[✉] and Reiner Kolla

Department of Computer Science, University of Wuerzburg, Wuerzburg, Germany
{runge,kolla}@informatik.uni-wuerzburg.de

Abstract. Deflection routing is a promising approach for energy and hardware efficient Network-on-Chips (NoCs). As packet switching can not be deployed for deflection routing based NoCs, the appropriate link width for such NoCs is crucial. Further, the most appropriate link width can be considerably larger, compared to packet switched NoCs. In this paper, we present a new alternating transmission scheme for deflection routing which allows smaller link widths. Simulations and theoretical comparisons with existing basic transmission methods show that our approach outperforms the existing approaches for high injection rates and uniform packet sizes.

1 Introduction

Growing communication requirements as well as technology scaling lead to Network-on-Chips (NoCs) as the dominant communication infrastructure for many-core systems. NoCs consist of a number of routers and links, connecting two routers to each other. A frequently used topology is the 2D mesh. Most of the current NoC designs adopt buffered routers and packet switching, whereas this work focuses on bufferless deflection routing, which will be briefly described in Sect. 2. Besides the already mentioned design decisions, such as topology and buffering, there are several further parameters. As deflection routing based architectures do not allow packet switching (cf. Sect. 2), the link width is of particular importance for such NoCs. Wide links enable high throughputs and prevent large messages' fragmentation into too many sub-messages. However, these advantages are gained by higher hardware requirements. The hardware requirements for one switch increase quadratically with the number of ports and linearly with the link width or flit size [5]. Besides of hardware limits there are further reasons for smaller link and router sizes. First, the saved area and energy can be used for other components. The authors in [7] found, that the performance improvements achieved by widening the link width does not outweigh the increase in costs. Second, router design and wiring is much simpler, as a high number of wires is difficult to place and route. For off-chip routing, the limited number of pins plays a further crucial role.

In this work we investigate transmission schemes for deflection routing based NoCs, which allow the transmission of messages that exceed the link width.

© Springer International Publishing Switzerland 2016
F. Hannig et al. (Eds.): ARCS 2016, LNCS 9637, pp. 48–59, 2016.
DOI: 10.1007/978-3-319-30695-7_4

Our main contribution is *TwoPhases*, an alternating transmission scheme, which enables packets, that consist of several flits, for deflection routing. Thereby smaller links and a significant reduction of the routing overhead is achieved.

The remainder of this paper is organized as follows. In Sect. 2, we briefly introduce the concept of deflection routing and motivate for the need of large flit sizes at deflection routing. In Sect. 3, we introduce our new transmission scheme *TwoPhases*. More obvious transmission schemes, that can handle flit sizes which exceed the link width, are explained in Sect. 4. An evaluation and comparison of these approaches to *TwoPhases* follows in Sect. 5. In Sect. 6, we present related work. This paper closes with a summary in Sect. 7.

2   Bufferless Deflection Routing

At deflection routing based NoCs, flits are not stored or discarded in case of collisions. They can be deflected even to possibly non-shortest paths. A routing decision is basically a permutation between all input- and output-ports. Using this principle, input buffers as well as the allocation of buffers are avoided. This allows a simple and local flow control. Hence, deflection routing enables small and energy efficient router architectures with a short latency and low complexity. A further advantage of deflection routing is the adaptivity of routing. Flits are automatically routed away from hot spots, as flits are deflected away from those regions, along potentially non-shortest paths. For further information to deflection routing, please refer to [3,10]. For moderate injection rates, as it is the case for most real applications, it was shown that deflection routing enables significant energy reductions and only modest performance losses compared to buffered NoCs [8]. As flits are not stored by routers, deflection routing is inherently free of routing-dependent deadlocks. Therefore, livelocks have to be avoided. A common method to avoid livelocks is the prioritization by hop-count or age of a flit. This ensures that every flit arrives eventually at its destination.

An important disadvantage of deflection routing, which is addressed below, is the fact that deflection routing allows no distinction between packets and flits. Frequently deployed buffered NoCs route messages usually according to the wormhole flow control scheme. Messages are decomposed into packets, the data units for routing and sequencing [2]. Packets are further divided into flow control units (flits). A flit is the data unit for bandwidth and buffer allocation. There are three types of flits to be distinguished: head, body, and tail flits. Only head flits contain routing information. Body and tail flits follow the path of the head flits towards the destination. Flits can be further divided into physical units (phits). A phit is the data unit which can be transmitted over a link within one clock cycle. The flit size normally corresponds to the phit size.

This decomposition is not possible for deflection routing based NoCs. A basic prerequisite to avoid livelocks at deflection routing is, to transmit the highest prioritized flit to a productive port at every router[1]. As there are no flit-buffers

---

[1] If a flit is transmitted to a productive port, the flit gets one hop closer to its destination.

and each router has to calculate a new routing decision every time a new flit arrives, the flits of one packet could be separated by deflection routing. Thus, it can not be ensured that e.g. body flits can follow their head flit. Every flit either has to carry routing information or be a head flit. Hence, the overhead for routing information and sequencing is considerably higher than for buffered NoCs with packet switching. Further, in contrast to buffered NoCs, it is not possible for deflection routing based NoCs to packetize large messages into packets with many flits. It is therefore particularly important for deflection routing based architectures to determine the appropriate flit size and link width, which are usually significantly higher than for buffered NoCs. In this work, we present the transmission scheme *TwoPhases* for deflection routing, which enables smaller link and router widths for the same payload size and additionally reduces the above mentioned overhead.

3   TwoPhases

At deflection routing, there is generally no distinction between packets and flits, as every flit has to carry routing information. This is different at the new transmission scheme *TwoPhases*. Here, every packet consists of exactly two flits, the head flit *hf*, which carries the routing information, and a data flit *df*, which follows its head flit.

3.1   Prerequisites and General Operating Mode

In order to apply *TwoPhases*, some prerequisites have to be fulfilled. First, as *TwoPhases* is based on deflection routing, every router must have the same number of input- and output-ports. Second, if the routers represent vertices and the links represent edges, the corresponding graph has to be bipartite. In other words, all routers have to be divisible into two disjoint sets S_0 and S_1, so that every router of S_0 is only neighbored to routers of S_1 and vice versa. Third, the link and router width has to be at least as wide as the header information. Furthermore, we assume a single-cycle router architecture. Multi-cycle router architectures are investigated in Sect. 3.4. All the requirements mentioned above can be fulfilled for a 2D mesh topology, which we assume as the chosen topology. Here, the division into two disjoint sets corresponds to a checkerboard pattern, with $S_0 := \{R_{id} \mid id \bmod 2 \equiv 0\}$ and $S_1 := \{R_{id} \mid id \bmod 2 \equiv 1\}$, whereas R_{id} denotes a router with the ID *id* (cf. Fig. 1).

As shown in Sect. 2, deflection routing usually does not allow packet switching. Every network clock cycle, every router calculates a new permutation, which transmits the highest prioritized flit one hop closer to its destination. In contrast, packets with one head flit and one data flit are used at *TwoPhases*, even though deflection routing is deployed. Furthermore, the abstinence of livelocks can still be guaranteed. Assigning the preferred direction to the highest prioritized flit is an important requirement for livelock freeness. This is achieved at *TwoPhases* by the division of all routers into two sets, as described above. Every router from set

S_x is allowed to inject head flits only at clock cycles c with $c \bmod 2 \equiv x$. Hence, the routers from S_0 (S_1) expect only head flits at clock cycles with $c \bmod 2 \equiv 0$ $(c \bmod 2 \equiv 1)$ and only data flits at clock cycles with $c \bmod 2 \equiv 1$ $(c \bmod 2 \equiv 0)$. This ensures that in every clock cycle at every router either head flits or data flits arrive. All routers alternate between these two states, whereas two neighbored routers are always in different states. Routers determine new routing decisions only if the head flits hf arrive and hold their state (e.g. the routing decision as well as the injection and ejection state) for the next clock cycle, in which the data flits df traverse these routers.

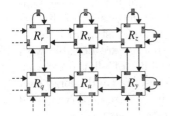

Fig. 1. Mesh topology with *TwoPhases*. Routers from S_0 (S_1) are colored in red (blue) (Color figure online).

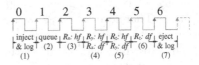

Fig. 2. Flit transmission/latency of one flit, which is transmitted from R_x to R_z via R_y (2 hops) with TwoPhases.

Generally, the output ports of routers, which are placed at the border of a 2D mesh topology, are fed back to the corresponding inputs ports. This ensures that the same number of input and output ports are used and the same router architecture can be deployed independently of the router position. As routers in *TwoPhases* alternate between head- and data-state, a flit which is sent to such a loop link would arrive one clock cycle later at the same router. A head flit would now arrive in the data-state and vice versa. To prevent this, a simple register has to be inserted in every loop link (cf. Fig. 1). These registers delay every flit by one clock cycle. Thus it is ensured that head- / data-flits arrive only if the router is in head- /data-state.

3.2   Performance

In this section, we compare the theoretical performance and costs of *TwoPhases* to standard deflection routing. The latency for one specific flit with standard deflection routing is $l_{DR} = hc + 1$. At *TwoPhases*, flits can only be injected if the corresponding router is in head-state, which is the case in half of the clock cycles. Further, after the head flit arrived at its destination, one additional clock cycle is required to transmit the corresponding data-flit to the destination. Thus, the theoretical latency for one specific flit, which arrives with a hop-count of hc, is given by:

$$l_{TP} = l_{DR} + 1.5 = hc + 2.5 \tag{1}$$

Simulated results are presented in Sect. 5. An example for a flit transmission is depicted in Fig. 2. Here, a flit is transmitted from R_x to its two hop neighbor R_z. The flit is injected (1) in clock cycle 0 and the core outputs the log message. In cycle 1, the flit has to stay in the queue (2), as $R_x \in S_0$ and therefore head flits can only be accepted in clock cycles with $c \bmod 2 \equiv 0$. In cycle 2, the head flit hf traverses the router R_x (3) and hf will arrive at R_y with the next clock pulse edge. In cycle 3, the data flit df traverses R_x and hf traverses R_y (4). In cycle 4, df traverses R_y, whereas hf traverses R_z (5). In cycle 5, the data flit traverses R_z, whereby the complete packet arrived at R_z (6). Finally, the packet is ejected (7) and the core prints the log message in cycle 6.

Conversely, the header overhead decreases by more than half the size compared to standard deflection routing. For a link width of lw bits and h header bits, only $lw - h$ payload bits can be transmitted per flit with standard deflection routing. In contrast, $2 \cdot lw - h$ payload bits per packet are possible with *TwoPhases*. Therefore, the link width and also the width of all the internal router architecture parts can be reduced, which allows resource and energy savings. If the same link width is used, the throughput can be increased, compared to standard deflection routing. This will more than offset the increased average latency. The benefits of *TwoPhases* compared to standard deflection routing gain in importance if small flits, and therefore small links and router widths, are deployed. For such small flit widths, which can be necessary due to resource constraints, the header overhead is particularly significant.

3.3   Optimality of Decomposition into Flits

TwoPhases enables the use of packets which consist of exactly two flits. The head flits arbitrate the paths, whereas the data flits follow the head flits. Legitimately, one may ask why not more than two flits are used. Unfortunately, it is not possible to split packets into more than two flits at deflection routing based NoCs. This can be proved by a counter-example.

We consider two neighbored routers R_x and R_y. It is assumed that these routers have a single-cycle router architecture and packets consist of at least three flits, a head flit hf and at least two data flits df_1, df_2. To avoid livelocks, all head flits have to arrive at the same clock cycle at one specific router. This assumes that only head flits and no data are allowed to arrive at the inputs of router R_x in clock cycle 0. As R_x could transmit one of those head flits to router R_y, R_y expects only head flits in clock cycle 1. At the same time, router R_x processes the first data flit df_1, which follows the head flits hf Now, it is possible that R_y decides to transmit one of the just received head flits to R_x. It is even possible that the head flit hf, that was sent from R_x to R_y, is deflected back to R_x. This is the case if all other output ports of R_y are occupied by higher prioritized flits. In cycle 2 (when R_x should process the second data flit df_2, as all packets consist of at least three flits following the adoption), a head flit arrives again at router R_x. This is not allowed, as in every clock cycle at every router solely head flits or solely data flits are permitted. Therefore, a decomposition of packets into more than two flits is not possible.

3.4   Pipelined Router Architectures

For single-cycle router architectures packets can not consist of more than two flits. This is not the case if the router architecture is pipelined. At pipelined routers with n stages it takes exactly n cycles to transmit a flit from an input port to an output port. Therefore, a head flit will arrive at a router of the same set exactly $2n$ cycles later. Thus, routers from S_0 can inject head flits at clock cycles with $c \bmod 2n \equiv 0$ and routers from S_1 at $c \bmod 2n \equiv n$. Accordingly, data flits can be injected at clock cycles with $c \bmod 2n \not\equiv 0$ and $c \bmod 2n \not\equiv n$, respectively. The abstinence of livelocks is still guaranteed, as in every network clock cycle at every router either head flits or data flits arrive. In contrast to *TwoPhases*, for single-cycle router architectures, where two neighbored routers are always in different states, here, both of the two neighbored routers can be in the state to receive data flits. However, two neighbored routers can never be both in the state to receive head flits. Thus, through the deployment of pipelining, the header overhead can be reduced even more. At n pipeline stages, n flits per packet and $n \cdot lw - h$ payload bits per packet are possible. As a result, the throughput can be enhanced or the link width can be reduced, respectively.

4   Transmission Methods

In this section, we give an overview of existing and more obvious methods to transmit messages which exceed the link width, and show their performance characteristics.

4.1   MultiFlit

The most obvious method to transmit data which exceeds the size of one flit is the transmission in multiple portions, hereinafter referred to as *MultiFlit*. For *MultiFlit*, the message to be transferred is divided into as many flits as necessary, whereas all flits are routed independently from sender to receiver. The advantage of this method is that the number of flits is variable. However, these flits can arrive out of order at their destination, as they are routed independently from each other and some may make a detour because of deflections. Hence, all flit parts of one message have to be received, to be able to assemble the complete message. Further, the flit structure has to be extended by a flit-ID field, which determines the sequence of the flits of one message, as the original message is distributed over several flits. As every flit has to carry routing information and additionally, the flit-ID field has to be appended, the overhead (transmitted data, which is not payload) can be significant depending on the flit width. If a message, which consists of pl payload bits, should be transmitted over a link with lw bits width, then in total $\#f = \lceil \frac{pl}{lw - h - f_{id}} \rceil$ flits have to be transferred. Here, h is the number of header bits and f_{id} gives the number of bits for the flit-ID. The number of required bits for the flit-ID field depends in turn on the

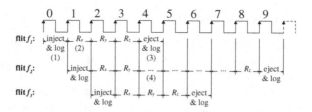

Fig. 3. Transmission of three flits between two hop neighbors with *MultiFlit*

maximum number of flits per packet. Thus the number of flits is given by:

$$\#f = \left\lceil \frac{pl}{lw - h - \lceil \log_2 \#f \rceil} \right\rceil . \tag{2}$$

The transferred overhead is hence $\#f \cdot (h + f_{id})$. Further, the links have to be as wide as the flits ($fw = lw$).

The latency for one message which is transferred with *MultiFlit* is given by the time difference of the last received flit and the injection time of the first flit. Please note that the last received flit does not necessarily have to be the last injected flit. Figure 3 shows an example of one message that consists of three flits being transmitted from R_x to its two hop neighbor R_z. In clock cycle 0, the first flit is injected (1) from the core and the log message is printed. In the next cycle, the first flit f_1 traverses router R_x and the second flit f_2 is injected (2). In clock cycle 2, f_1 traverses R_y, whereas f_2 traverses R_x and f_3 is injected. In clock cycle 4, flit f_1 is ejected at R_z. It is assumed that flit f_2, which has to traverse R_z in this cycle to follow the shortest path between R_x and R_z, is deflected (4) because of contention and arrives only in clock cycle 8. Hence, flit f_3 has overtaken the second flit, as f_3 followed the direct path to R_z. Generally, the latency l_{MF} for one packet which consists of $\#f$ flits is given by:

$$l_{MF} = \max_{1 \le i \le \#f} (l_i + i - 1) \tag{3}$$

whereas l_i denotes the latency of the i-th flit.

4.2   Serialization

Another method to transfer large amounts of data over smaller links and additionally avoid the separation into several flits, is the serialization and deserialization of all flits. For buffered NoCs, this method has been investigated extensively [1,4,13]. Unfortunately, the results for buffered NoCs can not be transferred to bufferless deflection routing based NoCs. For buffered wormhole flow control based NoCs, the routing decision can be calculated as soon as the routing information and in particular the destination address of the packet has arrived at a router. In case of a successful buffer arbitration, even the data transfer to the next router can be performed immediately. This is not possible for deflection routing, at least not without major adaptions of the router architecture [8].

Bufferless deflection routing based router architectures merely permute all inputs and outputs. There is no arbitration of buffer space. Instead it is exploited that also the neighbored routers calculate a permutation and can hence receive the flit. Therefore, at *Serialization* every flit is indeed transmitted in several phits, but the routing decisions will nevertheless be calculated synchronously by all routers of the NoC in the same clock cycle. Thereby the abstinence of livelocks is guaranteed, as the highest prioritized flit always gets assigned to its preferred direction.

At *Serialization*, every flit is divided into $\lceil \frac{fw}{lw} \rceil$ phits of lw bits, which are serially transferred over the link. The router architecture has to be extended by additional buffers at every input and control logic, which controls the phit transmission and the sorting into the correct buffer space. The buffer width has to be $fw - lw$ as all phits except the last one must be stored. This method allows a reduction of the link width up to 1 bit, but the router architecture is still based on the complete flit width. The router architecture size can even increase due to the additional buffers and the control logic (cf. Sect. 5).

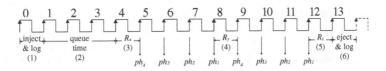

Fig. 4. Transmission of one message between two hop neighbors with Serialization.

Figure 4 shows the transmission of one packet sent from router R_x to R_z via R_y and which consists of four phits $ph_4 - ph_1$. In clock cycle 0, the whole packet is injected and the core prints the log message (1). As all routers operate synchronously and the last phit ph_1, which completes the whole packet, is expected in clock cycles with $c \bmod 4 \equiv 0$, the packet can not be transmitted to router R_x immediately. This is why the packet stays in the queue (2) until the fourth clock pulse edge. In the fourth clock cycle the whole packet traverses R_x, but only one phit can be transmitted to R_y in the next clock pulse edge. All four phits are transmitted to R_y after the eighth clock pulse edge. During clock cycle 8, the packet traverses R_y (4) and the phit transmission to R_z begins. In clock cycle 12, the whole packet arrives at R_z (5) and the packet can be ejected (6) in clock cycle 13.

In general, the latency of one packet, which arrives with a hop-count of hc and consists of $\#ph$ phits, is given by:

$$l_{SER} = \#ph \cdot (hc - 1) + 2 + \frac{\#ph - 1}{2} \tag{4}$$

The last term in this equation gives the average queue time. The constant 2 is added because it takes one cycle to traverse the last router and one clock cycle to transmit the flit to the core and print the log message. The most significant

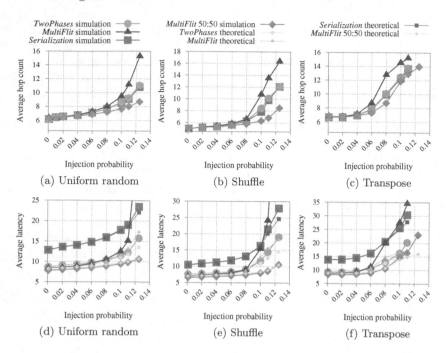

Fig. 5. Average hop-count ((a)–(c)) and latency ((d)–(f)) for a variable injection rate and different synthetic workloads.

term for the majority of the flits is the first term, which gives the serialization and deserialization time. As the packet is serialized at every router, except the router which receives the packet, this takes $\#ph \cdot (hc - 1)$ clock cycles.

5   Evaluation

In this section, we evaluate *TwoPhases* and compare it to the transmission schemes introduced in Sect. 4. All transmission schemes are simulated for a 8×8 NoC using our in-house cycle accurate simulator implemented in VHDL. Every router is connected to a traffic generator, which is able to generate different synthetic workloads. For further information regarding the router architecture, please refer to [10]. At every router, packets are injected with a given injection probability. If a flit could not be injected at a certain router due to congestion, the flit is stored in the injection queue, and is injected as soon as it is possible. The injection probability varied from 0.1 % up to the saturation point of the NoC. Simulations took 5000 clock cycles and every packet consists of 128 bit payload and 16 bit header information. For *TwoPhases* as well as for *Serialization*, hence, every packet has a length of 144 bit and we used link widths of 72 bits. As *MultiFlit* uses several independent flits to transmit larger messages, every flit has to carry routing information, and a flit-ID field for sequencing is required. In these simulations, every flit has a length of $64 + 16 + 1$ bit, whereas the last bit is the flit-ID. Therefore, the links are 81 bits width for *MultiFlit* and exactly two flits are transmitted per message.

Figure 5a–c shows the average hop-count for all three transmission methods, as well as for *MultiFlit* 50:50. In the latter, half of the packets have a payload of 128 bits (2 flits per message) and the other packets consist of only one flit. Real traffic for MPSoCs usually has no uniform length [14]. Instead it consists of larger messages (e.g. data fetch and data update packets) as well as shorter messages (e.g. memory access request packets). With *Serialization* as well as with *TwoPhases*, all messages have to have a uniform length, as it is the case for standard deflection routing. *MultiFlit* has the highest average hop-count as the deflection rate is higher due to the increased number of independent flits. This effect increases with the injection rate and occurs for all three traffic classes. The lowest average hop-count is achieved with *MultiFlit* 50:50, because of the lower network load. The latency of messages is even more important than the average hop-count, as all processing elements or cores have to reassemble the complete message before the data can be processed. The average latency, which was determined by our simulations, is depicted in Fig. 5d–f. The theoretical average latencies for every transmission method, which are based on the formulas (1), (3), and (4) given in Sects. 3 and 4 are also depicted (smaller point sizes and a brighter color). Please note that the theoretical values do not take congestion into account. It can be seen, that for all injection rates and all traffic scenarios, *Serialization* has a higher latency than the other approaches. For smaller injection rates, *MultiFlit* and *TwoPhases* perform equally well, but for higher injection rates the latency with *MultiFlit* increases significantly. With injection rates over 10 %, the theoretical average latency is higher, but the simulated latency is even much higher. The reason for this is the queue time, which increases drastically if the network is congested. Similar results have been achieved with different payload and link sizes, but are omitted because to the space restriction.

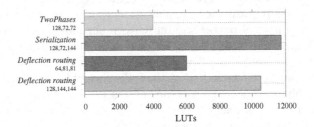

Fig. 6. Synthesis results for a 2 × 2 NoC and different router architectures.

To evaluate the hardware cost, we synthesized a 2 × 2 NoC using Xilinx's XST [12]. Please note that XST synthesizes a design for FPGAs and does not use a standard cell library like ASIC synthesis software. Nevertheless, this enables us to compare the hardware requirements and the achievable speed of our router architectures. Figure 6 shows the number of required look-up tables (LUTs) for the NoC of dimension 2×2. Underneath the name of the transmission scheme, the payload size, the link width, and the router width are depicted. With *TwoPhases* for example, each packet has 128 bit payload, the link width is 72 bit and the internal router structures also have a width of 72 bit. It can be seen that *TwoPhases* has the least hardware requirements of all presented transmission methods. *Serialization* has the highest requirements, because of the additional hardware for de-/serialization. The required LUTs for a NoC with standard deflection routing, as the case for *MultiFlit*, are depicted in blue. It can be seen that *MultiFlit* has higher hardware requirements than *TwoPhases*, as wider links (81 bits instead of 72 bits) have to be deployed to transmit the same amount of payload. The last bar in this plot shows the hardware requirements for a NoC with routers, which are able to transmit 128 bit payload in solely one flit.

6 Related Work

Moscibroda and Mutlu presented in [8] a router architecture which uses the wormhole principle and is still based on deflection routing. The livelock problem mentioned in Sect. 2 is solved by worm truncation. However, depending on the frequency of the truncations, the performance can be very similar to *MultiFlit*. Furthermore, additional buffers are required, as every router has to be able to create head flits out of data flits. Serialization has been investigated with different emphasis in the past, mainly for buffered NoCs. Serialization of the TSVs in 3D NoCs are investigated for packet switched routers in [4] and deflection routing in [6]. The authors in [1] proposed serialization to preserve partial defect links.

Most academic as well as industrial NoCs deploy a certain link width and flit size without justification or investigation. The optimal flit size, packet size, and link width is correlated to our investigations. However, these are also orthogonal problems as the transmission scheme affects these sizes and vice versa. Recently, the authors in [11] investigated the impact of the flit size on hardware requirements as well as on performance for deflection routing based NoCs. Ye et al. investigated the impact of packet size on performance and energy consumption for MPSoC designs [14]. In [7], Lee et al. gave a guideline how the appropriate flit or link width for wormhole flow control based router architectures can be determined. The authors conclude that the links should be as wide as the smallest packet size plus the header overhead. Ogras et al. presented equations for bandwidth and latency of packet switched NoCs in [9]. They also identified the optimal channel width as an open problem.

7 Summary

In this paper, we presented the new transmission method *TwoPhases* for deflection routing based NoCs. *TwoPhases* is an alternating transmission scheme which allows smaller link widths and a reduction of the routing overhead. We compared *TwoPhases* to basic transmission schemes, which are obvious solutions if the flit width exceeds the available link width. Theoretical as well as simulated results show that the latency for uniform message width can be reduced, in particular for high injection rates. Further, we found that *MultiFlit* could be a viable solution, if the message length is non-uniform.

References

1. Chen, C., Lu, Y., Cotofana, S.D.: A novel flit serialization strategy to utilize partially faulty links in networks-on-chip. In: 2012 Sixth IEEE/ACM International Symposium on Networks on Chip (NoCS), pp. 124–131. IEEE (2012)
2. Dally, W.J., Towles, B.P.: Principles and practices of interconnection networks. Access Online via Elsevier (2004)
3. Fallin, C., Craik, C., Mutlu, O.: Chipper: a low-complexity bufferless deflection router. Technical report, 2010-001, Carnegie Mellon University, December 2010
4. Ghidini, Y., Moreira, M., Brahm, L., Webber, T., Calazans, N., Marcon, C.: Lasio 3D NoC vertical links serialization: evaluation of latency and buffer occupancy. In: 2013 26th Symposium on Integrated Circuits and Systems Design (SBCCI), pp. 1–6. IEEE (2013)
5. Kahng, A., Lin, B., Nath, S.: Explicit modeling of control and data for improved NoC router estimation. In: Design Automation Conference (DAC), 2012 49th ACM/EDAC/IEEE, pp. 392–397, June 2012
6. Lee, J., Lee, D., Kim, S., Choi, K.: Deflection routing in 3D network-on-chip with TSV serialization. In: 2013 18th Asia and South Pacific Design Automation Conference (ASP-DAC) (2013)
7. Lee, J., Nicopoulos, C., Park, S.J., Swaminathan, M., Kim, J.: Do we need wide flits in networks-on-chip?. In: 2013 IEEE Computer Society Annual Symposium on VLSI (ISVLSI), pp. 2–7. IEEE (2013)
8. Moscibroda, T., Mutlu, O.: A case for bufferless routing in on-chip networks. In: Proceedings of the 36th Annual International Symposium on Computer Architecture, ISCA 2009, pp. 196–207. ACM (2009)
9. Ogras, U.Y., Hu, J., Marculescu, R.: Key research problems in noc design: a holistic perspective. In: Proceedings of the 3rd IEEE/ACM/IFIP International Conference on Hardware/Software Codesign and System Synthesis, pp. 69–74. ACM (2005)
10. Runge, A.: Fault-tolerant network-on-chip based on fault-aware flits and deflection routing. In: Proceedings of the 9th International Symposium on Networks-on-Chip, p. 9. ACM (2015)
11. Runge, A., Kolla, R.: Consideration of the flit size for deflection routing based network-on-chips. In: 1st International Workshop on Advanced Interconnect Solutions and Technologies for Emerging Computing Systems (AISTECS) (2016)
12. Xilinx: Ise webpack design software (2015). http://www.xilinx.com/products/design-tools/ise-design-suite/ise-webpack.htm. Accessed 23 October 2015
13. Yang, Z.J., Kumar, A., Ha, Y.: An area-efficient dynamically reconfigurable spatial division multiplexing network-on-chip with static throughput guarantee. In: 2010 International Conference on Field-Programmable Technology (FPT), pp. 389–392. IEEE (2010)
14. Ye, T.T., Benini, L., Micheli, G.D.: Packetized on-chip interconnect communication analysis for mpsoc. In: Design, Automation and Test in Europe Conference and Exhibition, pp. 344–349. IEEE (2003)

Exzess: Hardware-Based RAM Encryption Against Physical Memory Disclosure

Alexander Würstlein$^{(\boxtimes)}$, Michael Gernoth, Johannes Götzfried,
and Tilo Müller

Department of Computer Science,
Friedrich-Alexander-Universität Erlangen-Nürnberg (FAU), Erlangen, Germany
{alexander.wuerstlein,michael.gernoth,
johannes.goetzfried,tilo.mueller}@cs.fau.de

Abstract. The main memory of today's computers contains lots of sensitive data, in particular from applications that have been used recently. As data within RAM is stored in cleartext, it is exposed to attackers with physical access to a system. In this paper we introduce Exzess, a hardware-based mitigation against physical memory disclosure attacks such as, for example, cold boot and DMA attacks. Our FPGA-based prototype with accompanying software components demonstrates the viability, security and performance of our novel approach for partial main memory encryption via memory proxies. The memory proxy approach will be compared to other existing mitigation techniques and possible further uses beyond encryption will be discussed, as well. Exzess effectively protects against physical attacks on main memory while being transparent to applications and the operating system after initialization.

Keywords: Memory encryption · Memory disclosure · Physical attacks

1 Introduction

When protecting servers, desktop computers and notebooks against physical access, it is natural to draw on full disk encryption solutions. It is generally overlooked, however, that main memory contains lots of sensitive data, as well, from both the operating system and each process that was recently running. Physical access attacks against RAM range from exploitable Firewire devices that have direct memory access [1,2] to *cold boot attacks* which physically read RAM modules by first cooling them down [5,7]. The property of memory which allows cold boot attacks to work is referred to as the *remanence effect* [6,13]. RAM contents fade away gradually over time instead of being lost immediately after power is cut. Both kinds of attacks enable an attacker to completely recover arbitrary kernel and process memory. The fact that cryptographic keys in main memory are unsafe has been known for two decades now. Nevertheless, almost all vendors of software-based encryption solutions continue to store cryptographic keys inside RAM. Other sensitive data, such as cached passwords, credit card information and confidential emails are always stored in RAM in practice, too.

© Springer International Publishing Switzerland 2016
F. Hannig et al. (Eds.): ARCS 2016, LNCS 9637, pp. 60–71, 2016.
DOI: 10.1007/978-3-319-30695-7_5

The problem is hardware-related in nature, but almost all current attempts for a solution are software-based. Those solutions suffer from their limited scope – often only full disk encryption – or their poor performance. If encrypting RAM could be handled transparently in hardware, the problem of RAM extraction would be turned into the problem of extracting information from a dedicated piece of hardware that can be particularly protected.

Our Contribution

We created Exzess, a hardware-based device that is capable of transparently encrypting and decrypting portions of memory. Exzess is a PCI Express (PCIe) addon card which exploits direct memory access and acts as a transparent memory proxy to any operating system while performing certain functionality such as the encryption and decryption of data. During the development of Exzess, we designed and developed the hardware design for an FPGA-based prototype, wrote drivers and application software for Linux and performed evaluations regarding correctness and performance. In detail our contributions are threefold:

- We designed and implemented an FPGA-based prototype that acts as a transparent memory proxy to an operating system. A certain region of main memory can be accessed indirectly via PCI-Express through Exzess, while Exzess performs a given functionality on the data. We developed Exzess as a prototype to prevent physical memory disclosure attacks such as cold boot attacks by using an AES-128 IP core to encrypt all data that passes through Exzess.
- To be able to use Exzess, we provide device drivers and application software for Linux. Our host tools support the configuration of Exzess and our device driver offers an intuitive interface for using Exzess in end-user applications. Once configured, Exzess creates a number of special files and memory that should be accessed through Exzess. Protected memory can simply be read from and written to by usual system calls, i.e., access is semantically indistinguishable from the access to allocated RAM.
- We evaluated the prototype implementation regarding basic functionality, correctness and performance.

Although our prototype has primarily been developed against physical memory disclosure attacks, the generic design of Exzess as a transparent memory proxy allows for easy adoption to more application scenarios in future – such as error checking, checking the consistency of operating system structures and hardware-based malware detection, to name but a few.

2   Background

In this section, we give background information about the technologies that our work has been built on. Readers familiar with PCI Express (Sect. 2.1) and DMA transfers (Sect. 2.2) may safely skip this section.

2.1 PCI Express

Structure of a PCI Express System. PCIe forms a packet-switched, hierarchical, tree-shaped network as shown in Fig. 1. Inner nodes are called *switches*,
outer leaves are called *endpoint devices*. Examples of endpoint devices are plug-in
cards, such as a network interface card, or soldered-on chips on the mainboard
like an integrated graphics processor. The root node, called *root complex*, is
formed by the PCIe *root switch* and *root port*.

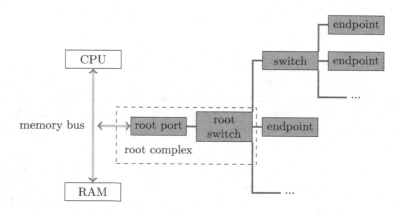

Fig. 1. Architecture of a PCI Express system

The root port has the special role of being the interface between the PCIe
bus, the CPU and the main memory of the computer system. Device discovery,
configuration and other *housekeeping tasks* are performed through it. Accesses
to main memory, referred to as DMA transfers, from PCIe devices are processed
by the root port. In the other direction, accesses from the CPU to device memory
are also issued via the root port. In both cases, the root port acts as a gateway
between the CPU and RAM on one side and the PCIe devices on the other side.

Transaction Layer Protocol. An important part of this work consists of
implementing the handling of *Transaction Layer Packets* (TLPs). The transaction layer protocol describes the routable topmost layer of the PCIe protocol.
This means that a TLP will travel across a number of links from one sending
endpoint to one or more receiving endpoints. As the name suggests, a sequence
of one or more exchanged TLPs is used to implement logical transactions.

Generally all transactions are initiated by a request TLP from the party
subsequently called *requester*. The receiving party, called *completer* performs the
request specified and, if necessary, answers the request with a *completion* TLP.
Posted requests like *memory write* (MWr) require no completion while *non-
posted* requests like *memory read* (MRd) have to be answered by a *completion
with data* (CplD).

2.2   DMA Transfers and Device Memory

There are two possible memory domains as well as directions for memory access between a PCIe endpoint, software running on the CPU and main memory:

1. Coming from and initiated by the software on the CPU, device memory can be accessed. Device memory is a memory area assigned to a specific endpoint for which that endpoint handles accesses. It is configured using the so-called *base address registers* (BARs) where size, address and access semantics are specified. Device memory accesses are accesses where the completer for a memory transaction is an endpoint and the requester for that transaction is the root port. The term *BAR* is a commonly used metonymy for *device memory*.
2. Coming from and initiated by an endpoint, a computer's main memory can be accessed as well. These accesses happen without interrupting normal program flow of the software running on the CPU. Such accesses, commonly known as *direct memory access* (DMA), are memory transactions where the requester is an endpoint and the completer is the root port. DMA memory areas are made known to the device via device-specific means.

3   Design and Implementation

In this section we will first explain the threat model (Sect. 3.1) with respect to which Exzess was desigend. Afterwards we justify our design choices (Sect. 3.2) before giving an overview of the Exzess architecture (Sect. 3.3). Finally we describe implementation details regarding the hardware design and the device driver (Sect. 3.4).

3.1   Threat Model

For the design of Exzess, we consider our protectable asset to be portions of RAM that are limited in size and that are flagged as such by the application or operating system component to which these memory areas have been allocated. The content of these memory areas is data that is considered more critical than other, unprotected data. Examples of such data are cryptographic keys, user passwords, credit card information, confidential emails and secret documents. By protecting full-disk-encryption keys, the encrypted contents of a hard disk can be considered an indirectly protected asset. The same principle applies to, for example, encrypted data within TLS connections and their respective keys stored within protected RAM on the communication endpoints.

We consider our attacker to be capable of physically accessing a machine running Exzess. In particular, the attacker is able to extract RAM modules from the system and read their contents, even after the system has been recently switched off. The attacker, however, is unable to perform more sophisticated attacks such as chip probing or fault injection as these attacks are by far more costly and technically difficult. Thus, he is not able to read CPU registers, CPU cache contents, and registers from the Exzess extension board.

We restrict ourselves to a physical attacker, i.e., software based attacks on applications or the operating system are out of scope for this work. Furthermore, we exclude the possibility of physically writing RAM from our attack model as writing RAM by extracting memory modules usually results in a system crash and is therefore not feasible in most scenarios. Observing bus transfers via direct electrical taps or electromagnetic emanations are excluded from our attack model as well.

3.2   Design Rationale

To mitigate physical memory disclosure we decided to encrypt a limited but sufficiently large portion of a computer's RAM. Any read access to the encrypted portion of the RAM is decrypted transparently when loading the respective data into the CPU's caches or registers. No unencrypted copy of this data can be found in physical main memory. Similarly, when writing CPU register or cache contents back to an encrypted portion of the RAM, encryption will happen transparently and without storing plaintext data in RAM. Userspace software and operating system components wishing to encrypt parts of their respective memory address space may allocate an appropriate address range through a special allocation function.

We decided to encrypt a limited portion of overall RAM. Although a cold boot attack exposes the complete contents of a computer's RAM to the attacker, not all data stored in RAM is equally sensitive as explained in Sect. 3.1. By only encrypting important portions of RAM, performance for the unencrypted parts is unaffected, thereby alleviating the severe performance problems of full memory encryption.

One consequence of encrypting selected portions of RAM is that userspace applications have to be modified to make use of our encrypted memory allocations. The modifications, however, only require limited effort: Cryptographic operations employ libraries that are therefore an obvious place to introduce our changes. Furthermore, many applications already identify the relevant parts of their RAM allocations by marking them non-swappable. To make the modifications of userspace applications as simple as possible we provide an easy to use library that offers the Exzess functionality to programmers.

3.3   Exzess Architecture

In Fig. 2 a schematic overview of a memory access with Exzess is shown. Exzess provides a readable and writeable memory window for the operating system. No additional memory beyond the available main memory is needed for Exzess to work. Instead, any read or write access to the memory window is redirected to a previously configured memory region in RAM via direct memory access. Exzess acts as proxy for those requests and encrypts or decrypts the data written to

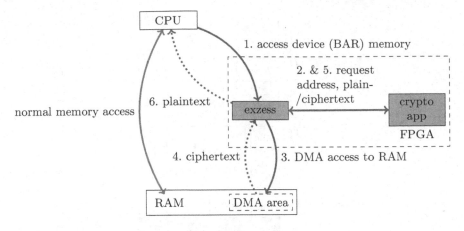

Fig. 2. Schematic overview of Exzess.

or read from the DMA area. Thus an encrypted memory area has the same semantics as usual memory accesses except for the transparent encryption.

Encryption Through a Memory Proxy. Exzess presents a PCI device memory area to the operating system which is a proxied cleartext view of a given memory window. The memory window can be configured in size and location with the help of our device driver. On each request encryption or decryption is performed on-the-fly. The encrypted data is stored in a DMA memory area which is a portion of regular main memory according to the previously configured memory window.

3.4   Exzess Implementation

In this section we will present the implementation of Exzess. We first will explain details of our hardware design and afterwards describe how the device driver is able to interact with our memory proxy.

FPGA Hardware with PCI Express Interface. Our prototype is implemented on an Enterpoint Raggedstone 2 board [4]. The Xilinx Spartan6 FPGA on this board includes a PCIe interface that is able to handle the physical layer and configuration portions of the PCIe protocol. The VHDL code written for our prototype handles the creation and sequencing of PCIe TLPs as well as encryption. To be able to encrypt data passing through Exzess, an open source AES core [12] has been utilized.

As shown in Fig. 3, the hardware is structured in a four-layered architecture: Physical PCIe interface and configuration tasks are performed by the hard IP core included on the FPGA. Above this lowermost layer, three layers were implemented in VHDL: (1) a basic, reusable generator and decoder for PCIe TLPs,

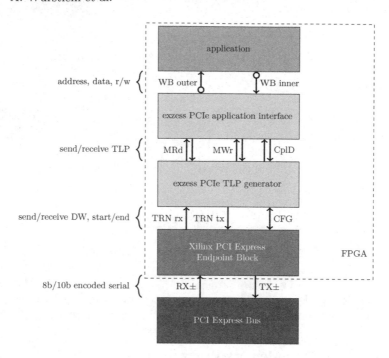

Fig. 3. Block diagram of the software stack of Exzess.

(2) an abstraction layer providing memory access primitives over the on-chip Whishbone bus as an abstraction to sending and receiving TLPs, and (3) the actual application responsible for encrypting and decrypting memory accesses.

PCI Express Communication. The memory proxy is implemented by a distinctive sequence of TLPs. After a request, e.g., a read request (MRd) addressing the BAR device memory, has arrived at the FPGA, a corresponding MRd for the encrypted data in the DMA area will be generated by the FPGA. After this second request has been answered by a CplD containing the encrypted data, decryption will take place within the FPGA. The decrypted data is then used to answer the initial MRd with a completion containing the decrypted data. As long as no timeout violations for the initial request occur, i.e., the final completion arrives in time, PCIe allows multiple larger or smaller requests between the initial and final TLP to be sent.

Exzess Encryption Applications. To be able to evaluate Exzess, especially regarding performance, two different applications have been implemented: The first one performs a simple "XOR encryption" with a configurable constant on all data passing through Exzess while the second actual application performs AES encryption on the data and thus effectively prevents physical memory disclosure.

For this prototype AES has been used in CTR mode of operation with the concatenation of a nonce and the currently requested address as start value. The key and the nonce can be set at configuration time, i.e., boot time, and are not readable by software afterwards. In real world scenarios, both the nonce and the key should be randomly generated on each boot.

Device Driver. The Linux device driver for Exzess is responsible for initializing the FPGA as well as for allocating and configuring the DMA and device memory areas, e.g., the current memory window. After configuration, Linux automatically exposes all device memory areas as special root-accessible files in the `/sys` filesystem (sysfs). The allocated DMA area is exposed by the driver via a character device `/dev/exzess` for debugging and verification purposes. Since it only enables access to the encrypted data, this device file would be unnecessary in a production environment.

Both the device memory areas and the DMA area can be accessed through the usual POSIX `read`/`write` and `mmap` system calls using the aforementioned files. For convenience, a library wrapping those calls with appropriate arguments into `secure_malloc` and `secure_free` routines is provided.

4   Evaluation

In this section we evaluate Exzess regarding basic functionality and correctness (Sect. 4.1) followed by performance (Sect. 4.2).

4.1   Correctness

Both applications, "XOR encryption" and AES encryption, were used to verify that the application interface, the device driver and the hardware are working together as expected: By inspecting both the contents of the encrypted DMA area and the plaintext device memory window using XOR encryption a first hint is given that the data is processed correctly by our memory proxy. To verify the correctness of our actual application, the AES encryption, OpenSSL was used. On the one hand, data has been encrypted by Exzess and decrypted by OpenSSL and on the other hand, it has been encrypted by OpenSSL and decrypted by Exzess. For both scenarios, a successful comparison of a large number of plain- and ciphertext pairs leads to the conclusion that the Exzess works as intended.

Furthermore, the device memory area was mapped into a Linux userspace application and known values were written to this area. By monitoring received and generated PCIe TLPs on the FPGA and viewing the contents of the DMA area, the correct functionality of the FPGA could be verified.

To examine the leakage of sensitive data, known patterns were written to the protected device memory area. Afterwards full physical memory dumps have been obtained via the `/dev/mem` special device. We searched for the previously written known patterns within these images and could not find a single pattern within one of the dumps. Note that obtaining a physical memory image via

`/dev/mem` is more strict then performing an actual cold boot attack, because the images do not contain bit errors and therefore no patterns can be missed.

4.2 Performance

To measure the performance of the AES and XOR application, a benchmarking application has been implemented which reads and writes device memory areas 100 times and calculates average measurements and error estimates. These measurements are shown in Fig. 4 and Table 1.

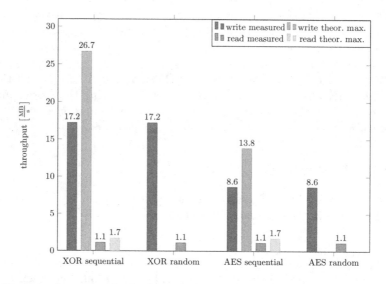

Fig. 4. Benchmark results for both applications, XOR and AES in read and write mode. The measured values are averaged over 100 iterations.

As expected, the measured values are lower than the calculated theoretical maximum values which are derived from transaction runtimes. The performance for read transactions, when comparing the XOR and AES applications, is equal within the precision of measurement. Performance values for write transactions are lower in the case of AES and the XOR application has roughly twice the write throughput of the AES application. This is also consistent with the predicted behaviour.

Random accesses have essentially the same performance as sequential accesses, at least for writes. In the case of reads, the performance is approximately 1 % lower for random reads than for sequential reads, both in the XOR and AES application. The difference is small but much larger than 5σ and therefore significant. While we have no definitive explanation, readahead behaviour is probably the most likely cause for this difference. Of course there are possibilities to improve performance and some of them will be discussed in Sect. 6.2.

Table 1. Benchmark results for both applications in read and write mode.

Application	Access pattern	Access direction	Theoretical maximum $\left[\frac{kB}{s}\right]$	Measured $\left[\frac{kB}{s}\right]$
XOR	sequential	write	26667	17223 ± 7
XOR	sequential	read	1739	1085 ± 1
XOR	random	write		17221 ± 6
XOR	random	read		1078 ± 1
AES	sequential	write	13793	8621 ± 3
AES	sequential	read	1739	1086 ± 1
AES	random	write		8620 ± 3
AES	random	read		1077 ± 1

5 Related Work

Theoretical approaches for *full memory encryption* [3] are described but practical implementations to encrypt, for example, swap space [10,11] are also available. Furthermore, a solution for use in embedded hardware [8] exists. All these solutions, however, are implemented in software and suffer from serious performance drawbacks while Exzess is a fast hardware solution that protects sensitive data on the users choice. For embedded hardware there exists work on hardware-based full memory encryption [9] as well, yet for the most critical and vulnerable species of personal computers no solution seems to be available.

6 Discussion

In this section, we will list current limitations (Sect. 6.1) of Exzess and give an outlook over future research directions (Sect. 6.2).

6.1 Limitations

The BAR memory area is generally limited in size by the hardware since all BAR memory areas of all PCI and PCIe devices in a system need to fit into the PCI address space which is a hardware-dependent fixed subset of the 32 bit address space, usually a few hundred megabytes in size. A switch to 64 bit addresses on the PCIe interface could diminish this limitation. This would also allow for DMA areas larger than what is addressable by 32 bit addresses.

The current interface to access BAR memory areas from a userspace program is not very convenient as root access privileges are necessary and the whole memory area can be accessed. To handle accesses for a *normal* user and to ensure the usual page-granular memory mapping and protection, an operating system interface to map these pages from the BAR memory area into process address spaces is necessary.

6.2 Future Work

An increase in performance to levels similar to normal RAM accesses could be achieved with some enhancements. Currently, the configuration of the BAR and DMA area forbids caching. This means that reads of previously accessed data are as slow as if accessed for the first time. With caching enabled, each access after the first one would access the cache, speeding up operations significantly. Additionally, read accesses are usually performed in cache-line-sized portions and following data would then be subject to read-ahead, possibly gaining even more speed.

PCIe TLPs not only contain the memory address subject to a read or write request but also the bus address of the requester to return data or error messages to. By only allowing requests from known-good bus addresses, i.e. the root complex where requests from the CPU originate, and rejecting all requests from other, possibly malicious PCIe devices, attacks from those devices could be mitigated as well.

The modular design of Exzess as a transparent memory proxy allows the development of a lot of different applications far beyond encrypting data to prevent physical memory disclosure and guarantee confidentiality. Possible applications include data integrity and authenticity by using, for example, an AEAD cipher mode. This is possible because both memory areas and the respective requests do not have to be equal in size. Furthermore, completely different application scenarios such as error checking, checking the consistency of operating system structures or hardware-based malware detection could be adopted.

In combination with those integrity checks, the Exzess threat model could be extended to include certain software-based attacks. When moving beyond the current FPGA prototype, e.g., towards an ASIC, certain limitations in the attacker model pertaining to the relative vulnerability of the FPGA could be replaced by those of a sufficiently hardened ASIC.

7 Conclusion

In this paper we presented Exzess, a hardware-based solution against physical memory disclosure attacks such as cold boot attacks. The design and implementation of Exzess as a transparent memory proxy with on-the-fly AES encryption for all data passing through allows applications and operating systems to transparently access sensitive data within main memory without leaving the data at risk. We have shown that Exzess successfully mitigates physical attacks on main memory while maintaining the overall performance of a computer system where other approaches either fall short or are very limited regarding the data they are able to protect.

Acknowledgment. This work was partly supported by the German Research Foundation (DFG) as part of the Transregional Collaborative Research Centre "Invasive Computing" (SFB/TR 89).

References

1. Becher, M., Dornseif, M., Klein, C.N.: FireWire - all your memory are belong to us. In: Proceedings of the Annual CanSecWest Applied Security Conference. Laboratory for Dependable Distributed Systems, RWTH Aachen University, Vancouver, British Columbia, Canada (2005)
2. Carrier, B.D., Grand, J.: A hardware-based memory acquisition procedure for digital investigations. Digit. Investig. **1**(1), 50–60 (2004)
3. Duc, G., Keryell, R.: Cryptopage: an efficient secure architecture with memory encryption, integrity and information leakage protection. In: 22nd Annual Computer Security Applications Conference ACSAC 2006, Miami Beach, Florida, USA, 11–15 December, pp. 483–492 (2006)
4. Enterpoint Ltd.: Raggedstone 2 - Xilinx Spartan 6 FPGA Development Board, Manufacturer Website. http://www.enterpoint.co.uk/products/spartan-6-development-boards/raggedstone-2/
5. Gruhn, M., Müller, T.: On the practicability of cold boot attacks. In: 2013 International Conference on Availability, Reliability and Security, ARES 2013, Regensburg, Germany, 2–6 September, pp. 390–397 (2013)
6. Gutmann, P.: Data remanence in semiconductor devices. In: 10th USENIX Security Symposium, Washington, D.C., USA, 13–17 August 2001 (2001)
7. Halderman, J.A., Schoen, S.D., Heninger, N., Clarkson, W., Paul, W., Calandrino, J.A., Feldman, A.J., Appelbaum, J., Felten, E.W.: Lest we remember: cold boot attacks on encryptions keys. In: Proceedings of the 17th USENIX Security Symposium. Princeton University, USENIX Association, San Jose, CA, August 2008
8. Henson, M., Taylor, S.: Beyond full disk encryption: protection on security-enhanced commodity processors. In: Jacobson, M., Locasto, M., Mohassel, P., Safavi-Naini, R. (eds.) ACNS 2013. LNCS, vol. 7954, pp. 307–321. Springer, Heidelberg (2013)
9. Kurdziel, M., Lukowiak, M., Sanfilippo, M.: Minimizing performance overhead in memory encryption. J. Cryptographic Eng. **3**(2), 129–138 (2013). http://dx.doi.org/10.1007/s13389-013-0047-5
10. Peterson, P.: Cryptkeeper: Improving security with encrypted RAM. In: Technologies for Homeland Security (HST), pp. 120–126. IEEE, November 2010
11. Provos, N.: Encrypting virtual memory. In: 9th USENIX Security Symposium, Denver, Colorado, USA, 14–17 August 2000 (2000)
12. Satyanarayana, H.: AES128 Crypto Core in VHDL, licensed under LGPL (2004). http://opencores.org/project,aes_crypto_core
13. Skorobogatov, S.: Data remanence in flash memory devices. In: Rao, J.R., Sunar, B. (eds.) CHES 2005. LNCS, vol. 3659, pp. 339–353. Springer, Heidelberg (2005)

Hardware-Assisted Context Management
for Accelerator Virtualization:
A Case Study with RSA

Ying Gao$^{(\boxtimes)}$ and Timothy Sherwood

University of California, Santa Barbara, CA 93106, USA
yinggao@ece.ucsb.edu, sherwood@cs.ucsb.edu

Abstract. The advantages of virtualization, including the ability to migrate, schedule, and manage software processes, continues to drive the demand for hardware and software support. However, the packaging of software state required by virtualization is in direct conflict with the trend toward accelerator-rich architectures where state is distributed between the processor and a set of heterogeneous devices – a problem that is particularly acute in the mobile SoC market. Virtualizing such systems requires that the VMM explicitly manage the internal state of all of the accelerators over which a process's computation may be spread. Public-key crypto engines are particularly problematic because of both the sensitivity of the information that they carry and the long compute times required to complete a single task.

In this paper we examine a set of hardware design approaches to public-key crypto accelerator virtualization and study the trade-off between sharing granularity and management overhead in time and space. Based on observations made during the design of several such systems, we propose a hybrid local-remote scheduling approach that promotes more intelligent decisions during hardware context switches and enables quick and safe state packaging. We find that performance can vary significantly among the examined approaches, and that our new design, with explicit accelerator support for state management and a modicum of scheduling flexibility, can allow highly contended resources to be efficiently shared with only moderate gains in area and power consumption.

1 Introduction

Virtualization has emerged as a common means by which one may share and more optimally utilize underlying physical resources. As custom hardware accelerators are called upon to take significant portions of the workload from traditional CPUs, the state of computing tasks is increasingly spread across a set of highly heterogeneous devices. Effective virtualization of a system with such distributed and heterogeneous memory elements can be extremely complicated as both fine-grained scheduling and the safe management of the underlying hardware state may be required [8,12,13]. For each distinct type of accelerator, the

© Springer International Publishing Switzerland 2016
F. Hannig et al. (Eds.): ARCS 2016, LNCS 9637, pp. 72–83, 2016.
DOI: 10.1007/978-3-319-30695-7_6

virtual machine monitor (VMM) must be aware of what subset of the machine state is critical to maintain correctness, which subset is potentially damaging if leaked to other VMs, and how critical parts of the hardware state can be managed and restored by the interface provided by that accelerator core.

This complexity also comes with a performance and system management cost, specifically in that it leads to an inability to coordinate the accelerators effectively. Switching the context for an accelerator can have a non-negligible cost (driver/OS and driver/device communication, cleanup, power management, etc.) and that cost can be variable based on time. If the VMM is to coordinate the accelerators it must have an accurate view of what resources are free for scheduling and what the costs of scheduling might be. The VMM must either be able to estimate those costs from models, gather them through further communication with the accelerators (which may be then subject to delay due to resource contention), or give up the opportunity for efficient coordinated control.

There are several ways in which a designer may approach this problem. First, they might consider fixed pass-through (e.g. Intel VT-d [9]) where an accelerator is exclusively assigned to one VM, but this exclusive relationship limits sharing. A second approach is for the hypervisor to arbitrate between several VMs with one VM having access at a time, where the hypervisor halts operation of the accelerator and restores it to a known state between guests [17]. This approach requires very little in the way of both additional memory and network communication, but carries a risk of significantly reduced throughput when interruptions cause the loss of interrupted but unfinished work. A third approach is to avoid dropping unfinished tasks, instead storing the intermediate results in memory for future retrieval. This method prevents wasting of allocated timing slots, but might incur heavy data communication [10, 11]. A fourth option is to involve the accelerator itself in the alleviation of context switch overhead. If the accelerator is granted some leeway in when the context switch occurs through a modicum of automation inside of a device, smarter switch timing might be possible saving both time and space. This might require an understanding of the computation and a careful re-architecting of the accelerator.

While performance is one important factor, the sharing of state also needs to be completed in a way that is secure. Given the importance of crypto operations, both in performance and security, they are a natural space in which to study accelerator design tradeoffs. To study the impact and suitability of different accelerator virtualization strategies and to provide optimizations for crypto devices, we implement a series of fast modular exponentiation engines. By making minimum changes to the device interface, we enable hardware assisted context management in such a way as to avoid exposing sensitive intermediate results to the upper system and as to involve local scheduling to improve performance. Our experimental results suggest that above certain switching frequencies, the local context switch approaches achieve significantly higher throughput rate than more traditional schemes and thus enable a new level of fine-grain and fair scheduling. The additional area overhead for our baseline and optimized design to implicitly accommodate four VMs is only 36 % and 15 %.

2   Related Work

The management of accelerator-rich architectures is a very active topic of research, but much of the work is focused on application partitioning and fair scheduling, but less with VM-level sharing. HiPPAI [20] alleviates the overheads of system calls and memory access by using a uniform virtual memory addressing model based on IOMMU support and direct user mode access to accelerators. While it is efficient in limiting overheads at the user/kernel boundary, it lacks support in resource sharing. Traditional accelerator scheduling schemes still rely heavily on usage statistics collected from hardware. Pegasus [8] manages accelerators as first class schedulable entities and uses coordinated scheduling methods to align accelerator resource usage with platform-level management. Disengaged scheduling [13] advocates a strategy in which the kernel intercedes between applications and the accelerator on an infrequent basis, with overuse control that guarantees fairness. Some work tackles the management problem by simplifying accelerator/application integration. VEAL [3] proposes a hybrid static-dynamic compilation approach to map a loop to a template for inner loop accelerators. DySER [7] utilizes program phase and integrates a configurable accelerator into specialized data-path to dynamically encode program regions into custom instructions. While these approaches are intelligent in software partitioning and mapping, they fail to take advantage of hardware assistance in resource managing. Some work starts to look into hardware device reusability: CHARM [6] and CAMEL [5] tackle the sharing and management problem mainly by automating composition of accelerator building blocks (ABBs), primarily stateless arithmetic units in ASICs.

Some projects favor managing hardware states implicitly. Task specific access structures(TSAS) [10] inserts a multiplexer as the input of each FF to select between updating its value from the combinational logic or from previously stored data, or simply remaining its value from the last cycle. This scheme takes the majority of the context switch workload within the device and enables fast switching, but at the sacrifice of non-negligible augmented logic and memory. Hardware checkpointing [11] where the hardware states of a device can be stored and be rolled back regarding checkpoint, hold the potential to minimize area overhead wisely. We recognize the value of hardware checkpointing - in fact we extend its role in coordinated resource management: for accelerators like an RSA engine that implements real-time requests, hardware support in context management will be of great help to fast and fine-grained accelerator sharing.

3   Baseline RSA Accelerator Architecture

3.1   Montgomery's Modular Multiplication and Exponentiation

The core computation in an RSA crypto engine is modular exponentiation, consisting of a number of modular multiplications. Montgomery's modular multiplication algorithm [15] employs simply additions, subtractions, and shift operations to avoid expensive divisions. In this paper we work with an extension to

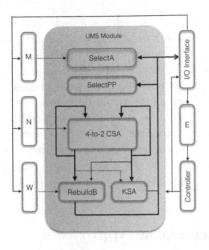

Fig. 1. Traditional RSA accelerator block architecture

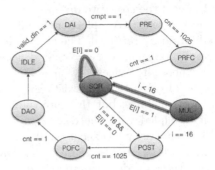

Fig. 2. State diagram of the original RSA accelerator design. PRE/PRFC and POST/POFC are the preprocessing and the post-processing states for domain format and carry-save format conversions. MUL and SQR stand for modular multiplication and square operation respectively.

this algorithm [18]. Three k-bit integers, the modulus N, the multiplicand A and the multiplier B are needed as inputs for computation.

Algorithm MM_UMS is defined as follows:

for i $= 0$ to i $=$ k -1 :

$$q = (S + A * B[i]) \ mod \ 2 \tag{1}$$

$$S = (S + A * B[i] + q * N) \ / \ 2 \tag{2}$$

S is restructured in carry-save form as (Sc, Ss) where Sc and Ss respectively denotes the carry and sum components of S. II-algorithm [2] transforms the computation of modular exponentiation into a sequence of squares and multiplications. Square operation could be performed when both multiplicand and multiplier are identical. The modular exponentiation algorithm, ME_UMS(M, E, N), iteratively applies a unified multiplication or square operation, where for each bit $E[i]$ in exponent E, both a single square operation and multiplication will be performed when $E[i] = 1$ while only a square operation will be performed otherwise.

Figure 1 shows the baseline design. The unified modular multiplication/square module is highlighted in the shadowed region. The nine states in Fig. 2 capture the major stages of the entire modular exponentiation process, as discussed in the algorithm ME_UMS.

3.2 Sharing an RSA Accelerator

One traditional method of device sharing is hard preemptive multitasking. The obvious drawback is that as the switching frequencies increase during heavy sharing, the throughput rate might suffer significant degradation.

To avoid the cost, two options are clear, either the OS relaxes its schedule to wait for the task to complete or the intermediate results from hardware have to be saved for future retrieval. The first option is becoming increasingly difficult since an application can occupy several accelerators simultaneously, thus a perfect point where all devices have just finished their current tasks can be extremely hard to identify or even exist. The latter option seems to comply well with software schedules, but the data movement required to store the intermediate results, coupled with the corresponding memory updates, making this option surprisingly tricky to execute well in practice. Moreover, exposing intermediate results to DMA are also risky due to DMA attacks [19]. A good solution should manage these burdens carefully and a new set of interfaces is needed to simplify the synchronization process.

4   Tightly Integrated Virtual Accelerator Approaches

The simplest tightly integrated design might store all local state in a set of D flip-flops sprinkled throughout the design. However, this approach is also prohibitively expensive. Simulation results suggest that regarding area (and power) efficiency, such virtualized accelerator can add up to a 78 % area overhead.

So what can we do if we want to maintain the accelerator's capability of being fast switched without giving up almost nearly all of our efficiency? We describe two different solutions – the simplest being to replace the local and distributed storage elements with a set of RAMs.

4.1   Baseline Virtual RSA Accelerator Design Overview

In general, most sharing patterns fall into one of the four categories:

- Double Vacancy. No VM is occupying the device.
- Single occupancy. The accelerator is currently dominated by one VM while another VM requires input data streaming for starting a new task.
- Double occupancy. One VM is scheduled to resume a previous uncompleted computation while the other VM is in the process of computing.
- Single occupancy. One VM requires to resume a suspended task while the other VM is performing output data streaming.

Note that in scenario 3, two whole sets of states need to be stored. Based on this, we include 2 KB of RAM alongside the core for temporary storage. We build a simple layer above the RSA accelerator to forward switching commands rather than changing the slave interface directly. We add a *switch* signal underneath the layer to help the controller determine the next state. In order to be able to interrupt a task in the middle of such computation, four more states are added to the FSM. We show the resulting state diagram in Fig. 3.

By enabling hardware preemption, the proposed accelerator virtualization approach successfully realizes the goal of abstracting away hardware details from software without abandoning tasks, at the sacrifice of increasing critical path delay by 16 %.

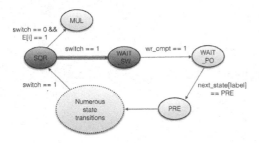

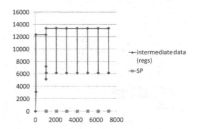

Fig. 3. State diagram of an example transition case in the baseline architecture. When receiving active switch signal in SQR state, it will jump to WAIT_SW state to store intermediate results in local RAM. label denotes VM ID. If the current requesting VM was in PRE state during last switch out, next_state will be set to PRE. After numerous state transitions, the VM that was switched off during SQR state might request again, and have a chance to restore its state

Fig. 4. The amount of local memory needed for storing intermediate results. The y-axis denotes the number of hardware registers and the x-axis denotes timeline measured by clock cycles during a single modular exponentiation operation

4.2 Optimized Accelerator Virtualization Strategy - Making Virtual Accelerator Out of Area Efficiency

In order to eliminate the increased critical path delay, we examine the registers that contain useful intermediate results along the entire process of a single modular exponentiation task. We measure the amount of memory needed to store these intermediate results against execution time cycle Fig. 4.

At the completion of a modular multiplication or a square computation, only the value of Sc and Ss (1025-bit register arrays) are a must-save among all the large register arrays. These transition points, which we informally call SP (*sweetspots*), can be intuitively pinned from the FSM inside the device controller. If we can make sure all switching operations happen at these sweet spots, we can significantly reduce the RAM size required.

To achieve this goal, the device controller is slightly modified to ensure switching always happens at these spots. Upon each major state transition, the contents of Sc and Ss will be forwarded to two designated register arrays Sc_SW and Ss_SW. Note that the contents of these two registers will be refreshed every time an SP is identified and will be flushed during switching operation Fig. 5.

We also want to make sure that the OS gets control of the preemption delay so that it can make scheduling decisions easily when it needs to context switch among a number of concurrent applications. Upon receiving the switching command, the device will compare the time bound to its backward counter and make a decision about whether to reach the next SP or to simply fall back to the last stored one. If the time bound is equal to or smaller than the value of the counter, the current multiplication computation will be abandoned and contents

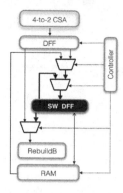

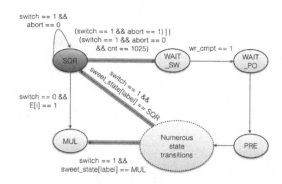

Fig. 5. Design of optimized context switch enforcement in detail. SW_DFF represents register arrays including Sc_SW and Ss_SW storing intermediate results at previous SP

Fig. 6. State diagram of an example transition case in optimized design. The abort signal calculated from time bound directs next_state when *switch* == 1. The current task is allowed to finish current square operation when *abort* == 0, sweet_state will be updated to its next square (SQR) or multiplication (MUL) operation judged by $E[i]$ for future state retrieval.

of Sc_SW and Ss_SW will be stored to RAM. An extra state, $SWEET$, is added to allow data transfers between registers and RAMs during task switching. The state that leads to $SWEET$ will be recorded. The relaxed timing bound can be very convenient for scheduling purposes, considering it is difficult for OS to decide the exact best timing to switch in a device. Granted with local scheduling power, the device can wisely help a task fully utilize its time slots. We show an example state transition scenario in Fig. 6 for illustration.

The design removes multiplexer arrays from the critical paths, significantly lowering area cost. Meanwhile responsiveness to interrupts or context switch commands is still guaranteed. Note that these modifications can be generally applied to public-key crypto accelerators. By simplifying the device interfaces, the VMM's scheduling becomes easier and more flexible. Tasks with higher priorities can always be ensured a quick access to hardware acceleration. The hardware accelerator manages to secure itself in a blackbox, without exposing hardware information unnecessarily.

5 Experimental Evaluation

Our evaluations are based on RTL prototypes of accelerators with standard AHB I/O interfaces written in Verilog under the ModelSim [14] environment. We test through the encryption process and use a Verilog testbench with a public exponent 65537 and modulus generated from OpenSSL [16] for encryption. We synthesize all of the RTL designs using the Synopsys Design Compiler [4] with a 45 nm library and collect critical path delays and executing clock frequencies.

The area and peak power models for our embedded memories are based on CACTI 5.3 [1] and for logic and registers based on the results from Design Compiler.

5.1 Relative Performance

One important measure of performance is the total virtualized device through-put as measured by the numbers of encryptions per second. We compare the virtualized throughput rate from each of the designs to the upper bound of per-formance where each VM is given a completely independent copy of the device (i.e. no interference at all). We simulate three scenarios representing light (con-currently running two VMs while requests from each VM fills 10 % of its time-line), medium (two VMs with 20 % requests) and near-saturating workloads (four VMs with 20 % requests) respectively. The only contention for the crypto accel-erator is from multiple VMs attempting to access the engine at the same time. Figure 7a–c depict the relative performance of virtualized devices under these loads respectively.

The y-axis of each of these plots is the relative performance of the different schemes (as compared to our ideal case). The x-axis is the time slice granular-ities under which the VMs are driving our accelerators. To simulate the fact that one does not switch between VMs instantaneously, a running task will not attempt to switch in a period smaller than a defined time slice. In real-time, latency sensitive, or reactive systems a design may be called upon to switch very quickly. To quantify the suitability of each of the previously described acceler-ator virtualization under various different switching speeds, we inject requests with the size of one task (for us, the crypto operation) but constrain the mini-mum window under which those switches might occur. The courser the minimum time between switches, the less we would expect to lose in wasted cycles as com-putation is abandoned on a switch, but more applications will have to wait to get their computation onto the accelerator. On each of the graphs there are 3 different bars labeled "Tra" for "Traditional" which drops unfinished tasks on a switch. "Base" saves all of the hardware state as described in Sect. 4.1. Finally, "Opti" adds the hardware necessary to allow the accelerator to delay the switching under a fixed bound as described in Sect. 4.2.

As can be seen in these graphs, when the request workload is comparatively low, the performance disparities among the three approaches are not as sig-nificant as those when task workload is heavier. However, the performance of the optimized design is consistently the highest throughout all the switching frequencies simulated. The base design has a slight advantage over traditional design when the time slice is smaller than the time for one encryption operation. The advantage more fully manifests when the amount of requests increases. The performance of all three approaches in all the scenarios reaches a peak around and slightly above 25 μs time slice. However, when we compare 25 μs to 100 μs granularities of the three figures, we can clearly see that the peak period tends to shrink as the workload increases. When reaching a comparatively coarse grain

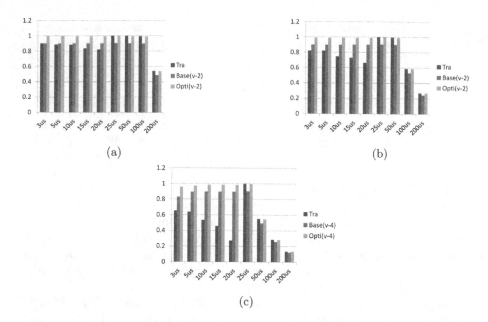

(a)   (b)

(c)

Fig. 7. Relative performance under light (a), medium (b) and near-saturating (c) workload scenarios. V-2 and v-4 denotes the default maximum number of VMs allowed to concurrently occupy the device.

scenario around $200\,\mu s$ the performance of all of the virtual devices suffer significantly. In these situations the bounds on switching time is large enough to cause a significant amount of idle time in the hardware. The optimized design outperforms the baseline consistently because the more restricted save points limit the hardware needed and the longer paths they cause.

One interesting observation is the non-monotonic performance of the traditional design. The throughput rate drops as the switching frequency rises until it reaches around $1/25\,\mu s$. The reason behind this pattern is that when a task is switched off and dropped, the device is more likely to waste more computation cycles when the device is only allowed to be switched at a granularity slightly smaller than time of one operation. Provided that the v-4 optimized design shows at most a 3.6X performance improvement compared to the traditional design, in 20 % workload scenario and reliably high efficiency throughout fine-grain granularities, the optimized design appears to be a clear choice in systems requiring very fine-grain switching when we consider performance alone.

5.2   Area Cost and Power Consumption

To model the area overhead and power consumption of the three virtual accelerators, we synthesized our RTL design in the TSMC 45 nm technology. Results show that the original accelerator occupies $0.11\,mm^2$ with a peak power consumption of 54.7 mW at 1.6 GHz. Due to the lack of publicly available SRAM

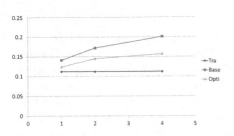
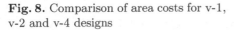
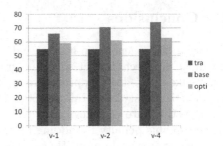

Fig. 8. Comparison of area costs for v-1, v-2 and v-4 designs

Fig. 9. Comparison of peak power consumption for v-1, v-2 and v-4 designs

compilers in this technology, we use CACTI 5.3 [1] to estimate the area and power of RAMs.

The area cost is shown in Fig. 8. The y-axis of the area plot is the absolute area costs measured in mm^2 unit of the different schemes. The x-axis is the number bounds of VMs that are allowed to be running concurrently on the accelerator (e.g. 2 corresponds to v-2 design). As we can see in the graph, the additional area overhead of the baseline design compared to the traditional design can increase area by up to 29 % for v-2 and up to 36 % for v-4. This extra price paid is primarily due to the additional arrays of multiplexers needed to switch between states and the additional RAMs needed to store the contents of all registers. Note that the optimized design scales better than the baseline. The area overhead is merely 12 % and 15 % for v-2 and v-4 respectively.

Similar to the area costs trends, plots of the peak power consumption present an increasing pattern somewhat proportional to area costs. As we can see from Fig. 9, where the y-axis denotes the absolute peak power consumption measured in mW unit of the different devices, the optimized design scales better from v-1 to v-4 than the baseline design as the default bounds of running VMs increase. The traditional design stands out due to its more uniform power consumption.

An important conclusion is that the baseline design performs slightly worse than both the traditional and the optimized design regarding power consumption, whereas the traditional one suffers significantly reduced throughput/watt rate for near saturating workloads when the time slice is small. While baseline and optimized design already provide with most responsiveness, it is as well likely that energy consumption can be compensated from simplified software level synchronization. Moreover, the internal memory read/write structure guarantees a quick and safe access to intermediate data without dealing with I/O hazards.

Due to its performance and power-friendly benefits, the optimized design improves the throughput/watt rate by at most 3.1X over traditional design when above switching frequency of 45 KHz magnitude and remains competitive to traditional design throughout all sharing granularity range under examination.

6 Conclusions

Growing heterogeneity in hardware devices continues to put easy and safe management in direct conflict with fine-grain scheduling and virtualization. Rather than take a top-down approach requiring that all accelerators be implemented in a particular style, we take a bottom up approach, looking at what it takes to manage the state of a device. In particular we found that there is a small but non-negligible penalty for adding in explicit access to the accelerator state both in terms of area and power. However, we also observe that there is an interesting and previously unexplored trade-off between the scheduling power one imbues the accelerator with and the efficiency with which the schedule can be managed to minimize the waste of timing slots.

With that said, under these limitations we presented comparisons of three different accelerator virtualization schemes working to manage a critical device - an RSA accelerator. When a high degree of sharing and switching is required, the traditional task-dropping scheme can suffer significant performance degradation. If such conditions are expected, a hardware preemption scheme can be adopted, and with a bit of analysis, is able to alleviate the burden of resource scheduling and context management, and to prevent sensitive intermediate data exposure. Results show that our proposed approach manages to dramatically diminish the performance degradation of the traditional scheme and to compensate a naive TSAS in a low-overhead manner both in area and power.

References

1. 5.3, C.: http://quid.hpl.hp.com:9081/cacti
2. Chen, J.H., Wu, H.S., Shieh, M.D., Lin, W.C.: A new montgomery modular multiplication algorithm and its vlsi design for rsa cryptosystem. In: IEEE International Symposium on Circuits and Systems, ISCAS 2007, pp. 3780–3783. IEEE (2007)
3. Clark, N., Hormati, A., Mahlke, S.: Veal: Virtualized execution accelerator for loops. In: 35th International Symposium on Computer Architecture, ISCA 2008, pp. 389–400. IEEE (2008)
4. Compiler, D.: https://www.synopsys.com/tools/implementation/rtlsynthesis
5. Cong, J., Ghodrat, M.A., Gill, M., Grigorian, B., Huang, H., Reinman, G.: Composable accelerator-rich microprocessor enhanced for adaptivity and longevity. In: 2013 IEEE International Symposium on Low Power Electronics and Design (ISLPED), pp. 305–310. IEEE (2013)
6. Cong, J., Ghodrat, M.A., Gill, M., Grigorian, B., Reinman, G.: Charm: a composable heterogeneous accelerator-rich microprocessor. In: Proceedings of the 2012 ACM/IEEE international symposium on Low power electronics and design, pp. 379–384. ACM (2012)
7. Govindaraju, V., Ho, C.H., Sankaralingam, K.: Dynamically specialized datapaths for energy efficient computing. In: 2011 IEEE 17th International Symposium on High Performance Computer Architecture (HPCA), pp. 503–514. IEEE (2011)
8. Gupta, V., Schwan, K., Tolia, N., Talwar, V., Ranganathan, P.: Pegasus: Coordinated scheduling for virtualized accelerator-based systems. In: 2011 USENIX Annual Technical Conference (USENIX ATC 2011), p. 31 (2011)

9. Hiremane, R.: Intel virtualization technology for directed i/o(intel vt-d). Technology@ Intel Magazine 4(10) (2007)
10. Jovanovic, S., Tanougast, C., Weber, S.: A hardware preemptive multitasking mechanism based on scan-path register structure for fpga-based reconfigurable systems. In: Second NASA/ESA Conference on Adaptive Hardware and Systems, AHS 2007, pp. 358–364. IEEE (2007)
11. Koch, D., Haubelt, C., Teich, J.: Efficient hardware checkpointing: concepts, overhead analysis, and implementation. In: Proceedings of the 2007 ACM/SIGDA 15th international symposium on Field programmable gate arrays, pp. 188–196. ACM (2007)
12. Liu, J., Abali, B.: Virtualization polling engine (vpe): using dedicated cpu cores to accelerate i/o virtualization. In: Proceedings of the 23rd International Conference on Supercomputing, pp. 225–234. ACM (2009)
13. Menychtas, K., Shen, K., Scott, M.L.: Disengaged scheduling for fair, protected access to fast computational accelerators. In: Proceedings of the 19th International Conference on Architectural Support for Programming Languages and Operating Systems, pp. 301–316. ACM (2014)
14. ModelSim: http://www.mentor.com/products/fv/modelsim
15. Montgomery, P.L.: Modular multiplication without trial division. Math. Comput. **44**(170), 519–521 (1985)
16. OpenSSL: https://www.openssl.org
17. Rupnow, K., Fu, W., Compton, K.: Block, drop or roll (back): Alternative preemption methods for rh multi-tasking. In: 17th IEEE Symposium on Field Programmable Custom Computing Machines, FCCM 2009, pp. 63–70. IEEE (2009)
18. Shieh, M.D., Chen, J.H., Wu, H.H., Lin, W.C.: A new modular exponentiation architecture for efficient design of rsa cryptosystem. IEEE Trans. Very Large Scale Integr. (VLSI) Syst. **16**(9), 1151–1161 (2008)
19. Stewin, P., Bystrov, I.: Understanding DMA malware. In: Flegel, U., Markatos, E., Robertson, W. (eds.) DIMVA 2012. LNCS, vol. 7591, pp. 21–41. Springer, Heidelberg (2013)
20. Stillwell, P.M., Chadha, V., Tickoo, O., Zhang, S., Illikkal, R.,Iyer, R., Newell, D.: Hippai: high performance portable accelerator interface for socs. In: 2009 International Conference on High Performance Computing (HiPC), pp.109–118. IEEE (2009)

Cache Architectures and Protocols

Adaptive Cache Structures

Carsten Tradowsky[✉], Enrique Cordero, Christoph Orsinger,
Malte Vesper, and Jürgen Becker

Institute for Information Processing Technologies,
Karlsruhe Institute of Technology, Karlsruhe, Germany
{tradowsky,becker}@kit.edu,
{enrique.cordero,christoph.orsinger,malte.vesper}@student.kit.edu

Abstract. Novel programming paradigms enable the concurrent execution and the dynamic run-time rescheduling of several competing applications on large heterogeneous multi-core systems. However, today the cache memory is still statically allocated at design time. This leads to a distribution of memory resources that is optimized for an average use case. This paper introduces adaptive cache structures to be able to cope with the agility of dynamic run-time systems on future heterogeneous multi-core platforms. To go beyond the state of the art, the cache model is an implemented HDL realization capable of dynamic run-time adaptations of various cache strategies, parameters and settings. Different design trade-offs are weighted against each other and a modular implementation is presented. This hardware representation makes it possible to deeply integrate the adaptive cache into an existing processor microarchitecture. The contribution of this paper is the application-specific run-time adaptation of the adaptive cache architecture that directly represents the available memory resources of the underlying hardware. The evaluation shows very efficient resource utilization while the cache set size is in- or decreased. Also, performance gains in terms of cache's miss rate and application's run-time are shown. The architecture's capabilities of performing in a multi-core use case and the potential for future power savings are also presented in an application scenario.

1 Introduction

Today's performance gains are mainly powered by a strict application of principles. Frequency gains are achieved by miniaturization of technology and making excessive use of parallelism through multi-core architectures. Since the possibilities for improvement are limited, it is time to turn to abstraction and generalization. Every abstraction or generalization comes at a cost in terms of performance or accuracy and hence has to be carefully weighted. It is necessary to take this one step further to unleash another quantum of performance from a multi-core system.

Performance gains by increasing frequency have hit the power-wall and the field has turned towards parallelism [6]. Today's multi-core systems exploit many heterogeneous resources that are allocated dynamically during run-time to different tasks [7]. The number of resources available on a chip can be varied with such adaptive architectures [8]. The benefits of reducing abstraction and giving

© Springer International Publishing Switzerland 2016
F. Hannig et al. (Eds.): ARCS 2016, LNCS 9637, pp. 87–99, 2016.
DOI: 10.1007/978-3-319-30695-7_7

the programmer control over hardware parameters is studied. This control allows the programmer to adapt the hardware to the application's needs. This paper presents this approach for adaptive caches in particular.

The cache design is a trade-off between power and performance, for which there is no general optimal solution [3]. However, there are optimal solutions for specific programs, in terms of power, performance, or performance per Watt [2]. One solution that is suggested by research projects like 'invasive computing' [7] is to relieve the chip designer of this burden and allow the application developer to unleash higher performance. Consequently, the application developer should choose the optimal cache configuration [4]. Further choices could be made either by the compiler or run-time system according to the current system state. This choice will be put beyond the silicon implementation stage to exploit performance gains that are higher than the cost arising from added complexity. While this strips an abstraction layer, which makes the cache truly transparent, it is a necessary step in uncovering additional performance. In parallel computing, caches are seen as something, for which cache oblivious algorithms could be written [5].

The paper is structured as follows: Sect. 2 then details the design of the adaptive cache structures. Afterwards, the adaptation possibilities are presented in Sect. 3. To prove our concept, we provide an evaluation of our adaptive cache structures in Sect. 4 Concluding, we summarize our contribution and provide an outlook for future work.

2   Designing Adaptive Cache Structures

Before explaining the actual concept, a summary of the requirements will be presented to justify and explain the following concept. The ultimate goal of this design is to target a silicon implementation as an Application-Specific Integrated Circuit (*ASIC*). Currently for prototyping and development purposes, the design has been implemented using the *Leon3* on Xilinx Virtex-5 Field Programmable Gate Arrays (*FPGA*). To allow future *ASIC* implementation, the proposed design run without any *FPGA*-specific techniques like run-time partial reconfiguration. Instead, the concept is based on run-time resource reallocation.

2.1   Basic Cache Model

Since caches are smaller than the memory cached by them, a mapping is required. Therefore, the cache is split in so called *lines*. A line is the smallest consecutive part that can be mapped. In the simplest case, referred to as *direct mapped* cache, the main memory is split into equal size regions and each region is mapped to one line. A group of lines is called a set. To loosen the restriction of direct mapped caches, *associativity* has been introduced. In associative caches multiple cache lines are mapped to the same set-bits. For this purpose a power of two number of lines are grouped to a *set*. The number of lines in a set is called *set size* s. The memory chunks are now mapped to the sets. Therefore, there are s possible lines, in which the data can be cached. By increasing the associativity and keeping the cache size the same, the number of sets $\#s$ is decreased.

For the concept, which we present in this paper, it is favorable to reinterpret the memory mapping. Figure 1 shows the memory mapping for a two-way cache. In Fig. 1a the two-way cache is shown as one large memory. This interpretation is favorable to explain the addressing of the cache memory. Figure 1b interprets a two-way cache as two parallel caches. This reinterpretation of the cache is favorable for our concept as it enables us to directly represent the underlying hardware memory resources.

Furthermore, when using the second interpretation, it is important that any value can only be cached in one of the two caches (ways), but for retrieval the value is looked up in both caches.

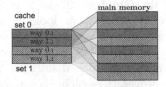

(a) Set partitioning

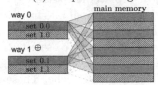

(b) Way partitioning

Fig. 1. Mapping for two-way cache - Memory mappings for a two-way associative cache. Figure a groups the cache by sets, while Fig. b groups the cache by way.

2.2 Modularization

To meet the requirements, the cache is divided into modules as shown in Fig. 2. The modules are: 1. the cache controller, 2. the cache memory, 3. the memory controller, 4. the transceiver, and 5. the adaptation controller.

Figure 2 also shows the minimal necessary connections between the different modules needed in order to exploit the parallelization capabilities of the cache subsystem to the fullest. Half-duplex connections support either read or write transfers, while full duplex connections support both at the same time. While the *CPU*-connection type is dictated by the *CPU*, and the connection between transceiver and memory controller is implicitly given by the bus capabilities, all internal connections can be adapted as needed. In the following sections the individual modules are presented.

2.3 Cache Controller

The cache controller is the heart of the system. In addition to the standard states, it has been expanded to include an adaptation state to change the configurations. All basic states are extended to account for the adaptation as well. From the *idle* state there are five states branching out: 1. read, 2. write, 3. flush, 4. discard, and 5. adapt. The added adaptation sequence will later be explained in more detail.

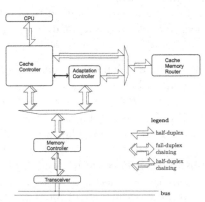

Fig. 2. Overview of the modules - Modules composing the cache system and their connections.

2.4 Cache Memory

The cache memory consists of two main parts: the tile cluster and the individual tiles.

Tile Cluster. The tile concept comes from looking at
caches with associativity n as
n parallel caches. Any memory
location is cached only once,
however, the cache is chosen
by a replacement strategy. If
we use additional bits from the
address instead of a replacement strategy to select the
cache, it behaves like a large
direct mapped cache. These n
caches are called *tiles*.

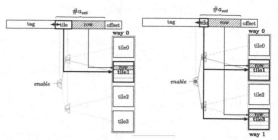

(a) direct mapped config-
uration

(b) two-way configura-
tion

Fig. 3. Tile network - The black arrows show
the schematic address-mapping, the grayed
out multiplier/multiplexer network shows the
implementation.

If the associativity is reduced, there is no need to query
all tiles, therefore a reduction
in the power consumption can be achieved. The connection of multiple tiles form
the actual memory of the cache.

The set address a_{set} is split into two parts like shown in Fig. 3. A static part,
the *row address* a_{row} that identifies the row inside a tile, and a dynamic part,
the *tile address* a_{tile}, that identifies the tile in the way. The tree of multiplexers
are controlled by the a_{tile} bits of the address as shown in Fig. 3. The multiplexer
on the highest level of the binary tree is controlled by the most significant bit
of a_{tile}. If the associativity is increased, meaning several stages of the tree act
as multipliers rather than multiplexers, the first level acting as multiplexer is
controlled by the most significant bit of a_{tile}. Since increasing the associativity
by n reduces the $\#a_{tile}$ ($\#a_{set}$) by n the mapping of the stages to the address
bits remains the same, regardless of the currently set associativity. This becomes
clear when comparing Fig. 3a with Fig. 3b. Note that all tiles are connected by
an internal bus relaying the tag and row, however, only those that are *enabled*
check for hits and output data on the data bus.

Tile. Three independent memory blocks are used to store the data, the tag and
the control bits.

The tag RAM and data RAM hold tag and data respectively. The control
bit RAM holds valid and dirty bits plus any per-line information needed by the
replacement strategy. The data is split to avoid unnecessary read-/write-accesses.

The separation in these three RAM blocks has a potential on reducing power
consumption because it avoids unnecessary read operations when only part of
a memory line needs to be updated. When updating a part of the line only
the data and the control bits (which are located in separate RAMs) need to be
updated and while the tag stays unchanged. This reduces the amount of write
operations because the tag will not be unnecessarily rewritten.

If power saving is a larger issue than performance, the access to the different
RAM cells can be serialized. For example instead of reading the tag, control

bits and data at the same time and having logic decide whether the data is put onto the data bus of the tile cluster one could first match the tag and compare the valid bit. The data RAM will only be accessed if it actually contains the value to be fetched. This costs an additional cycle, however there will only be one instead of s read operations executed on the data RAM.

3   Adaptation

The system supports different adaptation possibilities. The replacement strategy can be selected on the fly and cache memory parameters can be changed during run-time.

3.1   Configuration Register

All configuration information is stored in the *configuration register* located in the cache controller. A write to this register triggers an adaptation. Reading the register yields the current configuration.

The cache configuration register composition is described in the following paragraph but the actual sizes of the different components are omitted since they depend on the parametrization of the cache. To ease software development one should define fixed sizes independent of the parametrization.

The configuration register and its contents are shown in Fig. 4. Only powers of two values are accepted as line lengths, because otherwise irregularities are introduced in the memory mapping.

$ld_2(associativity)$	$ld_2(line\ length)$	blocks	flags	replacement strategy

Fig. 4. Adaptive cache configuration register

3.2   Cache Memory

There are three parameters that can be used to adapt the cache memory: 1. associativity s, 2. size $\#l^a$, and 3. line length L_W.

Using these parameters, all other configuration values for the cache can be computed. Adaptation of cache memory is broken down into base cases. Every base case has two subcases, increasing or decreasing one of the aforementioned cache memory parameters. Figure 5 gives an overview of the adaptation paths and the implied costs. The following subsections detail the different adaptive cache configurations and explain the cost of adaptively changing the cache configuration. It should be emphasized that all these possibilities do not require a full cache flush.

Associativity. Associativity is quantized by the tile-concept. While the direct mapped configuration offers only one valid location, the two-way associative configuration has two. This implies that by changing the associativity, values might end up in invalid locations.

Reducing associativity requires sorting. An associativity of 2^n has 2^n lines that are allowed to store values from a set address. If the associativity is decreased from 2^n to 2^m then 2^{n-m} cells might hold values which they are not allowed to hold. Due to the mapping chosen, the 2^m new lines are a subset of the 2^n lines. Therefore, those lines can remain untouched. The valid locations of any address a for a lower associativity form a true subset of those for a higher associativity. Thus, decreasing the associativity can yield wrongly placed data regarding the new associativity.

Increasing associativity does not require sorting. As shown under the decrease of associativity, the valid locations for higher associativities form a superset for those of lower associativities. Thus, all data remains valid and no scrubbing is required.

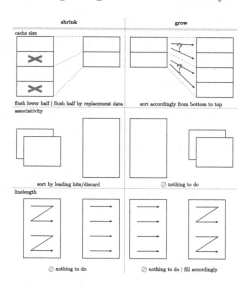

Cache Size. Like associativity, we quantize cache size based on the size of a tile. The reason behind this is that tiles can be powered off to conserve energy or be reused as a whole. To make changes in cache size perpendicular to changes in associativity we assume that they are achieved by reducing/increasing the number of lines in a direct mapped cache. This concept can be applied to an s-way associative cache by looking at it as s parallel caches as explained in Sub-

Fig. 5. Overview of the basic adaptation cases. Combining these spans the entire configuration space.

sect. 2.1. There are two possibilities to reduce the cache size based on this model: either all n-caches are reduced in size by an equal amount or m-ways are shut down. Increasing the cache size works by adding ways or increasing the set number. To increase the granularity a number of ways unequal to a power of two are allowed [1]. To achieve this the ways with the highest order identifier are shut down first. The corresponding hit, valid, and dirty signals are tied to 0.

Reducing ways requires different procedures depending on the cache configuration and on the further utilization of the reduced part. When operating in write-through mode, no further action is needed because of redundant data copies on lower cache hierarchy levels. For other operation modes, the tiles need to be flushed only if the stored values in the tile end will end up in invalid locations, or if they will be powered off.

Increasing/Reducing sets can be modelled as an increase or reduction of ways with a subsequent change in associativity. The same conditions explained in the previous sections apply for this cases.

Line Length. The line length variation works by constructing so called *virtual lines*. This means that for longer lines (multiples of the *base line length*) the line length can be simulated by the cache controller. By loading more than one line on every cache miss, the virtual line size can be increased. In order to avoid parts of the virtual line being spread over multiple sets, the way for each virtual line is determined once and then used as default for the next parts. This additional checking causes a slight overhead that can be hidden, if the tiles have a sufficient number of ports to enable checking for presence/free ways while other ways are written.

4   Evaluation of Adaptive Cache Structures

Different adaptive cache features have been presented that allow the variation of cache parameters depending on the application's current needs during run-time. This has been done with the goal of exploiting the faster run-time potential providing an optimized working point in each application by providing a more efficient individual cache setting at a given time.

As an evaluation of the proposed architecture, three main aspects will be considered. First, we will evaluate the amount of occupied hardware resources used by the adaptive cache design as well as the distribution of resources between all tiles and the tile controller based on three specific scenarios. Second, we will evaluate the impact of the adaptive cache structure on the application's and cache's performance. Third, the benefit of the adaptive cache structure in a multi-core case will be evaluated in terms of application performance.

4.1   Hardware Resources Evaluation

For utilization analysis we consider three different hardware configurations where the cache always contains 8 tiles. In each scenario the tile size is doubled with respect to the previous one, so that each design has 256, 512 and 1024 bytes per tile respectively.

Figure 6 shows the amount of reconfigurable hardware slices used for each case. It can be noted that the amount of resources used by the tile controller in each case is considerably lower (about 20 %) than the one of the tiles. In fact, considering that each scenario doubles the size of the tiles,

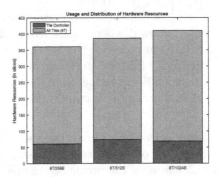

Fig. 6. Usage and distribution of hardware resources for tile controller and all tiles in three different scenarios: 256, 512 and 1024 bytes per tile with 8 tiles each.

the size of the tile controller can be considered to be almost constant with a small variation of ±10 slices. When looking at the total amount of tiles for each scenario we see increases of 4 % between the first and second scenario, and 9 % between the second and third scenario respectively.

These results show that the resources used on the FPGA for control and logic computations of the adaptive structure are comparably low considering the gain provided by each jump to the next scenario. The slices shown in Fig. 6 include all the resources used to control the cache. The actual cache memory is implemented using BRAMs. Even though the memory is being doubled in each scenario the BRAM utilization is constant for all three scenarios at 3 BRAMs per tile, thus 24 BRAMs in total. Despite the fact that the Virtex-5 XUPV5 contains BRAMs with sizes of 18 kB and 36 kB, each tile is using three separate blocks and the total amount is constant also for larger caches. This behavior can be explained by the high degree of parallel operations that need to be performed in an adaptive cache architecture. Since the BRAM blocks available are dual-port memory blocks, mapping an entire cache or an entire tile into the same BRAM would cause only an availability of two parallel access points into the memory. In the cache, however, more access points are needed in order to check in parallel all the tags depending on the associativity of the cache. This leads to an implementation of the cache in multiple blocks to allow this behavior.

4.2 Performance Evaluation

An adaptive cache reallocation architecture has the goal to provide performance gains for applications. In order to evaluate this gains we use the same three hardware scenarios explained before (256, 512 and 1024 bytes per tile).

These three scenarios will be analyzed in two different evaluations with focus on the cache performance improvements (cache miss rate) and the application's performance (run-time).

The software application running on each scenario is a Coremark benchmark. According to the benchmark's documentation a minimum of 10 s of run-time is necessary in order for the benchmark to produce meaningful results. We use a Coremark with 2000 iterations which in this architecture leads to a run-time of more than 35 s. The following tests are run on the real hardware implementation of the adaptive cache reallocation architecture on the Xilinx XUPV5.

Cache's Performance. For the analysis of the cache miss rate in this architecture, we perform two main tests: For the first test the software application is run 5 times on the previously defined hardware scenarios. Each time the application runs, a different cache configuration will be applied by the software. The configuration parameter to be changed is the amount of exclusive tiles available as cache memory for the processor. By changing the amount of tiles that the cache can use not only the cache's size will change depending on the size of each tile, but also the cache associativity will change. For each scenario we vary the amount of exclusive tiles from 4 to 8 in steps of 1 and we measure cache's miss rate during the application's run-time as a performance metric.

Figure 7 upper graph shows the behavior of the cache misses over the total cache size. We can notice a non-linear behavior and a performance gain that can be achieved when running the benchmark with a different cache configurations. For instance, a cache size of 3.5 kB built using 7 tiles of 512 bytes per tile would lead in this case to the lowest miss rate, hence the best cache performance.

In this test we selected always the same amount of tiles for each hardware scenario, which lead to different total cache sizes for each case. This is the case because each scenario has tiles of different sizes.

For the second test the same three hardware scenarios previously presented are being used. However, this time the total cache size will be varied from 2 to 6 kB in steps of 1 kB by adjusting the amount of tiles respectively for each hardware scenario. This has the advantage that the effect of the tile size and amount of tiles can be directly seen for all scenarios for each cache size. The hardware designs have been expanded to contain more available tiles as needed, however the amount of tiles to be used in each case is still configured on run-time by the software and varies depending on the hardware scenario. For example, to build a 5 kB cache in all three scenarios we would need 20 tiles of 256 bytes, 10 tiles of 512 bytes but only 5 tiles of 1024 bytes.

Figure 7 lower graph shows the different miss rates measured for each cache configuration on each hardware scenario. We see the miss rates staying in the range of 5 % to 8 % with variations in the miss rate in a range of about 2 %. The data shows that for this particular application a minimum miss rate can be achieved at a total cache size of $3.5\,kB$ with 7 tiles of 512 bytes per tile. The same analysis for other applications would provide different results, thus showing the importance of an adaptive cache structure that can match the individual application needs and that can be controlled by the software.

This analysis is intended as an example to show the impact that

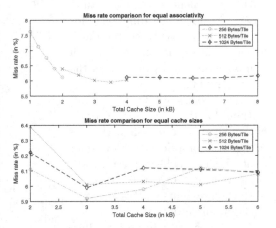

Fig. 7. Miss rate for the Coremark benchmark with 2000 iterations on three scenarios of the adaptive cache architecture with same associativity (upper graph) and with same cache size (lower graph).

the different adaptive parameters in the dynamic cache reallocation architecture can have on each individual application. Giving the developer the chance to adapt the underlying hardware characteristics to the current application, can allow the software to profit from a more suited architecture for a better performance.

Application's Performance. This second evaluation will investigate the effect of the adaptive architecture on the application's run-time of the same two tests previously described in the first evaluation. The software running in each of these tests is also the Coremark benchmark with 2000 iterations. First we consider the first test where in all three scenarios the amount of tiles is varied between 4 and 8 by the software.

Figure 8 upper graph shows the run-time in seconds over the total cache size for the three scenarios. The graph shows a strong improvement of the application run-time on small cache sizes and a much smaller variation for larger cache sizes. The graph also suggests that the performance can vary significantly with a constant cache size but with a different tile distribution or different bytes per tile. This can be seen more clearly at 2 kB cache size, where fewer tiles with 512 bytes per tile lead to a longer execution time than more tiles with 256 bytes per tile each.

Further, we consider the second test where the total cache size is varied equally among the three scenarios by adjusting the amount of tiles respectively.

Figure 8 lower graph shows the results for the amount of computation cycles used for each scenario with equal cache sizes. The results show a noticeable difference for small sized caches however much lower variation in the amount of computation cycles needed as the cache gets bigger.

The results of these two evaluations for the cache's and application's performance show that by giving the application developer control of the cache configuration a performance gain can be achieved with the flexibility of this adaptive cache architecture.

It is not only important how much improvement the architecture can bring to the application, but also the potential of this

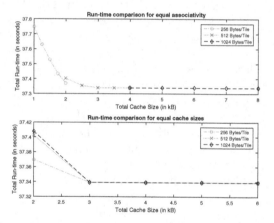

Fig. 8. Run-time for the Coremark benchmark with 2000 iterations on three scenarios of the adaptive cache architecture with same associativity (upper graph) and same cache size (lower graph).

architecture in a multi-core environment to provide benefits across multiple CPUs constantly increasing or reducing their momentary cache needs. This topic is more important than ever as every L1 cache miss has to go through a local bus to a 2nd level cache. If there is a miss in the 2nd level cache, which is most likely, the comparably slow DDR memory has to be accessed via the NoC, which costs a lot of time in shared memory multi-core scenarios. This aspects are considered in the following section.

4.3 Potential of the Adaptive Cache Architecture in a Multi-core Scenario

Reconfiguring the architecture to reallocate cache tiles with different parameters during run-time adds a reallocation overhead to the scenario. In order to evaluate the overhead and analyze the potential gain we simulate a dual-core system with each core featuring the adaptive cache architecture. The system parameters are provided in Table 1. We choose two applications, which have a different cache behaviour. The Coremark benchmark profits from more cache memory, while the MiBench

Table 1. Test system configuration parameters.

Parameter	Value
Amount CPUs	2
Clock frequency	80 MHz
I-Cache size	8 kB
I-Cache associativity	1
D-Cache amount tiles	8
D-Cache tile size	256 B, 512 B
D-Cache line length	32 Bit

(ADPCM) streaming Benchmark is not impacted by less cache memory.

The test scenario consists of two stages as shown in Fig. 9. In the first stage the Coremark benchmark runs in both CPUs simultaneously with the same cache resources. In the second stage the MiBench (ADPCM) benchmark is run in CPU1, while the Coremark is run again in CPU2 with additionally reallocated cache resources from CPU1. In order to avoid false results because of cache influences, the Coremark Benchmark exists in two separate copies in the memory, such that the CPU2 uses two different copies for both stages of the test.

We compare a static configuration design with the adaptive system containing an adaption sequence between both benchmarks. Test results have shown that for the first stage of the test (Coremark benchmark running on both CPUs) with 8 tiles, a distribution of 4:4 between both cores offers the best results. Similarly, for the second stage of the test (MiBench (ADPCM) running in CPU1 and Coremark running in CPU2) a distribution of 2:6

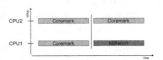

Fig. 9. Time flow of benchmarks in dual-core application scenario

provides the best results. The adaptive design will reallocate the resources between both test stages to compare the total run-time with a static design. The goal is to evaluate if the costs for the adaption sequence can achieve a shorter run-time because of a better distribution of resources. The static configuration will run with constant four tiles per CPU.

Table 2 shows an overview of the results for the second stage of the test. The first row presents the static case with an equal tile distribution across both CPUs and no adaption sequence. The second row shows the results for the reallocated resources with the corre-

Table 2. Run-time of the applications of second test stage benchmarks.

	Benchmark	Tiles	Adaption time	Run-time
CPU 1	MiBench	4	0 ns	13,31 ms
CPU 2	Coremark	4	0 ns	11,60 ms
CPU 1	MiBench	2	75 ns	13,38 ms
CPU 2	Coremark	6	880 ns	11,27 ms

sponding times for the adaption sequence. We notice a slight increase in the run-time for CPU1 and a larger decrease in the run-time for CPU2 for the adaptive design.

An overview of the absolute differences between the static and adaptive cases can be seen in Table 3. As expected the MiBench runs slower on CPU1 however the Coremark is accelerated. It is

Table 3. Relative run-time and performance gain of the dynamic cache reallocation.

	Benchmark	relative Run-time	Performance gain
CPU 1	MiBench	$+67\,\mu s$	$-0.5\,\%$
CPU 2	Coremark	$-329\,\mu s$	$+2.8\,\%$

important to note that the 853 ns of reallocation time is already included in the total run-time. Overall, we see a 2.8 % improvement after the resources reallocation.

5   Conclusion and Future Work

We provide a dynamic cache architecture, that for the first time has been described in a hardware description language and implemented on a Virtex-5 XUPV5. Our cache architecture exploits fine grain run-time adaption, which enables performance gains while keeping the hardware implementation overhead to a minimum. The presented concept provides the capability to adapt to different cache parameters on run-time and to redistribute vacant memory to other parallel processors. As the evaluation has shown, the architecture provides multiple advantages and performance gains with an expandable potential for multi-core architectures. It was shown that the hardware overhead introduced in the resource utilization of the adaptive architecture is small and slowly increasing while doubling the cache size. The evaluation also shows performance gains in both, the cache's miss rate and the application's run-time. Miss rate improvements and run-time reductions can be achieved by selecting an appropriate cache configuration through the software accessible cache configuration register. At last, the potential of the adaptive architecture in a multi-core scenario was shown by simulating a dual-core use case with adaptive cache architectures and running two different benchmarks in two CPUs. The results showed a 2.8 % improvement compared to the static case, as well as the feasibility of the adaptive architecture to reallocate tiles in a multi-core environment. Overall, this evaluation shows the importance of allowing the application developer to control hardware parameters of the underlying architecture to boost the applications performance.

For future work, the adaptive architecture will be expanded to a larger multi-core scenario running on the FPGA hardware, and tested using well established benchmarks for performance evaluations. Further, we will evaluate the power consumption as an important criterion for design decisions. Such an analysis would furthermore help to decide on which granularity cache size and associativity adjustments are sensible.

Acknowledgment. This research work is supported by the German Research Foundation (DFG) within the Transregio SFB *Invasive Computing* (DFG SFB/TRR89).

References

1. Albonesi, D.: Selective cache ways: on-demand cache resource allocation. In: MICRO-32, Proceedings of the 32nd Annual ACM/IEEE International Symposium on Microarchitecture, pp. 248–259 (1999)
2. Gordon-Ross, A., Lau, J., Calder, B.: Phase-based cache reconfiguration for a highly-configurable two-level cache hierarchy. In: Proceedings of the 18th ACM Great Lakes Symposium on VLSI - GLSVLSI 2008, pp. 379–382 (2008)
3. Malik, A., Moyer, B., Cermak, D.: A low power unified cache architecture providing power and performance flexibility (poster session). In: Proceedings of the International Symposium on Low Power Electronics and Design - ISLPED 2000, pp. 241–243 (2000)
4. Nowak, F., Buchty, R., Karl, W.: A run-time reconfigurable cache architecture. Adv. Parallel Comput. **15**, 757–766 (2008)
5. Prokop, H.: Cache-oblivious algorithms. Master's thesis, Massachusetts Institute of Technology (1999)
6. Sutter, H.: The free lunch is over: a fundamental turn toward concurrency in software. Dr. Dobb's J. **30**, 202–210 (2005)
7. Teich, J., Henkel, J., Herkersdorf, A., Schmitt-Landsiedel, D., Schröder-Preikschat, W., Snelting, G.: Invasive computing: an overview. In: Hübner, M., Becker, J. (eds.) Multiprocessor System-on-Chip, pp. 241–268. Springer, New York (2011)
8. Tradowsky, C., Thoma, F., Hubner, M., Becker, J.: Lisparc: using an architecture description language approach for modelling an adaptive processor microarchitecture. In: 7th IEEE International Symposium on Industrial Embedded Systems (SIES), pp. 279–282 (2012)

Optimization of a Linked Cache Coherence Protocol for Scalable Manycore Coherence

Ricardo Fernández-Pascual$^{(\boxtimes)}$, Alberto Ros, and Manuel E. Acacio

Dpto. de Ingeniería y Tecnología de Computadores,
Universidad de Murcia, Murcia, Spain
{rfernandez,aros,meacacio}@ditec.um.es

Abstract. Despite having been quite popular during the 1990 s because of their important advantages, linked cache coherence protocols have gone completely unnoticed in the multicore wave. In this work we bring them in the spotlight, demonstrating that they are a good alternative to other solutions being proposed nowadays. In particular, we consider in this work the case for a simply-linked list-based cache coherence protocol and propose two techniques, namely Concurrent Replacements (CR) and Opportunistic Replacements (OR), aimed at palliating the negative effects of replacements of clean data. Through detailed simulations of several SPLASH-2 and PARSEC applications, we demonstrate that, armed with CR and OR, simply-linked list-based protocols are able to offer the performance of a non-scalable bit-vector directory at the same time that scalability to larger core counts is preserved.

Keywords: Manycores · Cache coherence · Exact sharer enconding · Scalability · Singly-linked list · Area overhead · Execution time · Network traffic

1 Introduction

As technology allows the fabrication of chip-multiprocessors with dozens or even hundreds of cores, the organization of the coherence directory responsible for keeping track of the sharers of cached memory blocks becomes a first-class design concern. Ideally, a coherence directory should satisfy three basic requirements [15]: *(i)* small area, energy, and latency overheads that scale well with the number of cores; *(ii)* exact sharer representation to minimize resulting coherence traffic; and *(iii)* avoidance of directory-induced invalidations. The latter can arise with sparse directories due to their limited capacity and associativity, and could be reduced by doing a more efficient use of their entries [5,7,8]. However, ensuring exact sharer representation is usually hard, since it entails increased area

This work has been supported by the Spanish MINECO, as well as European Commission FEDER funds, under grants "TIN2012-38341-C04-03" and "TIN2015-66972-C5-3-R", and by the Fundación Séneca-Agencia de Ciencia y Tecnología de la Región de Murcia under grant "19295/PI/14".

© Springer International Publishing Switzerland 2016
F. Hannig et al. (Eds.): ARCS 2016, LNCS 9637, pp. 100–112, 2016.
DOI: 10.1007/978-3-319-30695-7_8

and energy requirements (if bit vectors are used), directory-induced invalidations (for limited pointers, when a pointer recycling overflow strategy is employed), or extra directory latency and/or non-conventional structures (e.g., SCD [15] requires a non-conventional ZCache architecture).

The design of scalable coherence directories for systems with a large number of cores has been extensively studied for traditional multiprocessors. In that context, the most scalable protocols —those which kept sharing information in a directory distributed among nodes— were classified in two categories [6]: those that store the sharing information about all the cached copies of each block in a single and fixed place, the home node of that block (we call them directories with *centralized* sharing codes), and those in which sharing information is distributed among the caches holding copies of each block and the home node, which only contains a pointer to one of the sharers (we call them directories with *distributed* sharing codes). Surprisingly, all recent proposals have concentrated on the first type of directories, and despite having been popular in the context of shared-memory multiprocessors during the 1990s [10,11,17], directories with distributed sharing codes have gone completely unnoticed in the multicore era.

Directories based on distributed sharing codes have several important advantages over their centralized counterparts. First of all, they ensure scalability since they employ pointers whose size increases logarithmically with the number of cores. Figure 1 shows that the amount of memory required by the simplest directory able to provide exact sharer representation based on a distributed sharing code (that using a simply-linked list, *List*) remains below 2 % as the number of cores is increased to 1024. The memory requirements of the recently proposed SCD [15] and two directories with centralized sharing codes (namely, *BitVector* and *1-Pointer*) are also shown for comparison purposes. *BitVector* does not scale because the number of bits per directory entry increases linearly with the number of cores, but it is able to offer the best performance. In [15], SCD has been shown to approximate the performance of *BitVector* but its area requirements do not scale as well as *List*. Finally, *1-Pointer* incurs an area penalty similar to *List* but it does not guarantee exact sharer representation, which compromises performance.

A second advantage of directories based on distributed sharing codes is that they naturally lead to more efficient use of the precious directory information, dynamically devoting more resources to those memory blocks with more sharers and less to those that do not need them (every cached data has at least one pointer assigned, which is the minimum to have its precise location, and at most as many pointers as sharers). And, finally, a third one is that conversely to other proposals based on the use of multi-hashing [15], directories based on distributed sharing codes do not require non-conventional cache structures. However, some disadvantages have been reported also, such as increased latency of write misses due to a sequential invalidation of sharers, high-latency replacements of shared blocks since the list structure must be preserved, and the necessity of modifying private caches to include pointers.

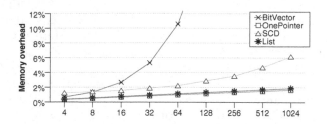

Fig. 1. Memory overhead as the number of cores increases.

In our previous work [9], we brought a singly-linked list-based directory similar to that described in [16] (*List*) to the multicore world. We found out that *List* was specially appealing since it entailed minimal additions to the critical private L1 caches (just one pointer per cache entry) and at the same time it was able to ensure scalability in terms of directory memory overhead (as shown in Fig. 1). However, we noticed important performance degradations (almost 20 % on average) when compared with *BitVector*. Particulary, we discovered that the most important source of inefficiency in *List* was due to the extra messages necessary to handle clean shared data replacements. Now, we propose in this work two novel techniques that minimize the negative impact that replacements of clean data in a simply-linked protocol have on performance: *Opportunistic replacements* (OR) and *Concurrent replacements* (CR). OR tries to mix pending replacements of clean data at the private caches with an on-going replacement (all referred to the same address), thus minimizing the number of replacements that the home node must manage. CR allows the home node to deal with load misses to a particular address whilst a replacement to the same address is progressing.

To the best of our knowledge, this is the first work showing how in manycores a directory with a distributed sharing code (*List*) can reach the performance of the most efficient but unfeasible (non-scalable) directory with a centralized bit-vector sharing code (*BitVector*) at the same time that scalability to larger core counts is guaranteed. The only overhead that we have observed in *List* is some increase in terms of average network traffic but it has no impact on final performance.

2   *List*: A Simply-Linked List Protocol

The *List* protocol analyzed in this work has been developed by modifying the base MESI protocol. Although different, *List* resembles previous proposals based on singly-linked lists like [16]. The complexity of the resulting protocol is very close to that of the base protocol from which it has been derived.

Distributed sharing codes store directory information for each memory block in a distributed way, instead of keeping it centralized in the home node. In *List*, the home node stores the identity of only one of the possibly many sharers of the memory block while the rest of sharers are represented using a linked list constructed through one pointer in each of the L1 cache entries[1]. Storing the sharing information this way implies that, to update it, some messages need to be exchanged between the sharers and the home node which would not be needed in a protocol using a centralized sharing code, but it achieves a much higher scalability in terms of memory overhead which results in lower area requirements and static energy consumption.

Whereas the amount of memory required per directory entry with a centralized bit-vector sharing code grows linearly with the number of processing cores (i.e., one bit per core), it grows logarithmically for distributed sharing codes (Fig. 1). Although distributed sharing codes need some additional information in each L1 entry (pointers), this is not a problem for scalability because the number of entries in the private caches is always much smaller than in the shared cache banks. Figure 1 shows the percentage of memory (in bits) added by each protocol with respect to the total number of bits dedicated to the L1 and L2 caches for different numbers of cores, assuming 4-way L1 caches with 128 sets and 16-way L2 caches with 256 sets per core and 64 byte blocks.

The starting point *List* protocol considered in this work is a slightly improved version of the one evaluated in [9]. The current version has one message less in the critical path of replacements (but still has the same total number of messages).

List stores the sharing information of a block in a distributed manner. The home L2 node keeps a pointer to the first sharer and each sharer keeps a pointer to another sharer, creating a linked list of sharers. The last sharer keeps a null pointer, which is codified as the identity of the sharer itself so that no additional bits are needed (i.e., the last node points to itself).

In *List*, without optimizations, updates to the list of sharers are serialized by the home node, which remains blocked (i.e., other requests for this block are not attended) until the modification of the list has been completed. This avoids races that could corrupt the list.

For requests to non-cached or private blocks, *List* behaves almost identically to a centralized protocol. The home L2 bank, after sending the data and receiving an *Unblock* message from the requester, stores the identity of the new and only sharer in the block's pointer. The differences come with read and write misses and replacements of shared blocks.

For read misses to blocks with at least one sharer, the new sharer is inserted at the beginning of the list (i.e., the new sharer will point to the previous first sharer and the L2 will point to the new sharer). The identity of the previous first sharer is sent to the requester along with the data, which can be sent by the L2 (for the S state) or by the previous first sharer after it receives the forwarded request (for the M or E state). No additional messages are required with respect to a centralized protocol in either case.

For write misses, the invalidation of all sharers is done in parallel to sending the data to the requester. But, while in a centralized protocol the home node can perform the invalidations in parallel by sending them directly to every sharer

---

[1] Without generality loss, we assume private L1 caches in each core and an inclusive, shared L2 cache distributed between them.

(because it has the complete sharing information), in *List* the L2 sends the invalidation only to the first sharer, which forwards it to the next sharer and so on until arriving to the last one, which sends an acknowledgment to the requester. This means that latency may increase specially for long lists of sharers because the invalidations are processed sequentially. On the other hand, while in a centralized protocol every sharer needs to send an acknowledgment to the requester, in *List* only the last sharer sends it, hence the number of messages used to resolve a write miss is the same or less than with a centralized protocol.

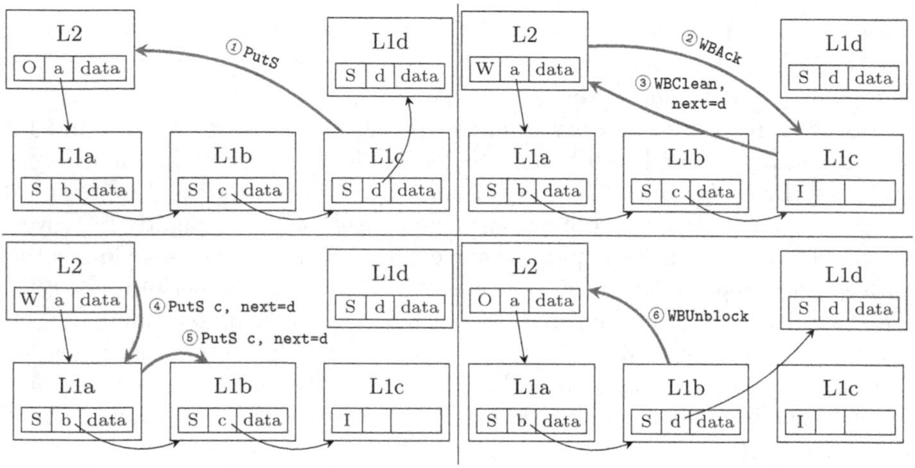

Fig. 2. Example of shared block replacement in *List*

Replacements of blocks shared by only one node are handled exactly the same as in a centralized protocol. However, the most determinant difference for performance is the way that replacements of shared blocks are done. In a centralized protocol, these replacements can happen silently (i.e., the sharer discards the data and does not inform the home node about it) while *List* needs to involve the home node and other sharers in a potentially long process. This is so because the sharing information (i.e., the pointer to the next sharer) is stored alongside the data, and discarding it would leave the list of sharers unconnected. Instead, as shown in Fig. 2, before a shared memory block can be replaced, a replacement request (①) is sent to the L2. When the L2 receives it and it is ready to handle it, it responds with a message authorizing the replacement (②). This message is answered by the replacing node with another one (③) that carries the value of the pointer kept at this L1, which indicates the *next sharer* in the list. After sending it, the L1 cache can discard the pointer from its cache and it will not be contacted again regarding this transaction. Upon receiving the message with the *next sharer*, the L2 needs to update the sharing list (which at this point is momentarily disconnected because the replacing node has discarded its pointer). For this, if the replacing node coincides with the sharer stored at the L2 (i.e., it is the first sharer of the list), then the value of the pointer at the L2 is changed to point to the *next sharer*. Otherwise, the L2 cache forwards the replacement request to the first sharer (④) and the message keeps propagating through the list of sharers until the node that preceded the replacing node in the list is reached (⑤). This is identified because its pointer to the next sharer will match the requester identity. At this point, the preceding node updates its pointer with the information included in the message (the *next sharer*), reconnecting the list of sharers. After updating its next pointer, the node sends an acknowledgment (⑥) to the L2 and the operation completes. Notice that the identity of the *next sharer* cannot be sent along with the first message of the transaction, because if the L2 receives another request for that line from a different node before the replacement request arrives, the information may become obsolete. The L2 will not attend other requests for that line while the replacement is being performed to avoid concurrent modifications to the list of sharers.

The fact that replacements for shared data in the *List* protocol cannot be done silently significantly increases the number of messages on the interconnection network (bandwidth requirements) and, what is more important, the occupancy of the directory controllers at the L2 cache. It is important to note that although write buffers are used at the L1 caches to prevent delaying unnecessarily the cache miss that caused the replacement, the fact that the directory controller "blocks" the memory block being replaced results in longer latencies for subsequent misses (from other nodes) to the replaced address because those misses cannot be attended by the L2 until the replacement has finished.

3   Optimizing Shared Replacements in *List*

The main reason for the execution time and traffic difference between *BitVector* and *List* is due to the replacement of shared blocks [9]. To mitigate this problem, we have designed two optimizations to *List* which can be used in combination or independently of each other: *Opportunistic replacements*, which mainly affect the behavior of L1 controllers, and *concurrent replacements*, which affect only the behavior of the L2 controller.

It is important to understand that shared replacements do not increase the latency of the miss that actually caused the replacement because all protocols considered in this work assume that the L1 caches have writeback buffers[2]. Instead, the replacement affects the latency of subsequent misses to the same or different addresses due to two reasons: the additional traffic, which can be absorbed by the network easily, and, more importantly, the additional time that the L2 controller needs to be blocked while handling the replacement.

---

[2] In the case of clean shared replacements, the writeback buffer only needs to store the sharing information, not the data. Due to its very small size in *List*, this information may alternatively be kept in a miss status holding register (MSHR) or similar structure.

3.1   Opportunistic Replacements (OR)

We noticed that, in some applications, several sharers of the same block frequently will request to replace it almost simultaneously. When this happens in *List*, the L2 has to process all these requests sequentially. Each replacement is a potentially long process because the list of sharers needs to be traversed (half of it, on average), and the L2 has to be blocked during the process, resulting in delaying other misses. *Opportunistic replacements* take advantage of the traversal of the list required for a shared replacement request to perform the replacement of other nodes that have also requested it. This way, fewer traversals are needed.

It works as follows. After an L1 requests a replacement, it keeps waiting until it receives permission from the L2, as previously described. If the L1 sees a message for a replacement requested by another L1 while it is waiting, instead of forwarding it to its next sharer it will send to the node who sent it (which may be either its previous sharer or the L2) an opportunistic replacement request including in the same message the identity of its next sharer and then it will discard the sharing information (the data had been discarded already), leaving the list temporarily unconnected.

Upon reception of the opportunistic replacement request message, the previous sharer will update its pointer to the next sharer, reconnecting the list, and then forward the original replacement request again to its new next sharer (or finish the transaction if the new next sharer happens to be the requester of the original replacement).

At this point, the L1 waiting to replace has been already disconnected from the list and when it eventually receives the authorization to replace from L2, it will answer with a *nack*, quickly unblocking the L2 without needing to traverse the list again. Notice that unblocking the L1 directly after it gets disconnected from the sharers list would lead to a protocol race and either deadlock or an incorrect list update because the L1 had already sent a replacement request to the L2 that it will eventually receive and process expecting some response.

This way, *Opportunistic replacements* reduce both the time that the L2 remains blocked and the traffic due to the replacements by means of avoiding repeated traversals of the list of sharers.

3.2   Concurrent Replacements (CR)

As stated before, the effect of shared replacements in the execution time of *List* is mainly due not to the increase in traffic neither to the increase in the time that L1 nodes spend performing replacements. Rather, what impacts performance the most is the time that the L2 stays blocked during the replacement, increasing the latency of other misses to the same block (from other nodes) which have to wait to be processed until the L2 is unblocked.

However, it is not strictly necessary that the L2 attends all requests sequentially. In particular, it is easy to modify *List* so that read misses are attended immediately by the L2 even when it is blocked due to a replacement as long as the replacing node is not the first of the list. *Concurrent replacements* allow the

L2 to process read requests concurrently to replacements, while other request combinations still need to be handled sequentially. Specifically, only one read request can be processed concurrently to one replacement at the same time.

This is possible because new sharers are always inserted at the beginning of the list in the *List* protocol. This means that, once the L2 has forwarded a replacement request, new nodes can be inserted in the list without risk because it would be impossible for them to be the predecessor of the replacing node, which is what the forwarded replacement message seeks.

The replacement of the first sharer cannot be done concurrently to an insertion due to races, no matter whether the read request or the replacement request is received first. As a consequence, to be able to detect this case, the L2 needs to update its pointer to the first sharer only when the insertion transaction is completed (i.e., after receiving the *Unblock* message). Note that this limitation is not important in practice because it is not necessary to actually traverse the list to replace the first sharer.

This optimization requires the addition of a new intermediate state to the L2 coherence controller which combines the intermediate states that deal with replacements and insertions. It improves miss latency by reducing the waiting time of requests at the L2 controller.

4   Evaluation Results

4.1   Simulation Methodology

We have done the evaluation of the cache coherence protocols mentioned in this work using the PIN [12] and GEMS 2.1 [13] simulators, which have been connected in a similar way as proposed in [14]. PIN obtains every data access performed by the applications while GEMS models the memory hierarchy and calculates the memory access latency for each processor request. We model the interconnection network with the Garnet [1] simulator. The simulated architecture corresponds to a single chip multiprocessor (*tiled*-CMP) with 64 cores. The most relevant simulation parameters are shown in Table 1.

We evaluate *List* with the two proposed optimizations (*OR* and *CR*), and we compare it to two protocols using centralized sharing codes. The first one, namely *1-Pointer*, resembles the AMD's *MagnyCours* [4] protocol and uses a single pointer to the owner as sharing information (therefore having similar area requirements than *List*). The other one, *BitVector*, employs as sharing code non-scalable bit-vectors in each directory entry.

Our simulations consider representative applications from both the SPLASH-2 [18] and the PARSEC 2.1 [3] benchmark suites. *Barnes, Cholesky, FFT, Ocean, Radix, Raytrace, Volrend,* and *Water-NSQ* use the input sizes used in the SPLASH-2 paper. *Bodytrack, Canneal, Streamcluster,* and *Swaptions* are from the PARSEC 2.1 suite and use the *simmedium* input sizes. We have accounted for the variability of parallel applications as discussed in [2]. To do so, we have performed a number of simulations for each application and configuration inserting

Table 1. System parameters.

Memory parameters	
Block size	64 bytes
L1 cache (data & instr.)	32 KiB, 4 ways
L1 access latency	1 cycle
L2 cache (shared)	256 KiB/tile, 16 ways
L2 access latency	6 cycle
Cache organization	Inclusive
Directory information	Included in L2
Memory access time	160 cycles
Network parameters	
Topology	2-D mesh (8×8)
Switching and routing	Wormhole and X-Y
Message size	4 flits (data), 1 flit (control)
Link time	2 cycles
Bandwidth	1 flit per cycle

random variations in each main memory access. All results in this work correspond to the parallel part of the applications.

4.2   Results

L1 Cache Miss Latency. L1 cache miss latency is a key performance aspect. The sharing code employed by the protocol can affect it significantly, specially for large core counts.

Figure 3 plots the average L1 miss latency split in five parts: the time spent in accessing the L1, accounting for stalls due to on-going coherence actions or exhausted MSHR capacity (*At_L1*); the time from L1 to L2 to access the directory information (*To_L2*); the time spent waiting at L2 until it can attend the request, mostly because of on-going transactions on the same block (*At_L2*); the time spent waiting to receive the data from main memory in case the block is not on-chip (*Main_memory*); and the time since the L2 sends the data or forwards the request until the requester receives the missing block (*To_L1*).

List experiences an increase in latency compared to the area-demanding *BitVector*, mainly because of the sharp increase in the *At_L2* latency. In effect, *List* "blocks" a memory block when updating the sharing list to ensure mutual exclusion and to avoid inconsistencies in the list. This forces the delay of subsequent cache misses to the same block. On average, *1-Pointer* experiences a significant but smaller increase in latency due to the broadcast that it requires to invalidate sharers upon write misses.

Replacements of shared blocks in a private cache in *List* require to sequentially traverse the list of sharers. Differently, in *BitVector* and *1-Pointer*, these

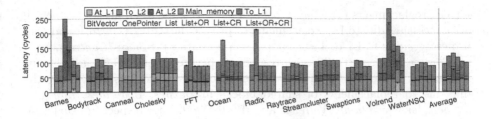

Fig. 3. L1 miss latency.

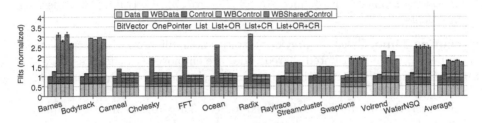

Fig. 4. Interconnection network traffic.

replacements are performed silently, without accessing nor blocking the L2 entry. Opportunistic replacements allow several replacements to happen at the same time, thus reducing the *At_L2* latency, notably in *Barnes* and *Volrend*. Concurrent replacements allow to resolve one read miss while performing a replacement, which further reduces miss latency down to a similar value as with *BitVector* and smaller than *1-Pointer*, making *List* a competitive protocol in terms of performance.

Despite the serial nature of invalidation in linked protocols, the *To_L1* latency is not affected. This counter-intuitive result is due to the low frequency of writes misses (23 %, on average), but most importantly to the low number of sharers found upon such write misses (54 % none, 41 % one, 3 % three, on average).

Network Traffic. Fig. 4 shows the network traffic, measured in flits, for each protocol. Traffic has been normalized with respect to *BitVector* and divided in the following categories: data messages due to L1 misses (*Data*); data messages

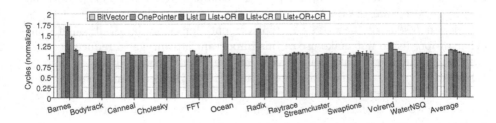

Fig. 5. Execution time.

due to L1 replacements (*WBData*); control messages due to L1 misses (*Control*); control messages due to L1 replacements of private data (*WBControl*); and control messages due to L1 replacements of shared data (*WBSharedControl*).

1-Pointer increases traffic with respect to *BitVector* in more than 50 % due to the use of broadcast for invalidating sharers. *List* notoriously increases the traffic due to replacements of shared blocks in *Barnes*, *Bodytrack*, *Raytrace*, *Streamcluster*, *Swaptions*, *Volrend*, and *WaterNSQ* with respect to *BitVector* since in *BitVector* these replacements are silent and do not generate traffic. This increase in traffic is even slightly larger than the increase suffered by *1-Pointer*. Oportunistic replacements reduce the *WBSharedControl* traffic by coalescing replacements.

Execution Time. Given the previous results, small differences in execution time are expected when distributed shared codes are employed. In effect, as shown in Fig. 5, *List* and *1-Pointer* both incur a similar slowdown of approximately 12 % with respect to *BitVector*.

However, the optimizations described in Sect. 3 are able to almost completely eliminate this slowdown when both are combined. *List+OR+CR* incurs in an average execution time degradation of 1.6 % with respect to *BitVector*, with a maximum reduction in execution time of 2.7 % (*Radix*) and maximum degradation of 3.8 % (*Barnes*).

Scalability. Three aspects reflect the scalability of a protocol: directory memory overhead, latency of cache misses, and network traffic. Since the first aspect has been addressed in Fig. 1, we now focus on the latter two. The latency of read misses in linked protocols is independent of the system size. However, the latency of write misses increases with the number of sharers per invalidation. Fortunately, this number grows more slowly than the system size (e.g., we have measured 0.52 sharers on average for 16 cores and 0.57 for 64 cores). Regarding traffic, the overhead comes from L1 replacements. In *List*, the number of messages per replacement depends on the size of the list which, as already mentioned, does not increase as fast as the total number of cores.

5   Conclusions and Opportunities

In this work, we show that a singly-list based linked protocol (*List*) has the potential of providing simultaneously both scalable directory memory overhead and high performance. We find out that the most remarkable source of inefficiencies in *List* is the lack of silent replacements for clean data (although some other proposals do not make use of this important advantage to reduce network traffic and directory controller activity) and we have presented two techniques (OR and CR) that remove completely the increase in execution time that otherwise would emerge. Regarding the disadvantages typically associated to these protocols, we see that the impact that list traversal operations have on average cache miss latency is minimal. This is because read misses are more frequent than write misses and because the number of sharers that need to be invalidated on every write miss (the length of the list to be traversed) is usually small. Also, *List* only requires the addition of one pointer to each private cache (although modifications to the private caches could be avoided by having per-core *pointers caches*).

All in all, we show that a simple implementation of a linked protocol is an interesting alternative to current proposals in the maycore arena, and therefore, linked protocols can constitute an attractive starting point for proposing further optimizations for (for example) reducing cache miss latencies and thus going beyond the performance of *BitVector*. We are currently exploring this direction.

References

1. Agarwal, N., Krishna, T., Peh, L.S., Jha, N.K.: GARNET: a detailed on-chip network model inside a full-system simulator. In: IEEE International Symposium on Performance Analysis of Systems and Software (ISPASS), pp. 33–42, April 2009
2. Alameldeen, A.R., Wood, D.A.: Variability in architectural simulations of multi-threaded workloads. In: 9th International Symposium on High-Performance Computer Architecture (HPCA), pp. 7–18, February 2003
3. Bienia, C., Kumar, S., Singh, J.P., Li, K.: The PARSEC benchmark suite: characterization and architectural implications. In: 17th International Conference on Parallel Architectures and Compilation Techniques (PACT), pp. 72–81, October 2008
4. Conway, P., Kalyanasundharam, N., Donley, G., Lepak, K., Hughes, B.: Blade computing with the AMD Opteron^TM processor ("Magny Cours"). In: 21st HotChips Symposium, August 2009
5. Cuesta, B., Ros, A., Gómez, M.E., Robles, A., Duato, J.: Increasing the effectiveness of directory caches by deactivating coherence for private memory blocks. In: 38th International Symposium on Computer Architecture (ISCA), pp. 93–103, June 2011
6. Culler, D.E., Singh, J.P., Gupta, A.: Parallel Computer Architecture: a Hardware/Software Approach. Morgan Kaufmann Inc., Burlington (1999)
7. Demetriades, S., Cho, S.: Stash directory: a scalable directory for many-core coherence. In: 20th International Symposium on High-Performance Computer Architecture (HPCA), pp. 177–188, February 2014
8. Fang, L., Liu, P., Hu, Q., Huang, M.C., Jiang, G.: Building expressive, area-efficient coherence directories. In: 22nd International Conference on Parallel Architectures and Compilation Techniques (PACT), pp. 299–308, September 2013
9. Fernández-Pascual, R., Ros, A., Acacio, M.E.: Characterization of a list-based directory cache coherence protocol for manycore CMPs. In: Lopes, L., Žilinskas, J., Costan, A., Cascella, R.G., Kecskemeti, G., Jeannot, E., Cannataro, M., Ricci, L., Benkner, S., Petit, S., Scarano, V., Gracia, J., Hunold, S., Scott, S.L., Lankes, S., Lengauer, C., Carretero, J., Breitbart, J., Alexander, M. (eds.) Euro-Par 2014, Part II. LNCS, vol. 8806, pp. 254–265. Springer, Heidelberg (2014)
10. James, D., Laundrie, A., Gjessing, S., Sohi, G.: Scalable coherent interface. Computer **23**(6), 74–77 (1990)
11. Lovett, T., Clapp, R.: STiNG: a CC-NUMA computer system for the commercial marketplace. In: 23rd International Symposium on Computer Architecture (ISCA), pp. 308–317, June 1996

12. Luk, C.K., Cohn, R., Muth, R., Patil, H., Klauser, A., Lowney, G., Wallace, S., Reddi, V.J., Hazelwood, K.: Pin: building customized program analysis tools with dynamic instrumentation. In: 2005 ACM SIGPLAN Conference on Programming Language Design and Implementation (PLDI), pp. 190–200, June 2005
13. Martin, M.M., Sorin, D.J., Beckmann, B.M., Marty, M.R., Xu, M., Alameldeen, A.R., Moore, K.E., Hill, M.D., Wood, D.A.: Multifacet's general execution-driven multiprocessor simulator (GEMS) toolset. Comput. Archit. News **33**(4), 92–99 (2005)
14. Monchiero, M., Ahn, J.H., Falcón, A., Ortega, D., Faraboschi, P.: How to simulate 1000 cores. Comput. Archit. News **37**(2), 10–19 (2009)
15. Sanchez, D., Kozyrakis, C.: SCD: a scalable coherence directory with flexible sharer set encoding. In: 18th International Symposium on High-Performance Computer Architecture (HPCA), pp. 129–140, February 2012
16. Thapar, M., Delagi, B.: Stanford distributed-directory protocol. Computer **23**(6), 78–80 (1990)
17. Thekkath, R., Singh, A.P., Singh, J.P., John, S., Hennessy, J.L.: An evaluation of a commercial CC-NUMA architecture: The CONVEX Exemplar SPP1200. In: 11th International Symposium on Parallel Processing (IPPS), pp. 8–17, April 1997
18. Woo, S.C., Ohara, M., Torrie, E., Singh, J.P., Gupta, A.: The SPLASH-2 programs: Characterization and methodological considerations. In: 22nd International Symposium on Computer Architecture (ISCA), pp. 24–36, June 1995

Mapping of Applications on Heterogeneous Architectures and Real-Time Tasks on Multiprocessors

Generic Algorithmic Scheme for 2D Stencil Applications on Hybrid Machines

Stephane Vialle[2]([⊠]), Sylvain Contassot-Vivier[1], and Patrick Mercier[2]

[1] Loria - UMR 7503, Université de Lorraine, Nancy, France
sylvain.contassotvivier@loria.fr
[2] UMI 2958, Georgia Tech - CNRS,
CentraleSupelec, University Paris-Saclay, Metz, France
Stephane.Vialle@centralesupelec.fr

Abstract. Hardware accelerators are classic scientific coprocessors in HPC machines. However, the number of CPU cores on the mother board is increasing and constitutes a non negligible part of the total computing power of the machine. So, running an application both on an accelerator (like a GPU or a Xeon-Phi device) and on the CPU cores can provide the highest performance. Moreover, it is now possible to include different accelerators in a machine, in order to support and to speedup a larger set of applications. Then, running an application part on the most suitable device allows to reach high performance, but using all unused devices in the machine should permit to improve even more the performance of that part. However, the overlapping of computations with inter-device data transfers is mandatory to limit the overhead of this approach, leading to complex asynchronous algorithms and multi-paradigm optimized codes. This article introduces our research and experiments on cooperation between several CPU and both a GPU and a Xeon-Phi accelerators, all included in a same machine.

1 Introduction and Objectives

Hardware accelerators have become classical scientific coprocessors but they still need a CPU to control the entire machine. Also, current standard CPU have a significant number of cores and computing power. Using both CPU and accelerator cores seems an interesting way to achieve the maximal computing speed on a computing node. But using both the CPU and accelerators leads to frequently transfer intermediate results between all those devices. So, asynchronous data transfers, overlapped with computations, are required to obtain significant speedups compared to mono-device executions.

In this study, we consider hybrid computing nodes: each node hosting one or more CPU, one GPU and one Xeon-Phi, allowing one to choose the most adapted architecture for each application, or application module. However, once the most adapted device has been identified for a computation in an algorithm, it may be interesting to cooperatively use any other kind of computing device available in the machine to concurrently process that computation, and then to

© Springer International Publishing Switzerland 2016
F. Hannig et al. (Eds.): ARCS 2016, LNCS 9637, pp. 115–129, 2016.
DOI: 10.1007/978-3-319-30695-7_9

increase the overall performance. In order to ease the use of our multi-devices and multi-architectures machines, we developed a generic parallel algorithmic scheme achieving an overlapping of data transfers with computations between two or three devices (simultaneously), for 2D stencil applications. This generic scheme has been implemented and optimized for GPU and Xeon-Phi devices, considering the specific features of their programming models and API.

Our approach has been validated in [3] with a Jacobi relaxation application. In this paper, we extend it to a more complex stencil application, more representative of real scientific applications: a shortest path computation. As in [3], that application has been tested on two different hybrid machines. We were able to experiment our different kernels (on CPU, GPU and Xeon-Phi), using one, two or three devices simultaneously, and to identify the most suited combination for each application.

2 Application Examples

Our parallel scheme (see Sect. 4) aims at running *2D stencil* applications, on hybrid machines. Two different applications have been used to test and validate our approach: a very classical *2D Jacobi relaxation* algorithm, and a *shortest path calculation on 2D+ ground* (taking the elevations into account). They both work on 2D regular grids of points. The reader is invited to see [3] for a detailed description of our *Jacobi* algorithm. Our *shortest path* algorithm computes *minimal paths costs* from a given position in the grid to all other positions. It is slightly different from the Jacobi algorithm as it is an adaptation of the Dijkstra's algorithm [5]. The path cost of each point $P_{i,j}$ is updated according to the previous costs of its eight neighbors in the 2D grid (denoted $N_8(P_{i,j})$). Indeed, for each neighbor, the 3D euclidian distance to the current point is computed and added to the current minimal cost of the neighbor. Then, the new cost of the current point is chosen as the minimal cost among the eight computations:

$$C^{n+1}(i,j) = \min_{P_{a,b} \in N_8(P_{i,j})} (C^n(a,b) + d(P_{i,j}, P_{a,b}))$$

Considering h, the side length of a grid cell (between two successive points in the grid), the distance between $P_{i,j}$ and $P_{a,b}$ is:

$$d(P_{i,j}, P_{a,b}) = \sqrt{((i-a).h)^2 + ((j-b).h)^2 + (z(i,j) - z(a,b))^2}$$

In fact, $N_8(P_{i,j})$, the neighboring of point $P_{i,j}$ in the 2D grid (see Fig. 1), contains less than eight neighbors when $P_{i,j}$ is located on a grid edge. This algorithm requires a 2D array of costs and a 2D array of elevations (z). Initially, a target point $T_{\alpha,\beta}$ is chosen and its cost is set to 0 while all others costs are set to $+\infty$. Then the algorithm starts to iterate until no cost changes during an entire iteration (convergence is reached). Finally, we get a 2D array of minimal costs (distances) and paths from every point $P_{i,j}$ to the target point $T_{\alpha,\beta}$.

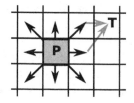

Fig. 1. Shortest path point neighboring

3   Related Work

Today, scientific computing on GPU accelerators is common, while using Xeon-Phi accelerators starts to be deeply investigated and some comparisons have been achieved. In [6], authors point out the need to optimize data storage and data accesses in different ways on GPU and Xeon Phi. In [2], authors optimize data storage for stencil applications on different CPU, GPU and APU (processors with both CPU and GPU cores). Several studies like [8,11] address the deep optimization of parallel stencil applications or other lattice based applications [12], for different types of devices. However, their programs use only one device at a time. Some authors use a generic programming model and tool to develop on different architectures, like OpenCL [7,10]. Nevertheless, such tool does not hide to the programmer the devices hardware specificities to be taken into account to attain optimal performance. Thus, an important algorithmic effort is still required to design codes efficiently running on different architectures.

Another approach consists in using the CPU memory to store data too large for the accelerator memory, and to efficiently send sub-parts of the problem to the accelerator [9]. Here again, there is no simultaneous use of the CPU and the accelerators.

Finally, some works propose general frameworks to use different devices by performing dynamic scheduling of tasks graphs or data flows [4]. However, the generality of such frameworks induces additional costs compared to application specific schemes.

In [3], we introduced our first algorithmic scheme of heterogeneous computing, successfully running a Jacobi relaxation on CPU, GPU and Xeon-Phi. In the current study, we generalize our approach to a more realistic scientific problem involving more complex and irregular computation.

4   Algorithmic Scheme

In our context, the GPU and the Xeon-Phi are used as scientific co-processors in *offload* mode. The Xeon-Phi could have been used via MPI but we chose the offload mode to get similar programming paradigms between the GPU and the Phi. So, our hybrid solution uses the CPU to launch and control the computation steps on the GPU, the Xeon-Phi and its own cores, and to manage data transfers between CPU and devices.

4.1   Global Strategy of the Parallel Scheme

Our global data distribution strategy is to partition the 2D grid in three horizontal strips (potentially of different heights), so that the first one is processed on the GPU, the second one, on the CPU, and the third one, on the Phi. Placing the CPU between the GPU and Phi in the logical organization is a strategic choice as direct data transfers between GPU and Phi are not currently possible. We name *CPU boundaries* the first and last lines computed by the CPU, *GPU boundary* the last line computed by the GPU, and *MIC boundary* the first line computed by the Xeon-Phi. We name *corpus* the other lines computed by a computing device. According to data dependencies in the application, each computing device must store, in addition to its strip of the grid, the adjacent boundary(ies) of its neighboring device(s). So, the top part of the grid is transferred to the GPU and the bottom part to the Xeon-Phi (see Fig. 2 left). Although the CPU memory may host only its associated part of the grid (and the required boundaries), for the sake of simplicity in the overall management of the system, we have chosen to store the entire current (`crt`) and previous (`prev`) relaxation grids. However, this could be easily optimized if the CPU memory were too small to store the entire grids.

At each iteration during the computation loop, the GPU boundary may be transferred to the CPU while the adjacent CPU boundary may be transferred to the GPU. Symmetrically, the CPU/Xeon-Phi boundaries may be transferred too. Indeed, as a frontier may remain unchanged during one iteration, our algorithm transfers a frontier to/from an accelerator only if it has undergone at least one modification. Also, in order to optimize the transfers, our algorithm is designed to allow direct transfers of the frontiers in their place in the local arrays on the destination device. So, no intermediate array is required to store the received frontiers coming from another device, and the CPU algorithm uses symmetric data structures and interactions for both accelerators.

4.2   Multi-device Algorithm

Figure 2 (right) details the three main parts of our generic multi-device algorithm (see [3] for a simplified version, with straightforward array allocation on accelerators and systematic frontier transfers):

Initialization Step: Memory allocation on accelerators and initial data transfers from CPU to accelerators can be long, so the initialization step is parallel. Firstly, input data are prepared on the CPU. Then, the other devices are initialized and they simultaneously receive their respective part of input data. Complementary allocations and initialization are performed concurrently between all devices. At last, synchronization barriers are used to ensure that each device is ready to enter the computation loop.

Computation Loop: We focused on maximizing the overlap of boundary(ies) computations, boundary(ies) transfers, and corpus computations on the different devices. Boundary transfers are performed simultaneously between devices that compute adjacent strips of the grid when boundaries are modified. On each device, boundaries computation and potential transfer are performed concurrently with the corpus computation in order to maximize the overlap of boundaries transfers with corpus computations. All the devices work concurrently thanks to asynchronous operations. Data transfers from/to the accelerators are fully efficient when two PCI express buses are present. Each iteration is ended by synchronization barriers to ensure that every device has all its newly updated data.

Final Step: Results retrieving from devices to the CPU can be long and have been also overlapped. The results from one accelerator are transferred asynchronously during the synchronous transfer from the other one. Thus, transfers overlap and only one synchronization barrier is required to ensure the complete reception on the CPU. Finally, the CPU cleans up the devices and its own memory and releases them. As this last operation never appeared to be time consuming, it is done sequentially.

5   Computing Kernels

The design of optimized multi-core or many-core kernels is out of scope of this article as we focus on the efficient interactions between cooperating kernels. However, as we developed the computing kernels for the three types of devices by adapting the Jacobi kernels to the shortests path problem, the reader should see [3] for further details.

On GPU, both for *Jacobi* and *Shortest Path* applications, we designed CUDA kernels using the fast (but small) *shared memory* of each stream-processor, in order to load and access sub-parts of the data arrays. This is a kind of cache memory explicitly managed by the developer, which is a classical optimization on NVIDIA GPU. For the *Shortest Path* program, we designed a first solution that pre-compute distances between all neighbors in the grid, in order to avoid recomputing $d(P_{i,j}, P_{a,b})$ (see Sect. 2). However, this version showed to be penalized by the induced larger data transfers between GPU memories. The adopted

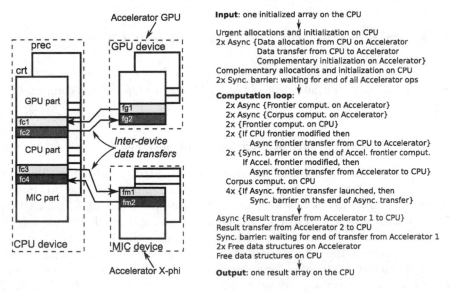

Fig. 2. Data structures (left) and asynchronous and overlapping algorithm (right) to obtain efficient simultaneous computations on the three devices (CPU, GPU and Xeon-phi)

solution, less memory consuming, consists in taking advantage of the regular structure of the grid cells by pre-computing only X and Y axis contributions to the distances between neighbors, which represents at most 8 values instead of four times the number of grid points. This implies an important reduction of data copies into the *shared memory* at each iteration. In compensation, distances have to be recomputed at each iteration, but only in a partial form (thanks to X and Y pre-computed contributions) that does not increase the computational load so much. This version has been used in all the experiments presented in Sect. 8.

Finally, we deployed 2D grids of 2D blocks of CUDA threads, and experimented different sizes of 2D blocks. The optimal solution depended on the GPU used: blocks of 16×16 ($Y \times X$) threads run faster on the *GeForce GTX Titan Black*, while blocks of 16×32 threads run faster on the *Tesla K40m* (both GPU have a Kepler architecture).

On CPU and Xeon-Phi, we designed basic and cache-blocking algorithms. When blocked in cache, the grid update was processed per small sub-grids filling only the amount of L2 cache available per thread. Moreover, we attempted to guide the compiler to vectorize computational loops by using the AVX units (but we did not implement *intrinsics* routine calls). On the basic calculations of the *Jacobi* algorithm, our cache blocking mechanism has been efficient. On the opposite, on the *Shortest Path* algorithm our cache blocking implementation had no effect but vectorization has been efficient. Using `#pragma ivdep` and `#pragma simd` directives and AVX compiler options, and achieving minor code modifications we succeeded to significantly improve performance on Xeon CPU and on Xeon-Phi accelerator (3120 and 5100 series).

6   Optimized Solution for Xeon-Phi and GPU Accelerators

We present below the optimization of the initialization step and the computation loop.

6.1   Initial Datastructure Allocations and Settings

Figure 3 introduces the actually implemented data-structures, not so different from the generic ones (see Fig. 2 right). Listing 1.1 illustrates how we implemented data-structures allocations and initialization by mixing GPU CUDA, CPU OpenMP and Xeon-Phi Offload semantics and syntax. This code implements and respects the initial step of our generic algorithm (see Sect. 4).

Main changes in the data-structures concern the Xeon-Phi (see Fig. 2 (right) and Fig. 3). In fact, we could observe during our developments that allocations of large arrays on the Xeon-Phi are very long when achieved from the CPU through a `#pragma offload in(...)` directive. However, this allocation mechanism is required to be able to transfer data between the CPU and the Xeon-Phi. So, we allocate the `micPrev` array and transfer CPU data with a `#pragma offload` directive (lines 4–5), but the `_micCrt` array is allocated as a pure Xeon-Phi variable (line 12), which is a fast mechanism. Then, it is initialized with a Xeon-Phi internal `memcpy` call (line 13). Obviously, the final results will have to be transferred from the Xeon-Phi to the CPU only through the `micPrev` array. This strategy significantly reduces the initialization step, but leads to allocate two additional small buffers to transfer the CPU and Xeon-Phi frontiers during each computation step, as shown in Fig. 3 (`fm1` and `fm2`). This allocation of a transferable 2-lines array is done at line 6. All this sequence of operations is run asynchronously due to the `signal` clause in line 9.

After launching the allocation and initialization sequence on the Xeon-Phi, the CPU immediately enters the GPU sequence at line 19. It allocates several *streams* to manage concurrent operations on the GPU, and several arrays on the GPU (lines 21 and 22). According to CUDA paradigm, the CPU allocates memory on the GPU calling a `cudaMalloc` function. At lines 24–26 the CPU runs another CUDA library function to lock in its memory the arrays that will be transferred to/from the GPU, in order to speedup the transfers and to do them asynchronously. All these memory allocations and locking operations are achieved synchronously but are fast. Then, the CPU launches long asynchronous data transfers to fill the

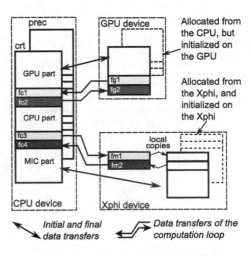

Fig. 3. Optimized data structures implemented on the three devices (CPU, Xphi and GPU)

allocated GPU arrays (lines 28–30), and an asynchronous GPU-to-GPU memory copy at lines 32–33. All these long operations are run asynchronously on stream 0 so that the CPU can concurrently perform its own initialization at lines 35–38 (running several threads to speedup a large memory copy).

Finally, we implemented the two synchronization barriers of our algorithm (Fig. 2 right). At line 40, the CPU waits for the end of all asynchronous GPU operations on stream 0, and at line 41, it waits for the end of all asynchronous Xeon-Phi operations. This implementation is very close to the initial step of our generic algorithm, save for some fast GPU memory allocation and CPU memory locking that remain synchronous.

Listing 1.1. Initial step implementation

```
1   // CPU allocation of data array
2   posix_memalign(&crt, ALIGN, TotCol * TotLin * sizeof(double));
3   // ASYNCHRONOUS XEON-PHI ALLOCATIONS AND INITIALIZATION
4   #pragma offload target(mic:0)                                    \
5     in(micPrev:length(micTotLin*TotCol) free_if(0) align(ALIGN)) \
6     in(micCrt:length(2*TotCol) free_if(0) align(ALIGN))          \
7     ...                                                          \
8     nocopy(micRes, _micCrt, micTopFront, micBotFront)            \
9     signal(&micPrev)
10  {
11    // Alloc and init of _micCrt array on Xeon-Phi (matching micPrev array)
12    posix_memalign(&_micCrt, ALIGN, micTotLin*TotCol*sizeof(double));
13    memcpy(_micCrt, micPrev, micTotLin*TotCol*sizeof(double));
14    // Init pointers on data arrays on Xeon-Phi
15    micRes = micPrev + TotCol;
16    ...
17  }
18  // Synchronous GPU Allocations
19  for (i=0; i<NBSTREAMS; ++i)   // 3 streams
20     cudaStreamCreate(&(streamTab[i]));
21  cudaMalloc(&gpuPrev, gpuTotLin*TotCol*sizeof(double));
22  ...
23  // Synchronous CPU memory lock (to speedup CPU-GPU data transfers)
24  cudaHostRegister(prev, gpuTotLin*TotCol*sizeof(double), // transferred
25                   cudaHostRegisterPortable);             // to gpuPrev
26  ...
27  // ASYNCHRONOUS GPU INIT: data transfer from CPU to GPU
28  cudaMemcpyAsync(GpuPrev, prev, gpuTotLin*TotCol*sizeof(double),
29                  cudaMemcpyHostToDevice, streamTab[0]);
30  ...
31  // ASYNCHRONOUS GPU INIT: data copy from GPU to GPU
32  cudaMemcpyAsync(GpuCrt, GpuPrev, gpuTotLin*TotCol*sizeof(double),
33                  cudaMemcpyDeviceToDevice, streamTab[0]);
34  // Complementary CPU init. (parallelized with OpenMP)
35  #pragma omp parallel num_threads(nbTHet) {
36    size_t idxFirstValTh = ...; size_t nbValTh = ...;
37    memcpy(crt+idxFirstValTh, prev+idxFirstValTh, nbValTh*sizeof(double));
38  }
39  // SYNCHRONIZATION BARRIERS on the end of the GPU and Xeon-Phi async. init.
40  cudaStreamSynchronize(streamTab[0]);          // GPU
41  #pragma offload_wait target(mic:0) wait(&micPrev) // Xeon-Phi
```

6.2   Asynchronous and Overlapped Computation Loop

Code snippet in Listing 1.2 summarizes our implementation of the computation loop of the generic algorithm (Fig. 2 right). Line 1 shows that the global loop is stopped as soon as no modification occurs during one iteration. Line 4 is an asynchronous CUDA kernel launch, running frontier computation on the GPU. Indeed, a CUDA kernel launch has a specific CUDA syntax, and requires to be implemented in a .cu source file, and to be compiled with the Nvidia CUDA compiler (nvcc), that cannot compile Intel offload or OpenMP directives. So, CUDA kernels launching operations have to be encapsulated into functions located in a .cu file. Line 5 transfers a *modification flag* of the GPU frontier onto the CPU. This asynchronous transfer uses the same CUDA *top frontier* stream (TF) as the previous kernel execution, so these two asynchronous operations are sequenced:

frontier computation is achieved and the modification flag set before it is transferred to the CPU. Lines 7 and 8 reproduce this kernel launch and modification flag transfer, focusing on the rest of the problem processed on the GPU, using the CUDA *corpus* stream.

Lines 11–16 perform a similar frontier and corpus computations on the Xeon-Phi (like on the GPU). Here, the modification flags are scalar boolean values automatically transferred between the CPU and the Xeon-Phi at the beginning and at the end of each `offload` directive. Moreover, when declared (at top of the source file) the `heterMIC` routine has been labeled to be a Xeon-Phi routine, in order the Intel compiler applies all the suited optimizations. In particular, it can take into account the vectorization directives embedded in the source code of this routine.

Lines 18–25 are the synchronous CPU computation of the two CPU frontiers (CPU/ GPU and CPU/Xeon-Phi), using OpenMP multithreading and Intel compiler vectorization on SSE or AVX units. The `CellUpdate` routine (lines 22–23) is compiled only for CPU, and Intel compiler can achieve vectorization optimization adapted to CPU cores. Lines 27–35 perform the asynchronous transfers of the CPU frontiers to the GPU, using a new CUDA *bottom frontier* stream (BF), and to the Xeon-Phi, using a new signal clause (`dummyTransfer`). According to our generic algorithm (see Sect. 4) these transfers are done only if the frontiers have been modified on the CPU.

At lines 37–40, the CPU waits for the end of the GPU frontier computation and modification flag transfer (TF CUDA stream) before to asynchronously transfer the GPU frontier to the CPU if it has been modified on the GPU. Lines 42–46 execute the same operations for the Xeon-Phi. Lines 48–61 correspond to the computation of the CPU part of the problem excepted its frontiers (the CPU *corpus*). Again, it is a multithreaded and vectorized computation, and a modification flag is raised when a modification occurs (line 60).

Lines 63–65 contain synchronization barriers for the end of the CPU/GPU frontier transfers and the end of the GPU corpus computation. Lines 67–71 perform the same operations on the Xeon-Phi. Lines 73–77 permute current and previous array pointers on the Xeon-Phi, the GPU, and the CPU. These permutations are not complex but their implementations differ: pointers on GPU memory are CPU variables managed by the CPU, while pointers on Xeon-Phi memory are stored on the Xeon-Phi and must be permuted by the Xeon-Phi. Finally, pointers on the Xeon-Phi memory have *mirror pointers* on the CPU (due to the offload semantics) that must be permuted too (line 77). Lines 78–81 compute global modification flags corresponding to each computing device.

Listing 1.2. Computation loop implementation

```
1  for(iter=0; iter<nbIters && (modifCPU || modifGPU || modifMIC); ++iter) {
2    ...
3    // ASYNCHRONOUS GPU computations and frontier transfer to the CPU -------------
4    gpuOneIterationLast(gpuPrec+..., gpuCrt+..., 1 /*1 line*/, nbCol, ..., TF);
5    cudaMemcpyFromSymbolAsync(&modifGPULast, pt_gpu_modif_hf, ...,
6                              cudaMemcpyDeviceToHost, streamTab[TF]);
7    gpuOneIteration(gpuPrev, gpuCrt, ..., nbLinsGPU-1, nbCol, ..., CORPUS);
8    cudaMemcpyFromSymbolAsync(&modifGPUCorpus, pt_gpu_modif_corpus, ...,
```

```
 9                                 cudaMemcpyDeviceToHost, streamTab[CORPUS]);
10    // ASYNCHRONOUS Xeon-Phi computations and frontier transfer to the CPU -------
11    #pragma offload target(mic:0) nocopy(botFrontMIC, micPrev, _micCrt, ...) \
12                               signal(&botFrontMIC)
13    { heterMIC(micPrev, _micCrt, ..., botFrontMIC, &modifMICFirst); }
14    #pragma offload target(mic:0)                                              \
15          nocopy(micPrev, _micCrt, micTer, ..., modifMICCorpus) signal(&_micCrt)
16    { heterMIC(micPrev, _micCrt, ..., &modifMICCorpus); }
17    // Synchronous CPU frontier computations ------------------------------------
18    #pragma omp parallel num_threads(nbTHet)
19    { #pragma omp for
20      #pragma simd
21      for (col=1; col <= nbCol; ++col) {
22        CellUpdate(prev, crt, ..., firstLine + col, &modifCPUFirst);
23        CellUpdate(prev, crt, ..., lastLine  + col, &modifCPULast);
24      }
25    }
26    // ASYNCHRONOUS CPU frontiers transfers to accelerators ---------------------
27    if (modifCPUFirst)
28      cudaMemcpyAsync(gpuCrt+..., cpuCrt+..., nbCol*sizeof(double),
29                        cudaMemcpyHostToDevice, streamTab[BF]);
30    if (modifCPULast) {
31      #pragma offload target(mic:0)                                            \
32          in(topFrontMIC:length(nbCol+1) alloc_if(0) free_if(0) align(ALIGN)) \
33          in(dummyTransfert) nocopy(_micCrt) signal(&dummyTransfer)
34      { memcpy(_micCrt+1, topFrontMIC+1, nbCol * sizeof(double)); }
35    }
36    // ASYNCHRONOUS GPU frontier transfer to the CPU ----------------------------
37    cudaStreamSynchronize(streamTab[TF]);
38    if (modifGPULast)
39      cudaMemcpyAsync(topFrontCPU, gpuCrt+..., nbCol*sizeof(double),
40                      cudaMemcpyDeviceToHost, streamTab[TF]);
41    // ASYNCHRONOUS Xeon-Phi frontier transfer to the CPU -----------------------
42    #pragma offload_wait target(mic:0) wait(&botFrontMIC)
43    if (modifMICFirst)
44      #pragma offload_transfer target(mic:0)                                   \
45          out(botFrontMIC:length(nbCol+1) alloc_if(0) free_if(0) align(ALIGN)) \
46          signal(&botFrontMIC)
47    // Synchronous CPU corpus computation ---------------------------------------
48    #pragma omp parallel for schedule(dynamic) num_threads(nbTHet)
49    for (lin=2; lin < nbLinesCPU; ++lin)         // multithreaded loop
50      #pragma simd                               // guided vectorization
51      for (col=1; col <= nbCol; ++col) {
52        size_t ind = lin*TotCol + col;
53        #pragma ivdep                            // guided vectorization
54        for (dl=-1; dl <= 1; ++dl)
55          for (dc=-1; dc <= 1; ++dc) {
56            cost = cpuPrev[ind + ...] + sqrt(...); // Compute the new distance
57            minCost = min(cost, minCost);          // Store current min distance
58          }
59        cpuCrt[ind] = minCost;                   // Store the min distance
60        if(minCost < cpuPrev[ind]) modifCPUCorpus = true; // Rise modif flag if
61      }                                          // min distance has changed
62    // SYNCHRONIZATION BARRIER on the end of GPU operations ---------------------
63    if (modifGPULast)  cudaStreamSynchronize(streamTab[TF]);
64    if (modifCPUFirst) cudaStreamSynchronize(streamTab[BF]);
65    cudaStreamSynchronize(streamTab[CORPUS]);
66    // SYNCHRONIZATION BARRIER on the end of Xeon-Phi operations ----------------
67    #pragma offload_wait target(mic:0) wait(&_micCrt)
68    if (modifMICFirst)
69      #pragma offload_wait target(mic:0) wait(&botFrontMIC)
70    if (modifCPULast)
71      #pragma offload_wait target(mic:0) wait(&dummyTransfer)
72    // SYNCHRONOUS PERMUTATION of current and previous arrays on each device -----
```

```
73   #pragma offload target(mic:0) nocopy(micPrev, _micCrt)
74   { double *tmp = _micCrt; _micCrt = micPrev; micPrev = tmp; }  // Phi ptr on Phi
75   tmp = gpuPrev; gpuPrev = gpuCrt; gpuCrt = tmp;                // GPU ptr on CPU
76   tmp = prev; prev = crt; crt = tmp;                           // CPU ptr on CPU
77   micCrt = crt + ...; micPrev = prev + ...; ...               // Mirror Phi ptr on CPU
78   // Modification flags computations
79   modifGPU = modifGPULast  | modifGPUCorpus;
80   modifMIC = modifMICPre   | modifMICCorpus;
81   modifCPU = modifCPUFirst | modifCPULast | modifCPUCorpus;
82   }
```

Finaly, mixing the Nvidia CUDA and Intel offload programming paradigm leads to a complex syntax, but we succeeded to implement our generic asynchronous parallel algorithm, including many *computations/data transfers* overlapping. Vectorization can be used on the CPU and Xeon-Phi kernels, but must be implemented in separated routines so that the compiler can easily generate efficient code for each architecture. Some different CUDA *streams* must be associated with the GPU kernel launches and data transfers, in order to concurrently run sequences of operations.

The final step of our generic algorithm mainly consists in retrieving the results from the accelerators. The mechanisms used to implement this are similar to the initialization step and consists in overlapping the results transfers from GPU and Xeon-Phi by using an asynchronous transfer from the GPU. So, we do not give code sample for that part. Instead, we mention that on the Xeon-Phi, it is necessary to copy the results into the transferable array (the one initialized with the *in* offload directive, line 5 in Listing 1.1) when the number of iterations is odd.

7   Testbeds and Benchmark Data for Shortest Path Computation

The machine used at CentraleSupelec is a Dell R720 server containing two 6-cores Intel(R) Xeon(R) CPU E5-2620 at 2.10 GHz, with two accelerators on separate PCIe buses. One accelerator is an Intel MIC *Xeon-Phi 3120* with 57 physical cores at 1.10 GHz, supporting 4 threads each. The second accelerator is a Nvidia GPU *GeForce GTX Titan Black* (Kepler architecture) with 2880 CUDA cores. The machine used at Loria is a Dell R720 server containing two 8-cores Intel(R) Xeon(R) CPU E5-2640 at 2.00 GHz, with two accelerators on separate PCIe buses. One accelerator is an Intel MIC *Xeon-Phi 5100* with 60 physical cores at 1.05 GHz supporting 4 threads each. The second accelerator is a Nvidia GPU *Tesla K40m* (Kepler architecture) with 2880 CUDA cores.

In order to get representative results with the shortest path problem, we used elevation data of a large area in the French and Italian Alps from the NASA SRTM project [1]. The 2D grid resolution is 30 m, with 10803 columns and 18005 lines ($\approx$324 Km$\times$540 Km), and the elevations range from -87 m to 4797 m. The overall calculation takes 9005 iterations with a target point located at the center of the area. In this study, we did not use larger datasets to be able to compare executions on single devices.

8   Benchmark Results with Different Hybrid Machines

In the following paragraphs, we present the performance results of our algorithm in several steps. Firstly, we present the performance of each device alone in order to give an idea of the relative computing powers of the devices inside each machine. These relative powers are useful to deduce the theoretical optimal partitioning of the 2D grid by using a simple static load balancing scheme. Then, we consider double device mixing, where two devices cooperate (GPU-CPU, CPU-PHI, GPU-PHI). Finally, the results with the three cooperating devices are presented. All the following experiments are averages of several executions although we observed a very limited standard deviation.

Standalone Performance. In Table 1 are presented the performance results for each device in both machines. Speeds are expressed in points per second instead of GFlops as the computation amount varies among the points. Relative computing powers are estimated according to the total power of each machine, deduced from the aggregation of the devices speeds. As expected, the CPU is the slowest device inside each machine and the GPU is the fastest one. However, strong differences between the two machines are observed, which is interesting as it provides significantly different hardware configurations. It allows us to see how our algorithm behaves in either cases. Absolute speeds are useful here to deduce the relative computing powers of the devices but they are omitted in the following tables as they are redundant information with gains.

Double Device Mixing. According to the single devices results, the relative computing powers of the devices in each machine are used to perform static load balancing. The optimal grid partitioning into two horizontal strips is computed for every couple of devices. For example, GPU is 4.7 times faster than CPU in the Loria machine, then the strip associated to the GPU will be 4.7 times larger

Table 1. Performance results of each device alone and relative computing powers

	Loria machine			CentralSupelec machine		
	CPU	PHI	GPU	CPU	PHI	GPU
Speed (pts/s)	6.35E+008	1.56E+009	3.00E+009	4.46E+008	1.74E+009	1.74E+009
Relative powers	12.20%	29.97%	57.83%	11.36%	44.32%	44.32%

Table 2. Performance results and gains around theoretical optimal cutting lines for both machines.

	Loria machine						CentraleSupelec machine					
	GPU-CPU		CPU-PHI		GPU-PHI		GPU-CPU		CPU-PHI		GPU-PHI	
	Cut line	gain	Cut line	gain	Cut line	gain	Cut line	gain	Cut line	gain	Cut line	gain
-1000	13900	-47.74%	4200	29.14%	10900	-14.80%	13300	-48.14%	1700	7.40%	8000	19.99%
-500	14400	-45.88%	4700	33.32%	11400	-13.27%	13800	-46.64%	2200	10.38%	8500	22.31%
opt. cut	14900	-42.92%	5200	37.19%	11900	-14.58%	14300	-44.66%	2700	13.97%	9000	23.01%
+500	15400	-37.03%	5700	28.37%	12400	-15.91%	14800	-41.61%	3200	13.94%	9500	22.32%
+1000	15900	-33.24%	6200	15.69%	12900	-17.59%	15300	-37.58%	3700	-0.92%	10000	19.29%

Table 3. Performance gains for the triple mixing on both machines.

CPU PHI cut line	Loria machine GPU-CPU cut line					CPU PHI cut line	CentraleSupelec machine GPU-CPU cut line					
	9400	9900	10400	10900	11400		7000	7500	8000	8500	9000	9500
11600	1.28%	-3.38%	-7.07%	-11.66%	-13.60%	9000	24.87%	28.94%	27.08%	25.63%	23.47%	
12100	-2.13%	1.55%	-2.31%	-5.70%	-9.57%	9500	3.05%	23.26%	32.60%	30.65%	28.41%	22.53%
12600	-12.73%	-5.19%	3.00%	-1.03%	-5.78%	10000	-9.33%	1.61%	21.92%	34.83%	32.30%	26.24%
13100	-21.84%	-16.00%	-9.32%	-4.51%	-2.01%	10500	-19.32%	-10.69%	0.07%	20.51%	37.01%	30.83%
13600	-30.68%	-23.83%	-20.22%	-12.83%	-7.13%	11000	-27.32%	-20.27%	-11.68%	-1.08%	19.08%	32.01%

than the CPU one, leading to a cutting line (opt. cut in Table 2) of 14900. The results are presented in Table 2 where the gains are computed relatively to the speed of the fastest device involved in the mixing.

First of all, we can see that some gains are negative and others are positive. Negative gains indicate that the mixing is less efficient than the fastest device alone. With both machines, the GPU-CPU mixing does not provide any gain. Indeed, even extremely imbalanced partitions with most of the grid on the GPU (17500 lines) provided a loss of 19.42 % on the Loria machine and 8.20 % on the CentralSupelec one. Those results show that the mixing overheads are never compensated by the computation gains with that grid size. Concerning the CPU-PHI mixing, we obtain significant gains on both machines, showing that our scheme is efficient for mixing those two devices. Finally, we obtain diverging results between the two machines for the GPU-PHI mixing. This mainly comes from the difference of powers between the two GPU devices. As the powers of the PHI and GPU are similar on the CS machine, their mixing is actually efficient whereas on the Loria machine the two devices have too different powers to compensate the mixing overheads. Also, it is surprising to get so different gains between GPU-CPU and CPU-PHI on the CS machine and this will require a deeper analyze.

Triple Device Mixing. For the sake of concision, we present in Table 3 only the percentage gains for both machine around their respective optimal cutting lines between GPU-CPU and CPU-PHI. For the CS machine, we added an extra column of GPU-CPU cutting line as the maximal performance was obtained at the limit of the initial set. It can be observed that our heterogeneous algorithm hardly obtains positive gains on the Loria machine whereas it obtains up to 37 % gain over the GPU on the CS machine (better than double mixing). The bad performance with the Loria machine is quite unexpected. It probably comes from the different hardware configuration as well as the older Intel compiler used. However, results with the CS machine show that our algorithmic scheme can provide significant gains. All those results show that the efficiency of our approach is sensitive to the hardware configuration as well as to the problem size. This will deserve a more complete investigation over the behavior of our scheme according to larger grid sizes.

9 Conclusion

An algorithmic scheme has been presented that enables the cooperation of several computing devices of different types (CPU, GPU, PHI) to process a stencil application on a single machine. Our scheme makes an intensive use of asynchronous computations and data transfers in order to obtain an efficient overlapping of both operations.

The scheme has been evaluated with different combinations of devices cooperation on a representative elevation map of the Alps region. Results show that our algorithm can provide significant gains either with two or three devices. It has been observed that better gains are obtained when the relative computing powers of the devices are closer.

Several extensions should be interesting such as studying the behavior of our scheme with larger grid sizes, including a dynamic load balancing by repartitioning the grid during the algorithm execution, as well as extending our scheme to cluster systems by adding explicit inter-machine communications.

References

1. Shuttle Radar Topography Mission (2000). https://lta.cr.usgs.gov/SRTM1Arc
2. Calandra, H., Dolbeau, R., Fortin, P., Lamotte, J.L., Said, I.: Evaluation of successive CPUs/APUs/GPUs based on an OpenCL finite difference stencil. In: 21st Euromicro International Conference on Parallel, Distributed and Network-Based Processing (PDP), February 2013
3. Contassot-Vivier, S., Vialle, S.: Algorithmic scheme for hybrid computing with CPU, Xeon-Phi/MIC and GPU devices on a single machine. In: ParCo 2015, Edinburgh, UK, September 2015
4. Courtès, L.: C language extensions for hybrid CPU/GPU programming with StarPU. Technical Report 8278, INRIA (2013)
5. Dijkstra, E.: A note on two problems in connexion with graphs. Numerische Mathematik **1**(1), 269–271 (1959). doi:10.1007/BF01386390
6. Fang, J., Varbanescu, A.L., Imbernon, B., Cecilia, J.M., Perez-Sanchez, H.: Parallel computation of non-bonded interactions in drug discovery: Nvidia GPUs vs. Intel Xeon Phi. In: 2nd International Work-Conference on Bioinformatics and Biomedical Engineering, Granada, Spain (2014)
7. Gaster, B., Howes, L., Kaeli, D., Mistry, P., Schaa, D.: Heterogeneous Computing with OpenCL, 2nd edn. Morgan Kaufmann, Burlington (2012). ISBN 9780124058941
8. Rao, J.S.: Optimization. In: Rao, J.S. (ed.) History of Rotating Machinery Dynamics. HMMS, vol. 20, pp. 341–351. Springer, Heidelberg (2011)
9. Jin, G., Lin, J., Endo, T.: Efficient utilization of memory hierarchy to enable the computation on bigger domains for stencil computation in CPU-GPU based systems. In: 2014 International Conference on High Performance Computing and Applications (ICHPCA), December 2014
10. Su, H., Wu, N., Wen, M., Zhang, C., Cai, X.: On the GPU-CPU performance portability of OpenCL for 3D stencil computations. In: Proceedings of the 2013 International Conference on Parallel and Distributed Systems, ICPADS 2013, Washington, DC, USA (2013)

11. Szustak, L., Rojek, K., Olas, T., Kuczynski, L., Halbiniak, K., Gepner, P.: Adaptation of MPDATA heterogeneous stencil computation to Intel Xeon Phi coprocessor. Sci. Prog. **2015**, Article ID 642705, 14 (2015). Doi:10.1155/2015/642705
12. Wende, F., Steinke, T.: Swendsen-Wang multi-cluster algorithm for the 2D/3D Ising model on Xeon Phi and GPU. In: Proceedings of the International Conference on High Performance Computing, Networking, Storage and Analysis, SC 2013, ACM, New York, NY, USA (2013)

GPU-Accelerated BWA-MEM Genomic Mapping Algorithm Using Adaptive Load Balancing

Ernst Joachim Houtgast[1]($\boxtimes$), Vlad-Mihai Sima[1],
Koen Bertels[2], and Zaid Al-Ars[2]

[1] Bluebee, Delft, The Netherlands
{ernst.houtgast,vlad.sima}@bluebee.com
[2] Faculty of EEMCS, Delft University of Technology, Delft, The Netherlands
{k.l.m.bertels,z.al-ars}@tudelft.nl

Abstract. Genomic sequencing is rapidly becoming a premier generator of Big Data, posing great computational challenges. Hence, acceleration of the algorithms used is of utmost importance. This paper presents a GPU-accelerated implementation of BWA-MEM, a widely used algorithm to map genomic sequences onto a reference genome. BWA-MEM contains three main computational functions: Seed Generation, Seed Extension and Output Generation. This paper discusses acceleration of the Seed Extension function on a GPU accelerator.

The GPU-based Extend kernel achieves three times higher performance and, by offloading the kernel onto an accelerator and overlapping its execution with the other functions, this results in an overall improvement to application-level execution time of up to 1.6x.

To ensure that using an accelerator always results in an overall performance improvement, especially when considering slower GPUs, an adaptive load balancing solution is introduced, which intelligently distributes work between host and GPU. This provides, compared to not using load balancing, up to +46 % more performance.

Keywords: Acceleration · BWA-MEM · GPU · High performance genomics

1 Introduction

Genomics information proves to be a valuable source of information to clinicians and researchers alike. The amount of data generated by Next Generation Sequencing (NGS) techniques is increasing at an explosive rate and will soon rival, if not overtake, other Big Data fields such as astronomy [14]. The raw sequenced data is processed by a complex pipeline of algorithms, a so-called genomics analysis pipeline. This data processing can require many days, even on a large cluster, and is becoming a bottleneck for applications dependent on

© Springer International Publishing Switzerland 2016
F. Hannig et al. (Eds.): ARCS 2016, LNCS 9637, pp. 130–142, 2016.
DOI: 10.1007/978-3-319-30695-7_10

genetic information. Hence, the challenges in genomics are shifting from sequencing towards data processing. Therefore, acceleration of bioinformatics algorithms is vital to relieve these bottlenecks.

One step in genomics analysis pipelines is to reconstruct the original genome from the millions of short reads produced using NGS. The purpose of subsequent steps in the pipeline is to find differences in the sequenced genetic material as compared to annotated reference material. The reconstruction step of a typical pipeline is represented by the mapping of the short reads onto a reference genome. BWA-MEM [9] is widely used in practice to this end.

This paper presents the following contributions:

- The first GPU-based implementation of the BWA-MEM algorithm.
- A load balancing algorithm to distribute reads between host and accelerator.
- A comparison of kernel and system-level results to an FPGA implementation.

The rest of this paper is organized as follows: Sect. 2 places this work into its context within related work. Section 3 discusses the BWA-MEM program operation and its main functions. Section 4 explains the modification of program scheduling to improve the acceleration potential. Section 5 describes the load balancing system. Section 6 discusses the GPU implementation. Section 7 presents the methods and results. The paper is concluded by Sect. 8.

2 Related Work

Although BWA-MEM [9] is one of the most popular mapping tools, there are numerous other mapping tools available. Most state-of-the-art mapping tools, such as [7], follow the Seed-and-Extend paradigm, explained below. Mapping tools generally differ in their mapping quality and speed. BWA-MEM offers a good compromise between mapping speed and quality. Many accelerated Seed-and-Extend-based mapping tools exist. However, in the field of bioinformatics, exactness of results is critical. To the authors' knowledge, the only accelerated versions of BWA-MEM are [1,5]. In [5], one of the BWA-MEM kernels is mapped onto a FPGA-based systolic array. This is further improved upon in [1], in which multiple BWA-MEM kernels are accelerated. The work here is similar to [5], but implements the systolic array on a GPU-based platform instead.

3 BWA-MEM Algorithm

BWA-MEM [9] is used to map sequenced reads onto a reference genome, such as the human genome. To illustrate the data sizes involved, a single run on a currently state-of-the-art sequencing platform, the Illumina HiSeq X, generates up to six billion pair-ended reads of 150 base pairs (or bp) in less than three days [6]. Even on a cluster, processing this data can take multiple days.

BWA-MEM is based on the Seed-and-Extend paradigm (refer to Fig. 1). For each read, *seed* locations on the genome are determined, exactly matching subsequences of the read and the reference. Then, Seed Extension is performed: an

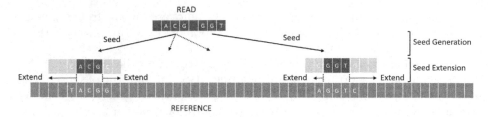

Fig. 1. BWA-MEM processes reads using the Seed-and-Extend paradigm: for each read, likely mapping locations on the reference are found by searching for exactly matching subsequences between the read and the reference, so called *seeds*. Then, these seeds are extended in both directions using a Smith-Waterman-like dynamic programming approach that allows for inexact matches. From all of these extended seeds, the best scoring alignment is selected.

attempt to extend these seeds in both directions using an alignment algorithm that allows for inexact matches. The best scoring alignment is chosen from all the resulting alignments. The final score is obtained by performing global alignment over the entire read against the chosen reference region.

3.1   BWA-MEM Profiling Results

The BWA-MEM algorithm main functions are: Seed Generation, Seed Extension, and Output Generation. To investigate the acceleration potential of BWA-MEM, the application has been profiled using the GCAT data set. The results are shown in Table 1, which reveals that acceleration of BWA-MEM is not trivial: processing is divided over multiple functions. As per Amdahl's law, speedup resulting from acceleration of any single function is limited. Greater speedup can only be achieved when accelerating multiple functions, such as in [1]. The table also shows that Seed Extension is the function limited by a computational bottleneck. For this reason, the Seed Extension function was chosen as initial optimization target. The other functions are not further analyzed in this paper.

Table 1. Results of BWA-MEM algorithm profiling (tests performed on Intel Core i7-4790 @ 4 GHz with the GCAT 150bp-se-small-indel data set)

Program kernel	Time	Bottleneck	Processing	Max speedup
Seed generation	46 %	Memory	Parallel	1.85x
Seed extension	43 %	Computation	Parallel	1.75x
Output generation	4 %	Memory	Parallel	1.04x
Other	7 %	I/O	Sequential	1.08x

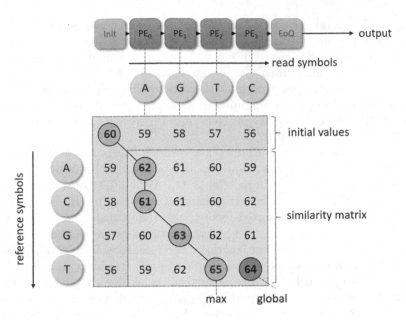

Fig. 2. Extend algorithm similarity matrix with initial score 60 showing local alignment with maximum score and global maximum score. Read symbols map one-to-one onto systolic array Processing Elements. Matrix entries only depend on top, top-left, and left neighbor. Thus, anti-diagonals can be processed in parallel. Differences compared to regular Smith-Waterman are: additional Initialization and End-of-Query blocks, non-zero initial values, and additional outputs, such as the global maximum (from [5]).

3.2   Seed Extension Functional Details

After Seed Generation, Seed Extension is invoked, which consists of two separate components: an outer function that loops over all seeds and determines whether it should be extended or not; and the actual Extend kernel. The number of times the Extend kernel is performed depends on the number of seeds found, which can range from none to thousands of seeds per short read. Since seeds generally only encompass a subsequence of the read, they may be extended in either direction, unless the seed includes the first and/or last symbol of the read.

The outer function keeps track of all earlier found extensions belonging to one read. If a later seed overlaps previous extensions by a certain amount, the seed is ignored. Seeds that are located close together on the reference are grouped into *chains*. Profiling shows that, in general, only one seed per chain is extended. Hence, a dependency exists between the extension of seeds. This dependency makes Extend less suitable for parallel execution: speculatively performing all extensions in parallel would cause significant work that would outweigh any benefit of parallelization. Therefore, Extend kernel executions for a read are performed serially. Instead, parallelism is extracted on two other levels: on the read-level by processing multiple reads at the same time, and by utilizing the parallelism inherent in the extension algorithm itself.

The extension algorithm is similar to the well-known Smith-Waterman dynamic programming algorithm [13], used to align two sequences to each other. Its basic operation is illustrated in Fig. 2. To compute the optimal alignment, a similarity matrix is filled, thus computing all possible alignments. The value of one cell in this matrix is only dependent on its top, top-left, and left- neighbor. Hence, anti-diagonals can be computed in parallel. A systolic array implementation is a natural way to map the problem onto Processing Elements when using an acceleration platform [10,15].

Most GPU-based Smith-Waterman acceleration efforts operate by mapping the complete processing of one alignment to a single core, in effect doing hundreds of sequence alignments in parallel [3,11]. As on a GPU the cores operate in lock-step, optimal performance is contingent on balancing the workload per core. Hence, alignments are sorted beforehand. Unfortunately, for BWA-MEM this method is unsuitable as Extend kernel invocations are generated dynamically and can have very different lengths. Therefore, to extract parallelism, the implementation described here operates in a systolic array-like manner.

As the Extend kernel is used to extend an earlier found match, in contrast to simply aligning sequences in complete isolation, it differs from regular Smith-Waterman in three ways, explained below. These differences are also illustrated in Fig. 2. The result is that the Extend kernel implementation is more complex than a normal Smith-Waterman implementation.

Non-zero Initial values: The initial values of the similarity matrix are not zero, but depend on the score of the seed that is being extended. Therefore, an Initial Value block is added in front of the systolic array.

Additional Outputs: The Extend kernel produces more outputs than the normal Smith-Waterman algorithm. Therefore, to obtain these, the output is post-processed by an additional End-of-Query block.

Partial Similarity Matrix Calculation: The algorithm uses a heuristic to restrict the similarity matrix calculations to only those cells that are likely to influence the end result.

4   Accelerated Program Architecture

In this section, changes made to enable an accelerated implementation of the BWA-MEM algorithm are described. The main goal was to drastically reduce the number of Seed Extension invocations. The original BWA-MEM algorithm works as shown in Algorithm 1. The input data is processed in batches. For each read in a batch, Seed Generation is performed first; then, Seed Extension; and finally, Output Generation. Note that for each read, Seed Generation and Seed Extension are performed directly after one another.

Applying heterogeneous acceleration of the Seed Extension function call directly to this structure would imply accelerator invocation for every individual read, along with the accompanying data transfers from and to the device's memory. As typically many millions of reads are processed, the resulting overhead

Algorithm 1. Original Program Structure

Input: a batch of n reads
Output: n aligned reads
1: **for** $i = 1$ to n **do**
2:     Seed Generation(read i)
3:     Seed Extension(read i)
4: **end for**
5: **for** $i = 1$ to n **do**
6:     Output Generation(read i)
7: **end for**

would be likely to nullify any gains resulting from more efficient execution. Moreover, acceleration of a single alignment may not even be faster than processing it on the host. Often, speedup is obtained by leveraging the massive parallelism inherent in the data set to be processed, which accelerators are able to exploit.

Therefore, the BWA-MEM program structure has been refactored in order to be more receptive to heterogeneous execution. The refactored structure is given in Algorithm 2. Note that the workload has been subdivided into chunks of reads. For each chunk, first, Seed Generation is performed for all reads in the chunk. Then, the Seed Extension function is executed for all the reads in the chunk. Then, the algorithm proceeds to the next chunk. After all chunks are finished, Output Generation is performed. This setup requires temporary data storage, which is in the order of tens of megabytes. However, this approach is far more suitable to acceleration, as in this situation a single accelerator invocation suffices to perform Seed Extension for the entire chunk, as opposed to one invocation per read. The reduction in number of invocations is on the same order of magnitude as the chunk size, which is typically in the order of tens of thousands.

Algorithm 2. Refactored Program Structure

Input: a batch of n reads
Output: n aligned reads
1: **for** $i = 1$ to $n/chunksize$ **do**
2:     **for** $j = 1$ to $chunksize$ **do**
3:         Seed Generation(read $j + (i - 1) \times chunksize$)
4:     **end for**
5:     **for** $j = 1$ to $chunksize$ **do**
6:         Seed Extension(read $j + (i - 1) \times chunksize$)
7:     **end for**
8: **end for**
9: **for** $i = 1$ to n **do**
10:     Output Generation(read i)
11: **end for**

Note that Algorithm 2 has been implemented in such a way that Seed Generation and Seed Extension are overlapped in a pipelined fashion. Hence, ideally, the execution of Seed Extension is almost completely hidden, resulting in a maximum theoretical speedup of 1.75x, as predicted by Amdahl's law.

5 Adaptive Load Balancing Strategy

To accelerate the Seed Extension function (lines 5–7 of Algorithm 2), a GPU is used to assist the host in processing the Seed Extension work. To ensure optimal speedup, even for slower GPUs, an adaptive load balancing strategy is used to determine the optimal division of work between host and GPU, controlled by a Load Balancing Factor parameter (LBF). The goal of this algorithm is to minimize the idle time on both host and GPU. Otherwise, simply offloading all the work onto a slower GPU might result in an application slowdown, instead of in an application speedup. The LBF is recalculated after each batch of reads as shown in Algorithm 3. As the amount of work per batch seems mostly stable, idle time is minimized by measuring the host and the GPU processing times to determine their respective busy percentage during the previous batch and modifying the LBF accordingly (similar to [2]). Given a sufficiently fast GPU, all the work can be offloaded from the host. However, for a slower GPU, only part of the work may be performed on the GPU, hence LBF will be less than 1. The load balancing should result in a speedup in all cases though. The algorithm uses smoothing in order to prevent oscillations of the LBF.

Algorithm 3. Adaptive Load Balancing Strategy

Input: HostBusyPct, GPUBusyPct, LBF_{old}
Output: LBF_{new}
 1: **for** each batch of reads **do**
 2:     $LBF_{old} = LBF_{new}$
 3:     $LBF_{new} = (HostBusyPct / GPUBusyPct) \times LBF_{old}$
 4:     $LBF_{new} = \min(1, (LBF_{new} + LBF_{old}) / 2)$
 5: **end for**

---

6 Implementation Details

The GPU implementation of Seed Extension consists of an outer loop and the actual Extend kernel. These have been implemented as separate kernels using the NVIDIA CUDA Runtime API. In this section, the GPU kernels and the optimizations that were applied are described in more detail.

6.1 Seed Extension Function Kernels

As discussed before (see Algorithm 2), reads are sent in large batches to the GPU. Each read is processed independently by the outer loop kernel, a control function that loops over the seeds and, using CUDA Dynamic Parallelism (available from

Table 2. Summary of NVIDIA CUDA compiler & profiling information

CUDA kernel	# Calls	Time	Registers	Shared memory	Threads
Outer loop	1	66 %	78	0 kB	1
Extend multipass long	24657	17 %	34	2.9 kB	32
Extend wide	17912	11 %	54	3.3 kB	1–131
Extend multipass short	9695	3 %	34	1.7 kB	32
Extend single pass	17640	3 %	30	0.5 kB	32

CUDA Compute Capability 3.5 onward), instantiates Extend kernels as needed. This function only runs as a single thread. For the Extend kernel itself, four versions of the kernel have been implemented to optimize register and shared memory usage to improve occupancy. These are described in the next section. Table 2 provides some information on the CUDA kernels in use.[1] From the table, it is clear that most time is spent in the outer loop, which is characterized by random memory accesses and branching operations.

6.2 Extend Systolic Array Kernels

The basic idea of all the Extend kernels is their implementation as a systolic array, similar to [5]. The largest advantage of using a systolic array is the possibility to extract the available parallelism on anti-diagonals while calculating the similarity matrix. Using a systolic array, calculation of the entire array takes $O(|\text{Reference}| + |\text{Extension}|)$ execution time, instead of $O(|\text{Reference}| \times |\text{Extension}|)$. For larger problem sizes, this can result in a large speedup compared to a serialized implementation. The drawback of a systolic implementation is the often low overall efficiency: in general, not all the Processing Elements (or PEs) of the array can be kept busy. Full utilization is only attained during calculation of the "widest" diagonals of the matrix. For the other diagonals, PEs at the start and/or at the end of the array will be idle, lowering overall efficiency. Moreover, for physically implemented systolic arrays, unnecessary latency is incurred when processing reads shorter than the array itself. Also, the number of PEs determines the maximum length of the extension that can be processed, as one PE is required for each read symbol that is to be extended. Longer reads can be processed by making multiple passes over the matrix, with temporary data stored between passes, as in [12]. The GPU implementation does not suffer from these issues as the systolic array length is dynamically instantiated.

The GPU implementation maps read symbols onto the systolic array PEs, similar to Fig. 2. The PEs are implemented as CUDA cores, where a CUDA thread performs the calculations of that PE. CUDA threads are grouped into blocks of 32 threads, a *warp*, which all perform exactly the same instruction.

---

[1] These numbers are obtained while executing the first 50,000 reads of the GCAT 150bp-se-small-indel data set using the *nvprof* and *nvcc* tools.

A warp is the basic unit of action in an NVIDIA GPU. The *Ext. wide* kernel is the most straightforward systolic array implementation. On the left of Fig. 3, is shown how the similarity matrix is processed over time. As many warps as necessary are allocated to process the matrix. After each cycle, PEs exchange data through the on-chip Shared Memory cache. For larger extension lengths, this can require a large amount of shared memory. Moreover, from Fig. 3 it is clear that many PEs will be idle for much of the time.

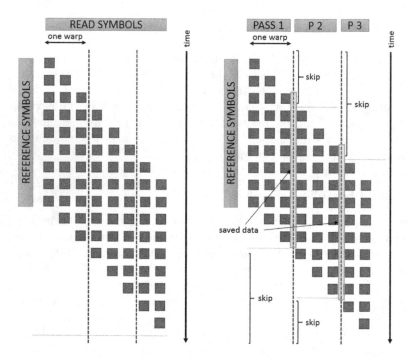

Fig. 3. Systolic array-based GPU Extend kernel implementation. Extension symbols are mapped one-to-one on CUDA cores, reference symbols are fed each iteration of the loop. After each iteration, data is exchanged through shared memory (left). The single warp-based implementation makes multiple passes over the array (right). Unnecessary iterations are skipped over and per-pass temporary data is saved in shared memory.

Therefore, a number of kernels have been implemented designed to process the matrix on a single warp, which corresponds to 32-symbol wide columns. This is shown on the right of Fig. 3. Multiple passes are made over the matrix, with intermediate data between passes saved into shared memory. Data exchange between cores is implemented using shuffle instructions, avoiding the use of shared memory. Unnecessary iterations per pass are skipped, drastically reducing idle time. For example, extending a size 150 reference against a size 100 extension would, in the simple implementation, result in on average 60 cores out of 100 being busy; however, for the warp-based implementation, 27 out of 32 are busy. Efficiency is 40 % higher. The *Ext. multipass long* and *Ext. multipass short* kernels differ in the available amount of statically allocated storage space. The *Ext. single pass* kernel is used when the entire matrix fits within a single warp (i.e., 32 read symbols or smaller), and hence only one pass is needed. In this case, no intermediate data from the matrix needs to be saved in shared memory. The use of the different kernels provides a 20 % improvement to performance.

6.3   GPU-Specific Optimizations

Apart from the multiple Extend kernel implementations, the following optimizations were applied and are worth mentioning:

Coalesced Memory Access: Memory accesses are coalesced as much as possible. In contrast to a normal systolic array, reference symbols are loaded in one large coalesced access. Read symbols are obtained similarly.

Shuffle Instructions: Shuffle instructions are used to remove the need to use shared memory for data exchange between PEs. This is only possible within a warp, hence the need for a multiple pass implementation.

Dynamic Parallelism: To reduce register pressure, the outer controlling function uses only a single thread, subsequently invoking Extend kernels with as many threads as needed using CUDA Dynamic Parallelism.

7   Results

Profiling and performance tests were performed on a machine with an Intel Core i7-4790 (four cores, Hyper-Threading enabled) running at 4.0 GHz, with 32 GB of DDR3 memory. The system contains two NVIDIA GeForce GTX TITAN X cards, with 3,072 CUDA cores each, running at up to 1,076 MHz, and offering Compute Capability 5.0. The GPU implementation requires at least Compute Capability 3.5 in order to be able to use dynamic parallelism. NVIDIA CUDA Runtime API version 7.5 was used.

The 150bp-se-small-indel data set from the Genome Comparison & Analytic Testing (GCAT) framework [4] was used to map about eight million 150 base pair reads onto the UCSC HG19 reference human genome. The GCAT online sequence alignment quality comparison service was used to verify that results of the GPU-accelerated version are similar to those obtained with the original BWA-MEM algorithm. BWA-MEM version 0.7.7 was used [8].

7.1   Performance Results and Scaling

Table 3 shows the Extend kernel execution time and overall application performance for single and dual GPU execution using eight CPU threads. The results of the FPGA implementation from [5] are also given. As the platforms are non-identical (they use 2x Intel Xeon E5-2643 at 3.3 GHz), relative Extend

140   E.J. Houtgast et al.

Table 3. Execution time and speedup on the GCAT alignment quality benchmark

Platform	Test	Extend kernel		Overall program		
		Time	Speedup	Time	Speedup	Throughput
GPU-Accelerated	CPU only	218 s	-	510 s	-	2.4 Mbp/s
	CPU+Single GPU	118 s	1.9x	468 s	1.09x	2.6 Mbp/s
	CPU+Dual GPU	73 s	3.0x	422 s	1.21x	2.9 Mbp/s
FPGA-Accelerated	CPU only	167 s	-	530 s	-	2.3 Mbp/s
	CPU+FPGA	62 s	2.7x	365 s	1.45x	3.3 Mbp/s

kernel times differ, mostly due to the different CPUs. Results are normalized to throughput in base pairs per second, to facilitate comparison of numbers.

The Extend dynamic programming kernel is three times faster compared to CPU-only execution. Even though execution of this kernel is overlapped with the functions executed on the host CPU, the results show that, in contrast to the FPGA implementation, the GPU-accelerated version is unable to hide the entire Seed Extension function time, due to the large overhead of the outer function. Performance results for varying CPU thread counts are given in Fig. 4. The dual GPU setup is able to achieve a speedup of 1.6x for up to two threads, or 1.5x for four threads. The maximum speedup of 1.75x is not achieved, due to batching overhead and since GPU on-chip memory limitations allow only 99.5 % of Seed Extensions to be processed on the GPU. The remaining reads, with thousands of seeds, are processed on the host and still require about 4 % of overall host execution time, reducing the maximum achievable speedup accordingly.

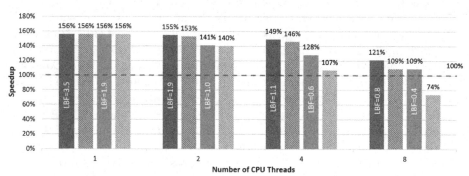

Fig. 4. Overall application speedup for varying number of CPU threads and single and dual GPUs. Results shown with load balancing enabled and disabled. The adaptive load balancing ensures efficient host and accelerator usage and provides an overall application speedup even for GPU-constrained scenarios, which might otherwise result in an overall application slowdown.

7.2 Load Balancing Results

An adaptive load balancing algorithm was implemented to ensure optimal benefit from the use of acceleration. Figure 4 shows that the load balancing is effective: for increasing number of CPU threads, the load balanced single GPU scenario provides similar or better performance as compared to non-load balanced execution, improving performance by up to 46 %. Note that execution using eight threads results in a slowdown on the non-load balanced situation, due to a mismatch in host and accelerator performance. For a dual GPU setup, load balancing still provides a benefit, but only when using eight threads. The unbounded LBF value is also given. This shows that the dual GPU setup is able to perform up to 90 % more work than a single GPU setup.

8 Conclusion

This paper describes a GPU-accelerated version of the BWA-MEM genomic mapping algorithm. It was possible to hide the execution time of the Seed Extension function, one of the three main computational functions, by overlapping its execution with the other program functions for up to four CPU threads. Speedup of up to three times is achieved for the Extend kernel, which translates in an overall improvement to BWA-MEM execution time of up to 1.6x. This can save days of processing time on real-world data sets.

A generally applicable adaptive load balancing strategy was implemented to ensure an efficient division of work between the host and the GPU, improving performance and ensuring application speedup even for mismatched host and accelerator performance. The load balancing algorithm provides an improvement to performance of up to 46 %, compared to non-load balanced execution.

Although the work here focuses on BWA-MEM, a widely used genomic mapping tool, the approach is valid for many similar Seed-and-Extend-based bioinformatics algorithms. Future work will focus on the reorganization of the outer Seed Extension function to make it better suitable towards parallel execution, and will also focus on porting other parts of BWA-MEM onto the GPU.

Acknowledgments. The authors would like to thank the people at the Neuroscience Department of the Erasmus Medical Center for kindly granting access to their computing facilities for performance tests.

References

1. Ahmed, N., Sima, V.M., Houtgast, E., Bertels, K., Al-Ars, Z.: Heterogeneous hardware/software acceleration of the BWA-MEM DNA alignment algorithm. In: Proceedings of the IEEE/ACM International Conference on Computer-Aided Design, ICCAD 2015, pp. 240–246. IEEE Press, Piscataway, NJ, USA (2015). http://dl.acm.org/citation.cfm?id=2840819.2840854

2. Augonnet, C., Thibault, S., Namyst, R., Wacrenier, P.A.: StarPU: a unified platform for task scheduling on heterogeneous multicore architectures. Concurrency Comput. Pract. Experience **23**(2), 187–198 (2011)
3. Hasan, L., Kentie, M., Al-Ars, Z.: DOPA: GPU-based protein alignment using database and memory access optimizations. BMC Res. Notes **4**(1), 261 (2011)
4. Highnam, G., Wang, J.J., Kusler, D., Zook, J., Vijayan, V., Leibovich, N., Mittelman, D.: An analytical framework for optimizing variant discovery from personal genomes. Nature Comm. **6** (2015)
5. Houtgast, E., Sima, V., Bertels, K., Al-Ars, Z.: An FPGA-based systolic array to accelerate the BWA-MEM genomic mapping algorithm. In: International Conference on Embedded Computer Systems: Architectures, Modeling, and Simulation (2015)
6. Illumina: HiSeq X Specification Sheet. http://www.illumina.com/content/dam/illumina-marketing/documents/products/datasheets/datasheet-hiseq-x-ten.pdf. Accessed 15 July 2015
7. Langmead, B., Salzberg, S.L.: Fast gapped-read alignment with Bowtie 2. Nat. Methods **9**(4), 357–359 (2012)
8. Li, H.: Burrows-Wheeler Aligner. http://bio-bwa.sourceforge.net/. Accessed 04 November 2014
9. Li, H.: Aligning Sequence Reads, Clone Sequences and Assembly Contigs with BWA-MEM. arXiv preprint arxiv:1303.3997 (2013)
10. Liu, W., Schmidt, B., Voss, G., Schroder, A., Muller-Wittig, W.: Bio-sequence database scanning on a GPU. In: 20th International Parallel and Distributed Processing Symposium, 2006, IPDPS 2006, p. 8. IEEE (2006)
11. Liu, Y., Wirawan, A., Schmidt, B.: CUDASW++ 3.0: accelerating Smith-Waterman protein database search by coupling CPU and GPU SIMD instructions. BMC Bioinformatics **14**(1), 117 (2013)
12. Oliver, T., Schmidt, B., Maskell, D.: Hyper customized processors for bio-sequence database scanning on FPGAs. In: Proceedings of the 2005 ACM/SIGDA 13th International Symposium on Field-Programmable Gate Arrays, pp. 229–237. ACM (2005)
13. Smith, T.F., Waterman, M.S.: Identification of common molecular subsequences. J. Mol. Biol. **147**(1), 195–197 (1981)
14. Stephens, Z., Lee, S., Faghri, F., Campbell, R., Zhai, C., Efron, M., et al.: Big data: astronomical or genomical? PLoS Biol. **13**(7), e1002195 (2015)
15. Yu, C.W., Kwong, K., Lee, K.H., Leong, P.H.W.: A Smith-Waterman systolic cell. In: Lysaght, P., Rosenstiel, W. (eds.) New Algorithms, Architectures and Applications for Reconfigurable Computing, pp. 291–300. Springer, Heidelberg (2005)

Task Variants with Different Scratchpad Memory Consumption in Multi-Task Environments

Martin Böhnert[✉] and Christoph Scholl

Department of Computer Science,
University of Freiburg, Freiburg im Breisgau, Germany
{boehnert,scholl}@informatik.uni-freiburg.de

Abstract. We present an approach which schedules task sets using scratchpad memory (*SPM*) in an embedded multi-task system with real-time constraints. A new task model is introduced, where each task is represented by different pre-compiled *variants* which differ in the amount of scratchpad memory used. A higher use of SPM leads to smaller run-times of a task. Moreover, the energy consumption is reduced by replacing memory accesses by SPM accesses. Our heuristic method assembles a task set of these variants by choosing one variant per task. After selecting candidates from the pre-computed set of task variants, the task set can be handled by a real-time scheduler like EDF. Our approach is able to build a new incremental task set and feasible transition in dynamically changing environments. Furthermore we show an extension of our approach to multicore environments.

1 Introduction

Designing embedded systems with minimal energy consumption is becoming increasingly important. The need for energy savings has manifold reasons. Apart from problems stemming from limited energy resources on earth, there are also problems with heat dissipation by processors and corresponding cooling problems. Moreover, embedded systems are used in more and more application areas where their energy supply has to rely on batteries.

There are several approaches to minimize energy in embedded processors and controllers. One particular aspect we consider in this paper is the usage of scratchpad memories (*SPM*) [3,15] instead of conventional caches. Scratchpad memories (*SPM*) are fast and located near to the CPU. Since they usually have no access penalty through wait states at accesses, they provide fast access to often used data. Moreover, SPM accesses need less energy than main memory accesses. In contrast to caches, SPMs are managed by the programmer / compiler, who decides which data is located in this memory. SPMs which are equal in memory size to caches, need no parallel comparison logic and therefore less chip area and less energy.

We use scratchpad memory to reduce processor utilization and energy consumption in a multi-task environment. More precisely, for each task we provide

© Springer International Publishing Switzerland 2016
F. Hannig et al. (Eds.): ARCS 2016, LNCS 9637, pp. 143–156, 2016.
DOI: 10.1007/978-3-319-30695-7_11

several pre-compiled *variants* using different amounts of scratchpad memory, i.e. we assume a framework like [24] which is able to map memory addresses either to main memory or scratchpad memory and produces different executables depending on a given upper limit to the amount of SPM provided to the task. Usually, the WCET (worst case execution time) of a task is shorter and its worst case energy consumption is lower, if it has more SPM at its disposal. [19], e.g., provides a heuristical method which minimizes run-times and energy consumption by analyzing the code of a task and by assigning code and/or data memory to available SPM of a given size. Thus, each tasks variant is connected with a triple of WCET, SPM, and energy consumption. Several tasks have to share both the CPU and the scratchpad memory. Given a certain amount of scratchpad memory in the system, we select for each task a *variant* such that

1. the sum of the SPM consumptions of all selected task variants does not exceed the available SPM,
2. the CPU utilization caused by the selected task variants does not exceed 1 and
3. the energy consumption is minimized under those constraints.

If the resulting CPU utilization factor is smaller than 1, then we have the additional opportunity to decrease the processor frequency (until the utilization factor is 1) which minimizes the energy consumption further.

The given problem resembles the Multiple Choice Knapsack Problem (*MCKP*) [10, 16] and can be solved exactly by 0-1-Integer-Linear-Programming. Since we need fast solutions in dynamically changing real-time system, we developed a heuristic which is much faster than the exact solution, and it compares well in quality though. Additionally our algorithm provides incremental solutions when a new task enters a system. This solution incorporates a feasible transition from the first set of task variants to the second without exceeding the available amount of SPM or processor resources. We extended our heuristics to multicore systems where exactly one task variant has to be allocated to exactly one processor.

Related Work. In [15] a first approach distributing data between SPM and external DRAM was presented which accelerates memory accesses for memory architectures using both SPM and caches. Later on, [3] showed, that SPMs have significant lower area and power consumption compared to caches. They also presented a simple SPM allocation method outperforming caches. [19] statically mapped global data memory objects and program code to SPM of a single task. They formulated a Knapsack problem with energy minimization as the optimization goal.

Many publications confirm that SPMs are useful for reducing of area, runtimes and energy consumptions. Most methods use profile runs to determine frequently accessed data and executed code as a basis for SPM allocation. *Static* SPM allocation is used in [2,18] for global data and stack variables, and in [1,23] for code. *Dynamic* SPM allocation is used in [5,21]. Here, global data, stack, or even heap variables are dynamically allocated to SPM at runtime.

More recent methods looked into the minimization of WCETs as well which is more important for embedded real-time systems [8,9,20]. The results show, that by increasing the amount of available SPM, it is possible to decrease the WCET and the energy consumption of a task. This is the basic assumption underlying our approach.

Our approach is neither restricted to any special method for assigning data and/or code to an SPM nor to the application of static or dynamic methods for allocating SPM. For our method it is only important that for each task variant there exists a fixed upper bound on the size of the SPM used by this variant; our method is completely orthogonal to the question *how* this amount of SPM is used by the task variant.

More recent methods consider SPM usage also in multi-task environments. A first approach was presented in [22]. In this work, a statically scheduled system with a fixed number of processes was considered. In the 'saving' approach, the whole SPM is given to the currently active task, the SPM contents are saved and restored at each context switch. Our method is closer to the so called 'non-saving' approach. Here, the SPM is split into disjoint regions, at most one for each task. In contrast to this method, our approach considers several task variants to select from instead of one, it can handle a dynamic number of tasks, it is integrated into the scheduler, and selects a schedulable set of variants for the tasks with the goal of minimizing the energy consumption.

The work in [7] uses the same SPM sharing strategies as [22], but is suitable for *dynamic* multitasking systems. The shares are redistributed whenever a task enters or leaves the system. This approach relies on the existence of an MMU in the memory architectures as it uses page faults to copy new pages into the SPM. In contrast to our approach, [7] has difficulties in real-time systems, since it is hard to provide tight WCET estimates with a strategy based on page faults. Furthermore, this approach is not designed to give guarantees regarding schedulability of a real-time task set.

[25,26] look into the 'saving approach' discussed above for sharing SPM between several tasks. They propose and analyze refined schemes for saving and restoring SPM data during context switches. An earlier work [17] proposes hardware support by DMA (Direct Memory Access) to reduce the cost of copying between scratchpad and main memory.

The remaining paper is structured as follows: We discuss the preliminaries of this work in Sect. 2. Section 3 presents our basic idea and gives an exact formulation of the resulting optimization problem. We give a heuristical solution to this problem in Sect. 4. In Sect. 7 the approach is evaluated by experiments. Finally, Sect. 8 concludes the paper with a summary.

2   Preliminaries

We assume a set of periodic tasks which can be preempted and are scheduled by the Earliest Deadline First (EDF) scheduler [13]. If we do not consider task *variants*, then a task τ_i is specified by its worst-case computation time C_i and its period T_i. We assume that the relative (hard) deadline D_i of a task is the same as the period T_i. The utilization factor U of a task set of n independent periodic tasks is defined as $U = \sum_{i=1}^{n} \frac{C_i}{T_i}$. Such a task set is schedulable with EDF if and only if $U \leq 1$. This holds for EDF scheduling for a single processor system. For simplicity we first assume a single processor in this work.

Our task variant selection problem is a generalization of the Multiple Choice Knapsack Problem (*MCKP*). In the Multiple Choice Knapsack Problem (*MCKP*) [16] exactly one item from each of n classes N_i is selected such that the profit is maximized:

Multiple Choice Knapsack Problem

Given: n classes N_i of items with weights $w_{ij} \in \mathbb{N}$ and profits $p_{ij} \in \mathbb{N}$ ($1 \leq i \leq n$, $j \in N_i$), a capacity $c \in \mathbb{N}$.

Find: Maximize $\sum_{i=1}^{n} \sum_{j \in N_i} x_{ij} p_{ij}$ with $\sum_{i=1}^{n} \sum_{j \in N_i} x_{ij} w_{ij} \leq c$, $\sum_{j \in N_i} x_{ij} = 1$ ($1 \leq i \leq n$), $x_{ij} \in \{0, 1\}$ ($1 \leq i \leq n$, $j \in N_i$).

($x_{ij} = 1$ iff the item j from class N_i is selected.)

MCKP is an NP-complete problem. There is a number of exact solution methods such as dynamic programming, branch-and-bound, or 0-1 Integer Linear Programming [6,12,16].

3   Basic Idea and Problem Formulation

As already mentioned in the introduction, our basic idea is to use different code variants for each task which differ in the amount of SPM that can be used. If a variant is allowed to use more SPM, this usually means that the energy consumption and the WCET is reduced [9]. The selection of variants for the different tasks has to be done in a way that *(a)* the sum of the SPM consumptions of all selected task variants does not exceed the available SPM, *(b)* the CPU utilization caused by the selected task variants does not exceed 1, and *(c)* the energy consumption is minimized under those constraints. If the utilization factor resulting from the selected variants is larger than 1, then the task set with its variants is not schedulable with the given amount of SPM in the system. If the utilization factor is smaller than 1, it may be possible to reduce the processor frequency in order to save even more energy.

In the following we assume that all computations are done with worst case execution times resulting from the maximal processor frequency. If a schedulable selection of task variants has been found, then the processor frequency can be adjusted accordingly. So our algorithm works with worst case execution *times* instead of cycles and we always mean the worst case execution times under the maximal processor frequency.

Furthermore, we assume a system without caches to avoid unstable WCET estimations for different task variant combinations and thus differing cache hit and miss patterns.

We assume a size M of the scratchpad memory in the system. Each task τ_i is connected with a task period T_i and a set of variants V_i. Each variant j in V_i is connected with the following properties:

- An SPM consumption M_{ij} which represents a fraction $s_{ij} = \frac{M_{ij}}{M}$ of the total SPM in the system.
- A (worst case) computation time C_{ij} leading to a contribution $u_{ij} = \frac{C_{ij}}{T_i}$ to the processor utilization factor.
- A (worst case) energy consumption E_{ij}. When computing the average energy consumption of the whole system, the energy consumptions of single task variants have to be weighted by the fraction of time the task variant is running on the processor, which is equal to u_{ij}. Thus, the task variant contributes $e_{ij} = u_{ij} \cdot E_{ij}$ to the average energy consumption.

Definition 1. *We call* $s_{ij} = \frac{M_{ij}}{M}$ *the* scratchpad memory share *(or* memory share *for short),* $u_{ij} = \frac{C_{ij}}{T_i}$ *the* utilization share, *and* $e_{ij} = u_{ij} \cdot E_{ij}$ *the* energy contribution *of the task variant.*

Altogether, if a task τ_i has v_i variants, it is represented by a set

$$V_i = \{(s_{ij}, u_{ij}, e_{ij}) \mid 1 \le j \le v_i\}.$$

Definition 2. *For all* $1 \le i \le n$ *let* $curr_i$ *(with* $1 \le curr_i \le v_i$*) be the selected task variant for task* τ_i. *By analogy to the processor utilization factor we define the* SPM utilization factor *of the selected task variants by* $S := \sum_{i=1}^{n} s_{i curr_i}$. *The* average energy consumption *is given by* $E := \sum_{i=1}^{n} e_{i curr_i}$.

Now we have the requirements that the sum of scratchpad memory shares s_{ij} and the sum of the utilization shares u_{ij} over all selected variants is ≤ 1. The average energy consumption has to be minimized. Thus, we arrive at the following problem formulation:

Task Variant Selection (TVS)
Given: n tasks τ_i with sets
$V_i = \{(s_{ij}, u_{ij}, e_{ij}) \mid 1 \le j \le v_i\}$ of task variants, $s_{ij}, u_{ij} \in (0, 1] \subseteq \mathbb{Q}$,
$e_{ij} \in \mathbb{Q}_{\ge 0}$ $(1 \le i \le n, 1 \le j \le v_i)$.
Find: Minimize $\sum_{i=1}^{n} \sum_{j=1}^{v_i} x_{ij} e_{ij}$ with
$\sum_{i=1}^{n} \sum_{j=1}^{v_i} x_{ij} s_{ij} \le 1$, $\sum_{i=1}^{n} \sum_{j=1}^{v_i} x_{ij} u_{ij} \le 1$, $\sum_{j=1}^{v_i} x_{ij} = 1$ $(1 \le i \le n)$,
$x_{ij} \in \{0, 1\}$ $(1 \le i \le n, 1 \le j \le v_i)$.
$(x_{ij} = 1$ iff variant j of task τ_i is selected.$)$

It is easy to see that the TVS problem generalizes the Multiple Choice Knapsack Problem, since it has two cost constraints (for processor *and* SPM utilization factors) instead of one. It can be solved exactly by 0-1-ILP.

4   Heuristical Solution

Especially if we apply our approach in the context of dynamically changing real-time embedded systems, we need a fast solution to the Task Variant Selection (TVS) problem. For this reason we present a fast heuristical solution here.

In a first step we compute a feasible solution, i.e., a solution where both the sum of selected s_{ij} and the sum of selected u_{ij} is less or equal to 1. If we find a feasible solution, then we further minimize the energy consumption while maintaining feasibility in step 2.

4.1   Step 1: Computing a Feasible Solution

In the first step we do not yet look at energy contributions e_{ij}, but concentrate on computing a feasible solution.

Step 1.1: Filtering Wrt. Pareto Optimality. At first, we remove all task variants which are not Pareto optimal wrt. (s_{ij}, u_{ij}). If the set $V_i = \{(s_{ij}, u_{ij}) \mid 1 \leq j \leq v_i\}$ of task variants for task τ_i contains a pair of variants x and y with $s_{ix} \geq s_{iy}$ and $u_{ix} \geq u_{iy}$, then we remove variant x from V_i, since variant x is not helpful in finding feasible solutions.

Step 1.2: Initial Solution. For a feasible solution, we have to competing goals: Reduction of the processor utilisation below 1, while staying inside the SPM limit.

So we construct a *balanced* initial solution which tries to avoid large scratch-pad memory and utilization shares *at the same time*. To do so, for a fixed task τ_i we compute the Euclidean lengths $l(s_{ij}, u_{ij}) := \sqrt{s_{ij}^2 + u_{ij}^2}$ of all vectors (s_{ij}, u_{ij}) $(1 \leq j \leq v_i)$, and select the task variant $start_i$ with the minimal length to be included into the initial solution.

The intuition is that we try to avoid long vectors which have a large memory share or a large utilization share or both. For this step to make sense, it is important that the memory and utilization shares are *normalized* in a way that we require both $\sum_{i=1}^{n} s_{i\,start_i} \leq 1$ and $\sum_{i=1}^{n} u_{i\,start_i} \leq 1$ with the same upper bound of 1 for a feasible solution. Nevertheless, this approach is only a heuristical method to obtain a good initial solution. It still may be the case that $\sum_{i=1}^{n} s_{i\,start_i} > 1$, $\sum_{i=1}^{n} u_{i\,start_i} > 1$ or both. For this reason, we try to improve the initial solution by exchanging task variants.

Step 1.3: Exchange Based Algorithm. The exchange based algorithm always holds a current solution consisting of one task variant $curr_i$ ($1 \leq curr_i \leq v_i$) for each task τ_i. It starts with the initial solution, i.e., with $curr_i := start_i$ for all $1 \leq i \leq n$. The exchange based algorithm is a greedy approach; a task variant which has previously been removed from the solution is never brought back into the solution.

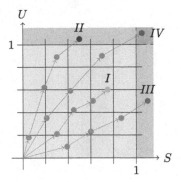

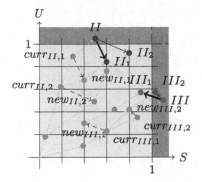

Fig. 1. The graph illustrates 4 different cases for the exchange based algorithm. *I* corresponds to a feasible solution, *II* and *III* violate only a single constraint (either the utilization U or the memory S), *IV* violates both.

Fig. 2. The choice of possible exchange partners is illustrated. In case *II* the two choices $curr_{II,1}$ and $curr_{II,2}$ are considered for exchange with either $new_{II,1}$ or $new_{II,2}$. Because the difference vector $diff_{new_{II,1},curr_{II,1}}$ has the minimum gradient, this exchange will be taken. Case *III* is analogous.

The algorithm differentiates between 4 cases for the current solution which are illustrated by Fig. 1. Each task variant $curr_i$ corresponds to a vector $(s_{i curr_i}, u_{i curr_i})$. The sum of all vectors over all tasks corresponds to the pair $(\sum_{i=1}^{n} s_{i curr_i}, \sum_{i=1}^{n} u_{i curr_i})$ which gives for the current solution the scratchpad memory utilization factor S and the processor utilization factor U. If we already have a feasible solution (case I), we stop exchanging in step 1 and continue with Step 2. Otherwise we are looking for a new exchange candidate.

An exchange candidate is rated by the difference vector $diff_{new_i, curr_i} := (s_{i new_i} - s_{i curr_i}, u_{i new_i} - u_{i curr_i})$, where new_i of task τ_i is considered a candidate for $curr_i$. Note that in all difference vectors $diff_{new_i, curr_i}$ either the first or the second component is negative. If both components were negative (positive), then variant $curr_i$ (new_i) would not be Pareto-optimal and would have been removed in Step 1.1. The next exchange is determined based on the gradients of vectors $diff_{new_i, curr_i}$ depending on the following cases II, III, and IV, see Fig. 2.

- Case II: $\sum_{i=1}^{n} s_{i curr_i} \leq 1$, $\sum_{i=1}^{n} u_{i curr_i} > 1$: We choose an exchange candidate which reduces the processor utilization factor, i.e., a candidate new_i with $u_{i new_i} - u_{i curr_i} < 0$. Among those candidates we choose the one with minimal (negative) gradient

$$\frac{u_{i new_i} - u_{i curr_i}}{s_{i new_i} - s_{i curr_i}} \tag{1}$$

of the difference vector $diff_{new_i, curr_i}$. The intuition for this decision is that the gain wrt. processor utilization factor U *relative to* the penalty wrt. SPM untilization factor S is maximized.
- Case III: $\sum_{i=1}^{n} s_{i curr_i} > 1$, $\sum_{i=1}^{n} u_{i curr_i} \leq 1$: Here we have to choose an exchange candidate which reduces the SPM utilization factor, i.e., a candidate

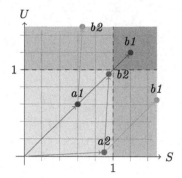

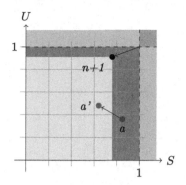

Fig. 3. Case IV of the initial solution: In the example task a has variants $a1$ and $a2$, task b variants $b1$ and $b2$. The initial solution consisting of $a1$ and $b1$ violates both constraints. After the first exchange of $a1$ with $a2$ only the U-constraint is violated, after the second exchange of $b1$ with $b2$ we obtain a feasible solution.

Fig. 4. Dynamic system case: We start from a feasible solution a. A new task $n+1$ is dynamically added to the task set. Our method tries to reach the green area with $0 \leq S \leq 1 - s_{n+1}start_{n+1}$ and $0 \leq U \leq 1 - u_{n+1}start_{n+1}$ without violation of the constraints $S \leq 1$ and $U \leq 1$ in the exchange process.

new_i with $s_{inew_i} - s_{icurr_i} < 0$. Similarly to case II, among those candidates we choose the one with minimal gradient

$$\frac{s_{inew_i} - s_{icurr_i}}{u_{inew_i} - u_{icurr_i}} \qquad (2)$$

of the difference vector $diff_{new_i, curr_i}$.

– Case IV: $\sum_{i=1}^{n} s_{icurr_i} > 1$, $\sum_{i=1}^{n} u_{icurr_i} > 1$: Since we cannot reduce SPM and processor utilization at the same time, we arbitrarily choose one component first and try to reduce the other one later on, depending on the following cases II, III and IV. Figure 3 illustrates an example with an initial solution violating both the processor utilization and the SPM utilization constraints (case IV). An exchange reducing S leads us into case II, a second exchange leads us to case I where both S and U are reduced to values ≤ 1.

In general, during the search for a feasible solution, it may happen that our algorithm switches back and forth between the exchange directions, towards more SPM usage or more processor usage, for several times. However, it always stops, if a feasible solution is found or at latest if all task variants have been moved once. If we have found a feasible solution, the solution is postprocessed in step 2 with the goal of further minimizing the average energy consumption.

4.2 Step 2: Postprocessing for Energy Minimization

We start with a feasible solution and perform further exchanges for energy minimization. We start with an application specific observation: As seen in step 1, there are only two cases wrt. exchanges: Either processor utilization is reduced and SPM utilization is increased or processor utilization is increased and SPM utilization is decreased. Increases in processor utilization and decreases in SPM utilization usually *both* increase the energy consumption. So we completely neglect exchange steps of the first type (i.e. we always proceed as in case II of step 1). There are only two differences compared to case II of step 1: (1) We omit exchanges which would produce an infeasible solution with SPM utilization larger 1. (2) For choosing exchange candidates we consider the gradients $\frac{e_{inew_i} - e_{icurr_i}}{s_{inew_i} - s_{icurr_i}}$ instead of $\frac{u_{inew_i} - u_{icurr_i}}{s_{inew_i} - s_{icurr_i}}$, since now our goal is to minimize the average energy. (Moreover, we remove task variants which are not Pareto-optimal wrt. (s_{ij}, e_{ij}) before we start exchanging in step 2.)

4.3 Complexity

Let $V = \sum_{i=1}^{n} v_i$ be the number of task instances in the original problem, $v_{max} = \max_{i=1}^{n} v_i$ the maximum number of variants per task. The main observation for worst case complexity estimation of step 1 or 2 is the fact that each of the V task instances is exchanged at most once. Each exchange step is in $O(v_{max} + n)$, leading to an overall worst case complexity of $O(V \cdot (v_{max} + n))$.

5 Dynamic Systems

Many real-time systems change behaviour dynamically over time. Our algorithm is suitable for an incremental use where a new task comes into the system. It exchanges task variants until a new feasible solution is found. If not, the newly arrived tasks is rejected.

However, there is an important additional constraint to be fulfilled: Even if we are able to compute a feasible solution including the new task, it is not guaranteed that there is a *transition* from the previous set of task variants to the new set of task variants (including a variant of the new task) which does not violate the processor utilization constraint or the SPM utilization constraint in between. Here we make the realistic assumption that task variants can not be exchanged instantaneously, but the code of one task variant i_j can only exchanged to the code of another variant $i_{j'}$, when the current instance of i_j has finished, i.e., no task variant of i_j is active.

In the following we present an approach that constructs a sequence of task instance exchanges guaranteeing $S \leq 1$ and $U \leq 1$ for the intermediate configurations as well. The 'schedule of task instance exchanges' follows the steps in a modified exchange algorithm.

In a first sequence of exchanges we try to 'make room' for the newly arriving task τ_{n+1}, such that adding a variant of τ_{n+1} leads to a feasible solution. Since we do not yet know which variant of τ_{n+1} will be selected in the end, we proceed similar to Step 1.2 in Sect. 4.1, i.e., we select the variant $start_{n+1}$ of τ_{n+1} with the smallest Euclidean vector length. Now we start from the current set of task variants and try to reach a pair (S, U) of SPM utilization factor and processor utilization factor with $S \leq 1 - s_{n+1start_{n+1}}$ and $U \leq 1 - u_{n+1start_{n+1}}$. Of course, we have to ensure that for each intermediate step on this way we have $S \leq 1$ and $U \leq 1$. Figure 4 illustrates the approach.

The implementation of the approach is similar to Step 1.3 in Sect. 4.1 with the difference that we replace the limit 1 for S by $1 - s_{n+1start_{n+1}}$ and the limit 1 for U by $1 - u_{n+1start_{n+1}}$. Moreover, we only accept exchange steps leading to an intermediate solution with $S \leq 1$ and $U \leq 1$. If we have finally reached the situation that $0 \leq S \leq 1 - s_{n+1start_{n+1}}$ and $0 \leq U \leq 1 - u_{n+1start_{n+1}}$, we add τ_{n+1} with the current variant $(s_{n+1start_{n+1}}, u_{n+1start_{n+1}})$ into the solution. Then, exactly the postprocessing step for energy minimization from Sect. 4.2 follows which minimizes the average energy further without violating $S \leq 1$ and $U \leq 1$.

6   Multicore Systems

Since many embedded systems feature multicore CPUs, we extend our approach to the use with these systems. We use a simple multicore system where each CPU has its own local SPM (of the same size) and there is a fixed assignment of the tasks to CPUs. For multicore CPUs, TVS is generalized to the following problem TVSM which can be solved exactly by 0-1-ILP:

Task Variant Selection Multicore (TVSM)

Given: m processor cores $p_1, \ldots, p_k$, n tasks τ_i with sets
$V_i = \{(s_{ij}, u_{ij}, e_{ij}) \mid 1 \leq j \leq v_i\}$ of task variants, $s_{ij}, u_{ij} \in (0,1] \subseteq \mathbb{Q}$, $e_{ij} \in \mathbb{Q}_{\geq 0}$ $(1 \leq i \leq n, 1 \leq j \leq v_i)$.
Find: Minimize $\sum_{k=1}^{m} \sum_{i=1}^{n} \sum_{j=1}^{v_i} x_{ijk} e_{ij}$ with
$\sum_{i=1}^{n} \sum_{j=1}^{v_i} x_{ijk} s_{ij} \leq 1$ $(1 \leq k \leq m)$,
$\sum_{i=1}^{n} \sum_{j=1}^{v_i} x_{ijk} u_{ij} \leq 1$ $(1 \leq k \leq m)$,
$\sum_{k=1}^{m} \sum_{j=1}^{v_i} x_{ijk} = 1$ $(1 \leq i \leq n)$,
$x_{ijk} \in \{0, 1\}$ $(1 \leq i \leq n, 1 \leq j \leq v_i, 1 \leq k \leq m)$.
$(x_{ijk} = 1$ iff variant j of task τ_i is selected and assigned to processor k. $)$

For the heuristical solution we adapt our heuristics from the single-core case: The initial task variant selection from Step 1.2, Sect. 4.1, is extended by a distribution over the m available processor cores. The tasks are assigned to the cores one by one. For each core we sum up the Euclidian lengths of task variant vectors which are already assigned to it and we always greedily assign the next task to the core with the smallest sum.

Then, each task set on each core is optimized individually as in the single-core case.

For the dynamic system case, the new task is added to the core with the smallest average energy consumption. This core will then be treated as in Sec. 5.

Table 1. Results MiBench data Benchmarks

Algorithm	SPM usage [%]	Processor utilization [%]	Energy share	Solution time [ms]
Baseline initial	0.00	54.54	168,971,415	—
Gurobi initial	99.45	48.38	142,724,205	2.9984
Heuristic initial	68.90	48.30	145,104,542	1.0592
Baseline	0.00	63.63	317,414,842	—
Gurobi dynamic	99.73	56.43	275,237,960	6.4964
Heuristic dynamic	69.85	56.55	277,601,029	0.1171

7   Experimental Results

To evaluate our algorithm, we considered benchmarks with data generated from the MiBench [11] benchmark suite. SPM allocations for the MiBench programs were made with the help of the MACC framework [24], which only allocates global data but also tries to relocate local data to global data. These SPM enabled variants are then run in the MPARM/MEMSIM simulator [4] to obtain the corresponding energy and runtime values. For our experiments we used seven programs with two to five obtained variants. These programs were *bitcount*, *dijkstra*, *stringsearch* (large and small), *rijndael*, *sha* and *crc*. *bitcount* acts as the task joining the system dynamically. For computing exact solutions to the task variant selection problem we used the 0-1-ILP solver Gurobi [14].

Table 1 shows the results of these experiments. The first three lines in Table 1 give results for the initial task set. The line labeled 'baseline' shows the processor utilization and the average energy for the task set without using the SPM at all. Our heuristics is able to compute a solution with an average energy which is only about 2 % higher than the energy obtained by the exact solution (Gurobi), but with only one third of the solution time.

Our solution for the dynamic system is within a 1 % range of the exact solution regarding the average energy. Here our heuristics is even faster with a factor of about 60. It is important to keep in mind, that our heuristics gives not only a feasible solution but also a feasible transition from the first task set to the second one. Gurobi only computes the new optimal task set without any guarantee that such a transition exists.

In order to set the evaluation onto a broader basis we also performed experiments with synthetic benchmarks. We randomly generated tasks with variants whose triplets of SPM usage, WCET, and energy consumption show characteristics derived from results in the literature discussed in Sect. 1, whereas SPM usage is reciprocal to runtime, and runtime correlates to energy. We generated initial task sets consisting of 15 tasks, each with 4 variants. Starting from a solution of such a task set, we added another task to evaluate the behavior for dynamic systems. 1000 of these task sets were created for the evaluation. Finally, we applied our approach also in a multicore setting, where 4 cores obtained a total of 60 tasks with 4 variants each. As before we add another task to the initial set to evaluate the dynamic behavior. Because of high run times of the exact solution we confined ourselves to 11 test runs with a multicore data set.

Table 2. Results synthetic Benchmarks

Algorithm	SPM usage [%]	Processor utilization [%]	Energy share	Solution time [ms]	Solutions
Gurobi initial	99.73	42.42	61.7597	56.2189	998
Heuristic initial	99.48	42.32	70.2280	0.7359	998
Gurobi dynamic	99.80	50.58	84.7071	114.9391	879
Heuristic dynamic	99.50	50.05	90.5008	0.4214	871
Gurobi (4 cores) initial	99.97	40.87	228.8178	492,301.5050	11
Heuristic (4 cores) initial	99.45	41.17	265.2159	4.1255	11
Gurobi (4 cores) dynamic	99.98	42.86	245.0765	1,528,642.3016	11
Heuristic (4 cores) dynamic	99.50	43.17	283.1873	0.4718	11

As we can see in Table 2, in 998 out of 1000 cases our algorithm finds a feasible solution for the initial task set. In the remaining 2 cases there exists no feasible solution as the exact result computed by Gurobi shows. On average the energy consumption in our solution is about 12 % higher than in the exact solution. SPM usage and processor utilization are almost equal to the values of Gurobi. However, our approach needs less than 2 % of the runtime of the exact solution.

In the dynamic system case, Gurobi finds 879 solutions, 8 more than our heuristics. However, we do not know whether there is a feasible transition between the old and the new task sets in these 8 cases. Again remember that our heuristics additionally guarantees a feasible transition from the initial task set with 15 tasks to the new one with 16 tasks. The solutions of our heuristics are still in a 10 % range of the exact ones regarding the average energy. The CPU times of our heuristics are by a factor of about 300 lower than those of Gurobi.

The last four rows in Table 2 show results for the multicore case. The values for SPM and processor utilization are the average values over all 4 cores. Both Gurobi and the heuristics found feasible solutions for all 11 multicore benchmarks. The energy values of the exact solutions are about 15 % better on average. The focus here lies on the run times, where our heuristical solution clearly outperforms the exact solution by several orders of magnitude in the initial, as well as in the dynamic case.

8 Conclusions

In this work we presented a new approach for using scratchpad memories in embedded systems with the goal of reducing the average energy consumption in a multi task environment.

We use a new task model, where a task can have multiple pre-compiled variants which differ in their use of scratchpad memories and therefore also in energy usage and worst-case execution times. Apart from an exact solution based on 0-1-Integer-Linear-Programming we presented a fast heuristics for the solution. The heuristical solution is well suited for incremental use in a dynamic environment when tasks enter or leave the system. It also computes a transition from an old to a new task set which guarantees that no system constraints regarding SPM usage and processor utilization are violated in between.

The algorithm presented here works completely *orthogonal* to the method for assigning data and / or code to an SPM.

The experiments show that the solutions computed by the heuristics are competitive to the exact solutions wrt. the energy consumptions. The CPU times for computing the solutions are much faster (sometimes by several orders of magnitude) than those for the exact method and are thus suitable for an application in embedded real-time systems.

References

1. Angiolini, F., Menichelli, F., Ferrero, A., Benini, L., Olivieri, M.: A post-compiler approach to scratchpad mapping of code. In: CASES (2004)
2. Avissar, O., Barua, R., Stewart, D.: An optimal memory allocation scheme for scratch-pad-based embedded systems. ACM Trans. Embed. Comput. Syst. **1**, 6–26 (2002)
3. Banakar, R., Steinke, S., Lee, B.S., Balakrishnan, M., Marwedel, P.: Scratchpad memory: a design alternative for cache on-chip memory in embedded systems. In: CODES (2002)
4. Benini, L., Bertozzi, D., Bogliolo, A., Menichelli, F., Olivieri, M.: MPARM: Exploring the multi-processor SOC design space with systemc. J. VLSI Signal Process. Syst. **41**, 169–182 (2005)
5. Dominguez, A., Udayakumaran, S., Barua, R.: Heap data allocation to scratch-pad memory in embedded systems. J. Embed. Comput. **1**, 521–540 (2005)
6. Dudziński, K., Walukiewicz, S.: Exact methods for the knapsack problem and its generalizations. Eur. J. Oper. Res. **28**, 2–3 (1987)
7. Egger, B., Lee, J., Shin, H.: Dynamic scratchpad memory management for code in portable systems with an MMU. ACM Trans. Embed. Comput. Syst. **7**, 11 (2008)
8. Falk, H., Kleinsorge, J.: Optimal static wcet-aware scratchpad allocation of program code. In: DAC (2009)
9. Falk, H., Lokuciejewski, P.: A compiler framework for the reduction of worst-case execution times. Real-Time Syst. **46**, 251–300 (2010)
10. Garey, M.R., Johnson, D.S.: Computers and Intractability: A Guide to the Theory of NP-Completeness. W. H. Freeman, New York (1979)
11. Guthaus, M.R., Ringenberg, J.S., Ernst, D., Austin, T.M., Mudge, T., Brown, R.B.: Mibench: A free, commercially representative embedded benchmark suite. In: WWC-4 (2001)
12. Kellerer, H., Pferschy, U., Pisinger, D.: Knapsack Problems. Springer, Heidelberg (2004)
13. Liu, C.L., Layland, J.W.: Scheduling algorithms for multiprogramming in a hard-real-time environment. J. ACM **20**, 46–61 (1973)
14. Optimization, G., et al.: Gurobi optimizer reference manual (2012). http://www.gurobi.com
15. Panda, P.R., Dutt, N.D., Nicolau, A.: Efficient utilization of scratch-pad memory in embedded processor applications. In: ED & TC (1997)

16. Pisinger, D.: Algorithms for Knapsack Problems. Ph.D. thesis, DIKU, University of Copenhagen, Denmark (1995)
17. Poletti, F., Marchal, P., Atienza, D., Benini, L., Catthoor, F., Mendias, J.M.: An integrated hardware/software approach for run-time scratchpad management. In: DAC (2004)
18. Sjödin, J., von Platen, C.: Storage allocation for embedded processors. In: CASES (2001)
19. Steinke, S., Wehmeyer, L., Lee, B., Marwedel, P.: Assigning program and data objects to scratchpad for energy reduction. In: DATE (2002)
20. Suhendra, V., Mitra, T., Roychoudhury, A., Chen, T.: WCET centric data allocation to scratchpad memory. In: RTSS (2005)
21. Udayakumaran, S., Barua, R.: Compiler-decided dynamic memory allocation for scratch-pad based embedded systems. In: CASES (2003)
22. Verma, M., Petzold, K., Wehmeyer, L., Falk, H., Marwedel, P.: Scratchpad sharing strategies for multiprocess embedded systems: a first approach. In: Embedded Systems for Real-Time Multimedia (2005)
23. Verma, M., Wehmeyer, L., Marwedel, P.: Cache-aware scratchpad allocation algorithm. In: DATE (2004)
24. Verma, M., Wehmeyer, L., Pyka, R., Marwedel, P., Benini, L.: Compilation and simulation tool chain for memory aware energy optimizations. In: Vassiliadis, S., Wong, S., Hämäläinen, T.D. (eds.) SAMOS 2006. LNCS, vol. 4017, pp. 279–288. Springer, Heidelberg (2006)
25. Whitham, J., Audsley, N.: Explicit reservation of local memory in a predictable, preemptive multitasking real-time system. In: RTAS (2012)
26. Whitham, J., Davis, R.I., Audsley, N.C., Altmeyer, S., Maiza, C.: Investigation of scratchpad memory for preemptive multitasking. In: RTSS (2012)

Feedback-Based Admission Control for Hard Real-Time Task Allocation Under Dynamic Workload on Many-Core Systems

Piotr Dziurzanski$^{(\boxtimes)}$, Amit Kumar Singh, and Leandro Soares Indrusiak

Department of Computer Science, University of York,
Deramore Lane, Heslington, York YO10 5GH, UK
{Piotr.Dziurzanski,Amit.Singh,Leandro.Indrusiak}@york.ac.uk

Abstract. In hard real-time systems, a computationally expensive schedulability analysis has to be performed for every task. Fulfilling this requirement is particularly tough when system workload and service capacity are not available a priori and thus the analysis has to be conducted at runtime. This paper presents an approach for applying control-theory-based admission control to predict the task schedulability so that the exact schedulability analysis is performed only to the tasks with positive prediction results. In case of a careful fine-tuning of parameters, the proposed approach can be successfully applied even to many-core embedded systems with hard real-time constraints and other time-critical systems. The provided experimental results demonstrate that, on average, only 62 % of the schedulability tests have to be performed in comparison with the traditional, open-loop approach. The proposed approach is particularly beneficial for heavier workloads, where the number of executed tasks is almost unchanged in comparison with the traditional open-loop approach. By our approach, only 32 % of exact schedulability tests have to be conducted. Moreover, for the analysed industrial workloads with dependent jobs, the proposed technique admitted and executed 11 % more tasks while not violating any timing constraints.

1 Introduction

The vast majority of existing research into hard real-time scheduling on many-core systems assumes workloads to be known in advance, so that traditional scheduling analysis can be applied to check statically whether a particular taskset is schedulable on a given platform [5]. The hard real-time scheduling is desired in several time critical systems such as automotive and aerospace domains [8]. Under dynamic workloads, admitting and executing all hard real-time (HRT) tasks belonging to a taskset can jeopardise system timeliness so that some task deadlines may be violated. The decision of a task admittance is made by an *admission controller*. Its role is to fetch a task from the task queue and check whether it can be executed by any core before its deadline and without forcing existing tasks to miss theirs. If the answer is positive, the task is admitted, and rejected otherwise. The benefits of this early task rejection are twofold: (*i*) the

© Springer International Publishing Switzerland 2016
F. Hannig et al. (Eds.): ARCS 2016, LNCS 9637, pp. 157–169, 2016.
DOI: 10.1007/978-3-319-30695-7_12

resource working time is not wasted for a task that will probably violate its deadline, and (ii) a possibility of early signalling the lack of admittance can be employed to perform an appropriate precaution measures in order to minimize the negative impact of the task rejection (for example, to execute the task outside the considered platform).

Dynamic workloads do not necessarily follow simple periodic or sporadic task models and it is rather difficult to find a many-core system scheduling analysis that relies on more sophisticated models [5,11]. Computationally-intensive workloads not following these basic models are more often analysed in High Performance Computing (HPC) domain, for example in [4]. The HPC community experience with these tasksets could help introducing novel workload models to many-core system schedulability analysis [5]. In HPC systems, tasks allocation and scheduling heuristics based on feedback control proved to be valuable for dynamic workloads [12], improving platform utilisation while meeting timing constraints. Despite a number of successful implementations in HPC, these heuristics are not exploited for many-core embedded platforms with hard real-time constraints.

The Roadmap on Control of Real-Time Computing Systems [1], one of the results of the EU/IST Network of Excellence ARTIST2 program, states clearly that feedback scheduling is not suitable for applications with hard real-time constraints, since feedback acts on errors. However, further research [13,14] shows that although the number of deadline misses must not be used as an observed value (since any positive error value would violate the hard real-time constraints), observing other system's parameters, such as dynamic slack, created when tasks are executed earlier than their worst-case execution time (WCET), or core utilisation, could help in allocating and scheduling tasks in a real-time system.

Contribution: In order to address aforementioned issues, we present a novel task resource allocation process, which is comprised of the *resource allocation* and *task scheduling*. The *resource allocation* process is executed on a particular core. Its role is to send the processes to be executed to other processing cores, putting them into the task queue of a particular core. Task scheduling is carried out locally on each core and selects the actual process to run on the core. The proposed approach adopts control-theory based techniques to perform runtime admission control and load balancing to cope with dynamic workloads having hard real-time constraints. It is worth stressing that, to the best of our knowledge, no control theory based allocation and scheduling method aiming at hard real-time systems has been proposed to operate in an embedded system with dynamic workloads.

This paper is structured as follows. Section 2 describes related work. The assumptions of the considered application and platform models are enumerated in Sect. 3. In Sect. 4, the proposed runtime admission control and load balancing approach dedicated to dynamic workloads are described. Section 5 presents the experimental results to demonstrate the performance of the proposed scheme under different workload conditions. Section 6 summarizes the paper.

2   Related Work

The majority of works that apply techniques from control-theory to map tasks to processing cores offers soft real-time guarantees only, which cannot be applied to time-critical systems [12]. Relatively little work is related to hard real-time systems, where the task dispatching should ensure admission control and guaranteed resource provisions, i.e. start a task's job (a task consists of many jobs, detailed model description in Sect. 3) only when the system can allocate a necessary resource budget to meet its timing requirements and guarantee that no access of a job being executed to its allocated resources is denied or blocked by any other jobs [1]. Providing such kind of guarantee facilitates to fulfill the requirements of time critical systems, e.g. avionic and automotive systems, where timing constraints must be satisfied [8].

Usually hard real-time scheduling requires a priori knowledge of the worst-case execution time (WCET) of each task to guarantee the schedulability of the whole system [5]. However, according to a number of experimental results [7], the difference between WCET and observed execution time (ET) can be rather substantial. Consequently, underutilization of resources can often be observed during hard real-time system run-time. The emerging dynamic slack can be used for various purposes, including energy conservation by means of dynamic voltage and frequency scaling (DVFS) or switching off the unused cores with clock or power gating and slack reclamation protocols [13,14].

In [6], a response time analysis (RTA) has been used to check the schedulability of real-time tasksets. This ensures meeting all hard deadlines despite assigning various execution frequencies to all real-time tasks to minimise energy consumption. In the approach proposed in this paper, RTA is also performed, but it is executed far less frequently due to the fast schedulability estimation based on controllers and thus its total execution time is shorter.

Some researchers highlight the role of a real-time manager (RTM) in scheduling hard real-time systems. In [10], it is described that after receiving a new allocation request, an RTM checks the resource availability using a simple predictor. Then the manager periodically monitors the progress of all running tasks and allocates more resources to the tasks with endangered deadlines. However, it is rather difficult to guarantee hard real-time requirements when no proper schedulability test is applied.

From the literature survey it follows that applying feedback-based controllers in hard real-time systems has been limited to determine the appropriate frequency benefiting from DVFS. According to the authors' knowledge, the feedback controller has not been yet used by an RTM to perform task allocation under dynamic workload on many-core systems.

3   System Model

In Fig. 1, the consecutive stages of a task life cycle in the proposed system are presented. The task τ_l is released at an arbitrary instant. Then an approximate

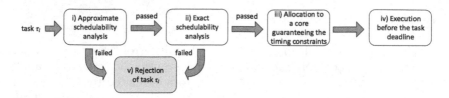

Fig. 1. Building blocks of the proposed approach

schedulability analysis is performed, which can return either fail or pass. If the approximate test is passed, the exact schedulability, characterised with a relatively high computational complexity [5], is performed. If this test is also passed, the task is assigned to the appropriate core, selected during the schedulability tests, where it is executed before its deadline.

3.1 Application Model

A taskset Γ is comprised of an arbitrary number of tasks, $\Gamma = \{\tau_1, \tau_2, \tau_3, \ldots\}$ with hard real-time constraints. The j-th job of task τ_i is denoted with $\tau_{i,j}$. If a *task* is comprised of only one *job*, these terms are used interchangeably in this paper. In case of tasks with job dependencies it is assumed that all jobs of a task are submitted at the same time, thus it is possible to identify the critical path at the instant of the task release, which can be viewed as a realistic assumption in assorted applications, e.g. industrial use cases [3]. Periodic or sporadic tasks can be modelled with an infinite series of jobs. Since the taskset is not known in advance, the tasks can be released at any instant.

3.2 Platform Model

The general architecture employed in our work is depicted in Fig. 2. The system is comprised of n processing cores, whose dynamic slacks (slack vector whose length $|slack| = n$) are observed constantly by the Monitor block.

In the PID Controllers block, one discrete-time PID controller for each core is invoked every dt time. Since small sampling intervals emulate continuous time

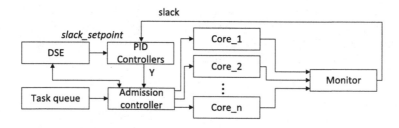

Fig. 2. Proposed many-core system architecture

algorithms more accurately [9], the PID controllers have been decided to be activated every clock tick.

The controllers use dynamic slacks of the corresponding cores as the observed values.

The Admission controller block receives a vector of PID controllers' outputs, $Y = [y_1(t), \ldots, y_n(t)]$, from the PID Controllers block. Based on its elements' values it performs, as shown in Fig. 1: *(i) approximate schedulability analysis.* If this analysis predicts that the workload is schedulable, an *(ii) exact schedulability analysis* is performed by the Design Space Exploration (DSE) block. If at the second stage the result of the task schedulability analysis is negative, the task is rejected. Otherwise it is *(iii) allocated to a core where the execution before the deadline is guaranteed* based on the schedulability analysis performed in block DSE.

3.3   Problem Formulation

Given an application and platform models, the problem is to quickly identify tasks whose hard timing constraints would be violated by the processing cores and then to reject such tasks without performing costly exact schedulability analysis. The number of rejected tasks should be reasonably close to the number of tasks rejected in a corresponding open-loop system, i.e. the system without the early rejection prediction. Meeting the deadlines for all admitted tasks shall be guaranteed.

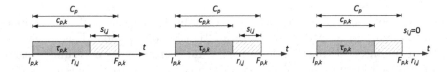

Fig. 3. Illustration of task $\tau_{i,j}$ slack in three cases from equation (1)

4   Performing Runtime Admission Control and Load Balancing to Cope with Dynamic Workloads

In dynamic workloads, admitting and executing all hard real-time (HRT) tasks belonging to a taskset can jeopardise system timeliness. The role of the admission control is to detect the potential deadline violation of a released task, τ_l, and to reject it in such a case. In doing so, the resource working time is not wasted for the task that would probably violate its deadline and early signaling of the rejection could be used for minimizing its negative impact.

The j-th job of task τ_i, $\tau_{i,j}$, is released at $r_{i,j}$, with the deadline $d_{i,j}$ and the relative deadline $D_{i,j} = d_{i,j} - r_{i,j}$. The slack for $\tau_{i,j}$ executed on core π_a, where $\tau_{p,k}$ was the immediate previous job executed by this core, is computed as follows:

$$s_{i,j} = \begin{cases} C_p - c_{p,k} & \text{if } r_{i,j} \leq I_{p,k} + c_{p,k}, \\ F_{p,k} - r_{i,j} & \text{if } I_{p,k} + c_{p,k} \leq r_{i,j} < F_{p,k}, \\ 0 & \text{if } r_{i,j} \geq F_{p,k}, \end{cases} \tag{1}$$

where $r_{i,j}$ is release time of $\tau_{i,j}$, $I_{p,k}$ - initiation time of $\tau_{p,k}$ (also known as the starting time of job execution), $c_{p,k}$ and C_p - computation time and worst-case execution time (WCET) of $\tau_{p,k}$, and $F_{p,k}$ - its worst-case completion time. A similar slack calculation approach is employed in [14]. The three possible slack cases (Eq. (1)) are illustrated in Fig. 3 (left, centre, right, respectively). In these figures the solid rectangle illustrates execution time (ET) of $\tau_{p,k}$, whereas the striped rectangle shows the difference between WCET and ET of this task.

The normalised value of slack of currently executed job $\tau_{i,j}$ on core π_a is computed as follows:

$$slack_a = \frac{D_{i,j} - s_{i,j}}{D_{i,j}}. \tag{2}$$

This value is returned by a monitor and compared by a PID controller with setpoint $slack\_setpoint$. An error $e_a(t) = slack_a - slack\_setpoint$ is computed for core π_a, as schematically shown in Fig. 2. Then the a-th output of the PID Controllers block, reflecting the past and previous dynamic slack values in core π_a, is computed with formula

$$y_a(t) = K_P e_a(t) + K_I \sum_{i=0}^{IW} e_a(t-i) + K_D \frac{e_a(t) - e_a(t-1)}{dt}, \tag{3}$$

where K_P, K_I and K_D are positive constant components of the proportional, integral and derivative terms of a PID controller, and IW is a selected length of the integral time window. Their values are usually determined using one of the well-known control theory methods, such as root locus technique, Ziegler-Nichols tuning method or many others, to obtain the desired control response and preserve the stability. In our research, we have applied Approximate M-constrained Integral Gain Optimisation (AMIGO), as it enables a reasonable compromise between load disturbance rejection and robustness [2].

The value of $slack\_setpoint$ is bounded between values: $min\_slack\_setpoint$ and $max\_slack\_setpoint$, which should be chosen appropriately during simulation of a particular system. Similarly, the initial value of $slack\_setpoint$ can influence (slightly, according to our experiments) the final results. In this paper, it is initialised with the average between its minimal and maximal allowed values to converge quickly with any value from the whole spectrum of possible controller responses.

The slacks of the tasks executed by a particular processing core accumulate as long as the release times of each task are lower than the worst-time completion time of the previous task, which correspond to the first two cases in Eq. (1) and are illustrated in Fig. 3 (left and centre). It means that the slacks of subsequent tasks executed on a given core can be used as a controller input value. However, previous values of dynamic slack are of no importance when the core becomes idle, i.e. the core finishes execution of a task and there are no more tasks in the queue to be processed, which corresponds to the third case in Eq. (1) illustrated in Fig. 3 (right). To reflect this situation, the current value of *slack_setpoint* is provided as an error $e_a(t)$, to enhance the task assignment to this idle core (since it corresponds to the situation that the normalised slack would be twice as large as the current setpoint value, i.e. behaves in the way the task would finish its execution two times earlier than expected). Substituting this value not only positively estimates the task schedulability at the given time instant, but also influences future computation of the PID controller output, as it appears as a prior error value in the integral part in Eq. (3).

The PID Controllers block output value $Y = [y_1(t), \ldots, y_n(t)]$ is provided as an input to the Admission controller block, where it is used to perform a task admittance decision. If all PID Controllers' outputs (errors) $y_a(t), a \in \{1, \ldots, n\}$ are negative, the task τ_l fetched from the Task queue is rejected. Otherwise, a further analysis is conducted by the Design Space Exploration (DSE) block to perform exact schedulability analysis. The available resources are checked according to any exact schedulability test (e.g. from [5]), which is performed for each core with task τ_l added to its taskset as long as a schedulable assignment is not found. If no resource is found that guarantees the task execution before its deadline, it is rejected.

The pseudo-code of the control strategy is presented in Algorithm 1. This algorithm is comprised of two parts, described respectively by lines 1–18 and 19–24, which are executed concurrently. The first part consists of the following steps.

- **Step 1. Invocation (lines 1, 17).**
  The block functionality is executed in an infinite loop (line 1), activated every time interval dt (line 17).
- **Step 2. Task fetching and schedulability analysis (lines 2–8).**
  All tasks present in the Task queue are fetched sequentially (line 2–3). For each task, the PID Controllers' outputs are browsed to find positive values, which are treated as an early estimation of schedulability (line 4). If such value is found in an a-th output, an exact schedulability test checks the schedulability of the taskset Γ_a of the corresponding core π_a extended with task τ_l using any exact schedulability test (line 5), e.g. from [5]. If the analysis proves that the taskset is schedulable, τ_l is assigned to π_a (line 6). Otherwise, the next core with the corresponding positive output value is looked for.
- **Step 3. Task rejection and setpoint increase (lines 9–15).**
  If all cores have been browsed and none of them can admit τ_l due to either a negative controller output value or the exact schedulability test failure, the task τ_l is rejected (line 10). In this case, if there exists at least one positive value in the PID Controllers' output vector, the *slack_setpoint* is increased by constant *slack_setpoint_add* provided that it is lower than constant *max_slack_setpoint* (lines 11–12) to improve the schedulability estimation in future.

The second part consists of two steps.

Algorithm 1. Pseudo-code of Admission controller involving DSE algorithm

---

inputs   : Task $\tau_l \in \Gamma$ (from Task queue)
            Vector of errors $Y[1..n]$ (from PID Controller)
            Controller invocation period dt
            $slack\_setpoint$ decrease period dt_1, $dt_1 > dt$
outputs   : Core $\pi_a \in \Pi$ executing τ_l or job rejection
            Value of $slack\_setpoint$
constants: $min\_slack\_setpoint$ - minimal allowed value of $slack\_setpoint$
            $max\_slack\_setpoint$ - maximal allowed value of $slack\_setpoint$
            $slack\_setpoint\_add$ - value to be added to $slack\_setpoint$
            $slack\_setpoint\_sub$ - value to be subtracted from $slack\_setpoint$

```
 1  while true do
 2  |   while task queue is not empty do
 3  |   |   fetch τl;
 4  |   |   forall the Ya > 0 do
 5  |   |   |   if taskset Γa ∪ τl is schedulable then
 6  |   |   |   |   assign τl to πa;
 7  |   |   |   |   break;
 8  |   |   |   end
 9  |   |   |   if τl not assigned then
10  |   |   |   |   reject τl;
11  |   |   |   |   if ∃Ya : Ya > 0 ∧ slack_setpoint < max_slack_setpoint then
12  |   |   |   |   |   increase slack_setpoint by slack_setpoint_add;
13  |   |   |   |   end
14  |   |   |   end
15  |   |   end
16  |   end
17  |   wait dt;
18  end
19  while true do
20  |   if slack_setpoint > min_slack_setpoint then
21  |   |   decrease slack_setpoint by slack_setpoint_sub;
22  |   end
23  |   wait dt1;
24  end
```

- **Step 1. Invocation (lines 19, 23).**
  The block functionality is executed in an infinite loop (line 19), activated every time interval dt_1, $dt_1 > dt$ (line 23).
- **Step 2. Setpoint decrease (lines 20–21).**
  The value of $slack\_setpoint$ is decreased by constant $slack\_setpoint\_sub$ (provided that it is higher than constant $min\_slack\_setpoint$), which encourages a higher number of tasks to be admitted in future.

5   Experimental Results

In order to check the efficiency of the proposed feedback-based admission control and real-time task allocation process, a Transaction-Level Modelling (TLM) simulation model has been developed in SystemC language. Firstly, the controller components K_P, K_I and K_D have to be tuned by analysing the corresponding open-loop system response to a bursty workload. Then two series of experiments have been performed. Firstly, workloads of various weight have been tested to observe the system behaviour under different conditions and to find the most beneficial operating region. Then industrial workloads with dependent jobs have been used to determine the applicability of the proposed approach in real-life scenarios. The details of these experiments are described below.

To tune the parameters of the controller, the task slack growth after applying a step-input in the open-loop system (i.e. without any feedback) has been analysed. This is a typical way in control-theory-based approaches [2]. As an input, a burst release of 500 tasks (each including only one single appearance job with execution time equal to $50\,\mu s$) has been chosen. The modelled platform has been comprised of 3 computing cores. However, any number of tasks can be released, their execution time may vary and the number of cores can be higher, which is shown in further experiments. The obtained results have confirmed the accumulating (integrating) nature of the process, and thus the accumulating process version of AMIGO tuning formulas have been applied to choose the proper values of PID controller components [2]. Using a technique similar to [9] (Chap. 15), the following constant values have been selected: $min\_slack\_setpoint = 0.05$, $max\_slack\_setpoint = 0.95$, $slack\_setpoint\_add = 0.01$, $slack\_setpoint\_sub = 0.05$, the first part of the proposed algorithm (Algorithm 1) is executed five times more often than the second one.

To check the system response to tasksets of various levels of load, eight sets, $W_1, \ldots, W_8$, of 10 random workloads each have been generated. Each workload is comprised of 100 tasks, including a random number (between 1 and 20) of independent jobs. The execution time of every job is selected randomly between 1 and $99\mu s$. All jobs of a task are released at the same instant, and the release time of the subsequent task is selected randomly between $r_i + range\_min \cdot C_i$ and $r_i + range\_max \cdot C_i$, where C_i is the total worst-case execution time of the current task τ_i released at r_i, and $range\_min, range\_max \in (0,1)$, $range\_min < range\_max$. The following parameters for pairs $(range\_min, range\_max)$ have been selected for workloads: W_1 - $(0.001, 0.01)$, W_2 - $(0.0025, 0.025)$, W_3 - $(0.005, 0.05)$, W_4 - $(0.0075, 0.075)$, W_5 - $(0.01, 0.1)$, W_6 - $(0.02, 0.2)$, W_7 - $(0.03, 0.3)$, W_8 - $(0.04, 0.4)$ to cover a wide spectrum of workload heaviness.

The numbers of executed tasks with respect to heaviness are presented in Fig. 4 (left). Both for the open-loop and closed-loop systems they are approximated better with power than linear regression (residual sum of squares is lower by one order of magnitude in case of power regression; logarithmic and exponential regression approximations were even more inaccurate). This regression model can be then used to determine the trend of executed task numbers with respect to different workload weights. Similarly, the difference between the number of admitted tasks by open and closed loop systems can be relatively accurately approximated with a power function (power regression result: $y = 960.87x^{-1.18}$, residual sum of squares $rss = 3646.06$, where x represents a workload weight computed as the total execution time of all jobs divided by the latest deadline of these jobs and y - the number of executed tasks). This relation implies that the closed-loop system admits relatively low number of tasks when the workload is light. In such lightweight condition, the number of schedulability tests to be performed is only 12 % lower in the extreme case of the set W_8 (Fig. 4 (right)).

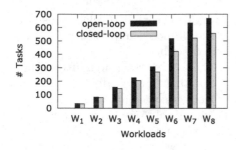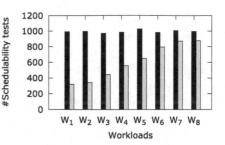

Fig. 4. Total number of tasks executed before their deadlines (left) and number of the exact schedulability test executions (right) in baseline open-loop and proposed closed-loop systems for the random workloads simulation scenario with workload sets $W_1, \ldots, W_8$ including 1000 tasks each

Thus, there is no reasonable benefit of using controllers and schedulability estimations. In heavier loaded systems, however, the number of admitted tasks in both configurations are more balanced, and the number of schedulability test executions is significantly varied. For example, for the two heaviest considered workload sets W_1 and W_2, the schedulability tests are executed about 65 % less frequently in the closed-loop system.

This experiment has been conducted for the number of processing cores ranging from 1 to 9. The number of executed tasks grows almost linearly with the number of cores in both configurations and the slopes of their linear regression approximations (both with correlation coefficients higher than 0.99) are almost equal. This implies that both configurations are scalable in a similar way and the difference between the number of executing tasks in open-loop and closed-loop systems is rather unvarying. The number of schedulability test executions is almost constant in the open-loop system regardless the number of cores. However, for the closed-loop configuration, it changes in a way relatively well approximated with a power regression model (power regression result: $y = 1476.29x^{-0.30}$, residual sum of squares $rss = 14216.21$, where x is the number of cores and y - the number of schedulability test executions). Since the growing number of processing cores corresponds to less computation on each of them, the conclusion is similar as in the $(range\_min, range\_max)$ variation case: the higher the load for the cores, the more beneficial is applying of the proposed scheme.

To analyse industrial workloads, 90 workloads have been generated whose dependency patterns are based on the grid workload of an engineering design department of a large aircraft manufacturer, as described in [3]. These workloads include 100 tasks of 827 to 962 jobs in total. The job execution time varies from 1 ms to 99 ms. Since the original workloads have no deadlines provided explicitly, relative deadline of each task has been set to its WCET increased by a certain constant (100ms).

In these workloads all jobs of any task are submitted at the same time, thus it is possible at the first stage to identify the critical path of each task and admit the task if there exists a core that is capable of executing the jobs belonging to the critical path before their deadlines. At the second stage, the remaining jobs of the task can be assigned to other cores so that the deadline of the critical path is not violated. The outputs from PID controllers can be used for choosing the core for the critical path jobs (during the first stage) or the cores for the remaining jobs (during the second stage). Four configurations can be then applied. We abbreviate them with four letter acronyms, where the two first letters denote whether the core selection for critical path tasks is done without (open loop - OL) or with (closed loop - CL) PID controllers and similarly the two remaining letters inform if the core selection for tasks outside the critical path is performed without (OL) or with (CL) PID controllers. For example, in configuration OLOL no PID controller is used and thus this configuration is treated as a baseline (only exact schedulability tests are used to select a core for a job execution).

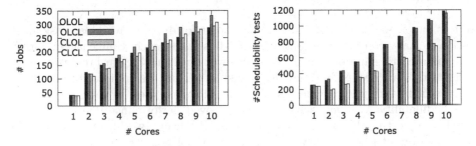

Fig. 5. Number of executed jobs (left) and number of schedulability test executions (right) for systems configured in four different ways for the industrial workloads simulation scenario

Figure 5 (left) shows the number of jobs executed before their deadlines. The cores are scanned in a lexicographical order as long as the first one capable of executing the job satisfying its timing constraints is not found, whereas in the closed-loop configurations the tasks are checked with regards to the decreasing value of the corresponding controller outputs. Notice that the number of cores is related to the processing cores only (Core_1, ..., Core_n in Fig. 2); the remaining functional blocks (e.g. Admission controller) are realised in additional cores.

The OLOL configuration approach seems to be particularly beneficial in the systems with lower number of cores (heavier loaded with tasks). However, in the systems with more than two cores, the OLCL configuration leads to the best results. Its superiority in comparison with CLCL stems from the fact that an over-pessimistic rejection of critical path jobs leads to fast rejection of the whole task. Thus the cost of a false negative estimation is rather high. Wrong estimation at the second stage usually results in choosing an idler core. The OLCL configuration admits 11 % more jobs than OLOL, whereas CLCL is only slightly (about 1.5 %) better than the baseline OLOL.

The main reason for introducing the control-theory based admittance is, however, decreasing the number of costly exact schedulability testing. The number of the exact test executions is presented in Fig. 5 (right). Not surprisingly, the wider the usage of controller outputs, the lower is the cost of schedulability testing. The difference between OLOL and OLCL is almost unnoticeable, but the configurations with control-theory-aided selection of a core for the critical path jobs leads to significant, over 30 % reduction.

From the results it follows that two configurations OLCL and CLCL dominate the others: the former in terms of number of executed jobs, the latter in terms of number of schedulability tests. Depending upon which goal is more important, one of them is advised to be selected. Interestingly, only in case of low number of processing cores, the baseline OLOL approach is slightly better than the remaining ones. For larger systems, applying PID controllers for task admissions seems to be quite beneficial.

6   Conclusions and Future Work

In this paper, we have presented a novel scheme for dynamic workload task allocation to many-cores using a control theory-based approach. Unlike the majority of similar existing approaches, we deal with workloads having hard real-time constraints that are desired in time-critical systems. Thus, we are forced to perform exact schedulability tests, whereas PID controllers are used for early estimation of schedulability. We have achieved an improved performance due to reduced number of costly scheduling test executions. For heavy workloads, up to 65 % lower number of schedulability tests are to be performed when compared to typical open-loop approach, whereas the number of admitted tasks is almost equal. For industrial workloads executed on larger systems, the number of admitted tasks is higher than the open-loop approach due to the selection of idler cores for computing jobs belonging to the critical path. In future, we plan to consider heterogeneous many-core system and extend the proposed approach for mixed criticality workloads.

Acknowledgments. The research leading to these results has received funding from the European Union's Seventh Framework Programme (FP7/2007-2013) under grant agreement no. 611411.

References

1. Bergami, Leonardo: Conclusion. In: Bergami, Leonardo (ed.) Smart Rotor Modeling. RTWE, vol. 3, pp. 155–157. Springer, Heidelberg (2014)
2. Astrom, K., Hagglund, T.: Revisiting the Ziegler-Nichols step response method for PID control. J. Process Control **14**, 635–650 (2004)
3. Burkimsher, A., Bate, I., Indrusiak, L.S.: A characterisation of the workload on an engineering design grid. In: Proceedings of the High Performance Computing Symposium (HPC 2014), Society for Computer Simulation International, Article 8 (2014)

 4. Cheveresan, R., Ramsay, M., Feucht, C., Sharapov, I.: Characteristics of workloads used in high performance and technical computing. In: Proceedings of the 21st Annual International Conference on Supercomputing (ICS 2007), pp. 73–82 (2007)
 5. Davis, R.I., Burns, A.: A survey of hard real-time scheduling for multiprocessor systems. ACM Comput. Surv. **43**(4), 35 (2011)
 6. Djosic, S., Jevtic, M.: Dynamic voltage scaling for real-time systems under fault tolerance constraints. In: 28th International Conference on Microelectronics (MIEL), pp. 375–378 (2012)
 7. Engblom, J., Ermedahl, A., Sjodin, M., Gustafsson, J., Hansson, H.: Worst-case execution-time analysis for em-bedded real-time systems. Int. J. Softw. Tools Technol. Transfer. **4**(4), 437–455 (2003)
 8. Giannopoulou, G., Stoimenov, N., Huang, P., Thiele, L.: Scheduling of mixed-criticality applications on resource-sharing multicore systems. In: International Conference on Embedded Software (EMSOFT 2013), pp. 1–15 (2013)
 9. Janert, P.K.: Feedback Control for Computer Systems. OReilly Media, Sebastopol (2013)
10. Kumar, A., Mesman, B., Theelen, B., Corporaal, H., Yajun, H.: Resource manager for non-preemptive heterogeneous multiprocessor system-on-chip. In: IEEE/ACM/IFIP Workshop on Embedded Systems for Real Time Multimedia (ESTMED 2006), pp. 33–38 (2006)
11. Kiasari, A.E., Jantsch, A., Lu, Z.: Mathematical formalisms for performance evaluation of networks-on-chip. ACM Comput. Surv. **45**(3), 38 (2013)
12. Lu, C., Stankovic, J.A., Son, S.H., Tao, G.: Feedback control real-time scheduling: framework, modeling, and algorithms. Real-Time Syst. **23**(1/2), 85–126 (2002)
13. Tavana, M.K., Salehi, M., Ejlali, A.: Feedback-Based Energy Management in a Standby-Sparing Scheme for Hard Real-Time Systems. In: 32nd IEEE Real-Time Systems Symposium (RTSS 2011), pp. 349–356 (2011)
14. Zhu, Y., Mueller, F.: Feedback EDF scheduling exploiting dynamic voltage scaling. In: 10th IEEE Real-Time and Embedded Technology and Applications Symposyum (RTAS 2004), pp. 84–93 (2004)

All About Time: Timing, Tracing,
and Performance Modeling

Data Age Diminution
in the Logical Execution Time Model

Christian Bradatsch$^{(\boxtimes)}$, Florian Kluge, and Theo Ungerer

University of Augsburg, Augsburg, Germany
{Christian.Bradatsch,Florian.Kluge,
Theo.Ungerer}@informatik.uni-augsburg.de

Abstract. The logical execution time (LET) model separates logical from physical execution times. Furthermore, tasks' input and output of data occurs at predictable times that are the tasks' arrival times and deadlines, respectively. The output of data is delayed until the period end meaning that output times have no jitter. The delayed output affects the freshness of data (respectively data age) between interacting tasks. Recently, critics from control theory arise that the LET approach provides outdated data. We analyze the data age of communicating tasks and propose an approach that reduces the data age. Therefore, we reduce the LET of tasks such that output data is provided earlier than at a task's deadline, but still preserve the predictability of output times. To confirm the improvement on the data age, we simulate 100 randomly generated task sets. Moreover, we also simulate a task set of a real-world automotive benchmark and show an enhancement of the average data age of approximately 33 % with our approach compared to the LET model.

1 Introduction

Nowadays, embedded real-time control systems interacting with their environment are omnipresent, for example in the automotive and avionic domains, in industrial control systems, or home automation. Due to continuously increasing demands on functionality, the complexity of software rises. In addition, the development of embedded software is highly platform dependent. On the one hand, engineers have to deal with the functional specification and on the other hand with the temporal behavior of software. High level programming languages help to implement the functional software requirements, but also abstract from many platform features. The temporal behavior is not covered in such high level languages and the engineer has to cope with hardware performance, scheduling policies, synchronization, and inter-process communication.

One solution for efficiently handling this circumstance is presented with Giotto, a time-triggered language for embedded programming [7]. Giotto introduces a logical execution time (LET) that abstracts from the physical execution time on a particular platform. Through the separation of logical and physical execution time, the application software is independent of the underlying hardware platform with regard to its temporal behavior. One key point of LET is that

© Springer International Publishing Switzerland 2016
F. Hannig et al. (Eds.): ARCS 2016, LNCS 9637, pp. 173–184, 2016.
DOI: 10.1007/978-3-319-30695-7_13

inputs to a task are read at the beginning and outputs are written at the end of the task's LET. So, LET provides a deterministic behavior regarding input and output times. Between start and end, the output has the value of the previous execution. The output value is updated when the end of the LET is reached. Thus, LET introduces a non-negligible delay for the observable output.

In real-time control systems, the overall performance of a system is measured by how accurate it regulates the controlled process variables despite changing operating conditions. Ideally, to achieve the best quality of control, the time between input, computation, and updating the actuating variables should be as close as possible to zero. With increasing latency, the accuracy and efficiency of a control system suffers. From this point of view, introducing the LET approach in an embedded control system is contradictory, since updating of task outputs is delayed by the LET model. Moreover, a producer task's output can drive an actuator or serve as input for other tasks. Since the visible output is delayed when applying the LET model, a consumer task may not read the most recent output of a producer task, but one of a former execution. In turn, this may have negative impact on the accuracy and robustness of real-time control, since the controller works on the basis of outdated input data.

The contribution of this paper is an approach to decrease the output delay in embedded control systems that are executed using the LET model. Therefor, we prepone the tasks' output times and shrink the LET with the help of a response time analysis. Our aim is to preserve the deterministic input and output times of the LET model and at the same time to minimize the output delay and thus also to improve the freshness of data.

The rest of the paper is structured as follows: Sect. 2 defines the system model of real-time tasks that will be used throughout the rest of the paper. In Sect. 3, we recap the two programming models, the bounded-execution-time (BET) and the logical-execution-time (LET) model, and in Sect. 4 we present our approach. In Sect. 5 we discuss some theoretical considerations. The evaluation methodology is explained in Sect. 6 and the obtained results are discussed. Subsequently, we show the applicability of our approach on the basis of a real-world automotive benchmark. In Sect. 7 we compare our approach to related work. We conclude the paper in Sect. 8.

2   System Model

In this work, we target synchronous task sets consisting of periodic real-time tasks with implicit deadlines. A task τ_i is represented by a tuple $\tau_i = (C_i, T_i)$ with worst-case execution time C_i, and period T_i. A task τ_i's relative deadline is equal to its period, i.e., each job must be finished before the next activation of the same task. All tasks in a task set $T = \{\tau_1, \tau_2, \ldots, \tau_n\}$ release their first job $\tau_{i,0}$ at time $t = 0$. Jobs $\tau_{i,k}$ with $k \geq 0$ are periodically released at times $a_{i,k} = k \cdot T_i$ and must finish execution until their absolute deadlines at time $d_{i,k} = (k+1)T_i$. Jobs are executed using FPP scheduling with priorities being assigned according to the rate monotonic algorithm [16]. In the following, we assume that the task set τ is schedulable. The starting time $s_{i,k}$ of a job $\tau_{i,k}$ is the time in the interval $[a_{i,k}, d_{i,k}]$ where $\tau_{i,k}$'s execution is started. Any job $\tau_{i,k}$ finishes execution at some time $f_{i,k}$ with $s_{i,k} < f_{i,k} \leq d_{i,k}$. The response time $R_{i,k}$ of a job is the interval between its arrival and its finishing time, i.e. $R_{i,k} = f_{i,k} - a_{i,k}$. The worst-case response time R_i of a task τ_i is the maximum of the response times of all of its jobs, i.e., $R_i = \max_{k \geq 0} R_{i,k}$. As $\mathcal{T}$ is schedulable, $R_i \leq T_i$. The hyper-period T of a task set is the least common multiple of all tasks' periods, $T = \mathrm{lcm}(T_1, T_2, \ldots, T_n)$. A special case are task sets with harmonic periods, i.e., $\mathcal{T} = \{\tau_1, \ldots, \tau_n\}, \forall i, j \leq n, i < j, T_i < T_j, \exists k \in \mathbb{N} : kT_i = T_j$.

For our following considerations throughout this paper, a task set $\mathcal{T}$ is partitioned into groups of *producer tasks* $\mathcal{P}$ and *consumer tasks* $\mathcal{C}$ with $\mathcal{T} = \mathcal{P} \cup \mathcal{C}$. Furthermore, there is a dependency between tasks of the two differing task groups. Each consumer task gets data from at least one producer task and at most the number of producer tasks in a task set. In turn, the data provided by a producer task is read by at least one consumer task. We define the *data age* as the time between writing data by a producer job at time t_w and reading data by a consumer job at time t_r.

Definition 1 (Data age). *To quantify the freshness of data, we define the data age $A_{i,k,j,l}$ of a communication between the k-th job $\tau_{i,k}$ of a producer task τ_i and the l-th job $\tau_{j,l}$ of a consumer task τ_j as follows:*

$$A_{i,k,j,l} = s_{j,l} - f_{i,k} \text{ with } i \neq j; k, l \geq 0$$

Actual indices k and l depend on the communication semantic. Reading of data at time t_r is possible, if data is available at any time $t_w \leq t_r$. We further assume that data will be initialized with default values, if no data is produced yet.

3   Baseline

In the following, a typical practice how inputs and outputs are handled in embedded control systems is introduced and compared to the LET model. In addition, the data age is characterized for both approaches.

3.1   Bounded-Execution-Time Model

The bounded-execution-time (BET) model is probably the most widely used programming model in real-time operating systems. In BET programming each task executes correctly, as long as reading input, computing states and output, and writing output is completed before its next activation, i.e., within its BET [9]. In the case of rate monotonic scheduled task sets, a task's BET can be set equal to its period T_i. Input is read before a job $\tau_{i,k}$'s computation that is at its starting time $t_{i,k}$ and output is written thereafter at its finishing time $f_{i,k}$. Figure 1a illustrates the data flow between two tasks in the BET model. Task τ_1 produces and writes data and task τ_2 reads and consumes data. The thick black arrows indicate data output and input.

Assumption 1 (Condition for data communication in BET model). *To quantify the data age $A_{i,k,j,l}$ (cf. Definition 1) between the time of the last produced output value by task τ_i and the time when the data is read by task τ_j, choose $k(l)$ so that:*

$$f_{i,k} \leq s_{j,l} < f_{i,k+1}$$

3.2   Logical-Execution-Time Model

The logical-execution-time (LET) model – first introduced in *Giotto* [6,7] – separates the functional part of a program from its timing. The underlying hardware platform can be exchanged without affecting the overall system behavior, even when migrating from a single-core to a multi-core platform. The logical execution of a job starts at a release event that is identical to its arrival time. Accordingly, a termination event symbolizes the end of the logical execution which corresponds to the job's deadline. Between these two events, the job is considered *active*. From the physical point of view, the job's execution can be anywhere between its arrival time and deadline as long as it completes before its deadline. So, a task's LET and period are equal. The input data of a job is read exactly at the beginning of the LET and the output data is made available exactly at the termination event even if the job finishes its computation before. Hence, data transfers happen at predictable times. Throughout the time the job is logically active, the output data produced by the prior instance remains visible to all other tasks. The output data is not updated until the termination event is reached. So, the LET model introduces a delay for the observable data output. Such an assumption leads to the fact that interactions between different tasks are deterministic due to the LET abstraction regardless of the underlying hardware platform.

Figure 1b shows the same task set extract as in Fig. 1a, but with the LET model applied. Here, the output data of $\tau_{1,k}$ is available at the end of τ_1's period (respectively LET) and the input data of τ_2 is read at the beginning of τ_2's period. The data received by τ_2 was actually produced earlier by a prior instance of τ_1.

Assumption 2 (Condition for data communication in LET model).
In the LET model, the data age $A_{i,k,j,l}$ (cf. Definition 1) is the difference between time $f_{i,k}$ when the data was actually produced and time $s_{j,l}$ when it is effectively read. Thus, choose $k(l)$ in such a way that:

$$d_{i,k} \leq a_{j,l} < d_{i,k+1}$$

In the example of Fig. 1b, the data age is greater using the LET model compared to the BET model. Obviously, the data age between tasks of a task set applying the LET model is at its best equal to the one using the BET model. This follows from the fact that almost always the output data is delayed depending on the completion time of the particular job.

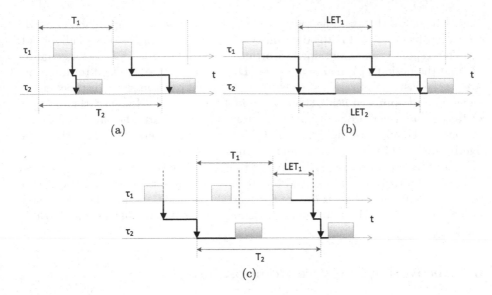

Fig. 1. Sample execution of two tasks on a single core. Thick black arrows symbolize observable data output from task τ_1 and data input to task τ_2, respectively, applying (a) bounded-execution-time (BET) model, (b) logical-execution-time (LET) model, and (c) adapted LET model via response time analysis (RTA).

4   Adapted LET Concept

Our aim is to keep the deterministic behavior of the LET approach, but to reduce the data age by moving the termination event of the producer job as close as possible to the job's finishing time. As a consequence, a task's LET and period will no longer be equal. The interesting point is the amount of time by which we can shift the termination event for each task and still guarantee the deterministic behavior of LET regarding well-defined input and output times. In the LET model, the output is made visible at the termination event respectively when the logical execution time elapses. There is no variation (or rather jitter) relating to the output point in time. So, for our approach, we are looking for a *new LET* at whose end any job of a task will be completed. This applies for the worst-case response time of a task. We choose the new LET_i of a task τ_i to be equal to R_i. To determine the worst-case response times of all tasks in a task set, a response time analysis (RTA) is performed for each task [1,2]. Due to the fact that the adapted LET model is based on a RTA, we abbreviate it LET-RTA approach.

Assumption 3 (Condition for data comm. in LET-RTA approach). *In the LET-RTA approach, the data age $A_{i,k,j,l}$ (cf. Definition 1) denotes the interval between the time when the data is published, i.e., at the end of producer job $\tau_{i,k}$'s response time $a_{i,k} + R_i$, and the time when the data is read. Choose $k(l)$ so that:*

$$a_{i,k} + R_i \le a_{j,l} < a_{i,k+1} + R_i$$

Figure 1c shows the example task set with the adapted LET approach applied. Consider the first job of τ_1 to be the one with the worst response time of all jobs of τ_1. The response time is obtained according to the RTA. So, LET_1 is set equal to R_1 and the period T_1 remains the same. Due to the forward shifted termination event, the last job of task τ_2 reads the output data of the same instance as in the standard approach using the BET model (cf. Fig. 1a). However, the first job of task τ_2 does not profit from the shorter LET and reads the same instance's output as the approach applying the LET model. So generally spoken, the data age between arbitrary producer and consumer jobs may be reduced.

One drawback of the LET-RTA approach is that each time parameters of any task of a task set are changed due to software modifications, a RTA has to be performed again. This is due to the fact that the WCRT may have changed and so the LET. So the software composability is limited in contrast to the LET model.

5   Recovering Software Composability

In embedded control systems task periods of a task set may also be harmonic. In this Section we examine such task sets regarding their software composability. Concerning the transfer of data between tasks with harmonic periods, a distinction can be made between fast-to-slow and slow-to-fast rate communication.

A fast-to-slow rate communication exists, if a higher priority task transfers data to a lower priority task. Since the higher priority task executes more frequently, it may happen that the lower priority task is interrupted and the output of the higher priority task is updated meanwhile. Concerning the LET model the input is read at the release of a task and the output is written at its deadline. Thus, an interim update of the higher priority task's output has no effect on the input data processed by the lower priority task. In the case of a task set with harmonic periods and LET-RTA approach applied, this means the following:

Theorem 1. *For all fast-to-slow rate communications with harmonic periods the data age in the LET-RTA approach is equal to the one in the LET model.*

Proof. For all consumer jobs $\tau_{j,l}$ with $l \neq 0$ there exists a value k, so that $\tau_{j,l}$ is reading from producer job $\tau_{i,k}$ under the condition of Assumption 3. As the periods are harmonic, each time consumer task τ_j is activated also producer task τ_i gets activated. More precisely, $\tau_{i,k}$ is the latest job instance before $\tau_{j,l}$ gets released and thus the period T_i of $\tau_{i,k}$ ends at $a_{j,l}$. This implicates that $a_{j,l} = d_{i,k}$ and so Assumption 2 is also met.   □

If τ_i has only consumer tasks τ_j with $T_j \geq T_i$, then we choose $LET_i = T_i$, since the data age remains the same.

In contrast, a slow-to-fast rate communication exists, if a lower priority task transfers data to a high priority task. Figure 2 shows two nearly identical task sets with a lower priority producer task τ_i and a higher priority consumer task τ_j except that the response time R_i of τ_i differs. As one can see, the longer R_i leads

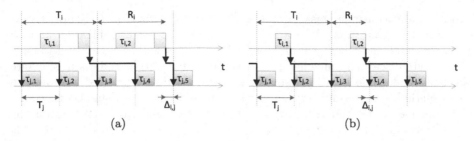

Fig. 2. Sample task execution in a multitasking environment with harmonic periods. Thick black arrows symbolize a slow-to-fast transition from lower priority task τ_i with (a) longer response time R_i and (b) shorter R_j to higher priority task τ_j, respectively.

to the fact that job $\tau_{j,4}$ gets its data from job $\tau_{i,1}$ (cf. Fig. 2a). On the contrary, in Fig. 2b $\tau_{j,4}$ receives more recent data of job $\tau_{i,2}$ due to the shorter R_i.

For all tasks involved in a slow-to-fast rate communication there may be a gap $\Delta_{i,j}$ between a producer task τ_i's response time R_i and a consumer task τ_j's arrival time a_j, which is released next after τ_i. Figure 2 shows the gap $\Delta_{i,j}$ between producer job $\tau_{i,2}$ and consumer job $\tau_{j,5}$ (respectively job $\tau_{j,4}$) exemplarily. Considering the LET-RTA approach, the idea is to postpone the termination event until $R_i + \Delta_{i,j}$. Therefore, the shortest $\Delta_{i,j}$ for each producer task τ_i and all its related consumer tasks τ_j has to be found. As we are focusing on FPP scheduling, the consumer task τ_j with the highest priority is of interest, since it is executed before all other consumer tasks. So, the new LET_i for a producer task τ_i is computed as follows: $LET_i = R_i + \Delta_i$ with $\Delta_i = a_{j,l} - (a_{i,k} + R_i)$ and l so that $a_{j,l-1} < a_{i,k} + R_i \le a_{j,l}$. This implicates that $LET_i = a_{j,l} - a_{i,k}$.

The advantage of postponing the termination event of producer tasks in slow-to-fast rate communications and setting the LET equal to the period for tasks in a fast-to-slow rate communication is that modifications on the software and hence changing tasks' execution times have no influence on the input and output times or rather data age to a certain extent. So, this increases software composability and facilitates testing due to deterministic input and output times.

6   Evaluation

We compare the data ages of the BET, LET, and LET-RTA approach. Thereby, we want to show that it is possible with the LET-RTA approach to reduce the data age in the LET model to a certain extent towards the data age when using BET model. The simulations were performed using *tms-sim* which is a C++ framework for the simulation and evaluation of scheduling algorithms [13].

For our evaluations, task sets composed of two task groups are required as stated in Sect. 2. Any time a consumer task is released or rather starts execution, it reads the data produced by former instances of its connected producer tasks and records the corresponding data age. The new task set generator is based on the generator used in [14], but additionally creates the dependencies between producer and consumer tasks. For each task set a utilization U is preset that lies within a given interval $U \pm d_U$. U represents the target utilization and d_U the maximum allowed deviation from U. Task sets with a utilization outside $U \pm d_U$ are discarded immediately. For significant results it suffices to simulate the task set for one hyper-period. If the task periods are selected randomly, a hyper-period can become very long, which in turn increases simulation times. We implement the approach proposed by Goossens and Macq [4] to limit the hyper-period of the task sets. Thus, simulations can be performed in a feasible time. The aim is to generate the periods of all tasks in a task set in such a manner that their least common multiple remains bounded. The schedulability of a task set is ensured by performing a RTA [1,2]. If the schedulability test fails, the respective task set will also be dropped. Beside the constraints on the task set generation, in our scenario, there is a dependency between tasks of the two differing task groups. Each consumer task gets data from at least one producer task and at most the number of producer tasks in a task set. In turn, the data provided by a producer task is read by at least one processing task.

6.1   Randomly Generated Task Sets

In our evaluation, we examine 100 task sets which operate at nearly full processor load with a total utilization of $U = 0.9$ subdivided in the producer tasks' utilization $U_p = 0.3$ and consumer tasks' utilization $U_c = 0.6$. The number of producer and consumer tasks is set equal to $n_p = n_c = 5$ representing a small to mid-sized work load on an embedded system. The task periods are within the interval $[7, 1664863200]$.

For each task set, we record the minimum, average, and maximum data age of the BET, LET, and LET-RTA approaches between related producer and consumer tasks. Figure 3 compares the means of the minimum, average, and maximum data ages of the BET, LET, and LET-RTA approaches of all interacting tasks from 100 evaluated task sets measured in simulated time steps. The obtained values for the average data ages of the BET, LET, and LET-RTA approaches are 5804, 14912, and 7731 and for the maximum data age 13319, 23109, and 15594. The results confirm that the average (respectively maximum) data age of the LET approach is lowered by $\approx 48.2\%$ (respectively $\approx 32.5\%$) when using the LET-RTA approach. At the same time, the average (respectively maximum) data age of the LET-RTA approach is about $\approx 33.2\%$ (respectively $\approx 17.1\%$) worse than compared to the BET model. As one can see from Fig. 3, on the average the maximum data age could be nearly diminished to the level when using the BET model.

But there are still outliers in the schedule where the data age between an interacting producer and consumer task in the LET-RTA approach is nearly as high as in the LET approach. This is due to the fact that if the producer task's period is short and the consumer task's period is long, the consumer task's scheduling priority is low and thus its computation starts relatively late in its period.

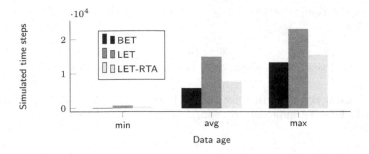

Fig. 3. Means of minimum/average/maximum data ages of all interacting tasks of all task sets.

6.2   Automotive Benchmark

To confirm our theoretical considerations and results obtained by simulation of randomly generated task sets, we applied the LET-RTA approach to a real-world automotive benchmark based on an engine management system. In [15], characteristics of a specific real-world automotive application are provided. We simulated a task set, which complies with the stated criteria. Table 1 shows the relevant task set properties. The task periods are pseudo-harmonic, i.e., most periods divided by every smaller period result in a natural number, but some periods are not divisible by every smaller period, in our case, the 5 ms/50 ms tasks are not divisible by the 2 ms/20 ms tasks. The task set's utilization is $U \approx 82.36\,\%$. For the angle-synchronous task we choose $T_i = 4\,\text{ms}$, which corresponds to an engine with 4 cylinders and a maximum of 7500 revolutions per minute. The communication matrix between the tasks is the same as in [15], with one exception that the angle-synchronous task is not communicating with any other task. This is due to the fact that the period of the angle-synchronous task is varying depending on the current revolutions per minute of the engine and we are focusing on strictly periodic tasks. To reflect the interruptions of all other tasks by the angle-synchronous task, it is still included in the task set.

The simulation results show that the average data age using the LET model is lowered by $\approx 33.0\,\%$, if applying the LET-RTA approach. At the same time, the average data age of the LET-RTA approach is about $\approx 14.3\,\%$ worse than in the case of using the BET model. The results also show that the data ages of the LET-RTA approach are nearly or the same as the ones using the LET model for fast-to-slow rate communications and the BET model for slow-to-fast rate communications, respectively. This is due to the fact, that the task periods are pseudo-harmonic.

Because of the pseudo-harmonic periods, we also extracted the smallest Δ for all tasks from the obtained results. Table 2 shows the LET of each task τ_i for the LET model ($LET_i = T_i$), the LET-RTA approach ($LET_i = R_i$), and the LET-RTA approach with relaxed response times ($LET_i = R_i + \Delta_i$). As one can see, for the 1 ms and 2 ms tasks the LET of the LET-RTA approach can be set equal to the one of the LET model and the average data ages remain still

Table 1. Period T_i and worst-case execution time C_i of the simulated real-world automotive task set

T_i in ms	1	2	5	10	20	50	100	200	1000	4	(angle-sync.)
C_i in ms	0.150	0.084	0.220	2.522	2.184	0.526	2.106	0.026	0.018	0.778	

Table 2. Logical execution time for the LET model (T_i), LET-RTA approach (R_i), and relaxed LET-RTA approach $(R_i + \Delta_i)$

T_i in ms	1	2	5	10	20	50	100	200	1000
R_i in ms	0.928	1.162	1.382	5.670	9.400	9.926	18.320	18.346	18.364
$R_i + \Delta_i$ in ms	1	2	2	6	10	10	20	20	20

the same for the LET-RTA approach. For all other tasks, the LET can also be increased without any disadvantages for the data ages.

7   Related Work

In Sect. 4 we already differentiated our approach from the original LET model [7]. With Giotto it shares the same basic idea of the LET model, but our focus lies more on the deterministic behavior of inputs and outputs than a complete programming language with support by an inherent compiler.

A successor of Giotto is a component model for real-time systems, named Timing Definition Language (TDL) [3]. However, Giotto is primarily an abstract mathematical model and TDL extends it by the notion of a *module*. Modules are named Giotto programs, which can be exported to other modules and vice versa import other modules. So, the TDL component model increases the composability of Giotto based programs and preserves the LET at the same time.

In [10], the authors give an overview of related and further work based on Giotto. Amongst others, they go into details on another real-time programming model, the synchronous model [8,9], also called synchronous reactive programming [5,17], which assumes that tasks have logically zero execution time. In contrast, the physical execution of a synchronous program is correct, if input is read at the occurrence of a triggering event and computation and writing output is finished before the next event occurs. Since output is written right after computation, it is subject to a certain jitter depending on varying computation times. In contrast, in the LET model, output is always written at the end of a period and thus does not underly any output jitter. From a logical time point of view, the synchronous model and LET approach have in common that reading input and writing output are assumed to be infinitely fast. On the other hand, in the LET approach the computation is performed within the LET whereas in synchronous programming it is assumed to be zero. Two prominent examples of synchronous reactive programming languages are Esterel and Lustre.

Another enhancement of LET or rather TDL is the extended timing definition language (E-TDL) [12]. Thereby, the LET is decoupled from the period meaning that the logical release and termination event is no longer at a period's start and end. Instead, the release event is moved forward by an offset ϕ allowing a later reading of inputs. Correspondingly, outputs are written at the termination event, which can be before or at the same time as the deadline. In [11] the applicability of E-TDL is shown for EDF scheduling. The E-TDL and the LET-RTA approach both have in common that the LET is no longer equal to the period. The E-TDL model goes one step further and also decouples the logical release event from the arrival time by a certain offset. But with E-TDL a task is constrained in advance whereas with LET-RTA the logical execution time is tightened afterwards without applying further restrictions. Currently, E-TDL is focusing on EDF scheduling in contrast to LET-RTA with its focus on FPP scheduled task sets.

8   Conclusion and Future Work

In this paper we presented an approach to reduce the tasks' output delay compared to the case of using the LET model. For this purpose, a response time analysis for each task of a task set was performed to obtain values for the new tasks' LETs and still guarantee predictable data output times. The main concern was to decrease the data age between communicating tasks. Our evaluations showed that the average (respectively maximum) data age between depending tasks were significantly reduced with our LET-RTA approach. Furthermore, we showed the applicability for real-world applications on the basis of an automotive benchmark.

The LET model permits exchanging the underlying hardware platform as long as the processing power suffices to do all tasks' computations within the corresponding LET. Due to the fact that our approach minimizes the LET, minimal changes on software parts or the task set require a new calculation of the RTA. For task sets with (pseudo-)harmonic periods we identified a possibility to relax the LET in the LET-RTA approach. So, small changes on the software may not require a new calculation of the RTA and the input and output times or rather the data age remains the same. This increases software composability and facilitates testing. The next step will be an investigation of the tasks' input times, whether an advantage arises for the data age by postponing the input times.

References

1. Audsley, N., Burns, A., Richardson, M., Tindell, K., Wellings, A.J.: Applying new scheduling theory to static priority pre-emptive scheduling. Softw. Eng. J. **8**(5), 284–292 (1993)
2. Audsley, N.C., Burns, A., Richardson, M.F., Wellings, A.J.: Hard real-time scheduling: the deadline-monotonic approach. In: Workshop on Real-Time Operating Systems and Software, pp. 133–137 (1991)

3. Farcas, E., Farcas, C., Pree, W., Templ, J.: Transparent distribution of real-time components based on logical execution time. ACM SIGPLAN Not. **40**(7), 31–39 (2005)
4. Goossens, J., Macq, C.: Limitation of the hyper-period in real-time periodic task set generation. In: RTS Embedded Systems, pp. 133–148 (2001)
5. Halbwachs, N.: Synchronous Programming of Reactive Systems. Kluwer Academic Publishers, Norwell (1992)
6. Henzinger, T.A., Horowitz, B., Kirsch, C.M.: Embedded control systems development with giotto. In: Workshop on Languages, Compilers and Tools for Embedded Systems (LCTES), LCTES 2001, pp. 64–72. ACM, New York, NY, USA (2001)
7. Henzinger, T.A., Horowitz, B., Kirsch, C.M.: Giotto: a time-triggered language for embedded programming. In: Henzinger, T.A., Kirsch, C.M. (eds.) EMSOFT 2001. LNCS, vol. 2211, pp. 166–184. Springer, Heidelberg (2001)
8. Kirsch, C.M.: Principles of real-time programming. In: Sangiovanni-Vincentelli, A., Sifakis, J. (eds.) EMSOFT 2002. LNCS, vol. 2491, pp. 61–75. Springer, Heidelberg (2002)
9. Kirsch, C.M., Sengupta, R.: The evolution of real-time programming. In: Handbook of Real-Time and Embedded Systems, pp. 11-1–11-23. Chapman & Hall/CRC Computer and Information Science Series, CRC Press, Boca Raton (2007)
10. Kirsch, C.M., Sokolova, A.: The logical execution time paradigm. In: Advances in Real-Time Systems, pp. 103–120. Springer, Heidelberg (2012)
11. Kloda, T., d'Ausbourg, B., Santinelli, L.: EDF schedulability analysis for an extended timing definition language. In: Symposium on Industrial Embedded Systems (SIES), pp. 30–40, June 2014
12. Kloda, T., d'Ausbourg, B., Santinelli, L.: Towards a more flexible timing definition language. In: Workshop on Quantitative Aspects of Programming Languages and Systems (QAPL) (2014)
13. Kluge, F.: `tms-sim` – timing models scheduling simulation framework. Technical Report 2014-07, Universität Augsburg, December 2014
14. Kluge, F., Neuerburg, M., Ungerer, T.: Utility-based scheduling of (m, k)-firm real-time task sets. In: Architecture of Computing Systems (ARCS), March 2015
15. Kramer, S., Ziegenbein, D., Hamann, A.: Real world automotive benchmarks for free. In: Workshop on Analysis Tools and Methodologies for Embedded and Real-Time Systems (WATERS), July 2015
16. Liu, C.L., Layland, J.W.: Scheduling algorithms for multiprogramming in a hard-real-time environment. J. ACM **20**(1), 46–61 (1973)
17. Potop-Butucaru, D., de Simone, R., Talpin, J.P.: The synchronous hypothesis and synchronous languages. In: Embedded Systems Handbook. pp. 8-1–8-23. CRC Press, Boca Raton, August 2005

Accurate Sample Time Reconstruction for Sensor Data Synchronization

Sebastian Stieber[1]([✉]), Rainer Dorsch[2], and Christian Haubelt[1]

[1] University of Rostock, Rostock, Germany
sebastian.stieber2@uni-rostock.de
[2] BOSCH Sensortec GmbH, Reutlingen, Germany

Abstract. In the context of cyber-physical systems the accuracy of a growing number of sensor systems plays an important role in data fusion and feature extraction. But the quality of the fusion of different sensor types and even multiple sensor devices directly depends on the sampling time information of the measured sensor samples. Due to potential clock drifts of the embedded sensor systems the fusion results of different sensor samples get worse. In this paper, we present an approach for an *accurate sample time reconstruction* independent of the actual clock drift with the help of an internal sensor counter, as it is already available in modern MEMS sensor systems. The presented approach focuses on calculating accurate timestamps with and without using the sensor FIFO interface.

Keywords: Sensor nodes · Sensor data synchronization · Sensor time · FIFO · MEMS

1 Introduction

MEMS (micro-electro-mechanical systems) have become the state-of-the-art technology for small, robust and energy efficient sensor devices in recent years [1]. They combine mechanical elements, measuring physical quantities, with traditional integrated circuit components on a single chip [2]. The sensor devices offer measured sensor data with up to several thousands of samples per second. In modern sensors, e.g. [4], data can be obtained one-by-one from dedicated sensor data registers. Additionally the sensor samples can be stored in a First-In-First-Out queue (FIFO) and be read periodically in burst mode. Fetching the samples from the data registers always returns the latest measured sample. This permits a low-latency processing, but also results in a higher communication overhead for high frequent data read-out, and, finally, leading to a higher power consumption of the host device.

However, collecting multiple sensor samples in the FIFO introduces an additional delay between the sampling time and the data acquisition by the host. Hence, the FIFO read-out mode is not suitable for low-latency applications like, e.g., image stabilization in cameras. On the other hand, using the FIFO prevents for data loss or double-acquisition of samples and can lower the power consumption by reducing the number of host/sensor interactions. As a consequence, it

F. Hannig et al. (Eds.): ARCS 2016, LNCS 9637, pp. 185–196, 2016.
DOI: 10.1007/978-3-319-30695-7_14

is used for many block-based sensor data processing applications like feature extraction for, e.g., step counting and gesture detection.

More and more gadgets and wearables contain an increasing number of MEMS sensors, measuring among others movement, pressure, sound, light and many more. These devices enable upcoming sensor data-based technologies, as activity recognition, indoor navigation, or augmented reality. For a precise calculation of the above mentioned applications, the fusion of the output of multiple sensor devices and sensor data types is necessary. This fusion needs usually time-aligned sensor data to produce high quality results. Due to unintended frequency drifts between the sensor system clocks and the host clock the fetched sensor samples are not synchronized as each sampling was triggered on its individually, and potentially, drifting timebase.

Many publications on sensor synchronization exist in literature [3]. However, most of them are concerned about clock synchronization or low-latency data acquisition based on register communication. For MEMS sensor devices that are not able to adapt their internal clock frequency the traditional clock synchronization approaches can not be applied. In this paper, we focus on the problem of sample time reconstruction for synchronizing sensor data, which is read via the FIFO interface of the sensor. In this scenario, the influence of different clock drifts on the sensor sampling times is shown in Fig. 1. If the host fetches the FIFO chunk at the dashed line, the resulting number of samples varies between (a), (b), and (c), representing the perfect clock, a slow clock, and a fast clock, respectively. From this figure, it is obvious that the sample time reconstruction without considering the individual sensor drift will become inaccurate.

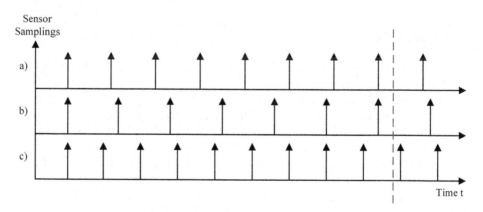

Fig. 1. Influence of different clock drifts on sampling times: Comparison of (a) ideal clock, (b) slower clock and (c) faster clock.

For our approach, we propose a sensor architecture, as it is shown in Fig. 2. Multiple sensor devices are connected to a host system. Each device has its own clock and runs unaligned to the host clock. As a consequence, their individual clocks may drift with respect to the clock of the host system. The sensor data is stored in a FIFO. Additionally, the internal sensor time is counted and returned by the FIFO on read-out. The host system fetches the sensor data from the different sensor devices and performs a reconstruction of the sensor sample times. Here, we assume deterministic communication times and constant clock drifts[1]. Based on the corrected timestamps, the data fusion can be calculated and further data processing can be done.

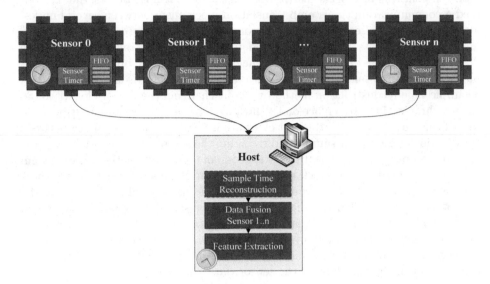

Fig. 2. Architecture overview: Multiple sensor nodes, containing sensor time counter and FIFO interface, are connected to a host system. Each device has its own timebase resulting in potential relative clock drifts between the sensor nodes and the host.

The paper is organized as follows. In Sect. 2, we present related work on sensor data synchronization. As most of the related work is based on clock synchronization and register-based data acquisition, we show in Sect. 3 a simple example of timestamp reconstruction when using the sensor FIFO and give a brief introduction into the FIFO interface of modern MEMS sensors. In Sect. 4, we present our approach for a more accurate sample time reconstruction. In Sect. 5, we describe and show the experimental setup and results.

2   Related Work

Synchronization in sensor networks has been discussed by many researchers in the last years. Sivrikaya et al. concludes different approaches for synchronization in wireless networks in [3]. The existing methods can be classified as *clock synchronization* and *sample time reconstruction* approaches. Elson et al. defined the Reference Broadcast Synchronization Scheme (RBS) [7] and Ganeriwal

---

[1] Our approach is also robust against variable clock drift to some extent, but this is not studied in this paper.

et al. proposed the Timing-Sync Protocol for Sensor Networks (TPSN) [10]. Both are based on adjusting the clock of the sensor nodes, while the synchronization protocol is different. In contrast, our approach is not focused on adjusting clocks, but on sample time reconstruction on the host device.

Later Römer and Elson presented several ideas for synchronization without modifying the timebase of the distributed sensors [8, 9]. Among others, they considered a communication timestamp translation mechanism between several nodes. Donovan et al. proposes a method for sensor synchronization by centralized triggering the measurements in a network with deterministic access times [6]. This can be done with some kinds of sensors, such as magnetic field sensors, but it is not applicable for continuously sensing devices, such as inertial sensors. Olson presented in [11] a sample time reconstruction method without changing the sensor clock, too. So the synchronization takes place on the host system only. Therefore multiple data sets of the sensor clock and the host clock are used to estimate the delay between the creation of the sensor sample and receiving the sample on the host.

Our approach operates near to the solution of Olson [11], as the sensor system clock is not changed and clock drift information is gained from multiple measurements of sensor data. In contrast to [11], we focus on block processing the sensor data from the FIFO, where not all sensor samples contain timestamps. Additionally, we use the internal sensor time counter of the sensor system to increase the timestamp accuracy in deterministic communication environments. In Sect. 4, we will show that our approach is independent of the actual time instance, when the host fetches the sensor data.

3   Background and Problem Statement

In this section, we introduce the FIFO interface, as well as the sensor time counter of the sensor nodes and we give a problem formulation.

3.1   Simple Timestamp Reconstruction of FIFO Data

Modern sensor systems provide sensor data not only via registers but also via a FIFO queue to buffer a specific amount of data. Using the FIFO of a sensor system can prevent data loss and reduce the energy consumption. When dealing with multiple sensors and high data rates, it might be the only solution for gathering the entire amount of sensor data. Here, we give a brief example of a simple timestamp reconstruction algorithm to explain the problem of using the FIFO interface in the presence of drifting clocks in the sensor system.

A typical usage of the FIFO interface is that the host reads all available data from the FIFO in burst mode. In order to configure a minimal amount of data to be read, the host can set a threshold within the sensor system. If the fill level of the FIFO exceeds this threshold, a *watermark* interrupt is issued to the host system. In response, the host reads a chunk of data from the FIFO interface.

When the host system reads a chunk of n sensor samples from the FIFO without any information about the drift between the host clock and the sensor system clock, the signal reconstruction is based on the ideal sampling period of the sensor. The individual sensor sample timestamps t_n can be calculated by Eq. (1).

$$t_n = t_0 + n \cdot period_{sensor} \tag{1}$$

Based on the time t_{wm} when the watermark interrupt is detected at the host, the initial timestamp t_0 of the next FIFO chunk can be calculated in a forward-only processing system. This kind of processing system parses the FIFO data from the beginning and does not allow modifications of already processed items. This behavior can reduce the latency for further processing steps, based on single sensor samples. In contrast, a post processing system can use the information of the whole FIFO chunk to modify the sensor sample timestamps. As a consequence, it has a higher processing delay.

$$t_0 = t_{wm-1} + period_{sensor} \tag{2}$$

Combining Eqs. (1) and (2), the timestamps for each sample of the FIFO stream can be calculated by

$$t_n = t_{wm-1} + (n+1) \cdot period_{sensor} \tag{3}$$

Figure 3 shows the signal reconstruction using Eq. (3). The clock of the sensor system in the upper part of the diagram runs slower than expected. The FIFO is filled with sensor samples until the configured fill level is reached and the watermark interrupt is issued. The host system reads immediately the FIFO data, but the sample time reconstruction of the fetched data, shown in the lower diagram, leads to increasing timing errors. The resulting jitter J directly depends on the clock drift of the sensor system and the fill level of the FIFO.

3.2 Sensor Time

To avoid the timing error of the reconstructed sensor signal, the sensor sample timestamps can be corrected with the help of timing information of the sensor system [12]. The inertial measurement unit in [4] provides such a sensor time.

It is implemented as a 24 bit wide free-running counter with a resolution of $1/25.6\,kHz$. The internal sensor data samples are strictly synchronized with the toggling rate of single bits of this counter. Table 1 shows a subset of the sensor time toggling rates.

The sensor data registers and the FIFO, respectively, get updated exactly with the appropriate sensor time bit m. E.g. an acceleration sensor with a configured data rate of $50\,Hz$ would be updated together with bit 9 of the sensor time. The actual sensor time value can be read by the host either from the dedicated sensor time registers or from the FIFO, where it is appended on an underflow. In both cases the sensor time value ST contains the timestamp, when the first byte of the latest sensor sample was read, with an accuracy of $39.0625\,\mu s$. Equation (4) can be used to calculate the delay t_{delay} between the sampling time and the read-out of the last frame.

$$t_{delay} = (ST \bmod 2^m) \cdot 39.0625\,\mu s \tag{4}$$

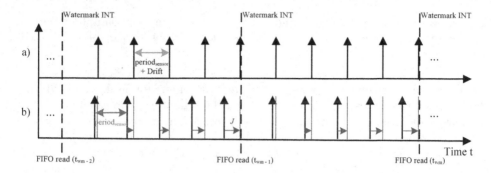

Fig. 3. Timing errors due to clock drift, where (a) represents the real sensor samplings affected by a drifting clock and (b) shows the reconstructed sampling times and the resulting jitter J.

Table 1. Sensor time aligned data rates.

Bit m in sensor time	...	10	9	8	7	6	5	4	3	...
Resolution [ms]	...	40	20	10	5	2.5	1.25	0.625	0.3125	...
Sensor sample rate [Hz]	...	25	50	100	200	400	800	1600	3200	...

4   Accurate Sample Time Reconstruction

In this section, we present our approach to calculate accurate sample timestamps by involving the relative drift between the host clock and sensor clock. The sensor time information of the sensor system is used on the host side to reconstruct the sensor signal accurately, without adjusting the sensor clock.

4.1   Using the FIFO Interface

To calculate the accurate timestamps for each sensor sample of a FIFO chunk, the relative drift $D_{H/S}$ between the host clock and the sensor system clock has to be determined. We present an algorithm in Fig. 4, which is able to calculate the relative drift $D_{H/S}$ by multiple timestamp observations. For this purpose, the delta of the sensor time values ST_{old} and ST_{new} and host timestamps HT_{old} and HT_{new} of consecutive FIFO read-outs are compared. The sensor system timestamps are taken directly from the sensor time frames, while the host timestamps are stored at the end of each burst access. The algorithm uses different fill level thresholds to reach a fast initialization of the sample time reconstruction algorithm.

While the algorithm is initializing, the FIFO fill level threshold is set to a minimum value. As a consequence, the FIFO chunk contains only a single sensor sample, when the watermark interrupt is activated. As soon as two pairs of HT and ST are available, the relative drift $D_{H/S}$ can be calculated by Algorithm 1. The host should take care about potential overflows of the sensor timer. Once the drift value is known, the FIFO fill level threshold can be increased. The repeated drift calculation with each FIFO read-out makes the algorithm robust against slow changing relative clock drifts.

if $ST_{new} >= ST_{old}$ **then**
  | $ST_{delta} = ST_{new} - ST_{old}$
else
  | $ST_{delta} = ST_{new} + 2^{24} - ST_{old}$
end
$HT_{delta} = HT_{new} - HT_{old}$
$D_{H/S} = HT_{delta} / (ST_{delta} \cdot 39.0625\,\mu s)$

Algorithm 1. Simple drift calculation.

The calculated relative drift can be used to modify the future sample timestamps in a forward-only system or even the past samples in a post processing system with Eq. (5). This way, the sensor period steps are scaled with the relative drift value to eliminate the jitter.

$$t_n = t_{n-1} + D_{H/S} \cdot period_{sensor} \tag{5}$$

Due to read-out latency after watermark interrupt notification and limited communication bandwidth while burst-read, the reconstructed timestamps might be influenced by an offset (phase). This offset can be calculated and corrected with the help of the sensor time value, too. The age of the last frame in the FIFO can be determined by the LSB below the toggling sensor time bit m, matching the currently selected data rate. Equation (4) is extended by the drift correction to get the accurate sample time t_{last} of the last sample of a FIFO chunk:

$$t_{last} = HT_{new} - (ST_{new} \bmod 2^m) \cdot D_{H/S} \cdot 39.0625\,\mu s \tag{6}$$

This timestamp can be used as initial timestamp for the next FIFO chunk. Combining Eqs. (5) and (6), the accurate sample times for all following sensor samples can be calculated. Equation (7) represents the calculation of accurate timestamps in a forward-only processing system.

$$t_n = t_{last} + (n+1) \cdot D_{H/S} \cdot period_{sensor} \tag{7}$$

In contrast to the simple timestamp reconstruction, presented in Sect. 3.1, we are now able to scale the timestamps of all samples of a FIFO chunk according to the relative drift between the sensor clock and the host clock. Additionally, we can eliminate the phase offset with an accuracy of approx. $39\,\mu s$.

4.2 Using the Register Interface

Without using the FIFO, the main reason for signal deviation is the phase offset, which is introduced by the delay between sample creation on the sensor system

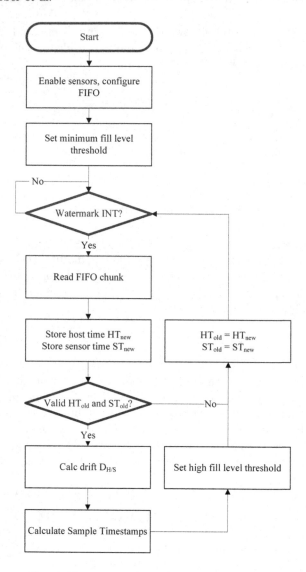

Fig. 4. Continuous drift calculation algorithm.

and read-out of the sample from the data register. However, to determine this delay and, as a result, to calculate the accurate sample timestamp using single sensor samples, the presented approach can be used, too.

The sensor time value can also be read from the register interface. This permits the calculation of the relative drift $D_{H/S}$ by multiple timestamp observations the same way as described in Algorithm 1. Using the drift information, the exact sample time of the single fetched sensor sample can easily be determined by Eq. (6).

5   Experimental Results

In this section, we present our simulation based test setup, as well as the performed experiments and results.

5.1   Test Setup

Our experiments are based on a virtual prototype of the sensor system mentioned in [4]. It was modeled with the $C++$ based simulation and modeling language *SystemC* [5]. The modeled sensor system provides accelerometer as well as gyroscope data, which can be stored in a FIFO queue. Also the sensor time counter, as described in Sect. 3.2, is contained. The host/sensor interface was simulated with an I^2C-protocol running with a frequency of 1MHz, resulting in a bandwidth of approx. 125 kbyte/s. Figure 5 shall explain the simulation setup.

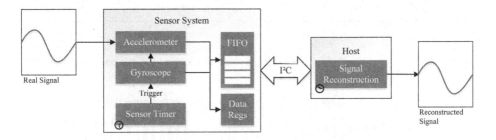

Fig. 5. SystemC based sensor/host test setup.

The accelerometer module is stimulated with an ideal 10 Hz sine signal on all axes. The sensor time counter triggers the sampling with a rate of 1.6 kHz and updates the FIFO and data registers with this rate respectively. The host reads the FIFO data and performs the signal reconstruction with and without using the presented approach for an accurate sample time calculation. The time between receiving the watermark interrupt and reading the FIFO data is annotated with a random jitter period with a maximum value of 500 μs.

5.2   Results

The test cases were performed with different relative drifts between the host clock and the sensor clock. For evaluation of the results, the reconstructed signal is compared to the input signal. The absolute error between the signals is considered as an noise signal, which is shown in the lower part of the Figs. 6 and 7. The relative drift is 5 % in both scenarios.

Figure 6 compares the error of the reconstructed sensor signals when using the register interface. On the left side, no timestamp correction was performed. Instead, the samples were annotated with the read times of the host. On the right side, the timestamps were corrected by the presented approach. The phase error has visibly be reduced by about 86 % with our approach.

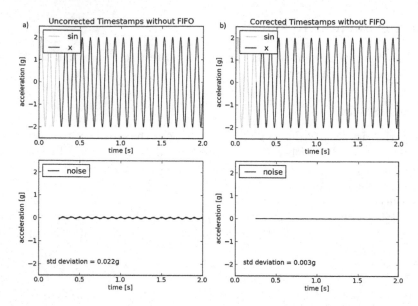

Fig. 6. Noise signal of a single sample based data processing (a) without and (b) with accurate sample time reconstruction

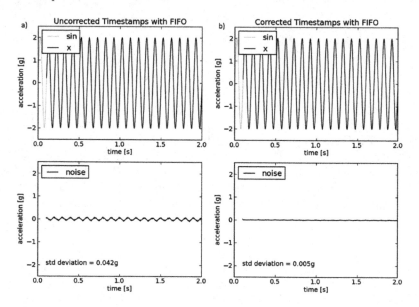

Fig. 7. Noise signal of a FIFO based data processing (a) without and (b) with accurate sample time reconstruction

The reconstructed signal, as well as the noise signal of the simple reconstruction algorithm from Sect. 3.1, is shown in Fig. 7. As expected, the error increases, when using the FIFO interface. Without paying attention to the relative clock drift, the timing jitter inside of a FIFO chunk increases with the

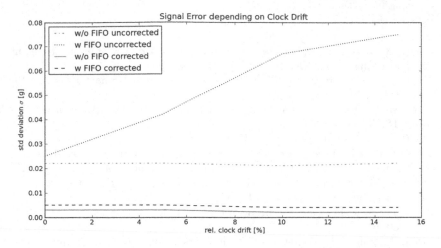

Fig. 8. Impact of different sensor drifts on noise signal

number of included sensor samples. In this scenario, we filled the FIFO with only 10 samples, so the result would become even worse, using a higher fill level. The accurate sample time reconstruction was able to reduce the noise level by 88 %.

Figure 8 shows the influence of different relative clock drifts on the resulting noise level of the reconstructed signals. The results show that our proposed accurate sample time reconstruction reaches significantly lower noise levels independent of the relative clock drifts between sensor and host. Furthermore, it becomes obvious that the uncorrected register based reconstruction is dominated by the phase offset error, while the simple FIFO based approach is not robust against drifting clocks, in any case. The remaining noise in the reconstructed signal is most likely an effect of quantization errors of the 16-bit sensor values and the limited precision of 39 μs of the sensor timer.

6   Conclusions

We presented an approach for an accurate sampling time reconstruction of sensor data fetched from FIFO based sensor systems. We assumed that the different clocks of sensor and host system introduces a relative drift, which results in asynchronous time bases. Without considering this drift, the FIFO based sensor signal reconstruction becomes inaccurate. Our approach was able to reduce the resulting noise of the reconstructed signal to a minimum, independent on the relative clock drift. This allows subsequent sensor data based applications, like sensor data fusion and feature extraction, to produce better results.

References

1. Bogue, R.: Recent developments in MEMS sensors: a review of applications, markets and technologies. Sens. Rev. **33**(4), 300–304 (2013)
2. Gardner, J.W., Varadan, V.K.: Microsensors, Mems and Smart Devices. Wiley, New York (2001)
3. Sivrikaya, F., Yener, B.: Time synchronization in sensor networks: a survey. IEEE Netw. **18**, 45–50 (2004)
4. BOSCH Sensortec: Data sheet BMI160, February 2015. https://ae-bst.resource. bosch.com/media/products/dokumente/bmi160/BST-BMI160-DS000-07.pdf
5. IEEE 1666–2011: Standard SystemC Language Reference Manual, January 2012
6. Donovan, M.J., Petrie, C.S., Kozomora, N., Doogue, M.C.: Systems and methods for synchronizing sensor data. US Patent 8,577,634 (2013)
7. Elson, J., Estrin, D.: Time synchronization for wireless sensor networks. In: IPDPS, p. 1 (2001)
8. Elson, J., Römer, K.: Wireless sensor networks: a new regime for time synchronization. SIGCOMM Comput. Commun. Rev. **33**(1), 149–154 (2003)
9. Römer, K.: Time synchronization in ad hoc networks. In: Proceedings of the 2nd ACM International Symposium on Mobile Ad Hoc Networking and Computing, pp. 173–182 (2001)
10. Ganeriwal, S., Kumar, R., Srivastava, M.B.: Timing-sync protocol for sensor networks. Center for Embedded Network Sensing. ACM, Los Angeles (2003)
11. Olson, E.: A passive solution to the sensor synchronization problem. In: 2010 IEEE/RSJ International Conference on Intelligent Robots and Systems (IROS), pp. 1059–1064 (2010)
12. Claus, T., Dorsch, R., Lammel, G.: Sensor Time. Patent WO2013159972A2 (2013)

DiaSys: On-Chip Trace Analysis
for Multi-processor System-on-Chip

Philipp Wagner$^{(\boxtimes)}$, Thomas Wild, and Andreas Herkersdorf

Lehrstuhl für Integrierte Systeme, Technische Universität München, Arcisstraße 21,
80333 Munich, Germany
{philipp.wagner,thomas.wild,herkersdorf}@tum.de
https://www.lis.ei.tum.de

Abstract. To find the cause of a functional or non-functional defect
(bug) in software running on multi-processor System-on-Chip (MPSoC),
developers need insight into the chip. For that, most of today's SoCs
have hardware tracing support. Unfortunately, insight is restricted by the
insufficient off-chip bandwidth, a problem which is expected to become
more severe in the future as more functionality is integrated on-chip. In
this paper, we present a novel tracing system architecture, the diagnosis system "DiaSys." It moves the analysis of the trace data from the
debugging tool on a host PC into the chip, avoiding the off-chip bandwidth bottleneck. To enable on-chip processing, we propose to move away
from trace data streams towards self-contained diagnosis events. These
events can then be transformed on-chip by processing nodes to increase
the information density, and then be transferred off-chip with less bandwidth. We evaluate the concept with a prototype hardware implementation, which we use to find a functional software bug. We show that
on-chip trace processing can significantly lower the off-chip bandwidth
requirements, while providing insight into the software execution equal
to existing tracing solutions.

Keywords: Debugging · Tracing · MPSoC · SoC architectures

1 Introduction

To write high-quality program code for a Multi-Processor System-on-Chip
(MPSoC), software developers must fully understand how their code will be
executed on-chip. Debugging or diagnosis tools can help developers to gain
this understanding. They are a keyhole through which developers can peek and
observe the software execution. Today, and even more in the future, this keyhole narrows as MPSoCs integrate more functionalities, at the same time as the
amount of software increases. Furthermore, the interaction between software and
hardware components increases beyond the instruction set architecture (ISA)
boundary. Therefore, more, not less, insight into the system is required to keep
up or even increase developer productivity.

© Springer International Publishing Switzerland 2016
F. Hannig et al. (Eds.): ARCS 2016, LNCS 9637, pp. 197–209, 2016.
DOI: 10.1007/978-3-319-30695-7_15

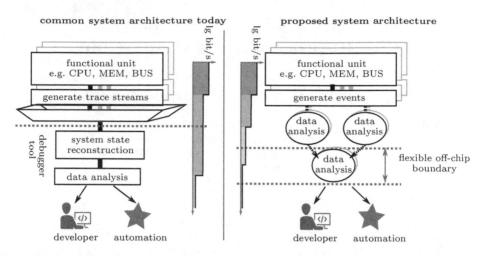

Fig. 1. Comparing a traditional SoC tracing system architecture (left) with our proposed architecture (right). Only the trace data path is shown.

Many of today's MPSoCs are executing concurrent code on multiple cores, interact with the physical environment (cyber-physical systems), or need to finish execution in a bounded amount of time (hard real-time). In these scenarios, non-intrusive observation of the software execution is required, which tracing provides. Instead of stopping the system for observation (as it is done in run-control debugging), the observed data is transferred off-chip for analysis. Unfortunately, observing a full system execution would generate data streams in the range of petabits per second [14, p. 16]. As the bandwidth of available I/O interfaces is limited, only a part of the system can be observed at any given time. In summary, the lack of sufficient off-chip bandwidth is the most significant drawback of tracing.

Today's tracing system architectures, like ARM CoreSight [1] or NEXUS 5001 [2] follow a design pattern as shown on the left in Fig. 1. The foremost design goal is the bandwidth-efficient transmission of data streams from CPUs, memories and interconnects through an off-chip interface to a host PC. This is achieved by configurable filtering, (cross-)triggering and compression methods. On the host PC a debugger tool reconstructs the SoC system state using the program binary and other static information. It then extracts useful information out of the data and presents it to a developer or to another tool, e.g. for runtime verification.

The **main idea** in this work is to move the trace data analysis (at least partially) from the host PC into the chip, as shown on the right side of Fig. 1. Bringing the computation closer to the data reduces the off-chip bandwidth requirements, and ultimately increases insight into the software execution.

To realize this idea, in this paper we present a novel tracing system architecture, the "diagnosis system" which enables on-chip trace data analysis. As part of this system we introduce a general-purpose programmable on-chip data analysis element, the "diagnosis processor." It executes a trace analysis program on-chip and increases the information density of the off-chip traffic.

The further paper is structured as follows. Based on the related work in the field of SoC tracing and scriptable and event-based debugging in Sect. 2, we present our concept of the diagnosis system in Sect. 3. The feasibility of the concept is shown with a hardware implementation presented in Sect. 4.1, which is used in Sect. 4.2 to find a functional bug in a software program.

2   Related Work

Our approach relates to works from two fields of research. First, trace-based debugging for SoCs, and second, scriptable debugging and trace analysis.

Today's **tracing solutions for SoCs** are structured as shown in Fig. 1. First, a trace data stream is obtained from various functional units in the system, like CPUs, buses and memories. Then, this data is spatially and temporally reduced through the use of filters and triggers. Finally, the redundancy in the data is removed by the use of compression algorithms. The resulting trace data stream is then transferred off-chip (live or delayed through an on-chip memory buffer). On a host PC, the original trace stream is reconstructed and analyzed by debuggers or profilers.

All major commercial SoC vendors offer tracing solutions based on this template. ARM provides its licensees the CoreSight intellectual property (IP) blocks [1], which are used in SoCs from Texas Instruments, Samsung and STMi-croelectronics, among others. Vendors such as Freescale/NXP include tracing solutions based on the IEEE-ISTO 5001 (Nexus) standard [2], while Infineon integrates the Multi-Core Debug Solution (MCDS) into its automotive microcon-trollers [9]. The main differentiator between the solutions is the configurability of the filter and trigger blocks.

Driven by the off-chip bottleneck, a major research focus are lossless trace compression schemes. Program trace compression available in commercial solu-tions typically requires 1 to 4 bit per executed instruction [8,12], while solutions proposed in academia claim compression ratios down to 0.036 bit per instruc-tion [13]. Even though data traces contain in general no redundancy, in practice compression rates of about 4:1 have been achieved [8].

Scriptable or programmable debugging applies the concept of event-driven programming to debugging. Whenever a defined *probe point* is hit, an event is triggered and an *event handler* executes. Common probe points are the execution of a specific part of the program (like entering a certain program function), or the access to a given memory location. The best-known current implementations of this concept are DTrace, SystemTap and ktap, which run on, or are part of, BSDs, Linux, and MacOS X (where it is integrated into the "Apple Instruments" product) [3,5]. The concept, however, is much older. Dalek [11] is built on top of the GNU Debugger (GDB) and uses a dataflow app-roach to combine events and generate higher-level events out of primitive events.

Marceau et al. extend the dataflow approach and apply it to the debugging of Java applications [10]. Coca [4], on the other hand, uses a language based on Prolog to define conditional breakpoints as a sequence of events described through predicates for debugging C programs.

However, all mentioned scriptable debugging solutions are implemented in software running as part of the debugged system and are therefore intrusive. The design decisions reflect the environment of desktop to high performance computers and need to be reconsidered when applying the concept to SoCs.

3   DiaSys: A System for On-Chip Trace Analysis

3.1   Requirements for the Diagnosis System

Before presenting the concept of the diagnosis system, we first formulate a set of requirements, which guide both the development of the general concept, as well as the specific hardware implementation.

First and foremost, the diagnosis system must be able to reduce the amount of trace data as close to the source, i.e. the functional units in the SoC, as possible. Since the data sources are distributed across the chip, the diagnosis system must also be distributed in the same way.

Second, the diagnosis system must be non-intrusive (passive). Non-intrusive observation preserves the event ordering and temporal relationships in non-deterministic concurrent executions, a requirement for debugging multi-core, real-time, or cyber-physical systems [6]. Non-intrusiveness also makes the diagnosis process repeatable, giving its user the confidence that he or she is searching for the bug in the functional code, not chasing a problem caused by the observation (a phenomen often called "Heisenbug" [7]).

Third, the design and implementation of a tracing system involves a trade-off between the provided level of observability and the system cost. The two main contributions to the system cost are the off-chip interface and the used chip area. The diagnosis system concept must be flexible enough to give the chip designer the freedom to configure the amount of chip resources, the off-chip bandwidth and the pin count in a way that fits the chips target market. At the same time, the system must be able to adapt to a wide range of bugs by being tunable at run-time to observe different locations in the SoC and execute different types of trace analysis.

3.2   The Concept of the Diagnosis System

The starting point for all observations is a functional unit in the SoC. A functional unit can be a CPU, a memory, an interconnect resource such as a bus or a NoC router, or a specialized hardware block, like a DMA controller or a cryptographic accelerator. Each of these components has a state, which changes during the execution of software. Capturing and analyzing this state is the goal of any debugging or diagnosis approach. In the following, we refer to the full state of a functional unit F at time t as $S(F,t)$, or, in short, S. A subset of this state is what we call a "partial state of F", $S_P(F,t) \subset S(F,t)$. P describes which elements of the full state S are included in the subset S_P.

Our diagnosis system architecture consists of three main components: event generators, processing nodes, and event sinks. Between these three components, events are exchanged.

A **diagnosis event** $E = (t,C,S_P)$ is described by the 3-tuple of a trigger condition C, a partial state snapshot $S_P(F,t)$ and the time t when the event was created. Together, the event answers three questions: when was the event generated, what caused its generation, and in which state was the functional unit at this moment in time.

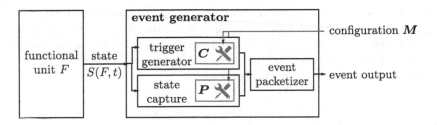

Fig. 2. A block diagram of a generic event generator.

Event generators produce events based on the observation of the state $S(F,t)$ of the functional unit F they are attached to. A schematic block diagram of an event generator is shown in Fig. 2. The event generators can be configured with configuration sets $\boldsymbol{M} = \{M_1, M_2, ..., M_n\}$ with $M = (C,P)$. The trigger condition C achieves temporal selection by defining a condition which causes an event to be generated. P describes which parts of the full state S are included in the event.

Event generators can be attached to all types of functional units, for example NoC routers, memories or CPUs. For example a CPU event generator generally supports trigger conditions based on the program counter (PC) value, which essentially describes the execution of a line of code. In this case, a specific example for a trigger condition C is `PC == 0x2020` which causes an event to be generated if the program counter reaches the value `0x2020`.

Processing nodes transform events by consuming a set of incoming events $\boldsymbol{E}_i = \{E_{i,1}, E_{i,2}, ..., E_{i,n}\}$, and possibly producing new events $\boldsymbol{E}_o = \{E_{o,1}, E_{o,2}, ..., E_{o,m}\}$ as result. The goal of this transformation is to increase the information density of the data contained in the events. The applied transformation function $f : \boldsymbol{E}_i \rightarrow \boldsymbol{E}_o$ depends on the type of the processing node, and possibly its run-time configuration.

For example, a simple processing node could just compare the $S_{P,i}$ of an incoming event with an expected value, and only produce a new event E_o if this value is not found. A more complex processing node could calculate statistical metrics out of the incoming data streams, such as averages or histograms. All processing nodes have in common that they provide a platform to apply knowledge about the system and the software execution to the events.

In this paper, we present a processing node called "diagnosis processor" which can be programmed by the user to perform a wide range of analysis tasks.

Event sinks consume events. They are the end of the event chain. Their purpose is to present the data either to a human user in a suitable form (e.g. as a simple log of events, or as visualization), or to format the events in a way that makes them suitable for consumption by an automated tool, or possibly even for usage by an on-chip component. An example usage scenario for an automated off-chip user is runtime validation, in which data collected during the runtime of the program is used to verify properties of the software.

Together, event generators, processing nodes and event sinks build a processing chain which provides powerful trace analysis according to the requirements outlined in the previous section. In the next section we present a specific type of a processing node, the diagnosis processor.

3.3   The Diagnosis Processor: A Multi-purpose Processing Node

The diagnosis processor is a freely programmable general-purpose processing node. Like any processor design, it sacrifices computational density for flexibility. Its design is inspired by existing scriptable debugging solutions, like SystemTap or DTrace, which have shown to provide a very useful tool for software developers in a growingly complex execution environment. The usage scenario for this processing node are custom or one-off trace data analysis tasks. This scenario is very common when searching for a bug in software. First, a hypothesis is formed by the developer why a problem might have occurred. Then, this hypothesis must be validated in the running system. For this validation, a custom data analysis script must be written, which is highly specific to the problem (or the system state is manually inspected). This process is repeated multiple times, until the root cause of the problem is found. As this process is approached differently by every developer (and often also influenced by experience and luck), a very flexible analysis runtime is required.

We present the hardware design of our diagnosis processor implementation in Sect. 4.1 (Diagnosis Processor).

We envision the programming of the diagnosis processor being done through scripts similar to the ones used by SystemTap or DTrace. They allow to write trace analysis tasks on a similar level of abstraction as the analyzed software itself, leading to good developer productivity.

4   Evaluation

In the following we show how to realize the diagnosis system concept in a hardware implementation. We then apply this hardware implementation in a use case showing how to find a functional bug in a software.

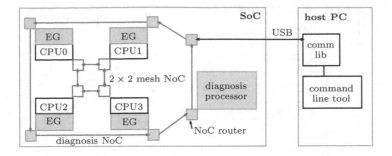

Fig. 3. Block diagram of the prototype implementation.

4.1 Prototype Implementation

Based on the concept of the diagnosis system as discussed in the previous section, we designed a diagnosis extension for a 2×2 tiled multi-core system. The functional system consists of four OpenRISC CPU cores with attached distributed memory components and a mesh NoC interconnect, as shown in Fig. 3 (components with white background). This system is representative of the multi- and many-core architecture template currently in research and available early products, such as the Intel SCC or the EZchip (formerly Tilera) Tile processors.

The diagnosis system, depicted in blue, consists of the following components.

– Four event generators attached to the CPUs (marked "EG" in Fig. 3).
– A single diagnosis processor.
– A 16 bit wide, unidirectional ring NoC, the "diagnosis NoC," to connect the components of the diagnosis system. It carries both the event packets as well as the configuration and control information for the event generators and processing nodes.
– A USB 2.0 off-chip interface.
– Software support on the host PC to control the diagnosis system, and display the results.

All components connected to the diagnosis NoC follow a common template to increase reusability. Common parts are the NoC interface and a configuration module, which exposes readable and writable configuration registers over the NoC. In the following, we explain the implementation of the main components in detail.

CPU Event Generator. The CPU event generator is attached to a single CPU core. Its main functionality is implemented in two modules, the trigger module and the system state snapshot unit. The trigger unit of the CPU event generator fires on two types of conditions: either the value of the program counter (PC), or the return from a function call (the jump back to the caller). At each point in time, 12 independent trigger conditions can be monitored. The number of monitored trigger conditions is proportional to the used hardware resources.

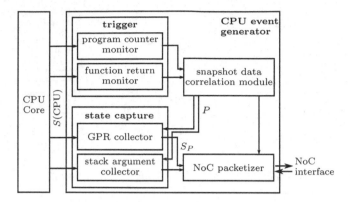

Fig. 4. Block diagram of the CPU event generator.

Our dimensioning was determined by statistical analysis of large collections of SystemTap and DTrace scripts: ≤ 9 concurrent probes are used in 95 % of SystemTap scripts, and ≤ 12 concurrent probes cover 92 % of the DTrace scripts. The partial system state snapshot $S_P(\text{CPU})$ can contain the CPU register contents and the function arguments passed to the function. A block diagram of the CPU event generator is shown in Fig. 4.

It is possible to associate an event with parts of the system state: the contents of the CPU general purpose registers (GPR), and the arguments passed to the currently executed function.

The passing of function arguments to functions depends on the calling convention. On OpenRISC, the first six data words passed to a function are available in CPU registers, all other arguments are pushed to the stack before calling the function. This is common for RISC architectures; other architectures and calling conventions might pass almost all arguments on the stack (such as x86). To record the function arguments as part of the system state we therefore need to create a copy of the stack memory that can be accessed non-intrusively. We do this by observing CPU writes to the stack memory location.

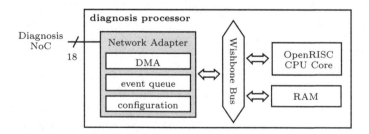

Fig. 5. Block diagram of the diagnosis processor.

Table 1. The resource usage of a CPU diagnosis unit.

Module	LUTS	REGS	RAMS
functional system	40625	29638	80
1 compute tile (system contains 4)	~7232	~4763	20
2 × 2 mesh NoC	10791	9964	0
support infrastructure (DRAM if, clock/reset mgr)	904	623	0
diagnosis system	19556	19140	147
1 CPU Event Generator	3603	6521	2
1 CPU Event Generator (CoreSight-like functionality)	1365	1594	0
1 Diagnosis Processor	8614	4549	145
diagnosis NoC	2520	2926	0

Diagnosis Processor. The diagnosis processor design (Fig. 5) is based on a standard processor template, which is extended towards the use case of event processing. The main components are a 32 bit in-order RISC processor core with the or1k instruction set (mor1kx) and a SRAM block as program and data memory. This system is extended with components to reduce the runtime overhead of processing event packets.

First, the network adapter, which connects the CPU to the diagnosis NoC, directly stores the incoming event packets in the memory through a DMA engine. All event packets are processed in a run-to-completion fashion. We can therefore avoid interrupting the CPU and instead store the address of the event to be processed next in a hardware "run queue". A "discard queue" signals the hardware scheduler which events have been processed and can be purged from memory.

Resource Usage. The prototype of the tiled MPSoC with the diagnosis extensions was synthesized for a ZTEX 1.15d board with a Xilinx Spartan-6 XC6SLX150 FPGA. The relevant hardware utilization numbers as obtained from a Synplify Premier FPGA synthesis are given in Table 1.

The functional system, even though it consists of four CPU cores, is relatively small, as the used mor1kx CPU cores are lightweight (comparable to small ARM Cortex M cores). The functional system contains no memory, but uses an external DDR memory.

In this scenario, the full diagnosis system rather large. We have implemented two types of CPU event generators. A "lite" variant of the event generator can trigger only on a program counter value, and not on the return from a function call. This reduced functionality makes the event generator comparable to the feature set of the ARM CoreSight ETM trace unit, which is said to use ~7,000 NAND gate equivalents [12], making it similarly sized as our event generator. The possibility to trigger also on the return from a function call significantly increases the size of the event generator, mostly due to additional memory. The diagnosis processor is about 20 % larger than a regular compute tile, as it contains an additional DMA engine and the packet queues. It also contains 30 kByte of SRAM as program and data memory, which is not present in a regular compute tile.

In summary, the resource usage of the diagnosis system is acceptable, especially if used in larger functional systems with more powerful CPU cores. At the same time, the implementation still contains many opportunities for optimization, which we plan to explore in the future. Also, a full system optimization to determine a suitable number of diagnosis processors for a given number of CPU cores is future work.

4.2   A Usage Example

In the previous section we described an implementation of our diagnosis system architecture containing a diagnosis processor. As discussed in Sect. 3.3, this processing node is especially suited for hypothesis testing in functional bugs. In the following, we show how to find a functional bug in the C program presented in Listing 1.1.

```
 1   void write_to_buf(char* string, uint32_t size) {
 2     struct {
 3       char buf[99];
 4       char var;
 5     } test;
 6     /* ... */
 7     strncpy(test.buf, string, size);
 8     /* ... */
 9   }
10
11   int main(int argc, char** argv) {
12     char teststr[100] ="string_100_chars_long...";
13
14     for (int i = 0; i < 10000000; i++) {
15       uint32_t len = (i
16       write_to_buf(teststr, len);
17     }
18
19     return 0;
20   }
```

Listing. 1.1. A buggy C program.

The program repeatedly calls the function write_to_buf with a string and the size of the string. The value of the size argument sweeps between 1 and 100. Inside write_to_buf, the string is copied into the buffer test.buf using the strncpy C library function.

The code contains a bug. The test.buf variable holds only 99 characters, while with size == 100 hundred characters are copied into it – a buffer overflow occurs. This causes the data in the variable `test.var` to be overwritten. In the best case this data corruption is annoying, whereas in the worst case this results in a critical security issue.

The debugging process might start with a bug report describing a data corruption on the `text.var` variable. To find the cause of such a defect, a developer might first rely on automated analysis tools. But since out-of-bounds errors on the stack (as in this case) are hard to find, neither the GCC compiler nor Valgrind (with the "exp-sgcheck" tool) issue any warning or error.

Since automated tools did not report anything suspicious, the developer needs to form a hypothesis what might have caused the defect, and test this hypothesis by collecting live data during the application run. The hypothesis in this case is "the value passed as `size` is greater than 99."

Using a traditional tracing system like ARM CoreSight ETM or Nexus 5001 Class 3, we would obtain a full program trace, together with a data trace of writes to the `size` variable.[1] The program trace is compressed to 2 bit/instruction, and the data trace is not compressed. Scaling to the same execution speed as in our prototype, which runs at 25 MHz and executes an average of one instruction every five cycles, this would result in an off-chip bandwidth requirement of 10 Mbit/s. It must be noted that in a faster system this number scales linearly, quickly reaching typically available off-chip interface speeds.

Now we turn to our implementation. First, we measured the execution time of the program by inserting program code to count the number of executed cycles between lines 12 and 16 in Listing 1.1. The measurement showed an equal number of executed cycles if the diagnosis system was enabled or disabled, i.e. that our solution is non-intrusive to the program execution.

Second, the on-chip traffic was analyzed. The event generator creates an event packet every time the function `write_to_buf` is executed. Every event packet consists of six NoC flits (each 16 bit wide): one header flit (with destination and packet type), a 32 bit wide time stamp, a 16 bit wide event identifier, and two flits containing the state snapshot, i.e. the value of the `size` variable. This leads to a NoC traffic of 4.3 Mbit/s, or 12 % of the theoretical NoC bandwidth. This shows two things: first, the NoC link was dimensioned wide enough to connect all four CPU event generators, and second, the event generators are sufficiently selective not to overwhelm the NoC with too many events, which are later discarded.

After processing in the diagnosis processor, only every 100th event generates an off-chip data packet. The off-chip packet is similar to the on-chip packets, but consists only of four flits: one header, a 32 bit time stamp, and a 16 bit event identifier. This results in 0.029 Mbit/s of off-chip traffic, which can easily be handled by cheap interfaces like JTAG. Compared to the compressed full trace, which required a bandwidth of 10 Mbit/s, the off-chip traffic was reduced by a factor of 345.

---

[1] We assume that a single memory location stores the `size` variable. In our compilation this is the case.

5   Conclusions

In this paper we presented a novel tracing system architecture for MPSoCs. We base our design on the observation that bringing the computation required for trace analysis closer to the data source can solve the off-chip bottleneck problem, which limits system observability in today's tracing solutions. The system architecture itself uses diagnosis events as method to transport data in a processing pipeline. Diagnosis events are transformed in a processing pipeline in order to increase their information density. The processing pipeline consists of event sources, which are attached to the SoC's functional units, processing nodes which transform the data to increase their information density, and event sinks, which are usually located on a developer's PC, but can also be on-chip. We also present a powerful processing node, the diagnosis processor. Based on a prototype implementation we show how our system architecture increases the insight into the software execution and makes it possible to find a bug in a program in an intuitive manner.

In the future, we plan to extend this system with more specialized processing nodes, which are suited for common analysis tasks. We also investigate how machine-learning approaches can be used to dynamically adjust the analysis tasks during runtime.

Acknowledgments. This work was funded by the Bayerisches Staatsministerium für Wirtschaft und Medien, Energie und Technologie (StMWi) as part of the project "SoC Doctor," and by the German Research Foundation (DFG) as part of the Transregional Collaborative Research Centre "Invasive Computing" (SFB/TR 89). The responsibility for the content remains with the authors.

References

1. CoreSight - ARM
2. The Nexus 5001 Forum Standard for a Global Embedded Processor Debug Interface, Version 2.0. Technical report, December 2003
3. Cantrill, B.M., Shapiro, M.W., Leventhal, A.H.: Dynamic instrumentation of production systems. In: Proceedings of the General Track: 2004 USENIX Annual Technical Conference, ATEC 2004. USENIX Association, Berkeley (2004)
4. Ducassé, M.: Coca: an automated debugger for C. In: Proceedings of the 21st International Conference on Software Engineering, ICSE 1999, pp. 504–513. ACM, New York (1999)
5. Eigler, F.C., Prasad, V., Cohen, W., Nguyen, H., Hunt, M., Keniston, J., Chen, B.: Architecture of systemtap: a Linux trace/probe tool (2005)
6. Fidge, C.: Fundamentals of distributed system observation. IEEE Softw. **13**(6), 77–83 (1996)
7. Gray, J.: Why do computers stop and what can be done about it? In: Symposium on Reliability in Distributed Software and Database Systems, Los Angeles, CA, USA, pp. 3–12 (1986)
8. Hopkins, A.B.T., McDonald-Maier, K.D.: Debug support strategy for systems-on-chips with multiple processor cores. IEEE Trans. Comput. **55**(2), 174–184 (2006)

9. IPextreme: Infineon Multi-Core Debug Solution: Product Brochure (2008)
10. Marceau, G., Cooper, G., Krishnamurthi, S., Reiss, S.: A dataflow language for scriptable debugging. In: Proceedings of the 19th International Conference on Automated Software Engineering, pp. 218–227, September 2004
11. Olsson, R.A., Crawford, R.H., Ho, W.W.: A dataflow approach to event-based debugging. Softw. Pract. Exper. **21**(2), 209–229 (1991)
12. Orme, W.: Debug and Trace for Multicore SoCs (ARM white paper), September 2008
13. Uzelac, V., Milenković, A., Burtscher, M., Milenković, M.: Real-time unobtrusive program execution trace compression using branch predictor events. In: Proceedings of the 2010 International Conference on Compilers, Architectures and Synthesis for Embedded Systems, CASES 2010, pp. 97–106. ACM, New York (2010)
14. Vermeulen, B., Goossens, K.: Debugging Systems-on-Chip: Communication-centric and Abstraction-based Techniques. Springer, New York (2014)

Analysis of Intel's Haswell Microarchitecture Using the ECM Model and Microbenchmarks

Johannes Hofmann[1]([✉]), Dietmar Fey[1], Jan Eitzinger[2], Georg Hager[2], and Gerhard Wellein[2]

[1] Computer Architecture, University Erlangen–Nuremberg, Erlangen, Germany
johannes.hofmann@fau.de
[2] Erlangen Regional Computing Center (RRZE),
University Erlangen–Nuremberg, Erlangen, Germany

Abstract. This paper presents an in-depth analysis of Intel's Haswell microarchitecture for streaming loop kernels. Among the new features examined are the dual-ring Uncore design, Cluster-on-Die mode, Uncore Frequency Scaling, enhancements such as new and improved execution units, as well as improvements throughout the memory hierarchy. The Execution-Cache-Memory diagnostic performance model is used together with a generic set of microbenchmarks to quantify the efficiency of the microarchitecture. The set of microbenchmarks is chosen in a way that it can serve as a blueprint for other streaming loop kernels.

Keywords: Intel Haswell · Architecture analysis · ECM model · Performance modeling

1 Introduction and Related Work

In accord with Intel's tick-tock model, where a tick corresponds to a shrinking of the process technology of an existing microarchitecture and a tock corresponds to a new microarchitecture, Haswell is a tock and thus represents a new microarchitecture. The major changes that come with a tock justify a thorough analysis of the new architecture. This paper demonstrates how the Execution-Cache-Memory (ECM) diagnostic performance model [2,3,10,11] can be used as a tool to evaluate and quantify the efficiency of a microarchitecture.

The ECM model is a resource-centric model that allows to quantify the runtime of a given loop kernel on a specific architecture. It requires detailed architectural specifications and an instruction throughput prediction as input. It assumes perfect instruction level parallelism for instruction execution as well as bandwidth-bound data transfers. The model yields a practical upper limit for single core performance. The only empirically determined input for the model is that of sustained memory bandwidth, which can be different for each benchmark. The model quantifies different runtime contributions from instruction execution and data transfers within the complete memory hierarchy as well as potential overlap between contributions. Runtime contributions are divided into two different categories: T_{nOL}, i.e. cycles in which the core executes instructions that

© Springer International Publishing Switzerland 2016
F. Hannig et al. (Eds.): ARCS 2016, LNCS 9637, pp. 210–222, 2016.
DOI: 10.1007/978-3-319-30695-7_16

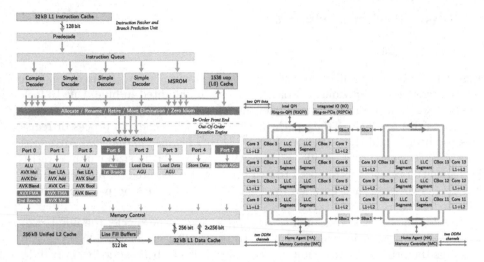

Fig. 1. Core design for the Haswell Microarchitecture

Fig. 2. Chip layout for the Haswell Microarchitecture

forbid simultaneous transfer of data between the L1 and L2 caches; and T_{OL}, i.e. cycles that do not contain non-overlapping instructions, thus allowing for simultaneous instruction execution and data transfers between L1 and L2 caches. One improvement to the original ECM model we make in this paper is that apart from load instructions, store instructions are now also considered non-overlapping. Instruction times as well as data transfer times, e.g. T_{L1L2} for the time required to transfer data between L1 and L2 caches, can be summarized in shorthand notation: $\{T_{\mathrm{OL}} \| T_{\mathrm{nOL}} \mid T_{\mathrm{L1L2}} \mid T_{\mathrm{L2L3}} \mid T_{\mathrm{L3Mem}}\}$. The in-core execution time T_{core} is the maximum of either overlapping or non-overlapping instructions. Predictions for cache/memory levels is given by $\max(T_{\mathrm{OL}}, T_{\mathrm{nOL}} + T_{\mathrm{data}})$ with T_{data} the sum of the individual contributions up to the cache/memory level under consideration, e.g. for the L3 cache $T_{\mathrm{data}} = T_{\mathrm{L1L2}} + T_{\mathrm{L2L3}}$. A similar shorthand notation exists for the model's prediction: $\{T_{\mathrm{core}} \rceil T_{\mathrm{L2}} \rceil T_{\mathrm{L3}} \rceil T_{\mathrm{Mem}}\}$. For details on the ECM model refer to the previously provided references.

Related work covers in-detail analysis of architectural features using microbenchmarks, e.g., [1,7,9]. We are not aware of any work though using an analytic model to quantify the efficiency of a microarchitecture.

Section 2 presents major improvements in Intel Haswell. In Sect. 3 we introduce a comprehensive set of microbenchmarks that serves as a blueprint for streaming loop kernels. To evaluate the hardware, obtained measurements are correlated with the performance predictions in Sect. 4.

2   Haswell Microarchitecture

2.1   Core Design

Figure 1 shows a simplified core design of the Haswell microarchitecture with selected changes to previous microarchitectures highlighted in blue. Due to lack of space we focus on new features relevant for streaming loop kernels.

The width of all three data paths between the L1 cache and processor registers has been doubled in size from 16 B to 32 B. This means that two Advanced Vector Extensions (AVX) loads and one AVX store (32 B in size) can now retire in a single clock cycle as opposed to two clock cycles required on previous architectures. The data path between the L1 and L2 caches has been widened from 32 B to 64 B.

While the core is still limited to retiring four μops per cycle, the number of issue ports has been increased from six to eight. The newly introduced port 6 contains the primary branch unit; a secondary unit has been added to port 0. In previous designs only a single branch unit was available and located on port 5. By moving it to a dedicated port, port 5—which is the only port that can perform AVX shuffle operations—is freed up. Adding a secondary branch unit benefits branch-intensive codes. The other new port is port 7, which houses a so-called simple Address Generation Unit (AGU). This unit was made necessary by the increase in register-L1 bandwidth. Using AVX on Sandy Bridge and Ivy Bridge, two AGUs were sufficient, because each load or store required two cycles to complete, not making it necessary to compute three new addresses every cycle, but only every second cycle. With Haswell this has changed, because potentially a maximum of three load/store operations can now retire in a single cycle, making a third AGU necessary. Unfortunately, this simple AGU can not perform the necessary addressing operations required for streaming kernels on its own (see Sect. 4.3 for more details).

Apart from adding additional ports, Intel also extended existing ones with new functionality. Instructions introduced by the Fused Multiply-Add (FMA) Instruction Set Architecture (ISA) extension are handled by two new, AVX-capable units on ports 0 and 1. Haswell is the first architecture to feature the AVX2 ISA extension and introduces a second AVX multiplication unit on port 1 while there is still just one low-latency add unit.

2.2   Package Layout

Figure 2 shows the layout of a 14-core Haswell processor package. Apart from the processor cores, the package consists of what Intel refers to as the Uncore. Attached to each core and its private L1 and L2 caches, there is a Last-Level Cache (LLC) segment, that can hold 2.5 MB of data. The physical proximity of core and cache segment does however not imply that data used by a core is stored exclusively or even preferably in its LLC segment. Data is placed in all LLC segments according to a proprietary hash function that is supposed to provide uniform distribution of data and prevent hotspots for a wide range of data access patterns. An added benefit of this design is that single-threaded applications can make use of the aggregated LLC capacity.

The cores and LLC segments are connected to a bidirectional ring interconnect that can transfer one Cache Line (CL) (64 B in size) every two cycles in each direction. In order to reduce latency, the cores are arranged to form two rings, which are connected via two queues. To each ring belongs a Home Agent (HA) which is responsible for cache snooping operations and reordering of memory requests to optimize memory performance. Attached to each HA is a Memory Controller (MC), each featuring two 8 byte-wide DDR4 memory channels. Also accessible via the ring interconnect are the on-die PCIe and QPI facilities.

Haswell introduces an on-die Fully Integrated Voltage Regulators (FIVR). This FIVR draws significantly less power than on previous microarchitectures, because it allows faster switching of power-saving states. It also enables a more fine-grained control of CPU states: instead of globally setting the CPU frequencies for all cores within a package, Haswell can now set core frequencies and sleep states individually.

2.3 Uncore Frequency Scaling

In the new Haswell microarchitecture, Intel reverted from Sandy and Ivy Bridges' unified clock domain for core and the Uncore to the Nehalem design of having two separate clock domains [4,5]. Haswell introduced a feature called Uncore Frequency Scaling (UFS), in which the Uncore frequency is dynamically scaled based on the number of stall cycles in the CPU cores. Despite reintroducing higher latencies, the separate clock domain for the Uncore offers a significant potential for power saving, especially for serial codes. Figure 3 shows the measured sustained bandwidth (left y-axis) for the Schönauer vector triad (cf. Table 1) using a single core along with the power consumption (right y-axis) for varying dataset sizes. As expected the performance is not influenced by whether UFS is active or not when data resides in a core's private caches; however, power requirements are reduced by about 30 %! Although we observe a difference in performance as soon as the LLC is involved, the performance impact is limited. The bandwidth drops from 24 to 21 GB/s (about 13 %) in the LLC, but power usage is reduced from 55 W to 40 W (about 27 %).

2.4 Memory

Intel's previous microarchitectures show a strong correlation between CPU frequency and sustained memory bandwidth. Figure 4 shows the measured chip bandwidth for the Stream Triad (cf. Table 1)—adjusted by a factor of 1.3 to account for the write-allocate when storing—on the Sandy Bridge, Ivy Bridge, and Haswell microarchitectures. For each system, the bandwidth was measured using the lowest possible frequency (1.2 GHz) and the advertised nominal clock speed. While we find differences around 33 % in the maximum achievable sustained memory bandwidth depending on the CPU frequency for Sandy and Ivy Bridge, on Haswell we can observe a frequency-independent sustained bandwidth

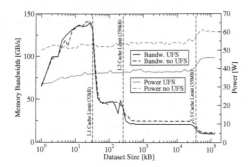

Fig. 3. Impact of UFS on bandwidth and power usage.

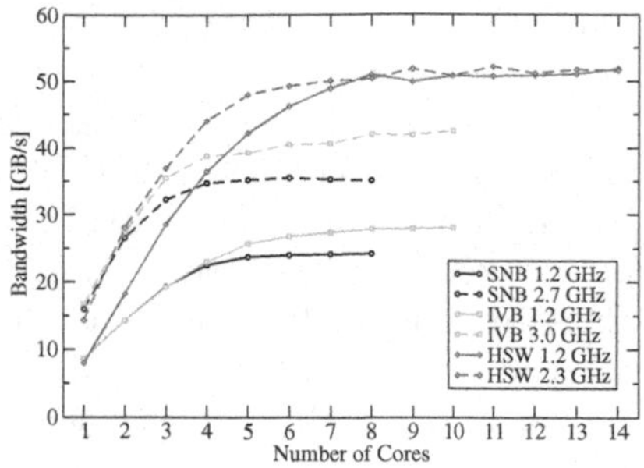

Fig. 4. Stream Triad bandwidth as function of frequency.

of 52.3 GB/s. On Haswell the CPU frequency can be lowered, thereby decreasing power consumption, while the memory bandwidth stays constant. Further research regarding the Stream Triad with a working set size of 10 GB has shown that Haswell offers an improvement of 23 % respectively 12 % over the Sandy and Ivy Bridge architectures when it comes to energy consumption and 55 % respectively 35 % in terms of Energy-Delay Product [3].

2.5   Cluster on Die

In Cluster on Die (CoD) mode, cores get equally separated into two ccNUMA memory domains. This means that instead of distributing requests between both memory controllers each core is assigned a dedicated memory controller. To keep latencies low, the strategy is to make a core access main memory through the memory controller attached to its ring. However, with memory domains being equal in size, the asymmetric core count on the two physical rings makes exceptions necessary. In the design shown in Fig. 2 the 14 cores are divided into two memory domains of 7 cores each. Using microbenchmarks and `likwid-perfctr` [12] to access performance counters in order to measure the number of memory accesses for each individual memory channel, we find that cores 0–6 access main memory through the memory channels associated with the memory controller on the left ring, and cores 7–13 those associated with the memory controller on ring 1. Thus, only core number 7 has to take a detour across rings to access data from main memory. Note that with CoD active the LLC also is divided. As each domain contains seven LLC segments (2.5 MB each), the total amount of LLC for each domain is only 17.5 MB instead of 35 MB.

CoD mode is intended for NUMA-optimized codes and serves two purposes: First latency is decreased by reducing the number of endpoints in the memory domain. Instead of 14 LLC segments, data will be distributed in only 7 segments inside each memory domain, thereby decreasing the mean hop count. Also, the requirement to pass through the two buffers connecting the rings is eliminated for all but one LLC segment. Second, bandwidth is increased by reducing the probability of ring collisions by lowering participant count from 14 to 7.

3   Microbenchmarks

A set of microbenchmarks chosen to provide a good coverage of relevant data access patterns was used to evaluate the Haswell microarchitecture and is summarized in Table 1. For each benchmark, the table lists the number of load and store streams—the former being divided into explicit and Read for Ownership (RFO) streams. RFO refers to implicit loads that occur whenever a store miss in the current cache triggers a write-allocate. On Intel architectures all cache levels use a write-allocate strategy on store misses. The table also includes the predictions of the ECM model and the actually measured runtimes in cycles along with a quantification of the model's error. In the following, we discuss the ECM model for each of the kernels and show how to arrive at the prediction shown in the table.

The sustained bandwidths used to derive the L3-memory cycles per CL inputs can be different for each benchmark, which is why for each individual kernel the sustained bandwidth is determined using a benchmark with the exact data access pattern that is modeled. For our measurements CoD mode was active and the measured bandwidth corresponds to that of a single memory domain; also, UFS was deactivated, so we assume a L2–L3 cache bandwidth of 32 B/c.

Table 1. Overview of microbenchmarks: Loop Body, Memory Streams, ECM prediction and Measurement in c/CL, and Model Error.

Benchmark	Description	Load Streams Explicit / RFO	Write Streams	ECM Prediction L1/L2/L3/Mem	Measurement L1/L2/L3/Mem	Model Error L1/L2/L3/Mem
ddot	s+=A[i]*B[i]	2 / 0	0	{2⌉4⌉8⌉17.1}	2.1⌉4.7⌉9.6⌉19.4	5%⌉17%⌉20%⌉13%
load	s+=A[i]	1 / 0	0	{2⌉2⌉4⌉8.5}	2⌉2.3⌉5⌉10.5	0%⌉15%⌉25%⌉23%
store	A[i]=s	0 / 1	1	{2⌉4⌉8⌉20.5}	2⌉6⌉8.2⌉17.7	0%⌉33%⌉3%⌉16%
update	A[i]=s*A[i]	1 / 0	1	{2⌉4⌉8⌉20.5}	2.1⌉6.5⌉8.3⌉17.6	5%⌉38%⌉4%⌉16%
copy	A[i]=B[i]	1 / 1	1	{2⌉5⌉11⌉27.8}	2.1⌉8⌉13⌉27	5%⌉38%⌉15%⌉3%
STREAM triad	A[i]=B[i]+s*C[i]	2 / 1	1	{3⌉7⌉15⌉36.7}	3.1⌉10⌉17.5⌉37	3%⌉30%⌉14%⌉1%
Schönauer triad	A[i]=B[i]+C[i]*D[i]	3 / 1	1	{4⌉9⌉19⌉45.5}	4.1⌉11.9⌉21.9⌉46.8	3%⌉24%⌉13%⌉3%

3.1   Dot Product and Load

The dot product benchmark *ddot* makes use of the new FMA instructions introduced in the FMA3 ISA extension implemented in the Haswell microarchitecture. T_{nOL} is two clock cycles, because the core has to load two CLs (A and B) from L1 to registers using four AVX loads (which can be processed in two clock cycles, because each individual AVX load can be retired in a single clock cycle and there are two load ports). Processing data from the CLs using two AVX FMA instructions only takes one clock cycle, because both issue ports 0 and 1 feature

AVX FMA units. A total of two CLs has to be transfered between the adjacent cache levels. At $64\,B/c$ this means $2\,c$ to transfer the CLs from L2 to L1. Transferring the CLs from L3 to L2 takes $4\,c$ at $32\,B/c$. The empirically determined sustained (memory domain) bandwidth is $32.4\,GB/s$. At $2.3\,GHz$, this corresponds to a bandwidth of about $64\,B/CL \cdot 2.3\,GHz/32.4\,GB/s \approx 4.5\,c/CL$ or $9.1\,c$ for two CLs. The ECM model input is thus $\{1\,\|\,2\,|\,2\,|\,4\,|\,9.1\}$ c and the corresponding prediction is $\{2\,\rceil\,4\,\rceil\,8\,\rceil\,17.1\}$ c.

For the *load* kernel the two AVX loads to get the CL containing A from L1 can be retired in a single cycle, yielding $T_{\mathrm{nOL}} = 1\,c$. With only a single AVX add unit available on port 1, processing the data takes $T_{\mathrm{OL}} = 2\,c$. Because only a single CL has to be transferred between adjacent cache levels and the measured bandwidth corresponds exactly to that of the *ddot* kernel, the time required is exactly half of that needed for the *ddot* benchmark. The ECM model input for this benchmark is $\{2\,\|\,1\,|\,1\,|\,2\,|\,4.5\}$ c, yielding a prediction of $\{2\,\rceil\,2\,\rceil\,4\,\rceil\,8.5\}$ c.

3.2   Store, Update, and Copy

For the *store* kernel, two AVX stores are required per CL. With only a single store unit available, $T_{\mathrm{nOL}} = 2\,c$; as there are no other instructions such as arithmetic operations, T_{nOL} is zero. When examining CL transfers along the cache hierarchy, we have to bear in mind that a store-miss will trigger a write-allocate, resulting in two CL transfers for each CL update: one to write-allocate the CL which data gets written to and one to evict the modified CL once the cache becomes full. This results in a transfer time of $2\,c$ to move the data between the L1 and L2 cache and a transfer time of $4\,c$ for L2 and L3. The sustained bandwidth of $23.6\,GB/s$ (corresponding to approximately $6.2\,c/CL$) for a kernel involving evictions is significantly worse than that of the previous load-only kernels. The resulting ECM input and prediction are $\{0\,\|\,2\,|\,2\,|\,4\,|\,12.5\}$ c respectively $\{2\,\rceil\,4\,\rceil\,8\,\rceil\,20.5\}$ c.

For the *update* kernel, two AVX stores and two AVX loads are required. Limited by a single store port, $T_{\mathrm{nOL}} = 2\,c$. The multiplications take $T_{\mathrm{OL}} = 2\,c.$[1] The number of CL transfers is identical to that of the *store* kernel, the only difference being that the CL load is caused by explicit loads and not a write-allocate. With a memory bandwidth almost identical to that of the *store* kernel, the time to transfer a CL between L3 and memory again is approximately $6.2\,c/CL$, yielding an ECM input of $\{2\,\|\,2\,|\,2\,|\,4\,|\,12.5\}$ c and a prediction that is identical to that of the *store* kernel.

The *copy* kernel has to perform two AVX loads and two AVX stores to copy one CL. The single store port is the bottleneck, yielding $T_{\mathrm{nOL}} = 2\,c$; absent arithmetic instructions T_{nOL} is zero. Three CLs have to be transferred between adjacent cache levels: load B, write-allocate and evict A. This results in a requirement of $3\,c$ for L1–L2 transfers and $6\,c$ for L2–L3 transfers. With a sustained

---

[1] Normally, with two AVX mul ports available, T_{OL} should be $1\,c$. However, the frontend can only retire 4 μops/c; this, along with the fact that stores count as 2 μops, means that if both multiplications were paired with the first store, there would not be enough full AGUs to retire the second store and the remaining AVX load instructions in the same cycle.

memory bandwidth of 26.3 GB/s the time to transfer one CL between main memory and LLC is approximately 5.6 c/CL or 16.8 c for three CLs. This results in the following input for the ECM model $\{0 \, \| \, 2 \, | \, 3 \, | \, 6 \, | \, 16.8\}$ c, which in turn yields a prediction of $\{2 \, \rceil \, 5 \, \rceil \, 11 \, \rceil \, 27.8\}$ c.

3.3 Stream Triad and Schönauer Triad

For the *STREAM Triad* [6], the AGUs prove to be the bottleneck: it is impossible to retire two AVX loads and an AVX store that use indexed addressing in the same cycle, because there are only two full AGUs available supporting this addressing mode. The resulting T_{nOL} thus is not 2 but 3 c to issue four AVX loads (two each for CLs containing B and C) and two AVX stores (two for CL A). Both FMAs can be retired in one cycle, because two AVX FMA units are available, yielding $T_{OL} = 1$ c. Traffic between adjacent cache levels is 4 CLs: load CLs containing B and C, write-allocate and evict the CL containing A. The measured sustained bandwidth of 27.1 GB/s corresponds to approximately 5.4 c/CL—or about 21.7 c for all four CLs. The input parameters for the ECM model are thus $\{1 \, \| \, 3 \, | \, 4 \, | \, 8 \, | \, 21.7\}$ c leading to the follow prediction: $\{3 \, \rceil \, 7 \, \rceil \, 15 \, \rceil \, 36.7\}$ c.

For the *Schönauer Triad* [8], again the AGUs are the bottleneck. Six AVX loads (CLs B, C, and D) and two AVX stores (CL A) have to be performed; these eight instructions have to share two AGUs, resulting in $T_{nOL} = 4$ c. The two AVX FMAs can be performed in a single cycle, yielding $T_{OL} = 1$ c. Data transfers between adjacent caches correspond to five CLs: B, C, and D require loading while CL A needs to be write-allocated and evicted. For the L1 cache, this results in a transfer time of 5 c. The L2 cache transfer time is 10 cycles. The measured sustained memory bandwidth of 27.8 GB/s corresponds to about 5.3 c/CL or 26.5 c for all five CLs. The resulting ECM input parameters are thus $\{1 \, \| \, 4 \, | \, 5 \, | \, 10 \, | \, 26.5\}$ c and the resulting prediction is $\{4 \, \rceil \, 9 \, \rceil \, 19 \, \rceil \, 45.5\}$ c.

4 Results

The results presented in this section were obtained using hand-written assembly kernels that were benchmarked using the `likwid-bench` tool [12]. No software prefetching was used in the code; the results therefore show the ability of the hardware prefetchers to hide data access latencies. The machine used for benchmarking was a standard two-socket server using Xeon E5-2695 v3 chips, featuring 14 cores each. Each core comes with its own 32 kB private L1 and 256 kB private L2 caches; the shared LLC is 35 MB in size. Each chip features four DDR4-2166 memory channels, adding up to a theoretical memory bandwidth of 69.3 GB/s per socket or 138.6 GB/s for the full node. For all benchmarks, the clock frequency was fixed at the nominal frequency of 2.3 GHz, CoD was activated, and UFS was disabled.

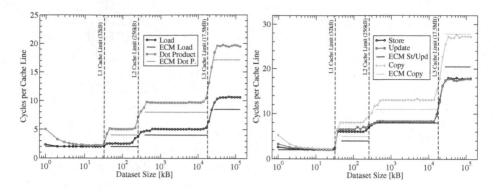

Fig. 5. ECM predictions and measurement results for load and dot product kernels.

Fig. 6. ECM predictions and measurement results for store, update, and copy kernels.

4.1 Dot Product and Load

Figure 5 illustrates ECM predictions and measurement results for both the *load* and *ddot* benchmarks. While core execution time for both benchmarks is two cycles as predicted by the model, *ddot* performance is slightly lower than predicted with data coming from the L2 cache. The worse than expected L2 cache performance has been a general problem with Haswell. In contrast to Haswell, Sandy and Ivy Bridge delivered the advertised bandwidth of 32 B/c [10]. On Haswell, in none of the cases the measured L2 bandwidth could live up to the advertised 64 B/c. For the *load* kernel, the performance in L2 is almost identical to that with data residing in the L1 cache: this is because the CL can theoretically be transfered from L2 to L1 a single cycle at 64 B/c, which is exactly the amount of slack that is the difference between $T_{OL} = 2$ c and $T_{nOL} = 1$ c. In practise, however, we observe a small penalty of 0.3 c/CL, so again, we do not observe the specified bandwidth of 64 B/c.

As soon as the working set becomes too large for the core-local L2 cache, the ECM prediction is slightly off. For kernels with a low number of cycles per CL an empirically determined penalty for transferring data from off-core locations was found to be one cycle per load stream and cache-level, e.g. 2 c for the *ddot* benchmark with data residing in L3 and 4 c with data from memory. In all likelihood, this can be attributed to latencies introduced when data is passing between different clock domains (e.g. core, cbox, mbox) that cannot be entirely hidden for kernels with a very low core cycle count.

4.2 Store, Update, and Copy

Figure 6 shows ECM predictions and measurements for the *store*, *update*, and *copy* kernels. With data in L1 cache, measurements for all three benchmarks match the prediction. In the L2 cache, measured performance is off about one

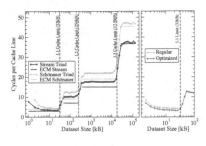

```
lea rbx, [r8+rax*8]                              1
vmovapd ymm0, [rsi+rax*8]                        2
vmovapd ymm1, [rsi+rax*8+32]                     3
vmovapd ymm8, [rdx+rax*8]                        4
vmovapd ymm9, [rdx+rax*8+32]                     5
vfmadd231pd ymm0,ymm8,[rcx+rax*8]                6
vfmadd231pd ymm1,ymm9,[rcx+rax*8+32]             7
vmovapd [rbx], ymm0                              8
vmovapd [rbx+32], ymm1                           9
```

Fig. 7. ECM predictions and measurement results for Stream and Schönauer Triads (left) and comparison of naive and optimized Schönauer Triad (right).

Listing 1.1. Shortened two-way unrolled, hand-optimized code for Schönauer Triad. Eight-way unrolling used in real benchmark kernel.

cycle per stream: two cycles for the *store* and *update* benchmarks, and four cycles for the *copy* benchmark. This means that it takes the data exactly twice as long to be transfered than what would be the case assuming a bandwidth of 64 B/c.

Measurements in L3 for the *store* and *update* kernel fit the prediction. This suggests either that either overlap between transfers is happening or some other undocumented optimization is taking place, as we would normally expect the poor L2 performance to trickle down to L3 and memory measurements (as is the case for the *copy* kernel). Suspicion about overlap or undocumented improvements is substantiated by better than expected in-memory performance.

4.3   Stream Triad and Schönauer Triad

Figure 7 shows model predictions and measurements for both the Stream and Schönauer Triads. The measurement fits the model's prediction for data in the L1 cache. We observe the same penalty for data in the L2 cache. This time, the penalty also propagates: measurement and prediction for data in L3 is still off. The match of measurement and prediction for the in-memory case suggests either overlap of transfers or other unknown optimization as was the case before for the *store*, *update*, and *copy* kernels.

In addition, Fig. 7 shows measurement results for the naive Schönauer Triad as it is currently generated by compilers (e.g. the Intel C Compiler 15.0.1) and an optimized version that makes use of the newly introduced simple AGU on port 7. The assembly for this optimized version is shown in Listing 1.1. Typically, address calculations in loop-unrolled streaming kernels require two steps: scaling and offset computation. Both AGUs on ports 2 and 3 support this addressing mode called "base plus index plus offset." The new simple AGU can only perform offset computations. However, it is possible to make use of this AGU by using one of the "fast LEA" units (which can perform *only* indexed and no offset addressing) to pre-compute an intermediary address (line 1 in Listing 1.1). This pre-computed address is fed to the simple AGU (lines 8–9 in Listing 1.1), which performs the outstanding offset addition. Using all three AGUs, the eight addressing operations can be completed in three instead of four cycles.

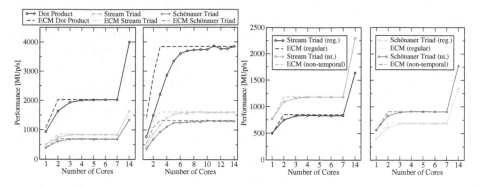

Fig. 8. Core-Scaling using CoD mode (left) and non-CoD mode (right).

Fig. 9. Performance using regular vs. non-temporal stores for Stream (left) and Schönauer Triads (right).

4.4   Multi-core Scaling and Cluster-on-Die Mode

When using the ECM model to estimate multi-core performance, single-core performance is scaled until a bottleneck is hit—which currently on Intel CPUs is main memory bandwidth. Figure 8 shows ECM predictions along with actual measurements for the *ddot, Stream Triad,* and *Schönauer Triad* kernels using both CoD and non-CoD modes. The L3-Memory CL transfer time used for each prediction is based on the sustained bandwidth of the CoD respectively non-CoD mode. While the measurement fits the prediction in CoD mode, we find a non-negligible discrepancy in non-CoD mode. This demonstrates how the ECM model can be used to uncover the source of performance deviations. In non-CoD mode, the kernel execution time is no longer just made up of in-core execution and bandwidth-limited data transfers as predicted by the model. Although we can only speculate, we attribute the penalty cycles encountered in non-CoD mode to higher latencies caused by longer ways to the memory controllers: due to equal distribution of memory requests, on average every second request has to go the "long way" across rings, which is not the case in CoD mode.

The measurements indicate that peak performance for both modes is nearly identical, e.g. for *ddot* performance saturates slightly below 4000 MUp/s for non-CoD mode while CoD saturates slightly above the 4000 mark. Although the plots indicate the bandwidth saturation point is reached earlier in CoD mode, this conclusion is deceiving. While it only takes four cores to saturate the memory bandwidth of an memory domain, a single domain is only using one of two memory controllers; thus, saturating chip bandwidth requires 2×4 threads to saturate *both* memory domains, the same amount of cores it takes to achieve the sustained bandwidth in non-CoD mode.

4.5 Non-temporal Stores

For streaming kernels with dataset sizes that do not fit into the LLC it is imperative to use non-temporal stores in order to achieve the best performance. Not only is the total amount of data to be transfered from memory reduced by getting rid of RFO stream(s), but in addition, unnecessary data no longer has to travel through the whole cache hierarchy. On Haswell, non-temporal stores are sent to the L1 cache by the core, just like regular stores; they do however not update any entries in the L1 cache but are relayed to core-private line fill buffers, from which data is transfered directly to main memory.

Figure 9 shows the performance gain offered by non-temporal stores. The left part shows the Stream Triad, which using regular stores is made up of two explicit load streams for arrays B and C plus a store and an implicit RFO stream for array A. Looking at transfered data volumes, we expect an performance increase by a factor of 1.33×, because using non-temporal stores gets rid of the RFO stream, thereby reducing streams count from four to three. However, the measured speedup is higher: 1181 vs. 831 MUp/s (1.42×) using a single memory domain respectively 2298 vs 1636 MUp/s (1.40×) when using a full chip. A possible explanation for this higher than anticipated speedup is that we have observed the efficiency of the memory subsystem degrade with an increasing number of streams. Vice verse, we could conclude that the efficiency increases by getting rid of the RFO stream.

A similar behavior is observed for the Schönauer Triad. Data volume analysis suggests a performance increase of 1.25× (4 streams instead of 5). However, the measured performance using non-temporal stores is 905 vs. 681 GUp/s (1.33×) using one memory domain resp. 1770 vs. 1339 MUp/s (1.32×) using a full chip.

5   Conclusion

This paper investigated new architectural features of the Intel Haswell microarchitecture with regard to the execution of streaming loop kernels. It demonstrated how to employ the ECM model together with microbenchmarking to quantify the efficiency of architectural features. On the example of a comprehensive set of streaming loop kernels deviations from official specifications as well as the overall efficiency was evaluated. Besides incremental improvements and core related things Haswell addresses two main areas: Energy efficiency and to provide low latency data access within the chip while increasing the core count. Sustained main memory bandwidth is no longer impaired by the selection of low clock frequencies, enabling power savings of more than 20 % respectively 10 % over the previous Sandy respectively Ivy Bridge architectures. Uncore Frequency Scaling can further improve power savings by more than 20 % for single-core workloads at no cost for data in core-private caches respectively a small performance penalty with data off-core. The new Cluster-on-Die mode offers performance improvements for single-threaded and parallel memory-bound codes, and has major benefits with regard to latency penalties.

References

1. Cache Coherence Protocol and Memory Performance of the Intel Haswell-EP Architecture. IEEE (2015)
2. Hager, G., Treibig, J., Habich, J., Wellein, G.: Exploring performance and power properties of modern multicore chips via simple machine models. Concurrency Computat: Pract. Exper. (2013). doi:10.1002/cpe.3180
3. Hofmann, J., Treibig, J., Fey, D.: Execution-cache-memory performance model: introduction and validation (2015)
4. Intel Corporation: Intel Xeon Processor E5-2600/4600 Product Family Technical Overview. https://www.software.intel.com/en-us/articles/intel-xeon-processor-e526004600-product-family-technical-overview
5. Intel Corporation: Intel Technology Journal **14**(3) (2010)
6. McCalpin, J.D.: Memory bandwidth and machine balance in current high performance computers. IEEE Computer Society Technical Committee on Computer Architecture (TCCA) Newsletter, pp. 19–25, December 1995
7. Molka, D., Hackenberg, D., Schöne, R.: Main memory and cache performance of intel sandy bridge and amd bulldozer. In: Proceedings of the Workshop on Memory Systems Performance and Correctness, MSPC 2014, pp. 4: 1–4:10. ACM (2014)
8. Schönauer, W.: Scientific Supercomputing: Architecture and Use of Shared and Distributed Memory Parallel Computers. Self-edition (2000)
9. Schöne, R., Hackenberg, D., Molka, D.: Memory performance at reduced cpu clock speeds: an analysis of current x86_64 processors. In: Proceedings of the 2012 USENIX Conference on Power-Aware Computing and Systems, HotPower 2012, p. 9. USENIX Association (2012)
10. Stengel, H., Treibig, J., Hager, G., Wellein, G.: Quantifying performance bottlenecks of stencil computations using the Execution-Cache-Memory model. In: Proceedings of the 29th ACM International Conference on Supercomputing, ICS 2015. ACM, New York (2015). http://doi.acm.org/10.1145/2751205.2751240
11. Treibig, J., Hager, G.: Introducing a performance model for bandwidth-limited loop kernels. In: Wyrzykowski, R., Dongarra, J., Karczewski, K., Wasniewski, J. (eds.) PPAM 2009, Part I. LNCS, vol. 6067, pp. 615–624. Springer, Heidelberg (2010)
12. Treibig, J., Hager, G., Wellein, G.: likwid-bench: an extensible microbenchmarking platform for x86 multicore compute nodes. In: Parallel Tools Workshop, pp. 27–36 (2011)

Measurement-Based Probabilistic Timing Analysis for Graphics Processor Units

Kostiantyn Berezovskyi[2]([envelope]), Fabrice Guet[1], Luca Santinelli[1],
Konstantinos Bletsas[2], and Eduardo Tovar[2]

[1] ONERA, Toulouse, France
[2] CISTER/INESC-TEC, ISEP, Porto, Portugal
kosbe@isep.ipp.pt

Abstract. Purely analytical worst-case execution time (WCET) estimation approaches for Graphics Processor Units (GPUs) cannot go far
because of insufficient public information for the hardware. Therefore
measurement-based probabilistic timing analysis (MBPTA) seems the
way forward. We recently demonstrated MBPTA for GPUs, based on
Extreme Value Theory (EVT) of the "Block Maxima" paradigm. In this
newer work, we formulate and experimentally evaluate a more robust
MBPTA approach based on the EVT "Peak over Threshold" paradigm
with a complete set of tests for verifying EVT applicability. It optimally
selects parameters to best-fit the input measurements for more accurate probabilistic WCET estimates. Different system configuration parameters (cache arrangements, thread block size) and their effect on the
pWCET are considered, enhancing models of worst-case GPU behavior.

1 Introduction

Programming models such as CUDA (Compute Unified Device Architecture)
facilitate harnessing the power of GPUs for general-purpose applications exhibit-
ing inherent parallelism, and even for embedded real-time systems. However,
such systems have timeliness constraints and currently no satisfactory worst-case
execution time (WCET) analysis technique for parallel applications on GPUs
exists. Techniques for CPUs are not portable because GPU applications consist
of thousands of identical ultra-lightweight threads (1-cycle context-switch) and
we are not interested in the execution time of any one of them; instead we want
to bound the time since the first thread starts until the last one completes.

Analytical approaches, relying on detailed GPU models [3, 15] have had limited success because the application has *no control* over how intra-GPU thread
scheduling, which is also a trade secret; and so is the GPU cache replacement
policy. Static measurement-based approaches [6] face the same challenges.

Therefore, a probabilistic measurement-based approach, relying on statistical analysis and Extreme Value Theory (EVT) seems a viable alternative, as it
can characterize the WCET even without this information. Many works insist

© Springer International Publishing Switzerland 2016
F. Hannig et al. (Eds.): ARCS 2016, LNCS 9637, pp. 223–236, 2016.
DOI: 10.1007/978-3-319-30695-7_17

on hardware randomization (e.g., random replacement caches) as a prerequisite for the application of Measurement-Based Probabilistic Timing Analysis (MBPTA) and EVT. Randomization indeed helps with certain properties, but with commercial-of-the-shelf GPUs it is not an option – and, as we will demonstrate, it is not strictly needed either, for WCET characterization via EVT.

GPU Architectures and CUDA. Modern GPUs contain several "Streaming Multiprocessors" (SMs), which are complex manycores in themselves. For example, the NVIDIA Kepler GK104 [30] has 8 SMs and a shared 1.5 MB L2 cache. Each SM has 192 CUDA cores, 32 load/store units, 32 special units (e.g., for cosines in H/W) and 64 double-precision units. Its 64-kB dedicated memory, with the latency of a register, is split into "shared memory" and L1.

CUDA programs running on GPUs are called "kernels". Under CUDA, at any time, groups of 32 threads (termed *warps*) execute in lockstep, i.e., during the same cycles as each other and also executing the same kernel instruction[1]. At run-time, warps are bundled together in groups termed *thread blocks* and each thread block is sent to one SM for execution. Each SM has a few thread blocks assigned to it at any time. Thread blocks do not migrate among SMs. The CUDA engine tries to keep each SM's processing units busy, but exactly how warps are dispatched is not publicly documented.

GPU Timing Analysis: State of the Art. Despite the lack of GPU documentation, effortts are made to analyse GPUs or make them more time-predictable. Many works attempted to make the scheduling on the GPU more predictable [2,18] and provide multitasking [19] among different GPU contexts and efficient resource sharing. In [17], CPU-GPU data transfers are made preemptible, to reduce blocking. The GPU management infrastructure in [31] supports data transfer and computation overlap and multi-GPU systems. The framework in [27] supports LDF and fixed-priority policies and uses the maximum execution time over a number of runs of a task as a WCET estimate. The lock-based management framework for multi-GPU systems in [12] also allocates GPU resources to tasks via a cost predictor that infers computation times and data transfer delay from a few runs. In [25] the adaptive scheduling of anytime algorithms is explored; worst-case scenarios for GPU kernels are empirically derived experimentally.

The ILP-based WCET estimation in [3] is intractable for longer kernels (due to control variable explosion) and it relies on an *optimistic* assumption about cache misses. The metaheuristic-based alternative in [4] for soft real-time systems is more tractable but its WCET estimates are not provably safe and the optimistic assumptions about cache misses remain. Since L1 misses take hundreds of cycles, extending [3] or [4] to tractably model caches is hard.

Betts *et al.* [6] employ the simulator GPGPU-sim [1]. Their first technique (*dynamic*) estimates from the respective high-water mark times the maximum

---

[1] Intra-warp control flow divergence is handled with predicates/masking and NOPs.

"release jitter" (delay in launch, measured from the kernel launch) and WCET (including the effects of contention for cache, GPU main memory, etc.) of the GPU warps. A second technique (*hybrid*) assumes a fixed delay for launching each additional warp and uses static analysis based on instrumentation point graphs annotated with execution times obtained from the measurements. This assumes thread blocks arriving in "waves" and processed in round-robin.

Recently [5], we applied Block-Maxima EVT to CUDA kernels, and explored the dependence of probabilistic WCETs (pWCETs) on the size of the problem instance. In this work, we apply the Peak Over Threshold variant of EVT aiming at providing a more complete view to the EVT and highlighting how these techniques can offer clues to the developer about optimizing performance wrt the pWCET. We fix the size of the problem instance, in order to explore how other factors (cache configuration, thread block size) affect the pWCET.

2   Statistical Modeling of Execution Time with GPUs

Whenever there is variability of task execution times, these may be defined as random variables (rvs)[2]. The rv C_i draws its values from the set of different execution times that task τ_i can experience, with respective observed probability; C_i is an empirical distribution obtained from actual measurements.

The Cumulative Distribution Function (CDF) $F_{C_i}(C_{i,x}) \overset{def}{=} \sum_{j=0}^{x} f_{C_i}(C_{i,j}) = P(C_i \le C_{i,x})$ and the inverse Cumulative Distribution Function (1-CDF) $F'_{C_i}(C_{i,x}) \overset{def}{=} 1 - \sum_{j=0}^{x} f_{C_i}(C_{i,j})$ are alternative representations to the pdf. In particular, the 1-CDF outlines the exceedence thresholds as $P\{C_i \ge C_{i,x}\}$. Each measurement $C_{i,k}$ is an execution time sample, stored in a trace $\mathcal{T}_{C_i}$ such that $\forall k, \mathcal{T}_{C_i}(k) = C_{i,k}$. We call C_i (calligraphic) the Execution Time Profile (ETP). Together with the traces, it describes the average execution-time behavior of τ_i.

CUDA Measurements. In this work we focus exclusively on the net CUDA kernel execution time, denoted as C^{DEV}. This corresponds to the time since the first warp executes its first instruction until the last one completes:

$$C^{DEV} = \max_p\{\text{end\_cycle}[p]\} - \min_p\{\text{start\_cycle}[p]\} \qquad (1)$$

where $p = 1, 2, \ldots, P$ is the index of the SM and the start_cycle/ end_cycle variables hold the value of special clock-register on each SM, recorded by extra-lighweight instrumentation assembly code injected into the kernel[3]. We collect execution time measurements for a sufficient (see below) number of runs of a given kernel, under the same execution conditions, and apply EVT to those.

---

[2] A random variable is a variable whose value is subject to variations due to chance; it can take on a set of possible different values, each with an associated probability.
[3] Admittedly, then the execution time is that of the *modified* kernel.

2.1   Worst-Case Profiling

Within a probabilistic paradigm, the pWCET is the worst possible distribution of task execution times. There should exist the exact pWCET C_i^* as the tightest upper bound distribution to any possible ETP in any possible execution condition or system scenario. Due to the overall complexity or cost of deriving the exact pWCET distribution, MBPTA approaches tend to infer pWCET estimates $\overline{C}_i$ which are safe in the sense that they are distributions greater than or equal to the exact (and potentially unknown) pWCET[4]. The partial ordering among distributions is defined such that, a distribution C_j is greater than or equal to a distribution C_k, $C_j \succeq C_k$, iff $P(C_j \leq d) \leq P(C_k \leq d)$ for any d and the two random variables are not identically distributed (two different distributions), [11].

The EVT deals with the extreme deviations from the median of probability distributions. It estimates the tails of distributions, where the worst case should lie, thus pWCET estimates $\overline{C}_i$. These are continuous worst-case distributions [9]

It is assumed that the safety of the worst-case estimates $\overline{C}_i$ with EVT relates only to the EVT applicability hypotheses, [10]. Ongoing research is investigating more formally both the safety and the robustness of EVT worst-case estimates.

The Fisher-Tippet-Gnedenko theorem [14] presents the EVT Block Maxima (BM) formulation where the tail distribution G_ξ is the possible limit law characterizing the sequence of the maxima $B_n = max\{C_{i,1}, C_{i,2}, \ldots, C_{i,n}\}$ of n independent identically distributed (i.i.d.) measurements $\{C_{i,n}\}$ as $n \to \infty$. In other words, the theorem says that whenever C_i belongs to the Maximum Domain of Attraction (MDA), $C_i \in MDA(G_\xi)$, then G_ξ is a good approximation of the extreme task behavior. G_ξ is the Generalized Extreme Value (GEV) distribution which is a family of continuous probability distributions combining the Gumbel, Frechet and Weibull families. The parameter ξ defines the shape of the GEV, such that $\xi = 0$, $\xi > 0$ and $\xi < 0$ correspond respectively to the Gumbel, Frechet and Weibull. The block size *block* plays a central role for the resulting pWCET estimation. In previous works, the pWCET estimates are achieved with the EVT BM approach applying Gumbel distributions, [9].

The second approach to the EVT is the Peaks Over Threshold (POT). It models the law of the execution time peaks in a trace that exceed a threshold.

Definition 1 (Generalized Pareto Distribution: Pickands theorem [13]). *The distribution function P_ξ of the peaks $C_u = C - u$ over a threshold u of the sequence T of execution time measurements from a distribution function C, $C \in MDA(G_\xi)$ whose G_ξ parameters are ξ, μ, σ, relatively to $C > u$, is a Generalized Pareto Distribution (GPD) defined as* $P_\xi(y) = \begin{cases} 1 - (1 + \xi y/\alpha_u)^{-1/\xi} \; if \; \xi \neq 0 \\ 1 - \exp(-y/\alpha_u) \; if \; \xi = 0 \end{cases}$, *with $\alpha_u = \mu - \xi(u - \sigma)$, and defined on $\{y, 1 + \xi y/\alpha_u > 0\}$. The conditional distribution function C_u of C above a certain threshold u, the conditional excess distribution function, is defined such as $C_u(y) = P(C - u \leq y | C > u) = \frac{C(u+y) - C(u)}{1 - C(u)}$.*

---

[4] The same holds for deterministic approaches, which derive safe WCET estimates from incomplete system models or assumptions about the system behavior.

Hence, P_ξ is the kind of distribution to use for estimating the pWCET distribution i.e. $F_{\overline{C}_i} = P_\xi$. The threshold u has a key role in the pWCET estimation.

As the threshold is chosen near the worst measured execution time, the law of the peaks tend to a GPD if and only if the measured empirical distribution (C_i) belongs to the maximum domain of attraction of $\mathcal{G}_\xi$, $C_i \in MDA(\mathcal{G}_\xi)$, i.e. iff the Fisher and Tippet theorem is verified. Formally there exists equivalence between the POT and the BM EVT approaches, as the law of extreme execution times given by G_ξ and the BM is closely linked to the law of peaks above the thresholds P_ξ. This translates into the equivalence of the distribution laws composing both the GEV and GPD distributions G_ξ and P_ξ, as they share the same value of ξ.

The meaning of independence looked for by the EVT is whether individual measurements $C_1, \ldots, C_n$ within the same trace are correlated with each other or not, i.e., the time history relationship. The identical distribution hypothesis assumes that all measurements follow the same distribution C_i.

Recent works show that independence is not a necessary hypothesis for EVT applicability. Leadbetter et al. [22], Hsing [16] and Northrop [28] developed EVT for stationary weakly dependent time series, extending EVT applicability. In particular, [5,32] demonstrated the *applicability* of the EVT to the worst-case execution time estimation problem in case of some low degree of dependence between measurements (non time-randomized, like the GPUs in our case). Even the identical distribution (i.d.) of random variables does not represent a limiting hypothesis to EVT applicability. Specifically, [26] states the applicability of EVT to non-i.d. random variables, by considering stationary measurements.

3   Measurement-Based Probabilistic GPU WCET Analysis

MBPTA uses the EVT for estimating pWCETs, [5,9,32]. In this work we apply the newly developed DIAGXTRM MBPTA framework in order to diagnose execution time traces and derive safe pWCET estimates with the EVT.

Figure 1 describes the logic flow with the basic steps that DIAGXTRM follows in order to verify measurements' independence, how to apply the EVT in the more generic and realistic case of extreme independence, and evaluating the reliability/confidence of the resulting worst-case estimates. In this work we make use of the EVT POT approach, for which we make use of the whole GPD distribution comparing the results of the $\xi \neq 0$ case (from the best-fit algorithm to select the ξ value that best-fit the input measurements) with the $\xi = 0$ (the Gumbel case). The Gumbel distribution is kept because it was considered in the past to better fit inferences at low probability levels with regard to measurements and the pessimism of the pWCET estimates, [5,9,32].

DIAGXTRM is automatic in the sense that it selects the parameters i.e. shape ξ, and threshold u, which best fit the input data T and reduce the pessimism of the pWCET estimates. Furthermore, DIAGXTRM offers a complete set of tests for verifying EVT applicability hypotheses and it considers confidence metrics for evaluating both the hypotheses and the pWCET estimates. If all the tests

Fig. 1. Decision diagram for DIAGXTRM: Actions and tests for EVT applicability.

are passed we can rely on the pWCETs from the EVT as safe estimation of task worst-case execution times. DIAGXTRM, unlike current measurement-based probabilistic timing analysis [9], may be applied also to non-time-randomized multi-core architectures as it evaluates the degree of dependence in T and defines the reliability/confidence of the worst-case estimates for specific parameters.

3.1   EVT Applicability for GPUs

With traces, one may study the relationship between measurements to evaluate (i) the distribution that every $C_{i,j}$ follows i.e. the i.d., and (ii) the impact that previous (in time) measurements would have on future ones, i.e., the degree of dependences between measurements. Such relationships can only be statistically verified. Hereby we describe the 3 main tests applied for EVT hypothesis verification, thus for validating EVT applicability and EVT reliability.

Stationarity. The EVT applicability (in its relaxed form, [22,32]) relates to strictly stationary traces. In a strictly stationary trace $(C_1, C_2,...)$, for any j, k, ℓ, the subtrace $C_j,...,C_{j+k}$ is governed by the same probabilistic law as subtrace $C_{\ell+j},...,C_{\ell+j+k}$. Statistical tests exist for checking if a trace is strictly stationary or not; one of the most reliable is the Kwiatowski Phillips Schmidt Shin (KPSS) test [20], where results below 0.74 guarantee the trace as stationary. The threshold of 0.74 is achieved for a 1 % confidence level: if the KPSS result value is below 0.74, then with a confidence of 0.99 the stationarity is acceptable. The KPSS test indirectly evaluates the i.d. hypothesis. The resulting confidence ρ^{KPSS} on the test translates into a confidence on the i.d. hypothesis.

Patterns and Correlation. The statistical dependence translates into correlated patterns of execution time measurements. One reliable statistical test for identifying correlated patterns is the Brock Dechert Scheinkman (BDS) test based on the correlation integral [7]. The test measures the degree of correlation between patterns of different lengths within a trace. For non-stationary traces the statistic diverges. The BDS results are expressed as the percentage of the independence hypothesis acceptance: the higher the percentage is, the more acceptable is the hypothesis to consider independent measurements. Implicit in the BDS result there is the confidence information on the i. hypothesis. ρ^{BDS} as the result of the BDS test defines the confidence on the independence hypothesis.

Extremal Independence. When overall independence does not hold, another way is to look for independence of extreme execution time measurements[5]. Leadbetter [21] introduced two formal conditions for stationary dependent sequences that guarantee the EVT application. Condition $D(u_n)$ means that for execution time measurements that are *distant enough* in the trace of measurements (e.g., $C_{i,j}$ and $C_{i,j+I}$ with the distance I), these measurements can be considered as independent. Condition $D'(u_n)$, if verified, prevents from the clustering of the extreme execution time measurements: if one measurement is over the threshold then the probability that the following measurements are over the threshold too must tend to zero, to not have clustering. Considering an independent measurement sequence, whose limit law is $\mathcal{P}_\xi$ and with the same distribution as the stationary dependent sequence whose limit law is $\mathcal{H}_\xi$, the relationship between the two is such that $\mathcal{H}_\xi(x) = \mathcal{P}_\xi^\theta(x)$.

The Extremal Index (EI) $\theta \in [0, 1]$ is an indicator of the dependence degree of extreme measurements for time series [28]. The worst-case profile produced in case of extreme dependence (ed) $\overline{C}_i^{ed}$ ($\theta < 1$) is greater than or equal to the one produced in case of extreme independence (ei) $\overline{C}_i^{ei}$: $\overline{C}_i^{\theta<1} \succeq \overline{C}_i^{\theta=1} \equiv \overline{C}_i^{ei}$. To note that the case $\theta = 1$ is equivalent to the independent case. The ordering of former equation is assured if and only if both extreme independence and independence cases follow the same average distribution. It describes a very important relationship between extremal dependence degrees and the independence of the execution times. The effects of extremal dependence are in the direction of adding pessimism to the pWCET estimates: the pWCETs with dependence between measurements are more pessimistic but safer as worst-case estimates. On the other end, papers like [23] that claim to artificially build the independence from dependent execution time should better consider the effects of that, as removing dependences could harm the safety of the pWCET estimates.

In practice, to validate the extremal independence, the EI is enough; with $\theta \sim 1$ either $D(u_n)$ and/or $D'(u_n)$ are valid, thus the extremal independence is guaranteed. The closer θ is to 1, the greater the confidence. $\rho^{EI} = \theta$ is the confidence measure on the extremal independence hypothesis.

EVT Confidence. The BDS test and the EI estimation jointly validate the EVT applicability wrt the independence, as $\max\{\rho^{BDS}, \rho^{EI}\}$. For a metric of confidence in *both* the i. and i.d. hypotheses, hence confidence in the full applicability of the EVT and the pWCET estimates from it, we can define ρ as

$$\rho = min\{\rho^{KPSS}, max\{\rho^{BDS}, \rho^{EI}\}\}. \tag{2}$$

4   Experiments

Our CUDA benchmark is the Voronoi diagram generator [5] inspired by the work of Majdandzic et al [24]. The raster size X by Y determines the number of

---

[5] By extreme execution time measurements we intend execution time relatively far from the average values or relatively separated in time.

threads. The per-thread workload scales linearly with K, the number of points (informally "tiles"), used as input. All experiments use $K = 32$ (for constant per-thread workload) and $X=Y=256$ (for constant overall workload) and we vary independently (i) the thread block size and (ii) the division of on-chip memory into L1 and "shared memory", to see the impact on the pWCET.

The four thread organization scenarios considered were: 64/256/512/1024 thread blocks (respectively, 1024/256/128/64 threads per thread block). Regarding the on-chip memory per SM, it is divided in two parts. The part used as L1 cache is managed by the driver. The other part, called "shared memory", is managed by the developer. The API provides three options for dividing the on-chip memory between these two parts: 75 %/25 %, 50 %/50 %, 25 %/75 %. Thus, we ran 4×3=12 sets of experiments on Kepler GK104 (8 SMs and 64 KB of on-chip memory per SM). We label each trace by the number of thread blocks and the fraction of shared memory used for L1, e.g. "512 TB 75 %". Our tool repeatedly cold-reboots, launches the kernel and records its timing measurements.

To later safely apply EVT and infer the pWCET estimate $\overline{C}_i$, we need enough measurements per trace. How many, we assess with the desired confidence level *a posteriori*, via the appropriate tests for stationarity, patterns and correlation, and extremal independence. If the tests fail, we add measurements to the trace, until they succeed. In our case, 50000 runs per trace proved sufficient (see below).

4.1 Timing Analysis

The GPU execution time traces show enough variability to be described by random variables. Even if it is a deterministic system (non time-randomized), the interactions between system elements, e.g., concurrent access to shared resources, create unpredictability from one execution to another. The average profiles $\mathcal{C}_i$ can be seen as discrete random variables because the time is measured in cycles.

The variability is quantified by applying KPSS, BDS and EI tests to the traces. From the results (Table 1), the variability is enough to have θ very close to 1, if not 1: the extremal independence of the execution times is guaranteed for all traces investigated. Moreover, the resulting pWCET estimates from the EVT would be the same as those with independent traces, since $\rho^{EI} \approx 1$. The confidence metric of Eq. (2) outlines the large confidence we would have on the EVT applicability, thus on the EVT pWCET estimates. In statistical hypothesis testing, a confidence of 0.99 for accepting a hypothesis is very large.

For two limit cases, 256 TB 75 % and 1024 TB 75 %, the stationarity and so the i.d. hypothesis are not guaranteed. The independence is still guaranteed by θ. Looking at their traces, we spot no patterns among the execution times, neither trends characterizing the task execution evolution. It is clear how they represent two false negatives from the KPSS test. Notably, the extremal independence of 256 TB 75 % and 1024 TB 75 % is very strong.

This first statistical analysis shows that EVT can also be applied with high confidence ($\rho{\approx}1$) even to some non-time-randomized systems (in this case, GPUs).

Table 1. Statistical results on the traces.

$\mathcal{T}$	ρ^{KPSS}	ρ^{BDS}	ρ^{EI}	u	ρ	ξ	ET-10^{-5}	GPD-10^{-9}	$a(GPD)$	Gumbel-10^{-9}	$a(Gumbel)$
1024 TB 75%	0	0	1	120594	0	0.06, NEG	132301	147056	0.112	177567	0.342
1024 TB 50%	0.645	0.574	0.999	95910	0.99	0.1, NEG	105627	118193	0.119	133150	0.261
1024 TB 25%	0.581	0.056	0.993	94302	0.99	0.1, NEG	104354	117461	0.126	133291	0.277
512 TB 75%	0.764	0.917	1	118650	0.99	0.04, NEG	139878	220798	0.579	187595	0.341
512 TB 50%	0.622	0.889	1	118161	0.99	0.04, POS	141671	193812	0.368	174113	0.229
512 TB 25%	0.876	0.935	0.995	116361	0.99	0.09, POS	137438	230602	0.678	165673	0.205
256 TB 75%	0	0.972	0.983	103168	0	0.02, POS	147773	164985	0.116	154373	0.045
256 TB 50%	0.508	0.972	0.995	104024	0.99	0.14, NEG	120882	129227	0.069	162471	0.344
256 TB 25%	0.891	0.75	0.965	102347	0.99	0.17, NEG	116650	124517	0.067	164717	0.412
64 TB 75%	0.936	1	1	152653	0.99	0.26, NEG	179799	183408	0.02	277551	0.544
64 TB 50%	0.543	0.741	0.989	153905	0.99	0.21, NEG	179426	187952	0.048	265640	0.48
64 TB 25%	0.905	0.667	0.911	152575	0.99	0.12, NEG	178781	197487	0.105	234506	0.312

4.2 pWCET with the EVT

Equation (3) defines the accuracy metric a through which we evaluate pWCET estimates with respect to the execution time measurements in $\mathcal{T}$:

$$a \stackrel{def}{=} \frac{\text{WCET thresholds at } 10^{-9} - \text{ maximum observed value}}{\text{WCET thresholds at } 10^{-9}}, \tag{3}$$

which translates into $a = (\overline{C}_i^{\sharp} - C_i^{\sharp})/\overline{C}_i^{\sharp}$, where $\overline{C}_i^{\sharp}$ is such that $P(\overline{C}_i > \overline{C}_i^{\sharp}) = 10^{-9}$, and $C_i^{\sharp}$ such that $P(C_i > C_i^{\sharp}) = 2 \cdot 10^{-5}$; $2 \cdot 10^{-5}$ is the minimum observable probability, as $\frac{1}{50000}$, from the size of the traces.

Figure 2 compares all the traces of measurements with their EVT pWCET estimates with both $\xi = 0$ (the Gumbel pWCET estimate) and ξ resulting from the best-fit procedure implemented within DIAGXTRM. It is worthy to note the difference that exists between the two estimates. This is motivated by the fact that the best-fit procedure best-fits the input traces, thus the known information, which do not necessarily follow a Gumbel distribution at the extremes. While with the best-fit procedure, the input measurements are best modeled, the tail of the distribution is not necessarily accurate; this is the case of $\xi > 0$. As we can see, there are also cases where $\xi < 0$ and the pWCET estimate is a Weibull distribution, which is more accurate than the Gumbel at the tail too.

With DIAGXTRM we are able to achieve a pWCET estimate accuracy of at worst 68 % with respect to the maximum measured value $C_i^{\sharp}$, see Table 1, with both Gumbel or GPD with $\xi \neq 0$. Most of the ξ resulting from the best-fit algorithm are negatives, thus the pWCET estimates take the form of Weibull distributions and a better accuracy. In a few cases, $\xi > 0$ (see Table 1). For those, the resulting pWCET is more conservative (potentially less accurate) by comparison with the other traces. In those cases the pWCET has a finite support and has a better accuracy than the Gumbel distribution. The positive values we obtain are close to 0, thus the GPD in those cases has a shape very close to the shape of Gumbel distributions: under a certain probability range they can be considered equivalent to the Gumbel pWCET estimates.

Figures 3 and 4 compare pWCET estimates in different execution scenarios. For the comparison, applied the EVT POT with the best threshold u selection was applied, in order to increase the accuracy of the pWCET estimates; k is the number of the measurements over the threshold u used to infer the pWCET

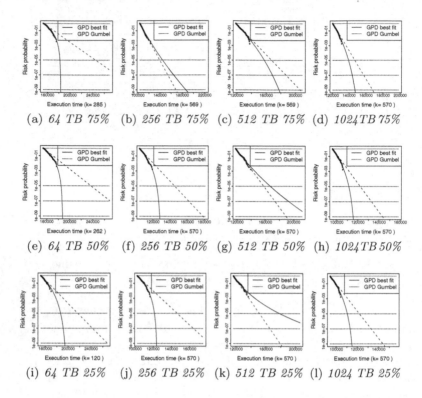

(a) *64 TB 75%* (b) *256 TB 75%* (c) *512 TB 75%* (d) *1024TB 75%*

(e) *64 TB 50%* (f) *256 TB 50%* (g) *512 TB 50%* (h) *1024TB 50%*

(i) *64 TB 25%* (j) *256 TB 25%* (k) *512 TB 25%* (l) *1024 TB 25%*

Fig. 2. Direct comparisons (# of thread blocks; % of on-chip memory used for L1).

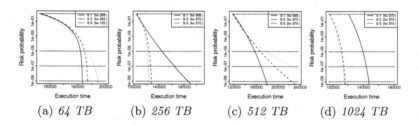

(a) *64 TB*   (b) *256 TB*   (c) *512 TB*   (d) *1024 TB*

Fig. 3. Comparison between on-chip memory splitting.

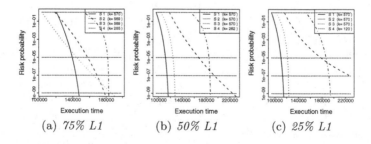

(a) *75% L1*   (b) *50% L1*   (c) *25% L1*

Fig. 4. Comparison between threads per thread block.

estimation. It depends on u as a direct result of the best-fit approach. The Gumbel distribution is chosen to compare with the best-fit resulting GPDs and to comply with previous works. It allows us also to outline that DIAGXTRM can face any resulting GPD shape. In most of the time, the resulting GPD is a Weibull distribution ($\xi < 0$), thus the pWCET estimates will have finite support and will be less pessimistic than the Gumbel distribution; this is the direct result of the best-fit approach which best-fits measurements and not necessarily concludes that Gumbel is the best approximation to the worst-case behaviors.

In Fig. 3, due to shortage of space, labels S1, S2 and S3 correspond to 75 %, 50 % and 25 % of the per-SM on-chip memory used as L1 cache (the rest being "shared memory"). In the case of Fig. 3(a) (which corresponds to 64 TBs), interestingly, the thread thresholds which maximizes the accuracy for S1, S2, S3 differ from each other; unlike what holds for the other three cases. The reason for that comes from the best-fit parameter selection algorithm we have implemented and the shape of the input traces: to best-fit the input traces the threshold could vary, and in this case it does so more than in others.

Figure 3 shows that, depending on the number of thread blocks in which the kernel is configured, a bigger L1 may have either a positive or a *negative* effect on both average-performance and the pWCET. For 64 TBs or 512 TBs, the pWCET is smaller with smaller L1, which is anomalous. But for "interleaved" cases of 256 TBs and 1024 TBs, a bigger L1 helps. Strikingly, there is no monotonic trade-off with the number of thread blocks. We attribute this to a strange interplay of various micro-architectural effects, most likely including the hit rate on the shared L2 (especially, since the cache hierarchy is not strictly inclusive but not exclusive either [8]). As for the number of thread blocks, NVIDIA acknowledges[6] that the thread block size is not a simple tradeoff. Our experiments demonstrate that this reality also extends to the pWCETs. Figure 4 organizes the same information as Fig. 3 differently, to highlight the effect of thread block organization. Here, again due to shortage of space, the labels S1 to S4 now correspond to the number of thread blocks (1024/512/256/64, respectively).

DIAGXTRM captures even such counter-intuitive performance dependencies and allows the designer to optimize according to the pWCET by choosing the best configuration. For example, if the exceedance probability of interest is 10^{-9}, the best-performing configuration is 1024 TBs and 25 % L1.

To conclude, apart from the two case limits, with non time-randomized architectures such as the GPUs considered, it is still possible to verify EVT applicability with extremely high confidence. Such confidence propagates to the pWCET estimates achieved with the EVT. Finally, with Eq. (2) we are able to relate test confidence to the confidence in the whole EVT approach.

---

[6] As stated in [29], p. 47: "There are many factors involved in selecting block size, and inevitably some experimentation is required."

5   Conclusions

This work applied the DIAGXTRM MBPTA approach to GPUs. The results show that hardware time-randomization is not strictly necessary for the applicability of EVT. Indeed the execution time traces, even when dependent, are all independent at the extremes, resulting in pWCET estimates as accurate as those from fully independent traces. Using generic GPDs or GEVs, not limiting the pWCET estimates to Gumbel distributions, allows for accurate pWCET estimates. The best-fit of the input measurements usually led to better extreme event estimation than the Gumbel assumption. We also compared GPU execution scenarios using DIAGXTRM to study system behavior with probabilistic models.

In the future, we will investigate other system configurations and/or other system elements and apply the sensitivity analysis to evaluate their effect on the pWCET estimates. Our goal is to develop an aided-design probabilistic framework for more deterministic GPU development. Concerning DIAGXTRM, we will enhance its tests to reduce both false positives and false negatives and increase the confidence in its tests and EVT estimates.

Acknowledgements. Work partially supported by National Funds through FCT/MEC (Portuguese Foundation for Science and Technology) and co-financed by ERDF (European Regional Development Fund) under the PT2020 Partnership, within project UID/CEC/04234/2013 (CISTER); also by FCT/MEC and the EU ARTEMIS JU within projects ARTEMIS/0003/2012 - JU grant 333053 (CONCERTO) and ARTEMIS/0001/2013 - JU grant 621429 (EMC2); by FCT/MEC and ESF (European Social Fund) through POPH (Portuguese Human Potential Operational Program), under PhD grant SFRH/BD/82069/2011.

References

1. Bakhoda, A., Yuan, G.L., Fung, W.W., Wong, H., Aamodt, T.M.: Analyzing CUDA workloads using a detailed GPU simulator. In: Proceedings of the IEEE ISPASS (2009)
2. Bautin, M., Dwarakinath, A., Chiueh, T.: Graphics engine resource management. In: Proceedings of the 15th ACM/SPIE MMCN (2008)
3. Berezovskyi, K., Bletsas, K., Andersson, B.: Makespan computation for GPU threads running on a single streaming multiprocessor. In: Proceedings of the 24th ECRTS (2012)
4. Berezovskyi, K., Bletsas, K., Petters, S.M.: Faster makespan estimation for GPU threads on a single streaming multiprocessor. In: Proceedings of the ETFA (2013)
5. Berezovskyi, K., Santinelli, L., Bletsas, K., Tovar, E.: WCET measurement-based and EVT characterisation of CUDA kernels. In: Proceedings of the RTNS (2014)
6. Betts, A., Donaldson, A.F.: Estimating the WCET of GPU-accelerated applications using hybrid analysis. In: Proceedings of the 25th ECRTS, pp. 193–202 (2013)
7. Brock, W., Scheinkman, J., Dechert, W., LeBaron, B.: A test for independence based on the correlation dimension. Econometric Rev. **15**(3), 197–235 (1996)
8. Chen, X., Chang, L.-W., Rodrigues, C.I., Lv, J., Wang, Z., Hwu, W.-M.: Adaptive cache management for energy-efficient gpu computing. In: Proceedings of the 47th IEEE/ACM International Symposium on Microarchitecture, pp. 343–355 (2014)

9. Cucu-Grosjean, L., Santinelli, L., Houston, M., Lo, C., Vardanega, T., Kosmidis, L., Abella, J., Mezzeti, E., Quinones, E., Cazorla, F.J.: Measurement-based probabilistic timing analysis for multi-path programs. In: Proceedings of the 23nd ECRTS (2012)

10. Davis, R.I., Santinelli, L., Altmeyer, S., Maiza, C., Cucu-Grosjean, L.: Analysis of probabilistic cache related pre-emption delays. In: Proceedings of the 25th IEEE Euromicro Conference on Real-Time Systems (ECRTS) (2013)

11. Díaz, J., Garcia, D., Kim, K., Lee, C., Bello, L., Lopez, J.M., Mirabella, O.: Stochastic analysis of periodic real-time systems. In: 23rd RTSS, pp. 289–300 (2002)

12. Elliott, G., Ward, B., Anderson, J.: GPUSync: architecture-aware management of GPUs for predictable multi-GPU real-time systems. In: Proceedings of the RTSS (2013)

13. Embrechts, P., Klüppelberg, C., Mikosch, T.: Modelling Extremal Events for Insurance and Finance. Applications of mathematics. Springer, Heidelberg (1997)

14. Gumbel, E.: Statistics of Extremes. Columbia University Press, New York (1958)

15. Hirvisalo, V.: On static timing analysis of GPU kernels. In: Proceedings of the WCET (2014)

16. Hsing, T.: On tail index estimation using dependent data. Ann. Stat. **19**(3), 1547–1569 (1991)

17. Kato, S., Lakshmanan, K., Kumar, A., Kelkar, M., Ishikawa, Y., Rajkumar, R.: RGEM: a responsive GPGPU execution model for runtime engines RTSS (2011)

18. Kato, S., Lakshmanan, K., Rajkumar, R., Ishikawa, Y.:Timegraph: GPU scheduling for real-time multi-tasking environments. In: USENIX ATC (2011)

19. Kato, S., McThrow, M., Maltzahn, C., Brandt, S.: Gdev: First-class GPU resource management in the operating system. In: Proceedings of the USENIX ATC (2012)

20. Kwiatkowski, D., Phillips, P.C.B., Schmidt, P., Shin, Y.: Testing the null hypothesis of stationarity against the alternative of a unit root: how sure are we that economic time series have a unit root? J. Econometrics **54**, 1–3 (1992)

21. Leadbetter, M.R., Lindgren, G., Rootzén, H.: Conditions for the convergence in distribution of maxima of stationary normal processes. Stoch. Process. Appl. **8**(2), 131–139 (1978)

22. Leadbetter, M.R., Lindgren, G., Rootzén, H.: Extremes and Related Properties of Random Sequences and Processes. Springer, New York (1983)

23. Lu, Y., Nolte, T., Bate, I., Cucu-Grosjean, L.: A statistical response-time analysis of real-time embedded systems. In: Proceedings of the RTSS, pp. 351–362 (2012)

24. Majdandzic, I., Trefftz, C., Wolffe, G.: Computation of voronoi diagrams using a graphics processing unit. In: IEEE International Conference on Electro/Information Technolog (EIT) (2008)

25. Mangharam, R., Saba, A.A.: Anytime algorithms for GPU architectures. In: Proceedings of the 32nd IEEE Real-Time Systems Symposium (RTSS) (2011)

26. Mejzler, D.: On the problem of the limit distribution for the maximal term of a variational series. Lvov. Politehn. Inst. Naucn Zap. Ser. Fiz. Mat. **38**, 90–109 (1956)

27. Membarth, R., Lupp, J.-H., Hannig, F., Teich, J., Körner, M., Eckert, W.: Dynamic task-scheduling and resource management for GPU accelerators in medical imaging. In: Herkersdorf, A., Römer, K., Brinkschulte, U. (eds.) ARCS 2012. LNCS, vol. 7179, pp. 147–159. Springer, Heidelberg (2012)

28. Northrop, P.: Semiparametric estimation of the extremal index using block maxima. Technical report, Dept of Statistical Science, UCL (2005)

29. NVIDIA Corp. CUDA C Best Practices Guide. DG-05603-001_v5.5

30. NVIDIA Corp. Whitepaper: Kepler GK110 (2012). www.nvidia.com/content/
    PDF/kepler/NVIDIA-Kepler-GK110-Architecture-Whitepaper.pdf
31. Rossbach, C.J., Currey, J., Silberstein, M., Ray, B., Witchel, E.: Ptask: Operating
    system abstractions to manage GPUs as computedevices. ACM SOSP (2011)
32. Santinelli, L., Morio, J., Dufour, G., Jacquemart, D.: On the sustainability of the
    extreme value theory for WCET estimation. In: International WCET Workshop
    (2014)

Approximate and Energy-Efficient Computing

Reducing Energy Consumption of Data Transfers Using Runtime Data Type Conversion

Michael Bromberger[1,2]($\boxtimes$), Vincent Heuveline[2], and Wolfgang Karl[1]

[1] Karlsruhe Institute of Technology, Karlsruhe, Germany
{bromberger,karl}@kit.edu, michael.bromberger@h-its.org
[2] Heidelberg Institute of Theoretical Studies, Heidelberg, Germany
vincent.heuveline@h-its.org

Abstract. Reducing the energy consumption of today's microprocessors, for which Approximate Computing (AC) is a promising candidate, is an important and challenging task. AC comprises approaches to relax the accuracy of computations in order to achieve a trade-off between energy efficiency and an acceptable remaining quality of the results. A high amount of energy is consumed by memory transfers. Therefore, we present an approach in this paper that saves energy by converting data before transferring it to memory. We introduce a static approach that can reduce the energy up to a factor of 4. We evaluate different methods to get the highest possible accuracy for a given data width. Extending this approach by a dynamic selection of different storage data types improves the accuracy for a 2D Fast Fourier Transformation by two orders of magnitude compared to the static approach using 16-bit data types, while still retaining the reduction in energy consumption. First results show that such a conversion unit can be integrated in low power processors with negligible impact on the power consumption.

Keywords: Energy reduction · Approximate computing · Data type conversion

1 Introduction

Due to the slowing of Moore's law as Dennard scaling reaches the physical lithographic limits at around 5 nm, new methods of increasing performance per watt will have to be found [4]. One possible answer is to support specialized hardware for particular applications, but this specialization results in so-called "dark silicon", i.e. silicon that is not used in all use-cases and presents a fixed cost overhead in such cases. Reducing the energy consumption is essential in low power processors and embedded systems where the battery or heat dissipation are often critical limitations. Memory accesses consume a considerable part of the energy in today's computing systems. An integer operation is $1{,}000\times$ less energy consuming than an access to a memory like DRAM [10]. The idea of approximate computing (AC) has been suggested as a possible means of increasing performance per watt across the gamut of computing systems. AC relaxes

© Springer International Publishing Switzerland 2016
F. Hannig et al. (Eds.): ARCS 2016, LNCS 9637, pp. 239–250, 2016.
DOI: 10.1007/978-3-319-30695-7_18

the accuracy of results produced by hard- and software in order to get an energy-efficient execution. Many algorithms from machine learning or image processing have an inherent resilience to such inexact operations.

We consider different approaches to reduce the amount of data that has to be transferred to memory, while getting the best achievable accuracy in each case. Our focus lies on conversion methods for a single data type rather than a bunch of data, because we want to improve energy efficiency of loads and stores inside a processor. Therefore, the first contribution of the paper is an evaluation of different conversion methods. A dynamic selection of data types provides a higher accuracy of results, while retaining the benefit of reducing the energy consumption. Secondly, a detailed measurement of the energy consumption of different embedded system platforms is given. We use memory footprints based on converted data for the measurements. Finally, we give preliminary results of a design that implements our results.

2   Related Work

Current approaches often focus on reducing the accuracy of hardware execution units [2]. An approximation of a software function with a certain number of inputs and outputs is given by a trained neural network (NN) [7]. Since software execution of a NN is slow, hardware support like a neural network processing unit is required. AC tools exist that lower the burden of programmers to decide which parts of an application can be executed approximately [5]. Hardware memoization techniques approximate mathematical and trigonometric functions [6] as well as fuzzy floating point (FP) operations [1]. Furthermore, there exist self-tuning off-line approaches, which use different AC kernels running on a GPU. Such approaches find the best available performance for a given result quality [16].

However, a considerable amount of energy is consumed by memories and memory transfers. Therefore, Sampson et al. have introduced EnerJ which uses approximated data types on a high level of abstraction [17]. Increasing the refresh cycle of certain DRAM memory regions raises the probability to read incorrect data, but reduces energy consumption [11,12]. Cache misses caused by loads are very expensive in terms of latency and energy consumption in modern architectures. Instead of loading a value that is missing in the cache, an approximated value is generated according to a history of loaded values [19]. Such approximated values have minor impact on the accuracy of output results for some applications. There exist approaches to store approximated data using Solid State Disks (SSD) [18] and Phase-Change Memory (PCM) [14]. Compressing data before storing it into memory reduces the overhead for transferring the data and increases the amount of data that fits into a certain memory region [20]. Block FP formats, in which several mantissae use the same exponent, also reduce the amount of data. Our approach reduces the size of data on a single data type level where we only consider information given by the current data type. Afterwards, several data types can be collected and compressed by above approaches. Such an approach requires domain-specific user knowledge. This issue has been addressed by Baek et al. [3].

3   Consideration of Different Conversion Methods

In this section, we evaluate which conversion methods are suitable for different algorithms. We used `Octave` to get a rapid prototype implementation. A statistical metric like the Mean Square Error (MSE) is sufficient enough for getting a deeper understanding of how different conversion methods influence the accuracy of results.

$$MSE(x_i, y_i) = \frac{1}{n} \sum_{i=0}^{n} (x_i - y_i)^2,$$

whereby x_i are results of a 64 bit FP implementation and y_i results of an approximated execution.

Instead of using an objective metric like MSE to evaluate the quality, several models exist, i.e. a mathematical formulation, which return a numerical value for a subjective quality. Task performance analysis is an approach that correlates the image quality to the success of a following operation on the data of the image. For example, the image quality of a radiography is good enough if a radiologist is able to see the bone fraction. Therefore, the required accuracy of the results depends strongly on the task that should be fulfilled by the application. In the absence of a general model that gets knowledge about the needed accuracy, knowledge from domain experts is required. This paper does not provide hints to the required accuracy of results. Instead, we give a domain expert the possibility to easily adapt the accuracy of the results of his application to get a performance improvement as well as an energy-efficient execution.

In the following, we use an IEEE 754-based 64-bit floating point (FP64) unit as execution unit. Internal architecture registers can store values in 64 bit. Our approach is similar to extending the accuracy to 80 bits inside a FP unit like in x86 architectures. This approach reduces errors, because internal calculations are performed with higher accuracy. But our approach also further reduces the overhead for transferring data from FP registers to memory in terms of energy and transfer time. Furthermore, such an approach avoids having FP units for different data types, which results in so-called dark silicon because not all units can be used at the same time. We do not consider additionally required data like loop counters, though such counters can be represented as FP values.

Methods which we consider for converting a FP64 value into one with 32, 21 or 16 bits are summarized in Table 1. The first method (opcode 0, op0) converts a FP64 value to one with less bits according to the IEEE-754 standard. Due to the absence of a FP21 data type, we assume 1 sign bit, 5 bits for the exponent and 15 bits for the mantissa. We investigate if such a data type is useful. The approach is to pack three FP21 values into a 64 bit word before transferring it to memory. It is tolerable for some applications to set values smaller than 1 to 0. Therefore, we can increase the data range by a factor of 2 for all FP data types, because we do not have to consider negative superscripts. This is implemented for opcode 1. Opcode 2 and 3 convert a FP64 value to a fixed point representation QX.Y or Q.Y, where X is the number of bits for the integer and Y for the

Table 1. Methods for converting a FP64 value to one with lower accuracy. Signed numbers are represented by a sign bit.

Opcode (op)	Conversion method	Applications
0	IEEE-754 standard	High data range
1	Values < 1 set to zero	Small numbers not needed
2	Unsigned/signed QX.Y	Small data range
3	Unsigned/signed Q0.Y	Small data range (adapting the scale value improves accuracy)

fractional part. The conversion is achieved by dividing the FP64 value by an adaptable scale value. Lines named with FP16, FP21, and FP32 in the following figures are based on opcode 0, lines with Q8.8, Q8.13 and Q8.24 are based on opcode 2, and Q.16, Q.21, and Q.32 are based on opcode 3. Opcode 1 was not used for the first two benchmarks. Additionally, an approach that changes dynamically between 16, 21 and 32 bit conversion data types is considered and corresponding lines are named with dynamic data type (*dyn dt (th=j)*, where j specifies a threshold). This threshold can be set by a programmer and specifies the maximum absolute error allowed for a conversion into a certain data type. The hardware itself, i.e. the conversion unit, checks whether a conversion into a lower data type is below this given threshold j or not. The conversion unit uses the smallest data type for which the resulting conversion error is less than the given threshold. A programmer can adapt the threshold during run-time, in order to trade off accuracy against energy consumption. This is useful if some parts of an algorithm need more accurate calculations. A line named with *Full FP32* means that all internal operations are executed in FP32 and not FP64. Due to the absence of a FP16 execution unit in the test system, we do not consider a *Full FP16* execution.

The first benchmark is a 2D convolution

$$I^{'}[x,y] = I[x,y] * f[x,y] = \sum_{m=-k/2}^{k/2} \sum_{n=-k/2}^{k/2} I[x,y] \cdot f[m-x,n-y],$$

where I is the original image, f is a $k \times k$ 2D Gaussian filter and $I^{'}$ is the de-blurred output image. The 2D convolution is executed up to 10 times, where the pixels of image $I^{'}$ are converted and used for following iterations. Pixel intensities are chosen randomly between 0 and 255 for a input image of size 1024×1024.

We specify for the first test that the values of a kernel are not preconverted before executing the first iteration and that the register set is large enough to store all kernel values (results see Fig. 1). Instead of a preconversion where values of a kernel are stored as converted values in the memory and have to be deconverted before transferring to the registers, kernel values are transferred as FP64 values to the FP register set. As mentioned above, image values are 8 bit integers, hence converting the image data is unnecessary. Therefore, the output of the first iteration is equal to a FP64 execution ($MSE = 0.0$). The MSE

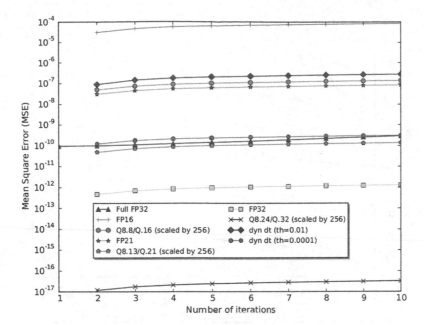

Fig. 1. MSE values of 2D convolutions using different conversion methods without preconversion. As input an image of size 1024×1024 with random values was used.

of a *Full FP32* execution is slightly higher than an execution using Q8.13 or Q.21, but about two orders of magnitude higher than our FP32 based approach and even seven orders of magnitude higher than Q8.24 and Q.32. Hence, our approach results in a much smaller MSE than a *Full FP32* execution, but has the same factor of data reduction. For the dynamic approach *dyn dt (th=0.01)*, the threshold 0.01 implies a usage of more FP16 data types, hence the MSE is closer to the MSE of the FP16 execution. More FP32 data types are used in the case of *dyn dt (th=0.0001)*, therefore the resulting MSE is closer to the MSE of the FP32 execution. For the second case, the kernel is preconverted into different conversion formats (see Fig. 2). The fixed point conversion formats (QY.X and Q.Y) are less accurate in terms of MSE than their FP relatives. According to the results in Figs. 1 and 2, higher accuracy is achieved in the first case. Hence, it turns out that for a higher accuracy of results frequently used data like the kernel values should be stored into the register set without conversion.

The second benchmark is a 2D `Richardson-Lucy Deconvolution`:

$$u^{(t+1)} = u^{(t)} \cdot \left(\frac{g}{u^{(t)} * K} * \widehat{K} \right),$$

where $u^{(t)}$ is the latent image, g the observed image, K a point spread function (PSF) and $\widehat{K}$ the flipped PSF. The Conversion method for the PSF values is fixed to FP16, FP21, and FP32 respectively (opcode 0). Conversion methods used for values of the intermediate results as well as the output image are shown in Fig. 3. Due to the higher data range of the algorithm, we have to adapt the

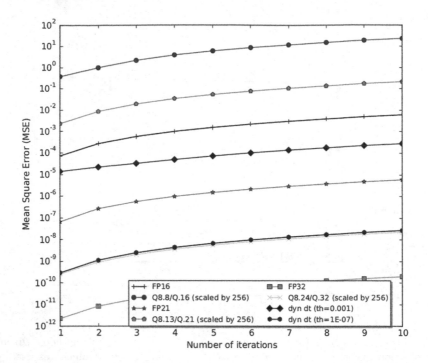

Fig. 2. MSE values of 2D convolutions using different conversion methods with pre-conversion. As input an image of size 1024×1024 with random values was used.

QX.Y conversion methods to Q.16, Q.21, Q.32, Q11.5, Q11.10, and Q11.21. Again the MSE of a *Full FP32* execution is higher than our FP32 approach. The FP approaches (FP16, FP21, FP32) have a smaller error than their fixed-point relatives (Q.16, Q.21, Q.32, Q11.5, Q11.10, and Q11.21). With the dynamic approach (*dyn dt (th=j)*) we can adapt the accuracy between FP16 and FP32 by adapting the threshold.

A 2D Fast Fourier Transformation[1] (FFT) is the last benchmark. As input we use an image with a size of 1024×1024, where the pixel intensities are chosen randomly between 0 and 255. A 2D FFT is done by row-wise 1D FFTs followed by column-wise 1D FFTs. The formula

$$X(n) = \sum_{k=0}^{N-1} x(k)e^{-jk2\pi\frac{n}{N}}, n = 0...N-1$$

is a forward FFT, where $x(k)$ is a complex series with N samples. We consider opcode 0, opcode 1, opcode 3, and the dynamic approach as conversion methods. The maximum absolute value during an execution has to be used as scale value for opcode 3. We also consider opcode 3 where we adapt the scale value by multiplying with 2 after each FFT butterfly beginning with 256.

---

[1] Code is based on the implementation of Paul Bourke http://paulbourke.net/miscellaneous/dft/.

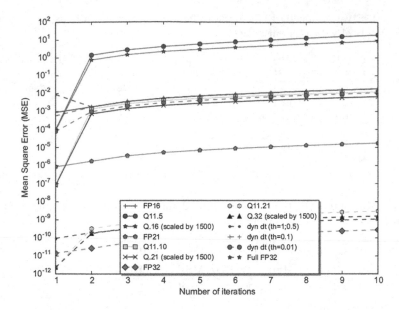

Fig. 3. MSE values for a 1024×1024 2D Richardson Lucy Deconvolution using different conversion methods for intermediate as well as the output image. The kernel values (psf) are converted using FP16, FP21 and FP32 (opcode 0), respectively.

The MSE and the factor of reduced data (RD) is shown in Table 2. Most of the static approaches using either 16 or 21 bits are assumedly not applicable in real applications. This is caused by the large codomain of the FFT algorithm. The only exception is opcode 1 using a 21 bit data type. A *Full FP32* execution has a higher MSE compared to FP32. Formats based on opcode 1 enable the reduction of the MSE compared to FP16 and FP21. Adapting the scale value for Q.32 results in a smaller MSE compared to FP32. Compared to a *Full FP32*, the dynamic approach with a threshold of 0.1 has roughly the same MSE, but reduces the amount of data by a factor of about 3. Hence, the dynamic approach is assumedly applicable for all used thresholds. We integrate the 2D FFT into an algorithm that reconstructs an image taken by a lens-free microscopy (see Table 3) [9]. The so-called spectral method is used to reconstruct holography images acquired by lens-free microscopy. Using FP32 yields to MSE of 0.0. The dynamic approach can reduce the MSE by two orders of magnitude while slightly decreasing the reduction of data transfers compared to FP16.

According to above benchmarks, it is sufficient for a conversion unit to have the conversion methods with opcode 0/1, because they achieve the best results in terms of MSE. It also turned out that Q.Y yields a lower MSE for algorithms with a small data range.

Table 2. MSE values for 2D FFTs using different conversion methods and an image of size 1024×1024 with random values.

	Full FP32		FP (op 0)		FP (op 1)		Q.Y (op 3)		Q.Y adapt. (op3)	
	MSE	RD	MSE	RD	MSE	RD	MSE	RD	MSE	RD
16 bit	-	-	∞	4	1.60E+05	4	2.00E+10	4	9.87E+07	4
21 bit	-	-	∞	3	2.84E+02	3	3.66E+09	3	9.53E+04	3
32 bit	1.63E+02	2	1.67E−04	2	-	2	9.02E+02	2	2.27E−05	2
Dynamic approach										
Threshhold	1E00		1E-01		1E-03		1E-05		1E-07	
	MSE	RD	MSE	RD	MSE	RD	MSE	RD	MSE	RD
	1.16E+03	3.65	1.85E+02	3.14	2.75E-02	2.34	1.67E-04	2.21	1.67E−04	2.21

Table 3. MSE values for the spectral method that reconstructs holography images using the above different FFT methods.

FP16 (Op 0)		FP21 (Op 0)		FP32 (Op 0)		
MSE	RD	MSE	RD	MSE	RD	
4.93E−02	4	4.78E−02	3	0.00E+00	2	
Dynamic approach						
Thesh = 1		Thesh = .5		Thresh = .1		Thresh = .01	
MSE	RD	MSE	RD	MSE	RD	MSE	RD
2.16E−04	3.94	1.63E−04	3.91	8.00E−05	3.77	1.40E−05	3.35

4 Measuring Energy Consumption

After the evaluation of promising conversion methods, we extract memory footprints of the 2D FFT benchmark that are created by using different FP conversion methods. Due to the fact that FP21 is not supported in current computing environments, we consider FP16, FP32 and FP64. The function memcpy, which is part of the standard C library, is used to transfer data according to the 2D FFT extracted memory footprints. We used memcpy, because we are only interested in the energy consumption of the data transfers. The used data is the result of a 2D FFT of a random image. Platforms used for the measurements are the Odriod-XU [8], the Parallela board [15], and the Myriad 1 development board [13]. An overview of the integrated compute units in each platform is given in Table 4. We selected these platforms because reducing energy consumption is especially important in embedded systems.

Table 4. Overview about the considered platforms.

Platform	Host processor [Technology]	Coprocessor [Technology]
Odriod-XU	Exsynos5 Octa (5410) [28 nm]	PowerVR SGX544MP3 GPU [28 nm]
Parallela	Zynq-7010 [28 nm]	E16G301 [65 nm]
Myriad 1	Leon 3 [65 nm]	SHAVEs [65 nm]

The Odriod-XU includes a Samsung Exsynos Octa processor that is based on the ARM big.LITTLE architecture and integrates a Cortex-A15 and a Cortex-A7. An operating system can switch between both clusters depending on the workload and the required performance, but the clusters cannot be used concurrently. We used a script to measure the energy consumption of the Odriod-XU. The script reads the values of different sensors for voltage, current, and power of the A7, A15 and the main memory. However, such a script influences the measurement. Therefore, we plan to use an external measuring setup using a GPIO pin of the Odriod-XU in the future. *POSIX Threads* (`Pthreads`) enable the usage of all four available cores. It is possible to decide on which cluster the benchmark is executed by specifying the frequency of the Exsynos5. We used an infinite loop around the `memcpy` calls to get a stable value of the electric power. We also measured the execution time in a different run.

The Parallela board, which includes a Dual-core ARM A9 (600 MHz) and a 16-core Epiphany (666 MHz), was developed for an energy efficient execution of high performance applications. We used the Odriod Smart Power, which is a deployable power supply to specify a fixed voltage and to measure the current as well as the electric power. The Odriod Smart Power measures the values for the entire board. For the first test, we used `Pthreads` again for starting two threads on the A9 and did not consider the energy consumption of the Epiphany. We measured the execution time in a second run and calculated the energy consumption. To measure the electric power of the A9 host processor together with the Epiphany, the A9 calls all 16 cores of the Epiphany. The 2D FFT data is transferred from the host memory to the local memory by Direct Memory Access (DMA). On each Epiphany core, `memcpy` transfers data to another region in the local memory of the core.

The Myriad I combines a Leon processor with eight Streaming Hybrid Architecture Vector Engines (SHAVEs). To measure the electric power of the Myriad 1, power cables are connected directly to supply the processor with electrical energy. A switched-mode power supply together with an ampere-meter enable to specify the voltage and to measure the current. To transfer the memory footprints inside the host memory, the function `memcpy` is used on the Leon processor. In the second test, eight DMA units, that are assigned to each SHAVEs, transfer data to the local memory. All SHAVES are used to transfer data inside the local memory according to the memory footprints.

The results of all setups are summarized in Table 5. Columns named with *Reduction* specify the factor of reduction in energy consumption compared to FP64. Energy consumptions are calculated by multiplying the execution time with the measured electric power. Our expectation is that a reduction of the amount of data, that has to be transferred, results in a reduction of the energy consumption of the same factor. According to the measurements, the expectation turned out to be true. The only exception is the dual-core A9 on the Parallela board, which is presumably caused by the underlying inefficient `memcpy` implementation.

Table 5. Measured energy consumption for a 2D FFT memory footprint.

	Size [MB]	Time [ms]	Power [W]	Energy [mJ]	Reduction	Time [ms]	Power [W]	Energy [mJ]	Reduction
		Odroid-XU							
		A15 & Global memory				A7 & Global memory			
FP64	16	5.503	4.849	26.682	1.0	11.226	0.702	7.881	1
FP32	8	2.588	4.875	12.618	2.1	5.104	0.724	3.695	2.1
FP16	4	1.185	4.962	5.880	4.5	2.503	0.729	1.825	4.3
		Parallela board							
		ARM A9				ARM A9 & Epiphany			
FP64	16	39.836	5.767	229.734	1.0	16513.133	6.179	102034.649	1.0
FP32	8	26.174	5.828	152.542	1.5	8257.387	6.026	49759.014	2.1
FP16	4	12.534	5.805	72.760	3.2	4135.034	4.034	16680.727	6.1
		Myriad I board							
		Leon 3				Leon 3 & SHAVES			
FP64	16	1826.062	0.190	346.952	1.0	168.571	0.499	84.117	1.0
FP32	8	910.723	0.187	170.305	2.0	83.152	0.482	40.079	2.1
FP16	4	456.516	0.188	85.825	4.0	40.162	0.478	19.197	4.4

5 Preliminary Design of a Conversion Unit

The Conversion Unit (CU) converts a FP64 value into a data type with fewer bits before storing it to memory (see Fig. 4). While reading the data, the value is converted back to FP64. The decision about the accuracy of the stored data is made statically using a conversion instruction. As a first step to realize such a CU, we described the *Converter* and *Deconverter* in Verilog. The *Converter* can convert a FP64 value to a FP16 or a FP32 value. This is realized by adapting the exponent part of the type and selecting the leading 10 or 23 bits of the mantissa. Instead of truncation, the round to nearest method is used for rounding. A FP64 value can also be converted to a FP format where no negative exponents are considered (opcode 1). If the exponent part of a FP64 value is smaller than the bias, the exponent part is set to 0. If the bias is equal to the exponent part, the exponent part is set to 1. 2 is added to the FP64 exponent for all other cases. The Q.16 and Q.32 data types are calculated by scaling the FP64 value. Such a scaling is only allowed for values $x_i = 2^i$, where $i = 0, 1, 2....$ Therefore, the scaling is

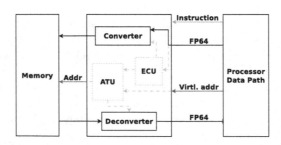

Fig. 4. Structure of the conversion unit.

performed by subtracting i from the exponent part. This avoids the use of a FP divider which increases the electric power as well as the latency of the unit. Each conversion is performed in a clock cycle. The *Deconverter* converts a conversion data type back to a FP64 value. Deconverting a FP value is always exact. As we restrict the factors to be a power of 2 for the scaling, the deconversion from a fixed point to the 64 bit floating point format is also exact. Using the Synopsis tools, we got an estimation about the electric power and the area of the units. We use the TSMC 28 nm HPM High Speed library for the synthesis. The results are summarized in Table 6. Compared to the measured values in Table 5, these units will not significantly increase the energy consumption. Supporting the dynamic approach will require an Address Translation Unit (ATU), as well as storing further information about the conversion method that was used for a specific data type. The ATU will avoid fragmentation inside memory. An Error Check Unit (ECU) decides, which conversion method is used depending on the error that will occur after the conversion. We will design and implement both units in future.

Table 6. Area and estimated power for the *Converter* and the *Deconverter*.

	500 MHz		600 MHz	
	Area	Power	Area	Power
	$[\mu m^2]$	$[\mu W]$	$[\mu m^2]$	$[\mu W]$
Converter	1958.681	336.900	2187.844	435.100
Deconverter	1199.812	188.300	1214.325	225.800

6   Conclusion

Memory accesses are expensive in terms of energy consumption and latency. Image processing applications can tolerate an execution on inaccurate hardware. Therefore, we presented an approach in this paper for a conversion unit (CU), that could be integrated in today's low power processors. Such a unit offers a static and a dynamic conversion of data types before the transfer to memory, which yields a reduction of the energy consumption for data transfers by a factor up to about 4. Using the dynamic approach, the accuracy of the results produced by a 2D FFT is improved by two orders of magnitude, while retaining the potential gain in the reduction of energy consumption. Dealing with different thresholds enables to trade off accuracy against energy consumption. In the future, we will integrate the implemented units into an existing processor design. Furthermore, we want to implement a CU that also supports the dynamic approach. Additionally, we will also design a memory architecture that enables an efficient transfer of data types for the dynamic approach.

Acknowledgements. The work was mainly performed during a HiPEAC internship at Movidius, Ireland. Special thanks to Fergal Connor and David Moloney. Additionally, this work was also funded by the Klaus Tschira Foundation.

References

1. Alvarez, C., Corbal, J., Valero, M.: Fuzzy memoization for floating-point multimedia applications. IEEE Trans. Comput. **54**(7), 922–927 (2005)
2. Avinash, L., Enz, C.C., Palem, K.V., Piguet, C.: Designing energy-efficient arithmetic operators using inexact computing. J. Low Power Electron. **9**(1), 141–153 (2013)
3. Baek, W., Chilimbi, T.M.: Green: a framework for supporting energy-conscious programming using controlled approximation. In: ACM Sigplan Notices, vol. 45, pp. 198–209. ACM (2010)
4. Borkar, S., Chien, A.A.: The future of microprocessors. Commun. ACM **54**(5), 67–77 (2011)
5. Chippa, V., Chakradhar, S., Roy, K., Raghunathan, A.: Analysis and characterization of inherent application resilience for approximate computing. In: DAC, pp. 1–9, May 2013
6. Citron, D., Feitelson, D.G.: Hardware Memoization of Mathematical and Trigonometric Functions. Hebrew University of Jerusalem, Technical report (2000)
7. Esmaeilzadeh, H., Sampson, A., Ceze, L., Burger, D.: Neural acceleration for general-purpose approximate programs. In: MICRO, pp. 449–460 (2012)
8. Hardkernel.: Odriod-XU. http://odroid.com/dokuwiki/doku.php?id=en:odroid-xu. Accessed 03 May 2015
9. Hennelly, B., Kelly, D., Pandey, N., Monaghan, D.: Zooming algorithms for digital holography. J. Phys: Conf. Ser. **206**(1), 012027 (2010)
10. Horowitz, M.: Computing energy problem: and what we can do about it. In: Keynote, International Solid-State Circuits Conference, February 2014. https://www.futurearchs.org/sites/default/files/horowitz-ComputingEnergyISSCC.pdf. Accessed 03 May 2015
11. Liu, S., Pattabiraman, K., Moscibroda, T., Zorn, B.: Flikker: saving DRAM refresh-power through critical data partitioning. In: ASPLOS, March 2011
12. Lucas, J., Alvarez-Mesa, M., Andersch, M., Juurlink, B.: Sparkk: Quality-scalable approximate storage in DRAM. In: The Memory Forum, June 2014
13. Movidius Ltd.: Myriad 1. http://www.hotchips.org/wp-content/uploads/hc_archives/hc23/HC23.19.8-Video/HC23.19.811-1TOPS-Media-Moloney-Movidius.pdf. Accessed 03 May 2015
14. Nelson, J., Sampson, A., Ceze, L.: Dense approximate storage in phase-change memory. In: ASPLOS (2011)
15. Parallela Project: Parallela board. http://www.parallella.org/board/. Accessed 03 May 2015
16. Samadi, M., Lee, J., Jamshidi, D.A., Hormati, A., Mahlke, S.: SAGE: self-tuning approximation for graphics engines. In: MICRO, pp. 13–24 (2013)
17. Sampson, A., Dietl, W., Fortuna, E., Gnanapragasam, D., Ceze, L., Grossman, D.: Enerj: approximate data types for safe and general low-power computation. In: ACM SIGPLAN Notices, vol. 46, pp. 164–174. ACM (2011)
18. Sampson, A., Nelson, J., Strauss, K., Ceze, L.: Approximate Storage in Solid-state Memories. In: Proceedings of the MICRO, MICRO-46, pp. 25–36. ACM, New York (2013)
19. San Miguel, J., Enright Jerger, N.: Load value approximation: approaching the ideal memory access latency. In: WACAS (2014)
20. Sardashti, S., Wood, D.A.: Decoupled compressed cache: exploiting spatial locality for energy-optimized compressed caching. In: MICRO, pp. 62–73 (2013)

Balancing High-Performance Parallelization and Accuracy in Canny Edge Detector

Valery Kritchallo[1](✉), Billy Braithwaite[2], Erik Vermij[3], Koen Bertels[1], and Zaid Al-Ars[1]

[1] Delft University of Technology, Mekelweg 4, 2628 CD Delft, The Netherlands
v.v.kritchallo@tudelft.nl
[2] University of Eastern Finland, Kuopio, Finland
[3] IBM Research, Dwingeloo, The Netherlands

Abstract. We present a novel approach to tradeoff accuracy against the degree of parallelization for the Canny edge detector, a well-known image-processing algorithm. At the heart of our method is a single top-level image-slicing loop incorporated into the sequential algorithm to process image segments concurrently, a parallelization technique allowing for breaks in the computational continuity in order to achieve high performance levels. By using the fidelity slider, a new approximate computing concept that we introduce, the user can exercise full control over the desired balance between accuracy of the output and parallel performance. The practical value and strong scalability of the presented method is demonstrated by extensive benchmarks performed on three evaluation platforms, showing speedups of up to 7x for an accuracy of 100 % and up to 19x for an accuracy of 99 % over the sequential version, as recorded on an Intel Xeon platform with 14 cores and 28 hardware threads.

1 Introduction

Three decades on since publication of the highly influential paper by John F. Canny [4], his edge detector algorithm (referred to as CED further on in the text) remains a standard and a basis of many efficient solutions in the fields of pattern recognition, computer vision, and a number of others. The algorithm is also known as computationally challenging due to its high latency that prevents a direct implementation from being employed in real-time applications [15]. And, while there exist numerous multi-core implementations of the algorithm, the issue of combining both high performance and quality of the edge detection in a single solution remains relevant as ever.

Among the previously published works on parallelization of the CED, [5] is, to our knowledge, the only one that could be meaningfully compared with our in terms of the recorded optimization levels. It reports a speedup of 11 times over sequential achieved on a 16-core CPU for a 2048 × 2048 pixels test image, but lacks, in our view, sufficient scalability analysis of the presented solution. All other previous efforts in parallelization of the CED have been carried

© Springer International Publishing Switzerland 2016
F. Hannig et al. (Eds.): ARCS 2016, LNCS 9637, pp. 251–262, 2016.
DOI: 10.1007/978-3-319-30695-7_19

out using a hardware acceleration platform of some sort, typically NVIDIA's GPU/CUDA [3,5,10,14,15]; furthermore, none of the works offered any user-defined scheme of tradeoff between the performance and quality of the traced output.

In contrast, the parallelization approach that we propose in this paper is not based on any particular hardware acceleration architecture, and thus can be implemented on a commodity multi-core platform equipped with an OpenMP-enabled GCC compiler. Similarly to the approach used in [5], in our parallelization of Canny edge we employ *domain decomposition* [11], a widely used data parallelization strategy that divides an image into equally-sized segments (with segments being in our case contiguous blocks of image pixel rows, or *slices*, as we call them), and processes them concurrently. However, unlike all previous approaches where the standard practice would dictate parallelizing the algorithm's sequential code on the laborious loop-by-loop basis, our method relies solely on incorporating a *single* image-slicing loop atop every other loop already existing in the code. This novel technique, besides being highly portable, requires minimal modification of the existing code and thus can be easily applied in a template manner to a wide range of image processing algorithms and applications.

Due to the enforced nature of the slicing loop-based parallelization, however, it is possible for our method to induce certain violation of the computational continuity of the sequential code, resulting in an output that is different from the sequential one. This issue is addressed in our method by introducing principles of approximate computing into the solution, such as the fully original *fidelity slider*, a mechanism that allows the user to maintain the desired level of edge detection quality in the parallel output by trading off a controlled amount of the achieved parallel performance.

Because of its universal character, our method of incorporating an image-slicing loop combined with the approximate computing-based tradeoff of accuracy against performance can be successfully applied to a wide range of image processing algorithms, particularly those not easily amenable to efficient parallelization due to their inherent constraints of computational continuity and internal data dependencies. As we estimate, such algorithms may vary from computer vision methods, such as Sobel's and Prewitt's edge detector method [7], anisotropic diffusion [13] and mean-shift filter [6], to more general data-processing ones, such as discrete wavelet transform [12], and many others.

To our knowledge, given the described above unique characteristics of our method, there are no existing analogues to compare it with.

The two major contributions of this paper are:

1. a novel efficient data parallelization technique based on introduction of a single top-level *image-slicing loop* into the application;
2. the *fidelity slider* as a new approximate computing concept to balance performance and precision in the parallelized application, such as the CED.

The rest of the paper is organized as follows. Section 2 describes the method we used to parallelize the CED. The achieved experimental results are shown and discussed in Sect. 3, followed by Sect. 4 that concludes this paper.

2 Parallelization of Canny Edge

2.1 Canny Edge Detection Algorithm

The Canny edge detection algorithm, developed by John F. Canny [4], is a well-known image processing algorithm used in many fields ranging from pattern recognition to computer vision. Description of this algorithm can be found in many introductory texts on image processing. Here, we only list the main stages of the algorithm:

1. noise reduction by filtering with a Gaussian-smoothing filter;
2. computing the gradients of an image to highlight regions with high spatial derivatives;
3. relating the edge gradients to directions that can be traced;
4. tracing valid edges using hysteresis thresholding to eliminate breaking up of edge contours.

The baseline sequential version that we used for parallelization, was the CED implementation by Heath et al. [1,8]. The function and variable names used throughout the text of this section, as well as included in the Fig. 2 and Table 1, refer to the source code of that implementation.

```
/* iterate over image slices */
for (row_ix=0; row_ix<rows; row_ix+=rows_slice) {
#pragma omp task shared(edge_file) if (do_async_tasking)
    {
        /* call the main filter function to process
         * the image slice as a concurrent task */
        canny_par(row_ix, rows_slice, cols, image, ...);
    }
}
```

Fig. 1. The source code fragment implementing the main image-slicing loop (simplified).

Table 1. Runtime breakdown by functions in the CED, percents

gaussian_smooth (Gaussian smoothing)	non_max_supp (non-maximum suppression)	apply_hysteresis (hysteresis edge thresholding)	derrivative_x_y (Gaussian derivative x & y)	magnitude_x_y (magnitude x & y)	follow_edges (edge tracing
76.7	8.2	4.4	4.4	3.8	2.3

2.2 Introduction of the Image-Slicing Loop

The domain decomposition-based strategy we employed to parallelize the sequential version enforces coarse-grained data parallelization onto the application through incorporating a top-level image-slicing loop into its code. In the case of the CED implementation, the slices are equally-sized, contiguous blocks of pixel rows that are processed concurrently by asynchronous tasks spawned by a dedicated OpenMP-driven loop (Fig. 1). The loop has been parallelized with a single

#pragma omp task OpenMP directive, which we chose over the more commonly used *#pragma omp for* due to its ability to parallelize non-canonical loops. To host the image-slicing loop, a separate function was added at the top of the program's logic; the (formerly) main function is called from within the loop to process a single slice, instead of the whole image, as before.

Figure 1 shows the (simplified) fragment of the source code implementing the image-slicing loop, with the *#pragma omp task* OpenMP directive launching concurrent slice-processing tasks.

Right choice of the slice size, denoted as the *rows_slice* variable in the source code fragment, is crucial for reaching the best parallel performance in our solution. It is controlled via a parameter in the application's command line that defines number of pixel rows in each slice. If the parameter is not specified, the optimal slice size will be calculated automatically by the application as simply the quotient of the image's vertical dimension divided by the current number of active threads. When the active thread count is equal to the maximal number of hardware threads supported by the system, the slice size calculated this way is nearly guaranteed to lead to the highest parallel performance for the host platform, since it effectuates an ideal workload balance between slice-processing tasks, with OpenMP efficiently distributing the tasks among active threads.

With the exception of the Gaussian-smoothing loops that we parallelized mostly for various testing and illustration reasons (see the *Earth, Gaussian smoothing loops only* curve in Fig. 3 showing modest overall speedup of 2.4 times over sequential achieved from a standalone parallelization of this loop), no other native loops in the application were explicitly parallelized. As the application profile data, as well as our analysis of the source code indicated, optimization benefits of such effort would have been minimal (see Table 1, which shows runtime breakdown by functions in the CED, as recorded during profiling of the sequential version).

2.3 Image-Slicing Challenges and Solutions

Due to the breaks in the computational continuity of the CED algorithm caused by the introduced image-slicing loop, the following issues have been observed in the edge-traced images rendered by the parallel version:

1. horizontal visual breaks appearing in the image, i.e. blank single-pixel rows between slices, as a result of broken continuity in the Gaussian-smoothing stage of the algorithm due to the smoothing filter now operating on separate image slices, instead of the whole image, as it was done by the sequential algorithm;
2. areas in the image rendered differently from the reference output due to the image histogram array no longer computed globally for the entire image, but computed piece-wise within each slice;
3. differently traced edges as a result of violating the logic of the recursive edge-tracing procedure used by the original code that allowed, in principle, for indefinitely long, contiguous edges traced from one arbitrary pixel in the image to another arbitrary one.

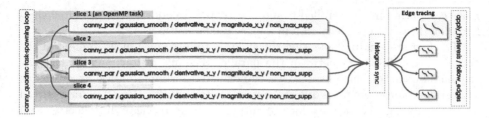

Fig. 2. OpenMP-based parallelization scheme, drawn as a simplified case of four asynchronous slice-processing tasks entering histogram synchronization before the edge-tracing stage.

To address the above-mentioned issues, we implemented the following additions to our solution.

The parallel code was adjusted such that the image slices included extra overlapping pixel rows blending into the neighbors, in order to mask the visual breaks that resulted from image-slicing. The thereby introduced vertical overlap size (expressed in pixel rows) is an integer parameter varying from 1 to τ_σ, where τ_σ is derived from σ, the input parameter of the Canny edge algorithm that defines the standard deviation of the Gaussian-smoothing filter. The vertical overlap size corresponds to the integer *windowsize* variable found in the sequential code of the filter, and is computed as follows:

$$\tau_\sigma = 2 * \lceil 2.5 * \sigma \rceil \tag{1}$$

For most typical use-cases where σ doesn't exceed 2.0, the value of 10 pixels calculated for τ_σ in accordance with Eq. 1 results in a Gaussian-smoothed output identical to that of the sequential version of the algorithm, while the default of 4 pixels provides adequate masking effect. This adjustment fully fixed issue (1), and partially addressed issue (3), with a performance penalty depending on the overlap size and number of slices.

To produce the precise – in respect to the sequential version that is – output, a modification in the parallel code was necessary that would allow using a single histogram of the entire image for all concurrent slice tasks. To implement this, a *histogram synchronization* scheme was developed, where slice tasks performed most of the work independently, and only synchronized with each other briefly (see "histogram sync" block in Fig. 2), to compute and share among themselves the single global histogram, before proceeding with edge-tracing within their individual image slices, again concurrently. The scheme (Fig. 2) allowed to retain most of the parallel performance, and partially solved issue (2) of divergence with the reference output. The complete solution for issue (2) and (3) could only be found as a part of the fidelity slider design (Sect. 2.5).

2.4   The Fidelity Slider: Balancing Performance and Accuracy

In order to fully address issue (2) and (3), a new feature which we call *fidelity slider* has been introduced into the solution. By means of adding elements of approximate computing in a controlled fashion, it allowed to address the principal challenges of the CED parallelization in a more fundamental way.

The first step in implementing the slider is to introduce measurement of the actual binary difference between the parallel version's output and that of the sequential one. For this purpose, we implemented a simple metric expressed as a total sum of average pixel difference between two images (Eq. 2), which proved a suitable divergence measure for the purposes of our application, reflecting well the degree of the observable visual difference, as well as more subtle deviations in rendered edges (see Fig. 6, explained in more detail in Sect. 3.4.)

The rendering error RE used to calculate the accuracy of the parallel output is computed as the image distance metric described above, that is the average pixel difference between the parallel-produced image p and the sequential image s (both grayscale, the only type of images the CED works with), and is defined as

$$RE(p,s) = \frac{\sum_{i=1}^{N} \sum_{j=1}^{M} \frac{|LPij - LSij|}{255.0}}{N * M} \tag{2}$$

where LPij and LSij are pixel intensity values, and N and M are the images vertical and horizontal dimensions in pixels. The corresponding accuracy percentage value is calculated as

$$AC = 100 * (1.0 - RE)$$

2.5 The Design of the Fidelity Slider

The fidelity slider is constructed as a composite parameter driving the strength of the following three factors, each moderating its own component of the aggregate divergence from the reference image induced by the computational discontinuity issues (1), (2) and (3):

1. the vertical slice overlap size in pixel rows, from 1 to τ_σ. This is the factor introduced to inhibit issue (1). It moderates the related component of the rendering error RE in a manner such that adding a pixel row to the slice overlap along incrementing the factor results in a steadily decreasing component of the rendering error;
2. the degree of the cross-slice histogram synchronization, expressed as the number of slice tasks synchronized before the algorithm's edge-tracing phase takes place, progressing from two to all slices synchronized. This is the factor introduced to inhibit issue (2). Advancing the slider value from 1 % to 100 % results in more and more slices using the globally synchronized histogram (as opposed to their locally computed one) and, correspondingly, decreasing component of the rendering error;
3. number of slices rendered in non-concurrent fashion during the last edge-tracing stage, progressing from two to all slices. This is the factor introduced to inhibit issue (3). This last-stage rendering is performed by the leading slice task, which is reflected in Fig. 2 by the slice on the top (drawn visibly larger than the rest). Advancing the slider value from 1 % to 100 % results in more and more slices jointly edge-traced as a single contiguous fragment of the input image and, correspondingly, decreasing component of the rendering error.

Further algorithmic details of the three introduced factors and the related to them moderation process can be found in [9].

3 Results

3.1 The Test and Development Platforms

In the course of benchmarking our CED implementation, we used the following three platforms. First, an IBM server equipped with two 4.2 GHz POWER8 CPUs both featuring six cores each supporting up to eight threads per core, running Ubuntu kernel v3.16, hereafter called "POWER8". Second, an HPC server with two 2.6 GHz Xeon E5-2697 CPUs, each having 14 cores supporting two threads per core, running Ubuntu kernel v3.13, hereafter called "Xeon E5-2697". And third, a Dell desktop with a 3.2 GHz Xeon E5-1650 CPU, having six cores supporting two threads per core, running Windows 7, hereafter called "Xeon E5-1650". In all our experiments on the dual-socket machines, only a single socket was used. The development platform on the three systems was GCC compiler v4.8.2, v4.9.1, and v4.8.2, respectively, with OpenMP v4.0 as the parallelization environment.

3.2 The Test Image Set and Benchmarking Routine

During the benchmarking stage, we used a wide variety of test images, ranging from 0.3 MB, 650×488 pixels size (*ThunderCloud* in Fig. 3), to 149 MB, 13985×11188 pixels (*Wrigley*), the size that, to all our knowledge, significantly

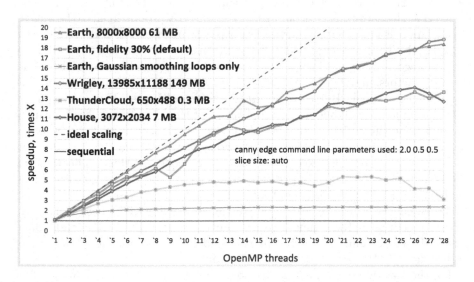

Fig. 3. Benchmark results for parallelized Canny edge, as registered for four test images at the fidelity level of 1 % (unless otherwise noted) with file output disabled. Test platform: Xeon E5-2697 with 14 cores and 28 hardware threads.

exceeds any previously reported one for an edge-traced image. The visual contents of the test images varied greatly as well, from natural (*Earth, ThunderCloud*) to mostly geometric (*House, Wrigley*) and entirely synthetic/computer-generated.

For benchmarking of the presented here CED solution, we used a custom benchmarking sub-system incorporated in the application's code. Based on principles of statistic sampling, this sub-system can execute long batches of test runs, objectively measuring the resulting speedup, and performance in general, against a user-selected range of threads, image-slicing-related parameters and ranges of application-specific numeric options in arbitrary combinations. Each test run, in turn, is typically comprised of 6 or 12 individual application executions, to produce statistically correct performance average. In the course of benchmarking our CED solution, we have performed some 900+ test batches to edge-trace a set of twenty images in total, of which a selected, most representative subset of four images was chosen for the illustration purposes of this paper, rendered as speedup and accuracy curves in Figs. 3 and 5.

The source images and the full compilation of produced benchmarks, as well as the code and other supplemental material used in this paper are available on the OSF site [2].

3.3   Recorded Speedups

Figure 3, displaying the range of speedups recorded when edge-tracing the representative sub-set of four test images on the Xeon E5-2697, demonstrates that our parallelization method performs the best when processing large-sized images (*Earth, Wrigley*), as compared to medium- and small-sized ones (*House, ThunderCloud*). Extensive benchmarking performed on the full test image set has confirmed that the performance of our method is generally proportional to the image's dimensions, although with a varying from platform to platform degree. On the other hand – as it was expected – the performance and method's scalability is affected negatively by the increased strength of the imposed by the fidelity slider accuracy factors, mainly by the histogram synchronization at 100 %. This is illustrated by the curve marked *Earth, fidelity 30 % (default)* in this Figure (the fidelity level that enforces maximum synchronization of the histogram slices), with the maximum speedup of 13.67 times over sequential, compared to 18.39 times for the same image at fidelity 1 %, which imposes no synchronization.

The maximal parallel execution speedup recorded for this application was 18.66 times over the sequential version, when processing the biggest test image on the Xeon E5-2697, with file output disabled and fidelity set at 1 % (*Wrigley* in Fig. 3). On the other two evaluation platforms, benchmarking has recorded the highest speedups of 13.33 times over sequential, for the POWER8 (test image: seven MB House.pgm, 3072 × 2034 pixels), and 7.74 times, for the Xeon E5-1650 (test image: 61 MB Earth.pgm, 8000 × 8000 pixels).

For the majority of the images we tested, rendering at the 1 % fidelity resulted in the accuracy of 98 %–99 % of the edge-traced output. The chart in Fig. 4 displays the highest absolute parallel performance in MBs per second registered for each

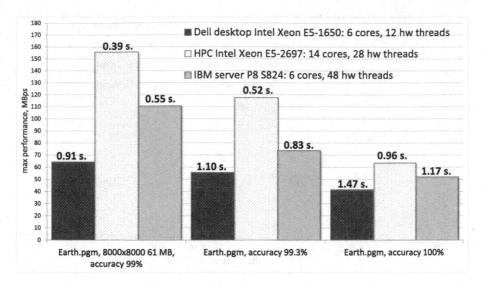

Fig. 4. Maximal parallel performance in MBs per second for the three test platforms at three accuracy levels. Test image: Earth, 8000 × 8000 pixels, 61 MB. The figures a top of every bar are the shortest runtime in seconds registered for the platform at each of the three accuracy levels.

of the three test platforms at three key accuracy levels (99 %, 99.3 % and 100 %), when rendering the main test image, with the shortest runtime in seconds atop of every bar. Although the Xeon E5-2697 appears a clear winner in the picture, the POWER8 comes out substantially better in the performance-per-core metric.

3.4   Fidelity Slider Benchmarks

In Fig. 5, the benchmark produced results for the four test images are displayed against the vertical speedup axis, with the accuracy value progressing from 99 % to 100 % along the horizontal one. The speedup is the highest (18.01 times over sequential for our main test image, 61 MB Earth.pgm of 8000 × 8000 pixel size) at the leftmost position of 99 percent accuracy.

To help in getting an idea of the degree of the edge detection divergence that can be expected at the lowest fidelity value of 1 %, Fig. 6 presents a fragment from another our test image, detail-rich Wrigley, with the original picture shown on the left and the output of the sequential version in the middle. The right side of this Figure (produced by an image-processing program in the layer difference mode) visualizes the edges traced spuriously by the parallel version; most of them, as can be observed, are concentrated along a horizontal row at about 1/3 height of the picture where a slice break happened. When comparing the two rendered outputs visually (without the help of such image-processing program that is), the difference of this scale is rather difficult to discover, unless one is hinted where to look first. The measured accuracy for this rendering was 98.01 %.

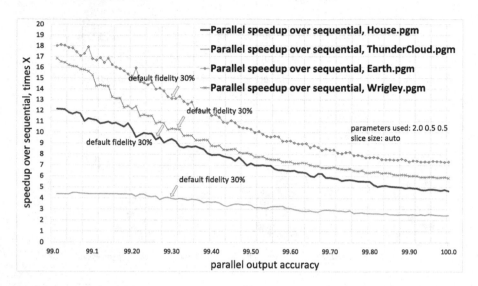

Fig. 5. Impact of the output accuracy on the parallel speedup, as recorded on the Xeon E5-2697 for four test images.

Fig. 6. A fragment from the Wrigley image (original picture on the left) with the sequential program's traced edge output (middle) and spurious edges rendered by the parallelized version at the lowest fidelity value of 1 % (right).

At the rightmost slider position of 100 %, where the performance is the lowest (7.32 times over sequential for Earth), the image difference is zero. In Fig. 3, the range of speedups recorded for the default slider value 30 % – chosen in our CED implementation for the best combination of speed and quality – can be seen, represented by the curve marked *Earth, fidelity 30 % (default)*.

4   Conclusions

The relevance and continued viability of the Canny edge detector as a robust computer vision algorithm remain undisputed, and there is no shortage of implementations of this venerable algorithm. What seems to be lacking among these implementations, however, is a consistent approach that would address the performance and edge detection quality in an equal and flexible manner, and that would not require using a proprietary acceleration platform to achieve its performance levels.

The two major contributions of this paper were:

1. a novel efficient data parallelization technique based on introduction of a single top-level *image-slicing loop* into the application;
2. the *fidelity slider* as a new approximate computing concept to balance performance and precision in the parallelized application, such as the CED.

In this paper, we demonstrated that a successful application of coarse-grained parallelization and innovative principles of approximate computing through incorporating an image-slicing loop into the CED algorithm allows to achieve highly scalable optimization without using any dedicated hardware acceleration equipment. On all three test platforms we used, benchmarking has registered strong multi-core performance, with highest speedups varying from 7.74 times over sequential, as recorded on the lowest platform (a 6-core, 12 hardware threads Intel Dell desktop), to 18.66 times, on the highest (a 14-core, 28-hardware thread Intel HPC Xeon server). The desired balance between the performance and quality of the output is maintained via the specially-introduced fidelity slider, yielding speedups varying from 18.66x at the accuracy level of 99 percent, down to 7.32x at the accuracy level of 100 percent, as recorded for the fastest benchmark.

References

1. Edge Detector Comparison (1996–2015). http://marathon.csee.usf.edu/edge/edge_detection.html
2. The Canny edge/QuadMC parallelization project (2015). https://osf.io/i725h/
3. Brethorst, A.Z., Desai, N., Enright, D.P., Scrofano, R.: Performance evaluation of canny edge detection on a tiled multicore architecture. In: Electronic Imaging, pp. 78720F–78720F. International Society for Optics and Photonics (2011)
4. Canny, J.: A computational approach to edge detection. IEEE Trans. Pattern Anal. Mach. Intell. **8**(6), 679–698 (1986)
5. Cheikh, L.B.T., Beltrame, G., Nicolescu, G., Cheriet, F., Tahar, S.: Parallelization strategies of the canny edge detector for multi-core CPUs and many-core GPUs. In: IEEE 10th International Conference on New Circuits and Systems, pp. 49–52. IEEE (2012)
6. Comaniciu, D., Meer, P.: Mean shift: a robust approach toward feature space analysis. IEEE Trans. Pattern Anal. Mach. Intell. **24**, 603–619 (2002)
7. Gongzalez, R.C., Woods, R.E.: Digital Image Processing. Prentice Hall, Upper Saddle River (2005)
8. Heath, M., Sarkar, S., Sanocki, T., Bowyer, K.: Comparison of edge detectors: a methodology and initial study. In: IEEE Computer Society Conference on Computer Vision and Pattern Recognition, pp. 143–148. IEEE (1996)
9. Kritchallo, V., Vermij, E., Bertels, K., Al-Ars, Z.: Fidelity slider: a user-defined method to trade off accuracy for performance in canny edge detector. In: 2nd Workshop On Approximate Computing, HiPEAC (2016)

10. Lourenćo, L.H., Perelman, D., Todt, E.: Efficient implementation of canny edge detection filter for ITK using CUDA. In: 13th Symposium on Computer Systems, pp. 33–40. IEEE (2012)
11. Papadrakakis, M., Stavroulakis, G., Karatarakis, A.: A new era in scientific computing: domain decomposition methods in hybrid CPU-GPU architectures. Comput. Meth. Appl. Mech. Eng. **200**, 1490–1508 (2011)
12. Park, I.K., Singhal, N., Lee, M.H., Cho, S., Kim, C.W.: Design and performance evaluation of image processing algorithms on GPUs. IEEE Trans. Parallel Distrib. Syst. **22**(1), 91–104 (2011)
13. Perona, P., Malik, J.: Scale-space and edge detection using anisotropic diffusion. IEEE Trans. Pattern Anal. Mach. Intell. **12**, 629–639 (1990)
14. Roodt, Y., Visser, W., Clarke, W.: Image processing on the GPU: implementing the canny edge detection algorithm. In: International Symposium of the Pattern Recognition Association of South Africa (2007)
15. Xu, Q., Varadarajan, S., Chakrabarti, C., Karam, L.J.: A distributed canny edge detector: algorithm and FPGA implementation. In: IEEE Transactions on Image Processing, pp. 2944–2960. IEEE (2014)

Analysis and Exploitation of CTU-Level Parallelism in the HEVC Mode Decision Process Using Actor-Based Modeling

Rafael Rosales(⊠), Christian Herglotz, Michael Glaß, André Kaup, and Jürgen Teich

Friedrich-Alexander-Universität Erlangen-Nürnberg (FAU), Erlangen, Germany
{rafael.rosales,christian.herglotz,michael.glass, andre.kaup,juergen.teich}@fau.de

Abstract. The new High-Efficiency Video Coding (HEVC) standard achieves much better compression ratios than previous ones by offering multiple coding modes, albeit with a significant increase over the required computational power especially at the encoder side. As the first major contribution, we propose a fine-grained parallelization of the encoding mode decision process using a SystemC actor-based model, exploiting multi-core platforms. Second, based on this model, we analyze achievable speedups compared to the single core sequential implementation of the HM-16.0 reference software. Using four different video sequences, we find that our approach achieves an equivalent rate-distortion performance for different quantization parameter values with a simulated encoding time improvement factor of up to $9\times$ for a maximally parallelized mode decision process. Third, an HEVC encoder has a huge number of different standard-complying encoding modes to choose from for each encoded frame, making the exploration space almost impossible to be fully covered by a brute-force search. Here, we systematically investigate the trade-off in encoding time versus required number of processor cores by proposing a multi-objective Design Space Exploration (DSE) of the mapping of the parallelized mode decision tasks to processing resources, taking as optimization objectives the resulting bitrate, image quality, number of processor cores used, execution time, and total energy consumption.

Keywords: Video encoding · HEVC · ESL · DSE · Parallelization · Actor-based modeling · Hardware/software co-design

1 Introduction

In the High-Efficiency Video Coding standard (HEVC) [12,20], a high number of new prediction (coding) modes has been introduced. On the encoder side, the mode providing the best rate-distortion performance is chosen such that the decoder can reconstruct a picture block with a high visual quality using as few bits as possible. Hence, the greatest challenge in the encoding process

© Springer International Publishing Switzerland 2016
F. Hannig et al. (Eds.): ARCS 2016, LNCS 9637, pp. 263–276, 2016.
DOI: 10.1007/978-3-319-30695-7_20

is the mode decision, i. e., the search for the best coding mode. This search is extremely complex. Typically, each tested mode is checked for rate and distortion to minimize the so-called Lagrangian costs J

$$\min J = D + \lambda R, \tag{1}$$

where D is the distortion calculated as the sum of squared-errors of the recon- struction errors for each pixel, R the number of bits required for coding, and λ the Lagrangian multiplier. Consequently, a major issue in the encoder design is the algorithmic complexity of the search and, hence, the required encoding time.

In this paper, we present an orthogonal approach to existing paralleliza- tion techniques to accelerate the encoding of frames such as Wavefront Parallel Processing [11] and Tiling [8]. Our approach exploits the available parallelism in the mode decision process at a Coding Tree Unit (CTU) level and it may be combined without any restriction with these existing parallelization techniques.

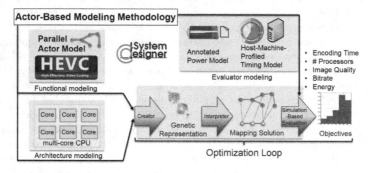

Fig. 1. SystemCoDesigner Methodology [9]. The parallelized actor-based model of the HEVC mode decision process is mapped to a multi-core architecture and a design space exploration is performed to optimize the mapping of actors to CPU cores. Performance models for power consumption and timing are used to evaluate achievable trade-offs through simulation in the five objectives of (a) encoding time, (b) number of CPU cores used, (c) image quality, (d) compression bitrate, and finally (e) energy consumption.

We propose an actor-based design, based on the SystemCoDesigner method- ology [9] depicted in Fig. 1, as a flexible model for the exploration of the par- allelization of the mode decision process which can then be mapped to multi- core CPU platforms with tens of CPU cores. In this work, we evaluate each explored multi-core CPU implementation using profile-based annotated virtual prototypes. Furthermore, this actor-based approach enables us to perform an automatic DSE of this mapping to search at design-time for the best implemen- tations with respect to different design objectives such as (a) number of employed CPU cores, (b) encoding time, (c) image quality, (d) compression rate, and (e) energy consumption. To demonstrate our approach, we actorize the mode deci- sion process of the available HM reference software [13], which contains the func- tionality of all encoding modes. To the best of our knowledge, this actor-based

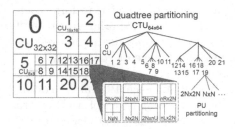

Fig. 2. Spatial partitioning and quadtree representation of a frame in HEVC. The CTU is the basis that is recursively split into square CUs as a quadtree. A CU can further be split into prediction units (PUs, shown in red at right-bottom) (Color figure online).

Table 1. Mode evaluation functions from the HM reference software [13]. All coding modes can be tested depending on the current depth of a block in the quadtree partitioning as indicated.

HM Mode Function	Tested Coding Modes	Tested PU Partitions	Depth
Inter$2N \times 2N$	Inter	$2N \times 2N$	0,1,2,3
Merge$2N \times 2N$	Merge, Skip	$2N \times 2N$	0,1,2,3
Inter$N \times 2N$	Merge, Inter	$N \times 2N$	0,1,2,3
Inter$2N \times N$	Merge, Inter	$2N \times N$	0,1,2,3
Inter$2N \times nU$	Merge, Inter	$2N \times nU$	0,1,2
Inter$2N \times nD$	Merge, Inter	$2N \times nD$	0,1,2
Inter$nL \times 2N$	Merge, Inter	$nL \times 2N$	0,1,2
Inter$nR \times 2N$	Merge, Inter	$nR \times 2N$	0,1,2
Intra$2N \times 2N$	Intra	$2N \times 2N$	0,1,2,3
Intra$N \times N$	Intra	$N \times N$	3
Split	All available at lower depth		0,1,2

modeling approach is the first that enables to analyze the potential parallelism of the mode decision process at a CTU-level and perform an automatic DSE to find the best mapping of HEVC encoding modes to a multi-core CPU platform.

The rest of the paper is structured as follows: We introduce the HEVC coding modes, discuss the state-of-the-art in the HEVC mode decision process, and review some recent work on encoding parallelization in subsects. 1.1 and 1.2 respectively. In Sect. 2, we present our design flow to parallelize the HEVC mode decision process, the architecture and performance models, as well as the DSE approach. Results on achievable trade-off curves of the five objectives of encoding time, number of CPU cores used, image quality, bitrate and energy consumption will be presented in Sect. 3 to finally come to conclusions in Sect. 4.

1.1 High Efficiency Video Coding

The main concepts important for our work are introduced in this next section. Afterwards, we give a short overview about state-of-the-art encoding techniques. In HEVC, a block of the picture is predicted from blocks that have already been decoded before. Therefore, at first, a suitable block partitioning has to be found. A frame is partitioned into so-called Coding Tree Units (CTUs), see Fig. 2. One CTU contains at most 64×64 pixels and can be further partitioned recursively into square coding units (CUs) like a quadtree. These CUs contain the explicit information of the prediction mode and the transformation coefficients. The CTUs are encoded in raster-scan order and the CUs in z-scan order. Hence, as a first major constraint to parallelization, each CU can only be encoded, and respectively decoded once all preceding CUs have been decoded and reconstructed. The CU size is described by the quadtree *depth*, where a depth of 0 typically corresponds to a CU size of 64×64 pixels and can go down to a depth of 3 with a size of 8×8 pixels. After CU partitioning, each CU obtains its own prediction mode (*inter* or *intra*). For inter-prediction, three modes are available:

inter which transmits explicit motion vector information and transform coefficients, *merge* which adopts the motion vectors from neighboring frames and transmits transform coefficients, and *skip* which only adopts the motion vectors from neighbouring frames and skips the transform coefficients completely.

The CU is further split into prediction units (PUs) according to the allowed PU partitionings of each coding mode. Note that for each PU, many coding modes can be evaluated, see Table 1. This hierarchical splitting of a CTU into CUs, and its further splitting into PUs for the different encoding modes results in a vast search space for the best encoding mode selection, and a high degree of freedom for the mode decision process.

1.2   State of the Art

For the encoder, a variety of different solutions exist. The official reference implementation is the HM software [13]. This software, implemented in C++, is a completely sequential implementation that tests individual coding modes presented in the last section by calling mode functions as shown in Table 1 and in the order shown in the flow graph in Fig. 3(a). In order to speed up this encoding process, branches are shown that may terminate the full search at an early stage. In Fig. 3(a), they are indicated by the grey boxes. The purpose of introducing these branches is to reduce encoding time by not testing for highly unlikely modes. They were determined by an empirical analysis and cause a very low loss in rate-distortion performance.

To overcome the limitation of sequential mode testing, several approaches exist that exploit parallelization. To this end, two new techniques were introduced in the standard: Wavefront Parallel Processing (WPP) [11] and tiling [8]. The former allows for encoding the CTUs in a wavefront manner. That means that every time the third CTU of a row is reached, a new thread starts coding the next row in parallel. With this approach, maximum speedups of around $9\times$ have been reported (resolution 2160p [6]), where several works improve upon this concept and even reach much higher speedups of up to $20\times$ [5,23]. Tiling splits each frame into multiple rectangular parts, where each tile can be processed independently from the others. Hence, the maximum speedup depends on the number of tiles that are created. However, tiling may affect the video quality by breaking the spatial dependencies between CTUs. A detailed analysis can be found in [15]. Furthermore, it was shown that tiling can successfully be exploited to reduce the processing power [18].

The work in [22] focuses on the parallel decision for neighboring CUs. To this end, they make use of a coding tool called Motion Estimation Region (MER), where all CUs in this region can only use predictors outside of this region. Hence, the constraint that all preceding CUs have to be decoded can be circumvented. Speedups of more than 14 have been reported on a 64 processor system.

A parallelization scheme for the motion-vector decision level is proposed by Wang et al. [21] and Radicke et al. [16]. In the HM motion vector search, a search range is defined in which a high number of different vectors is tested. The idea is to displace this search to the GPU. Furthermore, Wang et al. combine this approach with a wavefront processing which results in speedups of almost 30, but at the expense of rate-distortion performance.

Finally, a complete software-based parallelization approach is proposed by Heng et al. [10]. They also make use of GPU-driven motion estimation, but incorporate slice-level parallelism which uses a similar approach as tiling.

The HEVC mode decision process, however, can be further parallelized to cope with ever increasing video resolutions. In contrast to the discussed work, we present a solution for *parallelizing the mode decision process at a CTU-level*, i.e., for each CTU we parallelize the search for the best CTU's quadtree partitioning, sub-CU's best prediction modes and prediction unit partitioning. As this is performed on a CTU-level, it does not impair tiling or WPP and can hence be seen as an independent, additional parallelization method for the encoder. The x.265 software [1] has recently incorporated support to this kind of parallelism, but in contrast to this work, we not only allow the parallel processing of these modes, we can analyze the maximum speedups achievable with this fine-grained parallelism, as well as fully-automatically search for the best CPU mapping and optimize multiple criteria like encoding time, number of required cores, or energy consumption at the same time.

2   Proposed Parallelization

As our first contribution, we propose to fully parallelize the processing of Fig. 3(a), i.e., the testing of the different coding modes. In order to support all the coding modes available in the HEVC standard, we adopt the mode structure used in the HM reference implementation such that on a specific depth, a maximum of 10 modes as listed in Table 1 can be tested in parallel.

Figure 3(b) visualizes how these modes can be parallelized. Here, a red block corresponds to the workload of testing one mode. The upper three blocks refer to the modes on depth 0, the 4×3 blocks below to the modes on depth 1, and so forth. All modes that lie on the same vertical line can be processed in parallel. In contrast, due to the mandatory coding order, all modes on a horizontal line must be processed sequentially, which inherently limits the potential degree of parallelism. We obtain the non-trivial problem on how to distribute the testing of all modes to several CPUs. For formalizing and optimization of related mapping problems, we apply an actor-based methodology in the following.

2.1   Methodology

The general design flow of our methodology, based on the system level methodology for automatic design space exploration presented in [9], is as follows:

Each prediction mode evaluation of the HEVC encoder is specified by an individual actor in SystemC. Actors are natural entities to be mapped and executed on processing resources. They may communicate with each other only via so-called channels and are activated for execution based on the availability of data. Our multi-core platform architecture model consists of a set of CPU

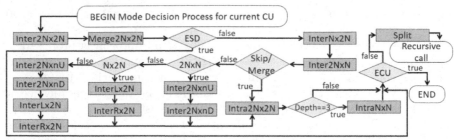

(a) Sequential mode decision process in the HM-16.0 reference software [13]. The grey blocks depict early exit points.

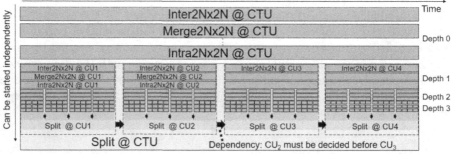

(b) Maximally parallelized mode decision process. The x-axis shows inevitable dependencies, the y-axis shows which modes can be processed in parallel.

Fig. 3. Mode decision processes for one CTU. The red blocks depict functions to test the prediction modes listed in Table 1 (Color figure online).

cores as processing resources which may be allocated to execute a set of actors mapped to them. Once the actor specification and architecture model have been created, mappings may be determined and evaluated for multiple objectives such as execution time by discrete-event simulation of the actor code, see Fig. 1.

Based on this model, we use a multi-objective evolutionary algorithm [7] for design space exploration of the achievable trade-offs such as encoding time vs. energy consumption for a given number of processing resources. The optimization loop separates the encoding of the optimization problem from its evaluation, enabling us to prune the search space for a more efficient design space exploration. To model the evaluators for the encoding time and power consumption of the CPU cores, we make use of the MPSoC simulation framework presented in [17].

The advantages of the proposed actor-based design of a HEVC encoder in SystemC are to obtain a modular, concurrent, standard-compliant executable specification and, thus, an ideal basis for design space exploration of mapping options as well as multi-objective trade-off analysis for multi-core platforms.

2.2 Design

In this section, we present the transformation of the HEVC mode decision process into an executable parallel actor model in SystemC. We also introduce the time model for the evaluation of the encoding time to analyze the achievable speedups, and we present our proposed multi-objective DSE approach for the mapping of the actor model to CPU cores to investigate the resulting trade-offs.

Actorized HEVC Mode Decision Process. The granularity of modeled actors has been chosen fine enough to encapsulate a single evaluation of an encoding mode. For full coverage of the HEVC standard, we applied our actorization to the HM-reference encoder [13]. As a major advantage, it provides the functionality for all prediction modes and provides a common reference to compare an encoder's video quality and compression rate. It enables an exhaustive search and, in addition to the existing fast mode decision schemes, can easily be extended by further fast mode decisions. Note that our actor-based approach can be applied to any HEVC encoder implementation.

In order to actorize the reference software, or any other implementation, the code must be first refactored to get rid of all shared variables between the prediction mode evaluators. We propose a hierarchical actor-based model to nicely capture the recursive aspect of the quadtree structure, where each encoding mode will be modeled by an actor, with the exception of the Split Mode, which will be modeled as an actor graph p. This allows us to embed the actor instances that evaluate the encoding modes of the sub-CUs into this actor graph, see Fig. 4.

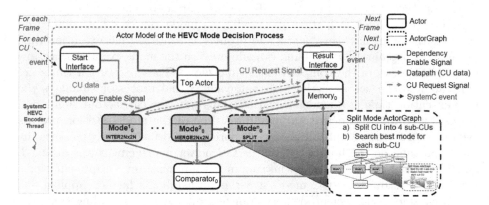

Fig. 4. Hierarchical actor-based HEVC mode decision process. The actor-model enables the evaluation of encoding modes concurrently at different CU depths. Dependency channels between the actors enable an ordered evaluation of encoding modes.

For the concurrent evaluation of all N encoding modes at a given CU depth level, we model the following actors: (I) A Memory actor Mem_{depth}, responsible to store the CU data to be evaluated for all encoding modes at depth level $depth$. (II) N instances of prediction mode evaluator actors $Mode^n_{depth}$, each capable of evaluating a single encoding mode. Each of these actors requests a copy of the CU data from the memory actor Mem_{depth} as it is not globally shared. (III) A Compare actor $Comp_{depth}$, which receives the evaluation of all mode evaluators and sends the best one to the memory actor Mem_{depth}.

To be able to respect the z-scan order dependencies of the standard, or induce an ordered evaluation of the modes, we propose a parameterizable mechanism to model all evaluation dependencies by interconnecting the prediction mode evaluator actors through so-called dependency ports. Only once all input dependency ports have received an enable token, the Mode evaluation can be performed.

The content of the SplitMode actor graph is defined recursively, i. e., a Split-Mode actor graph contains exactly one Memory actor $Mem_{depth+1}$, N instances of Mode evaluator actors $Mode_{depth+1}^n$, and one Compare actor $Comp_{depth+1}$. The SplitMode actor graph contains a special coordinating actor $SplitActor_{depth+1}$, which partitions the received copy of the CU data structure into four sub-CUs. It iteratively feeds its internal memory actor with one of the four sub-CUs, to search for its best encoding mode in z-scan order. At depth 0 a TopActor triggers the evaluation of all prediction modes. The modes as given in Table 1 result in total of 36 different mode evaluator actors.

Performance and Power Evaluation. For the evaluation of encoding time and energy consumption on a multi-core CPU, we simulate the execution of the encoder on virtual CPU cores as proposed in [19], where individual actor actions are annotated with static execution times when mapped to a given virtual processor. However, the fact that prediction modes are highly data dependent in HEVC prohibits static timing annotations. To obtain data-dependent timing annotations for the encoder evaluation of a prediction mode, our SystemC simulation executes the actor mode evaluators and profiles at runtime their execution time on the host machine. The profiling is made only on the mode evaluation actions in order to measure the computational time alone. These execution times are annotated to the actors' actions so that each virtual processor simulates the true execution time of a mode evaluation. This way, the carried out simulation derives the data-dependent total execution time of the mode decision process even when mapped to multiple processing cores. To most accurately measure the execution time on the host machine, the OS power management was disabled, and the thread priority is set to maximum to minimize any OS pre-emptions. During simulation, a First-Come-First-Served scheduling scheme is applied.

To consider the effect of memory transfers on the total encoding time, the memory actors are mapped to DDR3 memory resources. The read and write actions of the memory actors are annotated with static execution times according to the memory transfer size. The modeling of memories as resources enables to also consider the contention of simultaneous memory read requests and writes. The annotated static execution time for reading from a memory resource is the result of the multiplication of the number of eight-word burst reads $\Re$ needed to feed the evaluator actors times the latency L of an eight-word burst read. The number of bytes read B are calculated from the total amount of data that each mode evaluator requires, i. e., the CTU data structure, the context-adaptive binary arithmetic coding object, and a copy of the best prediction, residual and reconstruction YUV buffers. To determine $\Re$, we analyze the memory footprint of this data structures at all depth levels. We calculate then the annotated memory read time as: $\text{singleReadTime}(B) = \Re * L = \frac{B}{\text{WordSize} * 8} * L$

We use a system-level power model for our CPU cores and memory as proposed in [19]. We provide a static power consumption value for a CPU core in a `Running` and an `Idle state`. The total energy consumption is integrated for the time lapse the CPU core has been in the specified state.

The performance models introduced in this section, as well as the resulting bitrate and the image quality objectives computed in the encoding process itself, are integrated as *Objective Evaluators* in the optimization loop.

Mapping Exploration. Our multi-core platform is an architecture with a maximum number of 36 CPU cores, i. e., one CPU core for each prediction mode actor, and our application consists of the HEVC mode decision process actor graph. To optimize the mapping of actors to CPU cores, we make use of multi-objective genetic algorithms as available in the OPT4J framework [14]. A multi-objective optimization of the mapping problem can be defined as follows:

Let $x \in X$ be a possible mapping of application actors to CPU cores, and O_{min} the set of K objectives to be minimized without loss of generality.

$$\forall o_k(x) \in O_{min}$$

$$\min_x o_k(x) \quad s.t. \quad x \in X \tag{2}$$

Such an optimization problem can be transformed to a genetic representation as proposed in [3]. In our mapping problem, the genetic representation search space covers all possible mappings of HEVC actors to CPU cores. The evaluation of each explored implementation is performed by the set of user-defined functions called *Objective Evaluators*, one for each of the design objectives to be optimized, which take an implementation as input and return the respective objective.

The aforementioned application and architecture models, and mapping set enable us to perform a multi-objective DSE for finding a set of Pareto-optimal implementations with results reported next.

3 Results

Our experiments were executed in a Windows 8.1 environment running on an Intel i7-4770 CPU @ 3.40 GHz with 16 GB RAM host machine. The following four video test sequences, 10 frames each, from the JCT-VC common testing conditions [4] are used: (I) BasketballPass (416×240), (II) BlowingBubbles (416×240), (III) BQSquare (416×240), and (IV) BQTerrace (HD 1920×1080). First, to validate time estimates of the mode decision process of each actor, we reproduce the sequential evaluation of modes in HM in the actor model by inserting mode evaluation dependencies. The complete encoding time of the HM reference software for 10 frames of the HD sequence IV at a QP[1] of 20 was 11.8 min, of which the mode decision process took 11.7 min. Although the *simulation time* of the sequentialized actor model took considerably longer, i.e., 23.7 min, the *simulated time* of the pure mode decision process execution time of the actor model including the modeled memory transfers was quite accurate with 10.9 min. The difference between the simulated time of the sequentialized actor model and the mode decision process time of HM can be explained by the memory model. The separated profiling of time of actions and the memory transfers in the actor model introduces an inaccuracy of about 7 %.

Now, to estimate the encoding time speedup of a parallel execution of the mode decision process, we remove the dependencies introduced artificially to replicate the sequential evaluation of HM again, and initially map each mode evaluator actor to a dedicated CPU core, i.e., 36 CPU cores.

We execute the sequential and the parallel actor model on the four video sequences from I to IV at a range of QP values from 10 to 45 in steps of 5. The resulting curves of the calibrated mode decision process time in seconds vs. image quality in terms of the YUV-PSNR, a logarithmic representation of the pixel-average of the distortion D, are shown in Fig. 5(a). Comparing the plots of the parallel and sequential actor models it is possible to see an improvement of almost an order of magnitude independently of the resolution and video sequence. For the HD sequence IV at a QP=15, the simulated speedup is 9.6×. Note that this prediction is independent of the host-machine used for simulation.

In Fig. 5(b), the curves of bitrate vs. image quality are plotted to evaluate the compression performance of the parallel encoder. In order to quantitatively analyze our approach, we calculate bitrate differences and encoding time savings in terms of Bjøntegaard Delta [2]. The Bjøntegaard Delta was developed to allow for comparing different RD-curves in a single value. In our work, we give the delta

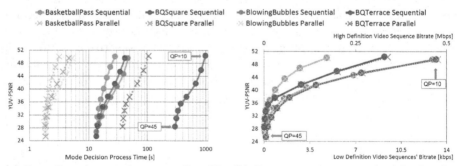

(a) Encoding time vs. image quality. The parallel model achieves a speedup of 7-9x.   (b) Bitrate vs. image quality. Both solutions show equivalent encoding curves.

Fig. 5. Plots for QP values [10:45] in steps of 5. The results of the sequential and the parallel version (using 36 cores) of the actor model are shown for sequences I to IV.

---

[1] QP denotes the quantization parameter. A low QP value corresponds to a fine quantization.

values for PSNR (BD-PSNR), bitrate (BD-rate), and encoding time (BD-time), where in the latter, we simply replace the bitrate by the encoding time values, see Table 2.

Table 2. Bjøntegaard Delta-Table for encoded video sequences.

id	Sequence	BD-PSNR	BD-Rate	BD-Time
I	BasketballPass	−0.10 dB	2.12 %	−88.19 %
II	BlowingBubbles	−0.05 dB	1.16 %	−88.90 %
III	BQSquare	−0.02 dB	0.47 %	−88.61 %
IV	BQTerrace (HD)	−0.03 dB	0.95 %	−89.02 %

3.1 Design Space Exploration

We use the Evolutionary Algorithm (EA) NSGA-II [7] to explore the mapping of Mode evaluator actors to different numbers of CPU cores for sequence I at QP=45, performing a 100 iteration exploration with a population size of 60 each, and creating 25 new implementations each iteration. The cross-over rate used is 0.95. We run the optimization on the range of [1:36] available CPU cores. Note that the DSE results are dependent on the input video sequence.

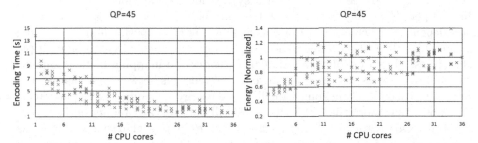

Fig. 6. Projection of the aproximate Pareto-front of the objectives CPU core number and encoding time for different mappings for sequence I in Table 1.

Fig. 7. Projection of the aproximate Pareto-front of the objectives CPU core number and total energy for different mappings for sequence I in Table 1.

A projection of the approximation of the 5D Pareto-front for different mappings with respect to the number of allocated CPU cores and encoding time is shown in Fig. 6. For a QP = 45, the DSE was able to find a mapping solution with 21 CPU cores with an estimated encoding time of 1.8 s. which is the same encoding time of the platform using 36 CPU cores. This is primarily due to a better utilization of CPU cores, as not all encoding modes are neither equally complex nor evaluated on all CUs. The parallelization of the mode decision is, however, limited by the z-order dependencies in the evaluation of the modes.

To compare the relative energy consumption of the different implementations, Fig. 7 shows the plot of the 2D projection of the obtained approximated Pareto-front of the number of allocated CPU cores and the total energy consumed normalized to the energy consumed with the maximum number of CPU cores. An increase in energy after increasing the amount of CPU cores reflects the amount of wasted time on a CPU in the Idle state. A CPU core might be idle if the workload of the prediction modes are not equal. Although we are speeding up the encoding time, the total energy consumed increases when the extra CPU cores are not being used efficiently. As it can be seen in Fig. 7, there is an inflection point in the energy consumed when allocating 21 CPU cores for sequence I. This is due to the fact, that adding more CPU cores provides no benefit in terms of encoding time.

4   Conclusions

We have proposed (i) a solution to the parallelization of the HEVC mode decision process based on an actor-based methodology and (ii) performed a design space exploration to find the best implementations with respect to the five design objectives of (a) number of employed CPU cores, (b) encoding time, (c) image quality, (d) compression rate, and (e) energy consumption. The proposed profile-based timing model lets us perform a system-level evaluation of the encoding time, explicitly taking into account the variable execution times arising from data-dependent calculations. As we have shown in the experimental results, the proposed parallelization provides up to a 9× speedup when executed on multiple CPU cores. Moreover, our DSE that investigates the mapping of functionality onto multiple processing resources unveils the trade-offs between number of CPU cores used, execution time, image quality, and energy consumption. In particular, it is shown that more than 21 CPU cores will not gain any reduction in execution time. Our actor-based approach also opens potential research directions to investigate different parallelizations of the HEVC mode decision process, as well as apply this analysis to different architecture implementations through the use of different objective evaluators, explore different memory architectures or explore trade-offs such as quality vs. encoding time by combining the proposed CTU-level parallelization with Tiling or WPP. Furthermore, our actor-based approach can be applied to other HEVC encoder implementations, and other coding standards that have multiple encoding modes.

Acknowledgments. This work was supported by the Research Training Group 1773 Heterogeneous Image Systems, funded by the German Research Foundation (DFG). We would also like to thank Dr. Muhammad Shafique, researcher at the Karlsruhe Institute of Technology for his valuable feedback.

References

1. x265 (2014). x265.org, Accessed 22 January 2015
2. Bjontegaard, G.: Calculation of average PSNR differences between RD curves, April 2001
3. Blickle, T., Teich, J., Thiele, L.: System-level synthesis using evolutionary algorithms. Des. Autom. Embedded Syst. **3**(1), 23–58 (1998)
4. Bossen, F.: Common test conditions and software reference configurations. Joint Collaborative Team on Video Coding (JCT-VC), JCTVC-F900 (2011)
5. Chen, K., Duan, Y., Sun, J., Guo, Z.: Towards efficient wavefront parallel encoding of HEVC: parallelism analysis and improvement. In: Proceedings of the IEEE 16th International Workshop on Multimedia Signal Processing (MMSP), pp. 1–6, September 2014
6. Chi, C.C., Alvarez-Mesa, M., Juurlink, B., Clare, G., Henry, F., Pateux, S., Schierl, T.: Parallel scalability and efficiency of HEVC parallelization approaches. IEEE Trans. Circ. Syst. Video Technol. **22**(12), 1827–1838 (2012)
7. Deb, K., Pratap, A., Agarwal, S., Meyarivan, T.: A fast and elitist multiobjective genetic algorithm: NSGA-II. IEEE Trans. Evol. Comput. **6**(2), 182–197 (2002)
8. Fuldseth, A., Horowitz, M., Xu, S., Segall, A., Zhou, M.: Tiles. JCTVC-F335, July 2011
9. Haubelt, C., Falk, J., Keinert, J., Schlichter, T., Streubühr, M., Deyhle, A., Hadert, A., Teich, J.: A SystemC-based design methodology for digital signal processing systems. EURASIP J. Embedded Syst. **2007**(1), 15 (2007)
10. Heng, T.K., Asano, W., Itoh, T., Tanizawa, A., Yamaguchi, J., Matsuo, T., Kodama, T.: A highly parallelized H.265/HEVC real-time UHD software encoder. In: Proceedings of the IEEE International Conference on Image Processing (ICIP), pp. 1213–1217, October 2014
11. Henry, F., Pateux, S.: Wavefront parallel processing. Joint Collaborative Team on Video Coding (JCT-VC), Document JCTVC-E196, Geneva (2011)
12. ITU-T: Recommendation H.265, April 2013. http://www.itu.int/rec/T-REC-H.265-201304-S/en
13. ITU/ISO/IEC: HEVC Test Model IIM16.0 (2014). https://hevc.hhi.fraunhofer.de/
14. Lukasiewycz, M., Glaß, M., Reimann, F., Teich, J.: Opt4J - a modular framework for meta-heuristic optimization. In: Proceedings of the Genetic and Evolutionary Computing Conference (GECCO 2011), Dublin, Ireland, pp. 1723–1730 (2011)
15. Misra, K., Segall, A., Horowitz, M., Xu, S., Fuldseth, A., Zhou, M.: An overview of tiles in HEVC. IEEE J. Sel. Top. Sign. Proces. **7**(6), 969–977 (2013)
16. Radicke, S., Hahn, J., Grecos, C., Wang, Q.: A highly-parallel approach on motion estimation for high efficiency video coding (HEVC). In: Proceedings of the IEEE International Conference on Consumer Electronics (ICCE), pp. 187–188, January 2014
17. Rosales, R., Glass, M., Teich, J., Wang, B., Xu, Y., Hasholzner, R.: MAESTRO-holistic actor-oriented modeling of nonfunctional properties and firmware behavior for MPSoCs. ACM Trans. Des. Autom. Electron. Syst. **19**(3), 23:1–23:26 (2014)
18. Shafique, M., Khan, M., Henkel, J.: Power efficient and workload balanced tiling for parallelized high efficiency video coding. In: Proceedings of the IEEE International Conference on Image Processing (ICIP), pp. 1253–1257, October 2014
19. Streubühr, M., Rosales, R., Hasholzner, R., Haubelt, C., Teich, J.: ESL power and performance estimation for heterogeneous MPSoCS using SystemC. In: FDL, pp. 1–8 (2011)

20. Sullivan, G., Ohm, J., Han, W.J., Wiegand, T.: Overview of the high efficiency video coding (HEVC) standard. IEEE Trans. Circ. Syst. Video Technol. **22**(12), 1649–1668 (2012)
21. Wang, X., Song, L., Chen, M., Yang, J.: Paralleling variable block size motion estimation of HEVC on multi-core CPU plus GPU platform. In: Proceedings of the IEEE International Conference on Image Processing (ICIP), pp. 1836–1839, September 2013
22. Zhang, J., Dai, F., Ma, Y., Zhang, Y.: Highly parallel mode decision method for HEVC. In: Proceedings of the Picture Coding Symposium (PCS), pp. 281–284, December 2013
23. Zhang, S., Zhang, X., Gao, Z.: Implementation and improvement of wavefront parallel processing for HEVC encoding on many-core platform. In: Proceedings of the IEEE International Conference on Multimedia and Expo Workshops (ICMEW), pp. 1–6, July 2014

Low-Cost Hardware Infrastructure for Runtime Thread Level Energy Accounting

Marius Marcu[1(✉)], Oana Boncalo[1], Madalin Ghenea[1], Alexandru Amaricai[1],
Jan Weinstock[2], Rainer Leupers[2], Zheng Wang[2], Giorgis Georgakoudis[3],
Dimitrios S. Nikolopoulos[3], Cosmin Cernazanu-Glavan[1], Lucian Bara[1],
and Marian Ionascu[1]

[1] Politehnica University of Timisoara, 2 V. Parvan Blv, 300223 Timisora, Romania
mmarcu@cs.upt.ro
[2] Institute for Communication Technologies and Embedded Systems, RWTH Aachen,
Templergraben 55, Aachen, Germany
[3] Queen's University Belfast, 10 Malone Road, Belfast, UK

Abstract. The ever-growing need for energy efficient computation requires adequate support for energy-aware thread scheduling that offers insight into a systems behavior for improved application energy/performance optimizations. Runtime accurate monitoring of energy consumed by every component of a multi-core embedded system is an important feature to be considered for future designs. Although, important steps have been made in this direction, the problem of distributing energy consumption among threads executed on different cores for shared components remains an ongoing struggle. We aim at designing a generic low-cost and energy efficient hardware infrastructure which supports thread level energy accounting of hardware components in a multi-core system. The proposed infrastructure provides upper software layers with per thread and per component energy accounting API, similar with performance profiling functions. Implementation results indicate that the proposed solution adds around 10 % resource overhead to the monitored system. Regarding the power estimates, the one derived by our solution achieves a correlation degree of more than 95 % with the ones obtained from physical power measurements.

Keywords: Energy accounting · Energy interrupt · Per-thread energy accounting · Runtime monitoring · Multi-core system on chip

1 Introduction

Energy metering has been a major research topic during the last years. Measuring energy is needed to validate and calibrate energy models; to perform energy profiling of hardware and software applications, and to develop energy-aware applications based on runtime energy measurement. Based on their intrusiveness and required hardware support, these techniques span from software approaches [1], to solutions requiring dedicated hardware support within the system such as a customized token ring interconnect [2], or a network on a chip interconnect with monitors [3, 4]. Approaches such

© Springer International Publishing Switzerland 2016
F. Hannig et al. (Eds.): ARCS 2016, LNCS 9637, pp. 277–289, 2016.
DOI: 10.1007/978-3-319-30695-7_21

as HEMA (Hardware-assisted energy monitoring architecture) [5], are a trade-off that rely on software techniques and usage patterns, with some periodic calibration from hardware monitors. These approaches aim at evaluating and distributing total power consumption per core. However, finer grain power estimation and distribution is required [6]. Per thread metering [6] is a must in nowadays systems in order to facilitate: efficient resource allocation for task execution (dynamically assess at OS level resource allocation), system level energy/performance optimization, and billing in data-centres.

Developing fine grained energy estimates is a complex task, which requires support on both the monitoring side, and on the OS side. Most of the state-of-the-art approaches have focused on providing power estimates from the system level down to component level. Thus, the problem of per component energy accounting is well documented, with well understood constraints arising due to the limited time resolution and/or accuracy of the existing sensors. Due to the ever-increasing complexity of systems and system-level interactions, Per Thread Energy Accounting (PTEA), also referred to Per Task Energy Metering (PTEM) in [7], is required. PTEA performs energy estimation of the hardware components in response to the actions initiated by each specific thread in a multi-tasking environment. PTEA techniques are even more complex to accomplish because they have to split power consumed by shared components to threads that control them. This is only possible with dedicated hardware and software support.

The contributions of this work are as follows: (1) infrastructure for dynamic energy consumption monitoring in a heterogeneous multi-core system with PTEA; (2) energy interrupt specification and design; (3) a use case on the software side (OS and drivers) for run-time PTEA implementation on FPGA; and (4) validation of proposed infrastructure on a high-end FPGA board with physical energy measurements.

Briefly, PTEA can be achieved by splitting the whole energy into processing energy (consumed by cores), data movement energy (consumed by interconnects and memories to read and store data) and data storage energy (consumed by memories to keep data). The proposed infrastructure addresses all of these energy consumers: processing energy accounting, data movement energy accounting, and data storage accounting. Both processing and data movement accounting is performed per thread, but data storage is per component. However, data storage energy splitting per task can be further implemented in our infrastructure using the techniques proposed by [6].

This paper is organized as follows: Section 2 provides the description of previous related work on energy accounting; Sect. 3 presents the proposed energy accounting infrastructure; experimental results and system overhead is presented in Sect. 4. The conclusions are discussed in the last section.

2   Related Work

Hardware monitoring infrastructures have been proposed in the past, with results reported for both FPGAs and ASICs. These solutions have to provide several main features: power and performance meters (physical or model based sensors), data collection (interconnects), control unit (configuration and processing) and finally, software drivers (API).

The work presented in [2] uses a customized token ring interconnect for monitoring and actuation. Two lines are dedicated for communication control (token and valid), with as many as desired data lines possible (based on the transmission speed and/or resources committed for the infrastructure). This solution is simple, with a limitation for the transmission delay: it increases linearly with the number of nodes. Research in [3, 4], relies on a network on a chip (NoC). Hardcoded routing tables and two types of monitors (i.e. data pull and data push) try to limit the overhead introduced by the NoC. Another approach [7], proposes a light-weight monitoring system relying on a single-wire interconnect network, where monitoring components take turns to send data to centralize data.

Most of the solutions allow centralized control [1–7], with [2] also permitting distributed control and information aggregation. When addressing large platforms, these are broken into subsystems (in some works referred to as islands), with each subsystem having its own interconnect and having its own monitoring infrastructure. For example, for large systems, the authors of [2] divided the SoC on islands and use a customized ring for each island. Inter-subsystem messages can be exchanged by means of an interconnect on top of the aforementioned one [2–4]. This type of solution is also adopted in this work.

Sensor/monitor architecture is typically made of two parts: interface with the choice of interconnect, and processing part, where the data is being aggregated/actuated (sensing application dependent). Furthermore, on the processing side (which is connected to the system being monitored), the coupling between the sensors and the target system can be classified in two categories: tight (when actual instrumentation of the component design is required for introducing event counters and additional ports for reporting their activity [6]), and weak (when already built-in support exists – e.g. thermal sensors, performance counters, or some sort of non-intrusive way of accounting events is proposed [3, 4, 7]).

Previous work [11–13] on energy accounting in the OS layer relies on approximating per-thread energy consumption through modeling instead of direct measurements. Specifically, the OS leverages per-core performance monitoring counters and coarse-grain power consumption sensors on selected hardware components, such as the CPU socket or memory, to assign energy consumption to each thread. However, this approach may suffer from modeling inaccuracies. More importantly, it cannot accurately account for energy consumption on shared components, when accessed by more than one thread, such as the memory subsystem or buses. By contrast, our LEM approach enables accurate accounting at the granularity of individual hardware components, for both private and shared resources.

PTEM is discussed only by few papers [6, 8], most of them targeting x86 processor system architectures [8]. In [6] PTEM is achieved on the basis of resource utilization and occupancy tracking with dedicated hardware. Considering the state of the art, most of the recent efforts in energy accounting are directed toward component level energy modelling, profiling, or monitoring. However, energy consumed by data movement is not taken in consideration, due to its complexity and shared usage problem. In our work we address energy accounting of data movement in a multi-core system in conjunction with energy accounting of processing elements.

This work contributes to the state-of-the art by proposing a versatile low cost monitoring infrastructure with the software drivers that provide incentive for PTEM at OS level. Furthermore, it advances a novel scheduling concept – that of energy interrupt, that can bring the energy efficient processing in the foreground. Last, but not least, we have tested modern FPGA capabilities for measuring/monitoring energy consumption and compared our results against simulation-based switching activity measurements for ASIC technologies. In order to validate all these, we have implemented a multi-core system on a Zynq FPGA board.

3   Per-Thread Energy Accounting

3.1   PTEA Hardware Infrastructure

The proposed solution, called Load and Energy Monitor (LEM) can achieve PTEA in two steps: (1) Per core energy accounting (PCEA) of processing cores and shared resources based on hardware support; (2) Per thread energy accounting (PTEA) implemented at OS level during context switching, using the provided SW drivers. PCEA implemented in HW uses a distributed sensor network through a dedicated bus interconnect, which is both cost-effective and light-weight. It consists of a generic hardware monitoring infrastructure which is able to connect a number of distributed sensors attached to the components of a target MPSoC. LEM monitoring infrastructure allows software layers to access at runtime, both the component level usage and the energy estimates. LEM control and configuration is centralized, thus providing a unique interface to the upper layers.

The LEM infrastructure building blocks are: LEM sensors (S-LEM), LEM controller (C-LEM) and LEM interconnect (LEM Bus) (Fig. 1). S-LEM hardware components collect data from the underlying system at a programmable high-speed rate, performing component level performance or energy accounting computations. The sensors' primary sampled values may be switching activity, performance counters, transactions, and power physical measures. Based on primary measurements S-LEMs estimate components energy on the fly or they can even measure the power consumption for component level built-in sensors. Sensors can be attached to individual cores, accelerators, or shared component components of the target system such as memories or buses. C-LEM performs energy accounting at core level, collecting and summing energy consumption values from both local sensors, attached to cores' local buses and memories, and shared sensors, attached to shared components, such as DRAM memory or system busses. Sensors attached to shared components are able to account component energy at processing core level.

Two important features of LEM infrastructure are non-intrusiveness and energy interrupts. Non-intrusiveness is achieved by weak coupling between the monitoring infrastructure and the target system (Fig. 1), due to the special sensor design and generic interface. Energy interrupts are generated for each core in the target design when the energy budget corresponding to the core has been consumed, so that no dedicated processor is needed to poll the energy counters.

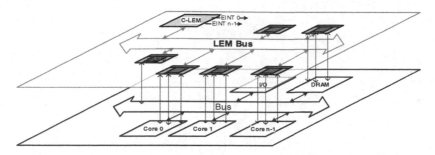

Fig. 1. Overall evaluation setup architecture

C-LEM (Fig. 2a) controls and collects sensor data from the LEM sensors and provides the OS with structured access to the accounting data. The OS communicates with the central LEM unit through the global memory address space for sensor control and sampling. Data received from S-LEM is aggregated into the C-LEM local memory. Each component of the target system has a reserved 128 bits memory structure, including timestamp, component usage, processing energy, and data movement energy. One or more sensors collect measurements for every component, while C-LEM aggregates these values at the core level. For each component two energy values are accounted: component operation energy and data moving energy. These values are collected from the sensors monitoring the respective component and its interfaces. Furthermore, C-LEM is also highly parameterized. Dedicated registers allow the programming of the LEM for: enabling/disabling monitoring for a component, enabling/disabling energy interrupt, changing the sampling rate, controlling the power model or selecting the sensors accounting mode.

LEM-bus is based on Wishbone standard [12], having one master (C-LEM) and several slaves (S-LEM, up to 256 in the current implementation). It has a configurable number of data lines for read and write channels, which provides C-LEM with efficient access to S_LEMs. As read operations are more frequent, we have selected an increased bus width for this channel (32 in the current implementation), with respect to the write channel (8 bits). Figure 2a highlights the C-LEM and its LEM-bus master and AXI slave interfaces [13]. The C-LEM AXI slave interface, provides cores with access for programming LEM. The cores can also poll C-LEM for their current load and energy counters through the AXI interface.

There are currently three classes of sensors used by LEM: (1) instruction sensors (core attached sensors), that monitor an instruction bus and calculate the energy of each instruction executed by a single core; (2) shared data sensors, that monitor a shared memory and calculate the energy consumption of data transfers for each processor monitored; (3) local data sensors, that monitors a local data memory. The C-LEM reads data from each sensor sequentially and aggregates the data depending on the type of the sensor and stores it in the energy counters of C-LEM memory.

Instruction sensors provide LEM with support to measure or estimate the processing energy of the cores they are attached to. These sensors are specific to the processing core they monitor and the instruction bus they are connected to. However, being modular, S-LEM sub-components have a high degree of flexibility: the S-LEM processing core can

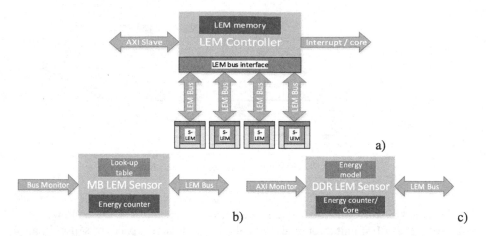

Fig. 2. LEM components: (a) C-LEM; (b) Instruction sensor; (c) DRAM shared data sensor

be connected to different busses only by changing the bus interface monitor. Instruction sensors included in the FPGA design target the Microblaze (uB) processor, a soft-core provided by Xilinx [14]. uB S-LEM is implemented as a virtual sensor that monitors the core's instruction bus and partially decodes the uB opcodes in order to associate estimates with the execution energy (Fig. 2b). Energy counter is incremented with the energy amount associated to the instructions executed by the processor. Energy values stored in the S-LEM look-up table have been computed through energy profiling on the target FPGA board.

Shared data sensors attached to the shared components of the target system allow per-core energy estimation of these components. These sensors are able to identify and dispatch the amount of energy consumed by the shared component to the core that is responsible for the energy consumed by the component (Fig. 2c). Shared data sensors implement internally one energy counter per core, whose contents are summed up at the core level, within the C-LEM, as described by next section.

3.2 PTEA Solution Use Case

LEM infrastructure is a hardware solution that can be customized for different applications. It has been further customized and used to implement PTEA in a multi-core system to account energy of shared components a core level.

In a multi-core system we consider three types of components: processing cores (could be homogeneous or heterogeneous), private resources and shared resources (e.g. memories and interconnects). In a multi-core hardware environment, every core has a unique core ID. Our idea is to use this ID in hardware transaction with shared components to identify the processing core which will be charged with the energy budget of the current transaction. The LEM sensors connected to these shared components will use master ID to account per core energy consumption.

Modern interconnects like Wishbone (open source) and AXI (ARM) allow system designers to attach meta-information to each transfer. For example, Wishbone bus standard specifies user-defined tags to apply extra information to each bus cycle [12]. On the other hand, AMBA open specification [13] associates implicitly hardware IDs of the master to each bus cycle. ARID, RID, AWID, WID and BID bus signals are carrying ID tags of the read address, read, write address, write and response bus transfers. Hence, it makes sense for the LEM sensors of shared resources to use the master ID of the access to split the energy consumed for shared components.

The LEM will account energy at core level. When a thread context switch occurs, the OS will store the energy counters of the current thread and will restart the counters for the next thread. While a thread is executed by a core, per core energy accounting implemented in HW will be used to account for the energy of a running thread. Considering that a core will execute only one thread at the time, the coordination between OS and HW will account for the thread level energy in a multi-core/multi-threading execution environment.

The reference system design for PTEA validation is presented in Fig. 3 and has two clusters of four Microblaze [14] soft cores. The clock frequency for the uB is 50 MHz. The cores include local interrupt controller, local instruction and data memory and local instruction and data buses. Local interrupt controllers serve two interrupt sources: time interrupt (1 ms) and energy interrupt (~100 nJ). The reference design implements one LEM infrastructure attached to the 4-cores cluster. The four uB cores cluster needs two shared DRAM sensors Fig. 3-1 (one for instruction bus and the second one for data bus) and three more local sensors per core (one DRAM instruction sensor Fig. 3-2, one BRAM data sensor and one BRAM instruction and data sensor Fig. 3-3). In total LEM implements 14 sensors and one C-LEM (4) with 16 ports. The presented LEM is replicated for the second cluster.

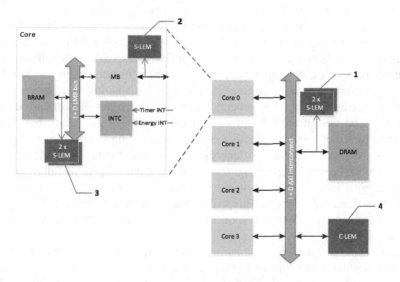

Fig. 3. Overall HW FPGA architecture

LEM HW comprises of bus sniffers (S-LEM) monitoring for the number and type of accesses for each shared component. Energy accounting is estimated in HW at runtime using look-up-tables which correlate the energy consumed with the number and type of accesses. In case core0, from cluster0, has a cache miss, the event is reported by the shared DRAM sensor. This event is accounted on behalf of core0. This behavior is a direct consequence of our proposed accounting method, being transparent for the supervised system. For example, a cache line eviction require a number of events on the system bus; the shared cache sensor for the processing core (identified by master ID) is notified by the sensor on the system bus that energy needs to be accounted on its behalf. This mechanism is hierarchical so that it can be extended to any number of memory layers.

3.3   PTEA Energy Interrupt

So far we discuss the possibility of using LEM as a passive monitoring component, much like the way performance monitoring counters are used by system software. In brief, at context switch dictated by scheduling time intervals, the OS kernel on each core queries C-LEM to retrieve energy sensor readings and attributes energy consumption to running threads. While this approach can accurately account energy consumption at the thread level, it provides limited support to implement energy budgeting policies which are crucial in optimizing energy efficiency of embedded platforms [11, 12]. This is because the OS can account of energy consumption only by sampling at time-based scheduling intervals. During such an interval, the OS has no control over how much energy a thread spends, thus it cannot enforce energy budget limits.

LEM implements what we refer to as the energy interrupt. In the same way a programmable timer generates an interrupt whenever its time slice depletes, LEM is extended with an energy slice and generates an energy interrupt when this energy slice depletes. Specifically, LEM stores a configurable energy budget per core (associated with a unique core ID). Recall core IDs uniquely identify thread IDs in the OS, since only one thread can be running on a core at a time. The OS sets LEM's energy slice register to the available budget for this core which corresponds to the allotted energy budget for the core's executing thread. LEM decreases the energy slice by monitoring the energy consumption due to the core's activity across all hardware components. When the energy slice is depleted, LEM generates an energy interrupt to the core, to be handled by the OS. The OS interrupt handler reads the LEM's sensor values per hardware component for a breakdown on thread's energy consumption and overwrites the LEM's energy slice register with the new energy budget value for the scheduled-in thread, according to the energy budgeting policy. A further extension, left as future work, is to enable energy slices for each hardware component instead of accumulating energy consumption across all of them. This will permit even finer control on distributing the energy budget among hardware components, to be leveraged in component-level energy budgeting policies.

This instantiation of energy accounting in hardware is new, to the best of our knowledge. We consider such an infrastructure as useful, because an OS now can implement PTEA, and applications can derive decisions based on energy consumption. Additionally, energy interrupts enable an OS to enforce energy policies in an efficient way.

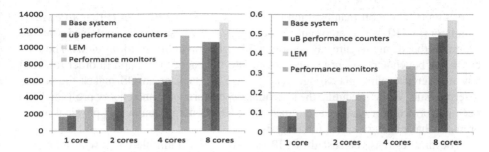

Fig. 4. Cost estimates for the system with different monitoring infrastructures:(a) Number of used slices (#); (b) Static power consumption (W) (*Performance monitors (using Xilinx PerfMon) component for 8 cores design exceeds the available board resources, the values are thus not available)

4 Experimental Results

The LEM infrastructure has been implemented on the Xilinx ZC702 evaluation kit, with Xilinx Zynq-7020 device. Xilinx Vivado 2014.4 toolset has been used for the implementation of the system. The development board has built-in power monitoring sensors for the power lines of the main components: processing system cores (ARM cores), programmable logic core (FPGA fabric), DRAM, I/O etc. Four target systems similar with the reference design have been analyzed in order to estimate the area/performance/ energy overhead of the LEM implementation compared with monitoring free situation. Furthermore, LEM implementation was compared with other solutions that can provide support for energy accounting implementation: existing Microblaze (MB) performance counters and Xilinx IP AXI PerfMon. The four systems feature 1, 2, 4, and 8 cores respectively, each being extended with all the infrastructure needed to estimate energy consumption per core.

The implementation overhead of the Microblaze SoC system featuring 1, 2, 4, and 8 cores respectively is presented in Fig. 4. Figure 4a presents the slice cost for the system with the following monitoring configurations: no monitoring, MB performance counters monitoring, Xillinx bus performance monitors, and the proposed monitoring infrastructure. The cost for the 8 core system with performance monitors did not fit the Zynq board resources. Compared to other monitoring solutions LEM infrastructure gives a better area/power consumption tradeoff (Fig. 4b). With respect to the Xilinx bus performance monitors, it presents up to 30.7 % less slice based resources, while offering the same degree of observability. Compared to the MB performance counters, it present 11.43 % increased cost. However, the proposed infrastructures has the following advantages: (1) it has increased observability, because it provides performance information for other components in the system (bus, memory controller, etc.), (2) it has better performance, as it requires less instruction cycles for configuration and reading; and (3) it provides PTEA.

To validate the LEM infrastructure, standalone benchmarks from the WCET project [15] have been selected. We have considered the following representative benchmark applications: a compression benchmark (COMPRESS), a CRC calculator (CRC), a FFT algorithm (FFT), a bit manipulation benchmark (BIT), a FIR filter (FIR), a Petri Net simulator (PETRI) and an auto generated code (AGC). These are self-contained software programs that do not require any additional libraries, operating or file systems. The self-contained benchmarks were needed to validate the energy interrupt, in order to avoid any interference with other programs, because the lack of an OS makes the results deterministic. While executing the benchmarks, performance and energy profiling have been performed. For each test set timer ticks, LEM energy quants and physical measurements have been recorded for analysis.

The first test case consisted of FIR benchmark on multiple cores with four tests changing the location of instructions and data: (1) both benchmark's instructions and data are executed from DRAM, (2) both instructions and data are in BRAM, (3) instructions are executed from DRAM and data are stored in BRAM, and (4) instructions are executed from BRAM and data are stored in DRAM. We aimed at determining the correlations between the power estimation provide by LEM infrastructure with the physical measurements on the Zynq board. The graphic in Fig. 5a depicts the correlation obtained for the FIR benchmark. Overall correlation value for this benchmark is 96.57 %. For this case, LEM sensors have implemented simple MB, DRAM and BRAM energy models based on look-up tables and linear regression, respectively. However, this result validates the LEM infrastructure both as (1) a mean for new energy models calibration

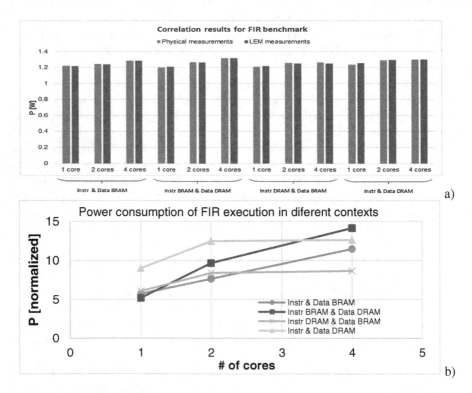

Fig. 5. Power consumption measurements for FIR benchmark: (a) correlation results (b) LEM normalized power

and evaluation based on runtime hardware measurements and (2) online system hardware profiling based on physical onboard sensors or virtual model based sensors. Figure 5b depicts an analysis for the online system hardware profiling for systems with 1 MB core, 2 MB cores and 4 MB cores which execute the FIR benchmark. When instructions are executed from local BRAM memories, the performance and the energy consumption of the system scales linearly with the number of cores. This remark shows the efficiency of L1 instruction caches (which for FPGA systems are implemented in BRAM); this result also validates the proposed monitoring environment. On the other hand, when instructions are executed from DRAM, the system is limited both in performance and power consumption at two cores.

The second test case aimed at emphasizing the energy efficiency of the benchmarks' executions in different system contexts: number of cores, location of instructions and data. In order to characterize benchmarks' executions in different contexts we accounted for runtime timer ticks and energy quanta needed to finalize the benchmarks. In Fig. 6, FIR benchmark performance and energy characterization is presented. Energy consumption and performance of the benchmark significantly depends on the data and instructions location. The system consumes more energy when executes instructions from DRAM memory. In this context, two cores shows the best energy efficiency, while 4 cores increase the penalty in energy and performance due to the DRAM bottleneck. Moving instructions from DRAM to BRAM increases the energy efficiency by a factor of 4.

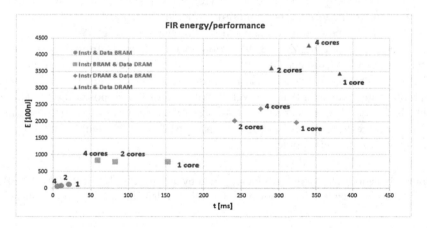

Fig. 6. Energy efficiency results for FIR benchmark

The third test case aimed at validating the LEM infrastructure ability to do software level profiling. Figure 7 shows normalized energy consumption of all WCET benchmarks executed from DRAM. Normalized energy is used in order to be able to compare different benchmarks. Differences between energy consumption results of benchmarks executions can be observed, which shows LEM infrastructure capability to profile software.

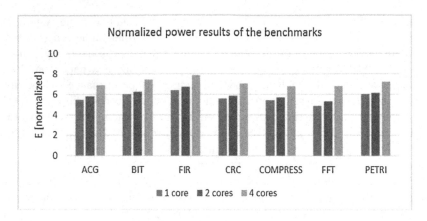

Fig. 7.   Energy profiling of WCET benchmarks

5   Conclusions

In this paper, we have introduced a cost effective LEM infrastructure for component level power and energy monitoring by providing adequate HW and SW support for PTEA and energy interrupt. The monitoring infrastructure implements two levels of energy accounting: processing energy and data movement energy. We have validated our infrastructure on a Zynq ZC702 evaluation board. The results from the execution of WCET benchmarks has indicated a strong correlation between the LEM based energy estimates and the physical power board measurements of more than 95 %. The implementation results indicated that the overall overhead of the proposed infrastructure is around 10 %, for 14 sensors attached to 4-cores reference design. The proposed LEM has lower cost with respect to the Xilinx based performance counters, while having increased flexibility and accuracy.

Acknowledgments.   This work has been supported by the project CHIST-ERA/1/01.10.2012 – "GEMSCLAIM: GreenEr Mobile Systems by Cross LAyer Integrated energy Management".

References

1. Weaver, V.M., Johnson, M., Kasichayanula, K., Ralph, J., Luszczek, P., Terpstra, D., Moore, S.: Measuring energy and power with PAPI. In: Proceedings of 41st International Conference on Parallel Processing Workshops (ICPPW 2012), September 2012
2. Bouajila, A., Lakhtel, A., Zeppenfeld, J., Stechele, W., Herkersdorf, A.: A low-overhead monitoring ring interconnect for MPSoC parameter optimization. In: Proceedings of IEEE International Symposium on Design and Diagnostics of Electronic Circuits & Systems (DDECS 2012), Tallinn, Estonia, April 2012

3. Madduri, S., Vadlamani, R., Burleson, W., Tessier, R.: A monitor interconnect and support subsystem for multicore processors. In: Proceedings of Design, Automation & Test Europe (DATE 2009) Nice, France, April 2009
4. Zhao, J., Madduri, S., Vadlamani, R., Burleson, W., Tessier, R.: A dedicated monitoring infrastructure for multicore processors. IEEE Trans. VLSI Syst. 19(6), 1011–1022 (2011)
5. Choi, S., Hwang, H., Song, B., Cha, H.: Hardware-assisted energy monitoring architecture for micro sensor nodes. J. Syst. Arch. 58(2), 73–85 (2012)
6. Lui, Q., Moreto, M., Jimenez, V., Abella, J., Cazorla, F.J., Valero, M.: Hardware support for accurate per-task energy metering in multicore systems. ACM Trans. Archit. Code Optim. 10(4), 34 (2013)
7. Ituero, P., López-Vallejo, M., Marcos, M.A.S., Osuna, C.G.: Light-weight on-chip monitoring network for dynamic adaptation and calibration. IEEE Sensors J. 12(6), 1736–1745 (2012)
8. Molka, D., Hackenberg, D., Schone, R., Millier, M.S.: Characterizing the energy consumption of data transfers and arithmetic operations on x86-64 processors. In: Proceedings of International Green Computing Conference, GreenComp2010, Chicago, USA, August 2010
9. Zeng, H., Ellis, C.S., Lebeck, A.R., Vahdat, A.: ECOSystem: managing energy as a first class operating system resource. In: Proceedings of the 10th International Conference On Architectural Support for Programming Languages and Operating Systems (ASPLOS X), pp. 123–132. ACM, New York, NY, USA (2002)
10. Snowdon, D.C., Le Sueur, E., Petters, S.M., Heiser, G.: Koala: a platform for OS-level power management. In: Proceedings of the 4th ACM European Conference on Computer Systems (EuroSys 2009), New York, USA (2009)
11. Roy, A., Rumble, S.M., Stutsman, R., Levis, P., Mazières, D., Zeldovich, N.: Energy management in mobile devices with the cinder OS. In: Proceedings of Conference on Computer Systems (EuroSys), New York, USA (2011)
12. OpenCores, WISHBONE System-on-Chip (SoC) Interconnection (2010)
13. ARM, AMBA Open Specifications (2003)
14. Xilinx Inc., MicroBlaze Processor Reference Guide, UG984 (v2014.1) (2014)
15. WCET benchmark: http://www.mrtc.mdh.se/projects/wcet/benchmarks.html

Allocation: From Memories to FPGA Hardware Modules

Reducing NoC and Memory Contention
for Manycores

Vishwanathan Chandru and Frank Mueller[✉]

North Carolina State University, Raleigh, NC, USA
mueller@cs.ncsu.edu

Abstract. Platforms consisting of many computing cores have become the mainstream in high performance computing, general purpose-computing and, lately, embedded systems. Such systems provide increased processing power and system availability, but often impose latencies and contention for memory accesses as multiple cores try to reference data at the same time. This may result in sub-optimal performance unless special allocation policies are employed. On a multi-processor board with 50 or more processing cores, the NoC (Network On Chip) adds to this challenge. This work evaluates the impact of bank-aware and controller-aware allocation on NoC contention. Experiments show that targeted memory allocation results in reduced execution times and NoC contention, the latter of which has not been studied before at this scale.

1 Introduction

On many-core platform(s), memory (DRAM) is a resource critical to performance. As applications share cores and become more and more memory intensive, DRAM tends to become a performance bottleneck that critically affects system performance [1].

Performance problems usually arise due to serialization of memory accesses. This can be avoided using bank-aware and controller-aware allocation. The DRAM in manycore platform(s) is divided among multiple memory controllers and, within a controller, ranks and banks. Controllers and banks can be accessed in parallel. Therefore, performance of an application varies significantly depending on how data is placed and how many cores/processors access a given bank at same time. In the best case, each core/processor accesses a different controller/bank. This ensures that contention of accesses does not occur and that accesses are resolved in parallel. One strategy to improve bank-level parallelism is to use bank interleaving. In case of single threaded applications it improves performance. However, when multiple programs or multiple threads are running simultaneously, it can cause cross-interference. The higher the degree of parallelism, the higher is the probability of bank sharing resulting in more cross-interference.

Linux on the Tilera platform can be configured to allocate memory on the closest NUMA node (physical memory controller) [2,3]. Since Linux on the Tilera

© Springer International Publishing Switzerland 2016
F. Hannig et al. (Eds.): ARCS 2016, LNCS 9637, pp. 293–305, 2016.
DOI: 10.1007/978-3-319-30695-7_22

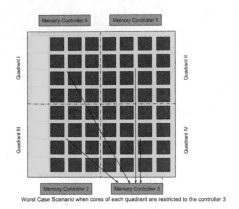

Worst Case Scenario when cores of each quadrant are restricted to the controller 3

Fig. 1. Worst case scenario   **Fig. 2.** Tilera architecture

platform handles DRAM as a single resource following a NUMA allocation policy (unless and until disabled), banks are not considered during allocation and it is not possible to predict the exact location of allocated memory over the banks.

The Tilera architecture features a mesh NoC (Network on Chip) instead of a bus. All data accesses and data exchanges go through the NoC. Given the large number of cores, traffic over the network can lead to high latencies. Therefore, NoC contention also becomes important for bandwidth and performance. Due to the large number of cores, controller contention also becomes a critical factor.

If all accesses are directed via a particular memory controller as depicted in Fig. 1, then the latencies increase since requests get queued at controller(s) and core(s) stall. Furthermore, cores in each quadrant may access all controllers, which leads to a high volume of traffic. Even though all controllers are being utilized, the latency is high.

Contributions: This work contributes a user space bank-aware and controller-aware allocator that keeps track of bank(s) and controller(s) of allocated memory, i.e., it returns memory addresses requested on a particular bank/controller. This allows users to bind a core/processor to a specific bank and controller reducing the contention and serialization, thus improving performance. Using the allocator, an extensive experimental study was performed to evaluate the impact of bank-aware and controller-aware allocation. It was observed that performance (in terms of execution time) improved with our allocator while its variance was reduced due to less NoC contention.

2   Background and Problems

The Tilera [4] architecture differs from most modern systems due to presence of a mesh NoC instead of a bus (see Fig. 2). Other platforms with large core count now use a mesh or ring NoC as well (Intel Xeon Phi [5], Intel SCC [6],

Adapteva [7] etc.). Like modern DRAM systems, the memory system is composed of a controller that handles the arbitration, scheduling and conversion of packets to external memory commands. Memory is organized into ranks (4 in our setup) and each rank has multiple banks (8 in our case). The systems may or may not have multiple independent memory controllers. The Tilera architecture supports four independent controllers that operate in parallel [8].

Tiles (similar to cores) do not have direct access to controllers as the architecture implements a DSM (Distributed Shared Memory) protocol to ensure coherence at the L2 level cache. Tilera utilizes a *mesh interconnect* for data exchange [9]. Dimension ordered routing is used in the network [8]. The interface to off-chip memory and I/O devices is done via *I/O shims* that interface the NoC to memory controllers and other I/O devices [9]. The memory controller is connected to the memory dynamic network (MDN, see Fig. 2) and has multiple ports [8] where requests arrive and are fulfilled.

NUMA allocation is the default policy. However, NUMA and STRIPE allocations might not be able to deliver the best possible performance by themselves as the accesses to data structures will be resolved by different memory controllers with different latencies (hops) over the NoC.

None of the policies are bank aware, i.e., they cannot restrict accesses of a task running on a tile to a particular bank or even controller if memory striping is enabled, where a page (64 kB size) is striped across all controllers in an interleaved way at 8 kB granularity to balance load and improve memory parallelism.

In this work, we present a user space allocator utilizing non-striped mode and using controller-interleaved page allocation instead of the default NUMA policy. We use the interleaved policy for allocating our memory pool as it ensures that an equal amount of memory per controller is available for allocation.

3   Bank Aware Allocator

We designed and implemented a user space bank-aware and controller-aware allocator. It exploits the virtual to physical address translation. After determining the bank and controller from bits within the physical address, the address is added to a specific list corresponding to the relevant controller and bank. When a user requests memory from a certain bank and controller, the corresponding list is searched and if memory is available, its address is returned.

Our allocator requires pre-allocation of a large pool of memory, which is then traversed at a granularity of 8 kB and chunks are added to the corresponding free list(s). The default behavior of the allocator is to try to find a memory chunk fitting the requested size, bank and controller. However, if the exact request cannot be full-filled, the allocator supports multiple modes as an automatic fallback from the default behavior, namely:

CONTROLLER RESTRICTED: If a requested bank is not found within the controller, the allocator defaults to the bank that has the most free memory.

CONTROLLER UNRESTRICTED: If a requested bank and the controller cannot be used to satisfy the request, the allocator defaults to the bank and controller that have the most free memory.

SPLIT: If the requested size is greater than 8 kB and this mode is enabled, then standard allocation is performed (i.e., find the first fitting contiguous chunk available) and its address is returned.

Algorithm 1 shows the implementation. Multiple modes can be configured via a bit-mask for finer control of the allocator. Multiple lists are used to improve the performance of the allocator. Multiple doubly linked list(s) are maintained, one for each bank within a controller. The head of the list is indexed using the controller number/bank number. For SPLIT allocation, a separate list is

---

Input: Request Size, Memory Controller, Bank, modes mask
block ⟵ NULL;
block ⟵ Memory from requested controller and bank;
if *block != NULL* **then**
  | return block;
end
if *CONTROLLER_RESTRICTED in modes_mask* **then**
  | Q ⟵ Banks corresponding to requested Memory Controller with banks in descending order of memory availability;
  | **for** *each bank in Q* **do**
  | | block ⟵ allocate memory from current bank if chunk of size greater than or equal to requested size is available;
  | | **if** *block != NULL* **then**
  | | | return block;
  | | **end**
  | **end**
end
if *CONTROLLER_UNRESTRICTED in modes_mask* **then**
  | ControllerQ ⟵ Get controllers in descending order of memory availability;
  | **for** *each controller in ControllerQ* **do**
  | | BankQ ⟵ Get banks from current controller (ordered in descending order of memory availability);
  | | **for** *each bank in BankQ* **do**
  | | | block ⟵ allocate memory from current bank if chunk of size greater than or equal to requested size is available;
  | | | **if** *block != NULL* **then**
  | | | | return block;
  | | | **end**
  | | **end**
  | **end**
end
block ⟵ NULL;
if *SPLIT_MODE in modes_mask* **then**
  | block ⟵ Allocate contiguous block of memory (may span across banks and controllers);
end
return block;

Algorithm 1. Bank aware algorithm allocator

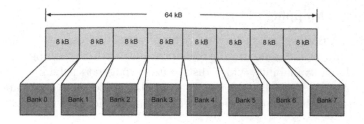

Fig. 3. Bank split up in a 64 kB page

maintained for quicker allocation. Each free memory chunk is part of both lists. Each memory chunk has four pointers, two pointers that are used to traverse the corresponding bank list and two pointers for the list used for SPLIT allocation.

Depending on the allocation modes, we track the memory available per bank/controller via a queue. Five such queues are maintained, one queue per controller to keep track of banks and one shared queue to keep track of memory available per controller.

This multiple-level design accelerates bank-aware allocation for allocations less than 8 kB. SPLIT allocation is slow as multiple data structures and free lists need to be updated. Hence, experiments exclude the allocation time and focus on real-time applications after they pre-allocate data during the initialization.

In contrast to PALLOC [10], a kernel-level allocator, and other software partitioning approaches [11,12], our allocator works targets manycores with mesh NoCs (not multicores with bus/ring NoCs) and operates in user space as a proof-of-concept implementation. It is more restrictive in terms of usage due to constraints imposed by manycores. Tilera supports a 64 kB page size and utilizes controller-interleaved page placement, i.e., we cannot allocate more than 64 kB of contiguous memory within a controller (see Fig. 3). As the bank varies every 13 address bits (explained in Sect. 4.1), a contiguous allocation cannot exceed 8 kB if it needs to be within the *same bank and controller*. Instead, our allocator allows medium allocations ($8KB < size \leq 64KB$) to span multiple banks while larger ones ($> 64KB$) even span multiple controllers.

4 Evaluation

The evaluation platform used is a Tilera TILEPro-64 with 64 tiles [13]. Each tile has $16 + 8$ kB private L1I+D cache(s), a 64 kB private L2 cache and a soft L3 cache of 5 MB, which is created by combining the private L2 caches of all tiles (see Fig. 2). There are 4 memory controllers, each capable of independent operation. Each controller can support up to 32 banks (4 ranks and 8 banks per rank). The configuration we utilize has 8 GB of DDR2 RAM, 2 GB per controller. Address hashing [8] is enabled to enhance the number of available banks.

4.1   Address Mapping

Address translation is straight forward. The physical address has 36 bits [8]. Per the documentation and configuration register values, address hashing is performed to increase bank availability, which distributes a page at cache line granularity among the available tiles. Bits 13, 14, 15 are used to determine banks and bits 34 and 35 are used to determine the controller (in combination covering all 32 banks).

4.2   Experimental Setup

To measure bank-level contention, we use two OpenMP benchmarks. The entire processor is divided into 4 quadrants with 16 tiles each, except 'quadrants 3 and 4 with only 12 tiles each as the bottom-most 8 tiles are reserved by Tilera's SDK in our setup. The primary aim of dividing tiles into quadrants is to restrict the access to memory via the closest memory controller. This allows us to remove controller contention across quadrants and to minimize NoC contention so that we can focus on measuring bank level contention. This also helps if we want to create pathological worst case scenarios, i.e., tiles from each quadrant accessing all four controllers to generate excessive memory contention. The execution time is indicative of contention. We refer to the controller-restricted policy as "colored allocation", i.e., choosing a page located at the closest controller to minimize NoC path length and this contention. The selection of c colors indicates that threads access controller-local banks shared by as few threads as possible depending on the configuration. Colored allocation results in lower execution time and better memory bandwidth compared to non-colored allocation. Non-colored, using tmc_alloc_map() from the Tilera Multicore Components (TMC) library, is subsequently referred to as the default allocator, which observes controller locality and uses address hashing (see Sect. 4.1) affecting banks, only, i.e., same or different banks may be chosen in an indeterminate manner.

During the entire experiment, threads were pinned to the respective tiles to prevent them from migrating and causing unintended interference. Benchmark data is explicitly allocated from the bank/controller-aware allocator using coloring.

5   Experiments and Results

Let us assess the impact of bank-aware allocation on performance. We use execution time to measure the performance impact of latency, bandwidth and contention. By running the same benchmark in multiple tile(s) and using an OpenMP enabled benchmark (where OpenMP constructs map to POSIX threads), the impact of bank-aware and controller-aware allocation is shown. The x-axis of the plots denotes the ith experiment/execution (experiment instance) and the y-axis shows overall memory bandwidth (MB per second) or execution time (seconds) depending on the plot.

Figure 4 depicts the execution time (y-axis) of the NAS IS OMP benchmark for 32 threads (8 threads per quadrant) for 15 runs. We obtain close to a 20 %

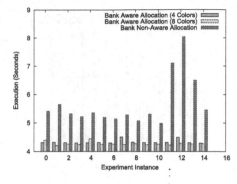
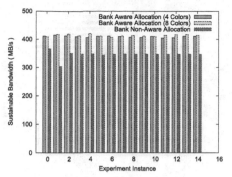

Fig. 4. NPB IS OMP (Class A)   **Fig. 5.** Stream add bandwidth

performance benefit with colored allocation, which improves as colors increase from four per controller (each color/bank shared by 2 threads) to eight (completely thread-private banks). We also observe significant performance variations when bank non-aware allocation is used. Figure 5 depicts the bandwidth on y-axis reported by the STREAM benchmark with 32 threads and 8 threads per quadrant. We observe a significant increase in sustainable bandwidth for the ADD kernel from the STREAM benchmark for 15 runs. Bank non-aware allocation results in higher variation again (for 1 of 15 experiments).

To further understand NoC contention and bank contention, composite benchmark executions (for bubblesort from the Mälardalen benchmark suite) with varied number of threads and memory traces were obtained. Bubblesort is the most memory bound of all integrated benchmarks. Composite benchmark runs are reported in terms of iterations. To get reliable data and account for outliers, multiple iterations are run per execution and experiments are repeated (reported as instances). Figure 6 shows the overall maximum execution time per experiment of the composite benchmark for 32 threads and 2 pages per thread. We observe that colored allocation always results in the best performance isolation. The two pathological worst case scenarios, tasks in each quadrant accessing all quadrants (labeled as circular allocation) or tasks restricted to a particular controller, always lead to the worst performance. This highlights the criticality of NoC contention and controller contention. Controller-local allocation is slightly slower than bank-aware allocation within a controller (colored allocation) as the latter reduces serializations of accesses.

The difference between 2, 4 and 8 color allocations is noticeable. This is due the fact that even though we are simulating two and four bank configuration(s) by wrapping around bank indices when populating free lists at user level, at hardware level we still have 8 banks, which is a higher bank level parallelism than can be exploited by a four or two color scheme.

To further analyze the impact of colored allocation, the following two sets of experiments were performed:

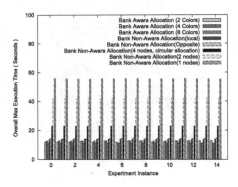
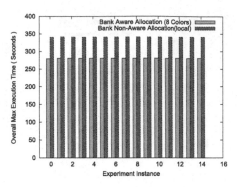

Fig. 6. Composite benchmark (32 threads, 2 pages per thread)

Fig. 7. Composite benchmark (32 threads, 10 pages per thread)

1. Constant memory footprint and variations in the number of threads.
2. Constant number of threads and variable memory footprint per thread.

Figure 7 shows the overall maximum execution time per experiment/execution of the composite benchmark for 32 threads and 10 pages per thread. As we compare the plots in Fig. 6 with Fig. 7, we observe an increase in execution time by a factor of 21, even though the input size increased five-fold. This is mainly due to memory boundedness of the latter vs. L2-boundedness of the former experiment. An improvement of 17 % to 20 % over non-bank aware controller-local allocation was observed on average.

For experimental case 1, we fixed the memory footprint to 10 pages per thread and varied the number of threads from 8 to 32 in steps of 8, i.e., increments of 2 threads per quadrant. We observe that the difference between colored allocation and bank non-aware controller-local allocation keeps increasing until 32 threads, and then remains close to 60 s (see Figs. 6, 7, and 8). This is due to the fact that each controller has 8 banks per rank, i.e., for up to 32 threads we were able to restrict each thread in the quadrant to a separate bank. However, as we exceed 8 threads per quadrant, more than one thread accesses a given bank leading to increased contention. Now, as we reduce the number of threads to 8, non-colored controller-local allocation provides good performance most of the times (see Fig. 9). There are two possible reasons for this behavior.

One is bank address hashing. In case of non-bank aware controller-local allocation, we perform 8 kB allocations using Tilera's API that allocates at 64 kB (page size) granularity. Effectively, we only access the first 8 kB of each page, for which the bank is randomized due to bank address hashing. Our colored allocation restricts thread 0 in each quadrant to bank 0 of the closest controller and thread 1 to bank 1 of the closest controller, effectively restricting accesses to 2 banks. But in case of non-colored allocation, due to bank address hashing, the first 8 kB of the page (which we access) can be any bank (from 0–4), so there is a high probability of more bank level parallelism. The second, less probable reason is that the number of threads per controller is less than the number of MDN ports per controller.

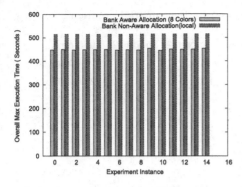
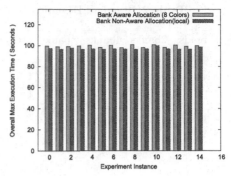

Fig. 8. Composite benchmark (48 threads, 10 pages per thread)

Fig. 9. Composite benchmark (8 threads, 10 pages per thread)

Table 1. Standard Deviations for IS and STREAM

Benchmark	4 Banks	8 Banks	Controller-local
NAS IS OMP	0.06824	0.06272	0.866052
STREAM	2.950072	3.919421	12.63999

There are two threads per quadrant and 3 MDN ports per controller. Therefore, any delay due to serialization at ports is avoided.

Table 1 shows the standard deviation of the execution times of IS and sustainable bandwidth reported by STREAM over 15 executions. We can observe that bank-aware allocation results in tighter bounds for IS and STREAM.

Table 2 shows the standard deviation over 15 experiments corresponding to the plots of each experiment having *5 iterations* for Composite Benchmarks. We observe increased jitter compared to controller-local allocation except for 8 banks. We can also observe that as we increase the number of threads from 32 to 48, the jitter decreases as we change the number of threads from 8 to 32, which is due to increased bank-level parallelism. However, as we increase the number for threads to 48, the increased NoC contention and bank sharing subsume the performance improvement. For controller-local allocation, a higher level of serialization exist as we increase the memory footprint, which causes lower performance at reduced jitter.

6   Related Work

Jeong et al. [11] propose to optimize power consumption, increase memory throughput and improve performance by means of bank-level partitioning but do not consider multiple controllers or NoC contention. Instead of actual hardware, the evaluation is based on a simulator. Fourth, the effect of the NUMA allocation policy is not considered. Park et al. [14], another software-based approach, propose

Table 2. Standard Deviation for Composite Benchmark Execution

threads, pages	2banks	4banks	8banks	ctrl-local	opposite-ctrl	1node	2nodes	circular-alloc
32,2	0.39	0.57	0.02	0.07	0.22	0.12	0.042	0.036
8,10	–	–	1.13	0.67	–	–	–	–
32,10	–	–	0.38	0.19	–	–	–	–
48,10	–	–	2.23	0.38	–	–	–	–

to increase memory bandwidth and reduce cross interference in a multicore system by dedicating multiple dedicated banks to different cores. Page allocation within the dedicated banks is randomized to reduce row-buffer conflicts and to further minimize unwarranted cross-interference. Due to the implicit assumption of more banks than cores, this approach excels when the number of banks is much larger than the number of cores. It can also be observed that none of the approaches focus specifically on improving worst-case execution time (WCET).

Since multicore systems have multiple memory channels, memory channel partitioning is one potential solution to improve performance isolation. Muralidhara et al. [15] propose an application-aware memory channel partitioning. They consider partitioning memory channels and prioritized request scheduling to minimize the interference between memory-bound tasks from cache bound tasks and CPU bound tasks. Apart from software based approaches, there are multiple works on improving predictability of memory controllers. PRET [16] employs a private banking scheme, which eliminates bank sharing interference. Wu et al. [17] take a similar approach but both approaches differ in scheduling policy and page policy. There are several other works closely related to our work [18–20]. AMC [20] focuses on improving the tightness of WCET estimation by reducing interference via bank interleaving and reducing inferences using a close-page policy. The drawback of this proposal is that instead of treating banks as resources, it treats memory as a resource. Akesson et al. [18] present a similar approach to guarantee a net bandwidth and provide an upper bound on latency. They use bank interleaving to increase the available bandwidth. For bounding latency, they use a Credit-Controlled Static-Priority arbiter [21]. The drawback of this approach is also is same as that of AMC.

Goossens et al. [19] presents a proposal to improve the average performance of hard and soft real time system(s) on a FRT (firm real-time) controller without sacrificing hard/firm real time guarantees. It utilizes bank interleaving and proposes a new conservative closed page policy to maintain locality within a certain window. The drawback of this approach is that it does not eliminate bank conflicts completely.

Caches also impact performance and there are several studies regarding the same at both hardware and software levels [22–30]. The basic idea behind software-based approaches is cache coloring.

Buono et al. [31] experiment with different Tilera allocations for their FastFlow framework that provides an abstraction for task-based programming.

In contrast to the above references, our work focuses on the impact of NoC contention for bank-aware and controller-aware allocation using multi-threaded codes. This makes it significantly different from prior studies and does not allow a direct comparison.

7 Conclusion

In this paper, we presented a prototype bank-aware and controller-aware user space allocator for increased memory performance on the Tilera architecture. It restricts tiles to access memory of specific banks in addition to a specific controller, thus minimizing bank sharing while balancing and enhancing available bandwidth and performance.

Using this allocator, we performed experiments with the STREAM and the NAS IS OMP benchmarks. Based on our results, we conclude that bank-aware allocation improves performance, increases memory bandwidth utilization, and reduces NoC contention, the latter of which has not been studied before and is becoming a problem for large-scale multicores with many memory controllers.

Acknowledgment. Tilera Corporation provided technical support of the research. This work was funded in part by NSF grants 1239246 and 1058779 as well as a grant from AFOSR via Securboration.

References

1. Wulf, W.A., McKee, S.A.: Hitting the memory wall: implications of the obvious. ACM SIGARCH Comput. Archit. News **23**(1), 20–24 (1995)
2. Programming The Tile Processor, Tilera. http://www.tilera.com/
3. Application Libraries Reference Manual, Tilera. http://www.tilera.com/
4. Tilera processor family. www.tilera.com
5. Intel xeon phi, April 2015. https://www-ssl.intel.com/content/www/us/en/processors/xeon/xeon-phi-coprocessor-datasheet.html
6. Single-chip cloud computer. blogs.intel.com/intellabs/2009/12/sccloudcomp.php
7. Adapteva processor family. www.adapteva.com/products/silicon-devices/e16g301/
8. Tile Processor I/O Device Guide, Tilera. http://www.tilera.com/
9. Tile Processor User Architecture Overview, Tilera. http://www.tilera.com/
10. Yun, H., Mancuso, R., Wu, Z.-P., Pellizzoni, R.: Palloc: dram bank-aware memory allocator for performance isolation on multicore platforms. In: IEEE Real-Time and Embedded Technology and Applications Symposium, vol. 356 (2014)
11. Jeong, M.K., Yoon, D.H., Sunwoo, D., Sullivan, M., Lee, I., Erez, M.: Balancing DRAM locality and parallelism in shared memory CMP systems. In: International Symposium on High Performance Computer Architecture, pp. 1–12 (2012)
12. Liu, L., Cui, Z., Xing, M., Bao, Y., Chen, M., Wu, C.: A software memory partition approach for eliminating bank-level interference in multicore systems. In: International Conference on Parallel Architectures and Compilation Techniques, pp. 367–376 (2012)

13. Tile Processor User Architecture Reference, Tilera. http://www.tilera.com/scm
14. Park, H., Baek, S., Choi, J., Lee, D., Noh, S.H.: Regularities considered harmful: forcing randomness to memory accesses to reduce row buffer conflicts for multi-core, multi-bank systems. ACM SIGPLAN Notices **48**(4), 181–192 (2013)
15. Muralidhara, S.P., Subramanian, L., Mutlu, O., Kandemir, M., Moscibroda, T.: Reducing memory interference in multicore systems via application-aware memory channel partitioning. In: International Symposium on Microarchitecture, pp. 374–385 (2011)
16. Reineke, J., Liu, I., Patel, H.D., Kim, S., Lee, E.A.: Pret dram controller: bank privatization for predictability and temporal isolation. In: International conference on Hardware/software codesign and system synthesis, pp. 99–108 (2011)
17. Wu, Z.P., Krish, Y., Pellizzoni, R.: Worst case analysis of DRAM latency in multi-requestor systems. In: 34th IEEE Real-Time Systems Symposium (RTSS), pp. 372–383 (2013)
18. Akesson, B., Goossens, K., Ringhofer, M.: Predator: a predictable SDRAM memory controller. In: International Conference on Hardware/Software Codesign and System Synthesis, pp. 251–256 (2007)
19. Goossens, S., Akesson, B., Goossens, K.: Conservative open-page policy for mixed time-criticality memory controllers. In: Conference on Design, Automation and Test in Europe, pp. 525–530 (2013)
20. Paolieri, M., Quiñones, E., Cazorla, F.J., Valero, M.: An analyzable memory controller for hard real-time CMPs. IEEE Embed. Syst. Lett. **1**(4), 86–90 (2009)
21. Åkesson, B., Steffens, L., Strooisma, E., Goossens, K. et al.: Real-time scheduling of hybrid systems using credit-controlled static-priority arbitration. In: RTCSA (2008)
22. Kim, S., Chandra, D., Solihin, Y.: Fair cache sharing and partitioning in a chip multiprocessor architecture. In: International Conference on Parallel Architectures and Compilation Techniques, pp. 111–122 (2004)
23. Nesbit, K.J., Laudon, J., Smith, J.E.: Virtual private caches. ACM SIGARCH Comput. Archit. News **35**(2), 57–68 (2007)
24. Liedtke, J., Hartig, H., Hohmuth, M.: OS-controlled cache predictability for real-time systems. In: Third IEEE Real-Time Technology and Applications Symposium, Proceedings, pp. 213–224 (1997)
25. Lin, J., Lu, Q., Ding, X., Zhang, Z., Zhang, X., Sadayappan, P.: Gaining insights into multicore cache partitioning: bridging the gap between simulation and real systems. In: IEEE 14th International Symposium on High Performance Computer Architecture, HPCA 2008, pp. 367–378 (2008)
26. Zhang, X., Dwarkadas, S., Shen, K.: Towards practical page coloring-based multicore cache management. In: European conference on Computer systems, pp. 89–102 (2009)
27. Soares, L., Tam, D., Stumm, M.: Reducing the harmful effects of last-level cache polluters with an OS-level, software-only pollute buffer. In: International Symposium on Microarchitecture, pp. 258–269 (2008)
28. Ding, X., Wang, K., Zhang, X.: SRM-Buffer,: an OS buffer management technique to prevent last level cache from thrashing in multicores. In: Conference on Computer systems, pp. 243–256 (2011)
29. Ward, B.C., Herman, J.L., Kenna, C.J., Anderson, J.H.: Outstanding paper award: making shared caches more predictable on multicore platforms. In: 25th Euromicro Conference on Real-Time Systems (ECRTS), pp. 157–167 (2013)

30. Mancuso, R., Dudko, R., Betti, E., Cesati, M., Caccamo, M., Pellizzoni, R.: Real-time cache management framework for multi-core architectures. In: IEEE 19th Real-Time and Embedded Technology and Applications Symposium (RTAS), pp. 45–54 (2013)
31. Buono, D., Danelutto, M., Lametti, S., Torquati, M.: Parallel patterns for general purpose many-core. In: Euromicro International Conference on Parallel, Distributed and Network-Based Processing (PDP), pp. 131–139 (2013)

An Efficient Data Structure for Dynamic Two-Dimensional Reconfiguration

Sándor P. Fekete, Jan-Marc Reinhardt$^{(\boxtimes)}$, and Christian Scheffer

Department of Computer Science, TU Braunschweig, Braunschweig, Germany
{s.fekete,j-m.reinhardt}@tu-bs.de, scheffer@ibr.cs.tu-bs.de

Abstract. In the presence of dynamic insertions and deletions into a partially reconfigurable FPGA, fragmentation is unavoidable. This poses the challenge of developing efficient approaches to dynamic defragmentation and reallocation. One key aspect is to develop efficient algorithms and data structures that exploit the two-dimensional geometry of a chip, instead of just one. We propose a new method for this task, based on the fractal structure of a quadtree, which allows dynamic segmentation of the chip area, along with dynamically adjusting the necessary communication infrastructure. We describe a number of algorithmic aspects, and present different solutions. We also provide experimental data for various scenarios, indicating practical usefulness of our approach.

Keywords: FPGAs · Partial reconfiguration · Two-dimensional reallocation · Defragmentation · Dynamic data structures · Insertions and deletions

1 Introduction

In recent years, a wide range of methodological developments on FPGAs have made it possible to combine the performance of an ASIC implementation with the flexibility of software realizations. One important development is partial run-time reconfiguration, which allows overcoming significant area overhead, monetary cost, higher power consumption, or speed penalties (see e.g. [20]). As described in [13], the idea is to load a sequence of different modules by partial runtime reconfiguration. In a general setting, we are faced with a dynamically changing set of modules, which may be modified by deletions and insertions. Typically, there is no full a-priori knowledge of the arrival or departure of modules, i.e., we have to deal with an online situation. The challenge is to ensure that arriving modules can be allocated. Because previously deleted modules may have been located in different areas of the layout, free space may be fragmented, making it necessary to *relocate* existing modules in order to provide sufficient area. In principle, this can be achieved by completely *defragmenting* the layout when necessary; however, the lack of control over the module sequence makes

---

This work was supported by the DFG Research Group FOR-1800, "Controlling Concurrent Change", under contract number FE407/17-1.

© Springer International Publishing Switzerland 2016
F. Hannig et al. (Eds.): ARCS 2016, LNCS 9637, pp. 306–318, 2016.
DOI: 10.1007/978-3-319-30695-7_23

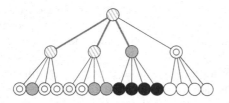 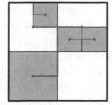

Fig. 1. A quadtree configuration (left) and the corresponding dynamically generated quadtree layout (right). Gray nodes are occupied, white ones with gray stripes fractional, black ones blocked, and white nodes without stripes empty. Maximally empty nodes have a circle inscribed. Red lines in the module layout indicate the dynamically produced communication infrastructure, induced by the quadtree structure (Color figure online).

it hard to avoid frequent full defragmentation, resulting in expensive operations for insertions if a naïve approach is used.

Dynamic insertion and deletion are classic problems of Computer Science. Many data structures (from simple to sophisticated) have been studied that result in low-cost operations and efficient maintenance of a changing set of objects. These data structures are mostly one-dimensional (or even dimensionless) by nature, making it hard to fully exploit the 2D nature of an FPGA. In this paper, we propose a 2D data structure based on a quadtree for maintaining the module layout under partial reconfiguration and reallocation. The key idea is to control the overall structure of the layout, such that future insertions can be performed with a limited amount of relocation, even when free space is limited.

Our main contribution is to introduce a 2D approach that is able to achieve provable constant-factor efficiency for different types of relocation cost. To this end, we give detailed mathematical proofs for a slightly simplified setting, along with sketches of extensions to the more general cases. We also provide experimental data for various scenarios, indicating practical usefulness of our approach.

The rest of this paper is organized as follows. The following Sect. 2 provides a survey of related work. For better accessiblity of the key ideas and due to limited space, our technical description in Sects. 3, 4, and 5 focuses on the case of discretized quadratic modules on a quadratic chip area. We discuss in Sect. 6 how general rectangles can be dealt with, with corresponding experimental data in Sect. 7. Along the same lines (and due to limited space), we do not explicitly elaborate on the dynamic maintenance of the communication infrastructure; see Fig. 1 for the basic idea.

2   Related Work

The problem considered in our paper has a resemblance to one-dimensional *dynamic storage allocation*, in which a sequence of storage requests of varying size have to be assigned to a block of memory cells, such that the length of each block corresponds to the size of the request. In its classic form (without virtual memory), this block needs to be contiguous; in our setting, contiguity of two-dimensional allocation is a must, as reconfigurable devices do not provide techniques such as paging and virtual memory. Once the allocation has been performed, it is static in space: after a block has been occupied, it will remain fixed until the corresponding data is no longer needed and the block is released. As a consequence, a sequence of allocations and releases can result in fragmentation of the memory array, making it hard or even impossible to store new data.

On the practical side, classic buddy systems partition the one-dimensional storage into a number of standard block sizes and allocate a block in a smallest free standard interval to contain it. Differing only in the choice of the standard size, various systems have been proposed [9,15–17,22]. Newer approaches based on cache-oblivious structures in memory hierarchies include Bender et al. [2,6]. Theoretical work on one-dimensional contiguous allocation includes Bender and Hu [7], who consider maintaining n elements in sorted order, with not more than $O(n)$ space. Bender et al. [5] aim at reducing fragmentation when maintaining n objects that require contiguous space. Fekete et al. [13] study complexity results and consider practical applications on FPGAs. Reallocations have also been studied in the context of heap allocation. Bendersky and Petrank [8] observe that full compaction is prohibitively expensive and consider partial compaction. Cohen and Petrank [11] extend these to practical applications. Bender et al. [3] describe a strategy that achieves good amortized movement costs for reallocations. Another paper by the same authors [4] deals with reallocations in the context of scheduling.

From within the FPGA community, there is a huge amount of related work dealing with relocation: Becker et al. [1] present a method for enhancing the relocability of partial bitstreams for FPGA runtime configuration, with a special focus on heterogeneities. They study the underlying prerequisites and technical conditions for dynamic relocation. Gericota et al. [14] present a relocation procedure for Configurable Logic Blocks (CLBs) that is able to carry out online rearrangements, defragmenting the available FPGA resources without disturbing functions currently running. Another relevant approach was given by Compton et al. [12], who present a new reconfigurable architecture design extension based on the ideas of relocation and defragmentation. Koch et al. [18] introduce efficient hardware extensions to typical FPGA architectures in order to allow hardware task preemption. These papers do not consider the algorithmic implications and how the relocation capabilities can be exploited to optimize module layout in a fast, practical fashion, which is what we consider in this paper. Koester et al. [19] also address the problem of defragmentation. Different defragmentation algorithms that minimize different types of costs are analyzed.

The general concept of defragmentation is well known, and has been applied to many fields, e.g., it is typically employed for memory management. Our approach is significantly different from defragmentation techniques which have been conceived so far: these require a freeze of the system, followed by a computation of the new layout and a complete reconfiguration of all modules at once. Instead, we just copy one module at a time, and simply switch the execution to the new module as soon as the move is complete. This leads to a *seamless, dynamic defragmentation of the module layout*, resulting in much better utilization of the available space for modules. All this makes our work a two-dimensional extension of the one-dimensional approach described in [13].

3 Preliminaries

We are faced with an (online) sequence of configuration requests that are to be carried out on a rectangular chip area. A request may consist of *deleting* an existing module, which simply means that the module may be terminated and its occupied area can be released to free space. On the other hand, a request may consist of *inserting* a new module, requiring an axis-aligned, rectangular module to be allocated to an unoccupied section of the chip; if necessary, this may require rearranging the allocated modules in order to create free space of the required dimensions, incurring some cost.

The rest of this section provides technical notation and descriptions. A square is called *aligned* if its size equals 2^{-r} for any $r \in \mathbb{N}_0$. It is called an *r-square* if its size is 2^{-r} for a specific $r \in \mathbb{N}_0$. A *quadtree* is a rooted tree in which every node has either four children or none. As a quadtree can be interpreted as the subdivision of the unit square into nested r-squares, we can use quadtrees to describe certain packings of aligned squares into the unit square.

Definition 1. *A (quadtree) configuration T assigns aligned squares to the nodes of a quadtree. The nodes with a distance j to the root of the quadtree form* layer *j. Nodes are also called* pixels *and pixels in layer j are called* j-pixels. *Thus, j-squares can only be assigned to j-pixels. A pixel p contains a square s if s is assigned to p or one of the children of p contains s. A j-pixel that has an assigned j-square is* occupied. *For a pixel p that is not occupied, with P the unique path from p to the root, we call p*

- blocked *if there is a $q \in P$ that is occupied,*
- free *if it is not blocked,*
- fractional *if it is free and contains a square,*
- empty *if it is free but not fractional,*
- maximally empty *if it is empty but its parent is not.*

The height h(T) *of a configuration T is defined as 0 if the root of T is empty. Otherwise, as the maximum $i + 1$ such that T contains an i-square.*

The *(remaining) capacity* $\mathrm{cap}(p)$ of a j-pixel p is defined as 0 if p is occupied or blocked and as 4^{-j} if p is empty. Otherwise, $\mathrm{cap}(p) := \sum_{p' \in C(p)} \mathrm{cap}(p')$, where $C(p)$ is the set of children of p. The *(remaining) capacity* of T, denoted $\mathrm{cap}(T)$, is the remaining capacity of the root of T.

See Fig. 1 for an example of a quadtree configuration and the corresponding packing of aligned squares in the unit square.

Quadtree configurations are transformed using *moves* (*reallocations*). A *j*-square *s* assigned to a *j*-pixel *p* can be *moved* (*reallocated*) to another *j*-pixel *q* by creating a new assignment from *q* to *s* and deleting the old assignment from *p* to *s*. *q* must have been empty for this to be allowed.

Definition 2. *A fractional pixel is* open *if at least one of its children is (maximally) empty. A configuration is called* compact *if there is at most one open j-pixel for every $j \in \mathbb{N}_0$.*

In (one-dimensional) storage allocation and scheduling, there are techniques that avoid reallocations by requiring more space than the sum of the sizes of the allocated pieces. See Bender et al. [4] for an example. From there we adopt the term *underallocation*. In particular, given two squares s_1 and s_2, s_2 is an *x*-underallocated copy of s_1, if $|s_2| = x \cdot |s_1|$ for $x > 1$.

Definition 3. *A request has one of the forms* INSERT(*x*) *or* DELETE(*x*), *where x is a unique identifier for a square. Let $v \in [0, 1]$ be the volume of the square x. The* volume *of a request σ is defined as*

$$\text{vol}(\sigma) = \begin{cases} v & \text{if } r = \text{INSERT}(x), \\ -v & \text{if } r = \text{DELETE}(x). \end{cases}$$

Definition 4. *A sequence of requests $\sigma_1, \sigma_2, \ldots, \sigma_k$ is* valid *if $\sum_{i=1}^{j} \text{vol}(\sigma_i) \le 1$ holds for every $j = 1, 2, \ldots, k$. It is called* aligned, *if $|\text{vol}(\sigma_j)| = 4^{-\ell_j}, \ell_j \in \mathbb{N}_0$, where $|.|$ denotes the absolute value, holds for every $j = 1, 2, \ldots, k$, i.e., if only aligned squares are packed.*

Our goal is to minimize the costs of reallocations. Costs can be measured in different ways, for example in the number of moves or the reallocated volume.

Definition 5. *Assume you fulfill a request σ and as a consequence reallocate a set of squares $\{s_1, s_2, \ldots, s_k\}$. The* movement cost *of σ is defined as $c_{\text{move}}(\sigma) = k$, the* total volume cost *of σ is defined as $c_{\text{total}}(\sigma) = \sum_{i=1}^{k} |s_i|$, and the (relative)* volume cost *of σ is defined as $c_{\text{vol}}(\sigma) = \frac{c_{\text{total}}(\sigma)}{|\text{vol}(\sigma)|}$.*

4 Inserting into a Given Configuration

In this section we examine the problem of rearranging a given configuration in such a way that the insertion of a new square is possible.

4.1 Coping with Fragmented Allocations

Our strategy follows one general idea: larger empty pixels can be built from smaller ones; e.g., four empty *i*-pixels can be combined into one empty $(i - 1)$-pixel. This can be iterated to build an empty pixel of suitable volume.

Lemma 6. *Let $p_1, p_2, \ldots, p_k$ be a sequence of empty pixels sorted by volume in descending order. Then $\sum_{i=1}^{k} \mathrm{cap}(p_i) \geq 4^{-\ell} > \sum_{i=1}^{k-1} \mathrm{cap}(p_i)$ implies the following properties:*

1. *$k < 4 \Leftrightarrow k = 1$*
2. *$k \geq 4 \Rightarrow \sum_{i=1}^{k} \mathrm{cap}(p_i) = 4^{-\ell}$*
3. *$k \geq 4 \Rightarrow \mathrm{cap}(p_k) = \mathrm{cap}(p_{k-1}) = \mathrm{cap}(p_{k-2}) = \mathrm{cap}(p_{k-3})$*

Lemma 7. *Given a quadtree configuration T with four maximally empty j-pixels. Then T can be transformed (using a sequence of moves) into a configuration T^* with one more maximally empty $(j-1)$-pixel and four fewer maximally empty j-pixels than T while retaining all its maximally empty i-pixels for $i < j - 1$.*

Theorem 8. *Given a quadtree configuration T with a remaining capacity of at least 4^{-j}, you can transform T into a quadtree configuration T^* with an empty j-pixel using a sequence of moves.*

Proof. Let $S = p_1, p_2, \ldots, p_n$ be the sequence containing all maximally empty pixels of T sorted by capacity in descending order. If the capacity of p_1 is at least 4^{-j}, then there already is an empty j-pixel in T and we can simply set $T^* = T$.

Assume $\mathrm{cap}(p_1) < 4^{-j}$. In this case we inductively build an empty j-pixel. Let $S' = p_1, p_2, \ldots, p_k$ be the shortest prefix of S satisfying $\sum_{i=1}^{k} \mathrm{cap}(p_i) \geq 4^{-j}$. Lemma 6 tells us $k \geq 4$ and the last four pixels in S', $p_{k-3}, p_{k-2}, p_{k-1}$ and p_k, are from the same layer, say layer ℓ. Thus, we can apply Lemma 7 to $p_{k-3}, p_{k-2}, p_{k-1}, p_k$ to get a new maximally empty $(\ell-1)$-pixel q. We remove $p_{k-3}, p_{k-2}, p_{k-1}, p_k$ from S' and insert q into S' according to its capacity.

We can repeat these steps until $k < 4$ holds. Then Lemma 6 implies that $k = 1$, i.e., the sequence contains only one pixel p_1, and because $\mathrm{cap}(p_1) = 4^{-j}$, p_1 is an empty j-pixel.

4.2   Reallocation Cost

Reallocation cost is made non-trivial by *cascading moves*: Reallocated squares may cause further reallocations, when there is no empty pixel of the required size available.

Observation 9. *In the worst case, reallocating an ℓ-square is not cheaper than reallocating four $(\ell + 1)$-squares – using any of the three defined cost types.*

Theorem 10. *The maximum total volume cost caused by the insertion of an i-square Q, $i \in \mathbb{N}_0$, into a quadtree configuration T with $\mathrm{cap}(T) \geq 4^{-i}$ is bounded by*

$$c_{\mathrm{total,max}} \leq \frac{3}{4} \cdot 4^{-i} \cdot \min\{(s - i), i\} \in O(|Q| \cdot h(T))$$

when the smallest previously inserted square is an s-square.

Proof. For $s \leq i$ there has to be an empty i-square in T, as $\text{cap}(T) \geq 4^{-i}$, and we can insert Q without any moves. In the following, we assume $s > i$. Let Q be the i-square to be inserted. We can assume that we do not choose an i-pixel with a remaining capacity of zero to pack Q – if there were no other pixels, $\text{cap}(T)$ would be zero as well. Therefore, the chosen pixel, say p, must have a remaining capacity of at least 4^{-s}. From Observation 9 follows that the worst case for p would be to be filled with 3 k-squares, for every $i < k \leq s$. Let v_i be the worst-case volume of a reallocated i-pixel. We get $v_i \leq \sum_{j=i+1}^{s} \frac{3}{4^j} = 4^{-i} - 4^{-s}$.

Now we have to consider cascading moves. Whenever we move an ℓ-square, $\ell > i$, to make room for Q, we might have to reallocate a volume of v_ℓ to make room for the ℓ-square. Let x_i be the total volume that is at most reallocated when inserting an i-square. Then we get the recurrence $x_i = v_i + \sum_{j=i+1}^{s} 3 \cdot x_j$ with $x_s = v_s = 0$. This resolves to $x_i = 3/4 \cdot 4^{-i} \cdot (s - i)$.

v_i cannot get arbitrarily large, as the remaining capacity must suffice to insert an i-square. Therefore, if all the possible i-pixels contain a volume of 4^{-s} (if some contained more, we would choose those and avoid the worst case), we can bound s by $4^i \cdot 4^{-s} \geq 4^{-i} \Leftrightarrow s \leq 2i$, which leads to $c_{\text{total,max}} \leq \frac{3}{4} \cdot 4^{-i} \cdot i$.

With $|Q| = 4^{-i}$ and $i < s < h(T)$ we get $c_{\text{total,max}} \in O(|Q| \cdot h(T))$.

Corollary 11. *Inserting a square into a quadtree configuration has a total volume cost of no more than $3/16 = 0.1875$.*

Proof. Looking at Theorem 10 it is easy to see that the worst case is attained for $i = 1$: $c_{\text{total}} = 3/4 \cdot 4^{-1} \cdot 1 = 3/16 = 0.1875$.

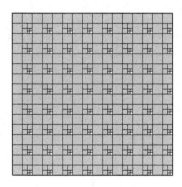

Fig. 2. The worst-case construction for volume cost for $s = 6$ and $i = 3$. Every 3-pixel contains three 4-, 5-, and 6-squares with only one remaining empty 6-pixel.

Theorem 12. *For every $i \in \mathbb{N}_0$ there are quadtree configurations T for which the insertion of an i-square Q causes a total volume cost of*

$$c_{\text{total,max}} \geq \frac{3}{4} \cdot 4^{-i} \cdot \min\{(s - i), i\} \in \Omega(|Q| \cdot h(T))$$

when the smallest previously inserted square is an s-square.

Proof. The worst case is attained for a quadtree configuration in which every i-pixel contains as many large squares as possible, while keeping the capacity of the configuration at 4^{-i}. This is achieved by a quadtree configuration containing three k-squares for every $i < k \leq 2i = s$. See Fig. 2 for an example with $i = 3$.

As a corollary we get an upper bound for the (relative) volume cost and a construction matching the bound: $c_{\text{vol,max}} \leq \frac{3}{4} \cdot \min\{(s-i), i\} \in \Theta(h(T))$.

The same methods we used to derive worst case bounds for volume cost can also be used to establish bounds for movement cost, which results in $c_{\text{move,max}} \leq 4^{\min\{s-i,i\}} - 1 \in O(4^{h(T)/2})$. A matching construction is the same as the one in the proof of Theorem 12.

5   Online Packing and Reallocation

We can avoid the worst cases presented in the previous section when we do not have to work with a given configuration and can handle all requests starting from the empty unit square.

5.1   First-Fit Packing

We present an algorithm that fulfills any valid, aligned sequence of requests and does not cause any reallocations on insertions. We call it *First Fit* in imitation of the well-known technique employed in one-dimensional allocation problems.

First Fit assigns items to be packed to the next available position in a certain order. For our 2D variant we use the z-order curve [21] to provide the order. We denote the position of a pixel p in z-order by $z(p)$, i.e., $z(p) < z(q)$ if and only if p comes before q in z-order.

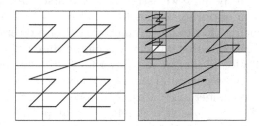

Fig. 3. The z-order for layer 2 pixels (left); a First Fit allocation and the z-order of the occupied pixels – which is not necessarily the insertion order (right).

First Fit proceeds as follows: A request to insert an i-square Q is handled by assigning Q to the first empty i-pixel in z-order; see Fig. 3. Deletions are more complicated. After unassigning a deleted square Q from a pixel p the following procedure handles reallocations (an example deletion can be seen in Fig. 4):

1: $S \leftarrow \{p'\}$, where p' is the maximally empty pixel containing p

2: **while** $S \neq \varnothing$ **do**
3:     Let a be the element of S that is first in z-order.
4:     $S \leftarrow S \setminus \{a\}$
5:     Let b be the last occupied pixel in z-order.
6:     **while** $z(b) > z(a)$ **do**
7:         **if** the square assigned to b, B, can be packed into a **then**
8:             Assign B to the first suitable descendant of a in z-order.
9:             Unassign B from b.
10:            Let b' be the maximally empty pixel containing b.
11:            $S \leftarrow S \cup \{b'\}$
12:            $S \leftarrow S \setminus \{b'' : b'' \text{ is child of } b'\}$
13:        **end if**
14:        Move the pointer z back in z-order to the next occupied pixel.
15:    **end while**
16: **end while**

Invariant 13. *For every empty i-pixel p in a quadtree configuration T there is no occupied i-pixel q with $z(q) > z(p)$.*

Lemma 14. *Every quadtree configuration T satisfying Invariant 13 is compact.*

Lemma 15. *Given an ℓ-square s and a compact quadtree configuration T, then s can be assigned to an empty ℓ-pixel in T, if and only if $\mathrm{cap}(T) \geq 4^{-l}$.*

Theorem 16. *The strategy presented above is correct. In particular,*

1. *every valid insertion request is fulfilled at zero cost,*
2. *every deletion request is fulfilled,*
3. *after every request Invariant 13 holds.*

Proof. The first part follows from Lemmas 14 and 15 and point 3. Insertions maintain the invariant, because we assign it to the first suitable empty pixel in z-order. Deletions can obviously always be fulfilled. We still need to prove the important part, which is that the invariant holds after a deletion.

We show this by proving that whenever the procedure reaches line 3 and sets a, the invariant holds for all squares in z-order up to a. As we only move squares in negative z-order, the sequence of pixels a refers to is increasing in z-order. Since we have a finite number of squares, the procedure terminates after a finite number of steps when no suitable a is left. At that point the invariant holds throughout the configuration.

Assume we are at step 3 of the procedure and the invariant holds for all squares up to a. None of the squares considered to be moved to a fit anywhere before a in z-order – otherwise the invariant would not hold for pixels before a. Afterwards, no square that has not been moved to a fits into a, because it would have been moved there otherwise. Once we reach line 3 again, and set the new a, say a', consider the pixels between a and a' in z-order. If any square after a' would fit somewhere into a pixel between a and a', then the invariant would not have held before the deletion. Therefore, the invariant holds up to a'.

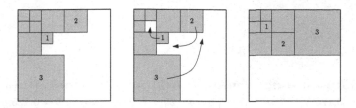

Fig. 4. Deleting a square causes several moves.

6 General Squares and Rectangles

Due to limited space and for clearer exposition, the description in the previous three sections considered aligned squares. We can adapt the technique to general squares and even rectangles at the expense of a constant factor.

Using 4-underallocation, we can pack any sequence of squares with total volume at most one into a 2×2 square, rounding the size of every square to the next power of two. An example is shown in Fig. 5. There, the solid gray areas are the packed squares and the shaded areas are space lost due to rounding. Note that even the best known result for merely packing squares – without considering deletions and reallocations – requires $5/2$-underallocation [10].

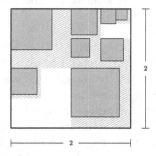

Fig. 5. Example of a dynamically generated quadtree layout.

Rectangles of bounded aspect ratio k are dealt with in the same way. Also accounting for intermodule communication, every rectangle is padded to the size of the next largest aligned square and assigned to the node of a quadtree, at a cost not exceeding a factor of $4k$ compared to the one we established for the worst case. As described in the following section, simulations show that the practical performance is even better.

7 Experimental Results

We carried out a number of experiments to evaluate the practical performance of our approach. For each test, we generated a random sequence of 1000 requests

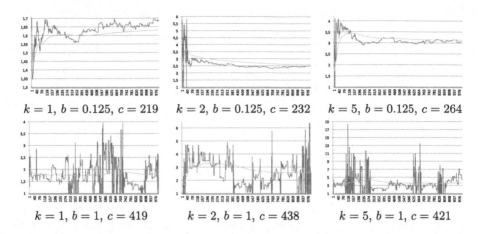

$k = 1$, $b = 0.125$, $c = 219$ $k = 2$, $b = 0.125$, $c = 232$ $k = 5$, $b = 0.125$, $c = 264$

$k = 1$, $b = 1$, $c = 419$ $k = 2$, $b = 1$, $c = 438$ $k = 5$, $b = 1$, $c = 421$

Fig. 6. Experimental evaluation of the First-Fit approach for different values of k and upper bounds of $b = 0.125$ and $b = 1$ for the side length of the considered squares: Each diagram illustrates the results of an experiment of 1000 requests that are randomly chosen as INSERT($\cdot$) (probability 0.7) or DELETE($\cdot$) (probability 0.3). We apply a larger probability for INSERT($\cdot$) to avoid the situation that repeatedly just a few rectangles are inserted and deleted. The red graph shows the total current underallocation after each request. The green graph shows the average of the total underallocation in the range between the first and the current request. We denote the number of collisions, i.e., the situations in that an INSERT($\cdot$) cannot be processed, by c (Color figure online).

that were chosen as INSERT($\cdot$) (probability 0.7) or DELETE($\cdot$) (probability 0.3). We apply a larger probability for INSERT($\cdot$) to avoid the (relatively simple) situation that repeatedly just a few rectangles are inserted and deleted, and in order to observe the effects of increasing congestion. The individual modules were generated by considering an upper bound $b \in [0, 1]$ for the side lengths of the considered squares. For $b = 0.125$, the value of the current underallocation seems to be stable except for the range of the first 50–150 requests. For $b = 1$, the current underallocation may be unstable, which could be caused by the following simple observation: A larger b allows larger rectangles that induce $4k$-underallocations.

Our experiments show that in practice, our approach achieves a much better underallocation than the theoretical worst-case bound of $1/4k$, see Fig. 6. Taking into account that a purely one-dimensional approach cannot provide an upper bound on the achievable underallocation, this indicates that our approach should be practically useful.

8   Conclusions

We have presented a data structure for exploiting the full dimensionality of dynamic geometric storage and reallocation tasks, such as online maintenance of the module layout for an FPGA. These first results indicate that our approach is suitable for making progress over purely one-dimensional approaches. There are several possible refinements and extensions, including a more sophisticated way of handling rectangles inside of square pieces of the subdivision, explicit self-refining communication infrastructures, handling heterogeneous chip areas, and advanced algorithmic methods. These will be addressed in future work.

References

1. Becker, T., Luk, W., Cheung, P.Y.: Enhancing relocatability of partial bitstreams for run-time reconfiguration. In: Proceedings of the 15th Annual Symposium on Field-Programmable Custom Computing Machines, pp. 35–44 (2007)
2. Bender, M.A., Demaine, E.D., Farach-Colton, M.: Cache-oblivious B-trees. SIAM J. Comput. **35**, 341–358 (2005)
3. Bender, M.A., Farach-Colton, M., Fekete, S.P., Fineman, J.T., Gilbert, S.: Cost-oblivious storage reallocation. In: Proceedings of the 33rd ACM SIGMOD-SIGACT-SIGART Symposium on Principles of Database Systems, PODS 2014, pp. 278–288. ACM (2014)
4. Bender, M.A., Farach-Colton, M., Fekete, S.P., Fineman, J.T., Gilbert, S.: Reallocation problems in scheduling. Algorithmica **73**(2), 389–409 (2014)
5. Bender, M.A., Fekete, S.P., Kamphans, T., Schweer, N.: Maintaining arrays of contiguous objects. In: Kutyłowski, M., Charatonik, W., Gębala, M. (eds.) FCT 2009. LNCS, vol. 5699, pp. 14–25. Springer, Heidelberg (2009)
6. Bender, M.A., Fineman, J.T., Gilbert, S., Kuszmaul, B.C.: Concurrent cache-oblivious B-trees. In: Proceedings of the 17th Annual ACM Symposium on Parallelism in Algorithms and Architectures, pp. 228–237 (2005)
7. Bender, M.A., Hu, H.: An adaptive packed-memory array. ACM Trans. Database Syst. **32**(4), 26:1–26:43 (2007)
8. Bendersky, A., Petrank, E.: Space overhead bounds for dynamic memory management with partial compaction. ACM Trans. Program. Lang. Syst. **34**(3), 13:1–13:43 (2012)
9. Bromley, G.: Memory fragmentation in buddy methods for dynamic storage allocation. Acta Informatica **14**, 107–117 (1980)
10. Brubach, B.: Improved bound for online square-into-square packing. In: Bampis, E., Svensson, O. (eds.) WAOA 2014. LNCS, vol. 8952, pp. 47–58. Springer, Heidelberg (2015)
11. Cohen, N., Petrank, E.: Limitations of partial compaction: towards practical bounds. In: Proceedings of the 34th ACM SIGPLAN Conference on Programming Language Design and Implementation, PLDI 2013, New York, NY, USA, pp. 309–320. ACM (2013)
12. Compton, K., Li, Z., Cooley, J., Knol, S., Hauck, S.: Configuration relocation and defragmentation for run-time reconfigurable systems. IEEE Trans. VLSI **10**, 209–220 (2002)
13. Fekete, S.P., Kamphans, T., Schweer, N., Tessars, C., van der Veen, J., Angermeier, J., Koch, D., Teich, J.: Dynamic defragmentation of reconfigurable devices. ACM Trans. Reconfigurable Technol. Syst. (TRETS) **5**(8), 8:1–8:20 (2012)
14. Gericota, M.G., Alves, G.R., Silva, M.L., Ferreira, J.M.: Run-time defragmentation for dynamically reconfigurable hardware. In: Lysaght, P., Rosenstiel, W. (eds.) New Algorithms, Architectures and Applications for Reconfigurable Computing, pp. 117–129. Springer, New York (2005)

318   S.P. Fekete et al.

15. Hinds, J.A.: An algorithm for locating adjacent storage blocks in the buddy system. Commun. ACM **18**, 221–222 (1975)
16. Hirschberg, D.S.: A class of dynamic memory allocation algorithms. Commun. ACM **16**, 615–618 (1973)
17. Knowlton, K.C.: A fast storage allocator. Commun. ACM **8**, 623–625 (1965)
18. Koch, D., Ahmadinia, A., Bobda, C., Kalte, H.: FPGA architecture extensions for preemptive multitasking and hardware defragmentation. In: Proceedings of the IEEE International Conference Field-Programmable Technology, Brisbane, Australia, pp. 433–436 (2004)
19. Koester, M., Kalte, H., Porrmann, M., Ruckert, U.: Defragmentation algorithms for partially reconfigurable hardware. In: Reis, R., Osseiran, A., Pfleiderer, H.-J. (eds.) Vlsi-Soc: From Systems To Silicon. IFIP International Federation for Information Proc, vol. 240, p. 41. Springer, Boston (2007)
20. Kuon, I., Rose, J.: Measuring the gap between FPGAs and ASICs. IEEE Trans. CAD Integr. Circ. Syst. **26**, 203–215 (2007)
21. Morton, G.: A computer oriented geodetic data base and a new technique in file-sequencing.Technical report, IBM Ltd., Ottawa, Ontario, March 1966
22. Shen, K.K., Peterson, J.L.: A weighted buddy method for dynamic storage allocation. Commun. ACM **17**, 558–562 (1974)

Organic Computing Systems

Runtime Clustering of Similarly Behaving Agents in Open Organic Computing Systems

Jan Kantert[1]([✉]), Richard Scharrer[1], Sven Tomforde[2], Sarah Edenhofer[2], and Christian Müller-Schloer[1]

[1] Institute of Systems Engineering,
Leibniz University of Hannover, Hannover, Germany
{kantert,scharrer,cms}@sra.uni-hannover.de
[2] Organic Computing Group, University of Augsburg, Augsburg, Germany
{sven.tomforde,sarah.edenhofer}@informatik.uni-augsburg.de

Abstract. Organic Computing systems are increasingly open for subsystems (or agents) to join and leave. Thereby, we can observe classes of similarly behaving agents, including those that try to exploit or even damage the system. In this paper, we describe a novel concept to cluster agent groups at runtime and to estimate their contribution to the system. The goal is to distinguish between good, suspicious and malicious agent groups to allow for counter measures. We demonstrate the potential benefit of our approach within simulations of a Desktop Grid Computing system that resembles typical Organic Computing characteristics such as self-organisation, adaptive behaviour of heterogeneous agents, and openness.

1 Introduction

Organic Computing (OC) is based on the insight that we are increasingly surrounded by large collections of autonomous systems, which are equipped with sensors and actuators. They are aware of their environment, communicate freely, and organise themselves in order to perform the actions and services that seem to be required (Muehl et al. 2007; Müller-Schloer 2004). Consequently, OC aims at designing technical systems which are equipped with sensors (to perceive their environment) and actuators (to manipulate it). Such an *organic* system adapts autonomously and dynamically to the current conditions of the perceived environment (Tomforde and Müller-Schloer 2014). This adaptation process has impact on the system's performance, which is continuously optimised by the organic system itself. OC systems are characterised by self-X properties (similar as, e.g., formulated for the Autonomic Computing initiative in (Kephart and Chess 2003)).

Recently, the focus of the OC initiative shifted towards handling complexity issues originating in the interaction processes of potentially large agent groups (Tomforde et al. 2014). In this context, a system-wide control following traditional hierarchically organised control structures is not feasible any more.

© Springer International Publishing Switzerland 2016
F. Hannig et al. (Eds.): ARCS 2016, LNCS 9637, pp. 321–333, 2016.
DOI: 10.1007/978-3-319-30695-7_24

Therefore, we introduced a concept for normative control that steers the behaviour of autonomous participants in terms of sanctions and incentives (Kantert et al. 2015), mostly working on the basis of externally observing trust and interaction relationships among distributed agents. In order to refine this approach, this paper develops a concept to cluster agents into groups that behave similarly. The approach works at runtime and maintains a robust agent-to-groups-mapping to allow for an efficient status estimation. With such an approach, we are able to analyse the robustness level and system structure from the outside and without the need of insights into the internal agents' logic (i.e., maintaining full autonomy according to (Schmeck et al. 2010)).

The remainder of this paper is organised as follows: Sect. 2 describes the Trusted Desktop Computing Grid as application scenario for this work. Afterwards, Sect. 3 defines the challenge investigated in this paper in more detail. This is accompanied by presenting the approach to solve the issue in Sect. 4. Section 5 analyses and evaluates the concept and demonstrates the benefit for the application scenario. Finally, Sect. 6 summarises the paper and gives an outlook to future work.

2   Application Scenario

As a possible application scenario, we investigate open grid computing systems which can host numerous distributable workloads, e.g., distributed rendering of films. The system is considered open since there is no central controlling entity and all communication is performed peer-to-peer. Worker nodes belong to different administrative domains. Thus, good behaviour cannot be assumed. Nodes participate voluntarily to submit work into the system and, thereby, increase the speedup of their jobs. However, the nodes also have to compute work units for other submitters (Bernard et al. 2010).

2.1   Agent Goal

To analyse such systems, we model nodes as agents and run a multi-agent system in simulation. Every agent works for a user and periodically receives a job, which contains multiple parallelisable work units. It aims to accomplish all work units as fast as possible by requesting other agents to work for it. Since we consider an open system, agents behave autonomously, and can join or leave at any time.

The system performance is measured by the speedup σ. In Eq. (1), t_{self} is the time an agent would require computing a job containing multiple work units without any cooperation. $t_{\text{distributed}}$ represents the time to compute all work units of one job with cooperation of other workers including all communication times. As a consequence, the speedup can only be determined after the results of the last work unit have been returned.

$$\sigma := \frac{t_{\text{self}}}{t_{\text{distributed}}} \tag{1}$$

If no cooperation partners can be found, agents need to compute their own work units and achieve a speedup value of at most one (i.e., no speedup at all).

Especially when a worker fails to finish a job or decides to cancel it, the speedup value will suffer and be less than one. Communication overhead also decreases the speedup. However, we assume that jobs require significantly more computing time than communication time and this overhead to be negligible. In general, agents behave selfishly and only cooperate if they can expect an advantage. They have to decide which agent they assign tasks to and for which agents they perform jobs themselves. We do not control the agent implementation, so they might behave uncooperatively or even maliciously.

2.2   Worker and Submitter Component

Each agent consists of a worker and a submitter component. The submitter component is responsible for distributing work units. When an agent receives a job containing multiple work units, it creates a list of trusted workers. It then requests workers from this list to cooperate and compute work units, until either no more work units or no more workers are left. If all workers were asked, but unprocessed work units remain, the agent computes them on its own.

The worker component decides whether an agent wants to work for a certain submitter. When the agent receives an offer, it computes its rewards for accepting or rejecting the job. There are different strategies based on reputation, workload, and environment. If the reward of accepting the job prevails, the agent accepts the job. It may cancel the job later on, but typically it computes the job and returns the results to the submitter (Klejnowski 2014).

2.3   Open Systems and Benevolence

In contrast to classical grid computing systems, we do not assume the benevolence of the agents (Wang and Vassileva 2004). In such an open system, we cannot control the implementation of agents and, therefore, the system is vulnerable to different kinds of attacks. For instance, a *Freerider* (see Sect. 2.5) could simply refuse to work for other agents and gain an advantage at the expense of cooperative agents. Another attacker might just pretend to work and return wrong results. Also, combinations of both or alternating behaviour are possible. Furthermore, attacker can collude to exploit the system.

2.4   Trust and Norms

To overcome such problems of an open system where no particular behaviour can be assumed, we introduce a trust metric. Agents receive ratings for all their actions from their particular interaction partners. This allows others to estimate the future behaviour of a certain agent based on its previous actions. To perform this reasoning, a series of ratings for a certain agent can be accumulated to a single reputation value using the trust metric.

Autonomous agents need to become aware of the expected behaviour in the system. Therefore, we influence the desired actions by norms. These norms are valid for an *Action* in a certain *Context* and, thereby, guide the agents. To enforce the behaviour, they impose a *Sanction* if violated, or offer an *Incentive* if fulfilled.

In this scenario, good trust ratings are used as an *Incentive* and, to the contrary, bad trust ratings impose a *Sanction*. Based on the norms, agents receive a good rating if they work for other agents and a bad rating if they reject or cancel work requests. As a result, the society isolates malevolent agents and maintains a good system utility in most cases. Generally, agents with higher reputation values have a higher chance to get their work units computed. We call this system a Trusted Desktop Grid (Klejnowski 2014).

Since agents are considered as black boxes, they cannot be controlled directly from the outside. Each agent is autonomous and selfish. However, we want to influence the system to optimise itself regarding performance and robustness. Therefore, we introduce norms to change the incentives and sanctions for all agents.

2.5   Agent Types

We consider the following agent types in our system:

- *Adaptive Agents* - These agents behave cooperatively. They perform tasks for other agents who earned good reputation in the system. The reputation value generally depends on the estimated current system load and how much the input queue of the agent is filled up.
- *Freeriders* - Such agents do not work for other agents and reject all work requests. However, they ask other agents to accomplish tasks for them. This increases the overall system load and decreases the utility for well-behaving agents.
- *Egoists* - These agents only pretend to work for other agents and only return correct results with a certain probability. They accept all work requests but return faked results to other agents, blocking other agents as they have to validate the results. On the other hand, if results are not validated, this may lead to wrong results. However, *Egoists* lower the utility of the system.
- *Cunning Agents* - These agents behave well in the beginning, but may change their behaviour later. Periodically, randomly, or under certain conditions, they behave like *Freeriders* or *Egoists*. Such behaviour is hard to detect and may lower the overall system utility.
- *Altruistic Agents* - Such agents will accept every job. In general, this behaviour is not malicious and increases the system performance. However, it hinders isolation of bad-behaving agents and impacts the system goals.

3   Problem Statement

In previous work (Kantert et al. 2014), we introduced a higher level Norm Manager (NM) which monitors the system and changes norms if attacks are detected

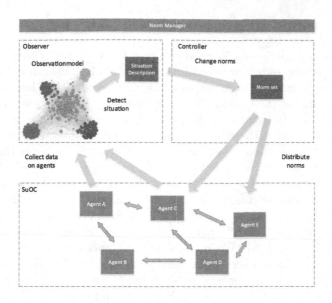

Fig. 1. An open distributed system (such as the TDG) is monitored and controlled by a higher-level Norm Manager. At the bottom, a System under Observation and Control (SuOC) consists of multiple agents which interact and perform actions. The observer on the top left monitors the interactions in the SuOC and creates a situation description. On the top right, the controller uses this description and changes norms which are passed to the SuOC.

(see Fig. 1). It consists of an observer component and a controller component. This work focuses on the observer component. We did initial work on the controller in Kantert et al. (2015).

In the observer we monitor the system using the reputation system and other externally accessible interactions between the agents. We build a *trust graph* which illustrates the resulting trust relationships, i.e., which agent trusts which other agent to which degree? In a second step, we analyse how an appropriate estimation of the current system conditions can be derived from the graphs. Therefore, we introduce a set of different graph-based metrics that are applied (Prestige, Actor Centrality, Degree Centrality, Clustering Coefficient, Authorities and Hubs; see Wasserman (1994).

Based on this metrics we want to cluster agents into groups of similar characteristics. For instance, we want to distinguish between benevolent and malicious agents in the first place. Furthermore, a detailed classification is desired that provides a basis for a sophisticated assessment of current conditions. The resulting information that is derived from this process then serves as input for the controller part.

4   Previous and Related Work

Our application scenario is a Trusted Desktop Grid system. These systems are used to share resources between multiple administrative authorities. The Share-Grid Project is an example for a peer-to-peer-based system (Anglano et al. 2008). A second approach is the Organic Grid, which is peer-to-peer-based with decentralised scheduling (Chakravarti et al. 2004). Compared to our system, these approaches assume that there are no malicious parties involved and each node behaves well. A similar implementation with a central tracker is the Berkeley Open Infrastructure for Network Computing project (BOINC) (Anderson and Fedak 2006). All those systems solve a distributed resource allocation problem. Since work units can be computed faster when agents cooperate, such systems reward and, thus, maximise cooperation. Additionally, a high fairness value ensures equal resource distribution (cf. Jain et al. 1996; Demers et al. 1989; Bennett and Zhang 1996). We model our grid nodes as agents. Agents follow a local goal which differs from the global system goal (Rosenschein and Zlotkin 1994). We consider agents as black boxes which means that we cannot observe their internal state. Thus, their actions and behaviour cannot be predicted (Hewitt 1991). Our Trusted Desktop Grid supports Bag-of-Tasks applications (Anglano et al. 2006). A classification of Desktop Grid Systems can be found in Choi et al. (2007). A taxonomy can be found in Choi et al. (2008). It is emphasised there that there has to be some mechanism to detect failures and malicious behaviour in large-scale systems. Nodes cannot be expected to act unselfishly and well-behaving. In contrast to other state-of-the-art works, we do not assume the benevolence of the agents (Wang and Vassileva 2004). To cope with this information uncertainty, we introduced a trust metric. A general overview about trust in Multi-Agent Systems can be found in Castelfranchi and Falcone (2010). A similar implementation of trust in a Desktop Grid System was evaluated in Domingues et al. (2007).

This work is part of wider research in the area of norms in multi-agent systems. However, we focus more on improving system performance by using norms than researching the characteristics of norms (Singh, 1999). Our scenario is similar to management of common pool resources. According to game theory, this leads to a "tragedy of the commons" (Hardin, 1968). However, Ostrom (1990) observed cases where this did not happen. She presented eight design principles for successful self-management of decentralised institutions. Pitt et al. (2011) adapted these to Normative Multi-Agent Systems (NMAS). NMAS are used in multiple fields: e.g. Governatori and Rotolo (2008) focuses on so-called policy-based intentions in the domain of business process design. Agents plan consecutive actions based on obligations, intentions, beliefs, and desires. Based on DL, social agents reason about norms and intentions.

To detect the system state, we use social network analysis. All algorithms used for this purpose can be found in Wasserman (1994). A survey of different analysed social networks was done by Newman (2003). In our implementation, we use *JGraphT* to run algorithms on graphs. A similar library is *JUNG* (O'Madadhain et al. 2005). To cluster similar behaving agents, we use clustering algorithms. An overview of traditional clustering algorithms can be found in Xu and Wunsch (2005).

5 Approach

To identify groups of similar behaving agents, we apply our metrics to the *trust graph* and evaluate them for every node (representing an agent) in the graph. Afterwards, we select a clustering algorithm which can find similar behaving agents (similar according to our metric). We capture this behaviour using our previously defined metrics and omit all connections in the graph. Therefore, every agent forms a data point in an n-dimensional space where n is the number of metrics considered. This allows us to use algorithms known from traditional clustering.

Requirements. To cluster similar-behaving agents, we need an algorithm which fulfils the following requirements:

- *Multi-dimensional Input*: We characterise every agent by multiple metrics, and the algorithm should be able to take all of them into account. Therefore, it has to cluster an n-dimensional vector for every agent.
- *Semi-deterministic/Order-invariant*: The clustering is performed periodically while the underlying graph slightly changes. However, the resulting groups should not change fundamentally.
- *Dynamic Group Count*: Typically, we do not know the number of different agent groups in advance. Therefore, we require an algorithm which can find a dynamic amount of groups.
- *Robust Against Outliers/Noise*: Single agents may behave differently from the rest of a group and the algorithm has to be robust against those outliers. Outliers should form a separate individual group or be ignored altogether.

Algorithm Selection. To find a suitable algorithm, we started with a survey (Xu and Wunsch 2005) and selected algorithms with different strategies:

- *Partitioning*: Those algorithms partition data points into groups while minimising the distances between all points in the group. Finding an optimal solution is NP-hard. However, heuristics exist which converge in polynomial time. We investigated Lloyd's algorithm (Lloyd 1982) (better known as k-means), since it is very well researched. Unfortunately, it does not meet our requirements (not semi-deterministic and cannot handle dynamic group count) and generated very bad results for our scenario. Therefore, we will no longer consider it in this work.
- *Density-based*: To handle noise effectively, those algorithms form groups based on the density of points in a certain area. The most popular algorithm in this area is *Density-Based Spatial Clustering of Applications with Noise* (DBSCAN) (Ester et al. 1996) which meets all requirements. However, we chose *DENsity-based CLUstEring* (DENCLUE) because it handles noise points more deterministically (Hinneburg and Gabriel 2007).

– *Hierarchical*: Those algorithms seek to build a hierarchy of groups which can be accomplished in two ways: Either top-down by starting with one group and splitting it up, or, alternatively, bottom-up by starting with one group per point and merging groups. The worst-case runtime of both approaches is rather high. However, fast algorithms exist which show a runtime better than quadratic. We choose *Balanced Iterative Reducing and Clustering using Hierarchies* (BIRCH) which meets all our requirements (Zhang et al. 1996). It is especially designed to handle noise/outliers effectively (i.e., it will not merge them into the nearest group if they are distant) and outperforms DBSCAN if comparing the runtime according to the *2006 ACM SIGMOD Test of Time Award*.

– *Grid-based*: This group of algorithms uses a multi-resolution grid to cluster points. We chose *WaveCluster* (Sheikholeslami et al. 2000) which is based on wavelet transformations and meets our requirements.

Based on our requirements and this discussion, we select BIRCH, DENCLUE and WaveCluster for further analysis. All three do not require any prior knowledge about the number of clusters or their size and should be robust against changes.

5.1   Rating of Results

To rate the results of the clustering process, we use metrics which are similar to Precision and Recall (Olson and Delen (2008) used in information retrieval systems. Additionally, we want to condense them to only one value. In an ideal clustering, every group (attackers, cooperating agents, etc.) has its own cluster which contains only agents of that group. First, we measure the share $ClusterShare_{t,i}$ of agents from group t in cluster i:

$$\text{ClusterShare}_{t,i} := \frac{|\{a : a \in \text{Cluster}_i \wedge a \in \text{Group}_t\}|}{|\text{Cluster}_i|}$$

Similarly, we calculate the share of the group t for cluster i in $\text{GroupShare}_{t,i}$:

$$\text{GroupShare}_{t,i} := \frac{|\{a : a \in \text{Group}_t \wedge a \in \text{Cluster}_i\}|}{|\text{Group}_t|}$$

To create a total measure, we weight the score of each group based on the amount of clusters a group is participating in using w_t:

$$w_t := \frac{|\text{Group}_t| - |\{i : a \in \text{Cluster}_i \wedge a \in \text{Group}_t\}|}{|\text{Group}_t|}$$

Based on that, we create the TotalShare_t of every group t:

$$\text{TotalShare}_t = \sum_{i=1}^{n} \text{ClusterShare}_{t,i} \cdot \text{GroupShare}_{t,i} \cdot w_t$$

To summarise the TotalShare metric: A value of one means that all agents of one group are in one cluster. If agents of a group are in multiple clusters, we calculate the GroupShare for every cluster and weight the GroupShare with the ClusterShare. At the end, we multiply a linear damping factor w to devalue solutions with too many clusters (e.g., 10 agents clustered into 10 clusters with 100 % GroupShare each is not a particularly good solution).

6 Evaluation

To evaluate the selected algorithms, we perform a simulation running 80,000 ticks and repeat it 50 times for each algorithm. Afterwards, we calculate the TotalShare for every group in the experiment.

6.1 Algorithm Selection

To find the best algorithm from our previous select, we perform 50 experiments with 100 agents for every algorithm and average the values. In the worst case, all agent group from Sect. 2.5 participate in the system and we need to identify five distinguished clusters.

Table 1. Average TotalShare for all algorithms and agent groups. Every experiment contains 20 Adaptive Agents, 20 Altruistic Agents, 20 Egoistic Agents, 20 Freeriders, and 20 Cunning Agents. Values range from 0 to 1 and higher is better.

Type	BIRCH	DENCLUE	WaveCluster
Adaptive	**51.53 %**	33.28 %	28.66 %
Altruistic	**94.53 %**	60.30 %	61.39 %
Egoistic	40.05 %	**45.70 %**	39.32 %
Freerider	40.65 %	**44.36 %**	41.59 %
Cunning	**46.65 %**	38.22 %	22.58 %

In Table 1, we show the average TotalShare for all groups per algorithm. BIRCH is best for Adaptive Agents, Altruistic Agents and Cunning Agents. For Egoistic Agents and Freerider the three algorithms perform similarly. We conducted additional experiments with less agent groups and BIRCH always performs best.

A TotalShare of 50 % per group may not be sufficient to find all groups. However, if we look at combined results to solve our initial problem of separating well-behaving and bad-behaving agents, the results are better: The group of Egoistic Agents and Freerider is larger than 80 %. Altruistic Agents can be singled out with more than 85 % share. Unfortunately, Cunning Agents behave like Adaptive Agents about half of the time. Therefore, this method cannot reliably separate them all the time and they form a combined group with a share or more than 90 %.

6.2   Independence from System Size

To verify that our approach works independent from the system size, we performed larger experiments with 500, 1,000 and 1,500 agents, each with 20 % of all agent types/groups.

Table 2. Average TotalShare for BIRCH with different system sizes. All values are stable. Values range from 0 to 1 and higher is better.

Type	500	1000	1500
Adaptive	52.44 %	51.13 %	55.40 %
Altruistic	92.70 %	94.98 %	88.20 %
Egoistic	55.33 %	40.11 %	54.38 %
Freerider	54.10 %	40.65 %	58.79 %
Cunning	39.50 %	47.07 %	38.45 %

In Table 2, we show the average TotalShare for BIRCH with increasing system size. The values are stable for all groups within the margin of error. Since BIRCH also has a linear complexity, the clustering should scale even for very large system.

7   Conclusion

Organic Computing systems typically consist of a variety of interacting agents. Due to the open character, uncertain or even malicious agents are free to join - which has large impact on the overall system's performance. This openness is combined with the missing possibilities to intervene from the outside – agents are autonomous and act selfishly. Consequently, this work investigates possibilities to monitor the system status from the outside by observing interaction and trust relationships. We propose a method to cluster agents at runtime according to their behaviour. As a result, we establish groups of similarly behaving agents. Based on this information, negative elements can be identified easily and isolated from the core system.

We use the Trusted Desktop Grid as example application for the considered system class. Based on simulations, we analysed the success of the clustering strategy. We observed that especially the BIRCH algorithm resulted in stable clusters of the considered stereo-type agent classes. Therefore, we found that this technique is the most promising candidate for consideration in OC systems.

Future work deals with questions of how this external and hierarchically organised concept can be augmented by decentralised solutions. For instance, a fully self-organised detection of malicious agents and their colluding partners can be combined with the presented technique to derive even faster and more robust clustering information.

Acknowledgements. This research is funded by the research unit "OC-Trust" (FOR 1085) of the German Research Foundation (DFG).

References

Anderson, D.P., Fedak, G.: The computational and storage potential of volunteer computing. In: Proceedings of CCGRID 2006, pp. 73–80. IEEE, Singapore (2006)

Anglano, C., Brevik, J., Canonico, M., Nurmi, D., Wolski, R.: Fault-aware scheduling for bag-of-tasks applications on desktop grids. In: Proceedings of GRID 2006, pp. 56–63. IEEE, Singapore (2006)

Anglano, C., Canonico, M., Guazzone, M., Botta, M., Rabellino, S., Arena, S., Girardi, G.: Peer-to-peer desktop grids in the real world: the ShareGrid project. In: Proceedings of CCGrid 2008, pp. 609–614 (2008)

Bennett, J.C., Zhang, H.: WF2Q: worst-case fair weighted fair queueing. In: INFOCOM 1996. Proceedings of Fifteenth Annual Joint Conference of the IEEE Computer Societies. Networking the Next Generation, vol. 1, pp. 120–128. IEEE, San Francisco, March 1996

Bernard, Y., Klejnowski, L., Hähner, J., Müller-Schloer, C.: Towards trust in desktop grid systems. In: Proceedings of CCGrid 2010, pp. 637–642 (2010)

Castelfranchi, C., Falcone, R.: Trust Theory: A Socio-Cognitive and Computational Model, vol. 18. John Wiley & Sons, Chichester (2010)

Chakravarti, A.J., Baumgartner, G., Lauria, M.: Application-specific scheduling for the organic grid. In: Proceedings of GRID 2004 Workshops, pp. 146–155. IEEE, Washington, DC (2004)

Choi, S., Buyya, R., Kim, H., Byun, E.: A taxonomy of desktop grids and its mapping to state of the art systems. Technical report, Grid Computing and Distributed System Integration, The University of Melbourne (2008)

Choi, S., Kim, H., Byun, E., Baik, M., Kim, S., Park, C., Hwang, C.: Characterizing and classifying desktop grid. In: Proceedings of CCGRID 2007, pp. 743–748. IEEE, Rio de Janeiro (2007)

Demers, A., Keshav, S., Shenker, S.: Analysis and simulation of a fair queueing algorithm. In: Symposium Proceedings on Communications Architectures and Protocols, pp. 1–12. SIGCOMM 1989. ACM, New York (1989)

Domingues, P., Sousa, B., Moura Silva, L.: Sabotage-tolerance and trustmanagement in desktop grid computing. Future Gener. Comput. Syst. 23(7), 904–912 (2007)

Ester, M., Kriegel, H.P., Sander, J., Xu, X.: A density-based algorithm for discovering clusters in large spatial databases with noise. In: Proceedings of the Second International Conference on Knowledge Discovery and Data Mining, vol. 96, pp. 226–231. The AAAI Press, Menlo Park (1996)

Governatori, G., Rotolo, A.: BIO logical agents: norms, beliefs, intentions in defeasible logic. Auton. Agents Multi-agent Syst. 17(1), 36–69 (2008)

Hardin, G.: The tragedy of the commons. Science 162(3859), 1243–1248 (1968)

Hewitt, C.: Open information systems semantics for distributed artificial intelligence. Artif. intell. 47(1), 79–106 (1991)

Hinneburg, Alexander, Gabriel, Hans-Henning: DENCLUE 2.0: fast clustering based on kernel density estimation. In: Berthold, Michael, Shawe-Taylor, John, Lavrač, Nada (eds.) IDA 2007. LNCS, vol. 4723, pp. 70–80. Springer, Heidelberg (2007)

Jain, R., Babic, G., Nagendra, B., Lam, C.C.: Fairness, call establishment latency and other performance metrics. ATM-Forum 96(1173), 1–6 (1996)

Kantert, J., Edenhofer, S., Tomforde, S., Hähner, J., Müller-Schloer, C.: Defending autonomous agents against attacks in multi-agent systems using norms. In: Proceedings of the 7th International Conference on Agents and Artificial Intelligence, pp. 149–156. INSTICC, SciTePress, Lisbon (2015)

Kantert, J., Scharf, H., Edenhofer, S., Tomforde, S., Hähner, J., Müller-Schloer, C.: A graph analysis approach to detect attacks in multi-agent-systems at runtime. In: 2014 IEEE Eighth International Conference on Self-Adaptive and Self-Organizing Systems, pp. 80–89. IEEE, London (2014)

Kephart, J.O., Chess, D.M.: The vision of autonomic computing. IEEE Comput. **36**(1), 41–50 (2003)

Klejnowski, L.: Trusted community: a novel multiagent organisation for OpenDistributed systems. Ph.D. thesis, Leibniz Universität Hannover (2014). http://edok01.tib.uni-hannover.de/edoks/e01dh11/668667427.pdf

Lloyd, S.: Least squares quantization in PCM. IEEE Trans. Inf. Theory **28**(2), 129–137 (1982)

Muehl, G., Werner, M., Jaeger, M.A., Herrmann, K., Parzyjegla, H.: On the definitions of self-managing and self-organizing systems. In: Communication in Distributed Systems (KiVS), 2007 ITG-GI Conference, pp. 1–11, February 2007

Müller-Schloer, C.: Organic computing: on the feasibility of controlled emergence. In: CODES and ISSS 2004 Proceedings, pp. 2–5. ACM Press, 8–10 September 2004

Newman, M.E.J.: The structure and function of complex networks. SIAM Rev. **45**(2), 167–256 (2003)

Olson, D.L., Delen, D.: Advanced Data Mining Techniques. Springer, Heidelberg (2008)

O'Madadhain, J., Fisher, D., Smyth, P., White, S., Boey, Y.B.: Analysis and visualization of network data using JUNG. J. Stat. Softw. **10**(2), 1–35 (2005)

Ostrom, E.: Governing the Commons: The Evolution of Institutions for Collective Action. Cambridge University Press, Cambridge (1990)

Pitt, J., Schaumeier, J., Artikis, A.: The axiomatisation of socio-economic principles for self-organising systems. In: 2011 Fifth IEEE International Conference on Self-Adaptive and Self-Organizing Systems (SASO), pp. 138–147. IEEE, Michigan, October 2011

Rosenschein, J.S., Zlotkin, G.: Rules of Encounter: Designing Conventions for Automated Negotiation Among Computers. MIT Press, Cambridge (1994)

Schmeck, H., Müller-Schloer, C., Çakar, E., Mnif, M., Richter, U.: Adaptivity and self-organization in organic computing systems. ACM Trans. Auton. Adapt. Syst. (TAAS) **5**(3), 1–32 (2010)

Sheikholeslami, G., Chatterjee, S., Zhang, A.: Wavecluster: a wavelet-based clustering approach for spatial data in very large databases. VLDB J. **8**(3–4), 289–304 (2000)

Singh, M.P.: An ontology for commitments in multiagent systems. Artif. Intell. Law **7**(1), 97–113 (1999)

Tomforde, S., Müller-Schloer, C.: Incremental design of adaptive systems. J. Ambient Intell. Smart Environ. **6**, 179–198 (2014)

Tomforde, S., Hähner, J., Seebach, H., Reif, W., Sick, B., Wacker, A., Scholtes, I.: Engineering and mastering interwoven systems. In: ARCS 2014–27th International Conference on Architecture of Computing Systems, Workshop Proceedings. Institute of Computer Engineering, University of Luebeck, Luebeck, pp. 1–8, 25–28 February 2014

Wang, Y., Vassileva, J.: Trust-based community formation in peer-to-peer file sharing networks. In: Proceedings on Web Intelligence, pp. 341–348. IEEE, Beijing, September 2004

Wasserman, S.: Social Network Analysis: Methods and Applications, vol. 8. Cambridge University Press, Cambridge (1994)

Xu, R., Wunsch, D.: Survey of clustering algorithms. IEEE Trans. Neural Netw. **16**(3), 645–678 (2005)

Zhang, T., Ramakrishnan, R., Livny, M.: BIRCH: an efficient data clustering method for very large databases. In: ACM SIGMOD Record, vol. 25, pp. 103–114. ACM, Montreal (1996)

Comparison of Dependency Measures for the Detection of Mutual Influences in Organic Computing Systems

Stefan Rudolph[(✉)], Rainer Hihn, Sven Tomforde, and Jörg Hähner

Organic Computing Group, University of Augsburg, 86159 Augsburg, Germany
{stefan.rudolph,sven.tomforde,joerg.haehner}@informatik.uni-augsburg.de

Abstract. Organic Computing (OC) postulates to tackle challenges arising from the increasing complexity in technical systems by means of self-organization and "life-like" properties. Recently, the arising complexity challenges have become even more severe due to the rapidly ongoing interweaving process – meaning that systems are directly and indirectly coupled and influencing each other. In order to be able to deal with such influences, they have to be identified and analyzed in the first place. Therefore, this paper reviews existing techniques to detect mutual influences among distributed entities at runtime. The goal is to compare the applicability of the varying concepts according to their applicability within Organic Computing systems. Therefore, we investigate two abstract (i.e., two simulated robots moving a crosscut saw and carrying a box) and a typical OC (i.e., smart camera network) example for evaluation purposes.

1 Introduction

Organic Computing (OC) [8] aims at handling complexity issues in Information and Communication Technology (ICT) by moving traditional design-time decisions to runtime and into the responsibility of systems themselves. As a result, OC develops distributed solutions that allow for adaptive, self-improving and consequently robust behavior even in the presence of disturbances or unanticipated conditions.

Typically, OC systems consist of a potentially large set of autonomous subsystems (or agents) that interact with each other. On the one hand, these interactions appear in a direct, explicit manner using protocols and well-defined interfaces. On the other hand, the continuous interweaving process of technical systems [19] entails indirect, mostly hidden influences that affect the agent's performance in achieving its goals. Consider two robots that cooperatively process a crosscut saw as example for the first aspect: The robots' behavior is only successful if both robots consider the current behavior of each other (i.e. push or pull) when deciding about their actions. The other aspect (i.e. a hidden, indirect influence) can be observed in smart camera networks [13]: The overall system benefit is higher if e.g. surveillance strategies allow the observation of interesting

© Springer International Publishing Switzerland 2016
F. Hannig et al. (Eds.): ARCS 2016, LNCS 9637, pp. 334–347, 2016.
DOI: 10.1007/978-3-319-30695-7_25

objects from different angles. The goal of current OC research is to detect such indirect influences at runtime and consider them within the control and learning mechanisms to achieve a higher performance [14].

This paper has the goal to analyze which stochastic dependency measures are most suitable for the mutual influence detection in OC systems. Therefore, we chose a set of dependency measures from the state-of-the-art that includes well-established measures that have been utilized over many years and rather new dependency measures that have recently got much attention because of their claim to even find more complex dependencies in a short time. These are evaluated by an empirical comparison when applying the most suitable candidates in simulations of the aforementioned exemplary applications. The remainder of this paper is organized as follows: Sect. 2 describes the considered system model and the approach to identify mutual influences in OC systems. The results are evaluated and analyzed in Sect. 3. Afterwards, Sect. 4 briefly summaries the state-of-the-art concerning detection of mutual influences and dependencies. Finally, Sect. 5 summarizes the paper and gives an outlook to future work.

2 Measuring Mutual Influences in Organic Computing Systems

As briefly scratched in the previous section, this work is about the identification of mutual influences. More precisely, we want to compare different dependency measures for a mutual influence detection algorithm in to order to identify the most powerful measures for this purpose. Therefore, we briefly define what is meant by mutual influence by introducing the system model in Sect. 2.1 which is inspired from standard machine learning notions. Despite the background in machine learning, the methodology is assumed to be applicable to all systems covering the basic system model. Afterwards, we continue this work with the presentation of the mutual influence detection algorithm in Sect. 2.2. The method of the measurement of mutual influences has originally been proposed in [14], therefore, we keep the description rather short in this work. Finally, we introduce the different dependency measures that can be utilized for the mutual influence detection algorithm and are compared in this work in Sect. 2.3.

2.1 System Model

We start with a set of agents $\{A_1, \ldots, A_n\}$, where each agent can assume different configurations. Such a configuration typically consists of different parts. Consider a router as a simple example: The router can take varying configurations into account, such as the processed network protocol or parameter settings (i.e. for time-out intervals, buffer sizes, etc.). We define the whole configuration space of an agent A_i as cartesian product $C_i = c_{i1} \times \cdots \times c_{im}$, where c_{ij} are the parts of the configuration. A further assumption is that the particular configurations of individual agents are non-overlapping, meaning each agent has its own set of configurations, $c_{ij} \neq c_{kl}$ for all defined $i \neq k, j, l$. This does not mean that the configuration parts have to be completely disjoint in structure and values of the contained variables. For instance, two routers might have the possibility to configure the time-out interval, which would lead to the same set of possible configurations in these attributes, but on different devices. Such a relation is explicitly allowed within the model.

Besides the configuration space, we need to consider a further element: the *local performance measurement*. In order to apply the proposed method, each agent has to estimate the success of its decisions at runtime – as a response to actions taken before. This is realized based on a feedback mechanism – with feedback possibly stemming from the environment of the agent (i.e. *direct* feedback) or from manual assignments (i.e. *indirect* feedback). This resembles the classic reinforcement model, where the existence of such a performance measurement (mostly called *reward*) is one of the basic assumptions, cf., e.g., [20].

2.2   Measurement of Mutual Influences

Given the described system model, we continue with the actual methodology for the measurement of mutual influences. The goal is to identify those parts of the configuration of the neighboring agents that have influence on the agent itself. Thereby, we focus on spatially neighbored agents (such as the cameras in the motivating example) – but the methodology is not restricted to this kind of neighborhood (i.e., "virtual neighborhoods" are also possible – for instance, routers in a data communication network). After the identification of influencing configuration parts, they can be addressed by a designer or by a self-adapting system itself.

In general, we are typically not interested in the question if an agent as a whole is influencing (some of) its neighbors, since the benefit of this information is negligible. In contrast, we want to detect specific configuration parameters whose optimal usage strategy is somehow influenced by the current settings of the neighbored agents. The basic idea of the algorithm is to make use of stochastic dependency measures that estimate associations and relations between the configuration parts of an agent and the performance of a second agent. These dependency measures are designed to find correlations between two random variables X and Y. It is possible to use several different dependency measures for this purpose. In previous works, the *Maximal Information Coefficient* [14] and the *Mutual Information* [15] have been utilized. These two and more dependency measures are introduced in Sect. 2.3.

If using this bare dependency measures, the proposed method does not completely tackle the previously introduced notion of mutual influence. This method alone has some issues since the configuration of the agent itself is not taken into account. We explain this problem and present a solution to resolve this issue in the following Section.

Consideration of Own Configuration. As mentioned before, the use of dependency measures for the detection of influences is not straight forward in some cases. The issue appears if the own configuration of the agent A is essential for the determination of the influence of an agent B on A. This is if the configuration of B and the performance of A without taking into account the configuration of A lead to a distribution that does not indicate a dependency between them, but, there is an influence of B on A. This influence can then by revealed by using multiple estimators of the influence for the different configurations of A. The effect can be observed in already rather simple examples. One is given with example calculations of the mutual influence in [14]. For the measurement, it is sufficient to use two estimators and group the samples of all available configurations to the two estimators. But, sometimes the usage of more estimators can lead to a faster detection, as shown in [15].

2.3   Dependency Measures

In this section, we present the different dependency measures that we chose for the comparison. We rely on a mix between some well-established measures, i.e., the Pearson Correlation Coefficient [11], the Spearman Rank Correlation [17], the Kendall Rank Correlation [3] and the Mutual Information [16], that are widely spread since several decades and two rather new measures that claim to be very powerful, i.e., the Distance Correlation [18] and the Maximal Information Coefficient [12].

Pearson Correlation Coefficient. The *Pearson Correlation Coefficient* (PCC) [11] (sometimes also *Pearson product-moment correlation coefficient, Bravais Pearson Correlation* or *Pearson's r*) is probably the most widely spread measure of association in statistics. It is defined as

$$\rho(X,Y) = \frac{\text{Cov}(X,Y)}{\sigma(X)\sigma(Y)}, \tag{1}$$

where X and Y are the random variables, $\text{Cov}(X,Y)$ denotes the covariance of X and Y and $\sigma(X)$ is the standard deviation. However, the above formula requires the knowledge of the distributions of X and Y in order to calculate the PCC. Since we rely on a sample for the calculation, we rely on the formula

$$r = \frac{\sum_{i=1}^{n}(x_i - \bar{x})(y_i - \bar{y})}{\sqrt{\sum_{i=1}^{n}(x_i - \bar{x})^2}\sqrt{\sum_{i=1}^{n}(y_i - \bar{y})^2}}, \tag{2}$$

where x_i and y_i are the samples and n the number of samples. The PCC gives values from $[-1, 1]$. If there is a full positive *linear* dependency between the random variables, it gives 1. In turn, it gives -1 if there is a full negative *linear* dependency. If there is no *linear* dependency it gives 0. Unfortunately, a result of 0 does not necessarily allow for concluding that there is no dependency, since other types of association are possible.

Spearman Rank Correlation. The *Spearman Rank Correlation* (SRC) (also *Spearman's rank correlation coefficient* or *Spearman's rho*) [17] introduces the idea of a rank-based correlation measurement. This means the samples are ordered and labels from $1, ..., n$ are allocated to them. Then the PCC is calculated for the resulting ranks. Shorter, the SRC can also be calculated as

$$\rho = 1 - \frac{6 \sum d_i^2}{n(n^2 - 1)}, \tag{3}$$

where d_i is the difference of the ranks of x_i and y_i.

Kendall Rank Correlation. The *Kendall Rank Correlation* (KRC) [3] (also *Kendall Rank Correlation Coefficient* or *Kendall's tau*) also uses a rank-based approach and is therefore a similar approach as Spearman's. The idea is to find *concordant* and *discordant pairs* and use them for the calculation of the association. A concordant pair is a pair (x_i, y_i) and (x_j, y_j) where $x_i > x_j$ and $y_i > y_j$ or $x_i < x_j$ and $y_i < y_j$. If this is not the case, the pair is called discordant. There are different variants of the KRC. Here, we rely on the τ_b. It can be calculated as

$$\tau_b = \frac{C - D}{\sqrt{(n_g - n_1)(n_g - n_2)}}, \tag{4}$$

where C is the number of concordant pairs and D is the number of discordant pairs. The variables n_g, n_1 and n_2 are necessary for handling duplicate values. They are defined as follows: $n_1 = \sum_i \frac{t_i(t_i-1)}{2}$, where t_i is number of occurrences of two samples with $x_i = x_j$. Similar, we have $n_2 = \sum_i \frac{u_i(u_i-1)}{2}$, where t_i is number of occurrences of two samples with $y_i = y_j$. At last, we define $n_g = \sum_i \frac{n(n-1)}{2}$, where n is the number of samples.

The KRC can give values from [-1,1], too. The values -1 and 1 imply a full negative or positive *monotone* dependency. A value of 0 implies that there is no monotone dependency, however, as for the dependency measures before this does not imply that there is no dependency at all.

Distance Correlation. The *Distance Correlation* (DC) [18] as a generalization of the PCC that also covers non-linear dependencies between the random variables by taking into account the distance between the sample points. The basic formula for the calculation is

$$\mathrm{dCor}(X, Y) = \frac{\mathrm{dCov}(X,Y)}{\sqrt{\mathrm{dVar}(X)\mathrm{dVar}(Y)}}, \tag{5}$$

i.e., similar to the PCC but with variants of the covariance and variance, dCov and dVar, that rely on the distance of the samples. If dCov has to be calculated from a sample, the formula

$$\mathrm{dCov}_n^2(X, Y) = \frac{1}{n^2} \sum_{j,k=1}^{n} A_{j,k} B_{j,k} \tag{6}$$

is used. dVar is given by $dVar_n^2(X) = dCov_n^2(X, X)$, where $A_{j,k}$ refer to the distance matrices defined by $A_{j,k} = a_{j,k} - \overline{a}_{j\cdot} - \overline{a}_{\cdot k} + \overline{a}_{\cdot\cdot}$. Here, $\overline{a}_{j\cdot}$ is the j-th row mean, $\overline{a}_{\cdot}$ the k-th column mean and $\overline{a}_{\cdot\cdot}$ the grand mean.

The DC gives values from $[0, 1]$. It is 0 if and only if the two random variables are stochastically independent.

Mutual Information. The *Mutual Information* (I) that goes back to Shannon [16] is closely related to Shannon's Entropy. The I is defined as:

$$I(X;Y) = \sum_{x \in X} \sum_{y \in Y} p(x,y) \log \left(\frac{p(x,y)}{p(x)p(y)} \right), \tag{7}$$

where $p(x, y)$ is the joint probability distribution of the discrete random variables X and Y. In addition, $p(x)$ and $p(y)$ are the corresponding marginal distributions. There is also a variant of the I for continuous random variables:

$$I(X;Y) = \int_{x \in X} \int_{y \in Y} p(x,y) \log \left(\frac{p(x,y)}{p(x)p(y)} \right), \tag{8}$$

Here, as often the case, the probability distributions $p(x)$, $p(y)$, and $p(x,y)$ are unknown and have to be estimated in order to calculate the I by the above formula. Therefore, in this work, we rely on an estimation of the I that does not require the knowledge of the distributions. This is the estimation using the k-nearest neighbor method as introduced in [4]. The I can measure stochastic dependencies between random variables and is only 0 if the random variables are independent.

Maximal Information Coefficient. The *Maximal Information Coefficient* (MIC) [12] is a measure of dependence between two real valued random variables. It has been introduced by Reshef et al. [12] and is based on the I. As depicted before, a common issue with the I is that the density is needed in order to calculate it. Besides the estimation by the before mentioned k-nearest neighbor method, the binning of the samples is common. Meaning that samples that are close to each other will collected in one bin. Afterwards, the probability distributions are estimated for the bins. This is an easy counting of frequency and the data is essentially discretized. The resulting distributions are used for the calculation of the discrete variant of the I. The problem is that the manual choice of the bins is time consuming and can lead to deceptive results if not appropriate. Therefore, MIC has been equipped with a concept of always using the bins that lead to the maximal I. Finding this bin configuration is computational heavy – which resulted in the utilization of a heuristic to tackle the problem. As a result, MIC is defined as:

$$MIC(X;Y) = \max_{n_x n_y < B} \frac{I(X;Y)}{\log(\min(n_x, n_y))}, \tag{9}$$

where n_x and n_y denote the number of bins for X and Y. The divisor $\log(\min(n_x, n_y))$ gives the maximal achievable I given the number of bins and thus is used as normalizing factor. B typically denotes a function of the sample size N and limits the number of bins. This is necessary to avoid *trivial* partitioning, such as creating a single bin for each data point that most of the time create relatively high values for the I. The initial paper introducing MIC proposes to use $B = N^{0.6}$ based on the described experiments.

The MIC gives values from $[0, 1]$. It equals 0 if and only if the random variables are completely independent.

3 Evaluation and Discussion

In this chapter, three applications are presented that are used for comparison of the different dependency measures. The first is presented in Sect. 3.1 and is considered to be very simple for the mutual influence detection algorithm. The second can be found in Sect. 3.2 and is similar to first, but, it requires to consider the own configuration (as explained in Sect. 2.2 (Consideration of Own Configuration)) in order to detect the influences. The last application, presented in Sect. 3.3 is from the smart camera network domain [13]. It is directly inspired by a real world application and therefore much more complex than the other two applications. We chose these scenarios since they are representatives of different characteristics that can be found in OC applications. Furthermore, each section also includes the comparison results for the corresponding application. A concluding discussion of all achieved results is given in Sect. 3.4.

3.1 Box Application

The *box application* is rather simple. It includes two robots and a heavy box. The robots can be configured to push or pull the box, but, none of them is able to move the box alone since it is too heavy. Therefore, the robots have to cooperate, i.e., both push or pull the box. The robots have a local performance measure that gives 1 if the box moves forward or 0 otherwise. We chose this scenario since it is used as an example for a simple scenario. We expect that the measures work very good on this application and there should only be a difference in the time that is needed to detect the mutual influence.

The result for the box application are depicted in Fig. 1. The values have been generated by averages of 20 independent runs of the application where the robots either push or pull randomly. The process is observed by the mutual influence detection using the different dependency measures. We compare the different measures by looking at the fraction of runs in which the algorithm detects the other robot as more influencing than a simulated robot that is not influencing it. In Fig. 1a, we see the results if the own configuration of the robot is not considered. The graph shows that nearly all considered techniques achieve the desired results, i.e., they find the influence in less than 50 steps. But, the I takes rather long. Even after 450 steps, it does not detect runs correctly. In

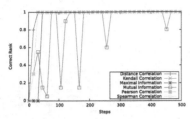
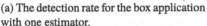
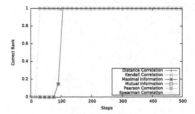

(a) The detection rate for the box application with one estimator.

(b) The detection rate for the box application with two estimators.

Fig. 1. The results of the influence measurement for the box application based on 20 independent runs. The graphs show the fraction of runs in which the other robot is detected as more influencing as the simulated independent robot.

Fig. 1b, we see the results if the own configuration is considered (cf. Sect. 2.2 (Consideration of Own Configuration)). Again, we see that most measures work well, but, the MIC a little worse by needing about 100 steps to detect every run correctly.

3.2 Two-Man Saw Application

The *two-man saw application* is similar to the box application. Again, it includes two robots, but, in comparison to Sect. 3.1, a two-man saw is operated instead of pushing a box. The robots can be configured to push or pull the two-man saw, but, they cannot operate the saw alone. Therefore, the robots have to cooperate, i.e., one push has to and the other one pull the saw or the other way around depending on the position of the saw. The robots have a local performance measure that gives 1 if the saw moves or 0 otherwise. We chose this scenario, since it is slightly more complex as the previous one: It additionally requires considering the own configuration. We expect that the measures does not work using one estimator. But, it should work very good with two estimators.

The results for the two-man saw application are depicted in Fig. 2. They are created by making 20 independent runs of the application where the robots either push or pull randomly. The process is observed by the mutual influence detection using the different dependency measures. We compare the different measures by looking at the fraction of runs in which the algorithm detects the other robot as more influencing than a simulated robot that is independent. In Fig. 2a, we see the results if the own configuration of the robot is not considered. The graph shows that all measures do not work at all, i.e., they cannot find the influence in the shown 500 steps and also not if more steps are considered. In Fig. 2b, we see the results if the own configuration is considered (cf. Sect. 2.2 (Consideration of Own Configuration)). Here, we see that most measures work well, but, the MIC and the I take longer that the rest with about 100 and 200 steps.

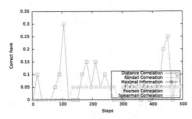 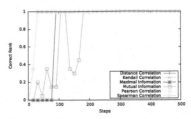

(a) The detection rate for the saw application with one estimator.

(b) The detection rate for the saw application with two estimators.

Fig. 2. The results of the influence measurement for the two-man saw application based on 20 independent runs. The graphs show the fraction of runs in which the other robot is detected as more influencing as the simulated independent robot.

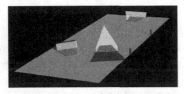 

(a) Scenario 1 in the smart camera application.

(b) Scenario 2 in the smart camera application.

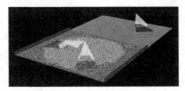

(c) Scenario 3 in the smart camera application.

Fig. 3. The picture shows the three scenarios in the smart camera application. The white pyramids represent the field of view of the cameras. The red dots mark undetected targets that switch to yellow when they have been detected. The blue pillars at the right border of the Scenario mark spawn points and the blue areas at the scene show the currently observed zones. The closest/left camera is Camera 0, followed by Camera 1 and the most remote camera is Camera 2(Color figure online).

3.3 Smart Camera Application

For the evaluation, we chose a Smart Camera application setting that requires a collaboration in order to reach an optimal result. Therefore, we define the goals: (i) detect new targets, and (ii) create 3D models of targets in an area (i.e., the goal is to provide a stereo reconstruction of suspicious persons). There is some research on techniques that allow to construct a 3D model from 2D pictures from different angles, see [6,7] for an example. In the performance measure, we reflect the goals mentioned before. We rate the detection of a before unobserved target with a performance of 1 and the observation of multiple cameras with a performance of 2.5 while one or multiple cameras could observe multiple targets which are then added up. We chose the difference between the two possible observations in order to reflect that a 3D reconstruction of a target is much more valuable. Experiments with other weightings between the two goals have shown only minor effects on the mutual influence detection.

Scenario 1. The first scenario (see Fig. 3a) shows a scene with three cameras. The cameras are represented by their pyramid-shaped fields of view and are named Camera 0, Camera 1 and Camera 2 from front to back, i.e., Camera 0 is the one pointing to the right. The green rectangle represents the observable space and shows three blue areas which is the currently observed space. The blue pillars at the right edges show spawn points for detectable targets. The targets are represented as yellow spots if they have already been detected and as red dots if they are still undetected. The spawning points create two streams of targets that are placed between Camera 0 and 1 and Camera 1 and 2, and are in the possible field of view of the two cameras each. A human considering the scenario can easily see that Camera 0 can be influenced by Camera 1, since they can potentially observe an overlapping area that is possibly populated by undetected targets. On the other hand, Camera 2 can not influence Camera 0, since it is not possible that their fields of view overlap.

Scenario 2. The second scenario (see Fig. 3b) shows significant differences to the first one. On the one hand, Camera 1 is now much closer to Camera 0, i.e. the cameras can nearly observe the same area of the scene. On the other hand, significantly more targets are created that appear on the entire observable area of Camera 0 and 1. Taking this into account, we expect that the influence of Camera 1 should be higher than the influence of Camera 2 since the influence of Camera 2 should remain unchanged and therefore should not exist.

Scenario 3. The third scenario (see Fig. 3c) is close to the first one, but there is a small difference. That is, there are additional spawning points at the left border of the scene creating two streams of targets that have opposite direction. Therefore, we expect that the influence occurs similar to the second scenario. But, we chose this scenario to find out if the measures behave differently if the additional targets occur.

Results. The result for the smart camera application are depicted in Fig. 4. They are created by averaging 20 independent runs of the application for each scenario where the cameras change their pan configuration randomly. For the purpose of the comparison of the measures, we limited the PTZ capabilities of the cameras, i.e., we fixed the zoom and tilt values to appropriate values.

The process is observed by the mutual influence detection using the different dependency measures. We compare the different measures by looking at the fraction of runs in which the algorithm applied on Camera 0 detects Camera

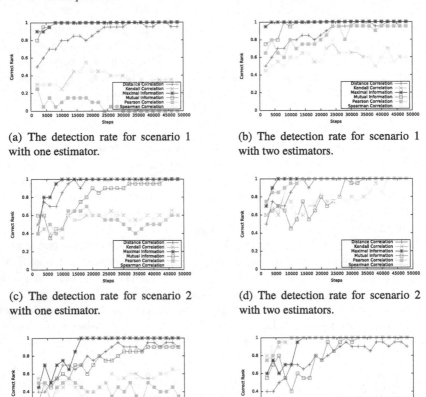

(a) The detection rate for scenario 1 with one estimator.

(b) The detection rate for scenario 1 with two estimators.

(c) The detection rate for scenario 2 with one estimator.

(d) The detection rate for scenario 2 with two estimators.

(e) The detection rate for scenario 3 with one estimator.

(f) The detection rate for scenario 3 with two estimators.

Fig. 4. The results of the influence measurement for the smart camera scenarios based on 20 independent runs. The graphs show the fraction of runs in which camera 1 is detected as more influencing as camera 2.

1 as more influencing than Camera 2 that is independent. In Figs. 4a, c and e, we see the results of the runs where the own configuration of Camera 1 is not considered. We can observe that PCC, KRC and SRC are not able to detect the influence correctly in the 50000 steps for each scenario. The MIC does perform best on each scenario. In scenario 1, the mutual influence can detect the influence on the same level as the MIC. In scenario 2, it takes much longer to find the influence in all runs and, in scenario 3, it is not able to recognize the influence in all runs even after the 50000 steps. The DC finds the influence in scenario 2 rather fast in all runs. But, it takes much more time in scenario 1 and 3 than the MIC.

In Fig. 4b, d and f, we can observe the results if the own configuration is considered (cf. Sect. 2.2 (Consideration of Own Configuration)). Here, we see that the DC, MIC have a similar behavior in all three scenarios. The PCC has improved greatly in all scenarios 1, but, it can still not detect the influences in all runs for scenario 1. The I, KRC, and SRC can improve in scenario 2 and 3, but, in scenario 1 and 2, the performance is still not convincing.

3.4 Discussion

Concluding the results, we can see that the MIC is the only dependency measure that has correctly detected all influences in every application and scenario. All other measures show weaknesses on one or the another scenario. Therefore, the MIC is the most suitable candidate if only one dependency has to be chosen for the detection of mutual influences. However, the results also imply that a mix of dependency measures can be suitable. This is especially due to the not fully satisfying results of the MIC in the box and two-man saw applications where it takes more time to recognize the influences. Therefore, a combination of the MIC and the DC seems to be most promising.

4   Related Work

In literature, several approaches that try to formalize mutual influences can be found. Most of these approaches focus on the influence through direct or indirect interactions. For instance, a model for interactions is proposed in [2], but a method to detect the implicit interactions is not provided. Another approach is to use *stit* logic for modeling the interactions in multi agent systems [1]. The focus of this work is on the system specification and verification and, therefore, differs much from the focus of our work. In [5], a data mining approach for the detection of mutual influences in multi agent systems is proposed, but, it does not provide concrete methods and results. The presented method has similarities with the feature selection approach that originates in supervised learning and, recently, there are some promising attempts for the adaption to systems with performance measurement, i.e. the reinforcement learning domain, such as [9,10]. All of these works have in common that they do not match the presented idea of a self-adapting and self-organizing system.

5   Conclusion

Based on the observation that OC systems are continuously interweaving with each other, we claimed that detecting and handling mutual influences becomes increasingly important within the next decade. Therefore, this paper investigated the applicability of a variety of available dependency and mutual influence measures. We considered three exemplary scenarios to evaluate the success and analyze the behavior of the particular techniques: A very simple box-moving example for two cooperating robots, a more complex two-man saw example with two robots having to move a cross-cut saw, and finally a sophisticated OC example from the smart camera domain. Within our simulations we were able to identify the MIC as most promising candidate, since this technique has been shown to outperform all other estimators. In future work, we will investigate the benefit of using the derived information in more established OC applications, such as vehicular traffic control or industry automation. Therein, we will further investigate the possible benefit of running several techniques in parallel in order to combine the advantages of the considered techniques[1].

References

1. Broersen, J.M.: CTL.STIT: enhancing ATL to express important multi-agent system verification properties. In: 9th International Conference on Autonomous Agents and Multiagent Systems (AAMAS), Toronto, Canada, vol. 1–3, pp. 683–690, 10–14 May, 2010
2. Keil, D., Goldin, D.Q.: Modeling indirect interaction in open computational systems. In: 12th IEEE International Workshops on Enabling Technologies (WETICE 2003), Infrastructure for Collaborative Enterprises, 9–11 , Linz, Austria, pp. 371–376 (2003)
3. Kendall, M.: Rank correlation methods. Griffin, London (1948)
4. Kraskov, A., Stögbauer, H., Grassberger, P.: Estimating mutual information. Phys. Rev. E **69**(6), 066138 (2004)
5. Logie, R., Hall, J.G., Waugh, K.G.: Towards mining for influence in a multi agent environment. In: Abraham, A. (ed.) IADIS European Conference Data Mining, pp. 97–101. IADIS (2008)
6. Menze, M., Muhle, D.: Using Stereo Vision to Support the Automated Analysis of Surveillance Videos. In: International Archives of the Photogrammetry, Remote Sensing and Spatial Information Sciences, ISPRS, pp. 47–51 (2012)
7. Menze, M., Klinger, T., Muhle, D., Metzler, J., Heipke, C.: A stereoscopic approach for the association of people tracks in video surveillance systems. PFG Photogrammetrie, Fernerkundung, Geoinformation **2013**(2), 83–92 (2013)
8. Müller-Schloer, C.: Organic Computing: On the Feasibility of Controlled Emergence. In: Proceedings of CODES and ISSS 2004, pp. 2–5 (2004)
9. Nguyen, T., Li, Z., Silander, T., Leong, T.Y.: Online feature selection for model-based reinforcement learning. In: Dasgupta, S., Mcallester, D. (eds.) Proceedings of the 30th International Conference on Machine Learning (ICML-13), JMLR Workshop, vol. 28, pp. 498–506 (2013)
10. Parr, R., Li, L., Taylor, G., Painter-Wakefield, C., Littman, M.L.: An analysis of linear models, linear value-function approximation, and feature selection for reinforcement learning. In: Proceedings of the 25th International Conference on Machine Learning, pp. 752–759, ICML 2008, NY, USA. ACM, New York (2008)
11. Pearson, K.: Notes on regression and inheritance in the case of two parents. Proc. R. Soc. Lond. **58**(1), 240–242 (1895)
12. Reshef, D.N., Reshef, Y.A., Finucane, H.K., Grossman, S.R., McVean, G., Turnbaugh, P.J., Lander, E.S., Mitzenmacher, M., Sabeti, P.C.: Detecting novel associations in large data sets. Science **334**(6062), 1518–1524 (2011)
13. Rinner, B., Winkler, T., Schriebl, W., Quaritsch, M., Wolf, W.: The evolution from single to pervasive smart cameras. In: Second ACM/IEEE International Conference on Distributed Smart Cameras, ICDSC 2008, pp. 1–10 (2008)

---

[1] This research is partially funded by the DFG (HA 5480/3-1) with the project CYPHOC.

14. Rudolph, S., Tomforde, S., Sick, B., Hähner, J.: A Mutual Influence Detection Algorithm for Systems with Local Performance Measurement. In: Proceedings of the 9th IEEE International Conference on Self-adapting and Self-organising Systems (SASO15), pp. 144–150, Boston, USA, 21-25 September, 2015
15. Rudolph, S., Tomforde, S., Sick, B., Heck, H., Wacker, A., Hähner, J.: An online influence detection algorithm for organic computing systems. In: Proceedings of the 28th GI/ITG International Conference on Architecture of Computing Systems - ARCS Workshops (2015)
16. Shannon, C., Weaver, W.: The Mathematical Theory of Communication. University of Illinois Press, Champaign (1949)
17. Spearman, C.: The proof and measurement of association between two things. Am. J. Psychol. **15**, 88–103 (1904)
18. Székely, G.J., Rizzo, M.L., Bakirov, N.K.: Measuring and testing dependence by correlation of distances. Ann. Statist. **35**(6), 2769–2794 (2007)
19. Tomforde, S., Hähner, J., Seebach, H., Reif, W., Sick, B., Wacker, A., Scholtes, I.: Engineering and Mastering Interwoven Systems. In: ARCS 2014–27th International Conference on Architecture of Computing Systems, Workshop Proceedings, University of Luebeck, Institute of Computer Engineering, pp. 1–8, Luebeck, Germany, 25–28 February, 2014
20. Wiering, M., van Otterlo, M. (eds.): Reinforcement Learning: State-of-the-Art. Adaptation, Learning, and Optimization. Springer, Heidelberg (2012). iSBN-13: 978-3642276446

Augmenting the Algorithmic Structure of XCS by Means of Interpolation

Anthony Stein[✉], Dominik Rauh, Sven Tomforde, and Jörg Hähner

Organic Computing Group, University of Augsburg,
Eichleitnerstr. 30, 86159 Augsburg, Germany
{anthony.stein,sven.tomforde,joerg.haehner}@informatik.uni-augsburg.de

Abstract. In this paper, first approaches for integrating interpolation techniques into XCS' algorithmic structure are discussed. We present extensions that focus on a specific challenge Organic Computing (OC) systems have to cope with, i.e. the non-uniform distribution of arising situations and the resulting sparseness of samples in the problem space. We draw a picture of how interpolation can be integrated into the well-studied structure of the XCS, initially proposed by Wilson in 1995. The design ideas and the resulting structure of a novel Interpolation Component (IC) will be described. Additionally, we point out two alternative architecture types that integrate the novel IC with XCS as well as concrete extensions concerning the internal calculations.

Keywords: Organic computing · XCS · Genetic algorithm · Action selection regime · Interpolation component · Inverse Distance Weighting

1 Introduction

Organic Computing (OC) is a recent paradigm of designing and developing technical systems acting in the real world. It makes heavy use of concepts drawn from the nature to overcome the complexity of technical systems. OC systems strive for adopting so-called self-x properties that allow them to act in a 'life-like' fashion. Principles of OC were integrated into a resilient traffic management system, called Organic Traffic Control (cf. [12]), an Organic Robot Control Architecture (ORCA) [2] which equips a six-legged robot with self-x properties to make it fault-tolerant and acting more 'life-like', or a two-stage method implementing a lightweight *Learning Classifier System* (LCS) to combine the advantages of software and hardware solutions [3,23]. During the first stage, the approach in [3,23] harnesses the adaptivity of a reduced LCS to learn a basic control strategy for a given problem based on simulation. Next, the learned rule set is transferred to a piece of high-performance hardware called 'Learning Classifier Table'. At this point, the classifiers are not updated any longer. This concept has been further refined and applied to an 'Autonomic System on Chip' (ASoC) to manage CPU workload [22]. For more examples and an en detail review of the Organic Computing initiative, we refer the reader to [1].

© Springer International Publishing Switzerland 2016
F. Hannig et al. (Eds.): ARCS 2016, LNCS 9637, pp. 348–360, 2016.
DOI: 10.1007/978-3-319-30695-7_26

One of the aforementioned self-x properties is the *self-learning* capability. According to that, OC systems are usually equipped with a designated learning component that learns adequate reactions on arising situations and improves them iteratively at runtime. Throughout this paper, we consider the rule-based *eXtended Classifier System* (XCS) as concrete learning component. As real world environments are highly dynamic, situations occur where the system is not able to respond with an already approved reaction due to lack of experience. We denote these experience lacks 'knowledge gaps', which can be considered as areas of a function or problem space where no sampling point exists yet. The existence of knowledge gaps, or the sparseness of samples, is but one of the following core challenges, we deem to be essential for applying online machine learning on real-world problems: (I) the *sparseness* and *non-uniform distribution* of samples, (II) the *inherent dynamics* of the problem space, (III) *high dimensionality* of the problem spaces, and (IV) *uncertainty* and *noise* regarding the samples. Although each of the identified core problems is essential from our point of view, in this paper we restrict our focus on problem (I).

The objective of this paper is two-fold. First, we want to give an idea of how interpolation techniques can generally be integrated in XCS' algorithmic structure to overcome the challenge of sparse non-uniformly distributed samples in the considered problem space. On the other hand, a novel *Interpolation Component* (IC) is presented that can be used to extend the architecture of a variety of learning systems, not necessarily restricted to extend XCS. Accordingly, two different ways of applying the general IC architecture to extend the XCS as well as the corresponding advantages and disadvantages of each are discussed.

The remainder of this paper is structured as follows: Sect. 2 provides an overview of related work in the field of XCS research. The fundamental architectural and algorithmic structure of XCS is briefly outlined in Sect. 3. Section 4 exemplarily describes a certain interpolation technique to give an idea of how interpolation works. Based on that, our novel IC will be introduced at the beginning of Sect. 5. Additionally, two alternative architectural approaches of how the XCS and the IC can be combined as well as concrete extensions of XCS' internal calculations are presented. Section 6 presents experimental results that show a promising potential of the proposed extensions. Finally, Sect. 7 concludes the paper with a further discussion and ongoing research topics that are currently under investigation.

2   Related Work

Interpolation can be considered as a more specific variant of approximation techniques. Approximating a function by means of interpolation guarantees that all sampling points are strictly passed by the approximation [13]. The approximation of functions is an application domain of Wilson's XCS that is often focused in the literature. The modified system is called XCSF and a first description can be found in [20]. Wilson integrates piecewise-linear approximation to resemble the shape of a function to be learned. The prediction value of a single classifier is no longer represented as a scalar, but as a linear function, which is modeled by a weighted function of the current situation's input vector. XCSF is very capable of learning complex sinusoidal functions, even of higher dimensions. Butz et al. in [6] presented very effective extensions to Wilson's initial approach that allows XCSF to be applied on more complex functions. The extensions range from hyper-ellipsoidal instead of interval-based condition structures, to alternative update rules for a faster and more accurate estimation of essential classifier attributes. Wilson also investigated the question how XCS in general can be extended to cope with a continuous action space. In [21] he presented three architectural approaches how this can be achieved. One particular architecture was called *Interpolating Classifier System* that suggests a relation to the research we are concerned with. However, what Wilson actually did was to apply his modified system, the XCSF, in a hierarchical fashion. With this technique, the system approximates between discrete action values on the second layer and applies the approximations on the environments that are observed by the XCSF instance on the first layer. Thus, his approach differs clearly from our proposed techniques, as our idea is to incorporate designated interpolation techniques as an integrated part of XCS' algorithmic structure. In our previous work, we have already investigated the extension of XCS' knowledge by means of neighborhood-based interpolation techniques that are based on *Voronoi* diagrams [15]. We found that there indeed exists a potential to improve the overall performance of an XCS when interpolation is incorporated. Beside the aforementioned efforts, further research striving for an increased learning performance can be found in the literature. For instance, Butz et al. in [5] applied gradient-descent techniques to XCS' reinforcement component to allow for a reliable, more accurate and less noisy evolution of payoff landscapes in complex multistep problems. Techniques to compact the classifier population after the system error has converged to a desired level can be found in [6]. In [7,8] Fredivianus et al. proposed a novel discovery mechanism called *rule combining* that supports XCS by generating maximally general rules and reduces the average number of classifiers. To draw a conclusion, the interest in the field of XCS research is widely spread and it focuses on several components. For a further view on current XCS research issues we refer the reader to [10].

3   XCS in a Nutshell

The XCS is a rule-based learning system that makes heavy use of a *genetic algorithm* (GA) and *reinforcement learning* techniques. XCS aims in constructing a complete, accurate and maximally general state-action map (*generalization hypothesis* [17]), more formally denoted as $X \times A \Rightarrow P$. X denotes the set of possible states $\mathbf{x}$ that can occur. The set of all possible actions is denoted as A and P represents the payoff space. To meet this aforementioned goal, XCS evolves rules, or rather *classifiers*, of the form $cl := (C, a, p, \epsilon, F)$, at which C represents a subspace of the input space X, a denotes a classifier's advocated action, and p, ϵ, F are ranking attributes described in a minute.

Initially in 1995, XCS and its predecessors where designed to act in a binary problem space, where the current situation $\sigma(t)$ was encoded as a binary string.

As OC systems are faced with application scenarios from the real world domain, throughout this paper we rely on an XCS extension called XCSR as proposed in [16,19], that allows to cope with real-valued inputs. That is, $\sigma(t)$ represents a situation vector $\mathbf{x} = (x_1, ..., x_n)$ with $\mathbf{x} \in \mathbb{R}^n$ for an n-dimensional problem space at time-step t. A classifier's condition part C that matches a particular subset of X is encoded as an interval-predicate (l_i, u_i), $i = 1 ... n$, with $l_i, u_i \in \mathbb{R}$. l_i and u_i serve as lower and upper bound and can be interpreted as axis-diagonal hyperrectangle in the situation space X. An action $cl.a$ advocated by a classifier cl can be seen as a reaction of XCS to a certain environmental state $\sigma(t)$. The aforementioned classifier attributes p, ϵ and F determine with which accuracy a classifier predicts a payoff from P. p is a scalar prediction of the expected payoff, ϵ is the absolute error of that prediction, and F is a measure of accuracy, i.e. some kind of inverse function of ϵ so that a higher value of ϵ decreases the accuracy exponentially (see e.g. [18] for more details). Besides the just mentioned attributes, other so-called *book-keeping* attributes are contained by a single classifier. For a more detailed description of these attributes, the reader is referred to [17–19].

Figure 1 depicts a schematic illustration of XCS' conventional structure. The set [P] of all evolved rules is called *classifier population*. The size of [P] is limited by N. An adequate choice for the size of N depends strongly on the underlying environment in terms of its dimensionality and the complexity of its surface [6]. When a new situation $\sigma(t)$ arrives, XCS forms a so-called *match set* [M] consisting of all matching classifiers from [P]. A classifier matches a certain situation if and only if $l_i \leq x_i <$

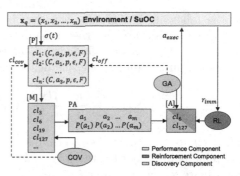

Fig. 1. XCS' architecture for single step problems, adapted from [18]

u_i for $i = 1 ... n$. If no matching classifier can be found or the number of distinct actions in [M] is less than θ_{mna}, a *covering mechanism* (depicted as COV in Fig. 1) creates a classifier that matches the input state. This generated classifier is initialized with predefined values for all attributes, except of its action. The action is drawn randomly from all actions not existing in [M]. When [M] contains at least θ_{mna} classifiers, a so-called prediction array PA is calculated. It has one entry for each action $a \in A$. Each entry is calculated as a fitness-weighted prediction value over all classifiers with the same action a_j, more formally $P(a_j) = \sum_{cl \in [M]|a_j} cl.p \cdot cl.F / \sum_{cl \in [M]|a_j} cl.F$. The value of $P(a_j)$ is called *system prediction* for action $a_j \in A$ and represents an estimate of the payoff that is expected when a_j is actualized. Based on an *action selection regime*, a certain action is selected for execution depending on the value in the PA. An action can be selected deterministically or probabilistically, depending on whether the already gained knowledge shall be exploited or further be extended by exploration of the problem space. After determining an action a_{exec} to be executed, a subset of [M], called *action set* $[A] := \{cl \in [M]|cl.a = a_{exec}\}$, is formed. a_{exec} is eventually executed on the environment which in turn delivers an immediate payoff or reward r_{imm} [1]. This reward is subsequently used to refine the attribute values $(p, \epsilon, F, ...)$ of each classifier present in [A]. This refinement is achieved by applying the *Widrow-Hoff delta rule* in conjunction with the *moyenne adaptive modifee* (MAM) technique (cf. [17] for more details). Besides the covering mechanism, a GA [9] is incorporated in XCS' main-loop. It generates two *offspring* classifiers cl_{off} from two *parents* selected from [A]. After copying the parents, crossover and mutation are probabilistically applied on both cl_{off}, so that with a certain probability two novel classifiers arise. The GA is invoked when the average time of all classifiers in [A] since the last GA invocation exceeds a threshold θ_{GA}. Again, for a more precise description of the GA or any other parts of XCS, we refer the reader to [17,18].

4   Inverse Distance Weighting Interpolation

In the following paragraphs, we describe a particular interpolation technique that we deem suitable for the problem field our research is concerned with. We elaborate on the *Inverse Distance Weighting* (IDW) method, a weighted global interpolation technique. Shepard defines the basic form of IDW as follows [14]:

$$f(\mathbf{x}_q) = \frac{\sum_i w_i \cdot f(\mathbf{x}_i)}{\sum_i w_i}, \text{ with } w_i = \left(\frac{1}{d(\mathbf{x}_q, \mathbf{x}_i)_2}\right)^p \tag{1}$$

The weights w_i denote the inverse distance from the query point $\mathbf{x}_q$ to the i-th sampling point's coordinate $\mathbf{x}_i$. We define the i-th sampling point comprising the coordinate $\mathbf{x}_i$ and the function value $f(\mathbf{x}_i)$ as tuple $s_i := (\mathbf{x}_i, f(\mathbf{x}_i))$. The term $d(\mathbf{x}_q, \mathbf{x}_i)_2$ denotes the L2-norm, i.e. the Euclidean distance between the query point $\mathbf{x}_q$ and the site $\mathbf{x}_i$ of the sampling point. The power parameter p controls to which degree the weights w_i decrease when the distance to $\mathbf{x}_q$ increases and vice versa. In essence, the IDW method interpolates any query point $\mathbf{x}_q \in \mathbb{R}^n$ by calculating a weighted average of the function values $f(\mathbf{x}_i)$ of already known sampling points s_i. Hence, it is theoretically not restricted to any dimension. Considering the time complexity of IDW, the calculation effort grows linear with the number m of s_i. An extension of the basic IDW technique toward a local interpolation method, also called *Modified Shepard's Method* in the literature, can be found in [11]. Besides IDW, we also experimented with local and *Voronoi-based Nearest* and *Natural Neighbor* interpolation techniques in [15], but for the sake of brevity, within this paper we limit our elaborations to IDW, as this method is simple and straightforward enough for discussing our general thoughts of incorporating interpolation within XCS' algorithmic structure.

---

[1] The description of XCS' main-loop and the remainder of this paper focus on single-step problems, where after each iteration a reward is provided and the rules are refined immediately. OC systems are generally faced with this kind of problems.

5 Architectural Approaches of Integrating IC with XCS

The preceding section introduced IDW as reference interpolation technique. In the next paragraphs, we present a novel generic Interpolation Component (IC) first and subsequently discuss two alternative architectural approaches of integration with XCS. In the same breath, we present two integration strategies that allow to involve the additionally gained interpolated 'knowledge' into XCS' internal calculations. Figure 2 illustrates the generic architecture of the IC. It comprises five components: (1) the *Machine Learning System Interface* (MLI) is responsible for communicating with the machine learning system (MLS) that should be extended by the IC (in this paper the XCS), i.e. it reports the interpolated output values o_{int} to, and receives feedback from the MLS. (2) the *SP* as set of sampling points which is more formally defined by $SP := \{s_i\}$, with $i \in \{1 \ldots m\}$. (3) the *Interpolant* defines an interpolation technique I such as IDW and generates the output values o_{int} that are subsequently reported to the MLS. (4) the *Adjustment* component alters the SP by deciding on the basis of a decision function A if and when a new sampling point s^* should be added, or rather if an obsolete one has to be deleted in favor of a new one. Finally, (5) the *Evaluation* component provides a metric E to track a so-called *trust-level* T_{IC}, that determines the accuracy of the interpolant.

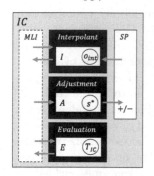

Fig. 2. Generic IC architecture

The generic IC is designed to extend any MLS where it is meaningful. The implementation details of components (3), (4) and (5) depend highly on the MLS and the underlying learning task. If the MLS is faced with a classification task, the IC can be used to interpolate the membership to different classes, and the evaluation component could track the accuracy, the precision or rather a combination of both. In the following, we go into more detail about the integration of IC and XCS as a concrete MLS. We compare two architectural approaches, XCS-IC and XCS-CIC, and discuss the corresponding advantages and disadvantages.

5.1 Loose Coupling - XCS-IC

The first approach follows the initial thoughts of the generic IC. It is schematically illustrated in Fig. 3 and depicts the XCS on the one hand, and the IC on the other. Both parts are connected by the MLI. Whenever a new situation $\sigma(t)$ arrives at the XCS, the MLI reports this value to the IC, which in turn interpolates a corresponding output value o_{int}. In this certain case, o_{int} can be any value that is independent from single classifier representation. Thus, e.g. the action to execute a_{exec} or the system prediction $P(a)$

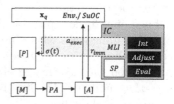

Fig. 3. XCS-IC, schematic illustration

can be interpolated. The latter makes more sense in the context of function approximation with XCSF, which is not part of this paper but a top priority on our current research agenda. For interpolating a_{exec}, we introduce the integration strategy *Action Selection Integration* (ASI), which works as follows: Whenever a new $\sigma(t)$ arrives at the XCS, the IC is asked to calculate the weights w_i as defined by Eq. 1. Since actions or rather classes are categorical values, we define $W_{a_j} := \{w_i | f(\mathbf{x}_i) = a_j\}$ as set of all weights w_i for corresponding sampling points s_i whose function value $f(\mathbf{x}_i)$ (encoding an action $a \in A$) equals a_j. Let $w_{acc}^{a_j} = \sum_{w_i \in W} w_i$ be the accumulated weight for action a_j, and normalized between [0,1]. Accordingly, we enhance the system prediction calculation (cf. Sect. 3) as follows:

$$P(a_j)' = \min[P(a_j) \cdot (1 + w_{acc}^{a_j} \cdot T_{IC}), maxPayoff] \qquad (2)$$

The constant *maxPayoff* determines the highest possible reward r_{imm} to be retrieved from the system. As can be seen, the initial system prediction value is increased by $w_{acc}^{a_j} \cdot 100\,\%$, discounted by the trust-level $T_{IC} \in [0,1]$. With that interpolation-based action-selection-regime, we extend XCS' available information to select an appropriate action a_{exec} to be executed.

Discussion. The XCS-IC approach follows the idea of loosely coupling two individual components, in this case the MLS and the IC. This approach yields chances, but also challenges that are discussed in the following lines. One advantage results from the interplay between the IC's subcomponents. The evaluation component continuously monitors the interpolant's quality in terms of T_{IC}, what becomes possible due to the output values that are feasible to be interpolated. These values, such as a_{exec} or $P(a_j)$ are global and classifier-independent, what makes them easier to be evaluated by considering the gained reward r_{imm} in combination with the actual values XCS has calculated or rather executed. With the evaluation metric E, the IC is enabled to decide whether or not the interpolated values would have been more appropriate than the actual ones yielded by XCS. The decision function A provided by the adjustment sub-component of IC is responsible for the extension of the available sampling points $s_i \in SP$. This automated decision acts like a preselection of suitable sampling point candidates s^* which in turn assures a certain level of quality regarding all s_i. However, the maintenance of SP is a highly problem-dependent and thus non-trivial task. Both, the evaluation metric E as well as the decision function A have to be defined once for any possible problem case. Furthermore, XCS involves a variety of algorithmic steps where interpolation can be meaningfully integrated, e.g. the covering mechanism for generating novel classifiers or the GA. Both parts of XCS operate on the classifier level, i.e. attributes such as C, p, ϵ and F are assigned or rather modified. To give an idea how to exploit these interesting points of IC integration, the following lines introduce an alternative architecture along with an additional integration strategy.

5.2   Classifiers Serving as Sampling Points - XCS-CIC

To overcome the aforementioned drawbacks of the XCS-IC approach, we will now introduce the second architectural concept of enriching XCS with interpolation techniques.

As Fig. 4 illustrates, we now interpret the population of classifiers [P] as current set of all available sampling points SP. Thus, at each timestep t we have a certain (sub-)set of $s_i \in SP$ represented by individual classifiers $cl_i \in [P]$. Therefore, we redefine $s_i := cl_i$ which implies that we now have a variety of possible function values to be interpolated. Let the coordinate $\mathbf{x}_i \in \mathbb{R}^n$ of s_i be represented by the center points of a classifier's (cl_i) interval predicates (l_j, u_j), i.e. $x_j = l_j + (u_j - l_j)/2$ for $j = 1 \ldots n$. For the integration strategies that are introduced in the following, we further define $f^p(cl_i) = cl_i.p$ to return the current prediction scalar p of classifier cl_i. Analogously, we further define $f^\epsilon(cl_i) = cl_i.\epsilon$ and $f^F(cl_i) = cl_i.F$. With these fundamental thoughts at hand we will now present an additional integration strategy, called *Offspring Initials Integration* (OII), that focuses the involved GA. Eq. 3 exemplarily formalizes the OII procedure for the prediction error ϵ:

$$cl_{off}.\epsilon = \frac{\sum_{i=1}^{|[A]|} w_i \cdot f^\epsilon(cl_i)}{\sum_{i=1}^{|[A]|} w_i}, \text{with } cl_i \in [A] \tag{3}$$

The set of considered sampling points is defined to be the action set [A], which assures to interpolate in between the environmental niche of interest.

In XCS' standard GA, values for the attributes p, ϵ and F are set to be the mean of both parents, partially discounted by a predefined factor. Although, this is a valid mindset from the genetics perspective, we believe that more than the 'knowledge' of the parents should be involved. This is exactly what OII assures by means of interpolating between the attribute values of all classifiers in the considered environmental niche (determined by [A]) and with an identical action a_{exec}.

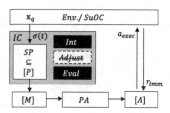

Fig. 4. XCS-CIC, schematic illustration

Discussion. With OII novel classifiers generated by the GA are assigned with attribute values that take already gained experience of existing classifiers into account. This makes the XCS more robust against possibly arbitrarily set design parameters and thus leads to a reduced configuration space. As Fig. 4 suggests, the adjustment component becomes obsolete, as now $SP \subseteq [P]$ and XCS itself takes care of deleting and adding classifiers to [P]. This also has a positive effect on the interpolation's time complexity, which grows linear with the number of $s_i \in SP$. Another clear advantage of XCS-CIC in comparison to the XCS-IC approach is the possibility to involve interpolation at nearly all sites of XCS' internal mechanisms. Accordingly, the IC is not limited to global and classifier-independent attributes such as a_{exec} or $P(a_j)$. However, also the ASI strategy is realizable with XCS-CIC. Furthermore, XCS-CIC does not learn on two sites as it is the case for the loose coupling approach XCS-IC, where knowledge is held in [P] and SP. On the other hand, a clear drawback is the challenge of selecting classifiers that constitute SP in the case of ASI. A preselection is necessary as [P] partially consists of classifiers that are not experienced enough to yield suitable information. According to that, especially at the beginning of a learning task the IC will presumably yield arbitrary outputs whose quality increases with runtime. Besides the measurable T_{IC} for the ASI strategy, a first proposal for increasing the initial quality of interpolation would be a preselection of $cl_i \in [P]$ by means of considering a form of quality metric for individual classifiers. Therefore, we define a classifier's quality as $Q(cl) = cl.p \cdot cl.F \cdot cl.exp$, where $cl.exp$ denotes a classifier's *experience*, i.e. how often it was member of an action set [A] since the beginning of the learning task. Thus, $Q(cl)$ considers not only the predicted payoff, but also how accurately it is predicted and how experienced cl is. With this metric at hand, only classifiers whose quality is greater than the mean quality of the entire classifier population [P] will be considered for the ASI strategy.

6   Experiments

In the following, the presented approaches are experimentally validated on a theoretical *checkerboard problem* (CBP) that is a well-known benchmark problem for XCS evaluation (cf. e.g. [16]). A CBP(n, n_d) instance is defined by two parameters: (1) the number of dimensions n, and (2) the number of divisions per dimension n_d. Hence, a classical chessboard would be a CBP(2,8) instance. Each dimension $x_i, i = 1 \ldots n$ is defined between [0,1]. According to that, a situation $\sigma(t)$ at time step t is an n-dimensional vector $\mathbf{x} \in \mathbb{R}^n$. The task of XCS is to learn of which color ('black' or 'white') the checkerboard field enclosing $\mathbf{x}$ is. If XCS guesses correct, $maxPayoff = 1000$ is retrieved as reward r_{imm}, 0 otherwise.

6.1   XCS on CBP(3,3)

In our first experiment, XCS is asked to learn a 3-dimensional hypercube with alternating colors 'black' and 'white'. First, we test the performance of an unmodified XCS on a CBP(3,3) instance, since this configuration is not a difficult challenge for standard XCS and we want to show that even for non-challenging problems, an increase in system performance can be achieved. If not stated differently, XCS is configured with standard parameters[2]. As we are confronted with a real-valued problem space, interval predicates are needed. We decided for the *unordered bound representation* [16] and set $r_0 = 1/n_d = 0.33$, where r_0 denotes a maximum span that is subtracted from a classifier's condition lower bound l_i

---

[2] $\alpha = 0.1$, $\beta = 0.2$, $\delta = 0.1$, $\nu = 5$, $\theta_{GA} = 12$, $\epsilon_0 = 10$, $\theta_{mna} = 2$, $\theta_{del} = 20$, $\theta_{sub} = 20$, $\chi = 0.8$, $\mu = 0.04$, $p_I = 10.0$, $\epsilon_I = 0.0$, $F_I = 0.01$, $m_0 = 0.1$. GA subsumption is activated and alternate explore and exploit trials are used. For a detailed description of the standard parameters the reader is referred to [4, 19].

and added to its upper bound u_i, respectively (cf. [20]). The maximum number N of *micro-classifiers* [17] in [P] is restricted to 2000. We decided to also set the maximum number of sampling points s_{max} to 2000, as it allows for a comparison between the XCS-IC and the XCS-CIC concept. This restriction only affects the XCS-IC approach, since for XCS-CIC holds $SP \subseteq [P]$. All experimental results are averaged over 30 runs. For CBP(3,3), XCS learns for 100000 iterations in each run. We also conducted paired t-tests with a significance-level α of 0.05 to substantiate the statistical expressiveness of our results.

Figures 5 (a) and (b) indicate that both of the presented concepts, XCS-IC and XCS-CIC, outperform the standard XCS variant in terms of the system error, which is an absolute error of the system's payoff prediction $P(a_{exec})$ and the actually received reward r_{imm}. More quantitatively, XCS-IC significantly

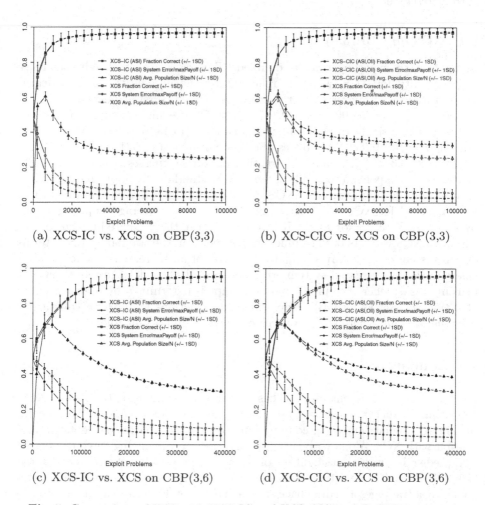

(a) XCS-IC vs. XCS on CBP(3,3)   (b) XCS-CIC vs. XCS on CBP(3,3)

(c) XCS-IC vs. XCS on CBP(3,6)   (d) XCS-CIC vs. XCS on CBP(3,6)

Fig. 5. Comparison of XCS with XCS-IC and XCS-CIC on 3-D CBP instances

($p \approx 2.13e^{-39}$) decreases the system error by $\sim$38 % (XCS-CIC actually by $\sim$41 % which is also highly significant for $p \approx 6.63e^{-38}$). The comparison of the variant's fractions of correct classifications ('black' or 'white') shows only marginal but still significant improvements (XCS-IC by $\sim$0.2 %, $p = 9.03e^{-23}$ and $\sim$0.27 %, $p = 8.08e^{-19}$ for XCS-CIC). Another observed metric is the average size of [P]. Since ASI is only an action-selection-regime for exploiting the current population, it has no effect on the size of [P]. Accordingly, the graphs overlap in Figs. 5 (a) and (c). In contrast, the OII strategy has a more far-reaching effect on the classifier evolution. This causes the obvious and significant increase of the average population size by $\sim$21 %. We attribute this effect to the offspring classifiers. A thorough investigation of the question how the ASI and OII strategy separately affect the classifier evolution is not part of this paper, but under current research.

6.2   XCS on CBP(3,6)

In the second experiment n_d is doubled. This causes a challenging increase of complexity for XCS, which is reflected by the necessity of 400000 learning iterations. Parameters are the same as for the first experiment, except of: $N = s_{max} = 20000$, $r_0 = 0.167$. Even for the more complex CBP(3,6) instance, the insights from the first experiment can be observed. XCS-IC significantly ($p \approx 1.75e^{-46}$) reduces the system error by $\sim$31 % (XCS-CIC by $\sim$35 %, $p \approx 3.37e^{-42}$). Again, the fraction of correct guesses is only marginally increased in comparison to a well-parametrized standard XCS, but indeed statistical relevant for both variants (XCS-IC by $\sim$0.32 %, $p = 2.47e^{-28}$ and $\sim$0.73 %, $p = 3.59e^{-20}$ for XCS-CIC). Also, an increase of the average population size by about 12 % occurs for XCS-CIC. To summarize, the presented interpolation-extended XCS variants both significantly outperform the standard XCS in terms of the system error – partially at the expense of an increased number of classifiers in [P]. A decreased system error is especially beneficial in more complex learning tasks, where the prediction landscape is determined by higher number of actions/classes as for CBP. Approximating functions with XCSF constitutes a further domain where the system error plays an important role.

7   Conclusion

In this paper, different approaches to integrate interpolation into XCS' algorithmic structure have been proposed. Therefore, a novel interpolation component IC was introduced in conjunction with two alternative concepts to integrate it with XCS. Along with that, two strategies for involving the interpolated 'knowledge' in internal mechanisms of XCS, more precisely (1) the incorporated GA (OII), and (2) the action selection regime (ASI), were presented. The corresponding advantages and drawbacks for each of the architectural approaches have been discussed. Significant improvements on a theoretical checkerboard problem quantitatively underpin the potential of incorporating interpolation techniques into the well-established structure of XCS. However, we deem the presented techniques especially valuable for problem scenarios from the real-world domain OC systems are usually faced with. Due to the inherent dynamics of real-world systems, an unforeseen event can change the current situation abruptly. Thus, situations arise where the learning component has not gained appropriate knowledge for this unforeseen incident. By means of using the IC, such rarely arising situations can be handled more effectively, as nearby and already covered areas of the problem space can be taken into account for generating a suitable reaction. Our current research activities are concerned with transferring the presented techniques to the problem domain of urban traffic control. Our preliminary findings show that with the incorporation of IC, quickly increasing traffic demands can be handled more appropriately in terms of a reduced average delay for the considered intersection. Furthermore, we are currently experimenting with enhancing the performance of XCSF for function approximation, which in turn constitutes an interesting testbed for OC systems in terms of the possibility to model functions that mimic real-world characteristics such as the core problems that were mentioned at the beginning of this paper.

References

1. Müller-Schloer, C., Schmeck, H., Ungerer, T. (eds.): Organic Computing - A Paradigm Shift for Complex Systems. Autonomic Systems, 1st edn. Birkhäuser, Basel (2011)
2. Auf, A.E.S., Litza, M., Maehle, E.: Distributed Fault-Tolerant Robot Control Architecture Based on Organic Computing Principles. In: Hinchey, M., Pagnoni, A., Rammig, F.J., Schmeck, H. (eds.) Biologically-Inspired Collaborative Computing. IFIP–The International Federation for Information Processing, vol. 268, pp. 115–124. Springer, New York (2008)
3. Bernauer, A., Zeppenfeld, J., Bringmann, O., Herkersdorf, A., Rosenstiel, W.: Combining software and hardware LCS for lightweight on-chip learning. In: Müller-Schloer, C., Schmeck, H., Ungerer, T. (eds.) Organic Computing – A Paradigm Shift for Complex, vol. 1, pp. 253–265. Birkäuser, Basel (2011)
4. Butz, M.V., Wilson, S.W.: An algorithmic description of XCS. In: Lanzi, P.L., Stolzmann, W., Wilson, S.W. (eds.) IWLCS 2000. LNCS (LNAI), vol. 1996, pp. 253–272. Springer, Heidelberg (2001)
5. Butz, M., Goldberg, D., Lanzi, P.: Gradient descent methods in learning classifier systems: improving XCS performance in multistep problems. IEEE Trans. Evol. Comput. **9**(5), 452–473 (2005)
6. Butz, M., Lanzi, P., Wilson, S.: Function approximation with XCS: hyperellipsoidal conditions, recursive least squares, and compaction. IEEE Trans. Evol. Comput. **12**(3), 355–376 (2008)
7. Fredivianus, N., Kara, K., Schmeck, H.: Stay real!: XCS with rule combining for real values. In: Proceedings of GECCO 2012, pp. 1493–1494. ACM, NY (2012)
8. Fredivianus, N., Prothmann, H., Schmeck, H.: XCS revisited: a novel discovery component for the eXtended classifier system. In: Deb, K. (ed.) SEAL 2010. LNCS, vol. 6457, pp. 289–298. Springer, Heidelberg (2010)
9. Holland, J.H.: Adaptation in Natural and Artificial Systems, 2nd edn. University of Michigan Press, Ann Arbor (1975)

10. Kovacs, T., Iqbal, M., Shafi, K., Urbanowicz, R.: Special issue on the 20th anniversary of XCS. Evol. Intell. **8**(2–3), 51–53 (2015)
11. Renka, R.J.: Multivariate interpolation of large sets of scattered data. ACM Trans. Math. Softw. **14**(2), 139–148 (1988)
12. Rochner, F., Prothmann, H., Branke, J., Müller-Schloer, C., Schmeck, H.: An organic architecture for traffic light controllers. In: GI Jahrestagung (1), LNI, vol. 93, pp. 120–127 (2006)
13. Schwarz, H.R., Köckler, N.: Numerische Mathematik. Interpolation und Approximation. Teubner, Verlag (2011)
14. Shepard, D.: A Two-dimensional Interpolation Function for Irregularly-spaced Data. In: Proceedings of 23rd ACM National Confeference. pp. 517–524. ACM, NY, USA (1968)
15. Stein, A.: Neighborhood-based Interpolation for XCS Improvements. In: Organic Computing: Doctoral Dissertation Colloquium 2014, pp. 71–83. Kassel University Press, Kassel (2014)
16. Stone, C., Bull, L.: For Real! XCS with Continuous-Valued Inputs. Evol. Comp. **11**(3), 298–336 (2003)
17. Wilson, S.W.: Classifier fitness based on accuracy. Evol. Comp. **3**(2), 149–175 (1995)
18. Wilson, S.W.: Generalization in the XCS Classifier System. Genetic Programming 1998. In: Proceedings of the 3rd Annual Conference, Morgan Kaufmann, University of Wisconsin, Madison, Wisconsin, USA (1998)
19. Wilson, S.W.: Get real! XCS with continuous-valued inputs. In: Lanzi, P.L., Stolzmann, W., Wilson, S.W. (eds.) IWLCS 1999. LNCS (LNAI), vol. 1813, pp. 209–219. Springer, Heidelberg (2000)
20. Wilson, S.W.: Classifiers that approximate functions. Natural Comp. **1**(2–3), 211–234 (2002)
21. Wilson, S.W.: Three architectures for continuous action. In: Kovacs, T., Llorà, X., Takadama, K., Lanzi, P.L., Stolzmann, W., Wilson, S.W. (eds.) IWLCS 2003. LNCS (LNAI), vol. 4399, pp. 239–257. Springer, Heidelberg (2007)
22. Zeppenfeld, J., Bouajila, A., Stechele, W., Bernauer, A., Bringmann, O., Rosenstiel, W., Herkersdorf, A.: Applying ASoC to multi-core applications for workload. In: Müller-Schloer, C., Schmeck, H., Ungerer, T. (eds.) Organic Computing–A Paradigm Shift for Complex Systems. Autonomic Systems, vol. 1, pp. 461–472. Birkäuser, Basel (2011)
23. Zeppenfeld, J., Herkersdorf, A.: Applying autonomic principles for workload management in multi-core systems on chip. In: Proceedings of ICAC 2011, pp. 3–10 (2011)

Reliability Aspects in NoCs, Caches, and GPUs

Estimation of End-to-End Packet Error Rates for NoC Multicasts

Michael Vonbun$^{(\boxtimes)}$, Thomas Wild, and Andreas Herkersdorf

Institute for Integrated Systems, Technische Universität München,
Arcisstr. 21, 80290 Munich, Germany
{michael.vonbun,thomas.wild,herkersdorf}@tum.de
http://www.lis.ei.tum.de

Abstract. As the number of tiles in a System-on-Chip (SoC) increase, Network-on-Chip (NoC) becomes the favored interconnect. With an increased number of tiles, applications are subject to being partitioned and distributed to multiple tiles as well. To deal with the resulting traffic efficiently, the NoC needs to support network multicasts. On the other hand, advanced techniques like aggressive voltage scaling and feature size reduction in technology generations of 22 nm and below introduce new variability challenges to SoC designers in general. Especially for Network-on-Chip (NoC) as on-Chip communication backbone, the impact of bit flips in registers and on wires is of high importance. This paper focuses on the expected end-to-end bit and packet error rates for multicast groups. The estimations are based on the probabilities of single bit flips of NoC entities such as buffers or links. Being based on binary-symmetric-channels (BSCs), the proposed approach abstracts technology details and allows for fast design space exploration during early phases of HW/SW system design to assess the reliability of NoC including different application partitionings without time-consuming network simulations.

1 Introduction

Network-on-Chip (NoC) has become the standard for interconnecting many-processor System-on-Chip (MPSoC). As feature size decreases, the chip becomes more vulnerable to both persistent and soft-errors [1,3]. In addition, System-on-Chip (SoC) vulnerability is also increased by-design using techniques such as aggressive voltage scaling to address the reduction of power consumption [4].

Therefore, on-Chip communication has to be protected, providing the MPSoC with a reliable communication infrastructure [9]. The predominant technique used for protecting NoC communication is point-to-point coding, i.e. flits are encoded and decoded at every single router [5,8]. Treating an entire NoC as an unreliable communication channel and using end-to-end coding mechanisms might be more flexible.

In either case, as code design is based on the expected error rate, it is crucial to estimate the probabilities that a bit might flip or that a packet gets corrupted.

© Springer International Publishing Switzerland 2016
F. Hannig et al. (Eds.): ARCS 2016, LNCS 9637, pp. 363–374, 2016.
DOI: 10.1007/978-3-319-30695-7_27

1.1 Related Work

Existing approaches towards error rate estimation for NoCs are manifold. Running simulations or emulations, as has been demonstrated in [7], is a straight forward approach for system designers.

To overcome tedious, time and resource consuming simulations or emulations, analytic approaches have been proposed [2,11]. While [2] focuses on point-to-point coding schemes and models the links of NoCs as noisy channels, the focus of [11] is on end-to-end packet error rate estimation by modeling NoC communication as a cascade of binary-symmetric-channels (BSC) which addresses NoC unicast connections. The authors of both [2] and [11] did, however, not address a multicast communication setting. But, as has been emphasized by [6], adding multicast support in NoCs can result in an overall performance enhancement.

Our contribution is an approach to model NoC multicasts based on the ideas of [11] of modeling NoC resources such as buffers, switches and links as BSCs. We provide algorithms to calculate end-to-end multicast transition matrices retaining full system information, i.e. the error probability of every possible subset of a multicast group can be estimated. We further utilize these probabilities in basic cost functions to compare the performance of different multicast groups.

The paper is organized as follows. In Sect. 2 we will review the system model and provide the algorithms to compute the transition matrices which are used to obtain the end-to-end multicast bit error rate estimates. In Sect. 3 we utilize these estimates for packet error estimation and cost function derivation. We provide a hands-on example in Sect. 4 and evaluate both distinct multicast groups as well as randomly selected ones in terms of the derived cost functions. Section 5 concludes the paper.

2 Multicast Bit Error Probabilities

Before we proceed with the derivation of end-to-end multicast error estimates, we will briefly describe the system model of [11] for the sake of completeness.

2.1 System Model

An arbitrary entity k, such as a buffer in a router or a wire connecting two routers, is modeled as a binary-symmetric-channel (BSC) with conditional transition probabilities $w_{0|0}^{(k)}$, $w_{0|1}^{(k)}$, $w_{1|0}^{(k)}$, and $w_{1|1}^{(k)}$ as depicted in Fig. 1. $w_{x|y}^{(k)}$ denotes the conditionally transition probability of entity k, which is the probability that the input to entity k was an x and an y is observed at its output.

The transition vector, system input vector, and atomic 4×4 transition matrix of that entity k, deduced from Fig. 1 and given in detail in [11], is

$$\boldsymbol{p}_k = \begin{bmatrix} p_{k;0|0} \\ p_{k;0|1} \\ p_{k;1|0} \\ p_{k;1|1} \end{bmatrix}, \quad \boldsymbol{p}_0 = \begin{bmatrix} 1 \\ 0 \\ 0 \\ 1 \end{bmatrix}, \quad \boldsymbol{W}_k = \begin{bmatrix} w_{0|0}^{(k)} & 0 & w_{0|1}^{(k)} & 0 \\ 0 & w_{0|0}^{(k)} & 0 & w_{0|1}^{(k)} \\ w_{1|0}^{(k)} & 0 & w_{1|1}^{(k)} & 0 \\ 0 & w_{1|0}^{(k)} & 0 & w_{1|1}^{(k)} \end{bmatrix}, \forall\, k. \tag{1}$$

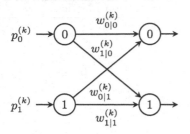

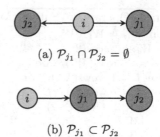

(a) $\mathcal{P}_{j_1} \cap \mathcal{P}_{j_2} = \emptyset$

(b) $\mathcal{P}_{j_1} \subset \mathcal{P}_{j_2}$

Fig. 1. Schematic of a binary-symmetric-channel (BSC) with conditional transition probabilities modeling an arbitrary NoC entity k.

Fig. 2. Multicast graph categories: (a) disjoint, (b) subset.

Algorithm 1. Operator $\|$: Disjoint Concatenation Transition Matrices

---

    function $\boldsymbol{W}_{ij} = \boldsymbol{W}_i \| \boldsymbol{W}_j$
        Init: $\boldsymbol{W}_{ij} = zeros(2^{(\log_2(\text{rows}(\boldsymbol{W}_i)\cdot\text{rows}(\boldsymbol{W}_j))-1)}, 4)$
        for $K = 1:\text{rows}(\boldsymbol{W}_i)/2$ do
            for $L = 1:\text{rows}(\boldsymbol{W}_j)/2$ do
5:               $m = \text{rows}(\boldsymbol{W}_j) \cdot (K-1) + 2 \cdot (L-1) + 1$
               $k = 2 \cdot (K-1) + 1, \; l = 2 \cdot (L-1) + 1$
               $[\boldsymbol{W}_{ij}]_{m,1} = [\boldsymbol{W}_{ij}]_{m+1,2} = [\boldsymbol{W}_i]_{k,1} \cdot [\boldsymbol{W}_j]_{l,1}$
               $[\boldsymbol{W}_{ij}]_{m,3} = [\boldsymbol{W}_{ij}]_{m+1,4} = [\boldsymbol{W}_i]_{k,3} \cdot [\boldsymbol{W}_j]_{l,3}$
            end for
10:      end for
    end function

2.2 Bit Error Probabilities

Let i be the source and $J = \{j_1, \ldots, j_n\}$ be the destinations of a multicast group. If the source naively injects n packets into the network, separated by time and routes taken, the calculation of the end-to-end error rate estimates is reduced to the calculation of n unicast connections and basically the results of [11] apply.

From the network perspective, splitting the multicast up into multiple unicasts greatly reduces the system performance, as common shared paths are used multiple times. More efficient multicast routing algorithms will share paths to a certain extent. In either case, we require algorithms that consistently combine the transition matrices of NoC entities.

Our approach towards multicast error rate estimation is based on arbitrary routing algorithms, retains full system information and provides structured probability computation.

Multicast Graph Decomposition Building Blocks. To derive the basic building blocks for decomposing every multicast group, we start with the minimum multicast group of two destinations j_1 and j_2 which are arranged such that

---

Algorithm 2. Operator ∘: Subset Combination of Transition Matrices

---

    function $W_{ij} = W_i \circ W_j$
      Init: $W_{ij} = zeros(2^{(\log_2(\text{rows}(W_i)\cdot\text{rows}(W_j))-1)}, 4)$
      for $K = 1:\text{rows}(W_j)/2$ **do**
          for $L = 1:\text{rows}(W_i)/2$ **do**
5:             $m = \text{rows}(W_i) \cdot (K-1) + 2 \cdot (L-1) + 1$
               $n = 2 \cdot (K + 1\%2) + 1,\ k = 2 \cdot K,\ l = 2 \cdot L$
               $[W_{ij}]_{m,1} = [W_i]_{l-1,n} \cdot [W_j]_{k-1,1}$
               $[W_{ij}]_{m,3} = [W_i]_{l-2,n} \cdot [W_j]_{k-1,3}$
               $[W_{ij}]_{m+1,2} = [W_i]_{l,n+1} \cdot [W_j]_{k,2}$
10:              $[W_{ij}]_{m+1,4} = [W_i]_{l,n+1} \cdot [W_j]_{k,4}$
          end for
      end for
    end function

---

they can be reached with two hops only. Clearly, there are exactly two possible cases depicted in Fig. 2: either both destinations are direct neighbors of the source, or one destination lies within the path of the other. Both cases result in different multicast transition matrices, accounting for the special structure.

Every multicast graph can be piecewise composed (or decomposed) of subgraphs which are either (1) a cascade of BSCs, (2) disjoint BSC paths, or (3) a subset graph. The operators needed to construct the final conditional transition matrix are (1) matrix multiplication, (2) matrix concatenation as provided by Algorithm 1, and (3) matrix subset-combination as provided by Algorithm 2.

Multicast Transition Matrix Generation. In a multicast group of n destinations, Algorithm 3 constructs the $2^{n+1} \times 4$-dimensional conditional multicast transition matrix $W_{iJ} \in [0,1]^{2^{n+1} \times 4}$ from the atomic entity transition matrices that describes the transition of a single bit to all n destinations. The core of this algorithm is the combination of matrix multiplication for BSC cascades in the multicast communication request (ll. 9 and 20) and a concatenation of transition matrices that accounts for disjoint (l. 15) and subset paths (ll. 7 and 18).

Multicast Conditional Transition Probability Vector. Left hand side multiplication with the input generating vector $p_{\text{in}} = [1,0,0,1]^{\text{T}}$ yields the vector of the 2^{n+1} conditional multicast transition probabilities

$$p_{iJ} = W_{iJ} \cdot p_{\text{in}}. \tag{2}$$

As this vector contains all conditional transition probabilities related to the multicast, by properly combining them, the success probabilities of all 2^n possible subsets $L_k \subset J$ of the multicast group can be calculated.

As can be seen from the sheer amount of probabilities generated, this method is only feasible for multicast groups of less than around 18 sinks (yielding more than half a million transition probabilities). This property is inherent to multicasting and can not be relaxed without sacrificing system information.

Algorithm 3. Get Multicast Transition Matrix

---

   function $[W] = \text{GET}(W, n, J)$
      if $n.num\_children == 0$ then
         return W
      else if $n.num\_children == 1$ then
5:       if $n \in J$ then
           $W_{\text{tmp}} \leftarrow \text{GET}(1, n.child(1), J)$
           $W \leftarrow W_{\text{tmp}} \circ W$
         else
           $W \leftarrow W_{n, n.child(1)} \cdot W$
10:         $W \leftarrow \text{GET}(W, n.child(1), J)$
         end if
      else
         $W_{\text{tmp}} \leftarrow \text{GET}(1, n.child(1), J)$
         for $k = 2: n.num\_children$ do
15:           $W_{\text{tmp}} \leftarrow W_{\text{tmp}} \,||\, \text{GET}(1, n.child(k), J)$
         end for
         if $n \in J$ then
           $W \leftarrow W_{\text{tmp}} \circ W$
         else
20:         $W \leftarrow W_{\text{tmp}} \cdot W$
         end if
      end if
   end function

Reduced Multicast Transition Matrix. Sacrificing system information for the sake of feasibility is straight forward if we keep the 2 top- and bottom-most rows of transition matrices only, as these lines account for the full- and empty-set only. Thus, all other information on one of the subsets of the multicast group is lost and exactly two probabilities are obtained, i.e. the probability that all destinations in the multicast group received the data correctly as well as its inverse probability. We are therefore still able to give performance measures for big multicast groups.

By issuing the reduced variant of the algorithms provided, it is more advantageous to provide proper operators instead of using the standard ones described in Algorithms 1 and 2 and keeping only the 2 top- and bottom-most rows. This is achieved by replacing the concatenation operator of Algorithm 1 by the elementwise (Hadamard) product, and the subset-combination operator of Algorithm 2 by the left-multiplication of the subset destination transition matrix with the diagonal of the superset transition matrix.

3 Efficiency and Cost of Packet Multicast

As there are n destinations involved in the multicast group J, there are 2^n possible subsets $L_k \subset J$ of these nodes. These 2^n subsets represent the 2^n atomic events that exactly the nodes in the subset observe the right bit, but the ones not in the subset observe a flipped bit. Calculating the probabilities that all nodes of a distinct subset L_k – or event – did or did not receive their data correctly, for every single subset, gives rise to simple cost models, which will be presented subsequently.

3.1   Event Probability Calculation

The probabilities of the atomic events can be directly obtained by combining distinct entries of the conditional transition probability vector p_{iJ}. The way we constructed p_{iJ}, we can use a structured matrix D to obtain the 2^n event probabilities.

Let D be the $2^n \times 2^{n+1}$ dimensional event probability generating matrix as

$$[D]_{k,l} = \begin{cases} p_0, & \text{if } k \text{ odd} \wedge l = k \vee k \text{ even} \wedge l = 2^n + 1 - k \\ p_1, & \text{if } k \text{ even} \wedge l = k \vee k \text{ odd} \wedge l = 2^n + 1 - k, \\ 0 & \text{otherwise} \end{cases} \tag{3}$$

where p_0 and p_1 are the probabilities, that the source injected a zero or a one, respectively. Then,

$$p_{L_k}{}_{\subset}^{\mathrm{T}} = \left(D p_{iJ}\right)^{\mathrm{T}} = \left[p_J, p_{\emptyset}, p_{J \setminus j_n}, p_{j_n}, \ldots, p_{j_1}, p_{J \setminus j_1}\right],$$

is the 2^n dimensional vector of success probabilities of the subsets, where p_{L_k} is the probability, that exactly the destinations in the subset L_k received the right data. The subset error probability vector $q_{L_k}{}_{\subset}$ is likewise calculated, as $q_{L_k} = p_{J \setminus L_k}$, i.e. the event success probabilities are merely relabeled to provide the equivalent event error probabilities.

$$q_{L_k}{}_{\subset}^{\mathrm{T}} = \left(D p_{iJ}\right)^{\mathrm{T}} = \left[q_{\emptyset}, q_J, q_{j_n}, q_{J \setminus j_n}, \ldots, q_{J \setminus j_1}, q_{j_1}\right], \tag{4}$$

where q_{L_k} is the probability that exactly the destinations in the subset L_k did not receive the right data.

Of course, the sum of all event probabilities, success or error, equals one.

3.2   Packet Multicast

So far, we followed a single bit through a network to get its end-to-end error rate. In an NoC, however, we transmit packets having F payload flits having B bit each. The estimation of the end-to-end packet success and error rate Q_{iL_k} and $\bar{Q}_{iL_k}$ for any subset L_k of the multicast group J is readily obtained once the success probabilities of the subsets are calculated (cf. [11]).

$$Q_{iL_k} = p_{L_k}^{FB}, \quad \bar{Q}_{iL_k} = \sum_{k=1}^{FB} \binom{FB}{k} p_{L_k}^{FB-k} q_{L_k}^{k} = \left(p_{L_k} + q_{L_k}\right)^{FB} - p_{L_k}^{FB}. \tag{5}$$

We assumed an uncorrelated error process to efficiently calculate estimates on the packet error rates. Although a more elaborate error model provides more accurate results, the deviation is only small, as has been pointed out in [11], but adds a huge increase in system model complexity.

3.3   Multicast Efficiency

In order to compare different multicast groups, we will first quantify the usefulness or efficiency of a multicast group. Deriving an efficiency function is straight forward and will be illustrated by an example.

Let the subset success probability of a distinct subset be close to one. Then, the nodes in this subset will receive the correct data almost certainly. Also, the more members the subset has, the more receivers get the correct data, thus sending to this very subset is more efficient than sending to a subset with equal success probability but with fewer members. These considerations give rise to a simple efficiency function λ_{L_k}, relating the cardinality of the subset L_k to its success probability:

$$\lambda_{L_k} = |L_k| \cdot Q_{iL_k} = |L_k| \cdot p_{L_k}^{FB}. \tag{6}$$

By a summation of the efficiency factors of all subsets, we get a measure of the overall multicast efficiency

$$\Lambda = \sum_{L \subset J} \lambda_L = \sum_{L \subset J} |L| \cdot Q_L = \sum_{L \subset J} |L| \cdot p_L^{FB}, \tag{7}$$

which accounts perfectly for describing the entire group, as the event success probabilities are related by the fact that $\sum_{L \subset J} p_L = 1$.

3.4   Multicast Cost Model

In addition to comparing the multicast by its efficiency, we also want to target the cost inflicted by multicasting. Sending to one or multiple destinations is, in general, related to a certain cost such as power consumption and latency. We do not put a constraint on these base costs here, but focus on the hop count in the results section, as it is strongly related to both power consumption, network resources and latency.

Based on the error probability of the subset L_k, the cost for serving the destinations in L_k will increase with increasing subset error probability. We model this cost by considering a simple retransmission based network. The cost of subset L_k computes as

$$\Gamma_{L_k} = \lim_{l \to \infty} \gamma_{L_k} + \gamma_{L_k} \bar{Q}_{iL_k} + \gamma_{L_k} \bar{Q}_{iL_k}^2 + \ldots + \gamma_{L_k} \bar{Q}_{iL_k}^l$$

$$= \gamma_{L_k} \sum_{l=0}^{\infty} \bar{Q}_{iL_k}^l = \frac{\gamma_{L_k}}{1 - \bar{Q}_{iL_k}}, \tag{8}$$

while serving the entire multicast group inflicts costs as

$$\Gamma = \gamma_J + \sum_{L \subset J:\, L \neq \emptyset} (\Gamma_L - \gamma_L) = \gamma_J + \sum_{L \subset J:\, L \neq \emptyset} \bar{Q}_L \Gamma_L = \gamma_J + \sum_{L \subset J:\, L \neq \emptyset} \frac{\bar{Q}_L \gamma_L}{1 - \bar{Q}_L}, \tag{9}$$

which is composed of the cost serving the group at the first transmission plus the retransmission costs of every subset of the multicast group.

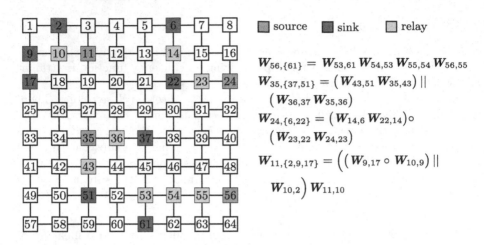

$$W_{56,\{61\}} = W_{53,61}\, W_{54,53}\, W_{55,54}\, W_{56,55}$$

$$W_{35,\{37,51\}} = \big(W_{43,51}\, W_{35,43}\big)\, \|$$
$$\big(W_{36,37}\, W_{35,36}\big)$$

$$W_{24,\{6,22\}} = \big(W_{14,6}\, W_{22,14}\big)\circ$$
$$\big(W_{23,22}\, W_{24,23}\big)$$

$$W_{11,\{2,9,17\}} = \Big(\big(W_{9,17}\circ W_{10,9}\big)\, \|$$
$$W_{10,2}\Big)\, W_{11,10}$$

Fig. 3. 8×8 2D-mesh NoC with four different multicast groups.

4   2D-mesh NoC Multicast Evaluation

We use the algorithms and cost functions derived so far to evaluate a 2D-mesh topology. For this, we assume that the routers of the NoC at hand is both input and output buffered and that errors can occur in buffers and links only. This means, when moving from one router to another, three entities have to be traversed: the output buffer, the link, and the input buffer.

We assume that in a single cycle a bit flip in either entity occurs with equal probability. Therefore, buffer-entities become position dependent, as the average service time of buffers differ in a 2D-mesh, and it is more likely for a bit to flip when it stays longer in a buffer. As a bit stays at most one cycle in a link-entity, links do not depend on the router position. We ran a short network simulation of uniform traffic using the popular event-driven network simulator Omnet++ to extract reasonable average service times of the buffers of the NoC.

Although we focus on a 8×8 2D-mesh topology using xy-routing, we have to emphasize that the algorithms provided are independent of both the topology and the routing mechanism, it is only the order in which entities are visited that is of importance. Our simulation files are available online at [10].

4.1   Distinct Multicast Groups

In a first experiment, we chose four distinct multicast groups within the 2D-mesh NoC, as can be seen from Fig. 3. For comparability, all multicast groups require four hops to reach all sinks, but differ in both the number and the position of the sinks. To give a hands-on example on the algorithms, we provided the four multicast transition matrices alongside the NoC schematic in Fig. 3.

In Fig. 4 we plotted the 18 resulting event probabilities on the bitlevel for these four multicast groups – two for $56, \{61\}$ (red), four for $35, \{37, 51\}$ and

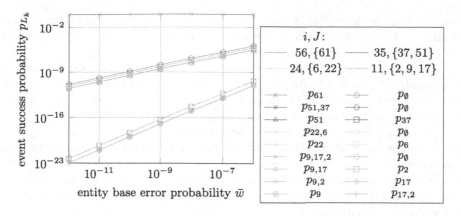

Fig. 4. End-to-end event probabilities p_{L_k} for the four multicast groups of Fig. 3(Color figure online).

$24, \{6, 22\}$ (blue and green), and eight for $11, \{2, 9, 17\}$ (purple) – over varying entity base error probabilities $\bar{w}$. The estimates were computed within $1.3\,\mathrm{s}$ on an Intel Core i5 M 560 clocked at $2.67\,\mathrm{GHz}$.

As can be seen, the probability that all sinks of the multicast group get the correct data is nearly 1 for all four groups (cross markers). Having chosen small entity base error probabilities, this is no surprise.

When we look at the empty set probabilities (circle markers), i.e. the probability that not a single sink received the correct data, we observe that 3 out of 4 groups behave very similar: the resulting probability is approximately the entity base error probability multiplied with the number of entities passed. For the single sink case $(56, \{61\})$, this behavior has already been reported in [11]. The blue circle line, however, is a dramatic outlier: it is decades lower than the entity base error probability. One might think at the first moment that this is because of the position within the NoC as it is the only multicast group in the center of the mesh and thus suffers more from hotspot traffic. But the difference is too big to be caused by an increased service time. The real reason is, that it is the only multicast group that is totally disjoint, i.e. both paths are statistically independent, so their joint error probability is the product of the single error probabilities.

For the same reason, the blue triangle and square lines behave just like unicast connections with 6 entities, having only a minor deviation due to their position in the mesh (triangles being slightly above the squares).

The green group has one outlier (squares) but the remaining lines are almost the same both being dominated by a 6 entity distance, for the circle line being the distance form source to sink 22, for the triangle line being the distance from sink 22 to sink 6, as 22 observed no error. The squares behavior is because it is very unlikely that a bit flips back.

The purple group finally combines the behavior of both disjoint and subset sinks. The triangle and square lines are again almost equal, this is because both describe the probability, that sink 2 and sink 9 and 17 have an error. As the distance of both node 2 and 9 are the same from the source, they yield the same error probability.

The star line again equals a 3-entity error probability, as node 9 observes no error, but 17 does. The diamond marker, on the other hand, has a very low probability, this is similar to the disjoint error case of the blue group (circle line), but now it is nodes 2 and 9 that shall jointly receive erroneous data.

The remaining two lines are in close proximity as well, as 2 and 17 are on disjoint paths (crossed circle line), and, as 9 observed an error, it is unlikely that this error is recovered for 17 (plus line).

Figure 5 additionally shows the cost and efficiency functions Γ and Λ, plotted again over different entity base error probabilities $\bar{w}$. The packets are assumed to have a 256 bit payload.

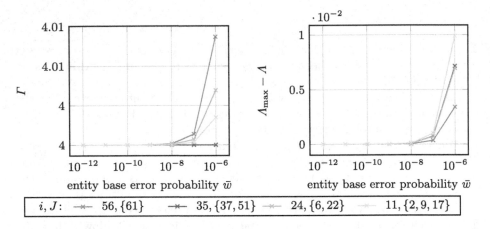

Fig. 5. Cost Γ and deviation form maximum efficiency $\Lambda_{\max} - \Lambda$ for the four multicast groups of Fig. 3 and a packet payload of 256 bit. (Color figure online)

The cost function clearly shows, that the relative position of the sinks to the source has the biggest impact on the inflicted cost. The red group is the worst, as it requires 4 hops to reach the sink. Next is the green group, although sink 6 has the same Manhattan Distance as the sink in the red group, the group cost is reduced because sink 22 is rather close to the source. The purple groups farthest sink has a distance of 3, so this dominating distance is the reason why it has less cost than red and green. Finally, in the blue group both sinks have a distance of 2, so this group is the best in terms of costs.

As for the deviation from the maximum efficiency, we can see that the advantage of a bigger multicast group is maintained and does not suffer significantly from the subset error probabilities.

4.2 Random Multicast Groups

To evaluate an entire NoC, we used a random approach by generating 10000 random multicast groups for 1, 3, and 5 sinks each (so 30000 random connections have been generated in total), and evaluating the cost and efficiency functions for various entity error probabilities. We kept modeling the buffers as before, but simulated packets with 1 bit of payload, thus, obtaining estimates on the cost and efficiency of a single bit instead of an entire packet. All estimates were computed within 12.6 h on an Intel Core i3-2120 clocked at 3.3 GHz.

At first, we fixed the number of sinks and evaluated the dependency on the length of the route from source to all sinks in Fig. 6. Afterwards, we fixed the length of the route to all sinks and evaluated the dependency on the number of sinks involved.

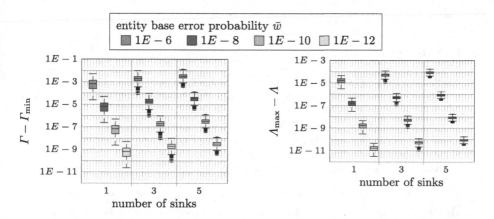

Fig. 6. Cost and efficiency comparison of a single bit for 10000 randomly selected multicast groups in an 8-by-8 2D-mesh with buffer and link modeling over different entity error probabilities $\bar{w}$.

As can be seen from Fig. 6, the median of the difference from the optimum cost and efficiency is increasing with the number of sinks served. This is mainly attributed to the fact, that bigger multicast groups require more hops on average.

On the other hand, the variance of bigger multicast groups is much less than it is in smaller multicast groups or even unicasts. Especially when comparing to the unicast, where one path alone determines the behavior of the entire cost and efficiency function, it is obvious that the variance must be big. For bigger multicast groups, the resulting cost and efficiency is obtained by a superposition of multiple affects, mainly the relative position of sinks to each other. This superposition is responsible for weakening the effect of poorly chosen sinks.

5 Conclusion

We have extended an analytic model intended for estimating end-to-end bit and packet error rates for unicast connections by introducing multicast capability.

Though getting full insight in terms of end-to-end transition probabilities into a multicast is an NP-hard problem which can not be relaxed, we are able to circumvent time- and resource-consuming system simulation or emulation by calculating end-to-end probabilities for meaningful sized multicast groups without sacrificing system information.

Our evaluation of a 2D-mesh NoC shows that the distance is the dominating factor in NoC communication reliability. We could also show, that at the same maximum distances, multicast groups have reduced cost values compared to unicasts, as sinks that are closer to the source reduce the overall cost.

As our algorithms are not tailored to specific topologies or routing algorithms, they provide a system designer with accurate estimates on to be expected bit errors and enables early design space exploration for various system and design parameters such as routing scheme, task allocation, technology node, and code strength.

References

1. Baumann, R.C.: The impact of technology scaling on soft error rate performance and limits to the efficacy of error correction. In: International Electron Devices Meeting, pp. 329–332 (2002)
2. Bertozzi, D., Benini, L., De Micheli, G.: Error control schemes for on-chip communication links: the energy-reliability tradeoff. IEEE Trans. Comput. Aided Des. Integr. Circuits Syst. **24**(6), 818–831 (2005)
3. Borkar, S.: Design challenges of technology scaling. IEEE Micro **19**(4), 23–29 (1999)
4. Dreslinski, R., Wieckowski, M., Blaauw, D., Sylvester, D., Mudge, T.: Near-threshold computing: reclaiming moore's law through energy efficient integrated circuits. Proc. IEEE **98**(2), 253–266 (2010)
5. Ganguly, A., Pande, P., Belzer, B.: Crosstalk-aware channel coding schemes for energy efficient and reliable NOC interconnects. IEEE Trans. VLSI Syst. **17**(11), 1626–1639 (2009)
6. Jerger, N., Peh, L.-S., Lipasti, M.: Virtual circuit tree multicasting: a case for on-chip hardware multicast support. In: International Symposium on Computer Architecture, pp. 229–240 (2008)
7. Kakoee, M., Bertacco, V., Benini, L.: ReliNoC: a reliable network for priority based on-chip communication. In: Design, Automation and Test in Europe Conference and Exhibition, pp. 1–6 (2011)
8. Maheswari, M., Seetharaman, G.: Enhanced low complex double error correction coding with crosstalk avoidance for reliable on-chip interconnection link. J. Electron. Test. **30**(4), 387–400 (2014)
9. Murali, S., Theocharides, T., Vijaykrishnan, N., Irwin, M.J., Benini, L., De Micheli, G.: Analysis of error recovery schemes for networks on chips. IEEE Des. Test Comput. **22**(5), 434–442 (2005)
10. Vonbun, M., Wallentowitz, S., Oeldemann, A.: An BSC based NoC simulator for end-to-end packet error rate estimation. https://github.com/TUM-LIS/nocbscsim
11. Vonbun, M., Wallentowitz, S., Oeldemann, A., Herkersdorf, A.: An analytic approach on end-to-end packet error rate estimation for network-on-chip. In: Euromicro Conference on Digital Systems Design (2015)

Protecting Code Regions on Asymmetrically Reliable Caches

Sanem Arslan[1], Haluk Rahmi Topcuoglu[2](✉), Mahmut Taylan Kandemir[3], and Oguz Tosun[1]

[1] Computer Engineering Department, Bogazici University, 34342 Istanbul, Turkey
sanem.arslan@boun.edu.tr, tosuno@boun.edu.tr
[2] Computer Engineering Department, Marmara University, 34722 Istanbul, Turkey
haluk@marmara.edu.tr
[3] Department of Computer Science and Engineering, Pennsylvania State University,
University Park, State College, PA 16802, USA
kandemir@cse.psu.edu

Abstract. Cache structures in a multicore system are considerably susceptible to soft errors. Protecting all caches using fault tolerance techniques has notable overheads on performance and power consumption. In this paper, we propose an enhanced protection mechanism for reliability-based critical code regions of the applications on asymmetrically reliable cores which have different error-tolerant cache structures. In this system, software threads which execute reliability-based critical code regions are mapped onto the protected cores, whereas the threads which execute non-critical regions are mapped to the unprotected ones, dynamically during the execution. Our experimental evaluations indicate that the proposed system improves Silent Data Corruption (SDC) rate by 66 % with 22 % performance loss and 1.2 % more power consumption for selected applications relative to the unprotected caches on average.

Keywords: Reliability · Selective protection · Fault injection · Asymmetric cores

1 Introduction

A soft error, a type of transient errors, results from a temporary condition in a semiconductor device that changes the stored data in memory [15]. This type of error randomly occurs and may corrupt the data or may cause the termination of the given program. Alpha particles, charged particles from radioactive materials, and high-energy cosmic rays are among the major reasons behind the occurrences of the soft errors [15].

Caches are increasingly susceptible to soft errors [3] since they have both large area of the logic compared to other parts of the chip and high transistor density. On the other hand, the effect of these types of errors can be considerably different and dramatic depending on the target application. For example, the result of a single transient error on a safety-critical application such as a

© Springer International Publishing Switzerland 2016
F. Hannig et al. (Eds.): ARCS 2016, LNCS 9637, pp. 375–387, 2016.
DOI: 10.1007/978-3-319-30695-7_28

program that controls a nuclear power plant or a missile can be disastrous. On the other hand, an error can considerably increase the execution cycles of the program in a molecular dynamics application with self-correcting capability (i.e., one that uses iterative solvers), although the application still finishes successfully [14]. Therefore, reliability should be considered as a primary metric of hardware/software design process for some applications.

Error Correcting Codes (ECCs) are widely deployed technology to protect cache memories. However applying ECC on each cache structure can be costly for performance, power and area sensitive systems. In this study, we propose a reliability framework by activating a minimum set of reliability enhancements using just enough extra hardware under the performance and power constraints.

The first contribution of this paper is designing and implementing a chip multiprocessor framework which has at least one protected, high-overhead core and a several number of unprotected, low-overhead cores. In our system, a programmer can annotate the reliability-based critical code regions of the application and it maps threads to asymmetrically reliable cores based on the annotated regions. The second contribution of this paper is designing a simulation-based fault injection model to evaluate reliability behaviour of applications on both proposed asymmetrically reliable caches and traditional caches. We present an experimental evaluation of our system, which validates the advantage of protecting only the reliability-based critical code regions of the applications; and offers significant reliability improvement under the performance and power constraints based on the applications considered. For the *Bodytrack* application, our scheme improves SDC rate by 51 % with 13 % more execution cycles and 0.8 % more power consumption compared to the unsafe configuration on average. Similarly, it improves reliability by 80 % with respect to SDC rate with 30 % more execution cycles and 1.5 % more power consumption on average, for *Fluidanimate* application.

2   Related Work

Various studies to enhance application fault tolerance on unreliable hardware are proposed in the literature. Kruijf et al. [7] propose *Relax* for software recovery of hardware faults. They mark code regions to indicate that code blocks are susceptible to failures and recover them by either re-execution of the relax block or discarding it. They do not differentiate the code regions as critical or non-critical, but they select applications which can discard computations in the event of an error. Sampson et al. [13] propose a programming language called *EnerJ* that allows the programmer to differentiate program data as approximate or critical. They guarantee that the operations on approximate data is processed with low-reliable way and critical data is processed with high reliable way. Arslan et al. [2] propose a framework which classifies input data as critical or non-critical and provides a protection mechanism for critical data by using asymmetrically reliable cores. Carbin et al. [6] propose a programming language that allows the programmer to express application-level properties for reliability issues and use probabilistic hardware models to satisfy these requirements running on unreliable hardware. Yetim et al. [16] propose a protection mechanism for inter-thread communication. They use application level information and convert potentially catastrophic communication errors to data errors. Rehman et al. [12] propose a system which improves task reliability of an application by selecting a task version among different versions and using heterogeneous error recovery cores. In their method, low resilient tasks are mapped to the fully protected cores and high resilient tasks are mapped to the unprotected ones. Luo et al. [11] propose heterogeneous-reliability memory where error tolerance of application data is differentiated. Their work is mainly based on memory partitioning of application data according to error tolerance to decrease the memory cost of data servers.

Our approach focuses on the code region criticality of the applications and provides an asymmetrically reliable system to assess reliability needs of the annotated regions. Multiple threads may execute critical code regions and need to run on the protected core(s). Therefore a dynamic allocation of application threads and a corresponding scheduling technique are required in our study which is the main contribution of our study.

3 Asymmetrically Reliable Caches for Critical Code Regions

In this study, we propose an enhanced protection mechanism for reliability-based critical code regions for utilizing asymmetric cores with different fault tolerance capabilities. Our proposed system consists of at least one protected, high-overhead core and several unprotected, low-overhead ones, where reliability-based criticality of the code regions should be differentiated a priori. Reliability-based critical code regions are the parts of the code that are critical from reliability perspective and to be protected. All instructions and memory accesses of an application do not have the same criticality. Some instructions or functions may need more reliability requirements than the others. Changes or corruptions in some regions of the application code may impact application execution behaviour or the output dramatically. These regions are called reliability-based critical code regions and should be annotated by the programmer in advance.

An effective way to utilize asymmetrically reliable cores is to map software threads executing reliability-based critical code regions to the protected core(s), and the other threads to the unprotected ones, dynamically during the execution. Therefore we can provide just enough reliability by using minimal extra hardware to eliminate potential overheads of reliability. If the reliability needs (criticality) of the instructions is not known, the system needs to be conservative to all memory accesses as having the same criticality which increases both cost and performance overheads. We can protect reliability-based critical regions more conservatively than the other non-critical parts from the possible transient errors, which provides only as much reliability as needed.

3.1   Architecture Model

Although our framework runs on cores with the same ISA and the same clock speed, asymmetrically reliable cores are differentiated with respect to different fault tolerant hardware in their caches. To test the effectiveness of our approach, we consider a 16-core system with dedicated L1 data and instruction caches and a unified L2 cache. There are three different cache protection configuration in our system: *unsafe*, *safe*, and *partially safe*. In *unsafe* configuration, 16 unprotected cores are used, whereas in *safe* configuration, 16 ECC protected cores are used. In *partially safe* configuration, 8 unprotected cores and several number of ECC protected cores (from 1 to 8 cores) are used. In this study, we assume that our cores are reconfigurable in terms of ECC protection. We can use them as either unsafe, safe or partially safe configuration according to our application needs. Both L1 instruction and data caches are protected with ECC mechanism for protected cores. Our goal for a partially safe configuration is to provide performance and power values close to the unsafe configuration, and fault rates (SDC rates) close to the safe configuration.

3.2   Execution Model

We assume that the reliability-based critical code regions of an application are determined beforehand. Initially, the application threads are mapped to the unprotected cores at the start of the execution. When a thread encounters a reliability-based critical code region, it sends a request for an execution on the protected core. Since several threads may send similar requests, the utilization of them is handled by a scheduler. As part of the framework, there is a single queue which collects pending requests sent by application threads. If a protected core is available, then the thread migrates to it, and executes the critical code region. After that, the thread is migrated back to the original requested core.

In Fig. 1, *funcA()* is a critical function for the user and it is annotated with *RCS_START* and *RCS_END* functions. The application should include the required files provided by our framework to call these functions. The execution scenario of application and queue threads can be seen in Algorithms 1 and 2. When an application thread encounters with a critical code region, it should add itself to the *requestList* for a protected core and wait response from a queue thread. In our system, each protected core has a queue thread that is responsible from getting the first request from the global request queue until *requestList* becomes empty. We consider a simple scheduling policy based on First Come First Served (FCFS) approach. When a queue thread takes a request from *requestList*, it notifies the corresponding application thread with its *protectedCoreID*. Then, the application thread binds itself onto it to execute reliability-based critical code region. After the completion of critical region, the thread binds itself to the initial core and notifies the corresponding queue thread about the completion. Then, the queue thread of the protected core dequeues the corresponding request from the queue. If the protected core is not available, its queue thread cannot get a request from the list since it is blocked at line 5 of

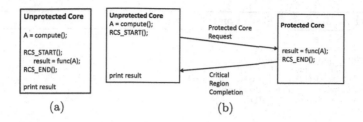

Fig. 1. Source code and its execution

Algorithm 1. Application Thread
___
Input: requestList, unprotectedCoreID
1 bindThread(unprotectedCoreID);
2   **A = compute();**
3 requestList.add(threadID);
4 protectedCoreID = **wait**ResponseFromQueueThread();
5 bindThread(protectedCoreID);
6   **func(A); //Critical function**
7 bindThread(initCoreID);
8 notifyQueueThread(threadID);
___

Algorithm 2 (*waitResponseFromThread*). The source code is executed by multiple threads at the same time and all operations on shared variables (i.e. *requestList*) are mutually exclusive.

3.3   Cache Protection Scheme

Error Correction Codes (ECCs), a widely deployed technology in the industry, are used on the cache memories of the protected core(s) in our framework. Single Error Correction and Double Error Detection (SEC-DED) can both correct single-bit errors and detect two bit errors. SEC-DED approach is implemented in our framework since most of the soft errors occurred as single-bit errors. ECC uses extra check bits to encrypt data and stores these check bits with the data. In our framework, SEC-DED can correct single bit errors and detect two bit errors by using additional 7 bits for 32-bit data. The additional cost of SEC-DED memory is 21.9 % in our system. Using SEC-DED for all cache memories has important performance, energy and area overheads [8]. Therefore we propose to use SEC-DED for the protected core(s) instead of protecting all of them.

3.4   Fault Injection Model

In our simulation-based fault injection model, six random numbers are generated to set a fault point in the execution: (1) a clock cycle of the running application (among number of clock cycles of the application), (2) a core number (among 16 cores), (3) a cache type (instruction or data cache), (4) a cache line (among 128 lines of the cache), (5) a cache index within a line (among 64 bytes), (6) a bit position (among 8 bits). Initially, uniformly distributed fault

---

Algorithm 2. Queue Thread on a protected core

Input: requestList
1 protectedCoreID = sched_getcpu(); //learn cpu id
2 **while** *requestList.isNotEmpty* **do**
3 | threadID = requestList.first();
4 | notifyThread(threadID, protectedCoreID);
5 | **wait**ResponseFromThread(threadID);
6 | requestList.delete(threadID);
7 └   **end while**

---

injection points are created. Then, an event is created and scheduled to the pre-determined clock cycle to inject a fault. We inject exactly one fault for each experiment, where the fault position and the faulty output are recorded on the host machine. It should be noted that every fault injected to the system does not hit to the application code. It can flip the bits when the system instructions are executed. *Event scheduling* mechanism of gem5 is used to implement our fault injection model.

In our framework, there is a controller mechanism on the host machine which evaluates the result of an experiment. Different types of cases may exist according to the results of fault injection experiments. The program finishes successfully and produces error-free output for the case of *correct execution*. In *Silent Data Corruption (SDC)*, the program finishes successfully, but it produces incorrect output. For the *program error* case, the program cannot terminate successfully due to an error such as a *segmentation fault* or it does not finish in logical time due to an unexpected situation such as an infinite loop.

4   Experimental Study

4.1   Simulation Platform

Gem5 system simulator [5] is used to implement our proposed framework by using ALPHA full system mode with *timing cpu* model. The *classical memory model* of gem5 is modified for ECC implementation on cache structures. Major characteristics of the simulated multicore are given in Table 1. We increase cache access latency values for cores which use SEC-DED check since it increases the memory access latency [11]. For the unprotected cores, cache access latency is left as 2 cycles. It is increased to 3 for protected cores, since an extra one cycle penalty is considered due to the SEC-DED encoding/decoding phases [1,8]. In addition to gem5, McPat [10] which models power, area and timing of desired architecture is used to estimate power consumption in the whole system. In order to differentiate power consumption values for ECC protected and unprotected cache structures, McPat source code was adapted.

4.2   Applications

We select applications from PARSEC [4] benchmark suite and profile them with *gprof*, which is a *GNU profiler*. According to the profiling results, function names

Table 1. Gem5 simulator parameters

Processor	
Number of cores	16
Processor type	ALPHA
Processor frequency	2 GHz
Simulation mode	Full system
Cache and Memory Hierarchy	
L1 instruction cache	32 KB, 2-way, 64 byte blocks, 2 cycle latency
L1 data cache	8 KB, 2-way, 64 byte blocks, 2 cycle latency
L2 cache	2 MB unified, 8-way, 64 byte blocks, 20 cycle latency
Memory	512 MB, 30 ns latency

that cover 90 % of total execution time are determined for each application. Then, each of these functions (might be 3–4 functions) is treated as a reliability-based critical code region, and they are executed one by one with the partially safe configuration. It is not important for our framework how the user annotates the code regions as critical. Any of the functions or regions in an application can be set critical from the user's perspective. We do not analyze the data dependencies between the reliability-based critical and non-critical sections so we assume that these parts are independent from each other. On the other hand, we only classify application's source code and do not interfere with the code of operating system.

In our experimental study we consider *Bodytrack* and *Fluidanimate* applications from PARSEC benchmark suite. *Bodytrack* is a computer vision application which tracks a human body with multiple cameras [4]. *Fluidanimate* is a computer animation application which simulates the underlying physics of fluid motion for real-time animation purposes [4]. In Table 2, we list the application

Table 2. Application functions, percentage of execution time, and total number of calls for each function

Application name	Function name	Ex. time percentage	# of calls	Serial or parallel	% of faults hit to this function
Bodytrack	*Exec*	50 %	96	Parallel	18.80 %
	OutputBMP	21.43 %	1	Serial	5.46 %
	InsideError	7.14 %	13045	Parallel	1.03 %
	EdgeError	7.14 %	13011	Parallel	1.11 %
	ImageProjections	7.14 %	13040	Parallel	0.59 %
	LoadSet	7.14 %	1	Serial	1.19 %
Fluidanimate	*ComputeForcesMT*	45 %	24	Parallel	14.74 %
	ComputeDensitiesMT	40 %	24	Parallel	12.46 %

name and the function name that belongs to the application in the first two columns. The third column displays the percentage of execution time which indicates how much time the protected core will be busy with this function. The fourth column shows the total number of calls for each function which directly affects the number of protected core requests and the queue overhead. The fifth column shows whether this function is executed serial or parallel, which indicates that how many threads compete for the protected core. Based on the fault injection experiments on an unsafe configuration, the fraction of the total number of faults that hit each function is shown in the last column. It should be noticed that the last column does not include the faults concerning other functions or system instructions. The faults listed in that table are totally eliminated by executing them on protected cores.

4.3 Experimental Results

We conducted a set of experiments to compare reliability, performance and power results of the partially safe with the unsafe and the safe configurations. *Bodytrack* and *Fluidanimate* applications are executed with 8 threads using *simdev* input set of PARSEC. Thread-to-core mapping is handled by Linux scheduler for the safe and unsafe configurations, but it is handled by our framework for the case of partially safe configurations. Execution time values contain both migration overhead and queue waiting overhead implicitly for the partially safe configurations. The number of fault injection tests for each function in an application is set to 2400, which is based on the calculation given in [9] with 95 % confidence level and 2 % error margin. We use SDC rate as a metric to compare our fault injection results since it is the most critical error type for the applications.

Performance and power consumption results of *Bodytrack* application are shown in Fig. 2. For this set of experiments, we utilize different number of protected cores for each function of the application. Figure 3 presents the results of fault injection experiments of the partially safe configurations by protecting single function at each case normalized to the unsafe configuration. The unsafe configuration has the smallest execution time and power consumption values and largest error rates (in terms of both SDC and program errors). Each bar in both figures already represent normalized values relative to the unsafe configuration. The greater part of the 2400 fault injection experiments result in correct execution. Therefore the bars related with correct execution do not increase dramatically for each case in Fig. 3. For example, the number of correct execution, program and SDC errors are 2120, 26, and 254, respectively for the unsafe configuration. On the other hand, these values change as 2153, 17 and 230 for protecting the *LoadSet* function. While the change of 33 number of correct execution yields 1.55 % increase in correct execution rate, the change of 9 number of faulty execution yields 35 % change in SDC rate. In this study, our goal is to decrease SDC error rates as much as possible.

Figure 2a shows the results with protecting *Exec* function which is a parallel function and cannot be executed serially by one thread at a time. All the threads are using only one protected core when executing this function in

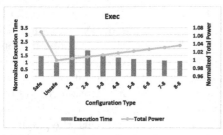

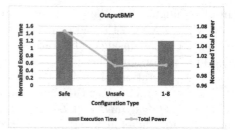

(a) Execution time and power consumption results with protecting *Exec* function

(b) Execution time and power consumption results with protecting *OutputBMP* function

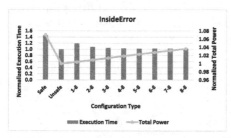

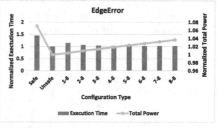

(c) Execution time and power consumption results with protecting *InsideError* function

(d) Execution time and power consumption results with protecting *EdgeError* function

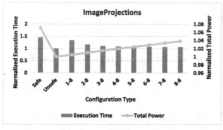

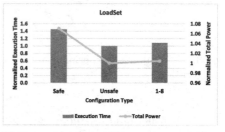

(e) Execution time and power consumption results with protecting *ImageProjections*

(f) Execution time and power consumption results with protecting *LoadSet* function

Fig. 2. Normalized values of execution time and power consumption for *Bodytrack*. (x-8) configuration: x protected and 8 unprotected cores

1–8 configuration. This configuration has the worst performance because of the resource contention among the threads. When we supply more protected core to the system, performance increase is observed, since the threads can execute their critical regions in parallel which decreases the queue waiting times of the threads. In contrast, the power consumption shows increasing behaviour since more ECC-protected cores consume more power. When we consider performance and power trade-off, supplying 5 protected cores for *Exec* function is suitable since it has execution time and power consumption values in between the safe and unsafe configurations. When we conduct fault injection experiments with protecting *Exec* function, SDC rate is considerably decreased compared to the unsafe configuration. We can improve reliability by 42 % with respect to SDC rate while having 24 % performance loss and 2.2 % more power consumption compared to the unsafe configuration. On the other hand, the safe configuration has 45 % performance loss and 7 % more power consumption compared to the unsafe configuration and it has no SDC since it can correct one bit errors.

Figure 2b and 2f show the execution time and power consumption results by protecting *OutputBMP* and *LoadSet* functions, which are executed serially by main thread. Therefore using only one protected core is enough with the partially safe configuration. We can improve reliability by 46 % with respect to SDC rate having 20 % performance loss and 0.14 % more power consumption relative to the unsafe configuration for *OutputBMP* function. Similarly, SDC rate is improved by 34 % with 8 % performance loss and 0.44 % more power consumption relative to the unsafe configuration for *LoadSet* function.

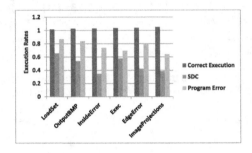

Fig. 3. Fault injection experiment results of *Bodytrack* functions relative to the *unsafe* configuration

On the other hand, *InsideError*, *EdgeError* and *ImageProjections* are thread-parallel functions that show very similar behaviour based on reliability, performance and power results (see Fig. 2c, 2d and 2e). Using 2 protected cores for *InsideError* and *EdgeError* functions and 3 protected cores for *ImageProjections* function are suitable, when we consider performance-power trade-off. SDC rates can be improved by 65 %, 57 % and 61 % for these functions while having 8 %, 6 % and 10 % performance loss and 0.9 %, 0.9 % and 1.5 % more power consumption compared to the unsafe configuration, for *InsideError*, *EdgeError* and *ImageProjections* functions, respectively. It can be noticed that the effect of each function on the application output is not equal.

Performance, power consumption and fault injection results of *Fluidanimate* application are shown in Fig. 4. *ComputeForces* and *ComputeDensities* functions are very similar functions and inherently show similar behaviour on the results. They are thread-parallel functions and there is a queuing overhead for both of them. They show best performance using 8 protected cores where the number of threads are equal to the number of protected cores. In other words, there is a protected core for each thread, which reduces the queue waiting overheads of the threads. The fault injection experiments are done with 4 protected cores where

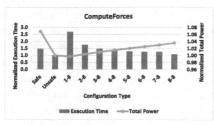

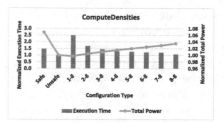

(a) Execution time and power consumption results with protecting *ComputeForces* function

(b) Execution time and power consumption results with protecting *ComputeDensities* function

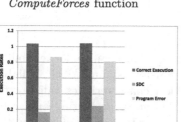

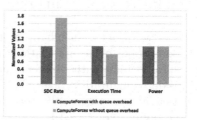

(c) Fault injection experiment results of Fluidanimate functions relative to the *unsafe* configuration

(d) Effect of queue waiting with *ComputeForces* function

Fig. 4. Normalized values of execution time, power and reliability results for *Fluidanimate*

the execution time converges in between safe and unsafe configurations and the power consumption is not high as in 8 protected cores. SDC rate of the unsafe configuration can be improved by 75 % with having 32 % performance loss and 1.5 % more power consumption for *ComputeForces* function. Similarly, SDC rate is improved by 83 % while having 26 % performance loss and 1.5 % more power consumption for *ComputeDensities* function.

In this set of experiments, we use different number of protected cores for each function of the applications. We present identical protection for each function by using different number of protected cores, where it only differs in performance and power results. We observe that there is not an ideal number of protected cores for each application, since each function has a different ideal number of protected cores under the performance and power constraints. The required number of protected cores for an application can be determined by considering reliability-based critical regions for the case of limited number of protected cores.

In order to measure the queuing overhead of our framework, we perform an additional test on a selected function from previous experiments, which is *ComputeForces* function of *Fluidanimate*. For this experiment, we again use additional 4 protected cores for the partially safe configuration; but in this case threads do not wait in the queue for a protected core and they continue to execute the critical code regions on the unprotected cores in case of protected cores are busy with other threads. Figure 4d shows SDC rate, execution time, and power consumption values which are normalized to the original case of the same function case (i.e., *ComputeForces* function by considering the queue overhead). Performance is improved by 21 % when queue-waiting overhead is eliminated, with the penalty of 75 % higher SDC rate, since only half of the threads are executed on the protected cores. Power consumption values are very close to each other since both configurations use the same number of protected cores. The user can select one of the configurations based on the priorities by considering reliability, performance and power trade-offs.

5 Conclusions and Future Work

In this paper, we propose an enhanced protection mechanism for reliability-based critical code regions of the applications with using asymmetrically reliable cores. Experimental studies with different function characteristics validate that our partially safe configuration takes the advantage of protecting only reliability-based critical code regions of the applications and offers significant performance and power savings compared to the safe configuration and lower failure rates compared to the unsafe configuration. Our adaptive approach can be applied in an environment where reliability is a major concern under the performance and power constraints. We plan to extend our framework by using different scheduling techniques which takes into consideration thread waiting times in the queue for the protected cores.

Acknowledgments. This research was supported by The Scientific and Technological Research Council of Turkey (TUBITAK) with a research grant (Project Number: 113E530).

References

1. Alameldeen, A.R., Wagner, I., Chishti, Z., Wu, W., Wilkerson, C., Lu, S.L.: Energy-efficient cache design using variable-strength error-correcting codes. In: Proceedings of the 38th Annual International Symposium on Computer Architecture, ISCA 2011, pp. 461–472 (2011)
2. Arslan, S., Topcuoglu, H.R., Kandemir, M.T., Tosun, O.: Performance and energy efficient asymmetrically reliable caches for multicore architectures. In: Parallel and Distributed Processing Symposium Workshop (IPDPSW), pp. 1025–1032 (2015)
3. Asadi, G., Sridharan, V., Tahoori, M.B., Kaeli, D.: Balancing performance and reliability in the memory hierarchy. In: Performance Analysis of Systems and Software, ISPASS 2005, pp. 269–279 (2005)
4. Bienia, C., Kumar, S., Singh, J.P., Li, K.: The PARSEC benchmark suite: characterization and architectural implications. In: Parallel Architectures and Compilation Techniques, PACT 2008, pp. 72–81 (2008)
5. Binkert, N., Beckmann, B., Black, G., Reinhardt, S.K., Saidi, A., Basu, A., et al.: The gem5 simulator. SIGARCH Comput. Archit. News **39**(2), 1–7 (2011)

6. Carbin, M., Misailovic, S., Rinard, M.C.: Verifying quantitative reliability for programs that execute on unreliable hardware. SIGPLAN Not. **48**(10), 33–52 (2013)
7. de Kruijf, M., Nomura, S., Sankaralingam, K.: Relax: an architectural framework for software recovery of hardware faults. In: Proceedings of the 37th Annual International Symposium on Computer Architecture, ISCA 2010, pp. 497–508 (2010)
8. Lee, K., Shrivastava, A., Issenin, I., Dutt, N., Venkatasubramanian, N.: Mitigating soft error failures for multimedia applications by selective data protection. In: Proceedings of the 2006 International Conference on Compilers, Architecture and Synthesis for Embedded Systems, CASES 2006, pp. 411–420 (2006)
9. Leveugle, R., Calvez, A., Maistri, P., Vanhauwaert, P.: Statistical fault injection: quantified error and confidence. In: Design, Automation Test in Europe Conference Exhibition, 2009, DATE 2009, pp. 502–506 (2009)
10. Li, S., Ahn, J., Strong, R.D., Brockman, J., Tullsen, D., Jouppi, N.: McPAT: an integrated power, area, and timing modeling framework for multicore and manycore architectures. In: 42nd Annual IEEE/ACM International Symposium on Microarchitecture, 2009, MICRO-42, pp. 469–480 (2009)
11. Luo, Y., Govindan, S., Sharma, B., Santaniello, M., Meza, J., Kansal, A., Liu, J., Khessib, B., Vaid, K., Mutlu, O.: Characterizing application memory error vulnerability to optimize datacenter cost via heterogeneous-reliability memory. In: Proceedings of the 2014 44th Annual IEEE/IFIP International Conference on Dependable Systems and Networks, DSN 2014, pp. 467–478 (2014)
12. Rehman, S., Kriebel, F., Shafique, M., Henkel, J.: Compiler-driven dynamic reliability management for on-chip systems under variabilities. In: Design, Automation and Test in Europe Conference and Exhibition (DATE), 2014, pp. 1–4 (2014)
13. Sampson, A., Dietl, W., Fortuna, E., Gnanapragasam, D., Ceze, L., Grossman, D.: EnerJ: approximate data types for safe and general low-power computation. SIGPLAN Not. **46**(6), 164–174 (2011)
14. Shantharam, M., Srinivasmurthy, S., Raghavan, P.: Characterizing the impact of soft errors on iterative methods in scientific computing. In: Proceedings of the International Conference on Supercomputing, ICS 2011, pp. 152–161 (2011)
15. Shivakumar, P., Kistler, M., Keckler, S., Burger, D., Alvisi, L.: Modeling the effect of technology trends on the soft error rate of combinational logic. In: Proceedings of the 2002 International Conference on Dependable Systems and Networks, DSN 2002, pp. 389–398 (2002)
16. Yetim, Y., Malik, S., Martonosi, M.: CommGuard: mitigating communication errors in error-prone parallel execution. In: Proceedings of the Twentieth International Conference on Architectural Support for Programming Languages and Operating Systems, ASPLOS 2015, pp. 311–323 (2015)

A New Simulation-Based Fault Injection Approach for the Evaluation of Transient Errors in GPGPUs

Sarah Azimi, Boyang Du, and Luca Sterpone$^{(\boxtimes)}$

Politecnico di Torino, Turin, Italy
{sarah.azimi,boyang.du,luca.sterpone}@polito.it

Abstract. General Purpose Graphics Processing Units (GPGPUs) are increasingly adopted thanks to their high computational capabilities. GPGPUs are preferable to CPUs for a large range of computationally intensive applications, not necessarily related to computer graphics. Within the high performance computing context, GPGPUs must require a large amount of resources and have plenty execution units. GPGPUs are becoming attractive for safety-critical applications where the phenomenon of transient errors is a major concern. In this paper we propose a novel transient error fault injection simulation methodology for the accurate simulation of GPGPUs applications during the occurrence of transient errors. The developed environment allows to inject transient errors within all the memory area of GPGPUs and into not user-accessible resources such as in streaming processors combinational logic and sequential elements. The capability of the fault injection simulation platform has been evaluated testing three benchmark applications including mitigation approaches. The amount of computational costs and time measured is minimal thus enabling the usage of the developed approach for effective transient errors evaluation.

1 Introduction

General Purpose Graphics Processing Units (GPGPUs) are high-performance oriented devices designed to execute stream-processing computations and perform high computational power combined with an overall low cost design cost thanks to their flexible development platform. Recently, these features are promoting the adoption of GPGPUs in various application fields like mission-critical applications including automotive, avionics, space and biomedical fields where the parallelism capabilities of GPGPUs would be very suitable [1]. Example of GPGPUs applications in these fields are the advanced driver assistance systems (ADAS), which are increasingly common in cars, are largely based on usage of images or radar signals coming from external camera and sensor devices to detect possible obstacles triggering the breaking system. Besides, in the space field, the European Space Agency (ESA) is nowadays employing low power GPGPUs for images compression on the COROT satellite [2] to minimize the bandwidth required to send data to ground, while the Airbus avionic company, within the framework of the ARAMIS project, integrates all the electronic used to deploy the Collision Avoidance System (CAS) into a single board including a GPGPU core [3].

© Springer International Publishing Switzerland 2016
F. Hannig et al. (Eds.): ARCS 2016, LNCS 9637, pp. 388–400, 2016.
DOI: 10.1007/978-3-319-30695-7_29

Considering their high degree of parallelism, in the GPGPUs environment is extremely easy to implement in software traditional soft error mitigation techniques such as duplication with comparison (DWC) and triple modular redundancy (TMR); however, the dimension of these software, their components organization and their complexity make them sensible to soft errors [4, 5]. Besides, while several soft-errors hardening techniques already exist for systems based on traditional CPUs, solutions and evaluations for GPGPUs are still under investigation and development [6]. Different methodologies have been proposed for evaluating the transient errors sensitivity of GPGPUs. Fault injection is a commonly adopted solution to validate the final application code and checks its detection and correction with respect to transient errors. Recently fault injection approaches have been applied to GPGPUs in two different methods: on one hand exposing the GPGPUs to accelerated radiation beams, on the other hand resorting to software fault injection using simulation-based methods. Several research activities have been recently developed in order to improve the efficiency of these methods, however the main limitations consisting of the elevated economical costs of experimental radiation beam and the excessive intrusiveness combined with ineffective fault models of simulation-based approaches still persists today.

In this paper we focus on the simulation-based fault injection methods, providing a solution that overcome the disadvantages of the state-of-the-art methods and giving novel insight on the behavior of GPGPUs when affected by transient errors. The main contribution of this paper is the development of a new simulation-based fault injection tool capable to inject transient errors within the architectural model of a GPGPU device and to evaluate its consequences on the executed application. The proposed method has two major advantages: the former consists in the accurate GPGPU fault model which allows to propagates transient errors from the affected location to the registers involved in the computation, modeling the transient error propagation and thus allowing to determine the right influence of the error in the GPGPU architecture; the latter consists in the low intrusiveness of the proposed approach when a software application is evaluated.

The analysis performed to evaluate the capability of the developed fault injection method has been done giving particular attention to the Streaming Processors (SPs), which are the elementary units where arithmetic and logic computations are executed. Consequently, an SP represent a critical component of GPGPUs computing, since an error may affect the execution code, the operands or the results thus compromising the whole algorithm execution.

The fault injection approach has been applied to the NVIDIA with Fermi architecture and the data has been acquired executing extensive fault injection campaigns on different types of applications including matrix multiplication, Fast Fourier Transform (FFT) and Sobel Filter using different type of mitigation approaches. The obtained results demonstrate the efficiency of the proposed fault injection method. The paper is organized as follow: Sect. 2 overviews some previous works in the area; Sect. 3 describes the developed fault injection approach describing the architectural level transient injector and the GPGPU-simulation based soft-error tool; Sect. 4 explains and comments experimental data. Finally, Sect. 5 depicts conclusions and outlines future activities.

2 Related Works

Reliability analysis of GPGPUs is nowadays a fundamental issue for enabling the usage of these devices in safety-critical applications. In particular, the usage of GPGPUs in the avionic and space fields require specific characterization of the fault tolerance techniques mitigation capabilities with respect to the errors induced by radiation effects. The research activities on this topic is nowadays still in its infancy [5]. Preliminary activities have performed through radiation test experiments where the GPGPUs operation is executed under the irradiation of the device with a neutron radiation source with energy above 10 MeV. While the application code is running, neutron particles may generate transient errors causing silent faults or functional interrupts. This approach has been effectively used to test software-based hardening strategies avoiding the propagation of soft-errors. Various paper reports the application of the Error Correction Code (ECC) mechanism applied to the most used applications in the High Performance Computing (HPC) and in safety-critical domain [7, 8]. Radiation analysis is a fundamental method for the evaluation the dependability although their executions require elevated economical cost. On the other hand, radiation tests experiment performed on GPGPUs relieve overall dependability data without a peculiar individuation of the error effects. Therefore different other methods have been developed to address this issue.

Fault injection by emulation has been recently developed in [9, 10]. These approaches were based on the NVIDIA CUDA-debugger (gdb), which, by means of ad-hoc software infrastructure, is able to inject transient faults in the accessible memory components, to mimic faults affecting ALUs and FPUs and to classify their effects.

These methods are characterized by the advantage of using a real device for the transient error characterization and to effectively evaluate the behavior of transient effects. However, they have two major drawbacks. At first, since based on debugger interface, the computational speed of the GPGPU under test is extremely low, nullifying the benefit of the emulation. Secondly, debugger interfaces have limited resource availability; therefore the fault injection is limited only on specific variables and memory elements of the architecture without any possibility of emulating transient effects affecting the GPGPU combinational resources.

Following the progressive availability of GPGPU Instruction Set Architectural (ISA) and hardware architectural models, several GPGPU simulators have been recently developed. In [11], the Barra GPGPU simulator has been presented. It is based on the UNISIM framework and it allows the Parallelization of the Thread eXecution (PTX) and the execution simulation of CUDA programs at the functional level. Moreover, the simulator can be customized reusing the module libraries and features proposed in the UNISIM repository and it allows the integration into the NVIDIA OpenCL software stack.

The performance execution of GPU simulation has been evaluated in [12] reporting a speedups below 50 times an equivalent CPU may obtain on a detailed performance simulator that simulated NVIDIA parallel thread execution, showing that for certain applications the reduction of the number of concurrent threads can improve the simulation performances.

A modern simulator, GPGPU-sim has been developed in [13, 14] in order to explore efficient mechanism in Single-Instruction Multiple-Data (SIMD) branch execution on GPUs. GPGPU-sim allows to have a detailed model of commercial GPGPU (especially the ones manufactured by NVIDIA) like Fermi and FT200. The simulator can be easily used with several applications due to the supported CUDA and OpenCL workloads. The architectural simulator GPGPU-sim offers the flexibility to modify the processor parameters and allows the integration of customized modules.

Recently, GPGPU-sim has been used in conjunction to hardware emulation for the execution of fault-injection analysis [15], although characterized by effective performances this method has the limitation of analyzing transient errors affecting exclusively variables and registers used by the tested applications without the possibility to analyze the effects of faults generated into the internal logic structure.

3 The Proposed Method

The proposed method consists in the flow diagram illustrated in Fig. 1. The method is based on the availability of the hardware model (i.e., by means of VHDL language) and the Instruction Set Architecture (ISA) of the considered GPGPU. The fault injection method is characterized by two phases: the injection of the transient errors and the GPGPU application simulation execution with the injected fault. During the first phases, transient phenomenon is injected in the hardware architectural model of the GPGPU under test; the transient pulse fault is propagated through the GPGPU resources up to computational registers. For each transient error injected a list of affected computational register cells is generated and stored into the GPGPU affected

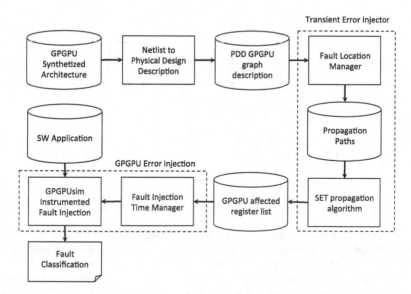

Fig. 1. The flow of the developed simulation-based fault injection for transient errors analysis on GPGPUs.

register list. The second phase consists of the software application execution using the GPGPU-sim framework, which has been instrumented with the injection of errors that simulates in a realistic way the radiation effects. In details, each error injection is performed using the GPGPU affected register list simulating the effective propagation of the original transient pulse to the GPGPU computation. The result of each fault injection is finally classified.

3.1   Architectural Level Transient Error Injector

The architectural level transient error injector has the main objective of simulating the Single Event Transient (SET) or transient error phenomena generated by radiation particles within the silicon structure of the GPGPU device. This process requires the description of the GPGPU architecture. Therefore, the preliminary phase consists in extracting the architectural graph description. A software tool elaborates the GPGPU netlist and translates it into a Physical Design Description (PDD) file containing a directed graph representation of the circuit where each vertex model a logic gate or sequential element while edges model the interconnection between them.

The transient error injector module consists in the following phases: the generation of the SET pulse phenomena which is modeled as transient pulse shape, the localization of all the combinational gates within the circuit description and finally the execution of the propagation of the SET pulse starting from the selected sensitive node of the GPGPU circuit and traversing logic gates and routing interconnections until a storage elements such as a Flip-Flop or a Memory bank is reached. As illustrated in Fig. 2, the propagation of the SET pulse may span over a large logic cone reaching several FFs resources on the final computational register.

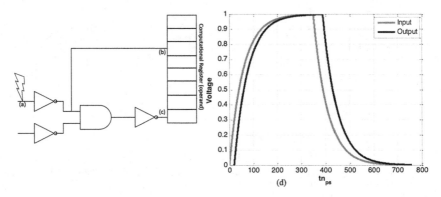

Fig. 2. An example of transient error injection and pulse propagation. A Single Event Transient pulse is applied at the fault location (a). The pulse is propagated on two different paths reaching two FFs: (b) and (c). Due to the different propagation effects on the two paths, the computational register is affected on two bits with two different SET shapes. The shape (d) represents an example of observed output at the register (c) with respect of a 700 ps transient error injected.

1. $if \left(T_n < kt_p\right) \to T_{n+1} = 0$
2. $if \left(T_n > (k+3)t_p\right) \to T_{n+1} = T_n + \Delta t_p$
3. $if \left((k+1)t_p < T_n < (k+3)t_p\right) \to T_{n+1} = \frac{(T_n^2 - T_p^2)}{T_n} + \Delta t_p$
4. $if \left(kt_p < T_n < (k+1)t_p\right) \to T_{n+1} = (k+1)t_p \left(1 - e^{\left(k - \left(\frac{T_n}{t_p}\right)\right)}\right) + \Delta t_p$

Fig. 3. The Single Event Transient pulse propagation model developed in [16].

In order to generate the SET pulse shape, we developed a model that elaborates the physical layout description of circuit logic gate. The model consists of three phases described in Fig. 3. The first phase generates the SET model according to the definition illustrated in Fig. 2d and developed in [16]; while the second phase executes the propagation on the basis of the resistive and capacitive load calculated on the hardware technology model of the circuit. The propagation coefficient is used in the model reported in Fig. 3 in order to generate the expected propagation coefficients for all the logic paths. In Fig. 2d is illustrated the pulse shape on the output obtained in case of broadening. The third phase includes the execution of the propagation to all the FFs of the involved register.

The architectural level transient error injection is executed for all the desired number of injected SETs. The generated outcome consists in a database of SET pulse events observed on all the GPGPU registers that will be selected for simulation-based fault injection. The main advantage provided by the transient injector module is the capability to individuate the effective propagation of the SET on the computational registers, which will determine a more accurate fault injection execution of the GPGPU soft error application simulation.

3.2   GPGPU Soft Error Simulator Injection

Architectural simulators offer a robust solution to verify the efficiency and the performance of applications through the detailed models of the most used commercial devices. In this paper we exploits the capability and the flexibility of the GPGPU-Sim [10] in order to develop a Soft-Error injector that simulates in a realistic way the radiation effects. An overview of the system model of the GPGPU architecture is illustrated in Fig. 4.

The GPGPU-sim simulator has been modified in order to cause a dynamic fault insertion in the thread executed by the GPGPU. The simulator executes GPGPU kernel and warps sequentially and accessing to a global memory it is possible to extract the information related to the execution timing. Exploiting the thread class interface, it was possible to obtain all the information to identify each thread executed in the simulator and the hardware associated to it. A fault free execution allows the extraction of the execution timing information of an application. This operation allows to know all the instruction executed from the simulator and therefore to identify the correspondent instruction registers and computational operand registers.

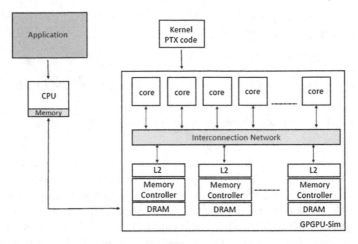

Fig. 4. GPGPU-sim modeled system [15].

The scheme of the soft-error injection tool integration in the GPGPU-sim is illustrated in Fig. 5. A fault injector module has been implemented to inject a specific fault inside an executed instruction. This module runs the applications of two distinct operational modes:

1. *Golden response mode*: it is a fault free execution. It provides at the output a profiling file containing a list of all the instructions executed with information related to the identification of the warp and of the thread in a specific execution time.
2. *Fault simulation mode*: it is able to inject a fault inside an instruction and for every fault generated is obtained a description of the fault.

The fault injection module operations can be managed through the usage of a configuration file. It allows to enable the fault injection module and consequently to select, using the fault list, the instruction in which the injection has to be performed. Every fault is identified from the following parameters:

1. *Instruction name*: the type of instruction affected from the injection
2. *Warp identification*: identify if the fault affects a specific warp or all the warps
3. *Kernel identification*: identify if the fault affects a specific kernel or all the kernels
4. *Bit mask*: it is a 32-bit integer representing the mask applied to the operands in order to invoke bit-flip. Each not-masked bit corresponds to the relative injected soft-errors.

The GPGPU soft error simulation module have been implemented to control the execution and to download the outputs of the executed applications and other information such as the monitor functions which allow the detection of functional interrupts caused by soft-errors. Besides, another tool has been developed to acquire and compare the golden response with the fault injected one.

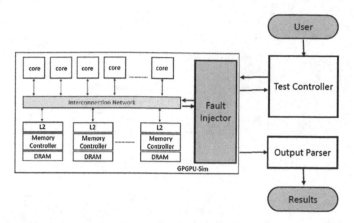

Fig. 5. Soft-error injection tool integration in the GPGPU-sim simulator.

3.3   Test Execution Flow

The fault injection environment integrates the architectural level transient injector and the GPGPU soft error simulator. As described in the previous sections the user may specify the number of injected transient faults as well as the number of parallel processes. The injection rate is automatically calculated on the basis of the GPGPU affected register list. Naturally, the time required for a test is directly proportional to the number of simulation required and the complexity of the application. The first operation performed in the test execution flow is to compile and build the application on the simulator. Once this operation is completed, the golden response mode is set and a first execution of the application is performed. This operation extracts the execution timing information for the kernel and warps, which allows to have the complete set of instructions and golden response of the applications. This is used to create an accurate timing fault list. The flow of the test execution is illustrated in Fig. 6.

The fault injection execution is performed while the main program runs the application and the injector module continuously checks the instruction execution in order to inject the error in the instruction and register defined in the GPGPU affected register list.

At the conclusion of the simulation a log file is generated; it reports the instructions executed during the application, the information on the faults injected and the final results. The output is a report that provides the number of affected simulation, which can be identified as follow:

1. *Silent simulations*: they have not been affected from the fault injection and the result corresponds to the golden one.
2. *Timed out simulations*: they have reported a functional interruption due to the time threshold.
3. *Corrupted simulations*: they have not reported a functional interruption, but their result is different from the expected one.

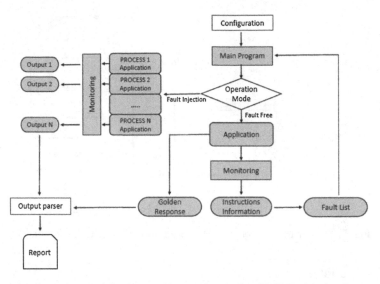

Fig. 6. Soft-error injection tool integration in the GPGPU-sim simulator.

4 Experimental Results

The developed fault injection method has been tested on the NVIDIA G80 GPGPU model architecture [17] using the hardware description of the FlexGrip GPGPU [18], which is directly implementing the Hardware Description Language of the NVIDIA G80 GPGPU. For the purpose of this work, we applied our fault injection method to its Streaming Multiprocessor (SM) architecture, which consists of a five-stage pipelined architecture including Fetch, Decode, Read, Execute and Write stages; supporting the execution of 27 CUDA instructions.

We synthesized the SM model using the Microsemi ProASIC gate library [19] and we performed two types of analysis. The first one consists in the evaluation of the overall transient error sensitivity of a single streaming processor, while the second consisted on the execution of various fault injection campaigns on some benchmark applications including the Matrix multiplication, FFT and Sobel filter.

4.1 Streaming Processor Transient Error Injection

The synthesis of the SM architecture generated a structure composed of more than 50 K gates organized in about 1.5 M logical paths. In order to perform a feasible evaluation we selected a single streaming processor, which counts around 4 K gates and registers organized in 238 K logical paths. We analyzed the sensitivity considering eight different types of single event transients ranging from 100 ps to 1 ns. We performed a fault injection experiments randomly injecting 1,000 errors for each type of pulses and classifying the data in filtered, partially filtered, equal and broadened SETs. The results of the SET sensitivity analysis are reported in Fig. 7. Please note that the majority of SET is filtered below 0.45 ns while they are progressively unfiltered by the intrinsic GPGPU circuitry with they increased width. Besides all of all SETs are broadened once their width is greater than 0.7 ns and all the SETs are reaching their respective logical cone outputs.

In order to have a better vision on the typology of propagation of SETs, the number of computational registers reached by the injection of each SET has been investigated, identifying a broadening of the SET pulses ranging from 5 to 10 % of their original width. The transient error profiles obtained by the error injection have been stored into the GPGPU affected register list.

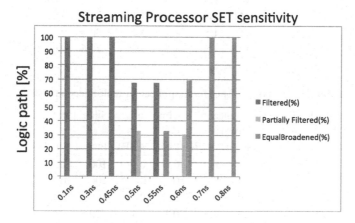

Fig. 7. Single Streaming Processor SET sensitivity overview.

4.2 Application Fault Injection Results

The fault injection campaigns have been performed on different type of applications such as: a Matrix multiplication between two 16 × 16 matrices of integer data, a Fast Fourier Transform (FFT) of a 16 × 16 matrix and Sobel filter on a 16 × 16 input matrix. The applications have been implemented in two different ways: not mitigated and using the Algorithm Based Fault Tolerance (ABFT) mitigation approach.

The results are illustrated in Tables 1, 2 and 3 showing the percentage of effects classified as: *application error*, once the application generates erroneous results; *Time out*, in case the application is blocked and never reach the generation of the data output and finally *Silent*, in case the injected errors do not generate any erroneous results on the executing application and the computed results correspond to normal execution without faults. Please consider that the average injection time ranges from 8 around 14 injected and simulated transient errors per minute of simulation.

The results provide a clear overview on the intrusiveness of the transient errors with respect on the SET original transient error's width. This phenomenon provokes two different scenario: on one side, the application errors increases with respect to the SET pulse widths; on the other side the increasing ratio is not linear since a wider transient pulse is not filtered on more logical paths than shorter ones thus exponentially increasing the application error percentage.

Table 1. Matrix multiplication application results fault injection results

SET pulse [ns]	Application error [%]		Time out [%]		Silent [%]	
	Plain	ABFT	Plain	ABFT	Plain	ABFT
0.10	0	0	0	0	100	100
0.30	0	0	0	0	100	100
0.45	0	0	0	0	100	100
0.50	8.5	1.3	4.2	2.9	87.3	95.8
0.55	10.6	1.5	4.3	3.0	85.1	95.5
0.60	12.8	1.6	4.3	3.0	82.9	95.4
0.70	14.0	1.7	4.3	3.1	81.7	95.2
0.80	15.3	1.8	4.4	3.1	80.4	95.1
1.00	16.9	1.8	4.5	3.2	78.6	95.0

Table 2. Fast Fourier Transform application fault injection results

SET pulse [ns]	Application error [%]		Time out [%]		Silent [%]	
	Plain	ABFT	Plain	ABFT	Plain	ABFT
0.10	0	0	0	0	100	100
0.30	0	0	0	0	100	100
0.45	0	0	0	0	100	100
0.50	20.1	1.8	0.1	0.1	79.8	98.1
0.55	20.3	2.1	0.1	0.1	79.6	97.9
0.60	24.5	2.9	0.1	0.1	75.4	97.0
0.70	27.4	3.6	0.2	0.1	72.4	96.3
0.80	31.4	4.4	0.2	0.2	68.4	95.4
1.00	36.4	5.6	0.3	0.2	63.3	94.2

Considering the mitigation approaches used, it is possible to notice the progressive reduction of the fault tolerance capability with respect to the injected transient errors. Please note that, in particular for the matrix multiplication algorithm, the ABFT approach should be able to mitigate all the injected faults. The obtained results demonstrate a different faults behavior, since a transient errors maybe propagated to several Flip-Flops in the computational registers, this nullifying the single fault scenario and confirming the radiation test data obtained in [20].

Table 3. Sobel application fault injection results.

SET pulse [ns]	Application error [%]		Time out [%]		Silent [%]	
	Plain	ABFT	Plain	ABFT	Plain	ABFT
0.10	0	0	0	0	100	100
0.30	0	0	0	0	100	100
0.45	0	0	0	0	100	100
0.50	9.1	2.1	0.1	0	90.8	97.9
0.55	10.4	3.4	0.1	0	89.5	96.6
0.60	14.5	5.6	0.1	0	85.4	94.4
0.70	24.4	8.4	0.1	0	75.5	91.6
0.80	25.4	12.5	0.1	0	74.5	87.5
1.00	25.8	14.5	0.1	0	74.1	85.5

5 Conclusions and Future Works

Simulation-based fault injection methods offer an effective and versatile analysis of soft-errors affecting the computation of GPGPUs. The introduction of the radiation-induced transient error analysis in the fault injection flow increases the capability and the efficiency of such kind of methodologies. In this paper, we developed a fault injection method with transient error propagation analysis. The results show that our methodology is accurate since effective and experimental results have been proposed comparing different applications and using traditional software-based mitigation solutions. As future works, we plan to extend the present analysis on further algorithms (e.g., BFS algorithm) and to provide a direct comparison with radiation-experiment analysis.

References

1. Sabena, D., Sonza Reorda, M., Sterpone, L., Rech, P., Carro, L.: On the evaluation of soft-errors detection techniques for GPGPUs. In: Proceedings of 8th Design and Test Symposium (IDT), pp. 1–6, December 2013
2. ESA COROT mission documentation (2014). http://www.esa.int/Our_Activities/Space_Science/COROT
3. Becker, J., Sander, O.: ARAMIS Project Overview (2013). http://www.across-project.eu/workshop2013/121108_ARAMIS_Introduction_HiPEAC_WS_V3.pdf
4. Sabena, D., Sonza Reorda, M., Sterpone, L., Rech, P., Carro, L.: Evaluating the radiation sensitivity of GPGPU caches: new algorithms and experimental results. Microelectron. Reliab. **54**(11), 2621–2628 (2014). Elsevier
5. Battista Gomez, L., Capello, F., Carro, L., DeBardeleben, N., Fang, B., Gurumurthi, S., Pattabiraman, K., Rech, P., Sonza Reorda, M.: GPGPUs: how to combine high computational power with high reliability. In: Proceedings of IEEE Design, Automation and Test in Europe (DATE), pp. 1–9 (2014)

6. Rech, P., Aguiar, C., Frost, C., Carro, L.: An efficient and experimentally tuned software-based hardening strategy for matrix multiplication on GPUs. IEEE Trans. Nucl. Sci. **60**(4), 2797–2804 (2013). Part. 1

7. Sabena, D., Sterpone, L., Carro, L., Rech, P.: Reliability evaluation of embedded GPGPUs for safety critical applications. IEEE Trans. Nucl. Sci. **61**(6), 3123–3129 (2014)

8. Sabena, D., Sonza Reorda, M., Sterpone, L., Rech, P., Carro, L.: On the evaluation of soft-errors detection techniques for GPGPUs. In: 8th International Design and Test Symposium (IDT 2013), pp. 1–6, 16–18 December 2013

9. Tan, J., Goswami, N., Li, T., Fu, X.: Analyzing soft-error vulnerability on GPGPU microarchitecture. In: 2011 IEEE International Symposium on Workload Characterization (IISWC), pp. 226–235 (2011)

10. Fang, B., Wei, J., Pattabiraman, K., Ripeanu, M.: Towards building error resilient GPGPU applications. In: SC Companion: High Performance Computing, Networking Storage and Analysis (2012)

11. Collange, S., Daumas, M., Defour, D., Parello, D.: Barra: a parallel functional simulator for GPGPU. In: 18th Annual IEEE/ACM International Symposium on Modeling, pp. 351–360 (2010)

12. Bakhoda, A., Yuan, G.L., Fung, W.W.L., Wong, H., Aamodt, T.M.: Analyzing CUDA workloads using a detailed GPU simulator. In: ISPASS (2009)

13. Fung, W.W.L., Sham, I., Yuan, G., Aamodt, T.M.: Dynamic warp formation and scheduling for efficient GPU control flow. In: 40th IEEE/ACM International Simposium on Microarchitecture (2014)

14. http://www.gpgpu-sim.org/

15. Fang, B., Pattabiraman, K., Ripeanu, M., Gurumurthi, S.: GPU-Qin: a methodology for evaluating the error resilience of GPGPU applications. In: IEEE International Symposium on Performance Analysis of Systems and Software (ISPASS), pp. 221–230 (2014)

16. Sterpone, L., Du, B., Azimi, S.: Radiation-induced single event transients modeling and testing on nanometric flash-based technology. Microelectron. Reliab. **55**(9–10), 2087–2091 (2015)

17. NVIDIA CUDA programming guide, version 2.3.1, August 2009

18. Andryc, K., Merchant, M., Tessier, R.: FlexGrip: a soft GPGPU for FPGAs. In: International Conference on Field Programmable Technology, Kyoto, Japan, pp. 230–237, December 2013

19. IGLOO, ProASIC3, Smartfusion and Fusion Macro Library Guide for Software 9.0, p. 193, February 2010

20. Olivera, D.A.G., Rech, P., Pilla, L.L., Navaux, P.O.A., Carro, L.: GPGPUs ECC efficiency and efficacy. In: International Symposium on Defect and Fault Tolerance in VLSI and Nanotechnology Systems (DFT), pp. 209–215 (2014)

Author Index

Printed in the United States
By Bookmasters